MEDIEVAL DUBLI

This volume is dedicated
by the Friends of Medieval Dublin
to the memory of
John Gallagher
(1933–2020)
'Legend of the Liberties', co-leader of Operation Sitric, 1979

Medieval Dublin XVIII

Seán Duffy

EDITOR

FOUR COURTS PRESS

Typeset in 10.5 pt on 12.5 pt Ehrhardt by
Carrigboy Typesetting Services for
FOUR COURTS PRESS LTD
7 Malpas Street, Dublin 8, Ireland
www.fourcourtspress.ie
and in North America for
FOUR COURTS PRESS
c/o IPG, 814 N Franklin St, Chicago, IL 60610.

A catalogue record for this title is available
from the British Library.

ISBN 978–1–84682–815–7 hbk
ISBN 978–1–84682–816–4 pbk

This book is published with the active support of
Dublin City Council/Comhairle Chathair Átha Cliath.

Dublin City
Baile Átha Cliath

Printed in England
by CPI Antony Rowe, Chippenham, Wilts.

Contents

Abbreviations

AClon	*The annals of Clonmacnoise, being the annals of Ireland from the earliest period to AD 1408 translated into English AD 1627 by Conell Mageoghagan*, ed. D. Murphy (Dublin, 1896)
AFM	*Annála ríoghachta Éireann: annals of the kingdom of Ireland by the Four Masters, from the earliest period to the year 1616*, ed. J. O'Donovan, 7 vols (Dublin, 1851)
AH	*Analecta Hibernica, including the report of the Irish Manuscripts Commission* (IMC, Dublin, 1930–)
AI	*The annals of Inisfallen (MS Rawlinson B. 503)*, ed. S. Mac Airt (DIAS, Dublin, 1951)
ALC	*The annals of Loch Cé: a chronicle of Irish affairs from AD 1014 to AD 1590*, ed. W.M. Hennessy, 2 vols (RS, London, 1871; repr. IMC, Dublin, 1939)
ATig	'Annals of Tigernach', ed. W. Stokes in *Revue Celtique*, 16 (1895) 374–419; 17 (1896) 6–33, 119–263, 337–420; 18 (1897) 9–59, 150–97, 267–303; reprinted in two vols (Felinfach, 1993).
AU	*Annála Uladh ('Annals of Ulster'), otherwise Annála Senait ('Annals of Senat'): a chronicle of Irish affairs AD 431 to AD 1540*, ed. W.M. Henessey and B. MacCarthy, 4 vols (Dublin, 1887–1901); *The annals of Ulster (to AD 1131)*, ed. S. Mac Airt and G. Mac Niocaill (Dublin, 1983)
BL	British Library, London
Bradley et al. (eds), *Dublin in the medieval world*	John Bradley, Alan J. Fletcher and Anngret Simms (eds), *Dublin in the medieval world: studies in honour of Howard B. Clarke* (Dublin, 2009)
Cal. S.P. Ire.	*Calendar of state papers relating to Ireland, 1509–73 [etc.]*, 24 vols (London, 1860–1911)
CARD	J.T. Gilbert (ed.), *Calendar of ancient records of Dublin*, 19 vols (Dublin, 1889–1944)
CCD	*Calendar of Christ Church deeds*, ed. M.J. McEnery and Raymond Refaussé (Dublin, 2001)
CCR	*Calendar of the close rolls [...], 1272–[1509]*, 47 vols (PRO, London, 1892–1963)
CDI	*Calendar of documents relating to Ireland, 1171–1307*, ed. H.S. Sweetman and G.F. Handcock, 5 vols (PRO, London, 1875–86)
CGG	*Cogadh Gaedhil re Gallaibh*, ed. and trans. James Henthorn Todd (London, 1867)

CIRCLE   Peter Crooks (ed.), *A calendar of Irish chancery letters*, c.*1244–*
                1509 (available at http://chancery.tcd.ie/)

Civil Survey The Civil Survey, AD *1654–56*, ed. R.C. Simington, 10 vols
                (Dublin, 1931–61)

Clarke et al. (eds), *Ireland and Scandinavia*
                H.B. Clarke, Máire Ní Mhaonaigh and Raghnall Ó Floinn (eds),
                Ireland and Scandinavia in the early Viking Age (Dublin, 1998)

Clarke, *Dublin, Pt 1* (IHTA)
                H.B. Clarke (ed.), *Dublin Part I, to 1610*, IHTA, no. 11 (RIA,
                Dublin, 2002)

CJRI   *Calendar of the justiciary rolls of Ireland*, ed. James Mills et al., 3
                vols (Dublin, 1905–56)

CPL   *Calendar of entries in the papal registers relating to Great Britain
                and Ireland: papal letters* (London, 1893–)

CPR   *Calendar of the patent rolls* [...], *1232–*[*1509*], 53 vols (PRO,
                London, 1911)

CPR Ire., Hen. VIII–Eliz.
                *Calendar of the patent and close rolls of chancery in Ireland, Henry
                VIII to 18th Elizabeth*, ed. J. Morrin (Dublin, 1862)

Crawford and Gillespie (eds), *St Patrick's*
                John Crawford and Raymond Gillespie (eds), *St Patrick's
                Cathedral, Dublin: a history* (Dublin, 2009)

CS   *Chronicum Scotorum*, ed. W.M. Hennessy (London, 1866)

CStM   *Chartularies of Saint Mary's Abbey, Dublin*, ed. J.T. Gilbert, 2
                vols (RS, London, 1884–6)

DGMR   Philomena Connolly and Geoffrey Martin (eds), *Dublin guild
                merchant roll* (Dublin, 1992)

DHR   *Dublin Historical Record*

DIB   *Dictionary of Irish biography*, ed. J. McGuire and J. Quinn, 9 vols
                (Cambridge, 2009)

eDIL   *Electronic Dictionary of the Irish language*, ed. Gregory Toner, Máire
                Ní Mhaonaigh, Sharon Arbuthnot, Marie-Luise Theuerkauf and
                Dagmar Wodtko (www.dil.ie 2019)

Extents Ir. mon. possessions
                Extents of Irish monastic possessions, 1540–1541 [...], ed. N.B.
                White (IMC, Dublin, 1943)

FAI   Joan Newlon Radner (ed.), *Fragmentary annals of Ireland*
                (Dublin, 1978)

Gilbert (ed.), *Hist. & mun. docs*
                J.T. Gilbert (ed.), *Historic and municipal documents of Ireland,
                AD 1172–1320, from the archives of the city of Dublin* (RS, London,
                1870)

Gillespie and Refaussé (eds), *Medieval manuscripts*
> Raymond Gillespie and Raymond Refaussé (eds), *The medieval manuscripts of Christ Church Cathedral, Dublin* (Dublin, 2006)

Griffith (ed.), *Cal. inquisitions*
> Margaret C. Griffith (ed.), *Calendar of inquisitions formerly in the office of the chief remembrance of the exchequer prepared from the MSS of the Irish Record Commission* (IMC, Dublin, 1991)

Hogan, *Onomasticon*
> Edmond Hogan (ed.), *Onomasticon Goedelicum: locorum et tribuum Hiberniae et Scotiae. An index, with identifications, to the Gaelic names of places and tribes* (Dublin, 1910)

IHS   *Irish Historical Studies*

IHTA   Irish Historic Towns Atlas (RIA, Dublin, 1986–)

IMC   *Coimisiún Láimhscríbhinní na hÉireann* (The Irish Manuscripts Commission)

JRSAI   *Journal of the Royal Society of Antiquaries of Ireland*

Mac Niocaill, *Buirgéisí*
> Gearóid Mac Niocaill, *Na Burgéisí, XII–XV aois*, 2 vols (Dublin, 1964)

Milne (ed.), *Christ Church*
> Kenneth Milne (ed.), *Christ Church Cathedral Dublin: a history* (Dublin, 2000)

NAI   National Archives of Ireland

NLI   National Library of Ireland, Dublin

O'Brien, *Corpus geneal. Hib.*
> M.A. O'Brien (ed.), *Corpus genealogiarum Hiberniae* (Dublin, 1962)

PRIA   *Proceedings of the Royal Irish Academy*

Reg. Alen   *A calendar of Archbishop Alen's register, c.1172–1534*, ed. C. McNeill (RSAI, Dublin, 1950)

Reg. All Hallows
> *Registrum prioratus Omnium Sanctorum juxta Dublin*, ed. R. Butler (IAS, Dublin, 1845)

Reg. St John   *Register of the Hospital of S. John the Baptist without the New Gate, Dublin*, ed. Eric St John Brooks (IMC, Dublin, 1936)

Reg. St Thomas   *Register of the abbey of St Thomas, Dublin*, ed. J.T. Gilbert (London, 1889)

Rep. DKPRI   *Reports of the deputy keeper of the public records in Ireland* (Dublin, 1869–)

RIA   Royal Irish Academy

RLC   *Rotuli litterarum clausarum, 1204–24 [etc.]*, ed. T.D. Hardy, 2 vols (London, 1833–44)

SGAC   Elizabeth Boyle and Liam Breatnach (eds), '*Senchas Gall Átha Cliath*: aspects of the cult of St Patrick in the twelfth century' in John Carey, Kevin Murray and Caitríona Ó Dochartaigh (eds), *Sacred histories: a festschrift for Máire Herbert* (Dublin, 2015), pp 22–55

Stat. rolls Ire. Edw. IV, i
             Statute rolls of the parliament of Ireland: 1st to 12th of King Edward IV, ed. H.F. Berry (Dublin, 1914)

Stat. rolls Ire. Edw. IV, ii
             Statute rolls of the parliament of Ireland: 12th & 13th to 21st & 22nd of King Edward IV, ed. James Morrissey (Dublin, 1939)

Stat. rolls Ire. Hen. VI
             Statute rolls of the parliament of Ireland: reign of King Henry VI, ed. by H.F. Berry (Dublin, 1910)

Stat. rolls Ire. Ric. III to Hen. VIII
             Statute rolls of the Irish parliament: Richard III–Henry VIII, ed. Philomena Connolly (Dublin, 2002)

TNA   The National Archives of the United Kingdom [including former PRO], Kew

Contributors

EDEL BHREATHNACH, who recently retired as CEO of the Discovery Programme, specializes in medieval Irish dynastic politics and monasticism.

DENIS CASEY holds a PhD from the University of Cambridge and is based at the Centre for Teaching and Learning, Maynooth University.

BRIAN COLEMAN is a civil servant and holds a PhD in medieval history from Trinity College Dublin.

PAUL DUFFY is a licensed archaeologist, working with Irish Archaeological Consultancy Ltd, and has excavated extensively in Dublin and elsewhere.

ANTOINE GIACOMETTI is a project manager with Archaeology Plan, Dublin.

LORCAN HARNEY has a specialism in early Irish ecclesiastical settlement and is a primary school teacher in Celbridge, Co. Kildare.

ALAN R. HAYDEN is an archaeological consultant and director of Archaeological Projects Ltd.

RANDOLPH JONES is an independent scholar, based in England, who has an interest in medieval Ireland.

MARK LAWLER is associate pro-vice-chancellor and Professor of Digital Health at Queen's University, Belfast; he is a nephew of the late Cllr John Gallagher.

JOHN NICHOLL is an independent researcher, leather finds specialist and experimental archaeologist.

THOMAS W. SMITH teaches history at Rugby School and is a fellow of the Royal Historical Society; he has published extensively on medieval ecclesiastical history and the Crusades.

JOHN WILLIAM SULLIVAN is an MA student at the University of St Andrews, and a former Erasmus exchange student in Trinity College Dublin.

CAOIMHE WHELAN is a research fellow at the Trinity Long Room Hub and honorary secretary of the Friends of Medieval Dublin.

Editor's preface

The year 2020 will live long in our memory, mostly for the wrong reasons. A minor casualty of this calamitous year has been the Medieval Dublin Symposium in Trinity College, which has been an annual May fixture for more than twenty years. We can only hope that 2021 offers fairer prospects and that, as life returns to normal, the delayed Symposium and other events habitually organized by the Friends of Medieval Dublin may proceed.

In the meantime, the Friends have been active in what is now called the digital space. Instead of the free walking tours of medieval Dublin previously held during Heritage Week, this year the Friends curated a number of 'virtual' walks in the form of playlists on the new 'Friends of Medieval Dublin' YouTube channel: https://www.youtube.com/channel/UCzbBWNoDdk1ly 631QfYF2KQ. The tours comprise short videos in which guides explore various locations in the city such as the site of the original *Dubh Linn*, or Dublin Castle, or Ship St, Castle St, Fishamble St, Cook St, and Lamb Alley, or Christ Church Cathedral, St John's Church, St Audoen's Church, and Isolde's Tower. We also have a tour dedicated to the city walls and another which transports the viewer to sites in County Dublin such as Rathfarnham Castle, Dundrum Castle and Drimnagh Castle.

These tours allow you to explore medieval Dublin without having to leave your own home and more content will be added over the coming months. So, I encourage you to subscribe to our channel (for free) to be notified of additional material. And I would like to thank all those members of the Friends who put so much effort into making, editing and uploading the videos. You can also watch our Q&A initiative, 'Ask a Friend (of Medieval Dublin)', also organized for Heritage Week 2020. In this video series, members of the Friends record answers to questions posed by the public on a wide array of matters to do with life in the medieval city. This can be seen on our twitter, @FMDublin, and our Facebook page: www.facebook.com/MedievalDublin. Those curious for more will see that the Friends also spent part of the lockdown creating a short quiz on medieval Dublin packed with reading suggestions and links to podcasts to help you learn more about the medieval city: https://qz.app.do/medieval-dublin-quiz. Details of all of the above are available on our website: http://fmd.ie/

For those who prefer rather more traditional fare we offer the present volume of papers, many of which originate in lectures given at our Medieval Dublin Symposium. Quite a number of the papers that follow have an ecclesiastical theme. Lorcan Harney examines early medieval ecclesiastical enclosures in Dublin and its hinterland as part of a major study of such sites nationwide, work that is sure to be a vital reference-point for years to come. Edel Bhreathnach studies the saints and Biblical figures to whom Dublin's churches were dedicated, to see what this tells us about the pre-Viking church there and how Christianization developed among the Hiberno-Norse of the city and suburbs. The internationally-acclaimed papal historian, Thomas W. Smith, turns his attention to Rome's intrusion into the affairs of the archdiocese of Dublin in the thirteenth century, while the up-an-coming young American scholar, John William Sullivan IV, looks again at the peculiar phenomenon of medieval Dublin's two cathedrals, pondering whether they may have served distinct functions in terms of Dubliners' lived religious experience.

What has been known for many years as Kevin Street Garda Station was in fact the archbishop's palace of St Sepulchre, and Alan Hayden was recently able to conduct archaeological investigations on both the grounds and the fabric of the building, the results of which may require a radical rethink of what the original palace looked like, and of how much of it survives. Paul Duffy also investigated part of the grounds of another of medieval Dublin's great ecclesiastical complexes, the abbey of St Thomas the Martyr, where he discovered, along the line of Thomas Street, much evidence for medieval tanneries, and this activity is reflected too in the report by Antoine Giacometti, also presented below, on one of the largest tanning complexes ever discovered in Ireland or Britain, which he unearthed in the area that still bears its name, Blackpitts.

Both these sites give an insight into an important industry – the production of leather – and so it is most appropriate that this volume also contains an analysis, by John Nicholl, of one of the largest collections of late-medieval footwear ever uncovered in Ireland, from a site in Chancery Lane. Such commercial activity is but one facet of economic life in the medieval city and therefore featured below is a ground-breaking study by Denis Casey of what exactly it was that constituted the economy of Dublin in the period immediately preceding the English conquest in 1170.

Among the descendants of those new English settlers were the Marewards, discussed by Randolph Jones below, who typified many a late-medieval nouveau riche family working their way up among the urban elite, to the extent of becoming mayor of Dublin, before marrying into the rural gentry of the hinterland in subsequent generations. They are precisely the class of individual elected to collect parliamentary taxes in Co. Dublin in the late Middle Ages and Brian Coleman investigates such county officials below. This is no doubt the English-speaking audience for whose entertainment – and perhaps for whose subtle political purposes – tales such as that of Tristan and Isolde were composed, which Caoimhe Whelan brilliantly explores in this volume.

The Symposia from which these papers emerge enjoyed capacity audiences of up to 200 members of the public, admission being entirely free, thanks to the contribution to costs by the Department of History, Trinity College, to whom the editor is exceedingly grateful. Similarly, it has only proved possible to publish this eighteenth volume in the *Medieval Dublin* series because of the ongoing commitment to the project by Dublin City Council. Here it is a pleasure to acknowledge the support of the City Heritage Officer, Charles Duggan, and the ceaseless encouragement of the City Archaeologist, Dr Ruth Johnson. The entire series has been published by Four Courts Press for whose collaboration the Friends of Medieval Dublin remain most grateful and the editor would like to thank Martin Fanning for the meticulous attention to detail which has characterized his work on the papers below. As we were going to press, news emerged of the death with Covid-19 of that indefatigable champion of Dublin's heritage, Cllr John Gallagher of The Coombe, and it is an honour to dedicate this volume to his memory.

SEÁN DUFFY
Chairman
Friends of Medieval Dublin

Councillor John Gallagher
Legend of the Liberties
(1933–2020)

On 29 March 2020, the people of the Liberties of Dublin lost their greatest hero, when John Gallagher sadly passed away. John was the colossus of the Coombe: one picture in a newspaper from the 1980s shows him outside the Liberties Community Information Centre on Patrick Street corner, with the caption 'JOHN GALLAGHER … as well known in the Liberties as Alfie Byrne [lord mayor, 1930–9] used to be in Dublin'. John's community work in the area was legendary, from the vital support delivered freely and wholeheartedly through the Liberties Community Information Centre to the St Nicholas of Myra Community Centre, which he set up over twenty-five years ago and which was a haven for the people of the Liberties, from dawn to dusk, and whether they were aged 3 or 103.

John Gallagher was not just a great campaigner for the people of the area in his fight against poverty, inequality and the scourge of drugs, he was also a powerful advocate for the area's heritage and culture. In 1979, he joined fellow activists including Fr F.X. Martin of the Friends of Medieval Dublin in defying a court order and occupying the Wood Quay site – the famous 'Operation Sitric' – to protect Dublin's Viking heritage from the short-sighted bulldozing mentality of Dublin Corporation. John was the last protestor to leave the site (even defying a second court order!), defending Dublin's heritage to the last. Ultimately, though, a great opportunity to preserve one of the most significant Viking settlements in Europe was missed, a disaster for our heritage and a great loss too in terms of Wood Quay's unrivalled tourism potential, something John emphasized at the time. One anecdote shared following John's sad passing highlights his hands-on involvement, and also his humour; in recalling his Wood Quay exploits, John remarked, 'You know what I learned when they arrested me, Jennifer? It's very hard to run fast and jump a fence when you have a crowbar in your belt!'

But John and his fellow protesters had the last laugh. The local elections in 1979 led to the people of Dublin kicking out the then Lord Mayor, Paddy Belton, and other councillors who had supported Dublin Corporation's anti-heritage philosophy. And through John's work with An Taisce, our heritage was not wholly lost, a good example being the restoration of Tailors' Hall off High Street in the Liberties (the 300-year-old home of the guild of tailors). Ironically, given his opposition to 'The Corpo' at the time, in 1999 John would be elected by the people of the Liberties to be their representative on what would soon be renamed Dublin City Council.

John Gallagher was also a Green before his time. He refused to use election posters because of their negative effect on the environment. Besides, the people of the Liberties didn't need a picture of John on a lamppost to know who he was and what he stood for, and they duly re-elected him as a poll topper in 2004 and 2009. His fellow councillors recognized his tireless work for the community and his integrity and elected him Deputy Lord Mayor in 2007. And that integrity was all encompassing. John regarded it as an honour to represent the people of the area and quietly but firmly refused to claim any daily expenses during his fifteen years on the City Council.

One of John's key areas of focus was on the young people of the Liberties. He gave them opportunities they would otherwise never have had. The Dublin Inner City Games allowed boys and girls to show their sporting athleticism in College Park, many of whom had never set foot inside Trinity College before. The Liberties Majorettes and a series of drama clubs gave youngsters an opportunity to display their talents, and some would go on to become stars of stage and screen (Imelda May being among those to remember him in a lovely tribute).

John Gallagher was a man of the people – everything he did in his life was to help people, and in particular the people of the Liberties whom he loved. And boy did they love him. The depth of emotion that arose when he died, particularly over social media, with countless messages and memories from far and wide shows that he had a very special place in the hearts of the people. The only regret was that all who loved and knew him couldn't be physically in the same place to pay tribute to a true colossus of the Liberties. But don't worry, when this public health crisis abates, there will be a celebration of John's life that will rival the funeral of Daniel O'Connell!

MARK LAWLER
8 September 2020

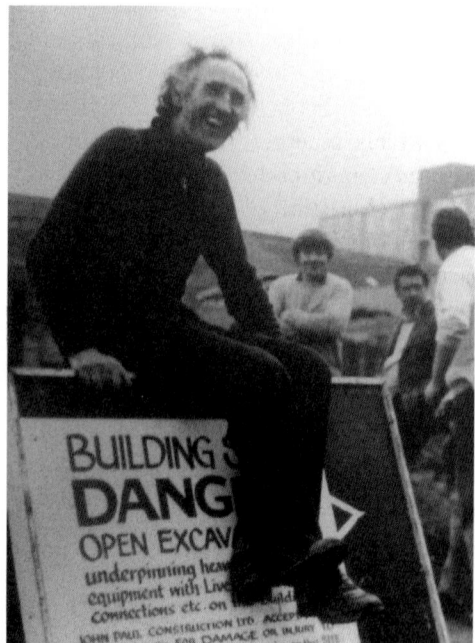

John Gallagher during
the Wood Quay
occupation, 1979.

The early medieval ecclesiastical enclosures of Dublin: exploring their character, chronology and evolving function in light of excavations across Ireland

LORCAN HARNEY

This study reviews the extensive archaeological excavation evidence for early medieval ecclesiastical enclosures both in Dublin and across Ireland to shed new light about their form and chronology. It establishes that ecclesiastical enclosures were primarily a feature of the early Christian period (sixth-to-ninth century) and that their layout was inspired by ancient canons of settlement organization, such as espoused in the eighth-century *Collectio canonum Hibernensis*. In addition, it reveals that ecclesiastical enclosure ditches were often larger than their counterparts on ringforts and cemetery settlements and that where multivallation occurs (the construction of two or more concentric enclosures), these tend to be constructed over time rather than built at the same time. The study tentatively posits a putative relationship between the decline of enclosure construction and a possible increase in the use of the inner *sanctum* cemetery space for craft activities in the later part of the early Middle Ages, as more functional concerns may have replaced an ideological desire to adhere to a prescribed enclosed organizational settlement *schema* in this period.

INTRODUCTION

It is widely accepted and commonly known that enclosures were integral features of both ecclesiastical and settlement sites in early medieval Ireland. These ecclesiastical enclosures primarily consisted of an external ditch and an internal earthen bank, but enclosures of stone occasionally occurred, particularly in western areas. Significantly, many of these ecclesiastical enclosures have been archaeologically investigated in recent decades (see Appendix). Despite all this considerable excavation, it must be noted that many of these excavations have yet to be published in detail, and that few studies have collated and reviewed the entire corpus of excavated ecclesiastical enclosures to explore trends and patterns from church sites nationally. It is fair to say that there has been much discussion about their function and origins (e.g., Doherty 1985; Swan 1985; Jenkins 2010), yet we have still much to learn about the character, form and chronologies of these enclosing elements, whether these enclosures were a fundamental aspect of these sites throughout the early medieval period (fifth-to-twelfth century) and how or why their role and function may have evolved over these many centuries.

This study seeks to address these research deficits: based on an extensive review of the excavation evidence, it has identified a provisional list of 126 ecclesiastical sites with potential early medieval enclosing features (table 1.1 and fig. 1.1); this does not include field- or internal-divisions or church sites where just a geophysical survey took place. As many of these enclosures have not been dated closely, a more detailed review of unpublished literature will be required in time to tighten up this dataset. Of these identified 126 church sites, the highest concentration is in Co. Dublin with 18 (14%), with other notable clusters in south-east Ulster, the Dublin commuter belt counties and Wexford and Kilkenny. Based on available sources – principally www.excavations.ie; published literature, and some unpublished reports – this study has compiled a catalogue (see Appendix below) which summarizes the information about these ecclesiastical enclosures (site location, enclosure size, form, chronology and dating evidence) as revealed in excavations.

The information from this provisional catalogue demonstrates that these ecclesiastical enclosures were primarily a feature of the 'early Christian' period – traditionally assigned to the period from the fifth to eighth century – and that these enclosing elements underwent much change before most gradually became obsolete in the later early medieval period. The study concludes with a short discussion on a few related topics – the evolution of the concept of 'ecclesiastical enclosure' in early medieval times, how enclosure construction was intimately bound up with the articulation of ritual and power on church sites, and how changing perceptions of cemetery space and craftwork zones may have ensured that church enclosures became increasingly obsolete towards the end of the early medieval period.

Table 1.1 Ecclesiastical sites with excavated evidence for potential early medieval enclosures

	Church Name	County	EASTING	NORTHING
1	Aghavea	Fermanagh	637494	838255
2	Ardfert	Kerry	478557	621182
3	Ardreigh	Kildare	668755	692463
4	Armagh	Armagh	687493	845243
5	Armoy	Antrim	707708	933233
6	Ballykilmore	Westmeath	641792	737279
7	Balrothery	Dublin	719867	761198
8	Butterfield	Dublin	713330	728459
9	Caherlehillan	Kerry	457218	583594

	Church Name	County	EASTING	NORTHING
10	Carns	Roscommon	583182	778297
11	Church Island	Kerry	442995	578627
12	Church of St Canice	Kilkenny	650249	656424
13	Church of St Michan	Dublin	714806	734311
14	Church of St Patrick	Kilkenny	650763	655438
15	Clonfad	Westmeath	640463	740568
16	Clonfert	Galway	595870	719500
17	Clonmacnoise	Offaly	600940	730668
18	Connor	Antrim	714927	896891
19	Dalkey Island	Dublin	727682	726422
20	Derryloran	Tyrone	679946	876746
21	Derrynaflan	Tipperary	610748	649045
22	Doras	Tyrone	681434	867798
23	Downpatrick	Down	748220	844502
24	Drumcliffe South	Sligo	567899	842058
25	Drumkay	Wicklow	731240	694282
26	Dunmisk	Tyrone	662738	870597
27	Dunshaughlin	Meath	696890	752584
28	Finglas	Dublin	713097	738860
29	Friar's Island	Clare	570582	671981
30	Glendalough	Wicklow	712258	696822
31	High Island	Galway	450154	757371
32	Illaunloughan	Kerry	436630	573137
33	Kells	Meath	673927	775906
34	Kilgobbin	Dublin	718924	724351
35	Kilhorne	Down	736922	819067
36	Kilkieran	Kilkenny	654329	660911
37	Kill St Lawrence	Waterford	661219	609215
38	Killeany	Laois	636781	687973
39	Killederdadrum	Tipperary	594752	672150
40	Killeen Demesne	Meath	693156	754930
41	Killegland	Meath	705823	751960
42	Kilmore	Armagh	694251	851161
43	Kilpatrick	Westmeath	657477	755892
44	Kiltiernan	Galway	543662	715620
45	Lorrha	Tipperary	591948	704552
46	Lusk	Dublin	721521	754467
47	Maghera	Down	737122	834105
48	Mullagh	Cavan	668171	785443
49	Nendrum	Down	752359	863628

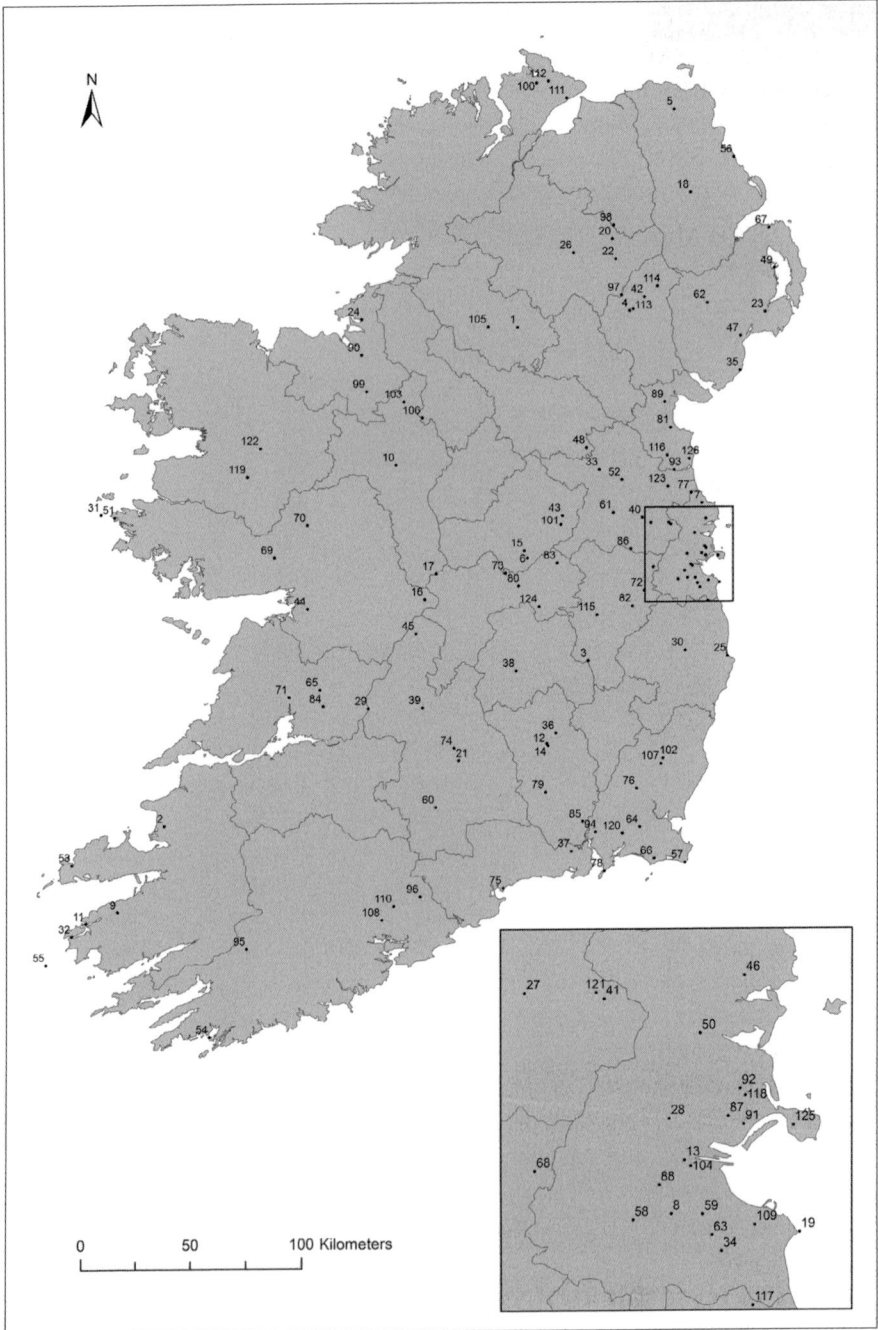

1.1 Map of Ireland showing the location of excavated ecclesiastical enclosures (numbers correspond with site names in table 1.1)

	Church Name	County	EASTING	NORTHING
50	Oldtown/Mooretown	Dublin	716582	748167
51	Omey Island	Galway	456304	756113
52	Randalstown	Meath	684070	771468
53	Reask	Kerry	436691	604405
54	Skeam West	Cork	498919	528920
55	Skellig Michael	Kerry	424803	560805
56	Solar	Antrim	734322	912188
57	St Vogue's	Wexford	711991	604070
58	Tallaght	Dublin	709024	727797
59	Taney	Dublin	716819	728414
60	Toureen Peakaun	Tipperary	600471	628590
61	Trim	Meath	680134	757189
62	Tullylish	Down	722225	848602
63	Balally	Dublin	717863	726097
64	Taghmon	Wexford	691788	619700
65	Tulla	Clare	548882	680189
66	Grange (Kilmore)	Wexford	698154	605944
67	Bangor	Down	749995	881190
68	Donaghcumper	Kildare	698014	733175
69	Annaghdown	Galway	528696	738107
70	Tuam	Galway	543648	752159
71	Doora	Clare	535300	677090
72	Kill	Kildare	694033	722899
73	Durrow	Offaly	632013	730711
74	Holycross	Tipperary	608718	654487
75	Kilgrovan	Waterford	630820	593225
76	Rossdroit	Wexford	690393	636610
77	Stamullin	Meath	714920	765744
78	Portersgate	Wexford	676000	600539
79	Aghaviller	Kilkenny	649677	635125
80	Cappancur	Offaly	637880	725125
81	Kilsaran	Louth	705843	794083
82	Killashee	Kildare	688748	716214
83	Ballyburley	Offaly	655137	735133
84	Clonlea	Clare	550315	673112
85	Graiguenakill	Kilkenny	666235	622158
86	Balfeaghan	Meath	687946	741142
87	Coolock	Dublin	719697	739096
88	Crumlin	Dublin	711962	731601

	Church Name	County	EASTING	NORTHING
89	Ballybarrack	Louth	703299	805221
90	Collooney	Sligo	567868	826450
91	Raheny	Dublin	721437	738213
92	St Doulagh's	Dublin	721035	742141
93	Loughboy	Louth	707235	775650
94	Kilmokea	Wexford	671995	617583
95	Kilmore	Cork	515982	567192
96	Ballynoe	Cork	593482	589665
97	Clonfeacle	Tyrone	683913	852041
98	Tullynure	Derry	680534	882794
99	Drumrat	Sligo	570064	810404
100	Carndonagh	Donegal	646239	944988
101	Glebe	Westmeath	656771	751863
102	Ferns	Wexford	702185	649758
103	Kilteasheen	Roscommon	586793	805795
104	Church of St Peter	Dublin	715512	733667
105	Cleenish	Fermanagh	624297	838498
106	Attirory	Leitrim	595049	798794
107	Clone	Wexford	701355	647389
108	Kilquane	Cork	576447	579559
109	Kill of the Grange	Dublin	722634	727250
110	Killamurren	Cork	581791	585577
111	Cooley	Donegal	659781	938370
112	Carrowmore	Donegal	651528	945749
113	Killuney	Armagh	689171	846055
114	Drumcree	Armagh	699974	855814
115	Kildare	Kildare	672798	712492
116	Monasterboice	Louth	704279	782071
117	Monastery	Wicklow	722421	718416
118	Balgriffin Park	Dublin	721611	741384
119	Kilkeeran	Mayo	516426	773532
120	Clongeen	Wexford	684087	616900
121	Cookstown	Meath	704900	752641
122	Creaghanboy	Mayo	522402	785928
123	Duleek	Meath	704502	768479
124	Sranure	Offaly	647089	716116
125	Sutton North	Dublin	726982	738079
126	Termonfeckin	Louth	714098	780473

THE CHARACTER AND FORM OF IRISH ECCLESIASTICAL ENCLOSURES

Exploring the shape and dimensions of ecclesiastical enclosures
Curvilinear enclosures were as integral an element of early church sites as they were for contemporary secular ringforts – the most ubiquitous field monument in the Irish landscape today. Church sites defined by one enclosing element are most common and these are invariably circular or oval-shaped in form with a church and cemetery, among other features, located in the interior. There is a general assumption that they are large, but in fact they vary in size, though most have diameters slightly or often considerably larger than the average ringfort (*c*.35–45m). For example, many small peninsular Kerry church sites have diameters around the same size as an average ringfort (see Cuppage 1986; O'Sullivan and Sheehan 1996), while some small-to-medium-sized church sites are broadly similar in size to contemporary cemetery settlements (O'Sullivan et al. 2014, 309–10), often measuring 50–80m in diameter. For example, the univallate enclosure at Ballykilmore had a projected internal diameter of 70m (Channing 2012, 85), while the Armoy boundary ditch measured 50m–60m by *c*.80m (Nelis et al. 2007, 111). Swan's (1983, 274) analysis has, however, indicated that the enclosure of a typical Irish ecclesiastical site was slightly larger again (roughly 90–120m in diameter), but that some of the most important church sites were substantially bigger, often boasting inner enclosures of up to 200m in diameter and concentric outer enclosures of up to 500m across (Swan 1985, 97).

This double enclosure arrangement is depicted in the later eighth-century *Book of Mulling* colophon (Henry 1965, 81) (see fig. 1.2), while the early eighth-century *Collectio canonum Hibernensis* describes a triple enclosure plan where church sites were organized according to defined spaces of increasing sanctity – *sanctus, sanctior* and *sanctissimus* (Doherty 1982, 302). Nendrum (Lawlor 1925; McErlean 2007, 335), Kilmacoo (Norman and St Joseph 1969, 66), Durrow (O'Brien 2012, 120) and probably Clonfad (Stevens 2006, 9; 2012, 120–24) are rare examples of ecclesiastical sites defined by trivallate enclosures, as described in the *Hibernensis*. The inner, middle and outermost enclosures at Nendrum (fig. 1.3) measured *c*.76m, 122m and 183m respectively (Edwards 1990, 107) and roughly similar dimensions of 180m by 150m have been posited for the outer enclosure at Killeany (Wiggins 2006, 33–5) and Toureen Peakaun (Ó Carragáin 2007:1738). Similarly, Clonfad's innermost enclosure measured 47–50m in diameter; outside it was the middle enclosure ditch (*c*.100–110m in diameter) and the outer enclosure ditch with an estimated diameter of 180–200m (Stevens 2006, 9; 2012, 117). Others are larger again; for example, Ó Drisceoil (2013, 35, 39) suggests that Kilkenny was defined by an inner enclosure with dimensions of *c*.110m and an outer enclosure of 270m

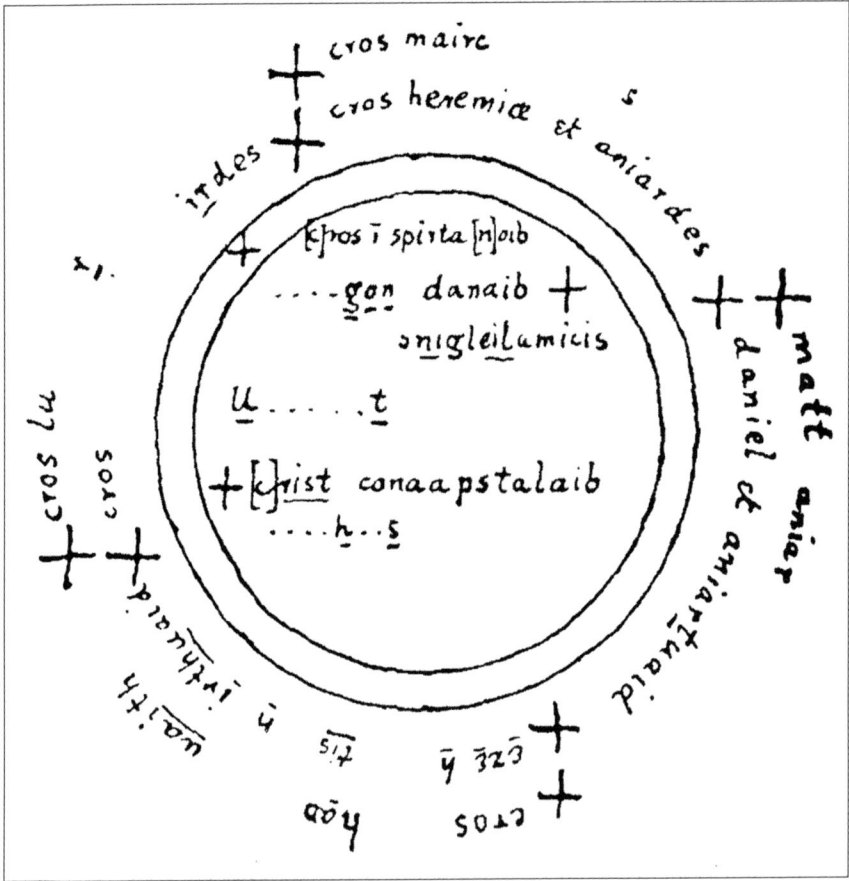

1.2 Suggested layout of an early medieval ecclesiastical enclosure, as depicted in the *Book of Mulling*, an Irish pocket gospel book dating to the late eighth century (Lawlor 1894–5, 37)

by 185m, while field and geophysical survey at Durrow has established that its outer enclosure (*c.*300m by 400m) contained about 30 acres (O'Brien 2012, 120). So, even a brief analysis reveals the scale and diversity of these features, and the large areas intended for enclosure, well beyond anything found in contemporary secular sites.

In Wales (Edwards 1996, 55–6; Ludlow 2009, 71–6; Silvester and Evans 2009, 22–31) and western Scotland (Smith 1996, 29; Blair 2005, 198; Lowe 2008, 250–2), large concentric enclosures resembling Irish multivallate church sites are also known. While curvilinear enclosures defining Anglo-Saxon minsters rarely survive in England, their outlines can sometimes be inferred in boundaries or road systems and typically measure 150–300m in diameter (Blair 2005, 198; Jenkins 2010, 48–9; Gittos 2011, 829). This evidence suggests that the supposedly distinctive Irish curvilinear ecclesiastical enclosure may have

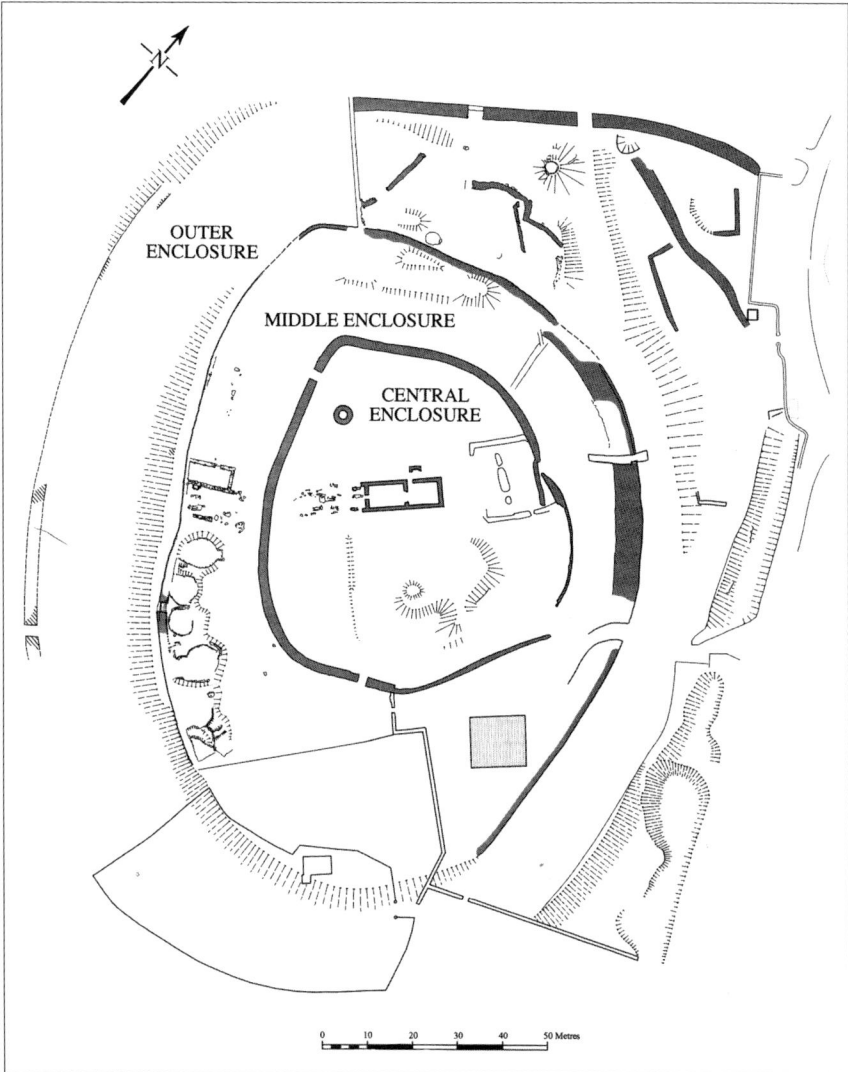

1.3 Plan of Nendrum showing its triple enclosure walled layout (J. Patience and D. Wilkinson, after McErlean 2007, 336)

been more common across Britain than traditionally assumed. However, many other Anglo-Saxon and Pictish church sites were organized according to square or rectilinear plans (Hall 2000, 77), perhaps based upon the prototype of the heavenly Jerusalem of Revelations with its square walls and gates (Smith 1996, 29–34; Blair 2005, 196). In Ireland, Thomas (1971, 29–32) has made the case for Irish rectangular-shaped ecclesiastical enclosures at Inch, Co. Down and Clonmacnoise, but more recent excavation and survey work suggests the

Inch example was associated with a later Cistercian abbey (Hamlin 1977, 85–7) and Clonmacnoise's enclosure had a more semi-circular shape (Murphy 2003, 21). However, we should note that rectangular stone enclosures are occasionally present and that these can sometimes represent the inner enclosing element as at Tulla (Myles 2012:086), Caher Island and Glaspatrick, Co. Mayo and High Island (Corlett 2014, 59). This evidence for a rectangular focal enclosure within a larger circular enclosure may then represent a building tradition unique to this western area or was perhaps simply informed by local topographic constraints.

Exploring the character and size of the enclosing element
These curvilinear enclosures on both secular and ecclesiastical sites were invariably defined by an internal bank and external ditch, or more rarely stone wall. Internal ditches and external banks are much rarer and more characteristic of prehistoric monuments such as ring-ditches – the presence of potential inner ditches at Lusk perhaps (O'Connell 2014, 178–80), Lullymore (Leigh 2016) and Armagh (Gaskell-Brown and Harper 1984, 109, 112–17, 156–9) could then indicate that these exceptional sites reused or were modelled on prehistoric ritual enclosures. There is much variation in the size of these enclosures on both secular and ecclesiastical sites. Although some ringforts like Béal Boru, Garryduff I and Rathbeg were defined by substantial banks and ditches (O'Sullivan et al. 2010, 57–8), the enclosure ditches of most ringforts 'seldom rise above 3m in width and 2m in depth' (Edwards 1990, 20). Some ecclesiastical enclosure ditches have broadly similar dimensions to ringfort ditches, but most cluster at the higher end, usually 2–4m wide and 1–2m deep. Such middle-range enclosure ditches are present, for example, at Maghera, Kilpatrick, Ballykilmore, Killederdadrum, Randalstown, Doras, Killeany, Killegland, Killeen Demesne and Clonfad (see Appendix), as well as at the Scottish sites at Hoddom (Lowe 2006, 32) and Inchmarnock (Lowe 2008, 85).

Some enclosure ditches were even shallower (<1m deep), and these probably may have had little functional use beyond symbolically defining the site boundaries (see Appendix). This was the case at Killeany whose small central cemetery area was marked by a ditch 1m wide and 0.5m deep (Wiggins 2006, 33–5). Other ecclesiastical enclosures were much wider but were still less than 1m deep, and on their own, these ditches would have had little functional or defensive use. Examples include the main ecclesiastical enclosure ditch (4) at Aghavea (3m wide x 0.8m deep) (Ó Baoill 2000, 15), the enclosure ditch at Kill St Lawrence (6m wide x 0.74m deep) (O'Connell 2004, 27, 39–43, 61), the inner ecclesiastical enclosure at St Canice's Cathedral, Kilkenny (6m wide x 0.9m) (Ó Drisceoil 2013, 36) and a ditched feature (*c.*4.6–5.9m wide x *c.*0.4–1m deep) at Lusk, which may have formed part of the outer ecclesiastical enclosure on the site (Moore 2001:448; Baker 2001:449; 2001, 5–7, 22).

However, excavations have shown that many other church sites were defined by wide, deep ditches measuring 4–7m wide and 2–4m deep. The digging of these enclosure ditches would have required access to, and control over, a great labour force and these naturally then tend to be found at important sites like Iona, Tullylish, Finglas, Tallaght, Lorrha, Armagh, Clonmacnoise and Glendalough (see Appendix) – indeed, the latter three church sites have revealed enclosure ditches of 6.4m wide and up to 3m deep (Gaskell-Brown and Harper 1984, 109, 112–17, 156–8), 5–6.2m wide and 3.8m deep (Murphy 2003, 16, 19) and *c.*8m wide and under 2m deep (Conor McDermott, pers. comm.) respectively. Like secular enclosed sites, the profile of ecclesiastical enclosure ditches could be V-shaped or U-shaped with flat or rounded bottoms. However, a V-shaped profile has often been revealed in many middle-to-large enclosure ditches, as were excavated at Armagh, Clonfad, Clonmacnoise, Doras, Kill St Lawrence, Ballykilmore, Downpatrick, Lusk, Kells, Taney, Killederdadrum and Maghera (see Appendix). These V-shaped ditches would have provided an effective deterrent from wandering livestock and also enemy attacks, if accompanied by internal banks and palisades.

Although both the enclosing ditches and banks of thousands of early medieval ringforts still survive, there is often little visible evidence for the enclosing ditches and banks of ecclesiastical sites today. Based on the paucity of this evidence, McCormick (1997, 51) suggested that ecclesiastical sites were generally enclosed by ditches (now generally infilled), rather than ditches and banks, implying that the upcast from these ditches must have been spread across the site's interior or exterior, rather than being used to create an internal bank. However, there is some good evidence to suggest that many ecclesiastical enclosure ditches were accompanied by internal banks constructed from the external ditch upcast. This evidence can often be inferred by the absence of features along the inner edge of enclosing ditches or the evidence for redeposited soil within the interior of the excavated ditches (see Appendix).

Traces of actual internal banks with stone-lined façades have been detected at Kilpatrick (Swan 1976, 90; 1997, 11–14), Tallaght (McConway 1994:102; 1994, 4–7, 12–13; Walsh 1997, 6–16, 25), St Vogue's (O'Kelly 1975, 23–4) and Killederdadrum (Manning 1984, 242), with the latter bank surviving to a height of 0.7m and width of 3m. Other church sites with traces of internal enclosure banks include Clonfad (Stevens 2012, 120–4), St Canice's, Kilkenny (Gittins 2002:1006; Ó Drisceoil 2006:1062; 2013, 9–10, 36), Ballykilmore (Channing 2012, 89), Kells (Byrne 1988, 9–10), Drumkay (O'Donovan 2014, 196), Tulla (Myles 2012:086), Kill of the Grange (Duffy 2018:634) and Dunshaughlin, where the bank was indicated by a series of redeposited clays along its internal side (Simpson 2005, 233–4). Most of these banks were clearly built from upcast from an accompanying external enclosure ditch, but some of these banks were stone- or timber-revetted (see Appendix) to prevent soil

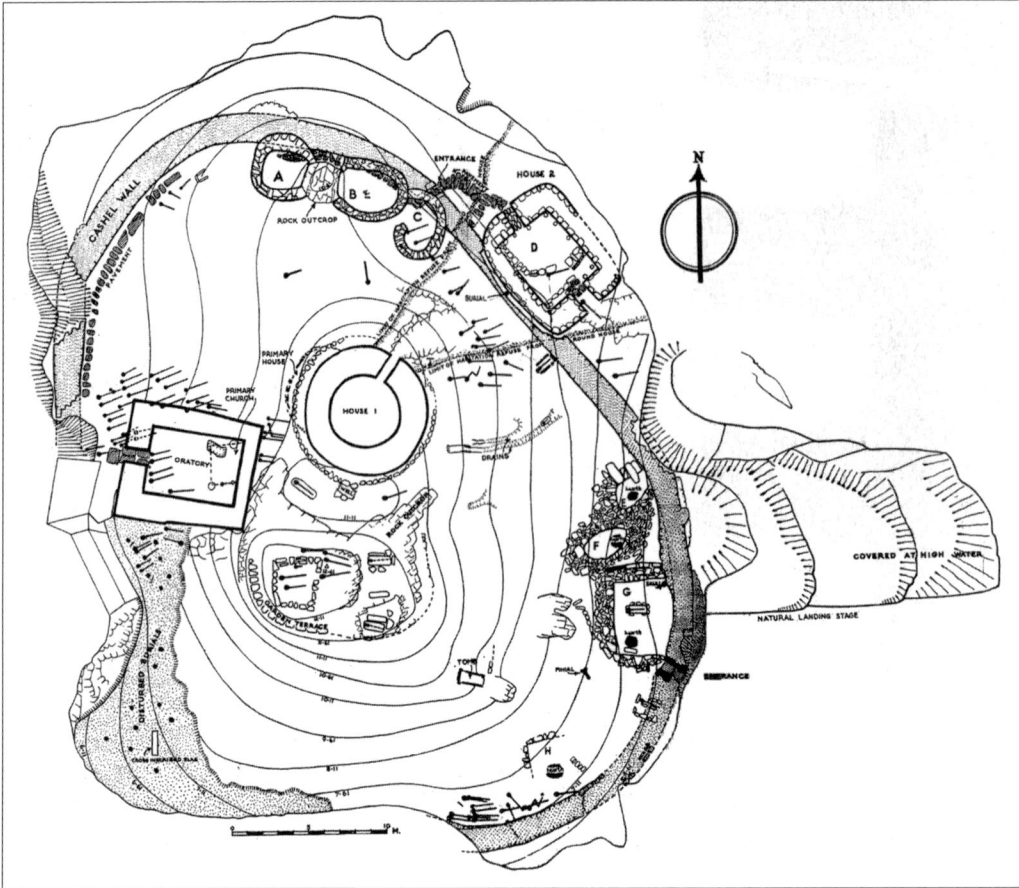

1.4 Plan of Church Island showing the 'cashel' wall enclosing almost the entire footprint of the small island (after O'Kelly 1958, plate XVII)

slippage into the ditch or internal *les* (the enclosed area within). These enclosure ditches and banks, then, display much variability in size and form.

Stone walls were used to enclose some church sites, particularly in western regions, but examples survive across the country as illustrated with the triple-enclosure 'cashel' at Nendrum (fig. 1.3). These walls varied in terms of their size and scale, but like secular cashels, the majority were stone-faced on either side of a rubble core (see Appendix). At Church Island, Co. Kerry (fig. 1.4), the wall (2m wide and up to 1m high) enclosed almost the complete habitable part of the island (O'Kelly 1958). The walls at Reask and Carns (Shanahan 2006, 7; McNeary and Shanahan 2009, 131) were also 2m thick, with the former surviving up to five or six courses high (Fanning 1981, 98–100), while the High Island enclosure was defined by a substantial wall containing inter-mural chambers (Marshall and Rourke 2000, 55–9; Scally 2015, 124).

1.5 Aerial view of the excavations at Taney looking south-east showing the complex of enclosures and other features (after O'Donovan 2012, 11, fig. 1.2)

Wooden palisades have also been excavated on both enclosed secular and ecclesiastical sites, but to a much lesser extent. These palisades were mostly accompanied by enclosure banks or ditches as found at Aghavea, where one enclosure ditch (3) was associated with an internal palisade trench running 0.40m parallel to it (Ó Baoill 2000, 12–13). Again, at Armoy, a parallel gully on the inner side of the original enclosure ditch was possibly intended as a palisade slot-trench (Nelis et al. 2007, 33–5; Nelis, McSparron and Gormley 2014, 149), while excavations at Cooley revealed that a palisade trench was potentially inserted into the actual stone-lined ditch base (Adams and O'Brien 2016:288). The sterile and homogenous nature of the ditch fills at Cooley suggests that they derived from the upcast of a now obliterated internal bank meaning that this site was defined by a bank, ditch and palisade as has been revealed in excavations at the seventh-century Northumbrian church of Hoddom (Lowe 2006, 32–8, 172).

Not all palisades, however, were associated with ditches or banks. Excavations at Toureen Peakaun revealed a palisaded structure on the inner side of a natural palaeochannel that initially defined the north-eastern side of the church site (Ó Carragáin 2006:1929; 2007:1738; 2008:1167). The footings for a palisade were also identified within the base of a gully to the north-east of

Clonfeacle ecclesiastical site, and it was suggested that it 'formed part of an early, outer enclosure of the monastery' (McHugh, Bell and MacDonald 2004, 60–2). Furthermore, it is interesting that the excavations at Taney (O'Donovan 2012, 32) and possibly Drumkay (O'Donovan 2014, 196) revealed timber palisades that pre-dated the early medieval enclosure ditches and appear to have been constructed to delineate these sites' boundaries when they were first established. At Taney (fig. 1.5), a small later seventh-/eighth-century palisaded enclosure (*c.*20–5m in diameter) was succeeded by a series of larger eighth- to tenth-century ditches enclosing the entire church site (O'Donovan 2012, 32). An early medieval cemetery apparently enclosed within a palisaded trench was also revealed in Rathfarnham (Butterfield Avenue) (Carroll 1997:184), but the ecclesiastical association of this site is far from certain. The palisades at Taney, Aghavea, Armoy and possibly Drumkay all had relatively small enclosing dimensions and it is then possible that timber palisades were more suited for defining the innermost precincts of church sites, than the much more substantial outer enclosing elements.

Symbolically defining sanctuary space on early medieval church sites
Most ecclesiastical sites were then defined by one or more curvilinear enclosures of ditches, banks or walls, which physically and legally demarcated the boundaries of the *termonn*, the area within the settlement in which right of sanctuary prevailed. However, we should briefly consider the possibility that the *termonn* was occasionally demarcated in a different way on some church sites, where 'the ideal of enclosure may have been as important as its monumentality' (Jenkins 2010, 35). In his analysis of Adomnán's *Life of Columba*, MacDonald (1997, 42) suggested that the purpose of enclosure was often primarily spiritual and legal and that such concerns to delimit church sites might have been as easily achieved by using wooden fences, hedges or natural topography as more permanent enclosure walls, banks and ditches. Such perishable hedgerow enclosures have been recorded at Wilfrid's seventh-century Anglo-Saxon monastery at Oundle (Colgrave 1927, 147; Blair 2005, 196), and may have been a feature of some Irish church sites for different economic, topographical or symbolic reasons. Indeed, Gerald of Wales describes a withy hedge enclosing the miraculous eternal fire at Kildare in the twelfth century (O'Meara 1982, 82), although this was perhaps only intended to define a small feature. Many centuries before, Cogitosus also asserted that the *suburbana* of later seventh-century Kildare was not bounded by physical walls, but instead 'delimited by signs going back to the time of Saint Brigit' (Bitel 1990, 63; Picard 2011, 57) – this despite potential evidence having been revealed for an outer ecclesiastical enclosure at Kildare recently (Taylor 2018:754).

Standing stones were also conceived as early Christian boundary markers (Kelly 2000, 409) and the location of crosses or cross-inscribed slabs on the peripheries of church sites suggests that they may have fulfilled a similar role as symbols of protection and sanctuary. This is certainly implied in the later eighth-century *Book of Mulling* colophon depiction (fig. 1.2), which provides an idealized representation of an early Christian curvilinear monastic enclosure surrounded by two compass-drawn concentric circles – representing an enclosure – and a number of crosses most of which were along the line of the enclosures at the four cardinal points (Stokes 1905, xxiv–vi; Henry 1965, 81). Some scholars have viewed this combination of circular enclosure and free-standing crosses as a common feature of eighth-century monasteries (Henry 1940, 102; Hurley 1982, 320; Bitel 1990, 59) and possible examples of this arrangement of crosses surrounding church sites have been identified at Kilkieran (Herity 1995, 42–8) and Temple Cronan, Co. Clare, where the stone crosses defining the site were complemented by a curvilinear enclosure (Sheehan 1982, 37). Jenkins (2010, 87, 152) has also noted that the *Collectio canonum Hibernensis* indicates that sanctuary space should be marked by crosses and/or boundary stones and views the colophon depiction as the embodiment of an Irish biblical ideal of holy space based upon the topography of the Temple of Jerusalem.

Very occasionally, crosses may have provided the sole means of symbolically defining the sanctuary area of an ecclesiastical settlement. This may have been the situation at the 'enclosure' of the Pictish monastery of Kilremont, St Andrews, which, according to one source, was defined by little more than stone crosses (Anderson 1976, 3). Similarly, excavations at another Pictish monastery at Portmahomack have found that both the churchyard and its setting within the Tarbat peninsula in Easter Ross were symbolically defined by stone crosses (Carver 2011, 928). A ninth-century Irish poem from Óengus the Culdee also describes a hermitage (*Dísert Bethech*) protected from the wilderness by nothing other than 'a circle of crosses' (Herity 1995, 48–9). Pillar-stones, as well as enclosures and high crosses, all appear to have marked the *termonn* extent of ecclesiastical sites including *Mainistir Chiaráin* and *Na Seacht dTeampaill* on the Aran Islands; some of these may have marked the *sanctissimus* or most sacred core, while others defined their outermost precincts (Ó Carragáin and Sheehan 2010, 221–2). Alongside other ritual functions (Bhreathnach 2015a, 17), crosses – probably more often together with physical enclosures – then appear to have played an important role in symbolically defining the sanctuary areas of church sites during the early medieval period.

Natural topography also influenced the organizational layout of ecclesiastical sites. Indeed, the builders at Killabuonia and Skellig Michael, Co. Kerry, were obliged to manipulate the local steep topography to create a series of inner and outer terraces ideal for organizing and demarcating these monastic spaces (Herity 1995, 58). It has been observed how the builders of Whithorn and Hoddom in Scotland, and perhaps High Island, utilized the natural topography when demarcating their church sites with enclosing elements

(Blair 2005, 196; Jenkins 2010, 48, 63). Similarly, excavations at Toureen Peakaun (above) revealed that the site was defined by an outer enclosure *c.*170m in diameter, part of whose perimeter was defined by a natural palaeochannel with internal palisade (Ó Carragáin 2006:1929; 2007:1738; 2008:1167).

In the case of small islands, it might not always have been necessary to enclose church sites there (except for practical reasons of shelter), as the island edges may have been understood as symbolically marking the outline of the site (Bitel 1990, 63). This might partly explain why the enclosing 'cashel' wall at Church Island was one of the last early medieval monastic features to be built on the island (O'Kelly 1958, 77). It may also have been the case on Iona where Adomnán possibly viewed the entire island landscape and not just the monastery as sacred space closely organized on the topography of the holy city of Jerusalem (MacDonald 2001, 23–9; Jenkins 2010, 36–7). Indeed, based on information from Adomnán's *Life of Columba*, and in the division of ecclesiastical space evident in the eighth-century *Hibernensis* into a sacred core (*sanctissimus*) and less sacred outer concentric enclosed spaces (*sanctus* and *sanctior*), MacDonald (2001, 15–19) suggests a biblical-inspired tripartite division of sacred space at Iona involving an outermost space marked by the island's boundaries, then the main monastic enclosure, and finally an innermost enclosure defining the church and cemetery – the *sanctissimus*. A similar tripartite plan may have existed at Clonmacnoise that involved an inner enclosure coterminous with the cemetery wall, a secondary enclosure represented by the backfilled ditch revealed by Murphy and an outermost enclosure utilizing the natural topography of the adjoining Esker Ridge (Murphy 2003, 20, 23; Jenkins 2010, 77–8).

THE LIFECYCLE AND CHRONOLOGY OF EARLY MEDIEVAL
ECCLESIASTICAL ENCLOSURES

Enclosure construction as an 'early Christian period' phenomenon
The enclosed settlement emerged as the standard vernacular settlement form for secular and religious communities during the conversion era (i.e., fifth to seventh century). Societal changes, climactic deterioration leading to crop failure, famines and plagues, as well as political upheavals and warfare (cattle-raiding), have been mooted as reasons for the appearance of these enclosed sites (O'Sullivan et al. 2014, 74–7). Early Irish secular and canon law also perceived the space within enclosed sites as affording protections of privacy, non-violence and sanctuary, perhaps building upon an earlier indigenous prehistoric tradition of curvilinear-shaped ritual complexes (i.e., passage tombs, stone circles, ring-barrows, ring-ditches, Iron Age ceremonial centres) as signifiers of sacred space (Harney 2016, 74, 400).

As these enclosed church sites, ringforts and cemetery settlements begin to proliferate in the conversion era, it is also conceivable that 'enclosure' became partly bound up with the process of Christianization. Many early Irish clerics envisaged enclosures as appropriate instruments for organizing and controlling the lives of dedicated monks committed to renouncing the secular world around them, or for organizing their church sites according to revered biblical settlement prototypes – the latter most eloquently articulated in the early eighth-century *Hibernensis* that described a hierarchical layout of curvilinear enclosed holy space around early Irish church sites, perhaps in imitation of the biblical Levitical Cities of Refuge (*civitates refugii*) (Doherty 1985, 58–9) or Ezekiel's Temple of Jerusalem (Jenkins 2010, 89–101). As already noted, this organization of hierarchical sacred space may not just have been reflected in physical concentric enclosures, but also in other boundary forms such as crosses/altars, the shoreline of islands or the natural topography of a site. However, as invisible boundaries were difficult to legally define and could not expect the type of trespass fines as visible boundary markers in early Irish law (Bitel 1990, 63–4), it is likely that enclosing banks and ditches or walls were invariably a distinctive feature of most early church sites.

As noted above, in relation to these early church sites, the sources often referred to their sacred, sanctuary space as the *termonn*, from the Latin *terminus* or boundary mark (Jenkins 2010, 96–7). The exact extent of the *termonn* has attracted much debate, particularly as some early *Lives* and sources such as the *Liber Angeli* (in relation to Armagh) suggest that the *termonn* could encompass a huge swathe of land, often several kilometres across (ibid., 87–8). However, other sources such as Cogitosus's late seventh-century description of Brigit's Kildare, the early eighth-century *Collectio canonum Hibernensis* – the key text for understanding the organization of early church sites – and the vernacular law tracts, all suggest a much more geographically limited understanding of the term *termonn*. Instead these sources suggest that the *termonn* should be viewed as a 'natural extension of the secular notion of sanctuary, which related to a freeman's *les* – i.e., the ring for a ringfort – to encompass ecclesial notions of sanctuary embodied in concepts such as the *civitas refugii*' (ibid., 88–9, 95). The restricted view of *termonn* in these early sources suggests that the *termonn* boundaries may have been usually synonymous with the ecclesiastical enclosure or outermost ecclesiastical enclosure, where multivallation occurred. The *termonn* could then vary considerably in size from 30m to 300m in diameter – and sometimes even larger – depending on the status and importance of the church site. The notion of the *termonn* as marking a 'finite area of enclosure and sanctuary' – as articulated in these seventh-/eighth-century sources – is then potentially crucial to understanding why early Christian ecclesiastical and secular sites were invariably enclosed.

The *vallum* was another Latin term for the physical enclosure itself, with the early Irish Lives often claiming that these boundary features (*vallum monasterii*) existed at the time of the founding saint. Thus it appears in Adomnán's late seventh-century *Life of Columba* of Iona when it describes how the Clonmacnoise community passed the boundary of the monastery when coming out to greet the visiting saint in the sixth century (Anderson and Anderson 1961, 214). The digging and marking out of the monastic enclosure at Lismore is described in the *Life of Mochuda* (Plummer 1922, ii, 290) where it is claimed that after advice from a virgin, the monks were inspired to build a substantial rampart, from which the name Lismore ('Great rampart') was derived. Jenkins (2010, 81–9) notes various other references to ecclesiastical enclosures and their symbolic marking out and construction in these early sources. However, just because hagiographies – which were often written in the centuries afterwards – claim that a boundary existed at the time of the founder, this does not mean it actually was there at that time. This is where archaeology can confirm the antiquity of an ecclesiastical enclosure.

And this archaeological evidence indicates that the vast majority of ecclesiastical enclosures were built between the sixth and the eighth century. There is emerging archaeological evidence that some of the earliest church sites, in particular, were established at or upon either pre-existing or ancient places of ritual, burial and settlement (Harney 2017, 105–17). In particular, it appears that some early missionaries may have targeted and Christianized certain existing ritual and political centres, such as potentially at Armagh, by incorporating ancient monuments (e.g., trees, groves, stone circles, standing stones) or existing physical enclosures into the design of their new church site. However, as church sites proliferated across the countryside in the later sixth and seventh centuries, it appears that most of these more recent foundations, whether for deliberate reasons or not, increasingly established their settlements in largely greenfield locations devoid of any pagan monuments or associations (Harney 2017, 121).

Given the substantial size and scale of some ecclesiastical enclosures, it is likely that many church sites were initially unenclosed or temporarily defined by boundary markers such as crosses until the church authorities were in a position to utilize the manpower for building these enclosing elements. Occupation evidence preceding these enclosures might also indicate temporary or makeshift religious settlements whilst plans were put in place to build the enclosing elements. For example, at Clonfad, the earliest feature consisted of a regularly maintained fifth- to sixth-century linear ditch (1.2–1.8m x 0.95m deep) predating the seventh-/eighth-century enclosure ditches (Stevens 2012, 118, 120). Its exact function is uncertain, but it may represent an initial partial delineation or outer enclosure dating to an early stage when the site did not have the resources to construct a more substantial boundary. Drainage activities were also sometimes necessary before enclosures were built. This was the case possibly at Kiltera, Co. Waterford (Macalister 1935, 6) and at Caherlehillan, where the earliest features consisted of substantial drainage trenches left open for a short period of time before the mid-fifth- to mid-sixth-century enclosure wall was built (Sheehan 2009, 194–6, 204).

Domestic activity preceding the construction of ecclesiastical enclosures have also been revealed in excavations. These include at Armoy (Nelis et al. 2007, 106); at Dunshaughlin, where a circular post-and-wattle building pre-dated the enclosure (Simpson 2005); at Kill St Lawrence, where a pit inside the inner enclosure returned a radiocarbon date of AD 370–540 (O'Connell 2004, 27); and at Kilgobbin, where the enclosures post-dated structural evidence consisting of a circular slot-trench and pit belonging to an apparently unenclosed (secular?) phase pre-dating AD 600 (Bolger 2008, 103). As mentioned above, excavations at Taney also uncovered a *c.*later seventh-/ eighth-century palisaded enclosure (*c.*20–5m diameter) preceding a series of eighth- to tenth-century ditches enclosing the entire site; this palisaded feature was interpreted as an outer adjoining enclosure containing a priest's house to the west of the pre-existing church and burial ground (O'Donovan 2012, 32), which was built before the community had the resources to mark out the entire site with an enclosing *vallum*.

Dating information from ecclesiastical enclosure ditches also confirms that these boundary features were mostly built between the sixth and eighth century, most probably in the decades or immediate centuries after the foundation of these church sites. For example, the enclosure ditch at Clonmacnoise was backfilled in the later eighth or early ninth century; but the great size and time involved in digging this feature implies that it was 'left open for a considerable length of time', perhaps suggesting that it was originally excavated in the sixth or seventh century (Murphy 2003, 19) – a suggestion potentially corroborated in Adomnán's *Life of Columba*. At St Canice's in Kilkenny city, the inner enclosure ditch was also apparently backfilled sometime before the late ninth century (Ó Drisceoil 2013, 9–10, 36), while a radiocarbon date from the lower fills of the enclosure ditch at Ballykilmore indicates 'the early use of the ditch in the sixth to seventh century' (Channing 2012, 85–6). Potential sixth-century ditches have been revealed at Carrowmore where following the recutting of the inner enclosure ditch, its first subsequent ditch fill was dated to AD 590–660 (O'Brien and Adams 2014, 4–5) and perhaps at Armoy, where the earliest silting evidence from the enclosure ditch yielded a date-range of AD 611–22 (2 sigma) (Nelis, McSparron and Gormley 2014, 148).

Clonfad was bounded by a stream and enclosing ditches dating to the seventh/eighth century (Stevens 2012, 120); charcoal from the second fill of the outer enclosure ditch at Lusk indicated a fifth-/sixth-century date or even earlier for its cutting (AD 420–600 – no Σ) (O'Connell 2009, 52–4); while a possible seventh-/eighth-century bronze ringed brooch from near the base of the ditch at Kells (Byrne 1988, 25–6) might provide a rough date for this feature. Two sections of the potential outer enclosure ditch at Kildare were examined – the ditch base was not reached in the excavations and animal bone from the lowest visible fill was dated to the late seventh or eighth century (Taylor 2018:754), thereby indicating that the ditch is most likely even earlier. Although a sample from the lower fills of the inner enclosure ditch at Tullylish produced a mid-fourth- to early seventh-century date, charcoal from a similar context of this feature was dated to the mid-fifth to mid-seventh century (Ivens 1987, 112–13, 119). In addition, twigs from the base of the inner enclosure ditch at Tallaght produced a date of AD 438–773 (2Σ) (Walsh 1997:187; 1997, 8), while charcoal from the primary fill of the outer enclosure ditch at Kill St Lawrence (1310±40 BP) (O'Connell 2004, 27, 39–43, 61) suggest that it was in use between the mid-seventh and later eighth century (2Σ). This dating evidence is replicated on Scottish church sites: the enclosure ditches on Iona (Barber 1981, 310), Inchmarnock (Lowe 2008, 85, 252–5) and Hoddom (Lowe 2006, 171–2, 186) were all viewed as seventh century in date, while the outer (and later) enclosure ditch at Portmahomack was dated to the later seventh to later eighth century (Carver 2008, 51; Spall 2009, 317).

Dating evidence from Irish ecclesiastical enclosure walls corroborates this chronological trend observed from excavated enclosure ditches and banks. Indeed, Caherlehillan's enclosure wall was a primary feature dating to the later fifth or sixth century (Sheehan 2009, 194–6, 204). While the Nendrum walls cannot be closely dated, a seventh-century date is not improbable given the construction of the tidal mill in the early seventh century (McErlean 2007, 395). Although the 'cashel' wall at Church Island was late in the sequence of building (above), the enclosure walls at Carns (McNeary and Shanahan 2009, 131), Illaunloughan (Marshall and Walsh 2005, 14) and Reask were also all deemed primary features, with the latter assigned to sometime during the sixth or seventh century (Fanning 1981, 98–100, 155).

The evolution and decline of enclosures on multivallate church sites
It is important to recognize that once these enclosure ditches were dug, it only ever took a few generations for these features to become infilled through either natural silting or anthropogenic (domestic dumping and craft activities) processes. These enclosures were then highly susceptible to change and could quickly become redundant without careful intervention and maintenance by the religious community. In many cases, there is evidence then that the infilling of these ditched features was followed by subsequent attempts to recut, modify, or replace these ecclesiastical boundaries at a later point. This is evident at Tullylish where the original inner ditch was recut twice, before being

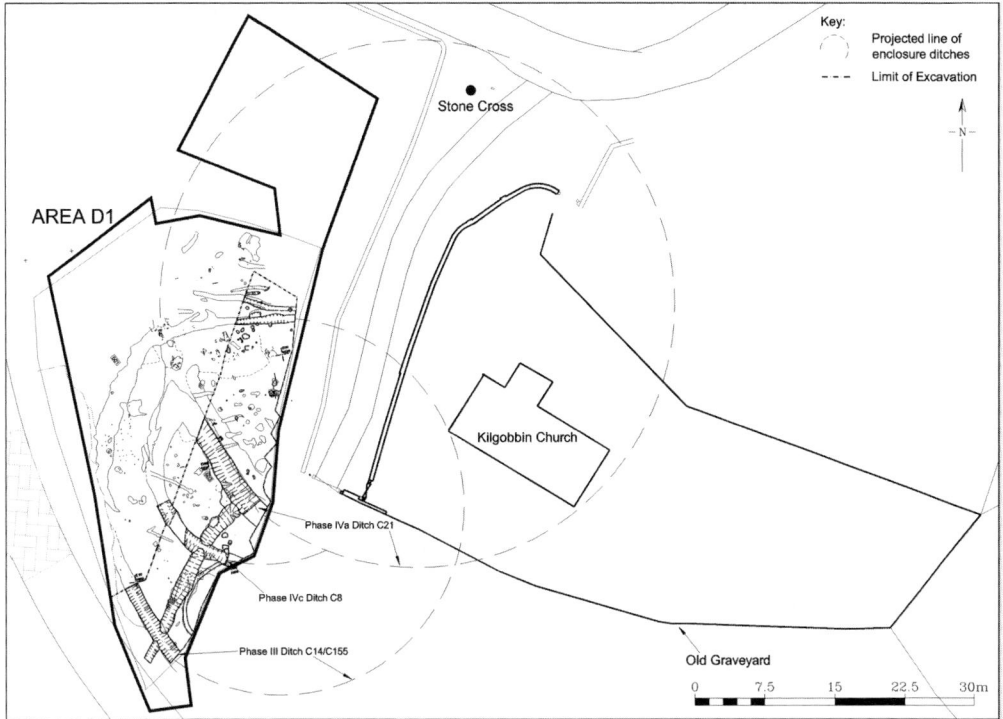

Key:
- Projected line of enclosure ditches
- --- Limit of Excavation

Stone Cross

AREA D1

Kilgobbin Church

Phase IVa Ditch C21

Phase IVc Ditch C8

Phase III Ditch C14/C155

Old Graveyard

0   7.5   15   22.5   30m

1.6 Excavation of area D1 at Kilgobbin showing alignment of enclosures (after Bolger 2014, 3)

replaced by the outer ditch which was again eventually allowed to fill up after being regularly cleaned out (Ivens 1987, 58–61).

Similar evidence for the maintenance and recutting of enclosure ditches has been identified at Cathedral Hill, Armagh (Gaskell-Brown and Harper 1984, 116), Clonfad (Stevens 2012, 120), Armoy (Nelis et al. 2007, 38–9), Killeen Demesne (Baker 2009, 59) and Taney (O'Donovan 2012, 28), while the absence of significant silting inside the Clonmacnoise ditch suggests that it was recut shortly before it was backfilled in the later eighth/early ninth century (Murphy 2003, 13). At Dunshaughlin, the original, water-filled ditch was finally deliberately infilled by the destruction of the bank, and then recut (Simpson 2005, 233–7), while both the inner and outer enclosure ditches at Tallaght were recut on a number of occasions before being eventually backfilled in the medieval period, perhaps from enclosure bank material (McConway 1994:102; 1994, 13–18; 1995, 5; Walsh 1997, 6–14).

Excavations have also shed light on the complex dating of enclosures within multivallate sites. Traditionally, it has often been assumed that all the enclosures on multivallate sites were built at the same time or were contemporary with each other. Indeed, McErlean (2007, 395) suggested that

the trivallate enclosure plan was put in place at Nendrum during the seventh
century, but while this is possible, he offered no hard evidence to confirm this.
Instead, closer investigation can often reveal that these multivallate enclosing
elements were built organically over the centuries as resources became
available and that they frequently represent successive enclosing features
indicative of the expansion or contraction of the ecclesiastical site over time.
Recent radiocarbon dates from Carrowmore (O'Brien and Adams 2014, 4–5)
potentially infer that the inner enclosure ditch (*c.*sixth/early seventh century)
may precede the outer enclosure (*c.*seventh/eighth century). At Kilgobbin (fig.
1.6), the earliest enclosure phases on this multivallate site were limited in scope
and focused more on the area to the west and south of the present graveyard,
but it was not until the phase IV enclosure ditch (C21), whose lower fills dated
from the late seventh to late ninth century, that a substantial portion of the
extant cemetery was actually incorporated within a boundary feature (Bolger
2008, 85, 107).

At Taney (fig. 1.5), a similar adjustment to the enclosure ditch layout was
identified involving the construction of successive, increasingly larger,
enclosing elements around the site between the later seventh and early tenth
century (O'Donovan 2012, 21–35). The gradual construction of such larger
enclosing elements is also demonstrated at Pictish Portmahomack in Scotland
and at Tullylish (Ivens 1987, 112–13, 119), where the outer enclosure was dated
to between the late seventh and mid-tenth century and was slightly later than
the inner enclosure, dug between the mid-fifth and mid-seventh century.
Similarly, animal bone from around the base of the outer enclosure ditch at
Tallaght is reported as yielding a radiocarbon date of AD 718–973 (Walsh 1997,
26), while twigs from the base of the inner enclosure ditch produced a
radiocarbon date range of AD 438–773 (Walsh 1997:187; 1997, 8). This
chronology at Tullylish and Tallaght suggests that the inner enclosure ditch
was dug sometime in the sixth to early eighth century as these sites were
beginning to develop, before outer, larger enclosures were subsequently
constructed between the eighth and tenth century.

The excavation evidence also indicates that the pace of ecclesiastical
enclosure construction substantially declined after the ninth century. Between
the ninth and twelfth century, often all traces of enclosure banks were removed
by being levelled, mined for soil/stone or backfilled into enclosure ditches. For
example, the enclosure ditches at Cathedral Hill, Armagh (Gaskell-Brown and
Harper 1984, 159) and Iona (McCormick 1997, 51) were backfilled in the later
early medieval period, while at Clonmacnoise, there is evidence that the
enclosure ditch was deliberately backfilled in one episode, presumably by the
demolition of its bank, most probably during the later eighth or early ninth
century (Murphy 2003, 13, 19), about the same time as the construction of the
bridge across the Shannon dating to AD 804 (Moore 1996; O'Sullivan and

Boland 2000), and the expansion of settlement into the 'New Graveyard' (King 2009, 336, 345). Similarly, the outer and middle enclosure ditches at Clonfad were deliberately backfilled as single events at roughly the same time in the later eighth or ninth century. Although this evidence might imply a site contraction, continued craft activity into the tenth century was revealed along the stream banks to the east of the church (Stevens 2012, 121–4).

At Armoy, the enclosure ditch (after one substantial recut) was also allowed to silt up before being infilled with a deposit that was introduced to raise the site level, perhaps around the eighth/ninth century. Most early medieval occupation activity at Armoy occurred between the ninth and twelfth century after this ditch had been infilled and had become irrelevant (Nelis et al. 2007, 4, 38–51, 111–12; Nelis, McSparron and Gormley 2014, 151). A similar process was evident at Tulla (Myles 2012:086) and Tullylish (Ivens 1987, 58–61, 112–15) where early medieval structures were built upon or cut into the backfilled enclosure ditches on these church sites. This situation was again replicated at Hoddom in Scotland, where its mid-seventh-century enclosure ditch had fallen out of use sometime before the later tenth century when a structure was built upon it (Lowe 2006, 186), and at Inchmarnock, Scotland, where material from the upper fill of the enclosure ditch indicated that the early seventh-century enclosure had been largely backfilled by the tenth century (Lowe 2008, 85, 252–5).

Between the ninth/tenth and twelfth century, many partly silted up enclosure ditches were also often reused for domestic or industrial dumps or as sheltered spaces for craft/agricultural activities. For example, a stone-lined hearth associated with small-scale ironworking dating to AD 1030–1160 was placed on top of the outer enclosure ditch fills at Carrowmore (O'Brien and Adams 2014, 5); bowl-furnaces were cut into the upper fills of the enclosure ditches at Clonfeacle (Long 2005, 27; Long 2006:133) and Creaghanboy (Guinan 2004:1144), while the outer enclosure ditch at Cooley was utilized for industrial purposes in its last phase (Adams and O'Brien 2016:288). The inner enclosure ditch at St Canice's Cathedral was backfilled by the late ninth century and was truncated by a corn-drying kiln dating to about the same time or a century or two later (Ó Drisceoil 2013, 9–10, 36). Similarly, the enclosure at Killederdadrum had largely silted up by the time a possible corn-drying kiln was cut into its inner face sometime between the tenth and early twelfth century (Manning 1984, 242, 261).

By the eleventh or twelfth century, some communities might then have even almost forgotten the location and former impressive nature of these ancient boundary markers, now barely perceptible as largely silted up/infilled undulations in the ground. At Skeam West, some memory of the enclosure may have been revived when the upper fill of the largely infilled ditch was cut by a *circa* eleventh- to thirteenth-century burial (Cotter 1995, 74–5). However,

1.7 Map of the possible ecclesiastical site at Oldtown, Finglas (see Appendix) showing the complex of enclosures revealed in the geophysical survey and excavation. Further continuations of enclosures belonging to this site were identified across the road in Mooretown but are not shown on this map (after Baker 2010, 10, fig. 1.12).

we should note that some enclosure ditches could have longer lifespans, in some cases remaining at least partly open until the thirteenth/fourteenth century. This is evident at St Michan's, Dublin city (Meenan 2004, 107–8) (Dawkes 2006:606; Hayden 2000, 9–11), Kilpatrick (Swan 1997, 5) and Tallaght (McConway 1994:102; 1994, 13–18; 1995, 5; Walsh 1997, 6–14), as well as the latest enclosures at Taney (O'Donovan 2012, 53) and Drumkay (O'Donovan 2014, 196, 209), but actual evidence that these enclosure ditches were carefully maintained and recut by church groups in the later early medieval centuries is often far from obvious.

Certainly, it is probable, however, that some enclosure ditches were dug or recut between the tenth and twelfth century, but it is perhaps unlikely that a desire to imitate an ancient seventh- /eighth-century settlement *schema* was the primary motivation for their construction. For example, at Dunshaughlin, the original enclosure ditch was backfilled around the tenth century or slightly later from material from the demolished enclosure bank. This ditch was subsequently recut, before being infilled sometime between the eleventh and mid-twelfth century (Simpson 2005, 233–7). Testing at Graiguenakill is reported as uncovering 'a ditched enclosure, which probably surrounded the monastic site in the tenth–twelfth century' (Ó Drisceoil 2004:0882), while at Annaghdown, animal bone from the basal fill of an enclosure ditch produced an eleventh- /twelfth-century date (Crumlish 2014:309), thereby implying a late date for this boundary feature. While a clear decline in enclosure construction appears to have occurred in the later early medieval period as discussed above, this evidence reminds us that it was sometimes deemed practical by certain religious communities to retain a curvilinear ecclesiastical enclosure for some symbolic, functional or defensive purpose in these centuries (fig. 1.7).

DISCUSSION

Mapping enclosure construction and decline in early medieval Ireland
Excavations have demonstrated that a physical enclosure was a fundamental aspect of secular and church sites – e.g., ringforts, church sites and cemetery settlements – in the conversion era and early Christian period. Both native and biblical views of sanctuary space, as well as monastic visions of claustration, all influenced the proliferation of enclosed settlement sites in the early Christian period, but to varying extents. There were many diverse forms of church sites in this period – monasteries, hermitages, pastoral churches, multifunctional pastoral and monastic sites and proprietary establishments – but this complexity in function was not always apparent in ecclesiastical layout, which generally conformed to a consistent plan, usually being situated within an enclosure, consisting of one, two and occasionally three concentric curvilinear banks, ditches and sometimes stone walls. Many small early Christian church sites were defined by just one enclosure with the area within often carefully organized according to an east–west division of sacred and profane space (Harney 2016, 406, 410).

However, by the seventh century at the very latest, it appears that Christian concepts of a hierarchy of holy space – drawing upon the templates of the biblical 'Cities of Refuge' and the Temple of Jerusalem – prompted a growing interest among clerical planners into reorganizing many church sites. Now sites like Clonmacnoise – whose churches, burials, dwellings and craft areas had all probably been formerly accommodated within a single enclosure in the fifth and even sixth centuries – were remodelled to contain an innermost enclosure *sanctum* exclusively boasting the church and burials around the saint's grave (if any), and newly created concentric outer enclosure zones associated with domestic activity, agriculture and craft. These developing church sites, however, never remained static in their layout, but underwent considerable site change in terms of their enclosing elements and the activities that took place within them between the seventh and tenth century. Indeed, where multivallation occurs, these enclosures were not always necessarily contemporary with each other, but indicative of the change and evolution of these settlements over many centuries.

Excavation evidence also indicates that the pace of enclosure construction substantially slowed in later early medieval times. Most ecclesiastical enclosure ditches dug in the sixth/seventh century, and flourishing in the early Christian period, appear to have naturally silted up or were deliberately infilled by the tenth/eleventh century at the latest, but we should note that exceptions to this trend clearly existed for different practical or symbolic reasons (above). The overall fall off in ecclesiastical enclosure construction was, however, part of a wider general societal trend where the importance and relevance of enclosed settlements such as the cemetery settlement or the ringfort – the archetypical monument of the clientship system of seventh- and eighth-century society – all significantly declined and had largely been abandoned by the tenth/ eleventh century (O'Sullivan et al. 2014, 328). Enclosure ditches and banks both tend to survive at these sites more often (despite later agricultural activity), but this was because these sites were now derelict in contrast to multi-period occupied church sites.

This societal change happened at a time when increasingly powerful kings were investing intensively in ecclesiastical art and architecture and as these church sites continued to develop and expand as centres of dwelling, craftwork and agricultural production, indicating that this process, far from signalling the decline of these sites, was more a testament to the increasingly obsolete role of enclosures as boundary markers towards the end of the early medieval period.

Why enclosures were often abandoned in the later early medieval centuries is not totally clear, but it might partly be the result of a shift from understanding the *termonn* as a clearly defined marker of restricted enclosed sanctuary space – as described in the seventh- /eighth-century sources – to the idea of the *termonn* as an indicator of a much larger (undefined) zone of protected space in the later early medieval period (Jenkins 2010, 89). The ideology underpinning the act of enclosure was then diminished significantly in meaning and purpose.

Enclosure construction and decline and changing perceptions of cemetery space in early medieval Ireland
In addition, it is possible that this decline in enclosure construction was part of a wider trend where church authorities became less preoccupied and concerned about the need to rigidly separate a clearly defined inner *sanctum* – utilized solely for ritual activities – from outer enclosed spaces reserved for craftworkers and agricultural tenants. It should be noted that craft activity, particularly ironworking, has been identified within Iron Age cemeteries (Dowling 2014, 168–9) and occasionally within the burial grounds of early medieval cemetery settlements and church sites (Bhreathnach 2013, 328;

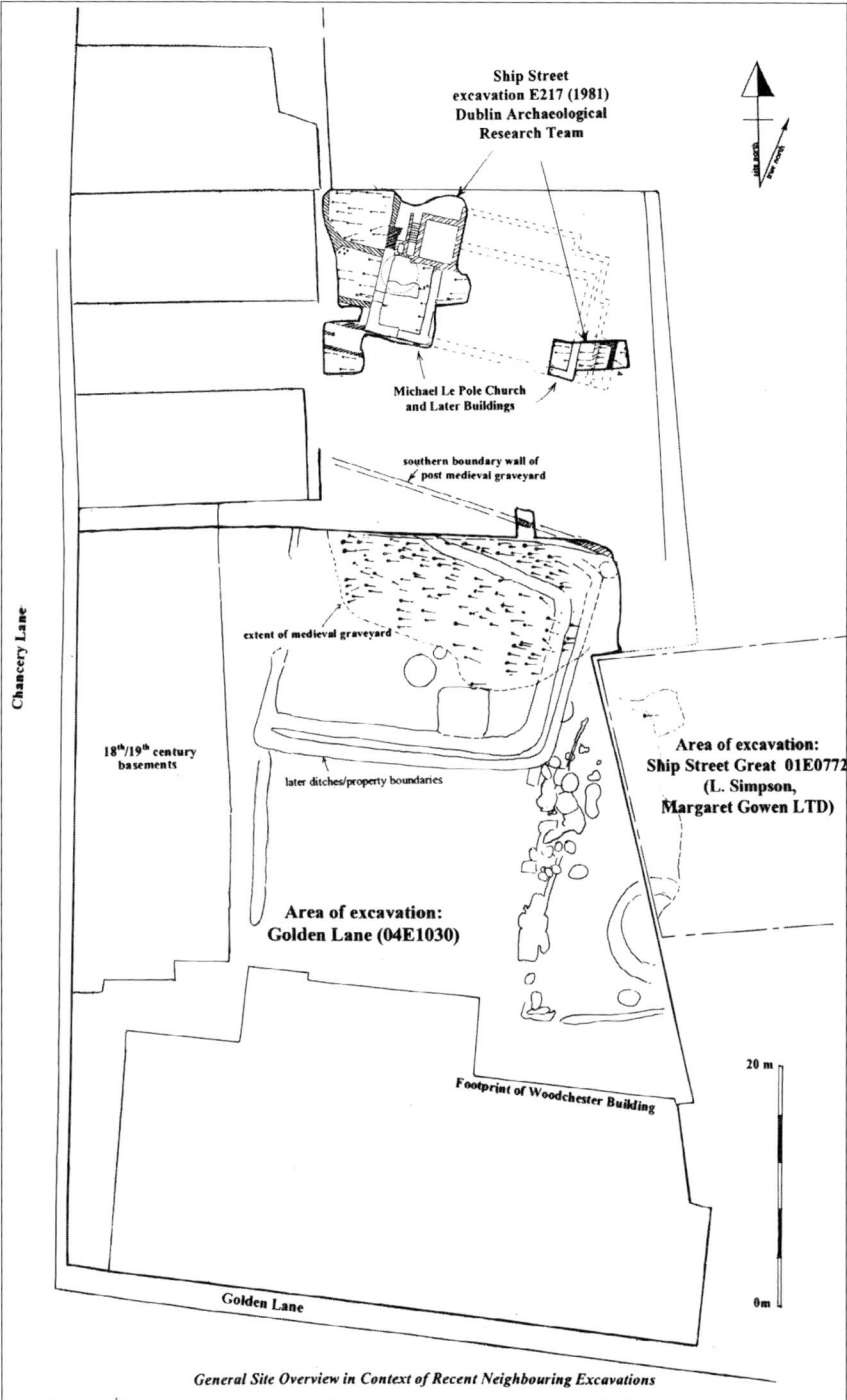

1.8 The church of St Michael le Pole, Dublin city, showing the church building and cemetery to the south (after O'Donovan 2008, 43)

O'Sullivan et al. 2014, 309). The early sources also confirm that early Christian cemeteries fulfilled other ritual and judicial roles such as the taking of oaths, often at the site of tombs and using relics (Binchy 1941, 80; Doherty 1982, 325; Lucas 1986, 24–5; Kelly 1988, 199), but it is noteworthy that Adomnán's later seventh-century *Vita Columbae* and certain *Céli Dé* sources from Tallaght tended to view the dead as unclean and something to be avoided. Indeed, these sources and the evidence for a deep ditch separating the cemetery at *Reilig Odhráin* from the rest of the monastery on Iona led McCormick (1997, 64–5) to posit that the monks wished to clearly separate areas of the dead from areas of the living on this island between the seventh to ninth century.

However, early medieval church cemeteries were not quiet or solemn places as they are today, and Fry (1999, 49–65) has documented their continued social roles as fair- or market-sites, areas for making contracts and swearing oaths and places for penance, habitation, games, contests and storage between the tenth and sixteenth century. Furthermore, Bhreathnach (2013, 238–9) has noted the practical reasons for undertaking craft activities close to the dead given that 'fires could be safely lit in a cemetery without endangering houses or animal pens'. So, were church cemeteries always utilized for craft activities, despite the best intentions of a prescribed settlement *schema* as outlined in the *Hibernensis* to protect the sacred core, or is there potential evidence for increasing craft activity within and around the inner cemetery precincts of some church sites towards the end of the early medieval period? A review of the evidence can often disclose craft or occupational activity pre-dating the use of the cemetery, as uncovered at the church of St Michael le Pole (fig. 1.8) (Gowen 2001, 28–33; O'Donovan 2008, 44–5) and Clonmacnoise (King 1997, 129–30; 2009, 345), and post-dating it as revealed at Scotch Street, Armagh, where the cemetery at *Temple na Ferta* was later reused for crafts from the eighth to tenth century (Matthews 2000, 107–15), but this is to be expected as we know that these settlements could considerably evolve in their layout during the early medieval period.

Clear indicators of economic activity (domestic evidence, animal bone or craft activity) within actual in-use ecclesiastical cemeteries is more difficult to identify, but we do know that partly infilled inner- and outer-enclosure ditches were strong candidates for the citing of kilns and ironworking between the ninth and twelfth century (above). In addition, it is noteworthy that Viking Age craft evidence has been revealed on the peripheries of the cemeteries at the church of St Michael le Pole (O'Donovan 2008, 44–5, 53–63; Walsh 2009, 15–25) and St Canice's, Kilkenny. At St Canice's, tenth- to twelfth-century antler- and bone-working was found within the inner precincts and along the line of the inner enclosure ditch; this economic activity post-dated the backfilling of the boundary ditches (Ó Drisceoil 2013, 46–8), and may indicate that such boundary features were increasingly viewed as impractical and symbolically unnecessary, particularly at expanding urban church sites in this later period where space was ever more at a premium. In addition, excavations at Iniscealtra also uncovered eleventh- to thirteenth-century craftwork – e.g., ironworking, bone-working, stone-working – around St Caimin's Church and the round tower (de Paor 1997, 79–81), as well as in the space north of the saint's graveyard (ibid., 78–9) and within St Brigid's Church enclosure (ibid., 57–8). Does both the decline in enclosure construction and the above evidence indicate the increasing use of the inner ecclesiastical precincts – i.e., the cemetery zone – for economic activity in later early medieval centuries, as the 'cemetery – rather than being removed from the daily life of the living community – was [ever more] at its centre' (Rodwell 1981, 135)? The evidence is still too tentative to determine, but this is certainly a research topic worth exploring in future.

Evolving ideologies and functions of ecclesiastical enclosures
Finally, this study reminds us that the building of early medieval ecclesiastical enclosures was intimately bound up with the articulation of power, ritual and control. It is clear that the construction of enclosures evoked different meanings for different people: for example, abbots may have viewed them as useful for organizing the lives of monastic subordinates; for monks and pagans, these may have been respectively viewed as instruments of segregation or exclusion; whilst for the agricultural tenants (*manaig*), these enclosures may have reminded them of the physical toil endured building them to honour the terms of their clientship agreements. Clearly, the substantial dimensions (*c.*100–400m in diameter) and size of the largest ecclesiastical enclosure ditches (*c.*4–8m wide; 2–4m deep) must have meant control over a considerable labour force, with several separate 'workgangs' responsible for excavating different portions as suggested at Tallaght (McConway 1994, 4–5). Furthermore, these impressive boundary features must have reminded all of the new Christian order, which was supplanting the old pagan past immortalized by the equally impressive but now derelict Iron Age royal sites.

As these church sites increased their influence in society, it appears that clerical planners of many larger sites, from at least the seventh century, drew upon the revered biblical prototypes of the 'Cities of Refuge' and the 'Temple of Jerusalem' in order to impose a new hierarchical organization of enclosure space that placed restrictions on how clerics, monks and the wider populace accessed these sites. Such a clear articulation of power may have been deemed necessary by a clerical elite, not just out of a concern to ensure that the ritual core did not get polluted by either profane activities or from pagan or not fully fledged Christian visitors, but also by the desire to heighten the mystery and intrigue of the sacred graves and relics of the founding saint that were being enshrined within purpose-built tombs in this period.

Nonetheless, the communities of many of these church sites were surely mindful that these settlements continued to undergo much change, particularly in terms of their enclosing elements and the diverse range of secular and profane activities that were taking place within them between the seventh and ninth century. Certainly, it is possible to envisage a growing tension among clerical planners on some church sites who wished to continue to expand the occupational, craft and agricultural zones within these sites, but who were cognisant of respecting the locations of their substantial enclosing elements, which were perceived as ancient symbolic site boundary markers. Unfortunately, many church authorities were not very effective at maintaining these enclosure ditches, but it is also possible that some important clerics were happy to allow these enclosure ditches become gradually infilled through natural silting or dumping to convey an illusion of wealth and feasting to outside communities visiting these church sites. In addition, the fact that these infilled enclosure ditches were often replaced by occupational and craft activity suggests that many Viking Age clerical planners were increasingly informed by more functional concerns, rather than by an ideological desire to closely adhere to a prescribed settlement *schema* envisioned many centuries before.

This continued settlement expansion at church sites like Clonmacnoise and the evidence for dwellings and craftwork post-dating backfilled enclosure ditches at Clonfad, Armoy and Armagh in the ninth and tenth centuries, suggests that the infilling of these enclosure ditches far from signalling the decline of these now developing settlement hubs, may instead attest to how the original symbolic meanings of these enclosures was increasingly lost and irrelevant. Certainly, enclosures were occasionally adapted for some functional purpose in this period as, for example, at Glendalough where the infilled enclosure ditch was transformed into a stone-revetted watermill race in the twelfth century (O'Reilly et al. 2019, 38). Occasionally, enclosures were even dug or recut in this later period and it has been posited that a recut ditch at Dunshaughlin 'may simply reflect efforts by the Uí Máel Sechnaill or their vassals to restore Dunshaughlin to its former glory' (Simpson 2005, 233–7). Learned church authorities were certainly cognisant of ancient seventh-/eighth-century ecclesiastical settlement *schema* in this period many centuries later, but contemporary ideological, political or functional considerations were now invariably paramount behind any enclosure modification or redesign.

ACKNOWLEDGMENTS

This paper is based on research completed for an Irish Research Council-funded PhD in the School of Archaeology, UCD, under the supervision of Aidan O'Sullivan. Sincere thanks to Teresa Bolger, Christine Baker and Ed O'Donovan (O'Donovan Digs) for permission to reproduce the illustrations above, to the editor Seán Duffy for his support in publishing the paper and full catalogue, to Conor McDermott for his advice and assistance, to Rob Sands for making the distribution map at late notice, and finally to Lisa and Cillian for their patience whilst I revised and updated the paper and catalogue this year. GRMA.

making the distribution map at late notice, and finally to Lisa and Cillian for their patience whilst I revised and updated the paper and catalogue this year. GRMA.

APPENDIX
CATALOGUE OF EXCAVATED ECCLESIASTICAL ENCLOSURES DATING
POTENTIALLY TO THE EARLY MEDIEVAL PERIOD

Aghavea, Co. Fermanagh

Enclosure: Enclosure ditches

Information and dating evidence: Excavated early medieval features included five ditches east of the nineteenth-century church. Three of these may have had an enclosing function, although their exact date/form was not definitely established. A steep-sided flat-bottomed ditch (1) – context 24 – with max. recorded width of 1.85m and depth of 0.80m. The ditch fill consisted of 'a mix of grey and brown organic and silty clays and soils'. Fragments of burnt bone and a blue glass bead were found in its uppermost fills while fragments of tooth enamel and two pieces of lignite were recovered from the fill immediately beneath. Burnt hazel nuts recovered from a fill beneath both these two fills. The finds suggest an early Christian date for this feature, which is likely to represent part of an enclosing ditch of the ecclesiastical site. A north-west–south-east aligned ditch (3) – context 309 – was possibly associated with an internal palisade trench running 0.40m parallel to it. The ditch (1.8m max. width 0.70m deep) was uncovered for 6m (only a 3m portion was excavated). The fills were artefact-free, except for the upper fill which produced 27 pieces of slag, one metal object and 7 sherds of souterrain ware pottery. The palisade slot – context 254 – associated with this external ditch (3) was constructed with interrupted stone-packed postholes and was uncovered below the wall slot of a medieval structure (context 208). This palisade was uncovered for a distance of 5.60m and was 0.20–0.40m wide and 0.10m–0.20m deep. Two dark grey sticky and friable clays filled the slot and fragments of slag were recovered from its lower fill. Together, palisade and ditch may represent the remains of an early medieval ecclesiastical enclosure. A section of the possible main enclosure (ditch 4) – context 303 – was revealed for 20m extending east–west from the direction of the modern church. It was *c.*3m wide x 0.80m deep and was filled with a number of sticky clays, some of which produced a 'high charcoal and organic content and redeposited natural'. These charcoal and organic-rich fills produced 19 pieces of slag, one metal object and large fragments of burnt bone. The ditch was probably the same feature as another ditch (103) and appears to pre-date the main medieval ditch (252) as it was truncated by this latter ditch and also the smaller medieval ditch (341). It appears then that this large ditch (4) – context 303 – 'may represent the main early Christian enclosure uncovered on site'. Two other early medieval ditches, ditches (2) – context 30 – and (5) – context 28 – were recorded, but these do not appear to have had an enclosing function.

References: Ó Baoill 2000:0352; Ó Baoill 2000, 12–15; Ó Baoill 2014

Aghaviller, Co. Kilkenny

Enclosure: Enclosure ditch
Information and dating evidence: Testing in close proximity to the ecclesiastical site revealed 'a sizeable ditch/boundary running north–south with stone revetting on its eastern side', which Devine identified as 'a small part of a ditch that delimited the extent of a second, outer enclosure' of the church site.

References: Devine 2005:791

Annaghdown, Co. Galway

Enclosure: Outer enclosure ditch
Information and dating evidence: Geophysical survey (13R86) by Roseanne Schot in 2013 revealed a series of anomalies. Testing by Ó Maoldúin in Janurary 2014 in the field north-east of the ecclesiastical site revealed 'the presence of subsurface archaeological remains and identified a probable outer *vallum* (enclosing ditch) of early medieval date'. This enclosure ditch was apparently 4m wide. Metalworking debris (slag) was also recovered from the upper fill of the backfilled *vallum*. Other finds included a bronze shank, possibly belonging to a dress pin or belt buckle. Testing by Crumlish in December 2014 in an area north-north-west of the graveyard revealed an east-north-east/west-south-west orientated ditch (4.2m wide and 1.55–1.8m deep). Its upper fill produced animal bone, one human bone (left humerus) and occasional charcoal. The fill below contained much animal bone, occasional flecks of charcoal and four pieces of slag. The basal fill contained a larger amount of animal bone than the two upper fills, as well as some charcoal and three pieces of iron slag. Animal bone from the basal fill of the ditch produced an eleventh-/twelfth-century date. This ditched feature correlated with anomalies identified in the geophysical survey and was of a similar dimension to that uncovered by Ó Maoldúin, with iron slag also found in Ó Maoldúin's ditch.

References: Ó Maoldúin 2014:050; Crumlish 2014:309

Ardfert, Co. Kerry

Enclosure: Enclosure ditch and possible causeway entrance
Information and dating evidence: Church site enclosed by a bank with an associated external wide, shallow ditch. The enclosure contained a possible

entrance causeway defined by two postholes on its northern terminal and was located to the east of the cathedral (*c*.20m east of the eleventh-century *damliac*). The causeway measured 1m wide and may have been wider originally. The causeway was cut by two pits. Fragments of bronze, animal bone and an iron chain with spike were found in their lower fill, with green-glazed Saintonge pottery and two pillow stone burials revealed in the upper fill. Two postholes, one at the northern terminal of the fosse and another between the two pits, suggest a structural feature connected with the entrance causeway. The enclosure ditch and bank could not be closely dated, although a medieval iron casket key was found within the fill of this ditched feature. A north–south flat-bottomed ditch (14.5m long, 1.3m–1.6m wide and up to 0.55m deep) also extended across the area of south aisle and west end of the nave, to the west of the *damliac* foundations. This feature contained animal bone and pre-dated the thirteenth-century cathedral, but it is unclear if it was related to the curving enclosing ditch to the east of the cathedral. There was no evidence for this feature in the excavations outside the north wall.

References: Moore 1991:062; Moore 2007, 39–41, 80–1

Ardreigh, Co. Kildare

Enclosure: Enclosure ditch
Information and dating evidence: Remains of inner and outer enclosure ditch uncovered during the excavations at the site.
References: Moloney, Baker, Millar and Shiels 2015

Armagh, Cathedral Hill (Castle Street), Co. Armagh

Enclosure: Enclosure ditch
Information and dating evidence: Excavations at Castle Street, Armagh to the south of the cathedral revealed an enclosure ditch and bank which may have enclosed Cathedral Hill (Gaskell-Brown and Harper 1984). The ditch was originally about 6.4m wide at the top, generally V-shaped in section and 1.68–2.25m deep (from beneath the topsoil). The excavators stated that it may have enclosed an area 50m in diameter with its centre to the south of the present cathedral, but this appears to have been a misprint and should have read 100m (Matthews 2000, 51). The first enclosure phase (1) involved the digging of the bank and ditch, followed by its primary and then secondary silting. A rough stone revetment, a substantial circular posthole on the north side of the ditch bottom and the vestiges of three wooden stakes driven into the ditch bottom, were associated with this phase. Twigs from organic matter from the secondary silting at the ditch bottom produced a date of 1660±80 B.P. (UB-283) which calibrates as AD 176–577 2Σ and provides a *terminus post quem* for the ditch's construction. Fragments of human bone and over 4kg of animal bone (cattle and pig) were found in the primary fill. The secondary silting

produced an iron knife, six lumps of slag, crucibles, fragments of human bone, and roughly 23.7kg of animal bone (Gaskell-Brown and Harper 1984, 112). The next phase (2) involved the end of the active use of the ditch and a deliberate infilling of red soil into the ditch which included a skeleton (D): this red soil layer appears to represent bank material deliberately pushed back into the ditch from its southern or outer side. Finds from this phase included several crucible fragments, ingot moulds, scrap bronze, a bone knife handle, slag, a whetstone and animal bone. Following the destruction and partial infilling of the ditch, a series of early medieval deposits and disturbances (i.e., pits) were cut into the ditch hollow (phase 3). Some localized recutting and silting up of the ditch were also identified. A charcoal-rich soil from one of these pits contained carbonized twigs (1432±85 BP) which produced a 2 sigma radiocarbon date range of AD 426–771. Finds from this layer (a bronze(?) shrine fitting) and other layers (bronze book fitting, iron loop, piece of fabric-impressed crucible, worked flints, slag) support the radiocarbon date range and provides a *terminus ante quem* for the demolition of the 'outer' bank. A rough stone causeway was built into the ditch hollow. The ditch was used for the disposal of early medieval metalworking rubbish, particularly in the area of the causeway. Finds from this ditch (stone ingot moulds, clay moulds, heating trays, crucibles, slag, scrap bronze, iron, bone and bronze objects, lumps of vitrified clay, sherds of E ware and sub-Roman pottery) imply a nearby workshop inside the ditch line. Phases 4 and 5 represented heterogeneous layers in the upper ditch fills dating to the early, late and post-medieval periods. The radiocarbon date of AD 176–577 from the ditch bottom has been used to suggest a potential pre-Christian ditch with external bank. However, Matthews (2000, 57–8, 156, 339–40) is not convinced that the ditch ever enclosed the entire hilltop summit and also that it may have had an external bank, although the latter suggestion is not pressed. Matthews (2000, 66, 72–3) is also cautious about the early dating of the ditch. She noted that the finds from the ditch dated from the fifth/sixth century to ninth century, but the fact that these were dispersed throughout the ditch fill might indicate that the ditch was dug and infilled within a relatively short period of time. She suggested that the ditch fill containing the artefacts consisted of redeposited material from nearby. This scenario might explain the broad 14C dates and the mixing of metalworking debris with animal and human bones. If the artefacts represented redeposited material, this might suggest that the sample used to provide an early date for the ditch might have also included residue material, and was therefore contaminated. Support for this might also come in the form of the disarticulated human remains as they appear to represent disturbed burials from a nearby early medieval cemetery which was deposited casually in the ditch. The exact date when this ditch was dug is therefore highly debatable.

References: Gaskell-Brown and Harper 1984, 109, 112–18, 156–8; Matthews 2000, 51, 57–8, 66, 72–3, 156, 339–40

Armoy (Glebe/Turnarobert td.), Co. Antrim

Enclosure: Enclosure ditch

Information and dating evidence: Excavation in 2004–5 at Armoy uncovered a substantial curving enclosure ditch (phase 2) north of the church. The upcast soil from the ditch was spread to the north and south of this feature, suggesting that no enclosure bank may have ever existed. The initial ditch cut was U-shaped, measuring 2–2.5m wide, and 1–1.5m deep. This initial ditch was accompanied by a parallel U-shaped gully to its south (1.0m in width, 0.5m in depth), and by a scarped walkway (c.1.5m in width) along its northern (exterior) side, which served to create a level ground surface by removing some of the gradient upslope to the north. The parallel gully south of the ditch may have been intended as a slot-trench for a palisade, but there was no evidence for packing or post- and stake-holes. Another portion of an enclosure ditch was uncovered in 1991 to the south of the church (Williams 1991:011) and may belong to the same boundary feature as it had a similar width (2.5–3m) to the ditch section excavated in 2005. This initial boundary feature may have been D-shaped and had projected dimensions of 50m–60m by c.80m. The ditch began to silt up during phase 3 and a sample of this silting was radiocarbon-dated to AD 611–622 (UB-12332 – 2 sigma: no BP date stated). The enclosure ditch was recut in phase 4 once it had substantially silted up. The recut was generally V-shaped. It was steeper, deeper and narrower than the original ditch, and cut deeply into the subsoil. This secondary ditch recut was soon open to refuse (i.e., animal bone) and may have partially filled up again over a relatively short period of time. A sample from the upper fill of this recut ditch produced a calibrated 2 sigma date of AD 717–883 (UB-12333 – no BP date stated). During this phase 4, the recut ditch was extended some 7m further than the phase 2 ditch, terminating 8m west of the eastern scarp of the site. The reason for the 8m gap in the phase 4 ditch and 15m gap in the phase 2 ditch is unclear, but it may indicate an entrance or causeway allowing access to the site. The ditch was almost completely infilled in phase 5 (c.ninth century), when a substantial soil deposit was spread across the site. The absence of souterrain ware and paucity of artefacts from phases 1 to 4 on the site suggests that this period of enclosure construction and recutting relates to the fifth to the eighth century AD. A fragmentary decorated bronze book clasp and a bi-facially decorated and perforated stone were found in phase 5 deposits sealing the phase 1–4 features and may date to around the eighth/ninth century.

References: Williams 1991:011; Ó Néill 2004:0008; Nelis 2005:0007; Nelis et al. 2007, 33–9, 86, 109–11; Nelis et al. 2014, 147–50

Attirory, Co. Leitrim

Enclosure: Enclosure ditch?

Information and dating evidence: Testing (5 trenches –18E0707) revealed two sections of a possible ditch 'likely to be the continuation of the ecclesiastical

enclosure (LE031–039003–) of Attirory'. 'Other features consisted of a series of post-holes and pits of various forms some containing animal bone and slag', all of which appear to have been located within the ecclesiastical enclosure.
References: McHugh 2019:075

Balally, Co. Dublin

Enclosure: Enclosure ditch
Information and dating evidence: In 2003, 'excavation in the townland of Balally, Co. Dublin, revealed a double-ditched enclosure probably associated with the nearby early Christian church. Both ditches had been heavily truncated during eighteenth-century landscaping when the area became part of the Moreen House demesne. Finds included a medieval rotary quern, as well as coarse local medieval ware. No structures were identified'. Portions of this bivallate enclosure were found by Desmond (2001:322) and Clinton (2000:0203). Previous to this, a shallow curving ditch (0.9m d.) was excavated by Mount (1990; 1990:029) on the site, but its antiquity was not clearly established.
References: Mount 1990; Mount 1990:029; Clinton 2000:0203; Desmond 2001:322; O'Donnchadha 2003:455

Balfeaghan, Co. Meath

Enclosure: Enclosure ditches?
Information and dating evidence: Excavation in advance of road realignment works at Site 14 revealed 'a series of medieval ditches which appeared to form a series of enclosures, which appear to be centred to the east of the eastern limit of excavation'. 'Balfeaghan church (ME049–017) was located directly across the R158 from the site, 15m to its north-east'. The excavator did not speculate about the function of these ditches.
References: Collins 2007:1256

Balgriffin Park, Co. Dublin

Enclosure: Enclosure ditch
Information and dating evidence: A church site in Balgriffin Park is located a small distance south-east of St Doulagh's Church (below). Testing in a field east of this church site in 2004 revealed a 'substantial curving ditch' that 'measured 4.75m wide and more than 1.3m deep and appeared to be enclosing the area to the west (i.e., the site of the church)'. Additional testing in 2004 to the west of the ditch revealed two smaller linear ditches that 'contained similar fills to the large curving ditch and may have been associated with it'. The excavator stated that 'it remains likely that this ditch is an enclosing feature related to the church'. No date was, however, advanced for it (McLoughlin 2004:0513).
References: McLoughlin 2004:0513

Ballybarrack, Co. Louth

Enclosure: Enclosure ditch and bank?

Information and dating evidence: Three souterrains were excavated at Ballybarrack within a large oval enclosure (maximum dimension of about 90m). The enclosure consisted of a 'deep ditch which formerly had an internal bank and a counterscarp bank, both of which appear to have been, at least partly, stone-faced'. As a medieval church is present within the south-west edge of the enclosure, might this feature form part of an outer ecclesiastical enclosure?

References: Kelly 1977–9:0052

Ballyburley, Co. Offaly

Enclosure: Enclosure ditch?

Information and dating evidence: Testing adjacent to the Ballyburley church, Rhode revealed a large ditched feature identified by the excavator as a possible ecclesiastical enclosure. The ditch was 3.4–3.8m across at the top and 1.8m deep.

References: Mullins 1997:443

Ballykilmore, Co. Westmeath

Enclosure: Enclosure ditch

Information and dating evidence: The exposed section of the enclosure ditch was V-shaped in profile and measured 2.43m–3.30m wide and 1.47m–1.61m deep. The curve of the exposed section suggests that the full enclosure formed a sub-circular or oval shape with a maximum internal diameter of *c.*70m. Three main ditch fill deposits were identified. Animal bone and some metalworking waste were recorded in the basal fills. Animal bone from the ditch basal fills produced a calibrated 2 sigma date from AD 538–682 (1425±51), implying 'the early use of the ditch in the sixth to seventh century'. Two small slag pit furnaces were cut into the partially infilled ditch. Bone from one of these furnaces returned a thirteenth-/fourteenth-century date, indicating that this feature had been largely infilled by this date, if not much earlier.

References: Channing 2012, 85–8; Channing 2014, 25, 26, 38

Ballynoe, Co. Cork

Enclosure: Enclosure ditch and bank

Information and dating evidence: A section of an enclosure ditch was identified in areas north and north-east of the church. It consisted of 'a U-shaped ditch 3.3m wide at the top, 0.8m wide at the base and 1.6m deep' (Cotter 1996:037). Based on the nature of the upper ditch fills and the small amount of silting, it was suggested that 'much of it was rapidly infilled, presumably shortly before the [thirteenth-century] church was built' (Cotter 2002, 115). Samples of hazel, willow/poplar and Rosaceae woods (e.g., blackthorn, hawthorn, cherry,

apple or pear) were recovered from near the ditch base, and might suggest that 'a wattle fence or a thorn hedge' existed close to the ditch in one area (E). The excavated section in area F north-east of the church revealed 'a lack of organic inclusions or sediment build-up' and 'a high content of clay' in the ditch layers, suggesting a 'deliberate backfilling of the ditch' (ibid., 120). It was suggested that this backfilled material probably derived from 'the levelling of an internal bank', which was recorded as 'spread over much of area F' (ibid.). The ditch 'extended in an arc under the wall of the vestry' and it was deemed 'most likely that this ditch is the enclosing element of an early ecclesiastical site which has been obliterated by the building of the thirteenth-century nave and the later addition of the chancel and vestry' (Cotter 1996:037). Only tiny amounts of charcoal were recovered from the ditch and these could not be dated.
References: Cotter 1996:037; Cotter 1999:074; Cotter 2002, 109, 115–21

Ballyovey (Kilkeeran td.), Co. Mayo

Enclosure: Enclosure wall
Information and dating evidence: A cutting along the south perimeter of the 'cashel-type enclosure' revealed 'a limestone wall 0.85m thick, very low internally and up to only 0.3–0.4m high externally. There is a drop of 1m from the top of the cashel wall to the outer ground level here, however'. No dateable evidence was recovered.
References: Morahan 1997:407

Balrothery (St Peter's Church), Co. Dublin

Enclosure: Enclosure ditch?
Information and dating evidence: 'Excavation revealed the presence of a curvilinear field ditch with stone along one edge' immediately outside the churchyard boundary wall. Bullaun stone recovered from topsoil nearby.
References: Stevens 2004:0470

Bangor, Co. Down

Enclosure: Enclosure ditches
Information and dating evidence: Excavations at Bangor revealed 'two medieval ditches, the latest of which had a tenth–thirteenth-century *terminus post quem*'. These may have been roughly contemporary with two linear channels, a stone linear feature, a well, a pit and two postholes. Artefacts recovered in association with these features included 'medieval pottery dating from the tenth to the thirteenth century, a metal stylus of medieval date, butchered animal bone, various stone artefacts, including a rotary quernstone, and organic material such as leather and hazelnuts'. These two ditches suggest that the original abbey was located within 'a large circular enclosure which

included the site of the present abbey church and probably extended to cover a portion of Cross Hill'. The earliest of the two ditches may have enclosed 'the site of the current parish church, thought to relate directly to the location of the original stone or wooden church. The later ditch did not appear to be an enclosing ditch but nevertheless could represent an internal division within the ecclesiastical site or a drainage feature running towards the stream to the east'.
References: Ward and Vuolteenaho 2011:152

Butterfield, Co. Dublin

Enclosure: Palisade trench
Information and dating evidence: An early medieval enclosed settlement with burial ground defined by a possible palisaded trench was found at Butterfield. The palisade trench dated to the earliest phase. Animal bone, a penannular brooch terminal, iron knives and a 'pig fibula' pin were found in the trench confirming an early medieval date for the palisade. It was suggested by the excavator that the site was probably ecclesiastical, but it could alternatively be a cemetery settlement type site.
References: Carroll 1997:0184

Caherlehillan, Co. Kerry

Enclosure: Enclosure wall
Information and dating evidence: The enclosing wall was found to represent a primary feature of the ecclesiastical site. Only a portion of the original enclosure survived along its southern and south-eastern sides with modern field walls overlying its western side and a roadway bisecting the site across its northern portion. It originally enclosed a space *c.*30m in diameter with an infilled entrance on east side. The surviving enclosure at the south end consisted of a rubble-built wall (1m high and 1.05m wide) with an outer facing of large horizontally-laid slabs and a 0.2m thick layer of internal stone collapse. Test trenches across a low tree-lined bank in the field north of the bisecting roadway revealed a stone wall with similar morphology and dimensions to the original ecclesiastical enclosure (Sheehan 2003). The enclosing wall directly overlay early drainage trenches and a sample from the enclosing wall yielded a BP date of 1445±70 BP (GrN-28343), dating this feature to the period from the early fifth to later seventh century (Sheehan 2009, 194).
References: Sheehan 2003; Sheehan 2009, 194–6, 204; Sheehan 2014, 250

Cappancur, Co. Offaly

Enclosure: Enclosure ditch and bank
Information and dating evidence: Testing adjacent to the church site at Cappancur revealed 'a flat/round-bottomed ditch, 2.9m wide and 0.75m deep' interpreted tentatively as an ecclesiastical enclosure. Animal bone and molluscs

were recovered from the fills, but no dateable finds. The remains of a possible levelled internal bank were also identified in the form of 'a deposit of orange, sandy clay, 0.4m thick'. A second ditch was revealed 6m to the south of the above ditch. It measured '1.8m wide, narrowing to 0.8m at the limit of excavation, which was 0.4m below the top of the ditch'. It contained a similar fill to that of the main ditch and it was therefore suggested that both features are probably contemporary.
References: Delany 1999:733

Carndonagh, Co. Donegal

Enclosure: Enclosure ditch
Information and dating evidence: Testing in Churchland Quarters townland revealed evidence for a slightly curving ditched feature 'in the general area where one would expect to find evidence of an enclosure associated with an ecclesiastical site'. This ditch was 3.2m wide within the trench (its east side was not fully uncovered within the trench) and at least 1.4m (west side) deep and was cut into the boulder clay. No dateable finds were recovered from the ditch fill.
References: King and Crumlish 1998:103

Carns, Co. Roscommon

Enclosure: Drystone enclosure wall
Information and dating evidence: A trench was opened up along the enclosure where it adjoined a relict field bank. The excavation confirmed that the circular church enclosure dated potentially to the late Iron Age/early Christian period and established that it was once 'bounded by a 2m thick drystone wall of a type that could be expected at an early medieval church site'. Finds of part of a lignite bracelet and a blue glass bead from this feature support an early medieval date. The drystone enclosure wall was also found to carefully enclose an earlier, smaller bivallate enclosure of potential prehistoric date, suggesting 'a deliberate attempt to incorporate the earlier site into Christian tradition'.
References: Shanahan 2006:1715; McNeary and Shanahan 2009, 131

Carrowmore, Co. Donegal

Enclosure: Enclosure ditches
Information and dating evidence: Geophysical survey in 2014 revealed a bivallate enclosure around the church. Follow-up trial trenches across both enclosures revealed the outer boundary ditch to be U-shaped in profile and 3.6m wide at the top and more than 1.6m deep. A thin turf layer above the basal fill produced a radiocarbon date of AD 670–870. A stone-lined hearth was

placed on the top of the ditch fills and this feature produced a calibrated radiocarbon date of AD 1030–1160. The inner ditch was V-shaped in profile and measured *c.*2m wide at the top and 1.55m deep. Primary fills were from natural silting, while organic matter was recovered in middle zones. The ditch was then recut and its first subsequent fill produced a calibrated radiocarbon date of AD 590–660. Metalworking debris was uncovered in the next zone of fills. The excavation also uncovered a revetment 'set back from its inner edge, with linear cut-features and stakeholes in between'.
References: O'Brien and Adams 2014, 4–5

Church Island, Co. Kerry

Enclosure: Enclosure wall
Information and dating evidence: The enclosing cashel wall (maximum width of 2m and height of 1m) is still present for two-thirds (83m long) of its original circuit (*c.*140m) and encloses almost the whole habitable top of the island. It was absent on the western and south-western sides of the island because of cliff-edge erosion. On the basis of the stone collapse around its surviving perimeter, it was suggested that it may have originally stood 1.5m high. Like the rectangular house on site, its walls comprised inner and outer stone faces with a rubble and earthen core. There were at least two entrances: one along the north-east which gave the occupants of the rectangular house access to the enclosure and another flagged entranceway along the eastern side affording access to the natural slipway and landing place. The cashel wall was built on top of two early burials (O'Kelly 1958, 92), which implies that it is not a primary feature. O'Kelly viewed it as the last major monastic structure on the island. It clearly post-dated the rectangular house as it curved to avoid it. Although O'Kelly (1958, 76) viewed the enclosure wall as later than the round stone house, Hayden argues that the latter house is the latest monastic structure built around the twelfth century. The enclosing cashel wall can be assigned to the eleventh/twelfth century following the revised chronology posited by Hayden.
References: O'Kelly 1958, 75–7, 82; Hayden 2013, 101, 104, 130

Cleenish, Co. Fermanagh

Enclosure: Enclosure ditches
Information and dating evidence: Geophysical survey revealed 'a large, D-shaped enclosure with internal sub-divisions, encompassing an area of *c.*160m by 125m'. Excavation across the main enclosure uncovered a V-shaped ditch 2.8m wide and 1.1m deep. No definite evidence for a bank was uncovered, though most of the ditch fill was 'derived from the inner, upslope, side'. Finds from the basal fill included animal bone, an iron needle and an iron knife blade. A second trench inside this enclosure uncovered 'a shallow pit and ditch, filled by charcoal-rich soil, fragments of burnt stone and animal bone'.
References: Ó Maoldúin 2014:310

Clone, Co. Wexford

Enclosure: Enclosure ditches
Information and dating evidence: Following the identification of anomalies in a geophysical survey, two cuttings revealed the inner and outer enclosures and two other ditches of indeterminate date. No artefacts recovered, except a single sherd of Leinster cooking ware from topsoil. Radiometric dates on charcoal were pending.
References: Shine 2019:451

Clonfad, Co. Westmeath

Enclosure: Enclosure ditches and possible bank
Information and dating evidence: The outermost enclosure ditch (C101) was oval in plan and had a projected diameter of 180–200m. It was excavated for 66m and had a V-shaped profile, with a narrow but flat base, 2.8m–3.4m wide and 1.8–2.5m deep. The ditch was left open for a period of time and there was evidence for repairs and reinforcements. The lower fills consisted of slumps or in-washed sands and gravels containing smithing waste and bone needles. A line of large boulders was identified in the initial backfilling along the ditch base and this may represent the remains of a possible revetting feature belonging to an internal bank. Furthermore, the later, upper levels of the enclosure ditch appear to have been backfilled from both sides as a single event, with possible indications also evident for an internal bank. A large number of artefacts from the backfill deposits inside the ditch were interepted as the discarded waste from one or a number of workshops in the area. The inner enclosure ditch (1.2m–2.8m wide and 0.72m–1.3m deep) was shallowest in the north-west where it was U-shaped in profile and was occasionally lined with large boulders, but achieved a broader, V-shaped profile towards the stream. The fills contained early medieval industrial refuse. A sample of oak charcoal from the basal fill of the inner enclosure ditch returned a radiocarbon range of AD 688–878. The inner enclosure ditch was cleaned out a number of times before being completely sealed sometime around the ninth century with the construction of a blacksmith's forge over it. Stratagraphic, artefactual and dating evidence suggests that the infilling of both enclosures was possibly simultaneous and that both ditches were already in the process of being backfilled during the eighth century. Geophysical survey identified the line of the two enclosures around the rest of the site.
References: Stevens 2012, 120–4; Stevens 2014, 259–72

Clonfeacle (Tullydowey td.), Co. Armagh

Enclosure: Enclosure ditch
Information and dating evidence: Excavation in 2003 in a field north-east of the demolished graveyard wall revealed a shallow, linear gully extending for 8.8m; this feature varied in width from 1.6m–2.4m. A distinct slot was found

within the base of the gully and was interpreted as 'the footing for a palisade' (McHugh, Bell and MacDonald 2004, 60). As this feature 'broadly respects the adjacent curvilinear field boundary, located approximately 18m to the south-east and identified above as a possible reflection of the line of the early monastery's outer enclosure', it was suggested that this gully 'formed part of an early, outer enclosure of the monastery' (ibid., 62). Excavation in 2004 by Long also revealed 'a short section of the probable outer enclosing ditch of the monastic site', which 'was *c*.3m wide and cut directly into subsoil to a depth of 1.5m' (Long 2006:133). This ditch was 'recut several times in antiquity' and a bowl furnace containing much slag was present within its upper fill (Long 2005, 27; Long 2006:133). A large ditch also bisected the excavation area in an approximate north-west/south-east direction; it contained early Christian pottery and was interpreted as 'an internal division within the monastic enclosure'.

References: McHugh, Bell and MacDonald 2004, 60, 62; Long 2005, 27; Long 2006:133

Clonfert, Co. Galway

Enclosure: Enclosure ditch

Information and dating evidence: Excavations in a field east of the church and graveyard revealed a ditch which was 'likely to be of early medieval date'. The excavators suggested that it may have formed part of the 'original enclosure around the monastery' and noted that these enclosing earthworks are still visible in 'the field on the opposite side of the roadway south of the church, curving towards the area where the trench was opened'.

References: Walsh and Hayden 2001:496

Clongeen, Co. Wexford

Enclosure: Enclosure ditch?

Information and dating evidence: 'A large ditch was uncovered, possibly marking the extent of the ecclesiastical enclosure of Clongeen.'

References: McLoughlin 2006:2095

Clonlea, Co. Clare

Enclosure: Enclosure ditch?

Information and dating evidence: 'Testing in advance of a graveyard extension located ditches, pits and post-holes that, while undated, are likely to represent enclosed medieval ecclesiastical occupation.'

References: Hull 2008:115

Clonmacnoise, Co. Offaly

Enclosure: Enclosure ditch

Information and dating evidence: A portion of the outer enclosure ditch was uncovered south-west of the ecclesiastical buildings near St Ciaran's

School. The enclosure ditch measured roughly 5m–6.2m wide x 3.8m deep. The ditch was roughly V-shaped in profile with a flat bottom. Animal bone from the bottom fill of the ditch produced a date of AD 674–891 2Σ. The absence of significant silting in the ditch suggests that it may have been recut shortly before it was deliberately infilled. It was suggested that the ditch was backfilled in the later eighth or early ninth century and that the great size and time involved in digging this feature might imply that it was 'left open for a considerable length of time', thereby suggesting that it was originally excavated in the sixth or seventh century. Finds from the ditch fill included a worked piece of bone, a piece of timber and a small fragment of an iron nail. Further excavations in 2019 at the carpark revealed a large north-west/south-east orientated ditch which measured *c.*5.5m in width. 'This is thought likely to represent part of the enclosure ditch around the monastic site, as seen in previous excavations at Clonmacnoise' (Murphy 2019:529).

References: Murphy 2003, 13, 16, 19, 26; Murphy 2019:529

Collooney, Co. Sligo

Enclosure: Enclosure ditch?

Information and dating evidence: Testing east of the church revealed a possible ditch 21m from the graveyard wall. It was identified in the form of 'a loose fill of yellow clay' and was interpreted as 'part of an enclosing ditch'. The ditch measured 5m east–west and was approximately 2m deep.

References: Simpson 1994:204

Connor, Co. Antrim

Enclosure: Outer enclosure ditch

Information and dating evidence: The enclosure ditch identified by Brannon in 1986 measured *c.*3m wide x 1.5m deep and was U-shaped in profile. Souterrain ware was recovered from the upper strata of the ditch fills, thereby possibly suggesting an early Christian date for its original cutting. The ditch extended in a 'slightly curving NW-SE course across the E half of the field' and the projection of the ditch line suggests that it 'circuited the church site, at least on the N, and that it might therefore be interpreted as a perimeter boundary for an early Christian monastic precinct'. Testing in 2006 at the Braefield Nursing Home also revealed a ditch over 3m wide and 1m deep containing medieval pottery within its fills. Further examinations in 2007 at the site of the Braefield Nursing Home investigated the southernmost end of this ditch, which was found to be a maximum of 5m in width. The ditch was cut by a modern ditch and was at least medieval in date. The ditch was located in Connor townland near the church site, but it was not stated by the excavator whether it represented a field ditch, or possibly an enclosing element of the nearby church site.

References: Brannon 1986:02; Kovacik 2006:60; Morton 2007:39

Cookstown, Co. Meath

Enclosure: Enclosure ditch?
Information and dating evidence: Testing in 2001 revealed a V-shaped cut, *c.*1.2m wide at the top and at least 1m deep below the present ground. This feature was filled with grey silt, but did not produce any finds. No evidence for a bank, though 'it is possible that the layer of silty loam recorded on the southern side of the cut may constitute the ploughed-out remains of such a feature' (Myles 2001:955). This testing suggested that 'the boundary as depicted on the first edition of the Ordnance Survey map survives under the disturbed ploughsoil'. Further testing in 2002 revealed 'a possible raised earthen bank with an external ditch, representing the boundary of the churchyard, at the northern and southern ends of the trench'. The excavator did not speculate about the date of this enclosure ditch and bank (O'Connor 2002:1444). Whether these sections of ditch formed part of an early ecclesiastical enclosure was not stated and the possibility must equally remain that these boundary features are later in date.
References: Myles 2001:955; O'Connor 2002:1444

Cooley, Co. Donegal

Enclosure: Enclosure ditch and palisade
Information and dating evidence: Excavations in a field north-west of the cemetery at Cooley, Moville revealed the line of the outer ecclesiastical enclosure. The homogenous fill of the enclosure ditch (*c.*3.6m wide and 1.5m deep) was 'apparently introduced in only two or three dumps after a recutting episode which may have removed a more complex stratigraphic sequence. The deposit was so apparently sterile that its inferred origin is material which once formed a bank to the ditch: its original upcast, perhaps'. The excavation also revealed that parallel linear stone settings edged the enclosure ditch on either side, while a palisade trench may have been inserted into the ditch base. The outer enclosure was utilized for industrial activity, including probable iron-working, in its later phase.
References: Adams and O'Brien 2016:288

Coolock, Co. Dublin

Enclosure: Enclosure ditches
Information and dating evidence: A research excavation was undertaken at the church site in 1990 following the discovery of the lower stone of a horizontal watermill. Excavations in the area to the south-east, where an earlier gateway had existed, revealed 'evidence for an outer ditch, with inner bank, and burial within the line of the bank' (Swan 1990:033). 'A curving linear feature (length 30m min.; width 1.2–1.5m), interpreted as the north extent of an ecclesiastical enclosure, was uncovered to the immediate north of the church grounds in

October 2017 (Delany 2017:617; Delany 2018:698). Further testing in 2018 revealed the ditch (1.9m wide and 0.9m deep), with evidence of a recut on the south. The original ditch was U-shaped with steeply-sloping sides and a narrow base (width *c.*1.5m; depth 0.9m) while the secondary cut had gently-sloping sides and an almost flat base (width *c.*1m; depth 0.7m). Moderate–frequent inclusions of animal bones (cattle, sheep/goat and pig, but also a couple of horse and cat bones) as well as shells were recovered from the ditch fills. This ditch appears to form part of the same enclosure excavated by Swan in 1990 (above) along the southern perimeter of the church site. Further excavation in 2019 by McGlade (2019:493) potentially revealed the same enclosure along the eastern perimeter. Only a small section of the western side of this large curving ditch was identified. The two ditch fills again contained animal bone and charcoal. Based on the location of the three excavated ditch sections (1990; 2017/18; 2019) and the possibility that they all form part of the same boundary, it was suggested that this enclosure was oval in plan and measured approximately 87m east-south-east/west-north-west by 72m.

References: Swan 1990:033; Delany 2017:617; Delany 2018:698; McGlade 2019:493

Creaghanboy, Co. Mayo

Enclosure: Enclosure ditch?

Information and dating evidence: Testing within the constraint area of possible ecclesiastical remains revealed a curving linear feature under a stone boundary wall. This feature was revealed as a substantial V-shaped ditch (*c.*1.4m deep), which pre-dated the field wall and ran under the existing road. The upper ditch fill consisted of a compact orange/brown silty clay with large amounts of animal bone throughout. Beneath this was a compact greyish-brown silty clay. This fill contained some animal bone and snail shells. The ditch base contained a linear deposit of large stones within a loose silty clay. A sub-circular bowl furnace cut into the north side of the ditch and upper ditch fill. It was not speculated what function the ditch may have had, but its role as an ecclesiastical enclosure is possible.

References: Guinan 2004:1144

Crumlin, Co. Dublin

Enclosure: Enclosure ditch

Information and dating evidence: Testing in 1998 in an open area to the rear of Nos 1–7 St Agnes Road 'revealed a ditch outside and concentric to the boundary of the churchyard'. No dateable finds were recovered. Two pits containing burnt material were found inside the ditch and these were deemed likely to be of medieval date. Further excavation in 1999 revealed that the ditch fill was fairly consistent – a natural grey silting near the bottom, followed by a stony, brown clay of late medieval date. It was suggested that the ditch represents the outer ecclesiastical enclosure and that it was 'purposely infilled in the later medieval period'. The inner enclosure may survive in the existing circular graveyard wall.

References: Hayden 1998:130; Murphy 1999:173

Dalkey Island (St Begnet's), Co. Dublin

Enclosure: Enclosure wall

Information and dating evidence: Remains of a substantial wall, roughly 10–12m long, was uncovered to the north of the church; this feature appears to have formed the boundary of the early church graveyard. The wall contained a stone core revetted on both sides by slabs placed on edge. An excavation trench was opened through the wall entrance and a posthole was uncovered in this area which was identified as a gate-post. Based on the assumption that roughly half of the stone core of this wall was still extant, it was calculated that the original wall height was probably less than 0.90m. The wall collapse debris was overlain by a slightly darkened earth containing animal bones and thirteenth-century pottery sherds. This indicated that the wall was in a ruinous condition when this midden layer extended over the remains of the wall core. The excavation evidence suggests that the wall must pre-date the thirteenth century, but by how much is unknown.

References: Liversage 1968, 126–7, 192

Derryloran, Co. Tyrone

Enclosure: Enclosure ditches

Information and dating evidence: Excavations 50m to the west of Derryloran church and graveyard revealed three ditches which were deemed to represent 'the remains of successive enclosures surrounding the higher portion of the ridge' where the church site was located. Ditch 1 was *c.*4m wide and 2m deep, with initially steep V-shaped sides falling to a box-shaped base. The upper fill appeared to represent a recut. Ditch 2 measured *c.*2m wide and 0.8–1m deep and again had a V-shaped profile. The fills appear to mainly represent silting, although there may have been some deliberate backfilling. A single sherd of everted rim ware was found in the basal fill of the ditch. Ditch 3 was *c.*2m in width and 0.6-0.1m deep, with a V-shaped profile. The fills again appeared to represent natural silting, and no finds were recovered from it. It was indicated that 'the archaeology uncovered at Derryloran would appear to represent the remains of an early Christian enclosure site probably related to an earlier monastic enclosure which is reputed to have existed within this area of Cookstown'.

References: MacManus 2003:1843

Derrynaflan (Lurgoe td.), Co. Tipperary

Enclosure: Enclosure ditch?

Information and dating evidence: Excavation in 1987 focused on the outer enclosure ditch on the eastern side of the site. Two cuttings revealed that the ditch was broad and shallow with dimensions of 3m in width and 0.7m in depth. No finds were recovered to date its period of use or abandonment. However, the ditch appears to have cut a row of stakes, perhaps associated with a wooden trackway or 'togher' on the site. Limited excavation on a rectangular enclosure (20m x 22m) on the eastern side of the site revealed that this feature was earlier than the inner enclosure bank on the site. When excavated, the inner enclosure bank consisted of a rubble-filled wall faced with limestone boulders. The wall contained fragments of rotary querns, suggesting that this bank might be late in date. Previous excavations in 1985 and 1986 also uncovered ditched features, but it is unclear whether these formed part of an enclosure of the site. Instead, these may represent internal boundary divisions or could have an agricultural function.

References: Ó Floinn 1985:53; Ó Floinn 1986:70; Ó Floinn 1987:44

Donaghcumper, Co. Kildare

Enclosure: Enclosure ditch?

Information and dating evidence: Testing revealed 'a section of an east–west-aligned, 4.6m wide x 1.05m deep ditch that is probably part of an enclosure that surrounded the church'. A sherd of medieval pottery was recovered from the fill of a recut, confirming a medieval date for this phase. Animal bone was recovered from the base of the ditch; a sample of animal bone has been submitted for radiocarbon dating and should provide a date when the ditch was originally cut.

References: Devine 2010:399

Doora (Ballaghboy td.), Co. Clare

Enclosure: Enclosure ditch

Information and dating evidence: 'Following geophysical survey (08R314), test-trenching prior to a proposed graveyard extension adjacent to Doora church located a 3–4m-wide and *c.*1.2m-deep ditch enclosing the church'. The excavation also revealed pits, gullies and other archaeological features outside the ditch. It was suggested that these deposits may 'represent an early medieval monastic enclosure and associated activity'. Animal bone was recovered from the base of the ditch but was not unfortunately in a condition suitable for radiocarbon dating.

References: Hull 2009:085

Doras, Co. Tyrone

Enclosure: Inner enclosure ditch and bank

Information and dating evidence: A possible enclosure ditch was recorded to the south-west of the extant church. This ditch (3.75m wide x 1.2m deep) was V-shaped in profile. Thirteen deposits were identified; these were fairly clean, except for a small patch of burnt bone and charcoal at the base of layer 7. A sample of twigs (1305±90 BP), preserved by waterlogging, from below the lowest layer (1) of the ditch fill, and directly upon the original ditch bottom, produced a radiocarbon date (2 sigma) from the late sixth century to mid-tenth century. A body sherd of coarse ware pottery, probably medieval everted rim ware, was recovered from layer 11, fairly high up in the ditch fill. This suggests that the ditch had been largely infilled by this date. The complete lack of post-medieval material from the ditch fills indicates that the ditch was infilled by the end of the medieval period. Although most of the ditch deposits probably derived from the upslope external (south) side of the ditch, some appear to have washed in from both sides. This might indicate that an internal bank once existed on the north side of the ditch, but was subsequently destroyed when it was infilled. The ditch was only traced for a short distance, but its curving nature suggests that it may have enclosed an area downhill to the north, perhaps around the extant church. Its relationship with the larger townland boundary ditch – originally believed to represent the remains of the ecclesiastical enclosure – was not resolved, and the role of the excavated ditch as a possible internal subdivision cannot be completely excluded either.

References: McDowell 1987, 146–7

Downpatrick, Cathedral Hill, Co. Down

Enclosure: Enclosure ditches and banks

Information and dating evidence: Excavations by Brannon on the south-western slopes of Cathedral Hill revealed a V-shaped enclosure ditch (3m wide x 2m deep). The primary layers produced 'few artefacts, but all were of early Christian date' (Brannon 1988a, 5). The ditch was filled with layers of eroded soils, dumped rubbish (ashes and butchered animal bone), iron slag from nearby ironworking and souterrain ware, indicating that it was gradually infilled during the early Christian and medieval periods. Much of the eroded soil, particularly along the northern upslope of the ditch, probably originated from a long-vanished bank built from subsoil upcast from the original digging of the ditch. When first completed, the enclosure bank and ditch must have represented a formidable barrier combining to form an obstacle, some 3m–3.56m in height. Geophysical survey (by the Time Team TV production) of almost the entire area of Cathedral Hill also revealed two strong curving anomalies which may represent boundary ditches (Taylor and Aston 1998, 32). Trenches were dug across the lines of the two curving anomalies revealing two early medieval ditches; the inner ditch was 2.6m wide, at least 1.5m deep and contained souterrain ware sherds in its bottom fill, while the less substantial outer ditch was 1.3m wide and 0.8m deep. A concentric medieval ditch, 1.3m wide and 0.6m deep, cut the outer ditch in places. A thirteenth-century socketed iron arrowhead was recovered from topsoil overlying the ditches. Halpin (1998:115) also excavated 'a sizeable ditch running downslope (south) and cutting the two lower curving ditches' which contained souterrain ware. The date of the ditch running downslope obviously post-dates the early medieval ecclesiastical enclosure, but by how much is unclear. It is possible that it may represent an internal division? Proudfoot uncovered a series of ditches, banks and palisades around the hilltop to the south-west of the Cathedral in 1953/54 which he suggested dated to the Iron Age (fourth century BC to first century AD). He suggested that these ramparts and palisade then fell into disuse before a further refortification involving the construction of a simple wooden palisade on the extant enclosing bank was undertaken 'by people using "souterrain ware" type pottery'. The enclosing defences then fell into disrepair by the thirteenth century when medieval glazed pottery came into use on the hilltop. The above excavations, however, imply that Proudfoot's fortified enclosure may have been dug no earlier than the early medieval period and may instead have formed part of one of the ecclesiastical enclosures. The implications of these excavations are that Cathedral Hill can no longer be securely claimed as the site of a prehistoric hillfort (Brannon 1988a, 4).

References: Proudfoot 1955, 6–11; Proudfoot 1956, 65–71; Brannon 1986, 50; Brannon 1986:02; Brannon 1988a, 4–5; Brannon 1988b, 63; Brannon 1997:071; Halpin 1998:115; Taylor and Aston 1998, 32

Drumcliffe South, Co. Sligo

Enclosure: Enclosure ditch
Information and dating evidence: A series of excavations were undertaken at the church site in the early 1980s. Ditches, interpreted as internal site divisions, were revealed. Also uncovered was a northern section of the 'inner monastic enclosure'. No further details were provided.
References: Enright 1985:48

Drumcree, Co. Armagh

Enclosure: Enclosure ditch
Information and dating evidence: Excavation in advance of a carpark extension revealed linear features comprising 'enclosure ditches and structure gullies'. Artefacts uncovered included part of an early medieval stone bracelet and large quantities of early medieval pottery.
References: Donaghy 2018:278

Drumkay (Glebe td.), Co. Wicklow

Enclosure: Enclosure ditches, banks and palisades

Information and dating evidence: The enclosure (50m east–west x 35m north–south) was reconstructed at least twice and was slightly expanded, before being eventually surrounded by a post-medieval field boundary on its southern side. The earliest enclosing element was represented by a short length (15.5m) of a linear trench which was recorded 3.5m south-east of the church and 2.2m inside the phase I enclosure (below) (O'Donovan 2014, 196). A gap of 3.3m was identified between the east and west ends of this east–west aligned trench, which was interpreted as a possible entrance. Two smaller linear trenches – also truncated by later features – were identified in the south-western portion of the site. Both of these trenches were not very long, but 'may have been intended to support timber palisades' (O'Donovan 2014, 196). 18m of the phase I enclosure (*c.*1.8m wide x 0.75m deep) was excavated, and it contained a distinct sub-circular terminal marking an entrance 0.85m wide. Two deposits were identified as 'truncated remains of an internal bank inside the enclosure ditch'. The earliest bank deposit was viewed as upcast from the original ditch cut. A deposit of burnt charcoal-rich silty material lay above the upcast and this deposit produced eight fragments of Dublin-type coarse ware. This phase I enclosure contained an entrance which truncated the earliest possible 'linear enclosure'. This entrance feature consisted of a linear trench (5.3m long, 0.56m–0.60m wide and 0.30m deep) and a large posthole. Both the posthole and trench formed an angular feature that may have supported a palisade fence extending through the ecclesiastical enclosure. This possible entranceway opened into the south-eastern quadrant of the site. About 19.45m of the phase II enclosure ditch (0.2m wide x 0.70m deep) was excavated. The basal deposits were sealed by a grey-brown clayey silt which produced several medieval artefacts, including a pierced stone pendant, late twelfth- to thirteenth-century pottery and two sherds of post-medieval pottery, most probably intrusive. The southern edge of the phase II enclosure ditch was cut by the phase III enclosure ditch. This latter U-shaped ditch (2.2m wide) was excavated for 32m. This enclosure ditch extended further east than the earlier enclosure ditches, before being replaced by post-medieval ditches or field boundaries. The main fill of this phase III enclosure ditch produced a sherd of Leinster cooking ware and a ferrous nail. Overlying this main fill was a silt deposit which produced finds including post-medieval pottery, eight clay pipe fragments, a glass bottle fragment, a ferrous nail, a partial horseshoe and a sherd of Dublin-type coarse ware. The medieval finds from the main fill of the phase II enclosure ditch suggest that this ditch was open about *c.*1000–1500, in the same period when the stone church was in use. The absence of finds from the phase I enclosure ditch may imply an early medieval date for this feature. The linear trench truncated by the phase I enclosure ditch may have originally delineated the site and may date to the early Christian period (O'Donovan 2014, 209).

References: O'Donovan 2014, 193, 196, 209

Drumrat (Knockbrack td.), Co. Sligo

Enclosure: Enclosure ditch and possible bank

Information and dating evidence: Testing in advance of an extension to Drumrat graveyard revealed 'sections of a ditch filled with plastic sandy clay loam with occasional charcoal flecks' in three of the trenches. 'The remains of a possible bank (inside the ditch)' were also identified. It was suggested that 'the ditch and possible bank were part of the early Christian enclosure, which was just visible in the field to the east of the graveyard'.

References: Crumlish 2007:1538

Duleek, Co. Meath

Enclosure: Enclosure ditch?

Information and dating evidence: Testing in 1993 between St Cianan's Church and the Navan Road revealed 'traces of a ditch cut into subsoil', which 'may indicate the line of the southern boundary of the early Christian enclosure'. No artefacts were found, though 'a green glazed medieval potsherd was recovered from the top of the subsoil' (Donaghy 1993:180). Testing in 1999 on the south side of Larrix Street, Duleek, crossed the line of the enclosure ditch (Murphy 1999:681). Trench 1 uncovered a section of ditch extending in a south-west/north-east direction, which was at least 3m wide and 1m deep. A small dump of loose stone was also identified at the north side of the ditch, which was tentatively interpreted as belonging to 'part of a collapsed drystone wall'. Trench 3 revealed a ditch cut into the natural boulder clay, which 'was 1.8m deep, 2.7m wide at the top and 1m at the base'. The fill consisted of 'a grey, boulder-clay-like, wet clay, and no finds were recovered'. Another ditch was revealed in trench 4. It was 1.3m deep and 5m wide and also cut into natural subsoil. It was suggested that the ditch exposed in trench 3 'may relate to the early Christian enclosure but in all likelihood is not an enclosing ditch but an old field drain'. However, 'the ditch exposed in trenches 1 and 4 would appear to follow the line of the early Christian enclosure'. This ditch may have been interfered with in the north-east corner of the site towards Larrix Street in the early twentieth century when it appears to have been backfilled, 'as indicated by the relatively modern finds that were recovered'. 'It is clear, therefore, that, while the ditch follows the line of the early Christian enclosure, it has been altered in the north-east corner, where it was probably used as a drain' (ibid.). Further testing in 2008 at Larrix Street and Main Street revealed 'a ditch and bank of potential medieval date, and other related features within the monastic enclosure around St Cianan's Church' (Elder 2008:955). The full extent of these features were not established due to the limited size of the trenches.

References: Donaghy 1993:180; Murphy 1999:681; Elder 2008:955

Dunmisk, Co. Tyrone

Enclosure: Enclosure ditches and banks

Information and dating evidence: fifth–seventh-century early Christian activity involving erection of enclosed terraced settlement on Dunmisk hill. Original dome-shaped hilltop was flattened, terraced and modified. The earliest feature was remnants of a small bank set on the old turf line on the eastern side, which might represent the 'last remnants of a bank or rampart built on the original ground surface' before the deposition of an early medieval occupation layer. Charcoal from this overlying occupation debris (23.30) produced a 2 sigma date of AD 649–944 (1260±70), indicating that this bank (at its latest) pre-dates the early tenth century, but is probably considerably earlier. The hilltop was flattened at some point in this early period and some subsoil was cut away and dumped on the hill edge. A number of other soil dumps were laid over the redeposited subsoil to create the surface from which the early medieval cemetery was used and to further steepen the edge of the site. The material for this steepening was derived from the flattening of the hilltop and from scarping out the terrace which cut into the edge of the hilltop. These modifications to the hilltop occurred in early Christian times as they sealed the first early medieval occupation layer and the earlier primary boundary bank (above), but were partially sealed by the remains of the early medieval cemetery. Charcoal from a turf line post-dating the terracing activity returned a 2 sigma date of AD 346–769 (1480±100) indicating that the terracing activity (and various earlier features such as gullies) occurred before the later eighth century, if not much earlier. This dating evidence might imply activity on the hilltop during the fifth, sixth or seventh century in the form of banks, ditches and a general terracing of the site. An excavation by Brennan on the south side of the site uncovered a complex of ditches which he (1987:48) viewed as 'at least contemporary with and most likely predating the early Christian cemetery on the summit'. An excavation in the north of a cutting to the south of the fort revealed a ditch which cut through into the underlying boulder clay and gravel. The ditch fill contained several very thin deposits of purple, orange and brown layers sealed beneath a 0.2m deposit of black charcoal-flecked humic soil. This soil 'abutted a ridge revetted by three rough courses of stonework, with evidence of a posthole cut into the ridge directly behind the revetment'. A layer of stones and rock sealed the black humic soil, but underlay the subsoil. It is unclear whether this feature was associated with the construction of the enclosed terraced site revealed by Ivens above.

References: Brennan 1987:48; Ivens 1989, 21, 28, 55–6

Dunshaughlin, Co. Meath

Enclosure: Enclosure ditches and banks

Information and dating evidence: Remains of a curving ditch identified by Meenan in August 1993 north of the church were later excavated by Simpson in 1994 (1995:230; 2005) and were believed to represent a possible inner ecclesiastical enclosure as the outer ecclesiastical enclosure was believed to be fossilized in the curving streetscape. Possible inner enclosure consisted of remains of a curving ditch and an internal levelled bank. The possible enclosure ditch post-dated an early Christian round house and industrial activity. Internal bank indicated by a series of redeposited clays on the southern (internal) side of ditch. The bank deposits consisted of a spread of clays, 6.5m–7m wide but only 0.4m deep. Some clays had heavy charcoal flecking with lenses of ash and burnt clay, indicating that they originated from preceding craft phase. Enclosure ditch measured 4m–5m wide at the upper levels, 1m–1.4m wide at the base and 2.2m–2.4m deep with sloping sides and flat base. Water was originally channelled into the water-filled enclosure ditch from a natural spring, 1.8m south of the ditch via a stone drain (0.2m wide x 0.1m high). The ditch maintained a continuous water presence as indicated from its primary fill which consisted of banded layers of silt and fine gravel. A sample from this primary infill produced a date of AD 785–975 (sigma and BP date not specified). This sample indicates a date when the ditch was open. The ditch fill also produced small quantities of animal bone. Enclosure bank was later demolished and infilled into ditch, perhaps sealing it completely. After the bank was levelled, some craft occurred in the area. The ditch was then recut. This new ditch was smaller and narrower than the original ditch (2.8m wide at top and 1.6m wide at base). It was not water-filled as the spring was now sealed and measured 1.6m to 1.8m deep. Although the date of the recut could not be established, the infill of this new ditch was dated AD 1010–1165 (sigma or BP date not specified), providing a *terminus post quem* for it. Much animal bone was recovered from the recut. Southern arc of this possible inner enclosure ditch was recorded by Kevin Weldon in 1995 while monitoring on the eastern side of the main gate into the church. Here, the ditch was at least 3m wide and at least 0.5m deep. A stony deposit on northern (internal) side of ditch may represent remains of the internal bank (Simpson 2005, 234). Testing off Main Street just west-south-west of an early ecclesiastical settlement in 2004 (04E0670) also uncovered the possible remains of the inner enclosure ditch (Sweetman 2004:1235). Excavations in February/March 2003 by Finola O'Carroll (03E0089; 03E0348) along Dunshaughlin Road (east side of church site) also revealed a ditch, although its date/function was not stated (Simpson 2005, 238). A ditch (*c*.4m wide and at least 1.7m deep) was exposed in trenches *c*.100m north-east of the church in 1999 (99E0114) (Meenan 1999:683). However, it was deeper as the lower levels in trench 2 were waterlogged. The ditch in this waterlogged area was *c*.2m wide at its lowest excavated levels. The ditch in one trench (6) did not lie in the same arc as formed by the ditch in trenches 2 and 4. This evidence may suggest that the ditch in trenches 2 and 4 represented an inner ditch and that in trench 6 an outer ditch. An alternative explanation is that the ditch may not have been originally excavated as a regular circle. This ditched feature recorded by Meenan appears to be the same ditched feature which Simpson (2005, 234) had noted had been discovered to the north-east of the church. Other ditches were uncovered to the north of the church in 1991 by Rosanne Meenan and Beth Cassidy from ADS Ltd (Meenan 1991:101). The trenches exposed seven ditches grouped into two series. The inner series were spaced out over 12m and comprised three ditches with a possible bank outside the innermost. The second group comprised four ditches spaced *c.*47m–65m north of the churchyard wall. A possible stone wall was exposed in one trench to the west which respected the line of the ditches and may have formed a boundary. Medieval pottery was found in the fill of the innermost ditch. A spindle whorl was found in loose soil near the wall (ibid). The function, date and relationship of these ditches to the possible inner enclosure ditch (excavated in this area to the north of the church) is unclear. It is unclear if these ditches formed part of the possible inner enclosure ditch, or another enclosure, or represented internal subdivisions of medieval or earlier date. A number of ditches, possibly identifiable as enclosure ditches, have then been excavated around the early ecclesiastical site at Dunshaughlin. The exact function and date of the ditches excavated in 1991 is not clear, but the others, particularly that revealed by Simpson (2005) to the north of the church, appear to have formed part of an inner enclosure ditch around the ecclesiastical site.

References: Meenan 1991:101; Simpson 1995:230; Meenan 1999:683; Sweetman 2004:1235; Simpson 2005, 233–5, 237–8

Durrow, Co. Offaly

Enclosure: Enclosure ditches and banks

Information and dating evidence: Excavation in a field in Durrow Demesne 'revealed a semi-circular double bank and ditch roughly 500m in diameter and enclosing the standing remains of the monastery of Durrow'. It was observed that 'the eastern edge of this enclosure is aligned with the base of a high cross confirming that this represents the vallum of the monastery' (Ó Floinn 1985:46). In advance of a proposed golf course, a geophysical survey at the site in 2000/1 by Margaret Gowen Ltd revealed the same outer boundary. This revealed that 'the outer boundary, which is roughly oval in shape, consists of two close parallel ditches and banks with a further possible inner revetment, enclosing an area approx. 300m x 400m in diameter, that is 12 hectares or 30 acres' (O'Brien 2012, 120). Geophysical survey also identified traces of two inner enclosures inside the outer boundary. The smallest of the three enclosures contained the ninth-century high cross and the disused church (ibid., 120–1). A further geophysical survey in 2006 revealed complex multi-phase archaeological activity north of the church (King 2012). This included a large enclosure with associated field ditches, which may lie to the north of the enclosure surrounding the church site. In 2018, two cuttings were opened along the supposed line of the ecclesiastical enclosure. Trench 1 revealed a ditch 6.8m wide, with the boulder clay along its east edge noticeably fire-reddened. A charcoal-filled small pit or large posthole was recorded 2.7m west of the ditch. Trench 2 revealed a double fosse. The east example was 2.6m wide and the west example was 1.5m wide. These ditches were separated by a baulk of natural boulder clay 0.7m wide. No dating evidence was recovered from any of the ditches.

References: Ó Floinn 1985:46; O'Brien 2012, 119–20; King 2012, 128–30; Collins 2018:009

Ferns, Co. Wexford

Enclosure: Enclosure ditch

Information and dating evidence: Bhreathnach (2015, 39) reported that geophysical survey at Ferns, Co. Wexford and Kilmacduagh, Co. Galway revealed 'portions of the boundary (*termonn/terminus*) of the early monastic foundations', which were both 'defined by two widely spaced concentric ditches that curve around the existing churchyard enclosure'. Largescale test excavation at the eastern end of Ferns village in 2006 on the opposite side of the N11 to the cathedral and priory revealed multi-period archaeological deposits. These included a possible bivallate ringfort overlooking the early medieval ecclesiastical complex to the south-west and a third substantial ditch. It was aligned east–west and not related to the bivallate ringfort. It was V-shaped and was 5m wide, 2m deep. No finds were recovered. Kavanagh (2006:2104) did not suggest a function or date for the feature.

References: Kavanagh 2006:2104; Bhreathnach 2015b, 39

Finglas, Co. Dublin

Enclosure: Enclosure ditches and banks

Information and dating evidence: Excavations in 1993 just north of Mellowes Road, north of St Canice's Church, revealed a substantial U-shaped rock-cut ditch (8m wide x 2m in maximum depth) with an associated, much denuded bank (7m wide x 0.50m maximum surviving depth) to its south. Possible evidence for at least two ditch phases were revealed, while a mortared stone face had been recut into the ditch fill. This evidence suggests the reuse of an early enclosure ditch (with associated bank) as a townland boundary during the post-medieval period (Halpin 1994:092; Halpin and Murphy 1994, 4–5). Excavation in 1994 in same general area north of Mellowes Road uncovered a truncated rock-cut ditch on either side of the Fionn Ghlas river, which had been reused as a quarry in the post-medieval period. The line of the ditched feature was also reused as the townland boundary in post-medieval period. No trace of this original rock-cut ditch survived due to quarrying; however, a substantial bank (*c.*5m wide and 0.40m in maximum surviving height) survived south of the rock-cut face on the west side of the Fionn Ghlas stream and may represent an internal bank associated with the enclosure ditch. This enclosure ditch possibly defined the north side of the church site (Halpin 1994:093; McConway 1994a, 3–12). Excavation in 1996 at the site of the demolished Spanish Convent, south of Wellmount Road to the south of the church site, revealed a substantial east–west fosse and associated gully. This fosse (over 2m wide and up to 1.36m deep) contained an original early medieval fosse cut (*c.*2.1m wide x 1.02m deep) filled with silty clays, deemed to be generally indicative of slow deposition within waterlogged conditions. A *c.*seventh-/eighth-century ring pin was recovered from upper fill of original fosse. No evidence for an associated bank. This fosse was recut at least once. Recut fosse (0.48m deep and in excess of 2.1m wide) followed original fosse cut and line of associated inner gully, and its organic fill produced animal bone and thirteenth-/fourteenth-century pottery. Although it had relatively small dimensions, the early medieval fosse probably functioned as an enclosing marker for the church to the north (Halpin 1996:120; McConway 1996:121; 1996, 4–14). Excavations in 2003/4 on south side (4–8) of Church Street to the west of St Canice's medieval church revealed a substantial rock-cut V-shaped ditch (5.5m wide x 2.7m deep) which was identified as the remnants of an outer early ecclesiastical enclosure (Kavanagh 2005, 22). This ditch pre-dated medieval ploughsoil but contained no dateable finds. No evidence for an associated internal bank along its north side. Kavanagh suggested that this putative 'outer ecclesiastical enclosure did not encircle the medieval church site, but rather enclosed an area to the south-east of the settlement'. However, this ditch formed part of the large outer enclosure, originally posited by Swan (1985, 91, 98). From analysis of nineteenth-century OS Maps, Swan (1985, 91, 98–9) suggested the line of a large, oval-shaped, outer ecclesiastical enclosure (*c.*400m NE/SW and 260m NW/SE) at Finglas. The sites to the north of Mellowes Lane were located well over 300m north of the medieval church and may form the northern extent of a large, outer enclosure. The 1996 excavations to the south of Wellmount Road, south of the medieval church, uncovered an enclosure ditch of smaller dimensions. Although orientated in a more linear direction, Wellmount Road is located in the same general area as former Barrack Street, identifiable in early OS maps of the area, and it is possible that this ditch formed the southern perimeter of the outer ecclesiastical enclosure. The 2004 excavations in the southern area of 4–8 Church Street revealed an enclosure ditch along the line of the former Barrack Street, south-west of the medieval church, which again formed a possible enclosure of the church site to the north. These suggestions are only tentatively advanced and it is not clear if all of these ditches formed part of the same outer enclosure. None of the ditches were closely dated.

References: Swan 1985, 91, 98–9; Halpin 1994:092; Halpin 1994:093; Halpin and Murphy 1994, 4–5; McConway 1994a, 3–12; Halpin 1996:120; McConway 1996:121; McConway 1996, 4–14; Kavanagh 2005, 22

Friar's Island, Co. Clare

Enclosure: Cashel wall
Information and dating evidence: The stone church was possibly enclosed by some form of revetment or 'cashel' wall. Excavation uncovered a roughly constructed curved wall or revetment (0.76m high x 1.5m wide at the top) along the northern and north-eastern sides of the stone church, though this feature disappeared towards the shore of the island at the eastern end of the church. The surviving revetment wall did not enclose the church and was almost completely absent on its southern side. However, an 'abraded' ridge was identified to the south of a rectangular platform, extending straight across the island. Its function was unknown, but it was tentatively suggested that it may have originally formed part of the revetment or 'cashel' wall. If this suggestion is correct, it would indicate that the church was originally enclosed by some form of wall. No archaeological remains survived on the island to the south of this ridge.
References: Macalister 1929, 17–18

Glebe (Killucan), Co. Westmeath

Enclosure: Enclosure ditch?
Information and dating evidence: Testing to the west of the church and graveyard revealed 'a cut for a ditch or pit in trench A, followed by a number of inhumations, seemingly in simple unlined graves, extensively disturbed by at least two sets of furrows'. This cut was not fully excavated and its function/antiquity was not established.
References: O'Carroll 1997:585

Glendalough, Co. Wicklow

Enclosure: Enclosure ditch
Information and dating evidence: UCD research excavations have been undertaken at Glendalough on an annual basis since 2012. The main focus has been the field between the main ecclesiastical site and St Mary's Church to the west. Geophysical survey revealed a substantial north–south ditch, a potential large rectangular structure and other ditches and anomalies. The latest stratigraphic report (O'Reilly, Seaver, McDermott and Warren 2019, 36–8) provides the most up-to-date information about the sequence of events. It indicates that a north–south aligned ecclesiastical enclosure ditch was dug most likely in the seventh or eighth century. Similar radiocarbon dates were

retrieved from the rectangular structure immediately inside the line of the enclosure – both the enclosure and this structure appear to be contemporary. The next phase witnessed the cutting of a channel 'to divert water from the Glendasan river to the north into the enclosure ditch and back out to the south to Glenealo river flowing from the lower lake'. Both the western and eastern side of the ditch were revetted. The ditch measured about 8–9m wide and its flooding appears to have provided an ideal water supply for a watermill nearby. The ditch appears to have become almost completely infilled by the twelfth century. In this period, a series of stone revetments were set into the enclosure ditch. A broken millstone was found built into the earliest of these secondary revetments. These stone revetments progressively narrowed the ditched feature until the correct flow-rate was achieved for milling. The mill subsequently fell out of use sometime between the mid-thirteenth to mid-fourteenth century and the water channel became silted up in this period. A cereal-drying kiln was constructed on the eastern side of the ditch in the fifteenth century. Testing in 2016 at the site of a small single-story community centre known as God's Cottage to the north of the main ecclesiastical complex uncovered 'a large ditch which was backfilled in the twelfth–thirteenth century' (Whitty 2016:844). This ditched feature may have formed part of the ecclesiastical enclosure uncovered in the UCD excavations, though this was not stated by any of the excavators.

References: McDermott, Warren and Seaver 2016:486; Whitty 2016:844; O'Reilly, Seaver, McDermott and Warren 2019, 36–8

Graiguenakill, Co. Kilkenny

Enclosure: Enclosure ditch

Information and dating evidence: Testing near the church site revealed 'a ditched enclosure, which probably surrounded the monastic site in the tenth–twelfth century; two field ditches of eighteenth- to nineteenth-century date and a pit containing chunks of iron slag, the waste from iron smelting'.

References: Ó Drisceoil 2004:0882

High Island, Co. Galway

Enclosure: Cashel walls

Information and dating evidence: The monastery may have been enclosed within three enclosure walls: the church enclosure wall, the monastic enclosure wall and a wall that extended from the east and west from the monastic enclosure towards the cliff edges. This latter wall may have essentially cut off the south-western part of the island – where the monastery was located – from the rest of the island (Scally 2015, 300). *Monastic enclosure wall:* consisted of a large ovoid-shaped wall with internal diameter from 24m to 37m. The wall was originally 2.5m to 3.2m thick. It has been speculated that the enclosure was originally used as secular late Iron Age site, but excavation does not support this. Two phases of early medieval construction were revealed. Excavation along northern monastic enclosure wall revealed that the primary enclosure consisted of 'an earthen bank of soil and small stones revetted on each side with a stone facing' (Scally 2015, 120). Only one to three courses of stone, up to 0.4m in height, remained *in situ*. This wall continued underneath the wall of Cell A and its annulus and its earthen fill produced two porphyry fragments and a dished grinding slab (ibid., 121). The wall was built on top of a number of pre-construction layers of schist and clay (ibid., 119–20). A shallow spread of charcoal-flecked silty clay abutted the outer face of the primary enclosure wall in places. Charcoal from this layer post-dating the construction of the primary enclosure was dated to the late eighth century to about the turn of the first millennium AD (1138±48 BP) (ibid., 121). A deposit of burnt debris containing food waste was revealed in an area along the inner face of the northern monastic enclosure wall, beside Cell A (ibid., 125). Charcoal from the burnt debris was dated to the mid-eleventh to early thirteenth century (888±30 BP). This charcoal was extracted from a position directly beneath and sealed by the southern wall face of the secondary enclosure wall; it therefore provides a *terminus post quem* for the construction of the secondary enclosure wall and for the extended wall to the north-west (below) (ibid., 126). It indicates that the primary wall must pre-date this date range. The secondary monastic enclosure wall also contained an earthen bank faced on both sides with stone (ibid.). This second phase of construction involved the extension of the primary enclosure wall to form a wider and more substantial wall during phase 2 (mid-eleventh to late twelfth century). This construction was undertaken to incorporate the phase 2 Cell A within its thickness. Finds from the fill of the secondary enclosure wall comprised a hone or rubbing stone, two perforated stone objects and iron nails and scraps, possibly deriving from nearby smithing (ibid., 128–9). Charcoal from burnt debris inside the core produced a date from the early eleventh to mid-twelfth century (888±41 BP) (ibid., 129). The excavations at the western end of the northern monastic enclosure wall revealed the entrance to this secondary monastic enclosure which it was suggested dates 'to the latest remodelling of the wall in the mid- to late twelfth century' (Scally 2015, 129; 1999:305). This stepped passage was built over the enclosure wall in contrast to the other three entrances extending through the wall (ibid., 129–30). The primary monastic enclosure could not be closely dated, though a radiocarbon date range (late eighth to late tenth century; above) from a deposit later than its construction, suggests a *terminus ante quem* of the late tenth century (ibid., 303). The secondary monastic enclosure wall alterations can be assigned to phase 2 (mid-eleventh to late twelfth century) as charcoal from a burnt deposit (above) sealed by its wall face returned a date from the mid-eleventh to early thirteenth century. A twelfth-century date is likely for these wall alterations. The monastic enclosure wall fell out of active use after the late twelfth or early thirteenth century. During phase 4 (mid-fifteenth to late twentieth century), the enclosure wall became generally obscured by collapsed rubble and deposits of peat and fragmented schist along both its sides (ibid., 130–1). *Church enclosure wall:* A small quadrangular drystone wall (*c.*9m x 7m internally) pre-dated but enclosed the existing stone church (Marshall and Rourke 2000a, 99–124). The walls were damaged, but the surviving evidence rises to a height of 1.10m on the southern side and 1.35m on the eastern side with a width varying from 1.0m–1.15m (ibid., 99–100). A cross-inscribed stone was also embedded in the church enclosure wall (ibid., 101). Excavations were undertaken along the external face of the church enclosure wall along its northern side. This revealed a deposit of dark brown/black peaty silt with charcoal fragments overlying the boulder clay. Radiocarbon dates from the charcoal within this deposit returned a number of early Iron Age dates deemed to be reliable (Scally 2015, 85, 87). These radiocarbon dates confirm Iron Age activity pre-dating construction of the church enclosure. Excavation of the church enclosure revealed two early medieval construction phases. An incomplete wall face (F91), surviving to a height of about 0.4m, outside the upstanding northern side of the church enclosure was deemed to belong to the earliest enclosure (ibid., 87). This early structure diverged by 13 degrees from the east–west orientation of most of the later northern enclosure wall. The earlier church enclosure wall (F91) was aligned with the southern church enclosure wall and may therefore belong to the same building phase as it (Scally 2015, 88). A cutting at the south-eastern corner of the church enclosure wall exposed the outer face of an earlier wall (*c.*0.3m high) (Scally 2015, 88; 2001:517). Remains of the original wall was also identified along the eastern church enclosure side, though this evidence was absent on the western side. It was suggested by the excavator that 'the first church enclosure at High Island was rectangular-shaped (*c.*8m north–south), with the corners rounded externally and angular internally' (Scally 2015, 88). The existing church enclosure wall also dated to phase 1 (eighth to mid-eleventh century). This existing structure is trapezoidal in plan with no two sides parallel to each other and with each of the four sides varying in length from each other (ibid.). Only the northern and western side of the existing church enclosure were aligned with the eleventh-century church. The existing church enclosure wall was built using random courses of mica-schist blocks and small packing stones. The space (7m x *c.*1m) between the early church enclosure wall along the northern side (F91) and the existing church enclosure revealed several layers of domestic refuse (redeposited ash and burnt debris) which may have derived from domestic hearths (Scally 2015, 90). These deposits were sealed by the earlier church enclosure wall (F91) which had partially collapsed onto them. A combined charcoal sample from a number of these deposits returned a date from the early eighth to later tenth century (1171±41 BP) (Scally 2015, 90). The church enclosure was modified during phase 2 (mid-eleventh to late twelfth century). These alterations included the adding of a buttress along the south-eastern corner of the wall, the elaboration of the phase 1 north-east entrance to the church enclosure and the bonding of the outer wall masonry with that of the phase 2 Cell B immediately on its outside eastern side (Scally 2015, 90–1, 312). To conclude, the primary enclosure was originally rectangular with rounded corners and enclosed an area 9m east–west by 8m north–south (ibid., 300). The church enclosure was then redesigned into a more trapeozoidal shape measuring 9m east–west by 7m north–south. This secondary church enclosure was slightly smaller than the primary enclosure as the northern side of this enclosure was rebuilt inside the line of the earlier church enclosure wall. The foundations of the primary church enclosure wall along the northern perimeter were, however, retained and the space between both structures was then used to dump residues from domestic hearths. Both phases were not closely dated. However, the radiocarbon date from the early eighth to late ninth century from the hearth debris in the space between the two walls along the northern perimeter provides a *terminus ante quem* for the primary wall (ibid.). The secondary church enclosure wall also appears to have been in place before the existing mid- to later eleventh-century stone church was built inside it. Both phases of wall construction may then date to the phase 1 period between the eighth to mid-eleventh century, with modifications to it continuing in the later eleventh and twelfth centuries (phase 2).

References: Marshall and Rourke 2000, 46–7, 55–60, 99–124, 180–2; Scally 2001:517; Scally 2002:0742; Scally 2014; Scally 2015, 85–94, 119–31

Holycross, Co. Tipperary

Enclosure: Enclosure ditch and bank?

Information and dating evidence: Geophysical survey and testing revealed a series of linear and curved ditches around the Church of Ireland church site in 2007 (07E0794). 'One of the concentric ditches was crossed by several trenches, and appeared to have traces of an internal upcast bank. No building remains were found between this ditch and one inside, or between this and one outside, to the north-east.' Further excavations in 2001 (01E0168) in the vicinity of the church revealed 'a shallow enclosing ditch, residual bank and interior occupation deposits'.

References: Pollock 2007:1684; Stevens 2001:1223

Illaunloughan, Co. Kerry

Enclosure: Cashel wall

Information and dating evidence: The enclosure wall dates to phase 1 (seventh–eighth century). Two conjoined huts (A and B) dating to phase 1 were built up against the inner face of the island's western enclosing perimeter, indicating that the enclosure was a primary feature. The enclosure wall extended from the natural rock ridge at the western end of the island which was heightened by the addition of large flat stones used as capstones. It is possible that this stone was quarried out to build the wall. The drystone wall, 0.5m high, was originally much higher as evident by the rubble and stone collapse on either side of the ridge. It measured 1.6m wide and was faced internally and externally with rectangular sandstone blocks. The core of the enclosing wall consisted of rubble and tightly packed shillet. Today, this western enclosing wall abruptly ends on the northern side of the island, but originally may have been longer as this is where the most extensive coastal damage occurs.

References: Marshall and Walsh 2005, 14; Walsh 2005, 171–2

Kells (Townparks td.), Co. Meath

Enclosure: Enclosure ditches and banks

Information and dating evidence: Excavations by Byrne revealed a portion of a curving rock-cut V-shaped ditch (20m length) directly to the north-west of St Columba's House, which would, if projected, have formed a circular enclosure about 22m (internal diameter) with St Columba's oratory sited a few meters immediately outside it. The western (primarily excavated) portion of this enclosure was originally located on a natural hilltop with the remaining eastern side dug into the hillside around the site. This V-shaped ditch was cut into the natural bedrock and averaged 2.2m–2.8m wide and 1.5m–1.7m deep. Much truncation had occurred and there was little evidence for an associated bank. The ditch expanded in width and depth at its northern end before terminating at a potential entrance along the north-west perimeter of the site. This entrance was defined by stake-holes, the majority of which formed two main alignments parallel to the ditch end: the southern line of these stake-holes followed the ditch edge and 'may have formed a funnel shaped entrance structure'. The northern ditch terminal was not located, but was probably just outside the northern end of the cutting. The stake-holes cut a spread of redeposited boulder clay which may represent the upcast from the digging of this enclosure ditch. Other features like a stone setting (F43) to the east of the 'entrance' may have 'formed some sort of pavement and compacted surface just inside the entrance'. The basal ditch fills consisted mostly of layers of silting containing varying (although usually small) amounts of occupation refuse. The central layers produced a large quantity of domestic refuse which was 'followed by either a deliberate infilling of soil material or possibly a collapse of bank material from the interior of the enclosure and finally what may have been deliberate infilling of what remained of the ditch' (Byrne 1988, 22). It was suggested that the ditch was used as 'a convenient refuse tip by the inhabitants' prior to the final infilling of this cut feature (Byrne 1988, 22). It is possible that there may have been a recutting of the original ditch prior to the deposition of this upper ditch fills. A relatively large quantity of domestic and industrial finds was recovered from the early medieval ditch fills. Many of these were diagnostic early medieval finds, but most were not closely dateable. A possible seventh-/eighth-century kidney-shaped bronze ringed brooch was found near the base of the early medieval ditch, which might suggest that the feature was cut around this period. The exact date the ditch was completely infilled is not known, though the presence of typical early medieval finds (i.e., hones, polished bone pin, antler tines, furnace bottoms, hollow bone cylinder and possible awl) from the upper fills suggest that this occurred towards the end of the early medieval period. Recent excavations in 2010 along Church Street, Townparks, Kells also uncovered the remains of a large double ditch in excess of 1.2m deep (Walsh and Bailey 2010:523). The width of the two ditches totalled 8m although the southern edge of these features lay beyond the limit of excavation to the south. The remains of a redeposited natural bank were also discovered between the two ditches. No dating evidence was obtained from the sterile fills of this double ditch. The ditch was orientated on a west–north-west/east–south-east direction at the junction of Church Street and Canon Street and it was suggested that it may have formed a boundary surrounding the early ecclesiastical site as it was only situated *c.*25m east-south-east of the existing graveyard. The relatively small size of the early medieval enclosure ditch (*c.*diameter of 22m) excavated by Byrne and the fact that it probably did not enclose St Columba's House, never mind the round tower 150m to the south, may suggest that it did not form part of a large site enclosure. However, it is possible that this ditch uncovered in 2010 may have delineated the inner boundary of the entire ritual zone. The limited nature of the excavation in 2010 means, however, that further excavation will be required to confirm whether this is the case. It is also likely that the outer ecclesiastical enclosure might be fossilized in the surrounding street-pattern of Carrick Street, Castle Street, Farrell Street and Fair Green. If some of the finds, particularly the kidney-shaped bronze ringed pin can be viewed as seventh/eighth century in date, it is likely that some settlement (ecclesiastical or otherwise) was in existence prior to the early ninth century when the Columban monks, fleeing the Vikings from Iona, are believed to have arrived.

References: Byrne 1987:41; Byrne 1988:57; Byrne 1988, 2–10, 21–6; Walsh and Bailey 2010:523

Kildare, Co. Kildare

Enclosure: Enclosure ditch
Information and dating evidence: Monitoring in 2018 revealed a series of ditches in the town. One ditch measured 1.7m wide at top and had steep sloping sides. The base was not reached (>1.2m deep). Three ditch fills were identified – the lowest contained charcoal inclusions and animal bone. A

second parallel ditch was identified 7m to the south. This ditch contained three identical fills, 'suggesting that the two ditches were contemporary and related. Animal bone from the northern ditch yielded a radiocarbon determination of cal. AD 686–799 (UBA-41076, 1246 BP±31, 2 sigma), placing the lower fill event in the late seventh to the late eighth century AD'. It is possible that the graveyard boundary wall represents the innermost enclosure at Kildare. The excavator suggested that 'the two ditches might represent sections of an outer enclosing element around the early ecclesiastical complex, which would be aligned east to west in this location'.

References: Taylor 2018:754

Kilgobbin, Co. Dublin

Enclosure: Enclosure ditches, banks and possible palisade

Information and dating evidence: Excavations in several fields to the west/south-west of the church uncovered a sequence of enclosures (D1) with associated corn-drying kilns and field ditches primarily dating from AD 650–950. The earliest phase (I) of activity in Bolger's excavation may pre-date AD 600; this phase pre-dated the enclosure ditches and comprised the remains of a circular slot-trench and pit, possibly unenclosed. The main phase II feature consisted of a ditch (C3) measuring 1.1m wide and 0.73m deep. This feature contained four main fills (C4, C5, C6, C40) and two localized deposits (C41/42, C52). The lowest fill (C4) produced no finds, but secondary fill (C5) revealed an iron loop-headed pin. A sample (1267±31 BP) from this secondary fill produced a 2 sigma date from AD 665–859. The uppermost fill (C40) consisted of a localized charcoal-rich deposit at the northern end, which produced finds including a clay mould and a furnace bottom. Phase III revealed another enclosure ditch indicated by the curving ditch section (C14/155), of which an 11.2m long section was excavated in the south measuring 1.75m wide and 1.3m deep. The northern ditch section was badly truncated by early modern quarrying; it measured a maximum of 0.65m wide and 0.45m deep and produced a piece of iron sheeting. Western curvature of this ditch was identified and recorded by Larsson during the initial assessment linking the two investigated sections together. Six fills were identified along the southern section. Primary fill was sterile and shallow. However, a sample (1285±32 BP) from the secondary fill (C16) produced a 2 sigma date of AD 659–801. Also recovered from this secondary fill (C16) was an iron knife, iron loop-headed pin and a copper-alloy tool. Phase IV – main occupation phase in area D1 – contained three sub-phases. A 10m long section of large curvilinear ditch (C21) was excavated. It measured 2.4m wide and 1.1m deep and contained nine deposits and is likely to have defined a circular or sub-circular enclosure. No finds or dateable material were recovered from phase IVa deposits. Phase IVb was associated with the deliberate backfilling of the ditch through levelling of a nearby bank. No finds were retrieved from the ditch fills from this phase, but a sample (1222±34 BP) from one fill (C27) produced a 2 sigma date range from AD 689–888. A clay mould fragment was recovered from deposit (C63) on the south side of the ditch. Phase IVc involved the digging of the latest in the sequence of ditches (C8). This feature (1.7m wide x 0.74m deep) contained five fills and was excavated for 10m. An iron awl and a lignite bracelet fragment were recovered from the ditch fills. A sample (1226±32 BP) from one of the fills (C10) produced a 2 sigma date range of AD 689–885. This ditch curved to the north towards C21 with the maximum distance between the two ditches being only 6m. It was suggested that C8 represented 'an alteration or adjustment to the enclosure defined by C21'. Bolger noted that C8 appeared to define the southern limit of a number of deposits and features associated with metalworking and other industrial activities. Phase V was associated with the final fills across the phase IVa enclosure ditch (C21). Two final fills of ditch (C21) were identified as occupation layers which had subsided into the ditch. Vitrified fuel ash slag, ferric slag, crucible fragments and copper-alloy artefacts including an unusual slotted tool were recovered from fill C92. A sample (970±33 BP) from this fill produced a 2 sigma date of AD 1015–1157. It is unclear if the phase II ditch (C3) represented a settlement enclosure or part of a field system. Phase III ditch curved to form a possible enclosure (c.37m in diameter). Bolger believed that this ditch was 'unlikely to have encompassed all or a substantial portion of the present church and graveyard'. This enclosure was more in the range of a rath and it is also possible, though less likely, that it formed part of a secular enclosure predating later enclosure activity associated with the church. Other ditches were also recorded in areas E, D2 and D3 by Larsson and Bolger, though these appear to have formed part of ancillary enclosures associated with this main site. Phase IVa (C21) was on a different alignment to phase III ditch and was defined by a larger circular or sub-circular space, which may have 'incorporated all or a substantial proportion of the present church and graveyard'. The phase IVc latest ditches (C8) was only a maximum distance of 6m from C21 and it was suggested that C8 represented 'an alteration or adjustment to the enclosure defined by C21'.

References: Bolger 2004:0647; Larson 2004:0644; Larson 2004:0645; Larson 2004:0646; Bolger 2008, 88–97, 104; Bolger 2014, 3–4

Kilgrovan, Co. Waterford

Enclosure: Enclosure ditch
Information and dating evidence: Geophysical survey was undertaken in 2003 on the church site over an area of 100m by 120m revealing a double-ditched sub-circular enclosure. The geophysical survey was followed by subsequent testing of the enclosing feature in 2007. These revealed a large north-east/south-west orientated ditch. It was suggested that this ditch may

represent the 'eastern extent of the ditch of an enclosure associated with the site of the church'.

References: Purcell 2003:1882; Kiely 2007:1819

Kilhorne, Co. Down

Enclosure: Enclosure ditches?

Information and dating evidence: Geophysical survey identified the possible remains of two enclosing ditches. One feature was interpreted as a ditched enclosure (R1, R2, M1, M2), *c.*50m in internal diameter. The excavation area was located to the south of and outside the projected line of this curving anomaly and therefore could not ascertain its exact form. A possible outlying circular anomaly (R3, R4) was also recorded in the resistivity survey and was interpreted as a possible (outer?) ditch partly enclosing an area of about 80m in internal diameter. The projected line of this curving outer anomaly was not, however, identified in the excavation, suggesting that, if it was a genuine feature, it was restricted to the northern and eastern sides of the circular enclosure (R1, R2, M1, M2) identified as the primary early ecclesiastical vallum. A possible interrupting curving feature (M4, M5) was also identified in the magnetometry survey. The poorly-defined edges of this feature might indicate that it represents a variation in the underlying geology, though it is also possible that it may have formed part of a larger ditched enclosure. The dates of these features are unknown but they could be of some antiquity as they pre-date both the field boundaries on the 1859 6-inch OS map and the Kilkeel Road.

References: MacDonald and McIlreavy 2007, 101–3, 111

Kilkenny (St Canice's Cathedral), Co. Kilkenny

Enclosure: Enclosure ditch and bank

Information and dating evidence: At least three separate excavations have revealed potential evidence for an early medieval inner ecclesiastical enclosure at St Canice's Cathedral, with projected dimensions of 110m (Ó Drisceoil 2013, 36, 49). The ecclesiastical site was also possibly defined by an outer ecclesiastical enclosure, which Ó Drisceoil (2013, 35) has recently revised as extending around the curving streetscape of Thomas Street, upper Dean Street and the natural contours of the gravel hill that the church was situated upon. This outer enclosure had possible dimensions of 270m by 185m, with its southern perimeter largely informed by the low-lying floodplains of the rivers Nore and Breagagh – wetlands which were not reclaimed until the late twelfth or early thirteenth century (Ó Drisceoil et al. 2008, 80; Ó Drisceoil 2013, 35, 49). Three separate excavations by Gittins, Ó Drisceoil and Neary have revealed evidence for the inner ecclesiastical enclosure at the Deanery Gardens and Coach Road. Excavations by Gittins (2002:1006) in the Deanery Orchard south of the Cathedral revealed three clay boulder layers, deemed to 'constitute the truncated remains of an earthen vallum delineating the boundary of the pre-Norman monastic precinct of St Canice's'. These clay features were then 'buried by what looks like a mass disposal of butchery waste' at some later stage (Gittins 2002:1006). Further excavations by Ó Drisceoil inside Deanery Orchard (06E0306) in 2006 revealed 'some evidence for this bank' (trench 4) and 'a section of the monastic ditch' (trench 5) (Ó Drisceoil 2006:1062). The fill of this possible inner enclosure ditch 'was truncated by a stone corn-dryer', whose lower backfill, a cess deposit, was radiocarbon-dated to the late seventh to late ninth century (no BP date available) (Beta 338558); this evidence was deemed as 'providing a *terminus ante quem* for ditch backfilling' of the late ninth century (Ó Drisceoil 2013, 9–10, 36). A Class 2 watch-winder stick pin (AD *c.*975–1100) and an antler tine were also recovered from the corn-dryer's backfill. This possible inner enclosure ditch (6m wide x 0.9m deep) was backfilled with gravels and clay layers with antler tines and was traced for a distance of 37m within the Deanery Orchard (Ó Drisceoil 2013, 10, 36). Monitoring by Neary (06E0075) in 2006 in advance of renovations to the streetscape at Coach Road also revealed 'traces of what had previously been identified by Gittins as part of an embankment', which appears to have belonged to part of an inner precinct enclosure bank right outside the main gate into the cathedral at the top of Coach Road. This evidence comprised 'a layer of orange clay, similar to that recorded in the adjacent Deanery Orchard', which 'was interpreted as a portion of the levelled early medieval enclosure bank' (Neary 2006:1053; Ó Drisceoil 2013, 10). No dating evidence was uncovered in Gittins's or Neary's excavations in the vicinity of St Canice's Cathedral, although Ó Drisceoil's excavations in 2006 did establish that the ditch was backfilled by the late ninth century. Based on this evidence, Ó Drisceoil (2013, 36, 47) has made the suggestion that the backfilling of this excavated inner enclosure ditch, 'as recorded at the Deanery Orchard', might have been linked 'to the late ninth-century growth in power of the kingdom of Ossory under Cerball mac Dúnlainge'. Another ditch was excavated in the Robing Room to the north of the cathedral; this ditch was dated to the eleventh or twelfth century and was interpreted as a subdivision (*trian*) for the outer ecclesiastical enclosure for St Canice's (Ó Drisceoil 2013, 46).

References: Gittins 2002:1006; Ó Drisceoil 2006:1062; Neary 2006:1053; Ó Drisceoil et al. 2008, 80; Ó Drisceoil 2013, 9–10, 35–6, 46–9

Kilkenny (St Patrick's Church – the *Domhnach Mór*), Co. Kilkenny

Enclosure: Enclosure ditch
Information and dating evidence: An archaeological assessment by Cóilín Ó Drisceoil at Fr Hayden's Road revealed potential evidence for an early medieval enclosure associated with the nearby St Patrick's graveyard – the

reputed site of the early ecclesiastical foundation at Kilkenny known as the *Domhnach Mór*. The site was located 'within the rear of a probable medieval burgage plot and 5m from the southern boundary wall of St Patrick's graveyard'. Testing uncovered 'what is likely to be a substantial section of the ditch of the inner ecclesiastical enclosure', 'beneath a deep garden soil deposit'. No dating evidence was recovered from the posited early medieval ditch.

References: Ó Drisceoil 2005:813; Ó Drisceoil et al. 2008, 80–1, 202

Kilkieran (Castletown), Co. Kilkenny

Enclosure: Enclosure ditch, bank and overlying wall

Information and dating evidence: Basal courses of an east–west aligned curving stone wall were excavated north of the old cemetery at Kilkieran. The wall was interpreted 'as an enclosing element, as there is a distinct difference between the features on either side, those on the outside (north) being a ditch and some field divisions and those on the inside (south) being features primarily associated with habitation'. The wall was 1.5m–2m thick and stood to a height of 0.2m–0.9m, with one or two courses of stone surviving *in situ*. The wall contained inner and outer dry-built faces of stones frequently set on edge and an interior filled with large boulders and rubble. The wall was not removed but it appears to have been set on a raised boulder clay area that possibly formed 'a natural terrace or pre-existing clay bank'. This 'bank' may then have formed part of an enclosure itself of early Christian or medieval date, which was then 'modified or increased in height by the addition of the stone wall'. A shallow west–east aligned ditch (10) was excavated outside of and running parallel to the wall (*c.*1.10m to the north of the wall). It was U-shaped in profile, *c.*0.84m deep and cut into the boulder clay to a depth of 0.34m. The ditch was *c.*1m wide at the level of the boulder clay. This ditch contained medieval pottery and was interpreted as a medieval field boundary. Ditch (10) cut into the fill of an earlier deeper ditch (9) and evidently post-dated the silting up of this earlier ditch. Ditch (9) had a maximum depth of 1.25m deep. Its lowest fill comprised a mixture of clay with large boulders – collapse from the wall (1) above. Charcoal flecks were recorded throughout the clay fill with a particular concentration recorded *c.*0.7m above the bottom of the ditch. Excavations on the site were limited, but revealed a drystone enclosure wall set on a possible pre-existing bank or natural terrace, which, along with the external ditch (9), may have formed part of an earlier enclosure of early Christian or medieval date. None of these features could be closely dated, but the two phases of enclosure construction were unlikely to have been separated by a long period 'since the trench [ditch 9] had not silted up when the stones began to collapse from the wall' (Hurley 1988, 132).

References: Hurley 1988, 126–9, 132

Kill, Co. Kildare

Enclosure: Enclosure ditch
Information and dating evidence: Initial testing (93E0059) to the west of the parish church site revealed a possible ditched feature. Further excavation in 1996 (96E0079) intersected this feature, revealing 'a large negative feature some 6m wide and apparently U-shaped in profile, reaching a depth of at least 1m below the natural gravel subsoil through which it was cut'. Danger of collapse prevented an examination of the basal layers. No pottery or dateable finds were recovered. These remains may form part of an enclosure associated with the church site to the north.
References: Halpin 1993:134; Halpin 1996:184

Killamurren, Co. Cork

Enclosure: Enclosure Bank
Information and dating evidence: Excavation in advance of the proposed removal of a 10m section of the enclosure bank revealed that it measured 3m wide at its base, 1.5m high and 1m wide at its crest. No evidence for a palisade along the top of the bank was identified, but 'some stone facing survived on the outer face, comprised of flat stones set on edge in a style typical of the field boundaries in this locality'. There was no evidence for an internal or external ditch, but these were presumably 'removed by earthmoving associated with previous farmyard expansion'.
References: Cotter 2016:687

Killashee, Co. Kildare

Enclosure: Enclosure ditches?
Information and dating evidence: Geophysical survey detected 'a number of sub-circular features in one specific area located to the west of an existing church and graveyard site'. Subsequent testing uncovered a number of ditches in this area, 'the locations of which broadly coincided with the geophysical anomalies'. The testing found that 'the fills of the ditches did not reveal anything that might be of use in dating the features'. However, the basal fill of one of the ditches produced 'a flint scraper and a twin-pronged bone object, of possible early historic date'. Also uncovered were 'a number of small areas of burning and possible post-holes'. It was suggested that 'the archaeological remains form part of a multi-period complex, probably associated with the fifth-century monastic site founded by St Auxilius'.
References: Byrne 2006:963

Kill of the Grange, Co. Dublin

Enclosure: Enclosure ditches and bank
Information and dating evidence: A pipeline passed within 6m of the graveyard. Excavation revealed 'six small pits, a shallow gully, two large ditches, the boulder core of an inner bank and two inhumation burials. The burials and curving ditch were dated through Accelerated Mass Spectroscopy (14C) to the sixth or seventh century, while the larger ditch, gully and inner bank were artefactually dated to the twelfth and thirteenth centuries'.
References: Duffy 2018:634

Kill St Lawrence, Co. Waterford

Enclosure: Enclosure bank and ditches
Information and dating evidence: The outer and inner enclosure ditches were revealed in excavation. Outer enclosure ditch had extrapolated diameter of *c.*110m and was excavated in two locations. Along southern enclosure side, outer ditch (6m wide at the top x 0.74m deep) contained two deposits and generally had a shallow stepped profile with a flat base. Along northern enclosure side, the ditch was 2.8m wide at the top and 1.38m deep and generally had steeply sloping sides and a V-shaped profile. It contained three deposits. Charcoal from basal fill of the outer enclosing ditch produced a 2 sigma radiocarbon date (1330±40 BP) of AD 647–778, suggesting that it was constructed between the mid-seventh and later eighth century. A portion of the outer enclosure ditch, 12.5m long by 2.5m wide, was also exposed during monitoring to the south of the site in May–June 2003. A bank of redeposited natural mottled clay (2.5m wide x 0.4m thick) was identified immediately north of the outer enclosure ditch on the southern side of the site. No evidence for the internal bank was uncovered along the northern enclosure side. However, in this area, a second ditch was uncovered parallel to and 1.3m south of the outer enclosure ditch. This internal ditch measured 1.8m wide at the top and 0.58m deep with steeply sloping sides and a concave base. Its basal fill contained some charcoal along with five pieces of slag. The line of the inner enclosure ditch was found to be roughly concentric with the outer enclosure. This inner enclosure had extrapolated diameter of 60m. There was no evidence for an associated bank, contrary to results of the previous geophysical survey. One excavated section of the inner enclosure ditch revealed that it measured 1.9m wide and 0.96m deep with gently sloping sides and a concave base. Here it contained three deposits, the uppermost of which produced a flint flake. The inner enclosure ditch in another excavated section measured 2.3m wide and 0.85m deep with steeply sloping sides and a concave base. It contained four deposits. Not enough charcoal was recovered from the inner enclosure ditch to submit for radiocarbon analysis.
References: O'Connell 2004, 27, 39–44, 47, 49, 61

Killeany 1, Co. Laois

Enclosure: Enclosure ditch

Information and dating evidence: Most of the south-eastern quadrant of a large bivallate enclosure was excavated at Killeany 1. The outer enclosure (1) measured *c.*185m by 150m and was delineated by a ditch, 3m wide by 1.5m deep. Approximately one third of its overall circumference was excavated. A break (3m wide) was identified midway along its excavated length and was interpreted as the south-east-facing entrance. Animal bone (UBA-8172) from the ditch fill produced a calibrated 2 sigma date of AD 600–57, which led the excavator to suggest that the ditch was dug in the first half of the seventh century. It was also suggested that ditch upcast was used to build an internal earthen bank; no surviving vestiges of this bank was discovered, though this feature – if it had existed – had most likely been levelled during the course of subsequent agricultural activities. Other radiocarbon dating evidence indicates that this ditch remained in use until some point in the twelfth century. Other excavated features on the site consisted of numerous postholes and pits. Several postholes were found in the entrance break of this outer enclosure ditch (1) and may relate to an arrangement of gates to secure the gap. A smaller ditched inner enclosure (2) defining an early medieval burial ground was located at the highest point of the site, roughly at the centre of the larger enclosure (ditch 1). Ditch (2) was excavated for *c.*35m and had dimensions of up to 1m wide and 0.5m deep. Only part of the south-eastern area of this burial ground was excavated. One burial was discovered in one of the entrance terminals of the outer enclosure ditch 1. The site has been identified as a possible early ecclesiastical foundation which had fallen out of use by the later medieval period.

References: Wiggins 2006, 33–5; Wiggins 2014, 273–4, 280

Killederdadrum (Lackenavorna), Co. Tipperary

Enclosure: Enclosure ditch and bank

Information and dating evidence: Cuttings revealed that the enclosure ditch was *c.*2.8m wide at the top and V-shaped in profile, varying from 1.4m– 1.8m deep below the surface. Ditch was apparently deliberately infilled on the western side, possibly from bank material, as fill was largely undifferentiated with scant evidence for charcoal or occupation debris. A small iron riveted mounting or punch was found in the ditch fill in this area. An iron shears, iron knife and iron awl (all probably of early medieval date) were recovered from the enclosure ditch fill along the southern perimeter. The enclosure bank survived best along the northern perimeter where it was about 3m wide and was a maximum of 0.7m high. Two stake-holes were cut into this bank material, but their function is unknown. A spindle whorl was recorded along the line of the enclosure bank beneath the sod, while an iron awl was recorded on natural clay inside the bank line. The enclosure entranceway was identified along the south-east perimeter. It consisted of an undug causeway extending across the ditch, 3.0m–3.5m wide. Two pairs of stone-packed postholes were revealed inside the causeway flanking the entrance. The centre of both sets of posts were set 2.5m apart, giving a width of *c.*2m for the entrance. These four postholes represented either successive gate-posts, or formed part of one set of gate-posts with attached fences flanking the entranceway. A pit-like feature cut into the inner slope of the enclosure ditch. This pit-like feature was interpreted as the remains of a corn-drying kiln bowl. A rough double row of stones extended west along the ditch and was interpreted as the demolished remains of the kiln's flue. Charcoal from the fill of this feature produced a 2 sigma date of AD 895–1172 (1000±60 BP), indicating that it was cut into the enclosure ditch sometime between the tenth to mid-twelfth century. The ecclesiastical enclosure was considerably silted up when it was cut by this possible kiln dating to the tenth–twelfth century. This suggests that this enclosure was originally cut much earlier in the early medieval period, and was considerably filled up by the tenth or eleventh century.

References: Manning 1984, 240–5, 256, 258, 261

Killeen Demesne (Killeen td.), Co. Meath

Enclosure: Enclosure ditches

Information and dating evidence: Two unrecorded early medieval ecclesiastical sites were identified in Killeen townland within the Killeen Castle demesne complex. Site B consisted of a series of enclosures and other anomalies covering an area of 300m north–south by 130m east–west on the northern limit of Killeen Demesne (Baker 2009, 28; 2010, 13–14). Three curvilinear enclosures were identified at Site B. The innermost enclosure (A) measured *c.*22m in diameter and revealed ten east–west burials. Its northern and southern ditches (1.6m wide) were partially exposed. Part of a second larger inner enclosure (B), *c.*40m in diameter, was also revealed. This enclosure was identified in the form of ditches (2.3m–3.4m wide) rich in animal bone and charcoal. The south-eastern quadrant (1.8m wide) contained a high content of unmortared stone. These two enclosures intersected to the north-east. A large outer enclosure (C) circumnavigating these two inner enclosures was also identified. It measured *c.*58m in diameter and intersected a possibly earlier enclosure and field annexe. The outer enclosure was identified on the ground as a ditch (*c.*3.5m wide) and the cleaning back of its upper surface yielded a decorated copper-alloy polyhedral-headed pin with a twin link motif on one side and a saltire on the other. It can be compared with pins from the seventh- to tenth-century layers at Lagore and from later tenth- to early eleventh-century contexts at Christchurch Place and Fishamble Street, Dublin. Several radial ditches (internal divisions) were also identified. The castle ditch site was situated within the centre of Killeen demesne, *c*.9m north of the northern I of Killeen Castle (Baker 2009, 58–60, 72). Phase I of this separate site comprised the remains of an early medieval bivallate enclosure and kilns, which may mark the site of an ecclesiastical establishment preceding the nearby extant fifteenth-century church. The inner enclosure ditch was exposed for 67m to the east and north of the extant church. It was severely truncated and varied from 1.1m–2.5m wide and from 0.5m–1.3m deep. Three main mottled silty clay fills were identified in the ditch, which produced a radiocarbon date of AD 657–781 (1284±34 BP), indicating that this ditch was in use from the second half of the seventh to the early ninth century. Finds from the inner enclosure ditch comprised animal bone, a type E whittle and a tang knife. The outer enclosure ditch probably had a diameter of *c*.110m and enclosed the space occupied by the fifteenth-century church. It was located *c*.12m from the inner enclosure and comprised two distinct ditches, both of which had rounded terminals that had been truncated by a later excavation which obliterated what was originally an entrance (4.1m wide) facing to the north-east. The entire outer enclosing ditch was exposed for 130m varying from 1.7m–4m wide and from 1m–1.9m deep and contained six major construction/backfill events. Event 1 at the south-eastern segment of the ditch produced a date of AD 433–634 (1512±40 BP), while Event 6 towards the western limit provided a date of AD 777–969 (1163±32 BP). The construction of the outer enclosure can then be dated to the fifth to the seventh century, with perhaps an extension to this feature occurring between the eighth to tenth century. A later ditch, 4.1m long, 2.1m wide and 1.2m deep, was cut into the entrance space between the *termini* of the outer enclosure ditches. The base of this ditch was higher than that of the *termini*, but the fills were similar. The construction of this ditch 'significantly improved the defensive properties of the enclosure, removing the north-eastern entrance and creating a continuous outer enclosure'. Alternatively, these boulder 'walls' at either end may have supported a wooden or draw bridge that could have been retracted when necessary. The outer enclosure ditch was truncated at its southern terminal by an Anglo-Norman ditch and medieval structure.

References: Baker 2009, 28, 58–60; Baker 2010, 13–14

Killegland, Co. Meath

Enclosure: Enclosure ditch

Information and dating evidence: Enclosure feature *c*.50m to the west of the early church site. Feature first identified during initial monitoring by Halliday. Excavations by Kavanagh revealed a U-shaped ditch, with a maximum depth of 1.9m and average width of 3.3m. There was little variation in the depth and width of this feature across the excavated portion. The ditch fills consisted of 'stratified deposits of compact mid- to dark-brown silts and clays which accumulated naturally over a substantial period of time'. An entrance was identified to the north-west and comprised a 3.8m wide causeway faced on each side with medium-sized stones. It was posited that it formed part of the outer enclosure of the early church. A souterrain, ditches, gullies and pits were recorded in the interior.

References: Kavanagh 2006:1499; Halliday 2006:1496

Killuney, Co. Armagh

Enclosure: Enclosure ditches

Information and dating evidence: The site of Kill-unche, a site associated with St Nectan, a disciple, and nephew of St Patrick, might be located in Killuney, immediately outside Armagh city. An excavation in 2009 in Killuney revealed evidence for two parallel and enclosing ditches which extended for some 110m across the site. The ditches had dimensions of 1.5–2m wide and over 1m deep in places. The ditches respect one another and it was suggested that 'at least the last phases of each ditch are thought to have been contemporary'. Excavations also revealed an earlier ditch below the outer ditch which it was suggested 'may represent an earlier phase of the same enclosure'. The excavator indicated that the parallel ditches may 'represent the northern extent of a large enclosure, which was only partially exposed during the 2009 excavations' and that they may form part of 'the outer boundaries of an ecclesiastical site known to have existed somewhere within the site'. Pottery dating from the early medieval period was recovered from these ditches.

References: Vuolteenaho and Baillie 2009:064

Kilmokea, Co. Wexford

Enclosure: Enclosure ditch and bank

Information and dating evidence: Testing just inside the eastern boundary of the ecclesiastical precincts revealed a ditch and bank interpreted as the 'enclosure earthworks'. The ditch measured 6.1m wide where exposed. The bank was disturbed but consisted of a compact, bright orange, sandy material (4.2m wide), which survived to a height of 0.6m above subsoil. No finds were recovered to date in the enclosure.

References: Stafford 2002:1916

Kilmore, Co. Armagh

Enclosure: Enclosure ditches?

Information and dating evidence: Excavations west of the church and graveyard uncovered four ditches. The innermost and largest ditch measured 2m wide x 1.5m deep and ran north–south along the line of the church boundary. It cut a large pit that ran below the perimeter wall and into the

church graveyard. A second north–south aligned ditch was uncovered 10m west of the inner ditch. It was 1.2m wide and a maximum of 0.9m deep and cut a large circular well. The outermost ditch was situated 2m west of the middle ditch and was 1.2m wide and a maximum of 0.8m deep. Unlike the other two ditches, the ditch fill was relatively clean, and it was probably infilled shortly after it was dug. The excavation also revealed a fourth ditch, aligned east–west, which was not excavated as it lay outside the limits of excavation. Although not stated, these north–south ditches may have formed part of an enclosure along the west side of the church.
References: Crothers 2002:0034

Kilmore, Co. Cork

Enclosure: Enclosure ditch?
Information and dating evidence: Geophysical survey and targeted excavation at Kilmore, Ballingeary revealed the 'backfilled ditch of a large earthwork enclosure'. No further information provided about the feature. It was suggested that the site had early ecclesiastical origins.
References: O'Sullivan 1997:043

Kilmore (Grange td.), Co. Wexford

Enclosure: Enclosure ditch?
Information and dating evidence: A Cambridge University aerial photograph of the site (CUCAP AVK 66) in 1968 identified a circular enclosure, defined by an earth-cut ditch, which may have once enclosed the church and graveyard. This enclosure was possibly bivallate. Excavation in Grange td. located this enclosure ditch for 57m. This ditch (3m wide) was located at a maximum internal distance of 23m from the existing graveyard boundary wall. No finds or dates were obtained from the ditch, though it is likely to represent the remains of an early medieval enclosure ditch.
References: Stafford 2011:624

Kilpatrick (Corbestown td.), Co. Westmeath

Enclosure: Enclosure bank and ditches
Information and dating evidence: Excavation established that the medieval stone church and its surrounding graveyard was located within the north-east quadrant of a larger, oval-shaped enclosure. Trial cuttings across the enclosure revealed a ditch flattened towards the north and slightly pointed to the south measuring 90m east–west by 80m north–south. Excavations revealed a well-defined U-shaped ditch with steeply sloping sides and a flat bottom. The ditch was cut into sandstone bedrock and measured 3m to 4.5m wide at the top and 2.5m and 3m deep (below present ground level). Traces of an internal bank

containing a stone-lined façade were also detected. The ditch was open for a long period and was not normally used for dumping. The primary silting represented a consolidation of the bank and ditch sides when it was originally constructed. The second phase involved a gradual silting up of clay from the bank during occupation. Much animal bone and charcoal were recovered from this fill, but the fragmentary nature of the bone suggests that it was not usually used as a dump. The upper deposit might be associated with the final silting up of the enclosure ditch during the later medieval period, as indicated by the discovery of a thirteenth-/fourteenth-century glazed pottery sherd from this layer. There was much less animal bone and charcoal from this upper fill. A substantial berm was identified in nearly all ditch cuttings, which may have been used to facilitate the cleaning of the ditch and the building of the stone revetment covering the outer face of the internal bank. Vestigial remains of the partly levelled inner enclosure bank were identified in all cuttings. The bank contained an outer stone facing or revetment resting on or close to the outer edge of the ditch berm. There was also some form of inner stone facing or revetment, but this was less well preserved. Nothing was found to indicate the height of the bank, though its original width at its base might be indicated by the termination of the earliest cultivation ridges 4m from the inner lip of the enclosing ditch. The bank was apparently built upon a habitation deposit, which was associated with the sixth- to eighth-century structures (1 and 2) on the site. The exact date and stratigraphic relationship between the enclosure and these structures is not completely clear. The enclosure is probably a primary feature associated with phase 1 (sixth- to eighth-century dwelling and industrial activity) and was certainly in existence when both the corn-drying kilns were built against it sometime perhaps between the ninth and thirteenth century. The ditch was probably fully infilled in the later medieval period, as attested by the finds of thirteenth-/fourteenth-century pottery from its upper fill. The enclosure bank was destroyed sometime in the late or post-medieval periods and its material distributed around the site, perhaps from cultivation. Cuttings closer to the graveyard wall in badly-disturbed ground also revealed a potential curving ditch that emerged from under the west wall of the churchyard curving around its south-western corner. This feature may indicate the presence of an inner enclosure or internal partition perhaps contemporary with the large outer oval enclosure. An iron hand-gouge and a bone pin, with an anthropomorphically carved head, were recovered from this area.

References: Swan 1976, 90, 92–3; Swan 1994–5, 4; Swan 1997, 4–5, 11, 14

Kilquane, Co. Cork

Enclosure: Enclosure ditch
Information and dating evidence: Testing in advance of a cemetery extension in 2014 uncovered 'two ditches outside the ecclesiastical enclosure

appearing to run concentric with the enclosure itself'. A section of one was partly examined and 'its width and steep sides suggested it was a substantial ditch'. Both ditches were interpreted as remains of ecclesiastical enclosures with 'a slight rise in ground level between them ... likely to be the remnant of a former earthen bank'.

References: Cotter 2014:528

Kilsaran, Co. Louth

Enclosure: Enclosure ditch

Information and dating evidence: Testing adjacent to Kilsaran graveyard revealed 'the internal cut of a large, slightly curving ditch', which may represent 'a large boundary enclosure'. 'The ditch contained six to seven deposits, two of which were natural redeposited boulder clay. The ditch cut also contained stone debris, which was interpreted as backfill, due to the mixed nature of the fills surrounding the stones.' No datable finds.

References: O'Connor 2007:1197

Kilteasheen, Co. Roscommon

Enclosure: Enclosure bank and ditches

Information and dating evidence: A research excavation from 2005–9 revealed evidence for the 'lost' church site at Kilteasheen. This site contained a large early medieval cemetery, but the excavation awaits full publication. It appears to have been surrounded by a large D-shaped enclosing earthen and stone bank with external ditch of probable early medieval date (Read 2007:1498; 2008:1034; 2010, 43, 49, 54). The D-shaped enclosure measured approximately 80m in diameter. A smaller kidney-shaped enclosure ditch was identified in the next field to the north (Read 2010, 43). Other ditches crisscrossed the site and maybe early medieval in date. These are mentioned in excavation summaries.

References: Read 2005:1339; Read 2006:1736; Read 2007:1498; Read 2008:1034; Read 2009:706; Read 2010, 43, 46, 49, 54, 64; Finan 2014, 356–61

Kiltiernan (Kiltiernan East td.), Co. Galway

Enclosure: Enclosure wall and possible ditch

Information and dating evidence: This ecclesiastical site was defined by a grass-covered enclosure wall with a modern field wall built on top of most of its perimeter, except the north-west section. The enclosure wall pre-dated the internal medieval buildings, but could not be closely dated. The enclosure wall at the entrance along the south-eastern perimeter survived to one or two courses high and measured 1.46m–1.95m wide. Where well-preserved, the wall was constructed with rubble masonry with their flat sides facing outwards. A low bank of light brown clay, 0.52m in maximum height, was identified beneath the enclosure wall and formed the core of this structure. A narrow V-sectioned ditch, 1.22m wide at the top, 0.18m wide at the base and 0.67m deep, dug into the yellow boulder clay, was revealed outside the enclosure wall to the east of House I. It was filled and overlain by a light brown clay which continued on westwards rising to make a low bank forming the core for the enclosure wall (above). The dimensions of this external ditch are not clear as limited excavations in another small trench outside the enclosure to the south of House I failed to uncover evidence for this external feature.

References: Duignan 1951; Waddell and Clyne 2005, 166–74

Lorrha, Co. Tipperary

Enclosure: Enclosure ditch

Information and dating evidence: A small portion of the ecclesiastical enclosure ditch was exposed 150–200m north-west of the church site. Excavations established that the ditch measured *c.*7m wide and had a probable minimum depth of about 3.5m deep. The full ditch depth was not uncovered, with the excavation ceasing at a depth of *c.*1m. The upper ditch fill consisted of a loose brown loam and finds from these upper fills suggest that the enclosure was still being backfilled as late as the seventeenth and eighteenth centuries. These upper ditch fill deposits produced large quantities of worked bone, implying that 'the material came from an area of high occupational activity (butchery) within the close vicinity'. The internal enclosure bank was not identified. The loose brown loam upper ditch fill deposits were not redeposited natural subsoil and do not appear to have formed part of the original enclosure bank if they had been backfilled into the ditch as part of ground-levelling activity. This enclosure ditch was not closely dated. Although not stated by the excavator, it is possible that it forms part of an outer enclosing element around the church site.

References: Linnane 2002:1738; Linnane 2002, 5; Linnane 2004, 19

Loughboy, Co. Louth

Enclosure: Enclosure ditch?

Information and dating evidence: Testing at the site in June 1998 revealed evidence for 'substantial ditches interpreted as an outer enclosure' of the church site. No dateable finds were recovered.

References: Cross 1999:576

Lusk, Co. Dublin

Enclosure: Enclosure ditches

Information and dating evidence: An archaeological assessment 200m west of the church uncovered a 5m potion of an outer enclosure ditch (O'Connell

2009, 52–3). This ditch (2.5m wide and 1.5m deep) had a V-shaped profile with straight sloping sides and a narrow flat base. The primary basal fill consisted of redeposited boulder clay along the base and western side of the ditch cut. It has been suggested that this originated from an eroded/flattened bank, situated externally to the ditch. However, this would be an unusual occurrence as banks along both early medieval ecclesiastical and secular settlements occur inside the enclosure ditch. The remaining fills appear to have silted up over time and produced animal bone and food refuse. The animal bone consisted of the remains of two cattle, four sheep/goats, three pigs, one horse and one domestic fowl. The only other finds from the ditch fills were an iron nail and a piece of slag. The slag came from the second ditch fill. A sample of hazel charcoal from the second fill of the ditch produced a radiocarbon date of AD 420–600 (1540±35), suggesting it was first dug in the fifth, or perhaps more likely, sixth century. Excavations to the south-west of the church at Chapel Farm also revealed the possible remains of this outermost enclosure ditch (Moore 2001:448; Baker 2001:449; Baker 2001, 5–7, 22). The ditched feature was wide, but shallow (*c*.4.6m–5.85m wide x *c*.0.4m–0.52m deep) and was cut into the natural subsoil (0.98m–1m below present ground level). An iron blade dateable to the tenth to twelfth century was recovered from the lower ditch fills. Other finds from the ditched feature at Chapel Farm dated from the tenth and fourteenth centuries, suggesting that the outer ecclesiastical enclosure was not completely backfilled until the medieval period (Giacometti 2008:475). This possible third, outermost enclosure may have measured 515m north–south by 280m east–west (O'Connell 2009, 59). Sherds of thirteenth-/fourteenth-century pottery were recovered from the upper fills of a large ditch to the south of the monastery along Church Road in 2008; this feature was not fully excavated, but was at least 0.6m deep and was interpreted as belonging to the early medieval monastic enclosure of Lusk based on its location, although it was not stated whether it formed part of the outermost enclosure potentially identified by the above excavators. A ditched feature (1.3m wide x 0.45m deep) was also excavated over 200m south of the church site at Barrack Lane, though it is unclear if it was associated with the third, outermost ecclesiastical enclosure (Stout 1991:051). Excavations by Whitty 132m from the ecclesiastical site (between the posited inner and outer enclosure ditches) revealed a number of ditches and linear features of probable early medieval date. The earliest feature comprised a truncated curvilinear ditch (C24) sealed beneath 0.6m of topsoil. The ditch had an exposed length of 6m and was 1.2m wide and 0.6m deep. It was truncated by a large ditch (C21) whose fill produced a possible grinding stone and a flint (Whitty 2009:350). A large ditch, which truncated the primary curvilinear ditch (C24), represented the second phase of activity. This ditch was aligned north–south. Initial analysis suggests that the ditch was left open after it was dug and was filled with water.

This ditch had exposed dimensions of 19m long, 3.25m wide and 1.5m deep. The third phase was indicated by the remains of a single shallow linear feature (C7) traversing the site from north-north-east to south-south-west and truncating the eastern end of the large ditch (phase II – C24). This ditch (C7) had an exposed length of 18.5m and measured 0.75m wide and 0.12m deep. These features were cut by medieval features including linear features and pits. The excavator did not speculate on the function of the probable early medieval ditches and they may either represent the remains of an enclosure or internal divisions. Finally, excavation at Church Road, Lusk uncovered 'a north–south aligned ditch' which was interpreted as 'part of the inner ecclesiastical enclosure ditch' (O'Connell 2017:654). The ditch consisted of 'a 2.25m wide band of grey silty clay that appeared to cut the natural boulder clay, although it was not possible to excavate an exploratory box-section due to the depth of the test trench'.

References: Stout 1991:051; Baker 2001:449; Baker 2001, 5–7, 22; Moore 2001:448; Giacometti 2008:475; Whitty 2009:349; Whitty 2009:350; O'Connell 2009, 52–4; O'Connell 2014, 175–80; O'Connell 2017:654.

Maghera (Carnacavill td.), Co. Down

Enclosure: Probable enclosure ditch
Information and dating evidence: The ditch was V-shaped in profile and traced for 25m east–west. The ditch measured 4m wide x 2m deep and contained a homogeneous gravelly fill, in which sherds of souterrain ware were found.
References: Lynn 1980–4:0086

Monasterboice, Co. Louth

Enclosure: Enclosure ditches?
Information and dating evidence: A geophysical survey in 2008 revealed a whole range of subsurface archaeological features around the graveyard at Monasterboice. The principle feature comprised at least two ecclesiastical enclosures. Potential internal site divisions and field systems were also identified within this survey. Two ditches of indeterminate date were revealed in test excavations in 2015. Ditch 1 was U-shaped, *c*.3m wide at the top and 1.1m deep. Ditch 2 was much shallower (maximum 0.3m in depth and 2m in width). Neither produced any finds and it was deemed unclear whether they formed part of an enclosure. Geophysical survey as well as separate test excavations in a field to the east of the church site in 2016 uncovered evidence for one of the enclosing elements around the church site. A second smaller and shallower ditch appears to run along the same alignment as the first ditch and 'may represent a second ditch running just outside the main one'.
References: Murphy 2015:103; Manning 2015; Murphy 2016:440

Monastery, Co. Wicklow

Enclosure: Enclosure ditch
Information and dating evidence: Geophysical survey in 2016 detected the
line of the ecclesiastical enclosure, as well as features within. Follow up
excavations uncovered the remains of the enclosure ditch 'at a location along
the detected enclosure anomaly, thereby proving its archaeological origins'.
References: Byrne 2016:420

Mullagh, Co. Cavan

Enclosure: Enclosure ditch
Information and dating evidence: Curving enclosure ditch measured
*c.*3.2m wide and 1.2m deep. This ditch enclosed burials. Finds from the ditch
fills included 'a large amount of slag, a possible furnace bottom and two *tuyère*
fragments. A possible entrance was identified to the east, which had been
backfilled and supported with a stone retaining wall or revetment' (Russell
2005:127).
References: Dempsey 2004:0123; Russell 2005:127

Nendrum, Co. Down

Enclosure: Enclosure wall revetment
Information and dating evidence: Nendrum is defined by three roughly
oval and concentric stone walls and has an overall diameter of about 190m
north–south by 159m east–west enclosing a total space of 2.46ha (6.08 acres).
The outer enclosure is defined by a low scarp on its north-west, west and
south-west sides with traces of stone revetting visible in some places.
Excavations along a short linear stone revetment of the outer enclosure
revealed that this feature survived to a height of *c.*0.7m and was 5m long
containing very large boulders. The excavation revealed a stratified occupation
deposit, *c.*0.14m deep, below its revetment which contained slag and charcoal,
the latter radiocarbon-dated from the late sixth to mid-eighth century
(1375±45 B.P. – UB-2365). Although this cannot be used to date the whole
outer enclosure, it might imply that this enclosure was built around the
seventh century. McErlean suggested that such a seventh-century date is not
inconceivable for the cashel walls given the construction of a large tidal mill in
the early seventh century.
References: Brannon 1977–9:0033; McErlean 2007, 378–87, 395

Oldtown and Mooretown, Co. Dublin (fig. 1.7)

Enclosure: Enclosure ditches
Information and dating evidence: Geophysical survey in 2003 revealed a
putative ecclesiastical site in the adjacent townlands of Oldtown and Mooretown.

The main features revealed in this excavation comprised a large outer enclosure (A), 200m in diameter, with an entranceway to the north. A middle enclosure (B), estimated as having a diameter of *c.*130m, was also identified containing within it a smaller enclosure (D), 70m in diameter. A water-course in a field to the south-east possibly defined the outer enclosure along its south-eastern side. A series of radial lines interpreted as formal internal divisions were recorded between the middle and outer enclosures, while a series of anomalies suggestive of field enclosures were identified on the northern side of the outer enclosure. A portion of the innermost enclosure (D) was exposed by Baker for a distance of *c.*8m; this measured 1.7m–2.6m wide and was hand excavated to a depth of 1.15m. It was not possible to reach its base, due to the constant influx of freshwater, possibly from a spring. A fragment of a bone comb ascribed to Dunlevy's Class F (ninth to twelfth century) was recovered from the top of this feature, proving a *terminus post-quem* date for this ditch. Probable intersections of the innermost enclosure (D) with the middle enclosure (B) were also excavated at their north-eastern angle. Within this section, the two features (4 and 5) measured 3.6m wide and were visible for a depth of 0.9m. Feature 6 was uncovered towards the eastern limit and may correspond with the outermost enclosure A. This feature measured 3.1m wide and was exposed for a depth of 1m. The middle enclosure ditch was recorded by Halliday in three trenches (1, 2 and 6) in the western field of Mooretown in 2004, corresponding exactly with the feature identified in the 2003 geophysical survey. It was only excavated to its base in trench 1 (037), where it contained two fills and measured 0.9m in maximum depth and 3m in width. The basal fill consisted of a thin layer of charcoal-rich sandy clay which produced animal bone and a sherd of possible souterrain ware. The upper ditch fill was interpreted as redeposited natural subsoil containing frequent charcoal and occasional animal bone. The fill of the partly excavated enclosure ditch in trenches 2 (072) and 6 (051) also produced charcoal and animal bone. A possible curvilinear feature was also recorded to the south-east of the enclosure complex in 2004, but its exact function is unclear. This ditch (066) – 3.6m wide – was excavated to a depth of 0.52m (trench 5) before being halted when the water table was met. The ditch fill produced animal bone and charcoal. Further geophysical survey and test excavations in 2005/6 was directed by Teresa Bolger in Oldtown and Mooretown on both sides of the Rathbeale Road. Geophysical survey identified potential features on the south side of the Rathbeale Road possibly associated with the ecclesiastical enclosure to the north of the road. Test-trenching in 2008 in Mooretown by Frazer also revealed what appears to be the southern part of the previously identified ecclesiastical complex. Features from this area included ditches and pits located within both the outer enclosure of the putative ecclesiastical complex and a southern annexe linked to it. Further monitoring and excavations in 2018 and 2019 (18E0718) to the immediate east of the ecclesiastical site revealed a series of features, including a large ditch, which was interpreted as 'forming part of an early medieval enclosure' (Coen 2019:238).

References: Baker 2004, 14; Halliday 2004:0651; Halliday 2004, 22–31; Bolger and Dennehy 2006:686; Frazer 2008:478; Baker 2010, 9–13; Coen 2019:238

Omey, Co. Galway

Enclosure: Enclosure wall

Information and dating evidence: All that survived of the earliest rectangular stone enclosure (13.5m long by at least 7.5m wide) was the lower course of walling at its east and west ends. Some of the stones in the south wall had collapsed, but most had been robbed, while the entire north side of the enclosure was destroyed by erosion. The discovery of a couple of postholes along the southern flank of the rectangular stone enclosure might indicate a preceding wooden enclosure associated with the earliest burials. The rectangular stone enclosure was associated with a seventh–ninth century ecclesiastical site. Part of the earliest rectangular stone enclosure was incorporated into the walls of a later trapezoidal-shaped enclosure during the eleventh to thirteenth century. This feature was not a free-standing wall but a revetment, only one stone-course thick with a pronounced batter, which could not have stood unaided. This revetment measured 11–12m east–west externally. Where it survived, the revetment contained rounded corners, both internally and externally, and stood to a height of 2m above foundation levels.

References: O'Keeffe 1992, 5; O'Keeffe 1993, 2–3; O'Keeffe 1994, 15

Portersgate, Co. Wexford

Enclosure: Enclosure ditch?

Information and dating evidence: This ruined church lies at the edge of a cliff and is being eroded by the sea. 'A round-bottomed fosse, 1.06m deep, which probably enclosed the area containing the church, was exposed at two points in the cliff face.' The fosse's inner face was 'revetted with stones, which later collapsed into the fosse'. A deep deposit of shells was found in one cutting. No finds were recovered to date the enclosure.

References: Breen 1987:57

Raheny, Co. Dublin

Enclosure: Enclosure ditch?

Information and dating evidence: Testing was undertaken in 1996 for Cahill Motors, Raheny Village, 20m to the north of the pear-shaped enclosure of the medieval church. This revealed 'a section of a V-shaped feature which may possibly be a truncated ditch'. It was suggested that this feature 'links up with, and is fairly similar in shape to, a ditch found by Leo Swan during roadworks in

1970. This ditch was interpreted by Swan as being the outer enclosure ditch of the medieval ecclesiastical site of Raheny'. However, the excavator cautioned that it could alternatively form part of a medieval boundary or defensive feature. Both medieval and post-medieval pottery were found in disturbed layers adjacent to the feature. More excavation is required to ascertain its function. Further testing near the church in 2009 revealed 'no archaeological features, but soil layers apparently undisturbed in modern times and containing butchered animal bone were encountered' (Ó Maeldúin 2009:356).
References: Carroll 1996:136; Ó Maeldúin 2009:356

Randalstown (St Anne's chapel), Co. Meath

Enclosure: Enclosure ditch
Information and dating evidence: Two excavations of sections along the enclosure ditch (*c.*90m in diameter) revealed that the ditch measured 4m wide and up to 2m deep. An Anglo-Saxon glass bead, a portion of a rotary quern and other finds were recorded within the ditch fill. Sections of a number of smaller curvilinear and linear ditches were also identified within the enclosure interior. Finds from the enclosure suggest that it was primarily occupied between the fifth and ninth century.
References: Kelly 1975:32; Kelly 1976:20

Reask, Co. Kerry

Enclosure: Enclosure wall
Information and dating evidence: The drystone-built enclosure wall was roughly sub-circular in shape (45m by 43m) and may have once originally stood at least 1.5m high. Only the wall foundations survived, though excavations in the best preserved sections in the north-east perimeter indicate that it contained substantial cashel-type walls, *c.*2.2m thick. Here a 14m segment was investigated which stood five-to-six courses high and was faced internally and externally by large slabs set on end at intervals in the basal course. These outer facing stones are large, but its core is mainly composed of small stones and soil. Removal of the collapse revealed that portions of the enclosure wall contained an internal terracing or revetment along its inner face, which added another 0.50m to the overall wall thickness. Although the full outline of the enclosure was identified, there was no evidence for an original entrance, but it may have been located in the northern sector of the site where the two conjoined huts A and B were subsequently built. No securely dated finds were recovered to closely date the enclosure wall. However, the enclosure wall was a primary feature of the site and dates to sometime from the fifth to seventh century. The enclosure wall was very broadly contemporary with the phase 1 drystone-built huts G and F and an extensive habitation deposit in the central area of the enclosure. Although the

earliest lintelled graves (phase 1) were inserted very close to the wall, none of these extended underneath it and there was no evidence for graves in any of the external cuttings outside the enclosure. This suggests that the enclosure wall pre-dated these early lintelled graves and was one of the first features built on the site.

References: Fanning 1981, 98–100, 155

Rossdroit (Moneytucker td.), Co. Wexford

Enclosure: Enclosure ditches?

Information and dating evidence: Excavation in Moneytucker townland (Site 1) on the opposite side of the road to the Church of Ireland church site of Rossdroit revealed six ditches and five structures. 'The plan of two of the ditches (C115 and C847) suggests that at different times they encircled the location of the medieval church.' A large amount of dating and environmental evidence were recovered from the ditches and will inform the dating of the site. If C115 encircled the church site, it would have had a diameter of *c.*350m by 200m. No dateable finds were recovered.

References: Ó Maoldúin 2004:1813

Skeam West, Co. Cork

Enclosure: Enclosure ditch

Information and dating evidence: Aerial photograph in 1980 indicated the possible existence of a bank or ditch along the northern sector of the early church site. The outline of a U-shaped ditch was clearly visible in the cliff face 9.5m south of the church. Only a short section of this ditch was excavated (*c.*1m in length), but the ditch (1.5m wide at the top, 0.4m at the base and roughly 1m deep) appears to curve north-westwards and may originally have enclosed the site. The bulk of the fill consisted of charcoal-flecked light brown stony soil. A thin deposit of charcoal along the bottom of the ditch contained fragments of burnt and semi-burnt bone. A phase 3 (*c.*eleventh to thirteenth century) burial had been inserted in its upper fill. The presence of this individual in this context suggests that the ditch had fallen out of use in this period. No definite evidence for an associated bank was found, although the excavation area was quite limited. No evidence was found to date this enclosure ditch.

References: Cotter 1990:021; Cotter 1995, 74–5

Skellig Michael, Co. Kerry

Enclosure: Enclosure wall

Information and dating evidence: The inner monastic enclosure defining the cells, large oratory and St Michael's Church was constructed sometime between the sixth to ninth century. The first phase of the enclosure wall pre-dated all the visible drystone-built eighth-/ninth-century cells and oratory within the inner enclosure. The earliest phase of the enclosure wall was located in the south-east corner (phase A). Here, the masonry was built with an inner stone face running parallel to the line of the wall and an outer stone face of large angular stones with their long axis at right angles to the line of the wall. This wall was repaired, revetted and reorganized at various points up until the twelfth century when the latest additions to St Michael's Church were completed. Remains of an outer monastic enclosure (lower monk's garden) was also uncovered, but this feature could not be closely dated.

References: Cotter 1991:071; Bourke 2005, 128–9, 133; Bourke, Hayden and Lynch 2011, 110–54

Solar, Co. Antrim

Enclosure: Enclosure ditch?

Information and dating evidence: A number of very early ditches were revealed in trenches 2 and 3 in the 1993 season of excavation north-east of the present church site. The ditch in trench 2 (up to 1.6m wide) consisted of 'two similar cuttings which joined at right angles to each other', while the feature in trench 3 comprised a wide and shallow ditch (3m wide x 0.6m deep) that was subsequently truncated by a thinner, deeper feature (2m wide x 1m deep), extending along the same course. Trench 2 and 3 were only 3m apart with the ditch features in trench 3 appearing to 'run directly to the junction of those in Tr 2'. These ditches belonged to the same phase, as the earliest burials in both trenches occurred directly after the respective ditches had been infilled. These ditches date to the earliest part of the early medieval period as a brooch recovered from the surface of the upper fill of the later ditch in trench 3 was assigned to the late eighth or early ninth century. It was in this period that the earliest individuals in trench 3 were buried. It was suggested that the evidence from this early phase indicates the presence of 'a rectilinear ditch on a terrace with possible drainage gullies and refuse pits on the lower ground around it'.

References: Hurl 2002, 55, 59–60

Sranure, Co. Offaly

Enclosure: Enclosure ditch?

Information and dating evidence: Testing to the east of the church site revealed 'a linear/curvilinear round-bottomed ditch, 2.55m wide and 0.9m deep, oriented north-east/south-west'. The fills of this ditch were similar to that of the topsoil 'although not as compacted and slightly darker in colour'. The upper fill (0.8m thick) produced a loose stone fill containing 'frequent lumps of iron slag, some of which were quite large and bowl-shaped' (furnace bottoms). The upper fill also revealed some animal bone (cattle, pig jaw) and an iron nail. The lower fill was slightly darker as it was mixed with the orange silty sand subsoil. No finds were recovered from this fill. A linear cut, 1.25m wide and 0.25m deep, was also orientated north-east/south-west, but did not extend parallel to the ditched feature. Three small fragments of burnt sheep/goat bone and a medieval potsherd were found in the upper fill. It was suggested that the ditched feature 'is probably part of an enclosure element associated with the ecclesiastical site at Sranure'. The extent of the ditch is unknown, but the discovery of 'significant quantities of iron slag in the ditch clearly indicates that iron-smelting was carried out in the vicinity'. The ditch perhaps provided a sheltered location for the ironworking. The function of the linear cut was not established, though 'the presence of charcoal, burnt clay and ash indicates intensive burning and suggests that it may be associated with the iron-smelting'.

References: Delany 2001:1104

Stamullin, Co. Meath

Enclosure: Enclosure ditch?

Information and dating evidence: Testing in an area south of the church revealed 'a single possible early feature'; this was the base of a ditch deeply cut into the underlying deposits, exposed at a point approximately 60m south from the present boundary wall of the churchyard and apparently extending east to west. No artefacts were found to date this feature.

References: Swan 1995:236

St Doulagh's (Kinsealy/ Balgriffin), Co. Dublin

Enclosure: Enclosure ditch

Information and dating evidence: Conservation excavations by Swan in 1989/90 on the remains of St Doulagh's Church site uncovered stratified occupation deposits indicative of both inner and outer enclosing ditches (Swan 1989:021). Further excavations in 1990 'revealed a well-defined ditch … best interpreted as part of the enclosure revealed to the south of the site in last year's excavations' (Swan 1990:031). Swan's ditch is reported as being V-shaped (Duffy 2015:274). Geophysical survey in 2009 by Ken Nicholls (09R165) in the environs of St Doulagh's Church revealed a series of enclosures. A test trench was opened across the posited ecclesiastical enclosure in 2015 revealing a V-shaped ditch (*c.*1.2m deep and 2.7m wide). No artefacts were recovered from it. The basal layer was 1.22m deep and 2m wide – one bone fragment (caprovid rib) from it was sent for dating and returned a date of BP 1122+/-42, or AD 853–935 (UBA-30540). Another radiocarbon date of 777–911 (C8th–C10th) has been recorded for this basal fill (Paul Duffy, pers. comm.) (O'Reilly, Seaver, McDermott and Warren 2019, 36). The ditch was sealed by a layer of sandy clay (0.4m deep) containing medieval pottery. Animal bone – a mix of cattle and sheep – were also identified with some fragments exhibiting cut and chop marks (Duffy 2015:274). A layer of sandy material (0.16m deep) was identified 1.8m upslope south of the ditch cut. This deposit overlay the subsoil and ran parallel to the ditch cut. It may represent the remnants of an internal bank. Animal bone, including that of pig or sheep/goat were recovered from this material (Duffy 2015:274). As no finds were recovered from the main fill of the ditch, it was suggested that this infill may have derived from the bank (Duffy 2016, 11–14).

References: Swan 1989:021; Swan 1990:031; Duffy 2015:274; Duffy 2016, 13; O'Reilly, Seaver, McDermott and Warren 2019, 36

St Michan's, Dublin City

Enclosure: Enclosure ditches and bank

Information and dating evidence: Portions of a possible enclosure ditch were uncovered at St Michan's Church in Oxmantown. The church is situated on the north side of the Liffey. A ditch excavated in 1997 by Meenan may have defined the northern perimeter of St Michan's Church. This ditch cut into the natural gravel. At the eastern end, the base of the ditch was square in profile, but elsewhere the base was V-shaped or U-shaped. The width of the ditch base measured 0.30m–0.60m. Due to truncation and the stepping out of baulks for security reasons, only one small ditch length (3m) was excavated where its original upper edges survived on both sides. This ditch portion measured 4m wide from edge to edge. There was no evidence for any upcast from the digging of the ditch. The lower ditch fill produced loose, large water-rolled stones, interpreted as having fallen in from the ditch sides. 169 sherds of medieval pottery were recovered from the ditch fill and these included Ham Green, Dublin-type coarse ware, Dublin-type ware, Dublin cooking ware and North Leinster cooking ware. A number of articulated and disarticulated human bone remains were either placed within the ditch base, or more commonly on the surface of the ditch slope. The bones from a child along the southern slopes (Area 1) of the ditch produced a 2 sigma date of AD 986–1155 (990±40 BP), while the remains of an adult along the south slopes of the ditch (Area 2) returned a 2 sigma date from AD 893–1021 (1072±39 BP). These indicate that these two burials (and probably all of the others) date to sometime around the late ninth to mid-twelfth century and that the ditch must pre-date this period. Meenan (2004, 99-100) suggested that these burials were 'placed in the ditch as a consequence of some calamitous event'. Excavations by Dawkes (2006:606) at 151–5 Church Street north-east of St Michan's Church revealed a truncated parallel double-ditch and a single ditch possibly defining the northern and eastern perimeters of the church site respectively. One of the double ditches formed part of the same enclosure discovered by Meenan on

the opposite side of May Lane, to the north. Following the silting up of the
ditches, the site reverted back to open ground and a number of extensive
medieval dark earth deposits were recorded across the area (Dawkes 2006:606).
Test excavations by Hayden to the rear of 161–8 Church Street, south of St
Michan's Church, uncovered two medieval ditches. These ditches cut into the
subsoil and were filled with organic material and silt. The northernmost ditch
consisted of a steep-sided feature cut into the subsoil measuring 2.3m–3m
wide and at least 1.2m deep. This ditch was filled with organic silt and
produced one sherd of locally produced medieval pottery. The remnants of a
possible internal bank, indicated by a large amount of redeposited subsoil,
were uncovered to the north of this ditch. This northernmost ditch (with
possible internal bank) was located *c.*80m south of the church and may have
formed part of the southern property boundary occupied by St Michan's. This
ditch was infilled during the medieval period. The second ditch was revealed to
the south of the first ditch and revealed local medieval pottery. This ditch was
at least 0.5m deep, but was again not fully excavated. Medieval pottery in their
ditch fills indicates that both were infilled in the medieval period. However,
both ditches might have been perhaps older as it was not stated when they were
originally cut. The ditch sections north of the church were too short to infer
the orientation and form of the putative ecclesiastical enclosure. The distance
between Meenan's ditch portion and the extant post-medieval church was 70–
80m, suggesting that this enclosure – assuming that it was circular in form and
located on the present church site – had an approximate diameter of 140–160m
(Meenan 2004, 105). If this is the case, it is likely to have straddled Church
Street, the possible site of an ancient thoroughfare in the medieval period.
Analysis of Rocque's map of AD 1756 tentatively suggests that the church of St
Michan was located at the core of an ecclesiastical enclosure (*c.*150m in
diameter) extending from Hammond Lane in the south, to Bow Lane in the
west and May Lane in the north. The location of this feature on the eastern
side is not clear, but the enclosure may have straddled Church Street and
might be represented in the curve of Pill Lane on this early map (McConway
and Dawkes 2005, 22). Meenan's excavation north of the church along the line
of the ecclesiastical enclosure uncovered early burials. The two dated burials
along the southern slopes of the enclosure ditch suggest that they were
interred in the (still open) ditch between the late ninth and mid-twelfth
century. The presence of these burials in the ditch may indicate that this ditch
had become obsolete by this time. If this ditch was an actual ecclesiastical
enclosure, this would suggest that a church was established here earlier than
the traditional date of AD 1090 (Meenan 2004, 107).

References: Hayden 2000, 9–12; Meenan 2004, 97–100, 105–9; Dawkes
2006:606; McConway and Dawkes 2005, 22

St Peter's, Dublin City

Enclosure: Enclosure ditch?

Information and dating evidence: The site of St Peter's Church is reputedly located slightly off-centre within a typical ecclesiastical enclosure, preserved in the street pattern, to the south of the putative Dubhlinn. Clarke (2004, 148) suggests that this site was associated with the abbots and bishops of Dubhlinn recorded in the annals for AD 790. Excavations in 2003 (Coughlan 2003, 19–23) in this area possibly uncovered 'two sections of a large ditch, which may represent a smaller, inner enclosure round St Peter's Church'. The outer main enclosure at St Peter's Church may have measured roughly 335m x 260m (Clarke 2004, 148). Excavation in 2004 was undertaken 'on the site of St Peter's churchyard on Peter Row, to the rear of the existing YMCA building on Aungier Street, Dublin 2'. The site's western boundary corresponded with the border of the twelfth-century parish of St Peter and it was suggested that this boundary was informed by the line of an early medieval ecclesiastical enclosure. A layer of medieval soil overlying subsoil and into which the first burials were cut may represent 'collapsed bank material related to the ecclesiastical enclosure that ran along the line of the western boundary', though it could equally belong to 'ordinary farm soil from within the former enclosure'. Medieval floor tile fragments from within the deposit indicate 'an ecclesiastical association for the layer'. The cut of a ditch associated with the ecclesiastical enclosure was also potentially uncovered, but 'the feature was too deep to safely excavate and was instead preserved in situ'. Further investigation required.

References: Coughlan 2003, 19–23; Clarke 2004, 148; Elliott 2004:0577

St Vogue's, Carnsore Point, Co. Wexford

Enclosure: Enclosure bank and ditch

Information and dating evidence: The church was originally contained within an oval-shaped enclosure (*c.*40.4m x 33.5m) consisting of an internal bank and external ditch. Three sections were excavated across the enclosing bank (2.5–3.5m thick and *c.*1m in maximum height). Excavations along the northern and western sections uncovered a wide, shallow, external ditch. The sections also established that the bank was constructed from spoils from the external ditch with granite boulders incorporated into it from adjacent areas. The bank also had a stone-built outer facing on its western side which was found in a collapsed condition. On its northern side, a modern stone facing had been built. It was difficult to establish a stratigraphic relationship between the enclosing bank and the internal features of the site. The general stratification within the enclosure comprised a thin turf layer overlying a grey/yellow sandy soil layer which in turn rested on the undisturbed yellow subsoil. The insertion of burials had caused considerable disturbance, particularly in the northern enclosure half and there was no stratigraphic way in which the enclosing bank could be definitely related to the early medieval phase I internal structures. However, on the basis of evidence from similar excavated sites, it was suggested that the enclosure was broadly contemporary with the phase 1 early medieval internal timber oratory and timber structures which may date from the sixth to tenth century based on radiocarbon dating evidence from the site.

References: O'Kelly 1975, 23–4; Lynch and Cahill 1976–7

Sutton North, Co. Dublin

Enclosure: Enclosure bank?
Information and dating evidence: Testing on land south and west of St Fintan's graveyard partly intercepted the enclosure bank. This excavation revealed 'evidence for a grey silty layer (700mm–1m deep) with charcoal and cockle-shells at the interface between the topsoil and the natural boulder clay. This layer could not be closely dated.

References: Meenan 1996:138

Taghmon, Co. Wexford

Enclosure: Enclosure ditch
Information and dating evidence: Excavation revealed a series of ditches near the church site. It was suggested that 'some of the smaller ditches in the north-west corner of the site, and possibly Ditch 1, date to the Iron Age/Early Christian period, while there is a twelfth–fifteenth-century date for Ditch 3, Ditch 2 and several of the discrete features'. Most of the activity on the site may date from the twelfth–fifteenth century, but the presence of a large seventh-/eighth-century pit confirms early medieval activity. Some of the smaller early Christian ditches were cut by the medieval ditch (3). It is possible that some of these ditches form part of an early ecclesiastical enclosure. A further cut feature belonging to a ditch or large pit was also excavated in 2000, but this feature was not closely dated.

References: Mullins 1998:677; Mullins 1999:888; Mullins 2000:1069

Tallaght, Co. Dublin

Enclosure: Enclosure ditches and bank
Information and dating evidence: A series of separate excavations uncovered the remains of two early medieval enclosing ditches at Tallaght, which were found to be spaced 3–6m apart. The inner enclosure ditch was excavated in two portions: the ditch to the south/south-east of the church was *c.*5m wide and 2.8m deep (Walsh 1997:187; 1997, 8), though the section

south/south-west of the church had a maximum width of 6m and depth of 4m (McConway 1994:102; 1994b, 3). Twigs from the base of the inner enclosure ditch (*c.*5m wide x 2.8m deep) south/south-east of the church at Tallaght produced a 2 sigma 14C date of AD 438–773 – 1410±72 BP (Walsh 1997:187; 1997, 8). This inner enclosure was recut on at least three occasions; the final backfilling consisted of a thick dump of redeposited boulder clay, perhaps deriving from the accompanying inner enclosure bank which contained a few sherds of medieval pottery (Walsh 1997, 6–14). The inner enclosure bank survived to a maximum height of 0.92m to the south/south-east of the church, but may have originally been up to 4m high given the considerable nature of the inner ditch (McConway 1994b, 4, 7, 13; Walsh 1997, 14, 16). Sizeable depths of natural silting within the lowest fills of this inner enclosure ditch in both McConway's and Walsh's excavated portions suggests that several centuries of material may have accumulated within this ditch before the deposition of the upper ditch fills in the medieval period (McConway 1994b, 17–18). The historic foundation date of the monastery (AD 769) just fits within the 2 sigma date (AD 531–773) secured by Walsh from the basal fill of the ditch. An outer enclosure ditch was also excavated. One section of this outer enclosure ditch measured at least 3m wide and 2.2m deep (McConway 1994:102), though another excavated section had maximum dimensions of *c.*5.35m wide and 1.6m deep (McConway 1995:111; 1995, 1). Further evidence for the continuous recutting and maintenance of the outer enclosure ditch was revealed in excavations by McConway (1995, 5). Other than some metal slag and medieval pottery sherds from the upper fills, there were few finds from the ditch (McConway 1994:102; 1994, 4–10, 15). Monitoring of pile caps by Christina Forrest south/south-east of the church uncovered the remnants of the outer enclosure bank and found that it was cut by a linear medieval ditch F4 (Walsh 1997, 26). The date of the outer enclosure ditch is unclear, though Walsh (1997, 26) reported that animal bone excavated by McConway in 1994 from around the outer ditch base yielded a 2 sigma date of AD 718–973 (No BP date provided). This evidence then indicates that the outer ditch was probably originally cut sometime from the eighth to the tenth century and that it remained at least partially open until around the fourteenth/fifteenth century, as implied from medieval pottery finds in the upper ditch fills (McConway 1994b, 13–18). The outer enclosure then appears to be later than the inner enclosure ditch; it was postulated that the recutting of the inner ditch may have been roughly contemporary with the excavation of the outer ditch and that this building work may have been inspired by a desire to refortify its defences and increase the status of the site (McConway 1994b, 17).

References: McConway 1994:102; McConway 1994; McConway 1995:111; McConway 1995; Walsh 1997:187; Walsh 1997

Taney, Co. Dublin

Enclosure: Enclosure ditches
Information and dating evidence: Remains of a number of early medieval
outer enclosures successively built around the site were uncovered in an
excavation west of the church. Phase I consisted of a possible palisade
enclosure (F118, F187) adjoining the church and graveyard. The palisade
enclosure was sub-circular in plan and enclosed an area *c.*20m–25m in
diameter. It had a U-shaped profile and varied from 0.6m–0.8m wide with an
average depth of 0.26m–0.42m deep along the western side. Large packing
stone were identified in the ditch base implying that the trench contained a
palisade/timber fence. Animal bone from the base of palisade trench dated
from the mid-seventh to early ninth century (1271±28 BP). Finds included
animal bone and three flint-flakes. The northern side of the palisade trench
was also U-shaped; it was recorded for 15m and was 0.76m wide and 0.46m
deep. Two sherds of medieval pottery were recovered from the upper ditch fill,
but these were considered intrusive. The *c.*eighth-century palisade enclosure
was interpreted as 'an outer adjoining enclosure to the west of the pre-existing
church and burial site' that may have 'enclosed a dwelling, such as the priest's
house for him or his retinue' (O'Donovan 2012, 32). Phase II enclosure ditch
(F297) consisted of a circular rampart (*c.*70m diameter) built outside the phase
I palisade trench, which enclosed the entire church site. It was V-shaped and
measured 2.26m to 2.8m wide and up to 1.6m deep with a narrow flat base
0.4m–0.55m wide. Its basal fill produced animal bone, though Leinster
cooking ware and Dublin-type ware were recovered from upper fills. This
V-shaped ditch was interpreted as later than the phase I palisade enclosure
(F118) due to the fact that 'an internal bank (inside the V-shaped ditch) would
have covered the southern end of the palisade enclosure'. The phase III
enclosure ditch (F101 – below) cut this V-shaped enclosure ditch and its basal
fill produced a date from the later seventh to later ninth century. The phase II
V-shaped enclosure ditch must then pre-date sometime in this date range.
Phase III witnessed the construction of a large U-shaped ditch (F101/F226)
surrounding the church site with an estimated diameter of *c.*100m. This ditch
had a flat base and was even more substantial than the phase II V-shaped ditch
and measured from 3.65m–4.36m wide and from 1.85m–2.2m deep. Small
pieces of animal bone and slag-like material were recovered from fills overlying
the lowest fills in the northern part of the ditch. A find from the basal fill of
this U-shaped ditch produced a 2 sigma date from later seventh to later ninth
century. After this large U-shaped ditch (F101/F226) had silted up, it was
recut (F106) and rebuilt in phase IV. The recut ditch contained a varying
profile and measured from 1.4m–2.7m wide and 1.4m–1.95m deep. Animal
bone and an alabaster stick pin (*c.*late twelfth to early fourteenth century) were
recovered from the basal fill. The basal fill of this recut ditch produced a

2 sigma date from the later eighth to mid-tenth century. The dating of the alabaster pin differs to the radiocarbon date, though the discovery of the pin close to the edge of a medieval pit (F317) cutting the ditch might indicate that it is intrusive. Animal bone, a human skullcap fragment, a piece of slag and two Dublin-type sherds of pottery were recorded from middle fills. The upper fills contained animal bone, several metal objects (strap-hinge, penannular iron-loop, nails, bone handle and iron tang) as well as a range of medieval pottery types. No evidence for enclosure banks were found associated with these enclosure ditches, but these had probably been entirely removed by land improvement works. It is possible that the curving form of the Churchtown Upper Road 'represents the alignment of another enclosure ditch, or internal subdivision, likely to have been the inner enclosure surrounding the church and graveyard'. It is then possible that the large U-shaped ditch (F101/F226) and its predecessor (F279) may represent the second, outer enclosure (O'Donovan 2012, 52).

References: O'Donovan 2012, 21–35, 52

Termonfeckin, Co. Louth

Enclosure: Enclosure ditch?

Information and dating evidence: Testing at Big Street, Termonfeckin revealed an east–west ditch; this feature was cut into the orange/brown boulder clay, which was exposed at a depth of 0.8–1.1m. The exposed ditch measured 2m wide and 'extended eastwards in line with the north side of the graveyard'. The ditch was found to be filled with a brown loam containing charcoal. It was suggested that the ditch may 'represent an early enclosure or vallum around the monastic site but could also be a later feature'. No finds were recovered, however, to date this feature.

References: Murphy 2008:859

Toureen Peakaun (Toureen td.), Co. Tipperary

Enclosure: Enclosure ditch, channel and palisade

Information and dating evidence: Ecclesiastical enclosure at Toureen Peakaun reported to measure *c.*170m in diameter. Part of the ecclesiastical enclosure along its north-eastern side was defined by a small west–east oriented natural palaeochannel feeding into the Toureen Stream. An internal palisade was identified immediately inside the channel. The palisade was situated about 1.2m from the channel bank (Ó Carragáin 2006:1929; 2007:1738; 2008:1167). Ecclesiastical enclosure reported to be of early medieval date (Ó Carragáin, pers. comm.).

References: Ó Carragáin 2005:1469; Ó Carragáin 2006:1929; Ó Carragáin 2007:1738; Ó Carragáin 2008:1167

Trim (St Patrick's Cathedral), Co. Meath

Enclosure: Enclosure ditch?
Information and dating evidence: A large ditch, 5.2m wide, cutting into the boulder clay was excavated along Loman Street west of St Patrick's Cathedral (Seaver 2014, 241). This ditch was revealed to the north-west of the church enclosure wall. The limited nature of the development meant that this feature was not fully assessed and that its northern limit was not found. Only 0.5m of the deposits within the ditch was excavated as the feature continued below the ground level required for the development. The soils filling the top of the ditch revealed a single charred elder seed and charcoal. The southern ditch side was partly stone-revetted. The small quantity of charred cereal and charcoal found in the ditch had not yet been submitted for dating in June 2014. It was therefore not possible to establish whether the ditch 'could represent an earlier stage in the defences of the medieval town or could be connected to an earlier enclosure of the ecclesiastical site'. The ditch was cut by a bowl-shaped pit with fire-reddened base, which may represent the remains of a charcoal clamp – a pit used to convert wood into charcoal for ironworking. A piece of iron slag was found beside this pit.
References: Seaver 2014, 241–4

Tuam, Co. Galway

Enclosure: Enclosure ditches?
Information and dating evidence: Excavations in 1992 in a field between Vicar Street and the grounds of St Mary's Church of Ireland Cathedral (Townparks) revealed a V-shaped canalized ditch (Higgins 1992:096). The ditch produced a complex series of organic layers of wood, bone and a portion of a small perforated amber bead. One interesting find was a piece of worked wood of uncertain function. Some of the sticks along the sides of the ditch were 'narrow and wattle-like, but only one or two apparently intertwined "woven" pieces were found'. The V-shaped ditch was deliberately cut, 'possibly on the site of a natural feature', which may correspond 'to the Srufan Bride [St Bridget's Stream] that runs across the field in the direction of Tober Jarlath'. The V-shaped ditch was discovered outside the remains of the robbed-out boundary of the ecclesiastical enclosure. The outer face of this enclosure was stone-faced, but the core consisted of earth and small stones and the inner face was that of a sloping embankment 'faced with small stones embedded at an angle in the inside face of the feature'. It was suggested that this wall was robbed out to build the present enclosing wall around the medieval cathedral. The exact function of the V-shaped ditch was not stated, though it is possible that it may have formed part of some boundary delineating the early medieval ecclesiastical site. Two other church sites were also investigated in 2009 and

2010. Excavations in 2009 were undertaken in close proximity to the ecclesiastical site of Templenascreen; excavations in 2010 were undertaken near the site of Temple Jarlath. Both excavations by Delaney. Excavations in July/August 2009 in the north-eastern quarter of Tuam town centre revealed the remains of a potential early medieval enclosure ditch (Delaney 2009:420). Four areas were investigated. Area 1 revealed the footings of a possible wall that may represent the boundary wall of a laneway marked on the first edition OS map, which may have followed the line of the ecclesiastical enclosure surrounding Templenascreen (GA029–68A). The excavation revealed a shallow ditch to the east of the wall, but this was not deemed to represent the ecclesiastical enclosure as it was too shallow. However, excavation also revealed a larger east–west orientated ditch in the area; this had been recut and measured 1m deep and had an exposed width of 2.2m. This large ditch was revealed below the garden soil and cut into the natural subsoil and it was suggested that it may 'represent a boundary contemporary with the medieval ecclesiastical enclosure'. Excavations in area 2 also revealed two ditches, but these appear to date to the post-medieval period (ibid.). Trenches were dug in 2010 at the junction between Sawpit Lane, The Mall and Church Lane and along the full length of Sawpit Lane south-west of the site excavated in 2009 (above), in close proximity to the ecclesiastical site of Temple Jarlath (Delaney 2010:367). One trench revealed a single skeleton. The second trench uncovered the truncated remains of a large ditch and possible bank, two large pits and four skeletons. Trench 3 revealed three ditches, a pit, a stone culvert, a boundary wall, a cobbled surface and eleven skeletons. It was not stated what date these ditches were and whether they may have potentially enclosed the nearby site of Temple Jarlath in the medieval period.

References: Higgins 1992:096; Delaney 2009:420; Delaney 2010:367

Tulla, Co. Clare

Enclosure: Enclosure ditch and bank

Information and dating evidence: Excavations revealed evidence for 'an inner enclosure ditch, presumably associated with the earliest church on the site, a tantalising glimpse of a stone-revetted embankment possibly creating a level platform for the early church on the summit of the hill and a fragment of a circular hut structure with a central post'. The ditch (F50) was interpreted as early medieval in date, though radiocarbon dates obtained from its lower fills were still awaiting. It was revealed for 35m and measured 1.25m–2.6m wide and 0.75m–1.45m deep. It had steep sides and a flat base. No evidence for an associated palisade was uncovered. The ditch contained three principle fills. The earliest fills comprised silt deposits, which had apparently accumulated when the ditch was functioning. Charcoal flecks were present in these lower fills and they were sampled for dating. A rotary sharpening stone – the only major find – was discovered at the interface between the lowermost silty fill (F47) and the main fill (F46). It does not appear that the lowermost silt deposits had been disturbed by a recut. The principle fill (F46) consisted of redeposited subsoil with the occasional stone boulder present. This subsoil forming the principle ditch fill 'is presumably derived from the upcast washing back in, or perhaps being deliberately redeposited to level out the ground'. The fact that 'three later drains terminated along the line of the ditch would suggest that despite its invisibility, it retained a drainage function long after it had been backfilled'. A dark line extending along the approximate southern extent of the ditch was recorded in Westropp's survey of the site and it was therefore suggested that this ditch survived on the ground surface at the turn of the twentieth century when Westropp had conducted this survey. The excavation also revealed 'ephemeral evidence for an internal bank to the east of the central portion of the excavated ditch'. This survived to 'no more than 0.25m in height, extending for 3.5m along the inner cut which tapered off into the natural gradient to the east'. The interpretation of this feature as the internal bank was not pressed as it was noted that there 'was a difficulty distinguishing this material from the underlying subsoil'. The arc of a curvilinear gully (F24) cut the upper fill of the F50 enclosure ditch. This gully survived for 3.25m and if extrapolated out would have formed a circle (*c.*4.8m diameter) over the F50 enclosure ditch. It was suggested that this structure might represent the remains of an early medieval round house, which was built after the earlier enclosure ditch had fallen out of use, 'although there was no indication of the structure cutting the enclosure's upper fill'. When extrapolated out, the inner enclosure formed 'a rectangular rather than an oval shape, with dimensions of approximately 76m (east–west) by 77m'. This enclosure ditch may have had 'a relatively short functional life', given 'the evidence for a single-phase backfill without recuts along with the absence of finds or industrial debris'.

References: Myles 2012:086

Tullylish, Co. Down

Enclosure: Enclosure ditches and bank
Information and dating evidence: A massive, wide, inner ditch (5m wide x 2.9m deep) with regular and steep sides and a flat-bottomed base cutting through the underlying boulder clay was excavated (Ivens 1987, 58–60). The ditch was recut on many occasions, but there was evidence for it naturally silting up over different periods of time. Charcoal from the lower fill produced a date of AD 433–658 2Σ (1475±60 BP – UB 2671) and AD 259–619 2Σ (1590±75 BP – UB 2673). The top of the inner, primary ditch may have been remodelled and used as an industrial area roughly around the time the outer enclosure ditch (below) was dug, probably around the later eighth- to tenth-century period. The

outer enclosure ditch originally consisted of a wide (*c.*5m) slightly irregular steep-sided and flat-bottomed feature (2.85m deep), which cut through the hard boulder clay and even the Silurian shale bedrock. The bottom 0.30m–0.40m of the ditch comprised a rock cut channel (0.80m wide) which extended along its southern side. The ditch was regularly cleaned out and recut during its earlier use, though the upper fills were much more uniform and indicative of more regular dumping of domestic debris. During this latter period, the ditch was allowed to silt up and was not regularly maintained. Charcoal from near the ditch bottom produced a 2 sigma date of AD 675–967 (1210±60 BP – UB 2672) (Ivens 1987, 113). Coins dating to the fourteenth century were recovered from the upper ditch fills, suggesting that the ditch was cut as early as the later seventh/eighth century, but was not fully backfilled until the fourteenth century (Ivens 1987, 60). Souterrain ware was recovered from the outer ditch fill. Possible remains of an internal bank were uncovered in the form of a layer of sterile yellow-brown boulder clay lying directly upon natural subsoil in the entire area between both ditches on the ecclesiastical site.
References: Ivens 1987, 58–61, 112–13, 119

Tullynure, Co. Derry

Enclosure: Enclosure ditch
Information and dating evidence: A trench (20m x 1.5m) was opened across the line of the posited ecclesiastical enclosure. This trench identified a ditch measuring *c.*3.5m wide at the subsoil surface and up to 1.5m deep. The ditch had a rounded 'U' profile and contained five layers. These comprised eroded subsoils that may have derived from the upslope, upcast bank and silts rich in vegetable matter. This ditch was recut once. The ditch was probably infilled in 'medieval times' due to the recovery of 'a few sherds of "everted rim" cooking pottery and a single body sherd of cream-coloured fabric'. There was no evidence, however, to date the cutting of the ditch. The ditch may have formed part of an oval-shaped enclosure with dimensions of *c.*140m north to south and *c.*190m east to west.
References: Brannon 1985:17

BIBLIOGRAPHY

Adams, M. and O'Brien, C. 2016:288 'Cooley ecclesiastical complex, Donegal'. www.excavations.ie.
Anderson, A.O. and Anderson, M.O. (eds) 1961 *Adomnán's Life of Columba*. London.
Anderson, M.O. 1976 'The Celtic church in Kinrimund'. In D. McRoberts (ed.), *The medieval church of St Andrews*, 1–10. Glasgow.
Baker, C. 2001:449 'Lusk, Co. Dublin'. www.excavations.ie.
Baker, C. 2001 'Report on archaeological testing at Lusk, Co. Dublin (01E0872 ext.)'. Unpublished report for the National Monuments Service, Dublin.

Baker, C. 2004 'A lost ecclesiastical site in Finglas'. *Archaeology Ireland* 18(3), 14–17.

Baker, C. (ed.) 2009 *The archaeology of Killeen Castle, Co. Meath.* Dublin.

Baker, C. 2010 'Occam's duck: three early medieval settlement cemeteries or ecclesiastical sites'. In C. Corlett and M. Potterton (eds), *Death and burial in early medieval Ireland in the light of recent archaeological excavations*, 1–21. Research papers in Irish archaeology 2. Dublin.

Barber, J.W. 1981 'Excavations on Iona 1979'. *Proceedings of the Society of Antiquaries of Scotland* 111, 282–380.

Bhreathnach, E. 2013 *Ireland in the medieval world, AD 400–1000: landscape, kingship and religion.* Dublin.

Bhreathnach, E. 2015a 'Observations on the context and landscape of the West Ossory crosses'. In E. Purcell, P. MacCotter, J. Nyhan and J. Sheehan (eds), *Clerics, kings and Vikings: essays on medieval Ireland in honour of Donnchadh Ó Corráin*, 11-20. Dublin.

Bhreathnach, E. 2015b 'Monastic Ireland AD 1100–1700: new directions'. *Archaeology Ireland* 29(3), 37–40.

Binchy, D.A. 1941 *Críth Gablach.* Mediaeval and Modern Series 11. Dublin.

Bitel, L.M. 1990 *Isle of the saints: monastic settlement and Christian community in early Ireland* Cork.

Blair, J. 2005 *The church in Anglo-Saxon Society.* Oxford.

Bolger, T. 2004:0647 'Kilgobbin, Stepaside, Co. Dublin'. www.excavations.ie.

Bolger, T. 2008 'Excavations at Kilgobbin church, Co. Dublin'. *Journal of Irish Archaeology.* 17, 85–112.

Bolger, T. 2014 'The metal-working evidence from Kilgobbin, Co. Dublin'. In C. Corlett and M. Potterton (eds), *The church in early medieval Ireland in the light of recent archaeological excavations*, 1–12. Research Papers in Irish Archaeology 5. Dublin.

Bolger, T. and Dennehy, E. 2006:686 'Oldtown/Mooretown, Co. Dublin'. www.excavations.ie.

Bourke, E. 2005 'A preliminary analysis of the inner enclosure of Skellig Michael, Co. Kerry'. In T. Condit and C. Corlett (eds), *Above and beyond: essays in memory of Leo Swan*, 121–37. Bray.

Bourke, E., Hayden, A. and Lynch, A. (eds) 2011 *Skellig Michael, Co. Kerry: the monastery and South Peak. Archaeological stratigraphic report: excavations 1986–2010.* Dublin.

Brannon, N.F. 1977-79:0033 'Nendrum, Down'. www.excavations.ie.

Brannon, N.F. 1985:17 'Tullynure, Co. Derry'. www.excavations.ie.

Brannon, N.F. 1986 'Archaeological excavations at Cathedral Hill, Downpatrick, 1985'. *Lecale Miscellany* 4, 50–2.

Brannon, N.F. 1986:02 'Rectory Field, Antrim'. www.excavations.ie.

Brannon, N.F. 1987:12 'Cathedral Hill, Downpatrick, Demesne of Down, Down'. www.excavations.ie.

Brannon, N.F. 1988a 'Archaeological excavations at Cathedral Hill, Downpatrick, 1987'. *Lecale Miscellany* 6, 3–9.

Brannon, N.F. 1988b 'Life and death in an early monastery: Cathedral Hill, Downpatrick, Co. Down'. In A. Hamlin and C.J. Lynn (eds), *Pieces of the past: archaeological excavations by the Department of the Environment for Northern Ireland, 1970–1986*, 61–4. Belfast.

Brannon, N.F. 1997:071 'Cathedral Hill, Downpatrick, Co. Down', www.excavations.ie

Breen, Thaddeus. 1987:57 '"Brecaun Church", Portersgate, Wexford'. www.excavations.ie

Brennan, M. 1987:48 '"Dunmisk", Dunmisk, Co. Tyrone'. www.excavations.ie.

Byrne, G. 1987:41 'Kells, Townparks, Co. Meath', www.excavations.ie.

Byrne, G. 1988:57 'Kells, Townparks, Co. Meath'. www.excavations.ie.

Byrne, G. 1988 'Report on archaeological excavation (E000428) at Townparks, Kells, Co. Meath'. Unpublished report for the National Monuments Service, Dublin.

Byrne, M. 2006:963 'Killashee Demesne, Kildare'. www.excavations.ie

Byrne, M. 2016:420 'Monastery, Wicklow'. www.excavations.ie.

Carroll, J. 1996:136 'Cahill Motors Ltd, Raheny, Dublin'. www.excavations.ie.

Carroll, J. 1997:184 'The Old Orchard Inn, Butterfield Avenue, Rathfarnham, Dublin'. www.excavations.ie.

Carver, M. 2008 *Portmahomack: monastery of the Picts*. Edinburgh.

Carver, M. 2011 'What were they thinking? Intellectual territories in Anglo-Saxon England'. In H. Hamerow, D.A. Hinton and S. Crawford (eds), *The Oxford handbook of Anglo-Saxon archaeology*, 914–47. Oxford.

Channing, J. 2012 Ballykilmore – living with the dead, the development and continuity of an early medieval graveyard. In P. Stevens and J. Channing (eds), *Settlement and community in the Fir Tulach Kingdom: archaeological excavation on the M6 and N52 road schemes*, 81–107. National Roads Authority Scheme Monographs. Dublin.

Channing, J. 2014 'Ballykilmore, Co. Westmeath: continuity of an early medieval graveyard'. In C. Corlett and M. Potterton (eds), *The church in early medieval Ireland in the light of recent archaeological excavations*, 23–38. Research Papers in Irish Archaeology 5. Dublin.

Clarke, H. 2004 'Christian cults and cult centers in Hiberno-Norse Dublin'. In A.S. MacShamhráin (ed.), *The island of St Patrick: church and ruling dynasties in Fingal and Meath, 400–1148*, 140–58. Dublin.

Clinton, M. 2000:0203 'Balally, Co. Dublin'. www.excavations.ie.

Coen, L. 2019:238 'Mooretown, Swords, Dublin'. www.excavations.ie.

Colgrave, B. (ed.) 1927 *The Life of Bishop Wilfrid by Eddius Stephanus*. Cambridge.

Collins, A. 2007:1256 'Site 14, Balfeaghan, Meath'. www.excavations.ie.

Collins, T. 2018:009 'Durrow Demesne, Offaly'. www.excavations.ie.

Corlett, C. 2014 'The early church in Umhall, west Mayo'. In C. Corlett and M. Potterton (eds), *The church in early medieval Ireland in the light of recent archaeological excavations*, 39–92. Research Papers in Irish Archaeology 5. Dublin.

Cotter, C. 1990:021 'Skeam West, Co. Cork'. www.excavations.ie.

Cotter, C. 1991:071 'Sceilig Michael, Co. Kerry'. www.excavations.ie.

Cotter, C. 1995 'Archaeological excavations at Skeam West'. *Mizen Journal* 3, 71–9.

Cotter, E. 1996:037 'Ballynoe, Cork'. www.excavations.ie

Cotter, E. 1999:074 'Ballynoe, Cork'. www.excavations.ie.

Cotter, E. 2002 'The medieval church at Ballynoe, Co. Cork'. *Journal of the Cork Historical and Archaeological Society* 107, 105–34.

Cotter, E. 2014:528 'Kilquane, Cork'. www.excavations.ie.

Cotter, E. 2016:687 'Killamurren, Cork'. www.excavations.ie.

Coughlan, T. 2003 'Excavations at the medieval cemetery of St Peter's Church, Dublin'. In S. Duffy (ed.), *Medieval Dublin IV*, 11–39. Dublin.

Cross, S. 1999:576 'Loughboy, Drogheda, Louth'. www.excavations.ie.

Crothers, N. 2002:0034 'Kilmore, Co. Armagh'. www.excavations.ie.

Crumlish, R. 2007:1538 'Knockbrack, Co. Sligo'. www.excavations.ie.

Crumlish, R. 2014:309 'Eanach Dhuin, Co. Galway'. www.excavations.ie.

Cuppage, J. 1986 *Archaeological survey of the Dingle peninsula: a description of the field antiquities of the barony of Corca Dhuibhne from the Mesolithic period to the 17th century AD*. Ballyferriter.

Dawkes, G. 2006:606 '152–155 Church Street, Co. Dublin'. www.excavations.ie.

de Paor, L. 1997 *Inis Cealtra: report on archaeological and other investigations of the monuments on the island*. Unpublished report for the Department of Environment. Dublin.

Delany, D. 1999:733 'Cappancur, Co. Offaly'. www.excavations.ie.

Delany, D. 2001:1104 'Sranure, Co. Offaly'. www.excavations.ie.

Delany, D. 2017:617 'Tonlegee Road, Coolock, Dublin 5, Dublin'. www.excavations.ie.

Delany, D. 2018:698 'Tonlegee Road, Coolock, Dublin 5, Dublin'. www.excavations.ie.

Delaney, F. 2009:420 'Bishop's Street, Tuam, Co. Galway'. www.excavations.ie.

Delaney, F. 2010:367 'Sawpit Lane, Tuam, Co. Galway'. www.excavations.ie.

Dempsey, J. 2004:0123 'Mullagh, Co. Cavan'. www.excavations.ie.

Desmond, S. 2001:322 'Balally, Co. Dublin'. www.excavations.ie.

Devine, E. 2005:791 'Aghaviller, Kilkenny'. www.excavations.ie.

Devine, E. 2010:399' Donaghcumper, Co. Kildare'. www.excavations.ie.

Doherty, C. 1982 'Some aspects of hagiography as a source for Irish economic history'. *Peritia* 1, 300–28.

Doherty, C. 1985 'The monastic town in early medieval Ireland'. In H. Clarke and A. Simms (eds), *The comparative history of urban origins in non-Roman Europe: Ireland, Wales, Denmark, Germany, Poland and Russia from the ninth to the thirteenth century, Vol. 1*, 45–75. British Archaeological Reports International Series 255. Oxford.

Donaghy, C. 1993:180 'Navan Road, Duleek, Co. Meath'. www.excavations.ie.

Donaghy, G. 2018:278 'Drumcree Parish Church, Drumcree, Armagh'. www.excavations.ie.

Dowling, G. 2014 'Landscape and settlement in late Iron Age Ireland: some emerging trends'. In *Discovery Programme Reports 8: Late Iron Age and 'Roman' Ireland*, 151–74. Dublin.

Duffy, P. 2015:274 'St Doulagh's, Kinsealy, Dublin'. www.excavations.ie.

Duffy, P. 2016 'Resurrecting monuments'. *Archaeology Ireland* 30(1), 11–14.

Duffy, P. 2018:634 'St Fintan's Park, Kill of the Grange, Dublin'. www.excavations.ie.

Duignan, M. 1951 'Early monastic site, Kiltiernan East townland, Co. Galway'. *JRSAI* 81, 73–5.

Edwards, N. 1990 *The archaeology of early medieval Ireland*. London.

Edwards, N. 1996 'Identifying the archaeology of the early church in Wales and Cornwall'. In J. Blair and C. Pyrah (eds), *Council for British Archaeology Research Report 104*, 49–62. London.

Elder, S. 2008:955 'Main Street/Larrix Street, Duleek, Co. Meath'. www.excavations.ie.

Elliott, R. 2004:0577 'St Peter, Dublin'. www.excavations.ie.

Fanning, T. 1981 'Excavation of an early Christian cemetery and settlement at Reask, County Kerry'. *PRIA* 81C, 67–172.

Finan, T. 2014 'The medieval bishops of Elphin and the lost church at Kilteasheen'. In S. Duffy (ed.), *Princes, prelates and poets in medieval Ireland: essays in honour of Katharine Simms*, 352–61. Dublin.

Frazer, W. 2008:478 'Mooretown, Co. Dublin'. www.excavations.ie.

Fry, S. 1999 *Burial in medieval Ireland 900–1500*. Dublin.

Gaskell-Brown, C. and Harper, A.E.T. 1984 'Excavations on Cathedral Hill, Armagh, 1968'. *Ulster Journal of Archaeology* 47, 109–61.

Giacometti, A. 2008:475 'Church Road and St Joseph's Avenue, Lusk, Co. Dublin'. www.excavations.ie.

Gittins, A. 2002:1006 'St Canice's Orchard, Coach Road, Co. Kilkenny'. www.excavations.ie.

Gittos, H. 2011 'Christian sacred spaces and places'. In H. Hamerow, D.A. Hinton and S. Crawford (eds), *The Oxford handbook of Anglo-Saxon archaeology*, 824–42. Oxford.

Gowen, M. 2001 'Excavations at the site of the church and tower of St Michael le Pole, Dublin'. In S. Duffy (ed.), *Medieval Dublin II*, 13–52. Dublin.

Guinan, B. 2004:1144 'Creaghanboy, Co. Mayo'. www.excavations.ie.

Hall, T. 2000 *Minster churches in the Dorset landscape*. British Archaeological Reports British Series 304. Oxford.

Halliday, S. 2004:0651 'Mooretown North, Swords, Co. Dublin'. www.excavations.ie.

Halliday, S. 2004 'Report on archaeological testing (04E0543) – Mooretown, Swords, Co. Dublin'. Unpublished report for the National Monuments Service, Dublin.

Halliday, S. 2006:1496 'Killegland, Ashbourne, Co. Meath'. www.excavations.ie.

Halpin, E. 1993:134 'Kill, Kildare'. www.excavations.ie.

Halpin, E. 1994:092 'Finglas by-pass, Finglas, Co. Dublin'. www.excavations.ie.

Halpin, E. 1994:093 'Finglas by-pass, Finglas, Co. Dublin'. www.excavations.ie.

Halpin, E. 1996:120 'Spanish Convent, Finglas, Co. Dublin'. www.excavations.ie.

Halpin, E. 1996:184 'Kill, Kildare'. www.excavations.ie.

Halpin, E. 1998:115 'Cathedral Hill, Downpatrick, Co. Down'. www.excavations.ie.

Halpin, E. and Murphy, D. 1994 'Archaeological site assessment of the proposed route of the Finglas by-pass (93E0193/94E0010)'. Unpublished ADS report for the National Monuments Service, Dublin.

Hamlin, A. 1977 'A recently discovered enclosure at Inch Abbey, County Down'. *Ulster Journal of Archaeology* 40, 85–8.

Harney, L. 2016 'Living with the church in early medieval Ireland, AD 400–1100: archaeological perspectives on the sacred and profane'. Unpublished PhD thesis, UCD.

Harney, L. 2017 'Christianising pagan worlds in conversion-era Ireland: archaeological evidence for the origins of Irish ecclesiastical sites'. *PRIA* 117C, 103–30.

Hayden, A. 1998:130 '1–7 (Rear of) St Agnes Road, Crumlin, Dublin'. www.excavations.ie.

Hayden, A. 2000 'Archaeological assessment and desk study for a proposed development site at Church St/Hammond Lane, Dublin'. Unpublished report for the National Monuments Service, Dublin.

Hayden, A. 2013 'Early medieval shrines in north-west Iveragh: new perspectives from Church Island, near Valentia, Co. Kerry'. *PRIA* 113C, 67–138.

Henry, F. 1940 *Irish art in the early Christian period*. London.

Henry, F. 1965 *Irish art in the early Christian period (to 800 AD)*. London.

Herity, M. 1995 *Studies in the layout, buildings, and art in stone of early Irish monasteries*. London.

Higgins, J. 1992:096 '"The Clareen", Townparks, Tuam, Co. Galway'. www.excavations.ie.

Hull, G. 2009:085 'Ballaghboy (Bunratty Upper), Co. Clare'. www.excavations.ie.

Hull, G. 2008:115 'Clonlea, Co. Clare'. www.excavations.ie.

Hurl, D.P. 2002 'Excavation of an early Christian cemetery at Solar, County Antrim'. *Ulster Journal of Archaeology* 61, 37–82.

Hurley, M.F. 1988 'Excavations at an early ecclesiastical enclosure at Kilkieran, Co. Kilkenny'. *JRSAI* 118, 124–34.

Hurley, V. 1982 'The early church in the south-west of Ireland'. In S.M. Pearce (ed.), *The early church in western Britain and Ireland: studies presented to C.A. Raleigh Radford*, 297–332. British Archaeological Reports British Series 102. Oxford.

Ivens, R.J. 1987 'The early Christian monastic enclosure at Tullylish, Co. Down'. *Ulster Journal of Archaeology* 50, 55–121.

Jenkins, D. 2010 *'Holy, holier, holiest': the sacred topography of the early medieval Irish church*. Studia Traditionis Theologiae: Explorations in Early and Medieval Theology. Turnhout.

Joyce, E. 1985:48 'Drumcliffe South, Sligo'. www.excavations.ie.

Kavanagh, J. 2005 'Preliminary archaeological excavation report at 4–8 Church Street, Finglas (03E0224)'. Unpublished report for the National Monuments Service, Dublin.

Kavanagh, J. 2006:1499 'Killegland, Ashbourne, Co. Meath'. www.excavations.ie.

Kavanagh, John. 2006:2104 'Ferns Upper, Ferns, Co. Wexford'. www.excavations.ie.

Kelly, E.P. 1975:32 'Randalstown, Co. Meath'. www.excavations.ie.

Kelly, E.P. 1976:20 'Randalstown, Co. Meath'. www.excavations.ie.

Kelly, E.P. 1977–9:0052. 'Ballybarrack, Louth'. www.excavations.ie.

Kelly, F. 1988 *A guide to early Irish law*. Early Irish Law 3. Dublin.

Kelly, F. 2000 *Early Irish farming: a study based mainly on the law-texts of the 7th and 8th centuries AD*. Early Irish Law 4. Dublin.

King, H. 1992 'Excavations at Clonmacnoise'. *Archaeology Ireland* 6(3), 12–14.

King, H. 1993:186 'Clonmacnoise, Co. Offaly'. www.excavations.ie.

King, H. 1994:196 'Clonmacnoise, Co. Offaly'. www.excavations.ie.

King, H. 1997 'Burials and high crosses at Clonmacnoise (Ireland)'. In G. de Boe and F. Vergaeghe (eds), *Death and burial in medieval Europe: papers of the medieval Europe Brugge 1997 Conference*, 127–31. Bruges.

King, H. 2009 'The economy and industry of early medieval Clonmacnoise: a preliminary view'. In N. Edwards (ed.), *The archaeology of the early medieval Celtic churches*, 333–49. Society for Medieval Archaeology Monograph 29. Leeds.

King, H. 2012 'St Columba's monastery at Durrow– some additional discoveries'. In P. Harbison and V.A. Hall (eds), *A carnival of learning: essays to honour George Cunningham and his 50 conferences on medieval Ireland in the Cistercian Abbey of Mount St Joseph, Roscrea, 1987–2012*, 125–32. Roscrea.

King, H. and Crumlish, R. 1998:103 'Churchland Quarters, Carndonagh, Donegal'. www.excavations.ie.

Kiely, J. 2007:1819. 'Kilgrovan, Waterford'. www.excavations.ie.

Kovacik, J. 2006:60 'Braefield Nursing Home, 2–6 Carncome Road, Connor, Co. Antrim'. www.excavations.ie.

Larsson, E. 2004:0644 'Kilgobbin Lane/Enniskerry Road, Stepaside, Co. Dublin'. www.excavations.ie.

Larsson, E. 2004:0645 'Kilgobbin Lane/Enniskerry Road, Stepaside, Co. Dublin'. www.excavations.ie.

Larsson, E. 2004:0646 'Kilgobbin Lane/Enniskerry Road, Stepaside, Co. Dublin'. www.excavations.ie.

Lawlor, H.C. 1925 *The monastery of Saint Mochaoi of Nendrum*. Belfast.

Lawlor, H.J. 1894–5 'Notes on some non-biblical matter in the MS of the Gospels known as the Book of Mulling'. *Proceedings of the Society of Antiquaries of Scotland* 29, 11–145.

Leigh, J. 2016 'Geophysical survey report: Lullymore East, ecclesiastical site, County Kildare (15R0103)'. Unpublished geophysical survey report by J.M. Leigh Surveys on behalf of Kilkenny Archaeology.

Linnane, S.J. 2002:1738. 'Lorrha, Tipperary'. www.excavations.ie.

Linnane, S.J. 2002 'Archaeological excavation: Lorrha, North Riding, Co. Tipperary'. Unpublished ACS report for the National Monuments Service, Dublin.

Linnane, S.J. 2004 'Archaeological excavation: Lorrha, North Riding, Co. Tipperary'. Unpublished ACS report for the National Monuments Service, Dublin.

Liversage, G.D. 1968 'Excavations at Dalkey Island, Co. Dublin 1956–1959'. *PRIA* 66C, 53–233.

Long, C. 2005 'Clonfeacle, an early monastic site'. *Seanchas Ardmhacha: Journal of the Armagh Diocesan Historical Society* 20(2), 23–33.

Long, C. 2006:133 'Clonfeacle Church, Armagh'. www.excavations.ie.

Lowe, C. 2006 *Excavations at Hoddom, Dumfriesshire*. Edinburgh.

Lowe, C. 2008 *Inchmarnock: an early historic island monastery and its archaeological landscape*. Edinburgh.

Lucas, A.T. 1986 'The social role of relics and reliquaries in ancient Ireland'. *JRSAI* 116, 5–37.

Ludlow, N. 2009 'Identifying early medieval ecclesiastical sites in south-west Wales'. In N. Edwards (ed.), *The archaeology of the early medieval Celtic churches*, 61–84. Society for Medieval Archaeology Monograph 29. Leeds.

Lynch, A. and Cahill, M. 1976–7 'The excavation of St Vogues well and dolmen (site of), at Carnsore, Co. Wexford'. *Journal of the Wexford Historical Society* 6, 55–60.

Lynn, C.J. 1980–4:0086. 'Maghera (Carnacavilla td.), Co. Down'. www.excavations.ie.

Macalister, R.A.S. 1929 'On some excavations recently conducted on Friar's Island, Killaloe'. *JRSAI* 59, 16–24.

Macalister, R.A.S. 1935 'The excavation of Kiltera, Co. Waterford'. *PRIA* 43C, 1–16.

MacDonald, A. 1997 'Adomnán's monastery of Iona'. In C. Bourke (ed.), *Studies in the cult of Saint Columba*, 24–44. Dublin.

MacDonald, A. 2001 'Aspects of the monastic landscape in Adomnán's Life of Columba'. In J. Carey, M. Herbert and P. Ó Riain (eds), *Saints and scholars: studies in Irish hagiography*, 15–30. Dublin.

MacDonald, P. and McIlreavy, D. 2007 'Archaeological investigations at Kilhorne, Moneydorragh, County Down'. *Ulster Journal of Archaeology* 66, 97–119.

MacManus, C. 2003:1843 'Derryloran, Tyrone'. www.excavations.ie.

McConway, C. 1994:102 'St Maelruan's, Tallaght, Co. Dublin'. www.excavations.ie.

McConway, C. 1994 'Excavations at the early Christian monastic enclosure, Tallaght, Co. Dublin (94E0135)'. Unpublished ADS report for the National Monuments Service, Dublin.

McConway, C. 1995:111 'St Maelruan's, Tallaght, Co. Dublin'. www.excavations.ie.

McConway, C. 1995 'Test-trenching at site to the west of St Maelruan's Church, Tallaght (95E0155)'. Unpublished ADS report for the National Monuments Service, Dublin.

McConway, C. 1996:121 'Spanish Convent, Finglas, Co. Dublin'. www.excavations.ie.

McConway, C. 1996 'Stratigraphic report. Excavations at Spanish Convent site, Finglas (96E0130)'. Unpublished ADS report for the National Monuments Service, Dublin.

McConway, C. and Dawkes, G. 2005 'Archaeological test excavations at 152 to 155 Church Street and south of May Lane, Dublin 7 1996, 2004, 2005, and archaeological impact assessment 2005'. Unpublished report for the National Monuments Service, Dublin.

McCormick, F. 1997 'Iona: the archaeology of the early monastery'. In C. Bourke (ed.), *Studies in the cult of Saint Columba*, 45–68. Dublin.

McDermott, C., Warren, G. and Seaver, M. 2016:486 'Seven Churches, Glendalough, Wicklow'. www.excavations.ie.

McDowell, J.A. 1987 'Excavation in an ecclesiastical enclosure at Doras, County Tyrone'. *Ulster Journal of Archaeology* 50, 137–54.

McErlean, T.C. 2007 'The mills in their monastic context, the archaeology of Nendrum reassessed'. In T.C. McErlean and N. Crothers (eds), *Harnessing the tides: the early medieval tide mill at Nendrum monastery, Strangford Lough*, 324–404. Norwich.

McGlade, S. 2019:493 'Environs of St John the Evangelist Church, Brookville, Coolock, Dublin'. www.excavations.ie.

McHugh, R., Bell, J. and MacDonald, P. 2004 'Excavations in the vicinity of St Jarlath's Church, Clonfeacle, County Tyrone'. *Ulster Journal of Archaeology* 63, 52–64.

McHugh, T. 2019:075 'Attirory, Leitrim'. www.excavations.ie.

McLoughlin, C. 2006:2095 'Clongeen, Co. Wexford'. www.excavations.ie.

McLoughlin, G. 2004:0513 'Balgriffin Park, Co. Dublin'. www.excavations.ie.

McNeary, R. and Shanahan, B. 2009 'Carns townland, Co. Roscommon: excavations by the Medieval Rural Settlement Project in 2006'. In C. Corlett and M. Potterton (eds), *Rural settlement in medieval Ireland in the light of recent archaeological excavations*, 125–37. Research Papers in Irish Archaeology 1. Dublin.

Manning, C. 1984 'The excavation of the early Christian enclosure of Killederdadrum in Lackenavorna, Co. Tipperary'. *PRIA* 84C, 237–68.

Manning, C. 1989:078 '"Clonmacnois", Clonmacnois, Co. Offaly'. www.excavations.ie.

Manning, C. 1990:096 '"Clonmacnoise", Clonmacnoise, Co. Offaly'. www.excavations.ie.

Manning, C. 1992 'The base of the North Cross at Clonmacnoise'. *Archaeology Ireland* 6(2), 8–9.

Manning, C. 2015 *Monasterboice*. Archaeology Ireland Heritage Guide, No. 71. Dublin.

Marshall, J.W. and Rourke, G.D. 2000 *High Island: an Irish monastery in the Atlantic*. Dublin.

Marshall, J.W. and Walsh, C. 2005 *Illaunloughan Island: an early medieval monastery in County Kerry*. Bray.

Matthews, G. 2000 'The early history and archaeology of Armagh City'. PhD, School of Archaeology, Queen's University Belfast.

Meenan, R. 1991:101 '"St Secundinus' Church", Dunshaughlin, Co. Meath'. www. excavations.ie.

Meenan, R. 1996:138 'Sutton North, Co. Dublin'. www.excavations.ie.

Meenan, R. 1999:683 'Dunshaughlin, Co. Meath'. www.excavations.ie.

Meenan, R. 2004 'The excavation of pre-Norman burials and ditch near St Michan's Church, Dublin'. In S. Duffy (ed.), *Medieval Dublin V*, 91–110. Dublin.

Moloney, C., Baker, L., Millar, J. and Shiels, D. 2015 *Guide to the excavations at Ardreigh, Co. Kildare*. Report produced by Rubicon Heritage. Cork.

Moore, E. 2001:448 'Lusk, Co. Dublin'. www.excavations.ie.

Moore, F. 1991:062 '"St Brendan's Cathedral", Ardfert, Co. Kerry'. www.excavations.ie.

Moore, F. 1996 'Ireland's oldest bridge at Clonmacnoise'. *Archaeology Ireland* 10(4), 24–7.

Moore, F. 2007 *Ardfert Cathedral: summary of excavation results*. Dublin.

Morahan, L. 1997:407 'Ballyovey Church, Kilkeeran, Co. Mayo'. www.excavations.ie.

Morton, L. 2007:39 'Braefield Nursing Home, Connor, Co. Antrim'. www.excavations.ie.

Mount, C. 1990 'An early medieval strap-tag from Balally, Co. Dublin'. *JRSAI* 120, 120–5.

Mount, C. 1990:029 '"Cross Church of Moreen", Balally, Co. Dublin'. www.excavations.ie.

Mullins, C. 1997:443 'Ballyburley, Offaly'. www.excavations.ie.

Mullins, C. 1998:677 'Main Street, Taghmon, Co. Wexford'. www.excavations.ie.

Mullins, C. 1999:888 'Taghmon, Co. Wexford'. www.excavations.ie.

Mullins, C. 2000:1069 'Taghmon, Co. Wexford'. www.excavations.ie.

Murphy, Deirdre. 1999:681 'Larrix Street, Duleek, Co. Meath'. www.excavations.ie.

Murphy, Donald. 1999:173 1–7 'St Agnes Road, Crumlin, Dublin'. www.excavations.ie.

Murphy, Donald. 2003 'Excavation of an early monastic enclosure at Clonmacnoise'. In H. King (ed.), *Clonmacnoise studies 2: seminar papers 1998*, 1–33. Dublin.

Murphy, Donald. 2008:859 'Big Street, Termonfeckin, Co. Louth'. www.excavations.ie.

Murphy, Donald. 2015:103 'Monasterboice, Louth'. www.excavations.ie.

Murphy, Donald. 2016:440 'Monasterboice, Louth'. www.excavations.ie.

Murphy, Donald. 2019:529 'Clonmacnoise, Offaly'. www.excavations.ie.

Myles, F. 2001:955 'Cookstown, Co. Meath'. www.excavations.ie.

Myles, F. 2012:086 'St Mochulla's Church, Fair Green, Tulla, Co. Clare'. www.excavations.ie.

Neary, P. 2006:1053 'Coach Road, Kilkenny, Co. Kilkenny'. www.excavations.ie.

Nelis, E. 2005:007 'St Patrick's Church, Armoy, Co. Antrim'. www.excavations.ie.

Nelis, E., Gormley, S., McSparron, J.C. and Kyle, A. 2007 'Excavations at St Patrick's Church, Armoy, County Antrim AE/04/155 and AE/05/50'. Unpublished Centre for Archaeological Fieldwork (CAF) Structure Report 044(Part 1). Belfast.

Nelis, E., McSparron, C. and Gormley, S. 2014 'Excavations at St Patrick's Church, Armoy, Co. Antrim'. In C. Corlett and M. Potterton (eds), *The church in early medieval Ireland in the light of recent archaeological excavations*, 143–58. Research Papers in Irish Archaeology 5. Dublin.

Norman, E.R. and St Joseph, J.K.S. 1969 *The early development of Irish society: the evidence of aerial photography.* Cambridge.

O'Brien, C. and Adams, M. 2014 'Early ecclesiastical precincts and landscapes of Inishowen: interim report of field work by the Bernician Studies Group 2012–2014'. Available at: http://www.bernicianstudies.eu/wp-content/uploads/2014/11/BSG-Inishowen-2012-14.pdf (accessed 31 August 2020).

O'Brien, E. 2012 'Re-discovering Columba's monastery at Durrow, Co. Offaly'. In P. Harbison and V.A. Hall (eds), *A carnival of learning: essays to honour George Cunningham and his 50 conferences on medieval Ireland in the Cistercian Abbey of Mount St Joseph, Roscrea, 1987–2012*, 111–24. Roscrea.

O'Carroll, F. 1997:585. 'Glebe, Westmeath'. www.excavations.ie.

O'Connell, A. 2004 'Recent archaeological investigations at Kill St Lawrence, Waterford, carried out as part of the realignment of the R708 airport road'. *Decies: Journal of the Waterford Archaeological and Historical Society* 60, 27–64.

O'Connell, A. 2009 'Excavations at Church Road and the early monastic foundation at Lusk, Co. Dublin'. In C. Baker (ed.), *Axes, warriors and windmills: recent archaeological discoveries in North Fingal*, 51–63. Dublin.

O'Connell, A. 2014 'The early church in Fingal: evidence from Church Road, Lusk, Co. Dublin'. In C. Corlett and M. Potterton (eds), *The church in early medieval Ireland in the light of recent archaeological excavations*, 173–86. Research Papers in Irish Archaeology 5. Dublin.

O'Connell, A. 2017:654 'St Macullin's Church, Lusk, Dublin'. www.excavations.ie.

O'Connor, D.J. 2002:1444 'Cookstown, Co. Meath'. www.excavations.ie.

O'Connor, D.J. 2007:1197. 'Kilsaran, Louth'. www.excavations.ie.

O'Donnchadha, B. 2003:455 'Balally, Co. Dublin'. www.excavations.ie.

O'Donovan, E. 2008 'The Irish, the Vikings and the English: new archaeological evidence from excavations at Golden Lane, Dublin'. In S. Duffy (ed.), *Medieval Dublin VIII*, 36–130. Dublin.

O'Donovan, E. 2012 'Early Christian and medieval excavations at Teach Naithí: the changing morphology of a church site in Dundrum, County Dublin'. In S. Duffy (ed.), *Medieval Dublin XII*, 9–93. Dublin.

O'Donovan, E. 2014 'Archaeological excavations at the lost church of Drumkay, Glebe, Co. Wicklow'. In C. Corlett and M. Potterton (eds), *The church in early medieval Ireland in the light of recent archaeological excavations*, 187–224. Research Papers in Irish Archaeology 5. Dublin.

O'Keeffe, T. 1992 'Early Christian hermitage discovered on Omey Island'. *Archaeology Ireland* 6(3), 5.

O'Keeffe, T. 1993 'Omey Island, Co. Galway: interim report on excavations, winter 1992–3'. Unpublished report for the National Monuments Service, Dublin.

O'Keeffe, T. 1994 'Omey and the sand of time'. *Archaeology Ireland* 8(2), 14–17.

O'Kelly, M.J. 1958 'Church Island near Valencia, Co. Kerry'. *PRIA* 59C, 57–136.

O'Kelly, M.J. 1975 *Archaeological survey and excavation of St Vogue's Church, enclosure and other monuments at Carnsore, Co. Wexford.* Dublin.

O'Meara, J.J. 1982 *The history and topography of Ireland (by Giraldus Cambrensis).* (First published in 1951). London.

O'Reilly, D., Seaver, M., McDermott, C. and Warren, G. 2019 'Archaeological excavations at the monastic complex, Sevenchurches or Camaderry townland, Glendalough, Co. Wicklow: 2018 Stratigraphic Report'. Unpublished report for the Heritage Council, Dublin.

O'Sullivan, A. and Boland, D. 2000 *The Clonmacnoise bridge: an early medieval river crossing in County Offaly.* Archaeology Ireland Heritage Guide, No. 11. Bray.

O'Sullivan, A., McCormick, F., Harney, L., Kinsella, J. and Kerr, T.R. 2010 *Early medieval dwellings and settlements in Ireland, AD 400–1100: vol. 1 Text.* Unpublished Early Medieval Archaeology Project (EMAP) Report 4.2 for the Heritage Council, Dublin.

O'Sullivan, A., McCormick, F., Kerr, T.R. and Harney, L. 2014 *Early medieval Ireland AD 400–1100: the evidence from archaeological excavations.* Dublin.

O'Sullivan, Ann and Sheehan, J. 1996 *The Iveragh Peninsula: an archaeological survey of south Kerry.* Cork.

O'Sullivan, J. 1997:043 'Kilmore, Cork'. www.excavations.ie.

Ó Baoill, R. 2000:0352 'Aghavea Church, Aghavea, Co. Fermanagh'. www.excavations.ie.

Ó Baoill, R. 2000 'Excavations at Aghavea, County Fermanagh'. Unpublished Centre for Archaeological Fieldwork (CAF) Structure Report 046. Belfast.

Ó Baoill, R. 2014 'Excavations at Aghavea, Co. Fermanagh'. In C. Corlett and M. Potterton (eds), *The church in early medieval Ireland in the light of recent archaeological excavations,* 159–72. Research Papers in Irish Archaeology 5. Dublin.

Ó Carragáin, T. 2005:1469 'Toureen, Co. Tipperary'. www.excavations.ie.

Ó Carragáin, T. 2006:1929 'Toureen, Co. Tipperary'. www.excavations.ie.

Ó Carragáin, T. 2007:1738 'Toureen, Co. Tipperary'. www.excavations.ie.

Ó Carragáin, T. 2008:1167 'Toureen, Co. Tipperary'. www.excavations.ie.

Ó Carragáin, T. and Sheehan, J. 2010 *Making Christian landscapes: settlement, society and regionality in early medieval Ireland.* Final unpublished report for the Heritage Council. Cork.

Ó Drisceoil, C. 2004:0882 'Graiguenakill, Kilkenny'. www.excavations.ie.

Ó Drisceoil, C. 2005:813 'Father Hayden Road, Kilkenny, Co. Kilkenny'. www.excavations.ie.

Ó Drisceoil, C. 2006:1062 'The Deanery Orchard, St Canice's Cathedral, Kilkenny, Co. Kilkenny'. www.excavations.ie.

Ó Drisceoil, C. 2013 'Excavation and archaeological building survey at the Robing Room, Heritage Council Headquarters (former Bishop's Palace), Church Lane, Kilkenny 2011 and 2012 (11E157 and 11E157 ext.): Final report'. Unpublished report for the National Monuments Service, Dublin.

Ó Drisceoil, C., Bradley, J., Jennings, R., McCullough, L. and Healy, J. 2008 'The Kilkenny Archaeological Project (KKAP)'. Unpublished INSTAR report for the Heritage Council. Kilkenny.

Ó Floinn, R. 1985:46 'Durrow Demesne, Co. Offaly'. www.excavations.ie.

Ó Floinn, R. 1985:53 'Lurgoe (Derrynaflan), Tipperary'. www.excavations.ie

Ó Floinn, R. 1986:70 '"Derrynaflan", Luroge, Tipperary'. www.excavations.ie.

Ó Floinn, R. 1987:44 '"Derrynaflan", Lurgoe, Tipperary'. www.excavations.ie.

Ó Maoldúin, R. 2004:1813 'Moneytucker, Wexford'. www.excavations.ie.

Ó Maoldúin, R. 2009:356 'St Assam's Church, Howth Road, Raheny, Dublin'. www.excavations.ie.

Ó Maoldúin, R. 2014:050 'Annaghdown, Co. Galway'. www.excavations.ie.

Ó Maoldúin, R. 2014:310 'Cleenish, Fermanagh'. www.excavations.ie.

Picard, J.M. 2011 'Space organisation in early Irish monasteries: the *platea*'. In C. Doherty, L. Doran and M. Kelly (eds), *Glendalough: city of God,* 54–63. Dublin.

Plummer, C. 1922 *Lives of the Irish saints.* Oxford.

Pollock, D. 2007:1684 'Holycross, Tipperary'. www.excavations.ie.

Proudfoot, V.B. 1955 *The Downpatrick gold find: the hoard of gold objects from the Cathedral Hill, Downpatrick.* Belfast.

Proudfoot, V.B. 1956 'Excavations at Cathedral Hill, Downpatrick, Co. Down: 1954'. *Ulster Journal of Archaeology* 19, 57–72.

Purcell, A. 2003:1882 'Kilgrovan, Waterford'. www.excavations.ie.

Read, C. 2005:1339 'Kilteasheen, Co. Roscommon'. www.excavations.ie.

Read, C. 2006:1736 'Kilteasheen, Co. Roscommon'. www.excavations.ie.

Read, C. 2007:1498 'Kilteasheen, Co. Roscommon'. www.excavations.ie.

Read, C. 2008:1034 'Kilteasheen, Co. Roscommon'. www.excavations.ie.

Read, C. 2009:706 'Kilteasheen, Co. Roscommon'. www.excavations.ie.

Read, C. 2010 'Remembering where the bishop sat: exploring perceptions of the past at the Bishop's Seat, Kilteasheen, Co. Roscommon'. In T. Finan (ed.), *Medieval Lough Cé: history, archaeology, and landscape*, 41–66. Dublin.

Rodwell, W. 1981 *The archaeology of the English church; the study of historic churches and churchyards*. London.

Russell, I. 2005:127 'Mullagh, Co. Cavan'. www.excavations.ie.

Scally, G. 2001:517 'High Island, Co. Galway'. www.excavations.ie.

Scally, G. 2002:0742 'High Island, Co. Galway'. www.excavations.ie.

Scally, G. 2014 'The church and earlier structures at High Island, Co. Galway'. In C. Corlett and M. Potterton (eds), *The church in early medieval Ireland in the light of recent archaeological excavations*, 225–40. Research Papers in Irish Archaeology 5. Dublin.

Scally, G. (ed.), 2015 *High Island (Ardoileán), Co. Galway: excavation of an early medieval monastery*. Archaeological Monograph Series 10. Dublin.

Seaver, M. 2014 'The earliest archaeological evidence for an ecclesiastical site at Trim, Co. Meath'. In C. Corlett and M. Potterton (eds), *The church in early medieval Ireland in the light of recent archaeological excavations*, 241–5. Research Papers in Irish Archaeology 5. Dublin.

Shanahan, B. 2006:1715 'Carns, Co. Roscommon'. www.excavations.ie.

Shanahan, B. 2006 'Recent research in Roscommon by the Discovery Programme's Medieval Rural Settlement Project'. *Group for the Study of Irish Historic Settlement Newsletter* 11, 1–9.

Sheehan, J. 1982 'The early historic church-sites of north Clare'. *North Munster Antiquarian Journal* 24, 29–47.

Sheehan, J. 2003 '2003 stratigraphic report on the archaeological excavations at Caherlehillan, Co. Kerry'. Unpublished report for the National Monuments Service, Dublin.

Sheehan, J. 2009 'A peacock's tale: excavations at Caherlehillan, Iveragh, Ireland'. In N. Edwards (ed.), *The archaeology of the early medieval Celtic churches*, 191–206. Society for Medieval Archaeology Monograph 29. Leeds.

Sheehan, J. 2014 'Caherlehillan, Co. Kerry: ritual, domestic and economic aspects of a Corcu Duibne ecclesiastical site'. In C. Corlett and M. Potterton (eds), *The church in early medieval Ireland in the light of recent archaeological excavations*, 247–58. Research Papers in Irish Archaeology 5. Dublin.

Shine, D. 2019:451. 'Clone, Wexford'. www.excavations.ie.

Silvester, R.J. and Evans, J.W. 2009 'Identifying the mother churches of north-east Wales'. In N. Edwards (ed.), *The archaeology of the early medieval Celtic churches*, 21–40. Society for Medieval Archaeology Monograph 29. Leeds.

Simpson, L. 1994:204 'Collooney, Sligo'. www.excavations.ie.

Simpson, L. 1995:230 'Church of St Secundinus, Dunshaughlin, Co. Meath'. www.excavations.ie.

Simpson, L. 2005 'The ecclesiastical enclosure at Dunshaughlin, Co. Meath; some dating evidence'. In T. Condit and C. Corlett (eds), *Above and beyond: essays in memory of Leo Swan*, 227–38. Bray.

Smith, I. 1996 'The origins and development of Christianity in north Britain and southern Pictland'. In J. Blair and C. Pyrah (eds), *Church archaeology: research directions for the future*, 19–36. Council for British Archaeology Research Report 104. London.

Spall, C.A. 2009 'Reflections on the monastic arts: recent discoveries at Portmahomack, Tarbat, Easter Ross'. In N. Edwards (ed.), *The archaeology of the early medieval Celtic churches*, 315–31. Society for Medieval Archaeology Monograph 29. Leeds.

Stafford, E. 2002:1916 'Kilmokea House, Kilmokea, Wexford'. www.excavations.ie.

Stafford, E. 2011:624 'Grange, Co. Wexford'. www.excavations.ie.

Stevens, P. 2001:1223 'Holycross, Tipperary'. www.excavations.ie

Stevens, P. 2004:0470 'St Peter's, Co. Dublin'. www.excavations.ie.

Stevens, P. 2006 'A monastic enclosure site at Clonfad, Co. Westmeath'. *Archaeology Ireland* 20(2), 8–11.

Stevens, P. 2012 'Clonfad – an industrious monastery'. In P. Stevens and J. Channing (eds), *Settlement and community in the Fir Tulach Kingdom: archaeological excavation on the M6 and N52 road schemes*, 109–36. National Roads Authority Scheme Monographs. Dublin.

Stevens, P. 2014 'Clonfad, Co. Westmeath: an early Irish monastic production centre'. In C. Corlett and M. Potterton (eds), *The church in early medieval Ireland in the light of recent archaeological excavations*, 259–72. Research Papers in Irish Archaeology 5. Dublin.

Stokes, W. 1905 *Félire Óengusso Céli Dé: The martyrology of Oengus the Culdee*. Henry Bradshaw Society 29. London.

Stout, G. 1991:051 'Barrack Lane, Lusk, Co. Dublin'. www.excavations.ie.

Swan, D.L. 1976 'Excavations at Kilpatrick churchyard, Killucan, Co. Westmeath, July/August 1973 and 1975'. *Ríocht na Mídhe* 6(2), 89–96.

Swan, D.L. 1983 'Enclosed ecclesiastical sites and their relevance to settlement patterns of the first millennium AD'. In T. Reeves-Smyth and F. Hammond (eds), *Landscape archaeology in Ireland*, 269–80. British Archaeological Reports British Series 116. Oxford.

Swan, D.L. 1985 'Monastic proto-towns in early medieval Ireland: the evidence of aerial photography, plan analysis and survey'. In H. Clarke and A. Simms (eds), *The comparative history of urban origins in non-Roman Europe: Ireland, Wales, Denmark, Germany, Poland and Russia from the ninth to the thirteenth century (2 parts; part 1)*, 77–102. British Archaeological Report International Series 255. Oxford.

Swan, D.L. 1989:021 '"St Doulagh's", Balgriffin, Dublin'. www.excavations.ie.

Swan, D.L. 1990:031 '"S. Doulagh's", Balgriffin, Dublin'. www.excavations.ie.

Swan, D.L. 1990:033 'Church of St John the Evangelist, Coolock, Dublin'. www.excavations.ie.

Swan, D.L. 1994–1995 'Excavations at Kilpatrick, Killucan, Co. Westmeath, evidence for bone, antler and iron working'. *Ríocht na Mídhe* 9(1), 1–21.

Swan, D.L. 1995:236 'Stamullin, Meath'. www.excavations.ie.

Swan, D.L. 1997 'Excavations of the early Christian enclosure at Kilpatrick in the townland of Corbetstown, Killucan, Co. Westmeath'. Unpublished report for the National Monuments Service, Dublin.

Sweetman, D.L. 2004:1235 'Dunshaughlin, Co. Meath'. www.excavations.ie.

Taylor, K. 2018:754 'Kildare Back Yard Services – Campion Crescent, Lourdesville and Cleamore Terrace, Kildare, Kildare'. www.excavations.ie.

Taylor, T. and Aston, M. 1998 'Time Team Dig Cathedral Hill'. *Lecale Miscellany* 16, 28–35.

Thomas, C. 1971 *The early Christian archaeology of North Britain*. Glasgow.

Vuolteenaho, J. and Baillie, W. 2009:064 'Killuney Park Road, Armagh, Co. Armagh'. www.excavations.ie.

Waddell, J. and Clyne, M. 1995 'M.V. Duignan's excavations at Kiltiernan, Co. Galway, 1950–1953'. *Journal of the Galway Archaeological and Historical Society* 47, 149–204.

Walsh, C. 1997:187 'St Maelruan's, Tallaght, Co. Dublin'. www.excavations.ie.

Walsh, C. 1997 'Archaeological excavation of a development site to the south-east of St Maelruan's, Tallaght, Co. Dublin (96E188)'. Unpublished report for the National Monuments Service, Dublin.

Walsh, C. 2005 'Stratigraphic report'. In J.W. Marshall and C. Walsh (eds), *Illaunloughan Island: an early medieval monastery in County Kerry*, 137–72. Bray.

Walsh, C. 2009 'An early medieval roadway at Chancery Lane: from Duibhlinn to Áth Cliath?'. In S. Duffy (ed.), *Medieval Dublin IX*, 9–37. Dublin.

Walsh, C. and Hayden, A. 2001:496 'Clonfert Cathedral, Galway'. www.excavations.ie.

Walsh, F. and Bailey, F. 2010:523 'Church Street, Townparks, Kells, Co. Meath'. www.excavations.ie.

Ward and Vuolteenaho 2011:152 'Bangor, Co. Down'. www.excavations.ie.

Whitty, Y. 2009:349 'Barrack Lane, Lusk, Dublin'. www.excavations.ie.

Whitty, Y. 2009:350 'Barrack Lane, Lusk, Dublin'. www.excavations.ie.

Whitty, Y. 2016:844 'God's Cottage, Glendalough, Wicklow'. www.excavations.ie.

Wiggins, K. 2006 'A tale of two cemeteries'. *Seanda: National Roads Authority Magazine* 1, 33–5.

Wiggins, K. 2014 'An early medieval ditched enclosure with burials and cereal-drying kilns at Killeany, Co. Laois'. In C. Corlett and M. Potterton (eds), *The church in early medieval Ireland in the light of recent archaeological excavations*, 273–86. Research Papers in Irish Archaeology 5. Dublin.

Williams, B.B. 1991:011 'Turnarobert, souterrain, Co. Antrim'. www.excavations.ie.

Dublin and the Gaelic Irish economy in the eleventh and twelfth centuries

DENIS CASEY

Despite a lack of documentary sources dealing with the internal affairs of the city prior to its conquest by the English in 1170, the fruits of archaeological excavations have demonstrated that Dublin was by that stage both the principal conduit through which exotic goods were imported into Ireland and an important Western European trading centre.[1] In addition, during the last thirty years the importance of economic hinterlands to Dublin's existence has also been highlighted, demonstrating that Dublin was no immured outpost of a foreign mercantile power unwilling or unable to engage with the locals in a meaningful way.[2] Rather it was a kingdom well-integrated into local and regional politics, with a town at its heart that was reliant on surrounding territories for foodstuffs, building materials and the raw materials necessary for many of its economic activities.[3]

However, the price of placing Dublin at the centre of analysis has been an under-appreciation of events and trends in Gaelic Ireland, in favour of a

In addition to the Friends of Medieval Dublin symposium, some of the material in this paper was presented at the 24th Irish Conference of Medievalists (NUI Galway, 2010) and at a workshop entitled 'Insular Economics', which I, Dr Andrew Woods and Dr Russell Ó Ríagáin organized (University of Cambridge, 2011). I am grateful to all who offered comments on those occasions, and to the Department of Anglo-Saxon, Norse and Celtic and the McDonald Institute for Archaeological Research who provided funding for the workshop. 1 For the archaeology of Dublin, see in particular, Linzi Simpson, 'Fifty years-a-digging: a synthesis of medieval archaeological investigations in Dublin city and suburbs' in Seán Duffy (ed.), *Medieval Dublin XI* (Dublin, 2011), pp 9–112 and Patrick F. Wallace, *Viking Dublin: the Wood Quay excavations* (Newbridge, 2016). 2 Notable publications in this area include John Bradley, 'The interpretation of Scandinavian settlement in Ireland' in idem (ed.), *Settlement and society in medieval Ireland: studies presented to F.X. Martin, o.s.a.* (Kilkenny, 1988), pp 49–78; Mary A. Valante, 'Dublin's economic relations with hinterland and periphery in the later Viking Age' in Seán Duffy (ed.), *Medieval Dublin I* (Dublin, 2000), pp 69–83; and John Bradley, 'Some reflections on the problem of Scandinavian settlement in the hinterland of Dublin during the ninth century' in Bradley et al. (eds), *Dublin in the medieval world*, pp 39–62. 3 An interesting light on Dublin's identity is expressed in two coins of Sitriuc Silkenbeard (*ob.* 1042) where he is styled SIHTRIC CVNVNG DYFL ('Sitriuc king of Dublin') using the Old Norse *cununc* ('king') and SITERIC REX IRVM ('Sitriuc king among the Irish'): Mark Blackburn, 'Currency under the Vikings. Part 4: the Dublin coinage *c.*995–1050' in Mark Blackburn [Rory Naismith and Elina Screen (eds)], *Viking coinage and currency in the British Isles*, The British Numismatic Society special publication 7 (London, 2011), pp 91–117, at p. 94. This was originally published in the *British Numismatic Journal*, 78 (2008), 111–37, at 114. On the question of

narrative of Dublin's economic power.[4] As a means of offering an alternative to this trend, this essay explores aspects of economic activity in eleventh- and twelfth-century Gaelic Ireland that may influence our understanding of medieval Dublin. To do so, it will begin with a very brief overview of Dublin's coinage in the eleventh and twelfth centuries, as the coinage of Hiberno-Scandinavian Dublin (first minted by King Sitriuc Silkenbeard *c.*995AD) is a useful proxy by which to measure Dublin's economic influence within Ireland and the Irish Sea region.[5] Following from that – this time using cattle prices as a proxy – it will be argued that there were periods of substantial economic stress in Gaelic Ireland, which caused cattle prices to grow considerably during the course of the twelfth century. Placing these two sets of analysis alongside one another offers an opportunity for considering the extent to which aspects of Dublin's economy were influenced by economic changes in Gaelic Ireland and *vice versa*.

THE DUBLIN COINAGE AND ECONOMY IN THE ELEVENTH AND TWELFTH CENTURIES

Recent research by Andrew Woods has done much to illuminate our understanding of Dublin's coinage.[6] Following in the footsteps of Mark Blackburn, Michael Dolley and Michael Kenny, he has shown that when Sitriuc Silkenbeard first minted his coinage he did so in a town already well-accustomed to the use of Anglo-Saxon coins,[7] and that the silver pennies minted in Dublin during the eleventh and twelfth centuries potentially circulated in the millions, rather than in the thousands.[8] This coinage quickly displaced almost all other coins in Ireland, and the post-1000AD finds of single

identities more broadly, see Clare Downham, 'Viking ethnicities: a historiographic overview', *History Compass*, 10:1 (2012), 1–12. **4** It has been argued that 'our understanding of the economy of early medieval Ireland is somewhat problematical, partly because it remains largely untheorised': Aidan O'Sullivan, Finbar McCormick, Thomas R. Kerr and Lorcan Harney, *Early medieval Ireland, AD 400–1100: the evidence from archaeological excavations*, Royal Irish Academy monographs (Dublin, 2013), p. 247. This is both a legitimate criticism of the lack of attention paid to economic history and a reflection of the prominence of theory in archaeology vis-à-vis history. **5** For reservations on approaching coinage in this fashion, see Michael Kenny, 'Coins and coinage in pre-Norman Ireland' in Dáibhí Ó Cróinín (ed.), *A new history of Ireland*, i: *prehistoric and early Ireland* (Oxford, 2005), pp 842–51, at pp 847–8. **6** For a good summary, see Andrew Woods, 'The coinage and economy of Hiberno-Scandinavian Dublin' in Seán Duffy (ed.), *Medieval Dublin XIII* (Dublin, 2013), pp 43–69. **7** Andrew Woods, 'Prelude to the Hiberno-Scandinavian coinage: the Castle Street and Werburgh Street hoards' in Howard B. Clarke and Ruth Johnson (eds), *The Vikings in Ireland and beyond*, Pathways to Our Past 4 (Dublin, 2015), pp 355–72, at pp 369–70. **8** Andrew R. Woods, 'Economy and authority: a study of the coinage of Hiberno-Scandinavian Dublin and Ireland', 2 vols (PhD, University of Cambridge, 2014), i, pp 121–37; available at: https://doi.org/10.17863/CAM.7489 (accessed 1 August 2019).

coins are predominantly of Dublin silver pennies. This is highly significant, as single coins are more indicative of regular commerce than coin hoards, meaning that the Dublin coinage became *the* coinage used in Ireland during the eleventh and twelfth centuries.

Dublin's coinage during this period is normally divided into seven phases, broadly following a typology devised by Michael Dolley, and revised by Woods.[9] Its silver penny became increasingly lighter over the course of the eleventh century, although its percentage silver remained high (at around 90%), which Michael Kenny suggests a progressive devaluation of the currency, rather than its debasement.[10] However, in the first quarter of the twelfth century a major change occurred, when Dublin switched to minting bracteates (*c.*1115; Dolley Phase VII, Woods Group Q) – a name given to very thin leaf-like coins that were only decorated on one side.[11] These coins were extremely light, and from the 1140s onward they had a very low silver content, marking a decisive shift in Dublin's minting that lasted until its capture by the English in 1170. This change was part of a wider European trend in response to a 'silver famine' of the late eleventh and early twelfth centuries.[12] Woods has suggested that since coinage was not abandoned in favour of other means of exchange at this time, but rather the supply of silver was stretched in response to shortages, it is apparent that 'a coin-using mentality was well entrenched across much of Europe', including Dublin.[13]

The authority behind Dublin's coinage during this period is quite unclear.[14] Certainly the first coins were produced under the auspices of Sitriuc, as testified by the legends they bear. Those quickly became garbled and subsequently illiterate, such that it is not possible to identify an issuing authority or moneyer from them (if indeed one was meant to be represented by their pseudo-epigraphy). Nonetheless, there are indications that this was not a coin-producing free-for-all. The absence of foreign coins suggests a reminting of silver locally, implying the ability to enforce the dominance of the local currency, while the hoarding patterns imply renewal of the coinage through organized withdrawal of old coins that were then melted down and reissued in a new form.[15] Who this issuing authority might have been, whether an individual or collective, is unknown. Attempts to link changes in the coinage

---

9 R.H.M. Dolley, *The Hiberno-Norse coins in the British Museum*, Sylloge of Coins of the British Isles 8 (London, 1966), pp 92–145; Woods, 'Economy and authority', i, pp 74–117; for a summary, see ibid., p. 88 (table 3.4). 10 Kenny, 'Coins and coinage in pre-Norman Ireland', p. 851. 11 Woods has proposed the existence of a semi-bracteate phase *c.*1110–15 (Woods Group P): Woods, 'Economy and authority', i, pp 105–7. 12 Andrew R. Woods, 'From Charlemagne to the commercial revolution (*c.*800–1150)' in Rory Naismith (ed.), *Money and coinage in the middle ages*, Reading Medieval Sources 1 (Boston, 2018), pp 93–121, at p. 108. 13 Ibid., p. 117. 14 As Michael Kenny notes, understanding of the monetary history of Dublin in the twelfth century is obscured by an unclear picture of the history of Dublin in general at this time: Kenny, 'Coins and coinage in pre-Norman Ireland', p. 850. 15 Woods, 'Economy and authority', i, pp 218–33.

with various Gaelic kings' control of the city in the eleventh and twelfth centuries have proven unsuccessful.[16] From the middle of the eleventh century, kings of Leinster, Munster and Connacht gained direct control over Dublin at various times, but unlike Sitriuc they did not place their own names or royal images on its coinage. In addition, the chronology of the hoards (which most likely coincide with the withdrawal and renewal of the coins) cannot be mapped onto changes in political leadership; there is no evidence for increased coin usage in the individual Gaelic kingdoms during their periods of dominance over Dublin; and the 'zone of monetary activity' did not change substantially between the tenth and twelfth centuries.[17] Woods has surmised that this points to mercantile rather than royal control of Dublin's coinage and that 'the agency behind changes within it must be sought elsewhere, quite probably in the transnational, mercantile community based in the emerging urban network of medieval Europe'.[18]

In any case, the economic influence of Gaelic Ireland should also be explored; it may not have exerted political authority over Dublin's coinage, but this does not preclude some economic agency. An understanding of the economic life of Gaelic Ireland during the period of Dublin's bracteate coinage (namely *c*.1115–*c*.1170) may aid interpretation of Dublin's coinage or at the very least flesh out the broader context within which it was produced.

THE ECONOMY OF GAELIC IRELAND

Small volumes of silver were sometimes used in transactions in Gaelic Ireland and in Middle Irish legal commentaries (written primarily during the eleventh and twelfth centuries), an ounce of silver was divided into 72 *pinginne*, where a *pinginn* ('penny') – despite being a loanword, borrowed either from Old English or Old Norse – appears to have denoted a measure of weight of precious metals (approximately 0.5g), rather than a coin.[19] One *pinginn* roughly corresponds to the weight of a Dublin silver penny of the 1090s and could even be sub-divided into 7–8 'grains'. Use of the term *pinginn* as a unit of weight and the subdivision into grains would suggest that in Gaelic areas silver pennies were treated as bullion (at least originally). In the *Annals of Ulster* for the 1030s and 1090s there is evidence for the use of *pinginne* in the buying and selling a variety of foodstuffs. Under 1032 a verse records:

---

16 For example, it has previously been speculated that the minting of bracteates might have been connected with the direct takeover of Dublin by Tairdelbach Ua Conchobair, but the grounds for thinking so are slim: see Kenny, 'Coins and coinage in pre-Norman Ireland', p. 849.   17 On this zone, see Woods, 'Economy and authority', i, pp 302–22.   18 Ibid., i, p. 364.   19 Three *pinginne* made a *screpul* ('scruple'), which in turn was one twenty-fourth of an ounce, therefore a *pinginn* of silver weighed one seventy-second of an ounce of silver (approximately 0.5g): Fergus Kelly, *Early Irish farming: a study based mainly on the law-texts*

> *Seissedhach do gran chorca*
> *no trian d'airnibh dubcorcra*
> *no do dercnaibh darach duinn*
> *no do chnoibh falach finncuill*
> *fo-gabhar cen tacha tinn*
> *(i nArd) Macha ar oen(pinginn.).*

A sixth-measure of oaten grain,
Or a third-measure of dark purple sloes,
Or of acorns of the brown oak,
Or of nuts of a fair hazel cluster–
All are to be had in full abundance
At Ard Macha for one penny.[20]

At the end of the same century (1097), the price of nuts following an exceptional harvest is recorded:

> *Cnomhes mor isin bliadhain-si: .xxx. bliadhan on chnómhes aile gusan cno mhessa .i. bliadhain na cnó finn .i. co fogaibthi sesedach cno ar aen pinginn.*

A great harvest of nuts in this year: thirty years since the other harvest of nuts to this harvest, i.e., the year of the white nuts, i.e. a 'sixth' of nuts could be had for one penny.[21]

Combined, these entries point to a market (in the broad sense) for preservable foodstuffs (oats and hazelnuts), perishable foodstuffs (sloes or possibly plums) and animal feed (acorns).[22] These products were cultivated rather than foraged

---

of the 7th and 8th centuries AD, Early Irish Law 4 (rev. ed. Dublin, 2000), pp 593–5. *eDIL, s.v. pinginn* (http://dil.ie/34350) (accessed 1 August 2019), suggests it is a Teutonic loanword, probably from Old English *penning*. Old Norse *penningr* is also a possibility: Kelly, *Early Irish farming*, p. 596. **20** *AU* 1032.8. The poem is an addition by hand *H¹*, but is absent from the R manuscript of AU (Bodleian Library, MS Rawlinson B. 489) and from the closely related Annals of Loch Cé, but this does not automatically imply that it is of a much later date. This verse is also found in *AFM* 1031, where O'Donovan translates the second-last line, *fogaibhthe gan tacha tinn*, as 'was got without stiff bargaining'. **21** *AU* 1097.8. The two explanatory clauses were additions to the main text, by the hand known as *H²* and are also in the R manuscript (Bodleian Library, MS Rawlinson B. 489, fo. 45v). The reference to thirty years previously corresponds with *AU* 1066.3: *Cnomhes mor i nErinn uile ut rebellat fluminibus* ('A great harvest of nuts in all Ireland, so that it hindered the rivers'). **22** Middle Irish legal commentaries differentiate between the *áirne cumra* (plum) and *áirne fiadain* (sloe): Kelly, *Early Irish farming*, p. 261. The second line of the poem could presumably be applied to either. Evidence for hazelnut and sloe consumption has been found at a number of archaeological sites: O'Sullivan et al., *Early medieval Ireland*, p. 212. On occasion acorns might be eaten by people when other foods were scarce: Kelly, *Early Irish farming*, p. 307. However, given the abundance of food indicated in the text, it is more likely they were put to their regular purpose, i.e., for fattening pigs. This is supported by

(careful management of woodland seems to have been a feature of medieval Irish life), which suggests that this was not necessarily impromptu, but that an annual trade in them was possible.[23]

When comparing the two entries, at first glance it would appear that in 1031 one *pinginn* could buy twice the amount of hazelnuts (*train*, 'a third') that it could in 1097 (*seisedach*, 'a sixth').[24] A number of explanations may be offered for this, including the available supply of nuts, supply of silver (if bullion), or whether actual Dublin pennies were used. If the latter, there may not have been any appreciable price difference in bullion, as between *c.*1031 (late Dolley Phase II; late Woods Group F) and *c.*1097 (cusp of Dolley Phase V and VI; cusp of Woods Group M and N) the Dublin penny had halved in weight from approximately 1.05g to approximately 0.5g.[25] Regardless, both entries imply that basic supply-and-demand economics existed in Gaelic areas in the eleventh century, suggesting the silver values that appear embedded in the law tracts did not dictate daily practice. This is an important consideration when looking at the price of cattle – the commodity that supplies the greatest evidence of price fluctuations – and whose price in silver provides a useful way of analysing the economy of Gaelic Ireland while simultaneously providing a link to that of Dublin.

THE PLACE OF CATTLE IN THE SOCIO-ECONOMIC GAELIC WORLD

At first glance, cattle appear ubiquitous in medieval Irish written sources.[26] Hagiographies abound with pastoral miracles, annals repeatedly refer to cattle handed over as tribute, legal texts show that cattle were the staple of fiefs and rents, and could be used to pay certain fines, and the greatest epic of medieval Irish literature, *Táin Bó Cúailnge*, is the story of a cattle raid. In medieval Irish law texts, dating mainly between the seventh and ninth century, a cow was normally valued at one ounce of silver; a consistent value that may partly be explained as a convenience for exercising legal judgments (where many payments were valued in cattle),[27] and an acknowledgment of 'their position at

---

AFM 1097, where it is claimed: *Cnói mhes mór ar fud Ereann a ccoitchinne isin mbliadhainsi, co ro mhéth muca Ereann, 7 ro mhair tiruairsi na ccnó hisin co cend dá bhliadhan iaramh. Bliadhain na ccnó bfionn do ghairthí dhi, 7 do gheibhthí seisedhadh cnó ar aon phinginn* ('Great abundance of nuts throughout Ireland in general this year, so that the swine of Ireland were fatted; and some of these nuts lasted to the end of two years afterwards. It was usually called the year of the white nuts, and a seiseadhach of nuts was got for one penny').   **23** On managing woodlands, see Kelly, *Early Irish farming*, pp 389–90.   **24** On these measures, see ibid., p. 583.   **25** For the former weight, see Blackburn, 'The Dublin coinage', p. 105 (table 4) [at 125 in the original] and, for the latter, Kenny, 'Coins and coinage in pre-Norman Ireland', p. 849.   **26** Dáibhí Ó Cróinín, *Early medieval Ireland, 400–1200*, Longman History of Ireland 1 (Harlow, 1995), p. 99; Donnchadh Ó Corráin, 'Ireland *c.*800: aspects of society' in Ó Cróinín (ed.), *A new history of Ireland*, i, p. 568.   **27** Kelly, *Early*

the core of the value system'.[28] However, their ideological importance need not have been matched by their economic value, as suggested in Chris Wickham's interesting and explicit comparison between the Nuer of southern Sudan and the medieval Irish, where the Nuer were:

> as cattle-obsessed as any ethnic group on earth, valuing their cattle above all else, capable of dividing them by colour into several *hundred* types, but in reality quite largely dependent on millet and fish for their actual diet. Ideology and economic activity are here virtually in direct opposition.[29]

Despite the omnipresence of cattle in literary sources, cattle in medieval Ireland were only one component of a mixed agricultural economy, not a primarily pastoral one.

Archaeological evidence, uneven though it is in terms of geographical and chronological cover, points toward changes in cattle production from *c.*800AD onwards, with an increased diversity in livestock.[30] How far cattle's decline in prominence was coupled with an expansion in grain-growing is unclear.[31] Nonetheless, thinking in terms of a pastoral/arable dichotomy is unhelpful, for, while cattle were important sources of dietary protein and fat through their milk products (and from their meat to a lesser degree), they were also vital for arable farming. Prior to the introduction of the large draught horse at the end of the twelfth century, it was oxen (castrated male cattle) that were used to provide the traction necessary for ploughing, without which cereal farming would have been impossible. The contribution of cattle dung as fertilizer was also appreciated in the legal sources, where it was assessed and valued depending on the type of animal producing it (e.g. cow, calf, ox, etc.).[32] In short, cattle were – and remained – indispensable for the vast majority of the people, regardless of their primary agricultural output.

Needless to say, such reliance had its perils. Medieval agricultural societies lived in the shadow of inclement climactic conditions and cereal and livestock

---

Irish farming, pp 57–8.   **28** O'Sullivan et al., *Early medieval Ireland*, p. 209.   **29** Chris Wickham, 'Pastoralism and underdevelopment in the early Middle Ages' in idem (ed.), *Land and power: studies in Italian and European social history, 400–1200* (London, 1994), pp 121–54, at p. 138 (his emphasis); contrary to the popular view of cattle as a medium of exchange, it appears that at all times the law tracts viewed silver as an appropriate and expected form of payment to people of high status: see Liam Breatnach, 'Forms of payment in the early Irish law tracts', *Cambrian Medieval Celtic Studies*, 68 (2014), 1–20. **30** O'Sullivan et al., *Early medieval Ireland*, p. 210.   **31** For an argument that cereal-growing was important at all times during the early medieval period and that caution needs to be exercised in seeing a shift from focusing on pastoral farming to cereal production, see Michael A. Monk, 'Early medieval agriculture in Ireland: the case for tillage' in Emer Purcell, Paul MacCotter, Julianne Nyhan and John Sheehan (eds), *Clerics, kings and vikings: essays on medieval Ireland in honour of Donnchadh Ó Corráin* (Dublin, 2015), pp 309–22. **32** Kelly, *Early Irish farming*, pp 229–30.

diseases, against which they had little or no protection. Near the beginning of the twelfth century (1114) a cattle mortality occurred that was 'great and sudden and most tormenting', according to the *Annals of Tigernach*,[33] and was followed by an extremely cold winter. Snow from the end of December to the middle of February 'inflicted slaughter on birds and beasts and men and, from this, great want arose throughout all Ireland, and particularly in Laigin'.[34] The dire consequences are seen in the report of *Chronicon Scotorum*: children sold into slavery for food and people resorting to cannibalism.[35] Extremes of weather at the other end of the spectrum could be just as punishing, like the parching hot summer of 1129.[36]

Unfortunately, it is not possible to quantify economically the effects of the cattle murrain of 1114–15 or the drought of 1129, but it is an interesting coincidence that the former occurred at roughly the same time that Dublin changed to minting the light and increasingly low-silver-content bracteate coinage. However, a further cattle murrain that began in 1133 was even worse than that which went before and was much better documented, offering a chink through which shines a good deal of light on the Gaelic economy of the first half of the twelfth century.

THE MURRAIN OF 1133

The murrain originated in England, in 1131, where the contemporary Anglo-Saxon Chronicle records in emotive terms:

> In the course of this same year, there was such a great cattle plague all over England as had never been before in the memory of man – that was among cattle and pigs, so that in a village that had ten or twelve ploughs in action, there was not one left, and the man who had two hundred or three hundred pigs had not one left. After that, the hens died, then the meat and cheese and butter ran short. May God amend it when it is his will![37]

By 1133 the cause of that murrain appears to have spread to Ireland; a series of annals for that year report a similarly devastatingly widespread death of cattle and pigs.[38] The *Annals of Loch Cé* note:

---

33 *ATig* 1114.   34 *AU* 1115.1.   35 *CS* 1116.   36 *CS* 1129; *AI* 1129.9.   37 Dorothy Whitelock, David C. Douglas and Susie I. Tucker (trans), *The Anglo-Saxon chronicle: a revised translation* (rev. ed., London, 1965), s.a. 1131.   38 Trade with Anglo-Saxon England was considerable during the early twelfth century, which could account for the spread but the precise mechanism by which it occurred is unknowable. It is suggested below that *rinderpest* was the cause, which is normally spread through direct contact between animals or drinking water contaminated by dung from infected animals.

Bó dhíbath ar dteacht i nErinn co huilidhe, dá ná frith samail ó thanic in
bódhíbhath mór roime sin i naimsir Flaithbertaigh mic Loingsigh, ocus dá
bliadhain .xxx. ar .cccc. etorra.

A great cow mortality occurred throughout all Erinn, for which no
likeness was found since the great cow mortality came before that in the
time of Flaithbhertach, son of Loingsech; and 432 years elapsed between
them.[39]

According to the *Annals of the Four Masters*:

Bo dhíth mhór ind Erinn, dá ngoirthí Maolgarbh, dá ná frith samhail ó
tháinic an bó díobhadh oile i naimsir Fhlaithbheartaigh mic Loingsigh, conar
fháccaibh acht tiruairsi becc do bhuaibh i nErinn, dia nebhradh,

Atrí sa triocha, na ceil
Céd ar mhile do bhliadhnaibh,
O ghein Críost i mBeithil bhinn
Gus an mbó díthsi i nErinn.

A great murrain of cows in Ireland, which was called Maelgarbh, the
likeness of which was not seen since the great cow mortality which
happened in the time of Flaithbheartach, son of Loingseach, and it left
but a small remnant of the cattle of Ireland; of which was said:

Three and thirty, do not conceal,
A hundred over a thousand years,
From the birth of Christ at sweet Bethlehem,
To this cow-mortality in Ireland.[40]

The entries in the *Annals of Loch Cé* and the seventeenth-century *Annals of the
Four Masters* are quite similar and both draw on a contemporary annalistic
text(s), probably kept in Armagh. The *Annals of Boyle*, a text surviving from
north Connacht (but related in part to the *Annals of Loch Cé*, although not in
this entry), also testify to its impact: *Maelgarb mór in hoc anno* ('A great murrain
in this year').[41] A short entry in *Chronicon Scotorum* – a Clonmacnoise-group
text (and therefore part of a different annalistic tradition) – notes, just as the
Anglo-Saxon chronicler did, that almost all the pigs died too: *Maolgarb isin
bliadain gur marb bu Erenn & a muca acht nemthni* ('A murrain in this year
which killed the cows of Ireland and almost all its pigs').[42] Such a high
mortality rate suggests an outbreak of something particularly virulent, such as
a virus like rinderpest, which can have a 90 per cent mortality rate.[43]

39 *ALC* 1133.   **40** *AFM* 1133.   **41** A.M. Freeman (ed. and trans.), 'The annals in Cotton
MS Titus A. XXV', *Revue Celtique*, 41 (1924), 301–30; 42 (1925), 283–305; 43 (1926), 358–
84 and 44 (1927), 336–61, s.a. 1133.   **42** *CS* 1133.   **43** The texts generally call this

Moreover, there was no let-up and the pestilence continued into 1134:

> *In bódhíbhadh cedna bhóss ag inredh na hErenn, conidh lan airgnigh sochaide in gach aird i nErinn.*

The same cow mortality again devastating Erinn, so that multitudes of people were completely ravaged in every locality in Erinn.[44]

Chronicon Scotorum suggests that it was particularly bad in the northern half of Ireland: *An dith cedna for innilibh Leithe Cuinn* ('The cattle of Leth Cuinn were still suffering the same murrain').[45] The economic and humanitarian effects were clearly devastating – many were 'completely ravaged', as the *Annals of Loch Cé* state – yet the annals do not claim that there was widespread famine.[46] It is difficult to argue that this was simply because it was possible to switch from pasture to arable farming. Both types would suffer from widespread cattle deaths with ploughs falling idle, as witnessed in the Anglo-Saxon Chronicle, while dietary deficiencies from lack of proteins and fats owing to the absence of dairy products might also be expected. It might be suggested that the Irish annals had overstated the extent of the cattle deaths, except that the Anglo-Saxon Chronicle offers corroborating evidence, as does another source, the *notitiae* recorded in the Book of Kells.

SILVER AND CATTLE

The *notitiae* in question are a small corpus of eleventh- and twelfth-century land transaction records, written into the margins and blank spaces of the Book of Kells. One *notitia*, recording a land donation within the community of Kells, dates it to *in bliadhain athbáthatar baí hErenn ocus a mucca* ('the year in

outbreak *máelgarb* ('bald rough'). Fergus Kelly has mooted the possibility that *máelgarb* may be equated with foot-and-mouth disease, whose symptoms include loss of coat (hence *máel*, 'bald') and skin sores (hence *garb*, 'rough'): Kelly, *Early Irish farming*, pp 195–6. However, foot-and-mouth, while debilitating, is rarely fatal, and never on a scale suggested by the Irish annals or the Anglo-Saxon Chronicle. In the annals the word *máelgarb* turns up occasionally over the centuries and by the twelfth century may have become a general term for any infectious bovine disease that caused widespread death. Notably, rinderpest can affect pigs as well as cattle.   **44** *ALC* 1134. I have altered Hennessy's translation slightly; he translates this as 'The same cow mortality again devastating Erinn, so that numbers of people were quite impoverished in every locality in Erinn', which does not do justice to the severity implied in the text, where the adjective *airgnigh* has the more violent meaning of 'given to ravaging or slaughter, aggressive, predatory': *eDIL, s.v. oirgnech, oircnech* (http://dil.ie/33727) (accessed 1 August 2019). The mortality was reported a second time in *ALC* for the same year: *Maolgarbh mór in hoc anno* ('A great murrain in this year').   **45** *CS* 1134. **46** Cherie Peters has argued that annalists employed distinctions in terminology for various forms of shortages and scarcities, recognizing famine as a separate and distinct phenomenon: Cherie N. Peters, 'Translating food shortages in the Irish chronicles, AD 500–1170', *Cambrian Medieval Celtic Studies*, 71 (2016), 29–58.

which the cattle and pigs of Ireland perished'): the floruits of the people named in it confirm that the year in question was 1133, suggesting that it was particularly noteworthy.[47] Another *notitia* records the subsequent reselling of land that had previously been granted to the *Céli Dé* of the community of Kells for the purpose of alleviating the effects of that epidemic.[48] The latter *notitia* is of particular importance, as it claims that the land was purchased two years after the murrain (i.e. 1135/6), using in-calf cows: *di bliadain d'aithli in mailgairb ro ceannaiged ocus tegtis .xx. penginne d'or ar in mboin in tan sin* ('two years after the murrain it was bought, and a cow fetched twenty penny-weights of gold at that time'), implying a substantial rise in cattle prices.[49] And while the Dublin coinage is a useful proxy for measuring economic activity and developments within that kingdom, it is these records of milch-cow prices in silver that afford the best means of illuminating economic activity in Gaelic Ireland.

The closest previous indicator of cattle prices is found in relation to a circuit of Cenél nEógain undertaken by Cellach, abbot of Armagh, in 1106 (admittedly thirty years prior to the *notitia*):

> *Ceallach comarba Patraic for cuairt Ceniuil Eogain cetna chur co tuc a óghreir .i. bó cech seisir no agh ndára cech trir no lethunga cech cethrair la taebh n-edbhart n-imda olchena.*

> Cellach, successor of Patrick, [went] on a visitation of Cenél nEógain for the first time and brought away his full due, i.e., a cow for every six persons or an in-calf heifer for every three or half an ounce for every four, along with many offerings also.[50]

This suggests that a milch cow was worth ¾ of an ounce of silver (or 54 *pinginne* of silver) at that time, i.e., less than the one ounce usually stipulated by the law texts. Naturally other events between 1106 and 1133 would have had

47 Gearóid Mac Niocaill (ed. and trans.), 'The Irish "Charters"' in Peter Fox (ed.), *The Book of Kells: MS 58 Trinity College Library Dublin* (Lucerne, 1990), pp 153–65, at pp 154–5 (§1). 48 On such responses to disasters, see Donnchadh Ó Corráin, *The Irish church, its reform and the English invasion*, Trinity Medieval Ireland Series 2 (Dublin, 2017), pp 27–8. 49 Mac Niocaill, 'The Irish "Charters"', pp 162–3 (§10). Mac Niocaill correctly interpreted *pinginn* as a unit of weight in his translation, although the text does not explicitly say this was a weight measurement. The use of in-calf cows to purchase this land is interesting. The law tracts claim that normally an in-calf cow was worth ¾ of a milch cow, but it appears that in 1106 it was worth just half a milch cow (see below). Fergus Kelly has suggested that the lower value of an in-calf cow is probably due to the danger it may abort or both the calf and mother may die during labour: Kelly, *Early Irish farming*, p. 64. The use of in-calf cows in the *notitia* transaction shortly after the murrain of 1133 suggests that they may have become particularly valued at the time, as they had survived the murrain with their reproductive capacity (and consequently milk-producing capacity) intact. The vendor probably wanted to restock a decimated herd and had more land than was necessary for his existing stock. 50 *AU* 1106.4.

an influence on the fluctuations in price (such as the cattle mortalities suffered in 1114 and 1129 mentioned earlier) but it is not possible to isolate their impact. Therefore, comparison of the post-1133 evidence with that of 1106 does not identify the consequences of a single event (i.e., the murrain of 1133) but rather indicates changes over a span of time.

The *notitia* refers to prices in *pinginne* of gold, but northern Europe was generally monometallic and Hiberno-Norse coins of the eleventh and twelfth centuries, like most European coins, were struck from silver, not gold although, as Michael Dolley pointed out, the role of uncoined gold in medieval commerce should not be ignored (and indeed the evidence of other *notitiae* supports this assertion).[51] But given the attested use of *pinginn* as a unit of weight and the absence of known gold coinage in Ireland, *pinginn* as a unit of mass is the most likely explanation for the *pinginne d'or* ('pennies of gold') mentioned in the *notitia*.[52] Consequently, in 1106 a cow was worth 54 *pinginne* of silver. The *notitia*, however, suggests that a cow would fetch 20 *pinginne* of gold in 1135/6. The value of gold to silver is unclear, but a pipe roll of 31 Henry I (1130) for Gloucestershire suggests a ratio of 1:9 operated in England at that time, and while caution is necessary in applying this to Ireland, it is almost exactly contemporary with the Irish evidence.[53] Applying this ratio to

---

See also *ALC* 1106.   **51** Dolley, *The Hiberno-Norse coins*, pp 30–1. The approach I have adopted of reducing all the precious metal calculations to units of silver, while necessary for comparative purposes, largely sidesteps questions of the economic and social intricacies of operating bimetallic monetary systems.   **52** An example of similarly flexible weight-coin terminology in Anglo-Saxon England may be seen in the will of the Anglo-Saxon king Eadred (d. 955); he specified that 2000 mancuses of gold (in weight) were to be minted into mancuses (coin): Mark Blackburn, 'Gold in England during the "Age of Silver" (eighth–eleventh centuries)' in James Graham-Campbell and Gareth Williams (eds), *Silver economy in the Viking Age* (Walnut Creek, CA, 2007), pp 55–98, at p. 58.   **53** Ratios of gold to silver are not easy to identify, and 1:10 or more is commonly suggested: Rory Naismith, 'Payments for land and privilege in Anglo-Saxon England', *Anglo-Saxon England*, 41 (2012), 277–342, at 308–9. A 1:8 ratio of gold:silver, suggested by Mac Niocaill in a *notitia* dating between 1129 and 1146, seems to me to be based upon unsupportable emendations to the text: Mac Niocaill, 'The Irish "Charters"', pp 161–2 (§9). For the pipe roll of 31 Henry I, containing an account for Gloucestershire at Michaelmas 1130, for the preceding twelve months, see David C. Douglas and George W. Greenaway (eds), *English historical documents: volume ii, 1042–1189* (2nd ed., London and New York, 1981), pp 611–14 (§71). It records: 'Roger, son of Osbert the priest, accounts for half a mark of gold in respect of the grant of the land and of the churches of his father. He has paid 60 shillings in the treasury in respect of this half mark of gold. And he is quit': ibid., p. 612. This implies a mark of gold was worth 120 shillings or 1,440 pence. A mark of silver was worth 160 pence (Peter Spufford, *Money and its use in medieval Europe* (Cambridge, 1988), p. 223), and here a mark of gold is nine times that amount. The underlying assumption is that Roger paid the exact equivalent of what was owed, neither being fined nor having part of his debt remitted. If the ratio adopted here is too conservative, then it suggests an even greater price jump from 1106 to the 1130s and a smaller one between the 1130s and 1160s. Coincidentally, that pipe roll also records a nefarious economic connection with Ireland: 'The burgesses of Gloucester owe 30 marks of silver if they can recover through the justice of the king the money which was

the 1135/6 figure shows that a cow was now worth 180 *pinginne* (2½ ounces) of silver, in other words running at 3⅓ times the amount that it did almost thirty years earlier, in 1106.

That increase appears to have been further exacerbated by another cattle plague that occurred in 1154,[54] which leads to the final point of reference, in 1161. In that year:

> *Cuairt Osraighi do dhenam la comarba Coluimcille, idon, la Flaithbertach hUa Brolcha[i]n : idon, secht fichit damh; acht as e a fiach rotaidhbedh ann,–idon, fiche 7 cethri cet uinge d'argut gil : idon, tri huinge i n-gach dam.*

> The circuit of Ossory was made by the successor of Colum Cille, namely, by Flaithbertach Ua Brolchá[i]n, that is, seven score oxen [were given], but it is their value that was presented there – namely, four hundred and twenty ounces of pure silver, to wit, three ounces for every ox.[55]

According to the early medieval *Cormac's Glossary*, a trained ox may achieve the value of a milch cow.[56] Applying this information to 1106 prices, an ox would also have been valued at ¾ of an ounce (54 *pinginne*) of silver. That an ox was worth three ounces (216 *pinginne*) of silver in 1161 indicates that cattle now cost four times the amount of silver they did in 1106 – even higher than they did in 1135/6 (see fig. 2.1).[57]

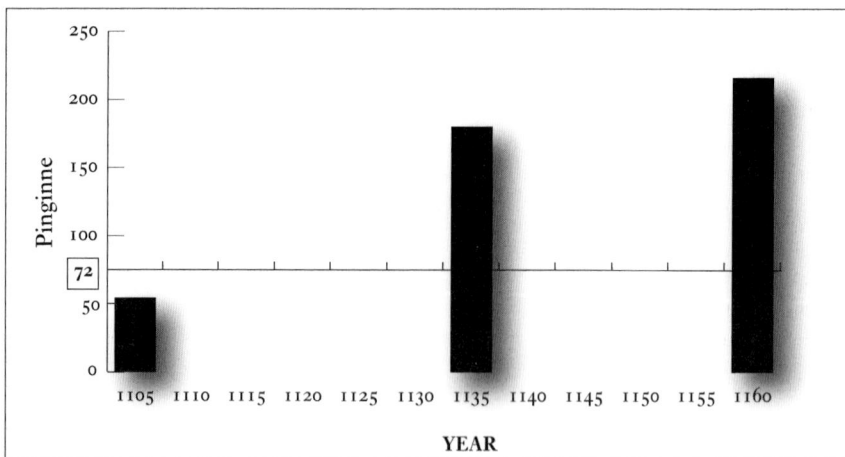

2.1 Cost of a milch cow in the twelfth century (72 *pinginne* = 1 oz)

taken from them in Ireland': Douglas and Greenaway, *English historical documents*, ii, p. 612. **54** *Ar mór for indilibh Ereann isin mbliadhainsi* ('There was a great destruction of the cattle of Ireland this year'): *AFM* 1154. **55** *AU* 1161. On some of the circumstances surrounding this circuit, see F.J. Byrne, 'Ireland and her neighbours, *c.*1014–*c.*1072' in Ó Cróinín (ed.), *A new history of Ireland*, i, pp 862–98, at p. 870. **56** Kelly, *Early Irish farming*, pp 65–6. For the importance of oxen and the necessity of adequately training them so that they attain this value, see ibid., pp 48–9. **57** When looking at the evidence for the value of cattle vis-à-vis

PUTTING THE PIECES TOGETHER

In the space of about fifty years the cost of a milch cow quadrupled, most likely in response to a series of cattle plagues. The first of these cattle murrains occurred in 1115, at approximately the same time that Dublin moved from minting silver pennies toward striking much lighter bracteates.[58] The second of these murrains occurred in the 1130s, just preceding a change in the bracteate composition; around 1140 their silver content dropped considerably and subsequently they were composed mainly of a copper alloy. In short, both cattle plagues were followed by changes in the Dublin coinage, during which it became lighter and more debased. If an international silver shortage was partly responsible for the changes in Dublin's coinage, it occurred at a period when the annals and *notitiae* suggest that transactions in small and large amounts of silver and gold bullion (ranging from fractions of an ounce to several pounds) were being conducted in Gaelic Ireland, all while the Hiberno-Norse coinage was becoming increasingly lighter. This is also the period in which something of a renaissance occurred in Irish gold- and silverwork, as witnessed by items like the Cross of Cong, which dates to the 1120s. In addition, there were differing reactions to the bracteate coinage in Gaelic Ireland and Dublin; single finds of bracteates are largely absent from Gaelic Ireland, indicating that they did not want them.[59] In contrast, in Dublin the bracteates appear to have been used and lost in greater quantities than the earlier pennies, which points toward 'a fairly deep-rooted, coin-using mentality'.[60] During the same period Gaelic Ireland seems to have had a fairly deep-rooted, bullion silver-using mentality.[61]

Is there a relationship between these cattle plagues and Dublin's economy? Slaughter evidence indicates that Dublin was a cattle consumer rather than a producer and a lack of cow hides would have hit Dublin's leather industry

---

silver or gold in 1106, 1135/6 and 1161, we must consider the possibility that values may also have differed in each of the areas in question, namely Cenél nEógain, Kells and Osraige respectively, owing to the availability of silver/gold and the extent of cattle raising. Analysis of cattle remains suggests that 'decline in cattle was more pronounced in Ulster and the western part of the country. The livestock economy tended to remain unchanged – traditional or conservative even – in the Meath–Dublin area; there is insufficient data from Munster as yet to allow similar analysis': O'Sullivan et al., *Early medieval Ireland*, p. 210. **58** Bracteates were not just a Dublin phenomenon, as other examples of this type of coinage emerged in parts of northern and central Europe, including Scandinavia, Germany and Poland: Kenny, 'Coins and coinage in pre-Norman Ireland', p. 849. **59** Andrew R. Woods, 'Monetary activity in Viking-Age Ireland: the evidence of the single-finds' in Rory Naismith, Martin Allen and Elina Screen (eds), *Early medieval monetary history: studies in memory of Mark Blackburn*, Studies in Early Medieval Britain and Ireland (Farnham, 2014), pp 295–330, at p. 312. **60** Woods, 'The coinage and economy of Hiberno-Scandinavian Dublin', p. 58. **61** A twelfth-century poem that seeks to assert Armagh's ecclesiastical dominance over Dublin suggests that among the items of tribute due are *screpall ó cach monatóir* ('a scruple from every moneyer'): *SGAC*, pp 38 and 43 (verse 13). That a moneyer

hard.[62] If there was a 'silver famine', then the increased bovine prices may have been a result of both shortages of cattle and of silver. In addition, it is possible that Gaelic Ireland's demand for bullion silver leeched Dublin's supply, further prompting production of bracteates – Dublin's silver stock was being drained from both ends and stretched in the middle. The specification of 'pure silver' in the record of Flaithbertach Ua Brolcháin's circuit in 1161 and of 'refined silver' (*d'airgead bruinnti*) in Tairdelbach Ua Conchobair's obit of 1156 point toward a growing eye for quality as well as quantity in Gaelic Ireland.[63]

At the very least, when taken together, the inflationary tendencies in Gaelic Ireland (as seen in cattle prices), the changes in Dublin's coinage and the differing reactions to that coinage in Dublin and Gaelic Ireland, all point to the complexity of the underexplored economic history of this period. In addition, this should warn us of the dangers of oversimplifying the political and social narrative of the eleventh and twelfth centuries and unquestioningly seeing Dublin as increasingly integrated into an Irish socio-political system. The economic complexities of the period paradoxically point toward interdependence and divergent responses to events.

CONCLUSION

A series of bovine plagues in twelfth-century Ireland, coupled with an international silver shortage, saw substantial rises in the price of cattle, which may have quadrupled in the course of fifty years. Two of these (1115 and 1133–4) coincide roughly with changes in the Dublin coinage, namely a move from pennies to bracteates (*c*.1115) and a substantial reduction in silver content (*c*.1140). The timing of these murrains and changes in the coinage could be coincidental, but these parallel developments, and the rejection of the bracteate currency in Gaelic Ireland – while it simultaneously expanded in Dublin – ought to be factored into discourse on the integration of the kingdom of Dublin into the Gaelic body politic in the twelfth century. Regardless of how culturally Gaelicized the Dubliners were growing, in some respects they were simultaneously becoming increasingly economically *Gaill*.

---

should be asked to provide bullion rather than his product (coins), when others such as shoemakers and combmakers provide theirs, indicates a potentially low regard for coinage, or at least a preference for uncoined silver.   **62** For Dublin as a consumer of cattle, see O'Sullivan et al., *Early medieval Ireland*, pp 209–10. Interestingly, there may be a link between certain types of craftsmen and coinage; bracteates and shoemakers (who worked with leather) are notable at High Street in Dublin: Woods, 'The coinage and economy of Hiberno-Scandinavian Dublin', p. 58 and Woods, 'Prelude to the Hiberno-Scandinavian coinage', p. 367.   **63** *ATig* 1156; *eDIL*, *s.v. bruinnte* (http://dil.ie/7127) (accessed 1 August 2019).

Saints' dedications and the ecclesiastical landscape of Hiberno-Norse Dublin: Irish, Scandinavian and others

EDEL BHREATHNACH

The role of the church in the physical development of urban landscapes forms an essential part of the international debate relating to the process of the spatial organization of towns during the medieval period from late antiquity to the Renaissance and Reformation. In a recent study on medieval monastic Europe that covers virtually the whole of Europe between AD1100 and 1600, a predictable central theme emerged around how the church and religious foundations shaped urban and rural landscapes.[1] Clearly regional differences, often determined by geography, size of population, scales of economy and wealth were important as was the reach of the authority and patronage of the papacy, emperors, kings, and of international monastic and mendicant orders. Nonetheless, common patterns of decision-making, relations between people with different cultural identities settling in one space, and the imposition of predetermined plans also feature in this extensive survey. This contribution is informed conceptually by the work of the scholars who contributed to the *Monastic Europe* volume and also by recent contacts with Scandinavian scholars, especially in Norway, and in the context of this paper, Bergen in particular.[2]

The wealth of archaeological and textual evidence for the ecclesiastical landscape of medieval Dublin has yet to be fully mined to understand the town's development. One has yet to consider in detail the spatial relationship between churches, great and small, the visibility of churches from the river, from roads, and from a distance; the physical dominance of the cathedral quarter and its constituent parts: cathedral, monks' or canons' quarters, the curia and the episcopal household; and the distance between the cathedral quarter and the king's residence, riverside and market places. Beyond these topics are questions of culture and of authority: for example, do church dedications signify associations with specific cultural/ethnic groups, occupations or ranks in society? What conditions led to the foundation of a

1 Edel Bhreathnach, Malgorzata Krasnodebska D'Aughton and Keith Smith (eds), *Monastic Europe: medieval communities, landscapes and settlements* (Turnhout, 2019). 2 I wish to acknowledge the active promotion of Irish-Norwegian cultural contacts by HE Ambassador Else Berit Eikeland, Norwegian Embassy Dublin, Dr Ruth Johnson, Dublin City Archaeologist, Dr Emer Purcell, National University of Ireland and Professor Alf Tore

cathedral or even the smallest church and to the choice of its dedication? An appraisal of the saints whose names occur in church dedications of eleventh- and twelfth-century Dublin requires an understanding of the origins and attributes of the saints, reasons for their appearance in Dublin, their occurrence in similar ecclesiastical landscapes elsewhere, and how the founding of various churches contributed to the process that drove the development of the medieval town. This essay largely concentrates on saints' dedications in pre-1200 Dublin and attempts to contextualize these dedications with reference to the local hinterland and to the greater scholarly debate about the role of saints' cults in the imposition of episcopal and royal power in growing urban landscapes, especially during the eleventh and twelfth centuries.[3]

THE EARLY SAINTS OF DUBLIN: *SENCHAS GALL ÁTHA CLIATH*

A review of saints' dedications in urban spaces or of the iconography of ecclesiastical architecture across medieval Europe testifies to the existence of an internationally-known company of saints that is supplemented by regional and local holy men and women. If, for example, one views the early thirteenth-century Portica di Gloria of the cathedral of St James in Santiago de Compostela – one of Europe's great medieval monuments – and contemplates its meaning, it is striking that some of the Portica's main figures are common to medieval dedications in Dublin. This monument is a tableau of medieval religious beliefs and devotion dealing as it does with judgment, redemption, condemnation and the apocalypse. It also represents the apex of sanctity in the corpus of saints. Among the figures represented on the Portica are:

- Christ the Redeemer showing his wounds as a symbol of triumph over pain and death
- Christ and St Michael separating the blessed from the damned
- the cathedral's patron, St James
- the apostles, most clearly represented by SS Peter, Paul, James, John and Andrew
- the Holy Trinity

The appearance of Christ in his various guises along with this panoply of saints is a standard combination found throughout Christendom, and especially in the church dedications of urban centres – and Dublin is no exception. It is as if any developing urban centre, no matter how small, needed to include a particular set of dedications for its ecclesiastical landscape to be regarded as

Hommedal, University of Bergen.   3 For a comparable study of saints' dedications in Scandinavian cathedrals, see Anna Minara Ciardi, 'Saints and cathedral culture in Scandinavia *c*.1000–*c*.1200' in Haki Antonsson and Ildar H. Garipzanov (eds), *Saints and their lives on the periphery: veneration of saints in Scandinavia and eastern Europe*

part of the culture of western Christendom. The prominent position given to St James on the Portica di Gloria represents, of course, his place as patron of Compostela and reflects both the town's and the church's need to promote him and the great pilgrimage to Compostela. Patron saints and their shrines were essential sources of veneration and income – Rome had St Peter and Cologne had the Three Kings. As will be discussed later, Dublin had a problem in that regard. In general, however, the ecclesiastical landscapes of medieval urban centres consisted of dedications to international and local saints who reflected the various cultural backgrounds of the local population. Dublin was no exception here either: universal saints appear as do a mix of Irish, Scandinavian and English saints. In a world in which saints were assigned particular miraculous powers, participated in the salvation or otherwise of humanity, or protected certain groups in society, their visibility to people – be it in church dedications, images, shrines or even holy wells – was a comfort and a constant reminder that there might be a better life in store after death, often gained through the intercession of the Virgin Mary or the saints, and the mercy of Christ.[4]

One particular source provides us with a glimpse of Dublin's ecclesiastical landscape from the perspective of the eleventh and twelfth centuries. This is the Middle Irish poem *Senchas Gall Átha Cliath* ('The history of the Foreigners of Dublin') (*SGAC*) which, according to its editors Elizabeth Boyle and Liam Breatnach, dates to sometime between AD1100 and 1180.[5] In his consideration of the poem and of Dublin's part in the eleventh- and twelfth-century 'reform' movement in Ireland, Martin Holland (following Donnchadh Ó Corráin) dates the poem to the period *c.*1121–9, when Bishop Cellach of Armagh attempted to impose Armagh's claim to supremacy over Dublin and usurp Canterbury's increasing power over its bishops.[6] A number of references in the poem may point to a more specific and different date for at least part of the poem. As with many such Middle Irish poems, *SGAC* may in fact be a series of verses relating to the same theme that have been strung together, and the section towards the end that lists the church dedications of Dublin could possibly form a separate fragment to the rest. It is likely that the part of the poem common to the Book of Uí Maine and *Lebor na Cert* versions of Patrick's conversion of the king of Dublin is the core text, extended to include other matters – details of Armagh's relationship with Dublin, a further tale about the

(*c.*1000–1200) (Turnhout, 2010), pp 39–66.   4 Robert Bartlett, *Why can the dead do such great things? Saints and worshippers from the martyrs to the Reformation* (Princeton and London).   5 Elizabeth Boyle and Liam Breatnach (eds), '*Senchas Gall Átha Cliath*: aspects of the cult of St Patrick in the twelfth century' in John Carey, Kevin Murray and Caitríona Ó Dochartaigh (eds), *Sacred histories. A festschrift for Máire Herbert* (Dublin, 2015), pp 22–55 [hereafter *SGAC*].   6 Donnchadh Ó Corráin, 'Ireland, Wales, Man and the Hebrides' in Peter Sawyer (ed.), *The Oxford illustrated history of the Vikings* (Oxford and New York, 1997), pp 83–109, at p. 107; Martin Holland, 'Dublin and the reform of the Irish church in

king of Dublin's daughter, the origin of St Patrick's well in Dublin, and a list of church dedications in Dublin.[7] Hence, sections of the poem are likely to have been composed for different reasons at various points during the twelfth century.

There are certain references in *SGAC* that may allude to specific historical episodes. The enmity between the kings of Mide (Tara) and Dublin (Liamuin) is mentioned when Patrick curses the king of Tara while he blesses the king of Dublin.[8] Conflict between the kings of Mide and Brega on the one hand and the kings of Dublin on the other was constant although, in the shifting alliances of early medieval Ireland, they could also be allies against other provincial kings. During the twelfth century there were certain periods of intense conflict, as in 1146 when the Dubliners were subjected to a slaughter by the men of East Meath (Brega) who killed Ragnall mac Torcaill, king (*mór máer*) of Dublin. In the same year Cellach úa Cellaig, king of Brega, was killed in revenge by the Dubliners with the assistance of the Uí Chathasaig, their subjects and their allies whose territory lay between Dublin and the kingdom of Brega.[9] In 1160, Brodur mac Torcaill was killed by Máelcrón mac Gillasechnaill, a lesser lord from Brega, and the latter's brother Domnall, in turn, was killed by Muirchertach Ua Máelsechlainn, a contender for the disputed kingship of Mide.[10] All these incidents were part of ongoing internecine and territorial disputes in the kingdoms of east Meath (Brega) and west Meath (Mide) during the twelfth century in which the Dubliners were participants, often at great cost to themselves.[11] This constant conflict may explain the comment made in *SGAC* verse 23:[12]

> As a result of that [the king of Tara being cursed by Patrick] the Foreigners used to give no peace to the king of Meath of the great blades, fighting every single year between Tara and Liamain.

This period of turmoil coincides with the incorporation of Dublin as a metropolitan see into the Irish diocesan structure. Martin Holland cogently argues that this decision was the outcome of a synod attended by St Malachy and Gréne (Gregorius), bishop of Dublin, on Inis Pádraig, off the coast of north Dublin, in 1148.[13] One particular detail quoted by Holland chimes with the sentiments of *SGAC*: the author stresses the need for a bishop from Armagh and a priest from Downpatrick to be in charge in Cell Phátraic,

the eleventh and twelfth centuries', *Peritia*, 14 (2000), 111–60, at 135.   7 Myles Dillon (ed.), *Lebor na Cert. The Book of Rights* (Dublin, 1962), pp 114–19.   8 *SGAC*, pp 39, 44 (verses 22–3).   9 *ATig, AFM* 1146.   10 *AFM* 1160.   11 Edel Bhreathnach, 'Authority and supremacy in Tara and its hinterland *c.*950–1200', *Discovery Programme Reports*, 5 (1999), 1–23; Ailbhe MacShamhráin, 'The battle of Glenn Máma, and the high-kingship of Ireland: a millennial commemoration' in Seán Duffy (ed.), *Medieval Dublin II* (Dublin, 2001), pp 53–64.   12 *SGAC*, pp 39, 44 (verse 23).   13 Holland, 'Dublin and the reform of

Patrick's Church in Dublin.[14] As Holland notes, Geoffrey Keating, quoting the lost annals of Cluain Eidnech, says that Armagh was not particularly pleased with the 1148 outcome 'and particularly it was in spite of the church of Ard Macha and the church of Dún Da Lethglas that other pallia [Dublin and Tuam] were given besides one to Ard Macha and one to Cashel'.[15] One might wonder if part of an agreement between Dublin and Armagh – and possibly Downpatrick – may be reflected among the Deeds of Christ Church Dublin that refers to the lands and tithes of the Cross of Holy Trinity Dublin at Lecale, Co. Down.[16] A deed dating to 1336 notes the appointment by the priory of the Holy Trinity (at Christ Church Dublin) of Nicholas Taaff 'to collect the tithes of New Town of Rath in Lechcaal; to build the said church at his discretion, and to collect the rents of the tenants who farm the land of the Cross of Holy Trinity, Dublin'.[17] This deed was based on an earlier transaction of *c*.1224 that was witnessed by among others Hugh de Lacy, earl of Ulster, Thomas, bishop of Down and William, prior of St Patrick's Down. Dublin's possession of land in Lecale may be reflected in one of John de Courcy's grants to the Benedictine foundation dedicated to St Patrick in Down where one charter dated to 1192–3 excludes the passage between Lecale (*Lethcathale*) and Ards, Co. Down.[18] Whether or not this provision points to some earlier agreement with Holy Trinity Dublin is not mentioned and can only be left in the realms of speculation.

What seems plausible is that at least part of *SGAC* expresses the interests of one or more propagandists writing in Irish during the twelfth century with the aim of promoting Patrick's patronage of Dublin and Armagh's primacy over the town. The poem lists in detail the materials to be given by the Dubliners as 'tribute' to Armagh, a list that accords with a similar list in Jocelin of Furness's late twelfth-century Life of Patrick:[19] apart from gold, the Dubliners were expected to provide apples, mead, combs, shoes, malt, salted meat, candles and a cloak fitting for the abbot of Armagh's status from every merchant vessel landing in Dublin.[20] In addition, the rights of the abbot of Armagh are clearly stated in *SGAC* (verse 15):[21]

---

the Irish church', 153–60.   **14** *SGAC*, pp 39, 44 (verses 25–6).   **15** Holland, 'Dublin and the reform of the Irish church', 156, quoting Keating, *Foras feasa ar Éirinn: the history of Ireland*, ed. David Comyn and P.S. Dineen, 4 vols, Irish Texts Society (London, 1902–14), iii, p. 314. **16** See in particular *CCD*, nos 35, 238(b) and (c). It is possible that the income from this land paid for the upkeep of the famous 'speaking' cross of Christ Church as land in Ballyboughal, Co. Dublin and St Patrick's on the Isle of Man paid for the upkeep of the Bachall Ísu in Armagh (Raghnall Ó Floinn, pers. comm.).   **17** *CCD*, no. 238.   **18** Gearóid MacNiocaill (ed.), 'Cartae Dunenses: XII–XIII céad', *Seanchas Ardmhacha* 5 (1970), 418–28, at 421 (8). **19** John Colgan, *Triadis thaumaturgae* (Louvain, 1647), p. 91 (correct to p. 81) (LXXXI); for the context of Jocelin's Life of Patrick, see Marie Therese Flanagan, 'Jocelin of Furness and the cult of St Patrick in twelfth-century Ulster' in Clare Downham (ed.), *Jocelin of Furness. Proceedings of the 2011 conference* (Donington, 2013), pp 45–66; *SGAC*, p. 33.   **20** *SGAC*, pp 33, 37–8, 43 (verses 11–14); 40, 44 (verses 31–2).   **21** *SGAC*, pp 38, 43 (verse 15).

Whether for a long or a short time the abbot of Armagh of the great lands will be in Dublin, the Foreigners without treachery are all in turn obliged to provide refection for him.

And there is a dire warning that if the Gaill refuse to pay his due tribute (*cáin*) to Patrick son of Calpurnius their sovereignty will perish as will their mast and sea-produce.[22]

ST PATRICK: PATRON OF DUBLIN?

Why Patrick and this strident claim by Armagh over Dublin? Much has been written, and disputed, about the rivalry between these two ecclesiastical entities and the role of English clerics, mainly from Canterbury, in promoting its counterclaims of supremacy over Dublin.[23] However, I want to draw attention in this essay to the apparent imposition – presumably by Armagh – of Patrick as the patron saint of Dublin. As far as we know, Dublin lacked a patron saint, although it had a cathedral dedicated to Christ and the Holy Trinity. Cities invariably had patron saints: one might point to St Werburgh in Chester or St Sunniva in Bergen, both of whose cults were revived during the eleventh century. *SGAC* implicitly declares Patrick as patron of Dublin especially in the tale relating to the origin of St Patrick's well and his church in Dublin.[24] An old woman meets Patrick on the seashore and she begs him to fill her mug with fresh water as her's is full of brine (verse 41):

> 'If I submit to you then [and become Christian], the Foreigners of the city will submit; o man who takes care of every tribulation, who gets water for me, Patrick'.

Patrick presses the butt of his crozier into the strand and a well of fresh water gushes forth: this is *Tipra Phátraic i nÁth Cliath*, 'Patrick's well in Dublin' (44a). And, of course, according to the poem there was also a *Cell Phátraic*, 'church of Patrick', in Dublin (47c).

Jocelin of Furness is explicit in his telling of the tale about Patrick's preeminence over Dublin. In listing the details of the tribute to be paid to Armagh from Dublin, he begins *Statuerunt ergo redditum suo sancto patrono Patricio*, 'And they determined a render to their holy patron Patrick'.[25] How early or late might this development have occurred? Elizabeth Boyle, in her consideration of the *SGAC*, alludes to the potential significance of the name of the eleventh-

22 *SGAC*, pp 40, 45 (verse 34).   23 For a comprehensive overview and bibliography relating to this topic, see Marie Therese Flanagan, *The transformation of the Irish church in the twelfth century* (Woodbridge, 2010).   24 *SGAC*, p. 45 (verses 40–44).   25 Colgan,

century bishop of Dublin, Patricius or Gilla Pátraic (d. 1084).[26] It may be no coincidence that Máel Ísu mac Amalgada, the *comarba Pátraic* (abbot of Armagh), one of the powerful hereditary family of Clann Sinaig, came to Dublin with his highly symbolic relic, the *bachall Ísu* ('staff of Jesus'), to join Tairdelbach ua Briain, the most powerful king in Ireland, in 1080, not alone to oversee the submission of one of Tairdelbach's rivals Máel Sechnaill mac Conchobair, but possibly, as Martin Holland has argued, to preside along with the king and with Bishop Patrick at an assembly of clergy and nobles.[27] The origin of a church dedicated to St Patrick outside the *dún* ('fortification') of Dublin may date to this period. It may be even earlier as reference is made in the Tripartite Life of Patrick to the saint reaching Áth Cliath and foretelling that it would be a place of honour,[28] although much depends on the date of this section of the life. And it should be recalled that unlike Irish kings of the period, and in particular provincial kings such as Muirchertach Ua Briain and Domnall Ua Lochlainn, the Norse had not attacked Armagh since the mid-tenth century, and therefore Armagh had every reason to come to an accommodation with the increasingly wealthy town. For the Dubliners, the protection that Armagh and its powerful abbot could afford them in the face of constant pressure on them from ambitious Irish kings wishing to rule them, was far more useful than distant prelates or kings and emperors, be they Ottonians in Cologne or archbishops in Canterbury.

CONVERSION-PERIOD DEDICATIONS: A SCOTTISH ORIGIN?

SGAC does not confine its interest to Patrick. The final section lists other churches or dedications, although it is not always clear, including whether, in some instances, their location lay in or outside the city. This provides an overview of the ecclesiastical landscape of Dublin at some point during the twelfth century and perhaps even before then.

Although we have no clear evidence of the process of christianisation among the Norse of Dublin – which may have begun in the tenth century[29] – part of that process may have involved an assimilation into the existing religious landscape, including assimilation of native saints or saints from the wider networks of the Norse of Dublin. I have argued elsewhere that Amlaíb

---

Triadis, p. 81; *SGAC*, p. 33.   **26** *SGAC*, p. 28.   **27** Martin Holland, 'The synod of Dublin in 1080' in Seán Duffy, *Medieval Dublin III* (Dublin, 2002), pp 81–94.   **28** Whitley Stokes (ed.), *The tripartite life of Patrick with other documents relating to that saint*, 2 vols, Rolls Series 89 (London, 1887), pt II, pp 466–7.   **29** David N. Dumville, 'St Patrick and the Scandinavians of Dublin' in idem and Leslie Abrams (eds), *Saint Patrick, AD 493–1993*. Studies in Celtic History 13 (Woodbridge, 1993), pp 259–64; Leslie Abrams, 'Conversion and the church in Viking-Age Ireland' in John Sheehan and Donnchadh Ó Corráin (eds), *The Viking Age: Ireland and the West: proceedings of the fifteenth Viking Congress* (Dublin,

Cúarán, king of Dublin (d. 980), seems to have associated himself with the cult of Colum Cille (Columba), to the point of dying in Iona.[30] Hence it could be argued that church dedications in Dublin may have reflected the variety of origins of its inhabitants that depended on cultural identity and the spiritual allegiances of different groups among the population.

The first church listed is Cell mac nÁeda, 'the church of the sons of Áed mac Bric': *the first fair church which was founded in Dublin, together with the church of Patrick.*[31] The sons of Áed of Áth Cliath are commemorated in the seventeenth-century Martyrology of Donegal along with their 'brother' Fionnbharr of *Inis Doimhle* who belonged to the Fothairt, to whom Brigit also belonged.[32] In the eleventh/twelfth-century notes to *Félire Óenguso*, the sons of Áed of Áth Cliath are the brothers Findbarr and Barrfhind of *Inis Teimle*, a duplicate of the same saint.[33] It should be noted, however, that *SGAC* associates the sons of Áed with Ailpín, a king of Dublin who in the tale is said to have submitted to St Patrick and converted to Christianity. The personal names of Ailpín's genealogy in the poem – Áed, Brec, Echaid and Domnall – have a remarkable similarity with some of the personal names among the ancestors of Máel Coluim mac Cináeda, king of Scotland (d. 1034), descendant of Ailpín mac Echdach (of the so-called Alpínid dynasty).[34]

It should come as no surprise that the author might draw on personal names from a Scottish dynasty, as fictitious links between Ireland and Scotland were constructed by the learned class in Ireland during the eleventh and particularly the twelfth century to reflect the interactions between ambitious Irish and Scottish kings, and also, of course, the common cultural ties that naturally linked the two kingdoms.[35] Furthermore, Dublin's interests stretched northwards to Galloway where a mixed Irish and Scandinavian population, the Gallgoídil, were settled.[36] There need not have been any historical truth that

2010), pp 1–10.   **30** *AFM* 980; Edel Bhreathnach, 'Columban churches in Brega and Leinster: relations with the Norse and the Anglo-Normans', *JRSAI*, 129 (1999), 5–18. **31** *SGAC*, pp 41, 45–6 (verses 45–7).   **32** John O'Donovan, James Henthorne Todd and Williams Reeves (eds), *The martyrology of Donegal. A calendar of the saints of Ireland* (Dublin, 1864), p. 187 (July 6). Inis Doimhle or Inis Teimle is identified as being located between the Uí Chennselaig and the Déssi, probably Great Island at the confluence of the rivers Nore, Suir and Barrow: see Máirín Ní Dhonnchadha, 'Inis Teimle, between the Uí Chennselaig and the Déissi', *Peritia*, 16 (2002), 451–8.   **33** Whitley Stokes (ed.), *Félire Óengusso Céli Dé. The martyrology of Oengus the Culdee* (London, 1905, repr. 1984), p. 166. **34** M.A. O'Brien (ed.), *Corpus genealogiarum Hiberniae* (Dublin, 1962, repr. 1976), p. 328: Genelach Ríg n-Alban:Máel Coluim macc Cináeda m. Máel Coluim m. Domnaill m. Causantín m. Cináeda m. **Alpín m. Echdach m. Áeda** Find m. Domongairt m. **Domnaill Bricc. 35** Máire Herbert, 'Sea-divided Gaels? Constructing relationships between Irish and Scots *c.*800–1169' in Brendan Smith (ed.), *Britain and Ireland, 900–1300. Insular responses to medieval European change* (Cambridge, 1999), pp 87–97; Patrick Wadden, '*Do feartaib Cairnich*, Ireland and Scotland in the twelfth century', *Proceedings of the Harvard Celtic Colloquium*, 33 (2013), 189–213.   **36** Clare Downham, 'The break-up of Dál Riata and the rise of the Gallgoídil' in Howard B. Clarke and Ruth Johnson (eds), *The*

the sons of Áed were Scottish or even Gallgoídil: this may have been a literary trope to indicate that their ancestry was not Irish but foreign, and perhaps even Scandinavians from Scotland. However, that the author comments that this church was the first one founded in Dublin – although conveniently on the same day as Cell Phátraic, 'Patrick's church' – may be significant. Could this have been a church founded by the Norse of Dublin themselves, possibly at the time of their conversion?

SGAC describes Cell mac nÁeda as being located *isin dún*, 'inside the [town's] enclosure/wall', and not necessarily near Cell Phátraic. If this church was an early Scandinavian foundation, perhaps it was located close to the residence of the king of Dublin, and even a royal *eigenkirche* established by Sitriuc Silkenbeard or his father Amlaíb Cúarán. It is tempting to place the foundation of this church in the context of Amlaíb's reign and especially during the period of his association with the cult of St Columba through Iona. Thomas Owen Clancy has made a persuasive argument that Mugrón, successor of Columba in Iona (d. 980, the same year as Amlaíb's death also in Iona), who is described as *suí epscop na Trí Rand*, 'eminent bishop of the Three Parts',[37] had episcopal jurisdiction over the three parts of Amlaíb Cúarán's dominion: Dublin and its hinterland, the Western Isles of Scotland and the Isle of Man.[38] If this was so, then a foundation with some form of Scottish connection might make sense, and would also explain the fleeting later references to a church in Dublin dedicated to St Columba which, if replaced by St Audeon's as suggested by Howard Clarke, was located inside the *dún*,[39] although archaeological excavations have not revealed any evidence of such an early church on the site.[40] If there was a cluster of Scottish dedications in Dublin, then the reference to 'the voyde grownd in the east end of Saint Molloye's chapell', fleetingly mentioned in a seventeenth-century source,[41] might not be all that fanciful: there may have been a church in Dublin dedicated to St Mo Luóc of Lismore whose cult was in Scotland and the Isle of Man,[42] and it may also have belonged to the conversion period.

Vikings in Ireland and beyond: before and after the Battle of Clontarf (Dublin, 2015), pp 189–205, at pp 203–4.   **37** *AFM* 978; *Annals of Roscrea* 980 (Bart Jaski and Daniel Mc Carthy, 'A facsimile edition of the Annals of Roscrea', available at http://www.scss.tcd.ie/misc/kronos/editions/AR_portal.htm.   **38** Thomas Owen Clancy, 'Iona v. Kells: succession, jurisdiction and politics in the Columban *familia* in the later tenth century' in Fiona Edmonds and Paul Russell (eds), *Tome: studies in medieval Celtic history and law in honour of Thomas Charles-Edwards* (Woodbridge, 2011), pp 89–101, at pp 94–5.   **39** *CCD*, no. 364; Clarke, *Dublin, Pt 1* (IHTA), p. 17.   **40** Mary McMahon, *St Audeon's Church, Cornmarket, Dublin: archaeology and architecture*, Archaeological Monograph Series, no. 2 (Dublin, 2006), pp 84–5.   **41** *CARD*, iii, p. 56 (dated 1615); Clarke, *Dublin, Pt 1* (IHTA), p. 1. **42** See *Saints in Scottish place-names* database: https://saintsplaces.gla.ac.uk, accessed 9 September 2019; Alex Woolf, 'The cult of Moluag, the see of Mortlach and church organisation in northern Scotland in the eleventh and twelfth centuries' in Sharon J. Arbuthnot and Kaarina Hollo (eds), *Fil súil nglais: a grey eye looks back: a festschrift in honour of Colm Ó Baoill* (Ceann Drochaid, Perthshire, 2007), pp 311–22.

IRISH SAINTS IN DUBLIN

The next four churches listed in *SGAC* were apparently located to the south and north of the *dún* and were dedicated to Irish saints. To the south of the *dún*, 'Máel Ruain and St Michael were settled' (verse 48). It is not specified if one or two churches are being described although the context would suggest that one church was dedicated to both saints. Máel Ruain was the eighth-century founder of the monastery of Tallaght, Co. Dublin, and his pairing with Michael the Archangel is not coincidental. There is much literature that links the two, including the foundation narrative of Tallaght itself in which Máel Ruain refused to take the land offered to his new church until Michael the Archangel agreed and 'because of that agreement (*cairde*) there are in Tamlachtu [Tallaght] relics consecrated to Michael'.[43] The space settled by Máel Ruain and Michael in Dublin is thought to be the church of St Michael le Pole with its attached round tower.[44] I have argued elsewhere that the same reflex of the pairing of Máel Ruain and Michael may explain the name of the church at Rathmichael in south Co. Dublin, a church with strong Hiberno-Norse connections given the number of Rathdown-type slabs surviving in its churchyard.[45] This affiliation between a church in Dublin and another in Dublin's hinterland – and an area with particularly strong Norse interests – is a pattern evident from other dedications mentioned in the poem.

To the north of the *dún* were churches dedicated to Cainnech and to Comgall. While it is assumed that these churches were located on the north side of the river Liffey, this is not stated in the poem. Cainnech, patron of Aghaboe, Co. Laois, and of Finglas, Co. Dublin, might just possibly be the same saint as Michen (as Mo-Chonnóc) whose church was situated on the north side of the river, although there are linguistic problems in equating the two saints.[46] Finglas lay on the road northwards from Dublin and like Máel Ruain's church at Tallaght was a *céli Dé* foundation. It may be that the Norse connection with Cainnech was similar to that of their connection with Máel Ruain of Tallaght. There is early thirteenth-century evidence that the community of Holy Trinity Dublin held lands at Finglas, highlighting a further link between the town and its greater hinterland.[47] While not necessarily part of this narrative, it should be noted nonetheless that a ninth-

---

43 *Félire Óengusso Céli Dé. The martyrology of Oengus the Culdee*, ed. Whitley Stokes (London, 1905, repr. 1984), pp 12–13.   44 Margaret Gowen, 'Excavations at the site of the church and tower of St Michael le Pole, Dublin' in Seán Duffy (ed.), *Medieval Dublin II* (Dublin, 2001), pp 13–52.   45 P. Ó hÉailidhe, 'The Rathdown slabs', *JRSAI*, 87 (1957), 75–88, at 77–9, 85–6; for a recent reassessment of the context of the Rathdown slabs, see Gill Boazman, 'Material culture and identity in the southern hinterland of Hiberno-Scandinavian Dublin' in Seán Duffy (ed.), *Medieval Dublin XVII* (Dublin, 2019), pp 15–62, at pp 53–60.   46 Emer Purcell, 'Michan: saint, cult and church' in Bradley et al. (eds), *Dublin in the medieval world*, pp 119–40, at pp 127–31.   47 *CCD*, no. 44.

century female Viking burial was discovered more than a decade ago close to St Canice's Church in Finglas.[48] Holy Trinity also had an interest in a church dedicated to St Canice at Kineagh near Kilcullen, Co. Kildare.[49]

One might assume that the reference to a church dedicated to St Comgall was associated with the founder of the early monastery of Bangor, Co. Down. But in his masterly study of Irish saints Pádraig Ó Riain notes that another Comgall (of Carrowmore, Co. Donegal) was a brother of Céile Críst (d. 727), patron of Kilteel, Co. Kildare.[50] This would make more sense as this was an area possibly occupied by Scandinavians from the ninth century.[51] The urban Dublin dedications to Comgall, Peter and Paul, as with Máel Ruain and Michael, appear to be also matched by churches in the greater Dublin hinterland, in this instance in Co. Wicklow. These are Kilcoole and Kilpedder, barony of Newcastle and Kilpoole, barony of Arklow. In 1179, Kilcoole was confirmed by Pope Alexander III to Lorcán Ua Tuathail as being in the possession of the archbishopric of Dublin (along with Rathmichael),[52] while possession of Kilpoole and other churches in Wicklow was disputed through the twelfth and thirteenth centuries with the Welsh Augustinian foundation of Llanthony.[53]

All the churches dedicated to Irish saints (Patrick, Brigit, Cóemgen (Kevin), Máel Ruain/Michael, Cainnech and Comgall) were located *outside* the *dún*. As noted by Linzi Simpson, four (Patrick, Brigit, Cóemgen (Kevin), Máel Ruain/Michael) along with St Peter's, were clustered in the southern suburbs, which in her estimation might 'reflect what must have been a strong Christian population in this location for which there is little archaeological evidence'.[54] The discovery of a large cemetery at Golden Lane and Ship Street Great, with the church of St Michael le Pole as its focal centre, is highly significant. This cemetery follows the established pattern of the many so called 'settlement' cemeteries or familial cemeteries that have been discovered throughout Ireland in recent decades, and which in general tend to have been in existence between the fifth and eighth century, with some continuity as late as the twelfth.[55] Apart from the orientation of the graves, the absence of grave goods, and the burial rite used, the Golden Lane cemetery also incorporated a

---

48 Maeve Sikora, 'The Finglas burial: archaeology and ethnicity in Viking-Age Dublin' in Sheehan and Ó Corráin (eds), *The Viking Age*, pp 402–17.   49 *CCD*, no. 379.   50 Pádraig Ó Riain, *A dictionary of Irish saints* (Dublin, 2011), p. 219.   51 John Bradley, 'Some reflections on the problem of Scandinavian settlement in the hinterland of Dublin during the ninth century' in Bradley et al. (eds), *Dublin in the medieval world*, pp 39–62, at p. 49. 52 *Reg. Alen*, p. 3 (20 April 1179).   53 Arlene Hogan, *The priory of Llanthony Prima and Secunda in Ireland, 1172–1541: lands, patronage and politics* (Dublin, 2008), pp 84, 166. 54 Linzi Simpson, 'Fifty years a-digging: a synthesis of medieval archaeological investigations in Dublin city and suburbs' in Seán Duffy (ed.), *Medieval Dublin XI* (Dublin, 2011), pp 9–112, at p. 47.   55 For descriptions of a series of excavations of such sites, see Christiaan Corlett and Michael Potterton (eds), *Death and burial in early medieval Ireland in light of recent archaeological excavations* (Dublin, 2010).

corn-drying kiln, a common feature of these cemeteries.[56] The existence of a cemetery that conformed with indigenous burial rites is not surprising. The pre-Anglo-Norman genealogies record that the Uí Dercmossaig, supposedly one of the minor dynasties of Leinster, were located *oc Áth Cliath*, 'at Áth Cliath'.[57] This was probably their cemetery. Five Viking graves, three of them furnished, were inserted just outside the boundaries of the indigenous cemetery, a pattern that is similar to the location of Viking burials at Donnybrook and Finglas.[58]

Although somewhat shadowy, there is fragmentary evidence that suggests that Dublin on the eve of the arrival of the Vikings may have belonged to a network of churches in the region associated with the *céli Dé*, and in particular with Máel Ruain's foundation at Tallaght. Máel Ruain died in 792, the same year as Áedán of Rahan and Áedán grandson of Cú Chumbu, all described as bishops and soldiers of Christ, and all presumably *céli Dé*.[59] During the period before and after Máel Ruain's death, the annals record a series of obits of *céli Dé* whose churches were located in the hinterland of Áth Cliath: Fer Fugaill, bishop of Clondalkin (AU 789), Caínchomrac, bishop of Finglas (AU 791), Dubliter of Finglas (AU 796), Airfhinnán, abbot of Tallaght (AU 803) and Echaid, bishop and anchorite of Tallaght (AU 812). The death of Siadail, abbot of Duiblinn, is mentioned in 790.[60] The feast day of Siadail son of Luath, bishop of Dublin, is mentioned in the Martyrology of Donegal under 12 February.[61] This entry conflates two individuals: Siadail of Dublin and the learned Siadail son of Luath, with no church affiliation, who died in 759.[62] But what about Siadail mac Testa of Ard Mór mentioned as part of the *céli Dé* circle in their rule?[63] An immediate assumption might be that Siadail belonged to St Declan's Church in Ardmore, Co. Waterford, but could it be that Siadail came from Ardmore, Co. Westmeath, and was a disciple of Máel Tuile of Dysart, Co. Westmeath? While this is highly speculative, there could have been a *céli Dé* foundation situated on a road between Tallaght and Finglas some-where near the strategic riverine crossing of Áth Cliath. It might also explain why a church in Dublin would have been dedicated to Máel Ruain of Tallaght.

The evidence from the excavations at the church of St Michael le Pole revealed the existence of a twelfth-century stone church and a conjoined round tower, similar to and probably contemporary with St Kevin's House or

56 Edmond O'Donovan, 'The Irish, the Vikings and the English: new archaeological evidence from excavations at Golden Lane, Dublin' in Seán Duffy (ed.), *Medieval Dublin VIII* (Dublin, 2008), pp 36–130, at pp 46–50; 53–7.   **57** O'Brien, *Corpus geneal. Hib.*, p. 44: 121a24; p. 69: 124a13.   **58** Stephen H. Harrison and Raghnall Ó Floinn, *Viking graves and grave-goods in Ireland*. Medieval Dublin excavations 1961–81. Ser. B, vol. 11 (Dublin, 2014), pp 529–43.   **59** *AU* 792.   **60** *AU*; *AFM*.   **61** John O'Donovan, James Henthorn Todd, and William Reeves (eds), *The martyrology of Donegal: a calendar of the saints of Ireland* (Dublin, 1864), p. 47.   **62** *AU*.   **63** Edward J. Gwynn and Walter J. Purton, 'The Monastery of Tallaght', *PRIA*, 29C (1911–12), 142–3, para. 40.

'kitchen' in Glendalough and St Mary's Abbey in Ferns.[64] In his study of the emergence of parishes in Anglo-Norman Dublin, Adrian Empey, comparing the profusion of churches in pre-Anglo-Norman Dublin with similar profiles in London, Winchester and Norwich, follows N.J.G. Pound in describing them as 'essentially lay foundations set up as private chapels for substantial households, serving more extensive local communities'.[65] If organization of a diocese was underway in the rural hinterlands of Dublin during the eleventh and twelfth centuries, as argued, for example, by Charles Doherty in relation to Clondalkin,[66] and by Tomás Ó Carragáin to explain the high density of stone churches in the south Dublin/north Wicklow region,[67] then the urban ecclesiastical landscape was undoubtedly being arranged gradually around focal nodes, most evident archaeologically in the construction of the church of St Michael le Pole, and possibly also the churches of St Peter and St John.[68] This urban/rural connection might also explain why a number of dedications – Comgall, Peter, Paul and indeed St Olaf – occur both in Dublin and in its hinterland, and one might wonder if the basis of the common dedications had something to do with the supply of pastoral care from an increasingly organized ecclesiastical urban centre to its rural hinterland, and receipt of foodstuffs and fuel from the hinterland. In reality, this was the essence of Armagh's contract with Dublin albeit on a grander scale.

PLANNING THE ECCLESIASTICAL LANDSCAPE OF DUBLIN: FOLLOWING INTERNATIONAL NORMS?

The next part of *SGAC*'s list reflects a different form of transmission of saints' cults, that of the international transfer of dedications. The poem (verse 49) declares that in the heart (*certlár*) of Dublin (Áth Cliath) stood the church of Peter and Paul, beside Cell Chríst (Christ Church) and Cell Muire (church of St Mary) and also the church of St Brigit *inside* the *dún*. This is a suite of dedications that appears in many places. Monastic foundations dedicated to SS

64 Gowen, 'Excavations at the site of the church and tower of St Michael le Pole, Dublin'.
65 Tomás Ó Carragáin, 'Church buildings and pastoral care in early medieval Ireland' in Elizabeth FitzPatrick and Raymond Gillespie (eds), *The parish in medieval and early modern Ireland. Community, territory and building* (Dublin, 2006), pp 91–123; Adrian Empey, 'The formation and development of intramural churches and communities in medieval Dublin in a European context' in Bradley et al. (eds), *Dublin in the medieval world*, pp 249–76.
66 Charles Doherty, 'Cluain Dolcáin: a brief note' in Alfred P. Smyth (ed.), *Seanchas. Studies in early and medieval Irish archaeology, history and literature in honour of Francis J. Byrne* (Dublin, 2000), pp 182–8.   67 Ó Carragáin, 'Church buildings and pastoral care', pp 101–8.   68 Tim Coughlan, 'Excavations at the medieval cemetery of St Peter's Church, Dublin' in Seán Duffy (ed.), *Medieval Dublin IV* (Dublin, 2003), pp 11–39; Linzi Simpson, 'Archaeological excavation of the medieval church of St John of Bothe Street, Dublin 8' in Seán Duffy (ed.), *Medieval Dublin XVII* (Dublin, 2019), 109–73.

Peter and Paul were in Armagh and Glendalough by the twelfth century.[69] There are close parallels with Dublin in the church dedications of towns such as Chester or Roskilde which raises the possibility of the transmission of a particular combination of dedications throughout urban settlements with Scandinavian connections. Hence by *c.*1170 *inside* the *dún* there were dedications to SS Mary, Michael, Nicholas, Martin, Werburgh, Olaf, John and Christ Church/Holy Trinity.[70] On the analogy of a town such as Worcester, one might speculate that the church dedicated to St Mary (*cell Muire*) associated in *SGAC* with Christ Church (*cell Chríst*) was a church for the monastic community – St Mary being a dedication favoured by medieval monastic communities to reflect their vow of chastity.[71] The dedication to St Brigit is not at all surprising as she appears in urban landscapes all over north-western Europe from Dublin to Chester to London to Cologne. Indeed, this is a phenomenon that requires separate detailed consideration elsewhere. Detaching St Brigit from her mythological associations and viewing her as a medieval saint of western Christendom, how did her cult spread so widely? For example, it would not have been surprising to find that Dublin's first bishop Dúnán (d. 1074) had a church dedicated to her in Dublin as she had one dedicated to her in Cologne where he seems to have received his formation; the Cologne dedication was probably due to strong connections with the eastern province of Leinster, at least in the eleventh century.[72] Nor should the presence of churches in Dublin dedicated to Brigit and Kevin be surprising, given that Kildare and Glendalough were so prominent in Leinster. No more than Armagh, these major churches undoubtedly sought to benefit from the growing wealth of the town, and there was no better way of doing so than by establishing churches dedicated to their patrons in the town or its environs.

Although *SGAC* does not mention it, these churches located in the heart of Dublin formed the town's cathedral quarter. Apart from the significance of the dedications – Christ, Mary, Peter, Paul and Brigit – this is where kings and bishops played their part in shaping Dublin's ecclesiastical landscape. The most important point is that Dublin's ecclesiastical landscape had many characteristics in common with towns and cities elsewhere, particularly in England, the Ottonian Empire and Scandinavia. In many ways those planning Dublin imitated international models of church dedications and the spatial accommodation between churches and monastic foundations within the urban scape. In some instances, this planning was executed through the joint efforts

---

69 Maurice P. Sheehy (ed.), *Pontificia Hibernica. Medieval papal chancery documents concerning Ireland, 640–1261*, 2 vols (Dublin, 1962), i, no. 97; ii, no. 273n (Armagh). 70 Clarke, *Dublin, Pt 1* (IHTA), p. 5 (fig. 4). 71 Francesca Tinti, *Sustaining belief: the church of Worcester from c.870 to c.1100* (Farnham and Burlington, 2010). 72 Bróen mac Máel Mórda, king of Leinster, was blinded by Sitriuc in Dublin in 1018 and he died in Cologne in 1052 (*AU*); this sequence of incidents suggests that ties with Cologne, at least between Dublin and Leinster, were fairly active throughout the eleventh century.

of kings and bishops, as in the case of Sitriuc Silkenbeard and the first bishop of Dublin, Dúnán.[73] It seems that Sitriuc, king of Dublin, sometime after his pilgrimage to Rome in 1028, established Christ Church as a cathedral church for Dublin, and arranged for a certain Donatus/Dúnán, likely to have been an Irishman and 'Benedictine' monk (in the Ottonian sense) who had received his formation in Cologne, to become the town's first bishop.[74] It would appear that a collection of relics with a distinctly Ottonian identity was brought to Dublin during Dúnán's episcopacy but more significantly in the context of foundational relics for a cathedral primarily consisting of apostolic and episcopal relics.[75] This symbolic transfer of relics from Cologne to Dublin during the eleventh century, including a relic of St Heribert, the archbishop of Cologne, who died in 1021, was a declaration that Dublin was part of a wider ecclesiastical network that centred on Cologne, an imperial city ruled by powerful archbishops.[76] Dúnán's formation as a Benedictine monk is probably reflected in the inclusion of relics of St Benedict (*de reliquiis sancti patris Benedicti*).[77]

The absence of native Irish relics listed among the contents of Dúnán's casket of relics has been remarked on by Ó Floinn,[78] but in a sense *SGAC* explains why they were absent: this cathedral was being founded as part of an international network linking it with Rome, Cologne and the Scandinavian world. At this juncture, native saints, even if there were existing associations with Iona and the cult of Columba, could not match the prestige of the staff of St Peter, a sandal of St Sylvester or a fragment of the garment of the Virgin that were included as part of the cathedral's collection of foundational relics. The Scandinavian character of the foundation is clearly declared by the inclusion of the garment of St Olaf who was not many years dead (d. 1030) when the cathedral's foundation relics were assembled, that is unless this item was added at a later stage.

Studies conducted elsewhere on the development of urban ecclesiastical landscapes suggest that saints' dedications were used by secular and religious authorities to shape their towns mindful of their own interests. In his study of Amiens between *c.*1050 and 1150, John S. Ott articulates how the city's bishops privileged above all others one group of patron saints – their own ancient predecessors and the great bishop, St Martin of Tours – and locations

73 Pádraig Ó Riain, 'Dublin's oldest book? A list of saints "made in Germany"' in Seán Duffy (ed.), *Medieval Dublin V* (Dublin, 2004), pp 52–72; Raghnall Ó Floinn, 'The foundation relics of Christ Church Cathedral and the origins of the diocese of Dublin' in Seán Duffy (ed.), *Medieval Dublin VII* (Dublin, 2006), pp 89–102.   74 Dagmar Ó Riain-Raedel, 'New light on the beginnings of Christ Church Cathedral, Dublin' in Sean Duffy (ed.), *Medieval Dublin XVII*, pp 63–80.   75 Ó Floinn, 'The foundation relics', p. 96.   76 Joseph P. Huffman, *The imperial city of Cologne. From Roman colony to medieval metropolis (19 BC to AD 1125)* (Amsterdam, 2018).   77 Ó Floinn, 'The foundation relics', p. 95.   78 Ó Floinn, 'The foundation relics', p. 96.

associated with their miracles, in order to maintain their authority against rival powers such as other religious communities, the counts of Flanders, the local castellan and the townspeople.[79] Ott's representation of the nature of Amiens's sacred, as opposed to its secular, geography offers a constructive guide towards understanding the strategy that may have sustained the development of Dublin's ecclesiastical landscape:

> The town's holy spaces loomed large in the collective identity and memory of the populace precisely through their association with the lives and deeds of the community's patron saints. At the centre of the city's network of sacred space stood the cathedral, the physical and meta-phorical representation of the Christian community. Surrounding the cathedral were buildings associated with the deeds of the community's first martyrs, confessors, and bishops.[80]

The early stages of Bergen's development also offer a potential model for the development of Dublin and Gitte Hansen's approach to early Bergen is a useful template with which to interrogate Dublin's landscape.[81] Hansen examined the archaeological and literary evidence for five chronological horizons covering that period and assessed Bergen's development on the basis of the central role of kings in organizing the settlement ('top down' initiatives) and the response of their subjects to their efforts ('bottom up' initiatives). A number of Hansen's conclusions are worth considering in the context of Dublin:

- kings were essential actors in choosing prominent sites, assigning plots to their subjects and founding and strengthening Bergen as an ecclesiastical centre;
- their reasons for developing the centre were primarily economic – for example, it strengthened the development of trade and crafts as well as a fishing post;
- the growth of the settlement was slow and kings had to intervene with new initiatives to maintain momentum – for example, the foundation of the cathedral and its associated quarter in Holmen and of other churches and monastic foundations in the emerging town were essential to Bergen's development as a town.

Unlike Bergen, there is evidence for a lot of activity in the pre-eleventh century horizons of Dublin. This includes evidence for Viking burials/

---

79 John S. Ott, *Bishops, authority and community in northwestern Europe*, c.*1050–1150* (Cambridge, 2015), pp 222–56.   80 Ott, *Bishops, authority and community*, pp 225–6. 81 Gitte Hansen, 'Bergen AD 1120/30–1170: between plans and reality' in James H. Barrett

cemeteries (e.g., Kilmainham/Islandbridge), Christian (assumed native Irish) burials/cemeteries (Golden Lane) and settlement (Chancery Lane), and from the ninth century onward a busy organization of the Viking settlement.[82] According to Hansen, the new ecclesiastical quarter of Holmen at Bergen began with the building of Christ Church Cathedral and a minor church also dedicated to Christ nearby by Óláfr Kyrre (d. 1093). King Øystein (d. 1123) added to the Holmen quarter by founding the church of the Apostles and a large timber hall – possibly a royal residence or assembly place – and he is reputed to have been one of the founders of the church of St Nicholas on the seashore and St Mary's in the middle of the settlement, and significantly Munkeliv, a monastery possibly dedicated to St Michael in Nordnes, at the other end of the settlement from Holmen.[83]

Building on Hansen's model for Bergen, we might speculate that the mid-eleventh-century houses excavated at Christchurch Place in Dublin, and especially the stave-built rectangular house dated by dendrochronology to *c.*1059 that produced a rich array of artefacts, were part of the royal and/or episcopal centre, perhaps even Dúnán's residence?[84] There was a well-developed settlement in existence when Sitriuc and Dúnán started to found their cathedral, and both would have had to identify a space for their church and plan its layout and its immediate surroundings. And as with a later generation of kings in Bergen, they chose what seems to have been a relatively undeveloped space: archaeological investigations in the vicinity of Christ Church and High Street (the western end of the settlement) suggest that this area was not settled or laid out until the early eleventh century.[85]

It is evident from Ott and Hansen's studies – among many others – that the development of urban ecclesiastical landscapes was determined by bishops and kings. When Sitriuc returned from his journey to Rome, possibly accompanied by Dúnán – although it is not certain that the latter became bishop at this early stage[86] – did they already have a plan for the burgeoning town's sacred geography in mind? Sitriuc could have been influenced by Cnut the Great who had discussed matters relating to the English church, and possibly also the Danish church, with Pope John XIX at the time of the coronation of Conrad II in Rome in 1027, a year before Sitriuc went to the Holy City. Cnut's involvement in the establishment of the Danish dioceses of Lund, Roskilde,

and Sarah Jane Gibbon (eds), *Maritime societies of the Viking and medieval world* (London and New York, 2016), pp 182–97. **82** Linzi Simpson, 'Forty years a-digging: a preliminary synthesis of archaeological investigations in medieval Dublin' in Seán Duffy (ed.), *Medieval Dublin I* (Dublin, 2000), pp 11–68; Simpson, 'Fifty years a-digging', pp 9–112. **83** Hansen, 'Bergen AD 1020/30', pp 188–90. **84** Simpson, 'Forty years a-digging', p. 34; a detailed study of the cultural material from this house and its environs at Christ Church Place might reveal its function and its cultural context. **85** Simpson, 'Fifty years a-digging', pp 41–2. **86** Dúnán's death is recorded in 1074 which would infer that his episcopacy lasted for over forty years; while not impossible, it is worth querying such a long episcopacy.

Odense, Hedeby-Schleswig, Ribe and Viborg and the development of these locations as urban sites, and also his sometimes fractious interaction with the archbishops of Hamburg-Bremen, may have been known to Sitriuc.[87]

Was the plan for Dublin based on Dúnán's knowledge of Cologne or on some other contemporary plan? A late fourteenth-/early fifteenth-century narrative on the foundation of Christ Church preserved in the manuscript known as the *Liber Niger* ('Black Book') of Christ Church which probably draws on an earlier source, includes details of Sitriuc and Dúnán's first foundation. Scholars working on cathedral dedications elsewhere have highlighted the significance of the idea and act of dedication of a cathedral, and in her essay on Scandinavian cathedral culture, Anna Minara Ciardi notes the proliferation of dedications to the Holy Trinity and Christ, as the highest ranking among saints, and the most powerful heavenly patrons and protectors: hence the Holy Trinity/Christ Church medieval cathedral dedications in Roskilde, Nidaros, Bergen, Oslo, Stavanger and Hamar and Orkney.[88]

Of course, the cathedral in Canterbury had been dedicated to Christ by its founder Augustine in the late sixth century but it is not evident that this influenced the dedication in Dublin. A cathedral's dedication was usually expressed visually in the building and Dublin was no exception as the *Liber Niger* text relates how Sitriuc and Dúnán – king and bishop, the key actors – built the nave of the church with two side aisles and an altar for the image of the Crucifixion (*edificauit nauem ecclesie cum duabus collatrallibus structuris et solium ymaginis crucifixi*).[89] In addition, a chapel dedicated to St Nicholas was incorporated into the northern part of Christ Church (*… cum capella sancti Nicholai in parte boriali*).[90] The dedication to St Nicholas is likely to be further evidence of Dúnán's connections with Ottonian Germany as the cult of this saint was possibly transferred there from Byzantium by Empress Theophanu (d. 990), which then spread to Scandinavia, France and England.[91] Theophanu was buried in the church of St Pantaleon in Cologne, the location of a Benedictine monastery founded in 955 by Archbishop Bruno, brother of Otto II and a church that Dúnán was no doubt familiar with during his time in Cologne. A later church dedicated to St Nicholas was in existence in Dublin by the late twelfth century, located to the south of Christ Church Cathedral. Clarke is probably correct in suggesting that the cult of St Nicholas was refocussed from the cathedral's side chapel to this new church.[92] The

---

87 For a survey of Cnut's role in creating an ecclesiastical structure in Denmark and his relations with the English and Danish churches, see Timothy Bolton, *The empire of Cnut the Great: conquest and the consolidation of power in northern Europe in the early eleventh century* (Leiden, 2009), pp 149–202.   88 Ciardi, 'Saints and cathedral culture in Scandinavia'. 89 Aubrey Gwynn, 'Some unpublished texts from the Black Book of Christ Church, Dublin', *AH*, 16 (1946), 281, 283–337, at 309.   90 Gwynn, 'Some unpublished texts', 309. 91 Ildar H. Garipzanov, 'The cult of St Nicholas in the early Christian north', *Scandinavian Journal of History*, 35 (2010), 229–46, at 230.   92 Howard B. Clarke, 'Conversion, church

circumstances in which this happened may be understood from the second part of the cathedral foundation narrative which claims that Lorcán Ua Tuathail as archbishop, along with Strongbow and other early Anglo-Norman adventurers, built a choir with a bell tower and two chapels, one dedicated to St Edmund the Martyr, the other to the Virgin Mary.[93]

A church dedicated to St Michael, which the first narrative explains was also built by Dúnán *in palacio suo*, 'in his [episcopal] palace/house',[94] was handed over to the canons of the newly founded Holy Trinity Priory.[95] This suggests that Dúnán had a plan in mind for an episcopal household. The bishops of Amiens planned the town's episcopal *burgus* in a manner not dissimilar from what is known of Dublin's episcopal quarter. Ott's schematic plan of the *burgus* and *civitas* – ruled by the castellan – shows the cathedral of SS Marie and Firmin at the north-eastern corner of the city wall with the collegiate church of Saint-Firmin-le Confesseur, the canons' houses and cloister, and the episcopal residence next to it. To the south of the cathedral lay the church of Saint Michel and beyond that to the south-west the church of Saint-Nicolas and Augustinian priory of Saint-Martin-aux-Jumeaux.[96]

The organization of an urban ecclesiastical landscape was thoroughly dependent on powerful bishops and Dúnán and his successors conformed with this norm. It is worth exploring references to the bishops of Dublin from Dúnán to Lorcán Ua Tuathail relating to building projects, dedications and the existence of an episcopal *curia*. As noted above, the earlier of the two narratives in the *Liber Niger* describes how Dúnán built a church dedicated to St Michael *in palacio suo*, while the second and later narrative maintains that Sitriuc gave Dúnán sufficient resources to build a church *cum tota curia*, which suggests that, like episcopal quarters elsewhere, Dúnán planned a street for his own household. Perhaps the layout of York's Minster Close might offer a starting point for us to look at the complex around Christ Church. By *c.*1070 the York Minster Close was 'largely occupied by the houses of the five senior officials of the chapter and by the houses of the first prebends established by Archbishop Thomas [of York], probably before 1086'.[97]

I have dealt elsewhere with the existence in Dublin by the late eleventh century of a Benedictine community that following an English model serviced the bishop and the cathedral.[98] The clearest evidence for this is found in a

and cathedral: the diocese of Dublin to 1152' in James Kelly and Dáire Keogh (eds), *History of the Catholic diocese of Dublin* (Dublin, 2000), pp 19–50, at p. 48.   **93** Gwynn, 'Some unpublished texts', 309; there are doubts about the accuracy of this text, as argued by Roger Stalley in his detailed architectural consideration of the construction of Christ Church Cathedral: 'The construction of the medieval cathedral, *c.*1030–1250' in Milne (ed.), *Christ Church*, pp 53–74, at pp 60–1.   **94** Gwynn, 'Some unpublished texts', 308.   **95** Gwynn, 'Some unpublished texts', 309.   **96** Ott, *Bishops, authority and community*, p. 227.   **97** Sarah Rees Jones, *York. The making of a city 1068–1350* (Oxford, 2013), p. 30.   **98** Edel Bhreathnach, 'Benedictine influence in Ireland in the late eleventh and early twelfth

letter of admonishment sent by Anselm of Canterbury to Bishop Samuel of Dublin (d. 1121). Among Anselm's complaints were that Samuel had expelled the monks – likely to have been Benedictines – who had been brought together [in community] in the church [Christ Church] to serve God (*Item audivi quod monachos, qui in ipsa ecclesia ad serviendum deo congregati erant, expellas et dispergas …*).[99] What the shape of the monastic precinct or cathedral close took in late eleventh-century Dublin is open to interpretation, although some ideas can be extracted by referring to contemporary cathedral complexes elsewhere, especially English cathedrals where it is likely that by the late eleventh century models for Dublin originated. Whereas it might be assumed that examples of pre twelfth-century English cloisters have survived, this is not the case. In his consideration of English Romanesque cloisters, John McNeill makes an interesting suggestion that might offer a template for the monastic/episcopal precinct in Dublin. He suggests that the earliest cloister at Westminster, where the claustral precinct was laid out between *c.*1060 and *c.*1080, may have been built of wood, like the *clôitre en bois* discovered at the French Augustinian foundation of St-Georges-de-Boscherville.[100] As in many English and continental cathedral complexes, a stone cloister may have been built at Christ Church only in the mid- to late twelfth century, possibly as part of the reconstruction of the city's ecclesiastical landscape during Lorcán Ua Tuathail's archiepiscopacy.[101]

IRISH KINGS IN DUBLIN

Sitriuc was deposed as king of Dublin in 1036 and he died in 1042, possibly overseas in the Scandinavian colony in Anglesey.[102] He was succeeded by Echmarcach mac Ragnaill perhaps at the instigation of the latter's brother-in-law, Donnchad mac Briain, king of Munster.[103] Echmarcach was deposed and exiled in 1052 by the powerful king of Leinster Diarmait mac Máel na mBó, who placed his own son Murchad in charge of Dublin. Murchad held that position until 1070 when he died there. From that period onwards, the provincial kings of Ireland in their attempts to claim the over-kingship of Ireland to the late twelfth century tended to seize Dublin and rule the town

centuries: a reflection', *Journal of Medieval Monastic Studies*, 1 (2012), 63–91. **99** Franciscus Salesius Schmitt (ed.), *S. Anselmi cantuariensis archiepiscopi opera omnia*, 6 vols (Edinburgh, 1946–61), iv, p. 190, no. 278. **100** John McNeill, 'The Romanesque cloister in England', *Journal of the British Archaeological Association*, 168 (2015), 34–76, at 64. **101** Rachel Moss, 'Tales from the crypt: the medieval stonework of Christ Church Cathedral, Dublin' in Seán Duffy (ed.), *Medieval Dublin III* (Dublin, 2002), pp 95–114, at pp 111–13; Stalley, 'The construction of the medieval cathedral', p. 57. **102** Howard B. Clarke, 'King Sitriuc Silkenbeard: a great survivor' in Clarke and Johnson (eds), *The Vikings in Ireland and beyond*, pp 253–67 at p. 264. **103** Clarke, 'King Sitriuc Silkenbeard', p. 264.

through their sons. External forces, primarily based around the Irish Sea –
Norse, Anglo-Saxon and finally Norman/Welsh – were also entwined in the
politics of Dublin of the period.[104] Nonetheless the Hiberno-Norse kings of
Dublin held considerable sway until the twelfth century. This intricate web of
internal and external control and intrusion shaped the ecclesiastical landscape
of what effectively was a new form of urban space in Ireland. The ecclesiastical
actors were stellar: Lanfranc, archbishop of Canterbury and a Benedictine; the
senior cleric of Munster, Domnall Ua hÉnna, bishop of Killaloe; the bishops
of Dublin, Patrick/Gilla Pátraic and Donatus/Donngus, both possibly trained
as Benedictine monks in England;[105] and last, but not least, the abbots of
Armagh. Their involvement must have intensified the foundation and
endowment of churches, and most likely saw the introduction of a Benedictine
cathedral chapter/episcopal household, perhaps modelled on the organisation
of English cathedrals. It is clear from Lanfranc's letter to Tairdelbach ua
Briain, written *c.*1074, that the archbishop of Canterbury – and no doubt
Bishop Patrick who had succeeded Dúnán – was concerned about episcopal
ordinations and the jurisdiction of bishops: 'Bishops are consecrated by a
single bishop; many are ordained to villages and small towns (*quod in uillis uel
ciuitatibus plures ordinantur*).'[106]

   If Dublin was to be the model episcopal seat, then it needed to emulate
international trends, with a cathedral chapter and churches dedicated to the
saints of western Christendom. How far Irish kings with their ecclesiastical
allies were instrumental in internationalizing Dublin is best illustrated by the
activities of Diarmait Mac Murchada, king of Leinster (d. 1171) and his
powerful brother-in-law Lorcán Ua Tuathail, abbot of Glendalough and
archbishop of Dublin (d. 1180). Diarmait was one of the most adventurous,
and ambitious, of all pre-Anglo-Norman Irish kings, and his influence on
Dublin reflects his resolve and his capacity to act on new ideas, often probably
recommended by individuals such as Archbishop Lorcán. Diarmait is
associated with the endowments of the nunnery of St Mary de Hogges and the
priory of All Saints/All Hallows, now part of Trinity College Dublin
(Augustinians) and possibly the first foundation of St Mary's Abbey (Savignac
Benedictines).[107]

   The motives behind all this activity were multi-faceted. It may be an
example of Gitte Hansen's theory concerning the intervention of kings in
urban planning: both St Mary's Abbey and All Saints' Priory had riverine
frontages with the latter strategically and probably deliberately built near an

---

104 Seán Duffy, 'Ostmen, Irish and Welsh in the eleventh century', *Peritia*, 9 (1996),
378–96.   **105** Ó Riain-Raedel, 'New light on the beginnings of Christ Church', pp 74–7.
106 Helen Clover and Margaret Gibson (eds), *The letters of Lanfranc, archbishop of
Canterbury* (Oxford, 1979), pp 70–1, no. 10.   **107** Linzi Simpson, 'The priory of All
Hallows and the Old College: archaeological investigations in Front Square, Trinity College
Dublin' in Seán Duffy (ed.), *Medieval Dublin XIII* (Dublin, 2013), pp 246–316.

important landing point on the river Liffey at the confluence with the tributary river Stein and close to Dublin's Viking ceremonial complex around the Long Stone and the Thingmoot. Mac Murchada's foundation of St Mary de Hogges was even closer to this ceremonial complex and may have even intruded on a Viking cemetery or on Hoggen Green which was part of Dublin's ceremonial complex.[108] Mac Murchada's intentions may have been twofold: to follow an age-old tactic of weakening or subduing the enemy by destroying or intruding on the physical site that represented the source of their power. But Mac Murchada was also emulating his friends elsewhere, such as Robert Fitz Harding of Bristol who had endowed an Augustinian house in 1148 (which later became Bristol Cathedral), in introducing monastic houses to expanding suburbs. Less than one hundred years later, some of the mendicant foundations were placed in similar strategic locations, St Saviour's Dominican Priory at the main river crossing in Dublin being a clear example.

This type of planning is evident elsewhere in Ireland, as in the case of Diarmait Mac Murchada's own caput at Ferns, Co. Wexford where around the same time as his endowment of All Saints' (*c.*1160–2), he granted a charter to St Mary's, another house of Augustinian canons.[109] The Ferns charter was witnessed by a list of eminent bishops and Lorcán Ua Tuathail as abbot of Glendalough. This charter finally brings us to Lorcán Ua Tuathail's installation at Christ Church, *c.*1163, of Augustinian canons following the Arrouasian rule as a cathedral chapter and part of the episcopal household with their claustral buildings incorporated into the cathedral complex.[110] This foundation is, like the foundation of Christ Church by Sitriuc and Dúnán, a milestone not alone in the collaboration between an archbishop and a king – Diarmait may have granted lands to Holy Trinity[111] – and in introducing a model that was taking root elsewhere of canons serving in cathedral chapters, but also in establishing a long-lasting monastic tradition in Dublin that expanded through the late medieval period and left a complex physical and onomastic legacy on the city's streets.

And what of the involvement of patrons other than provincial Irish kings in shaping Dublin's ecclesiastical landscape prior to 1200? A fair idea is gained from King John's grant to the prior and community of Holy Trinity of 6 March 1202 confirming all lands and possessions bestowed on that church before the English came to Ireland and after, and confirming them 'as best blessed Laurence, beloved archbishop of Dublin of good remembrance gave

108 Stephen Harrison, 'College Green – a neglected "Viking" cemetery at Dublin' in Andras Mortensen and Símun V. Arge (eds), *Viking and Norse in the North Atlantic. Select papers from the proceedings of the fourteenth Viking Congress, Tórshavn, 19–30 July 2001* (Tórshavn, 2005), pp 329–39. 109 Marie Therese Flanagan, *Irish royal charters: texts and contexts* (Oxford, 2005), pp 284–9. 110 Stalley, 'The construction of the medieval cathedral', pp 57–61. 111 Flanagan, *Irish royal charters*, p. 386.

them by his charters'.[112] The endowments granted within the town reflect the fact that Irish, Hiberno-Norse and English were patrons of the town's churches and provided their personnel.

The Hiberno-Norse patrons included their senior nobles such as Earl Ascall who granted 'the church of St Brigit and all the lands in the parish belonging anciently to Holy Trinity Church' or the apparently civic gift of the Ostmen of land between St Patrick's Church and the city wall. The gifts of Hiberno-Norse individuals of probable noble rank are instructive. Thorsin son of Torgair granted the land in which the masters of divinity resided (*accomodauerunt diuini*). The gift granted by Bastolian Gormelach, son of Pole, of St Michael's Church may explain the sobriquet 'le Pole' associated with this church.[113] This may have been a family church handed over to Holy Trinity as part of the creation of a permanent parish structure in Dublin in the late twelfth century. Grants of lands in the hinterland of Dublin by other members of the family, Dormlagh son of Pole, Pole son of Thorkill and Brodor son of Thorkyll, are also recorded in John's 1202 confirmation. Earl Ascall's gift of the church of St Brigit was also probably part of this organization of a parochial structure.[114] Isake the priest's gift of 'St Michen's Church with lands on each side' may equally be seen as a further example of the consolidation of a parochial system in the town.

Handing over of family churches was not confined to Hiberno-Norse families. The 1202 confirmation records that Gillamichell son of Gillamurri – ostensibly Irish from his personal name although perhaps more likely to be Hiberno-Norse – granted the churches of St John and St Paul to Holy Trinity.[115] Private parcels of land or enterprises were also handed over to Holy Trinity, presumably enabling the archbishop and the canons to pursue economically viable activities. Hence Gillamurra gave them a mill by the bridge and lands on both sides of the mill. Some land had existing tenants who presumably simply changed landlords as was the case with the gift of the Anglo-Norman William Brune of land in St Thomas's parish 'which Rolkysus and Sigena hold', the latter most likely being native Hiberno-Norse Dubliners. A variety of other inhabitants are also mentioned as grantees, thus providing a real insight into the landowning class of twelfth-century Dublin. These included Gillacormda, the wealthy man (*diuitis*); Soger the old (*senis*) who granted his burgage, possibly as part of his will for the salvation of his soul; Giffus the priest who granted the land between St John's church and Walter the goldsmith's house. Notably, women were also among Holy Trinity's

---

112 *CCD*, no. 364(a)–(c); Sheehy (ed.), *Pontificia Hibernica*, i, pp 26–9, no. 9 (Alexander to Lorcán Ua Tuathail, 20 April 1179); pp 41–4, no. 13 (Pope Urban III to prior and community of Holy Trinity, 2 July 1186).   **113** Alternatively, the suffix 'le Pole' may indicate the church's proximity to the pool of Dublin: Clarke, *Dublin, Pt 1* (IHTA), p. 5.   **114** Empey, 'Intramural churches and communities in Dublin', p. 250, n. 2.   **115** Sheehy (ed.), *Pontificia Hibernica*, i, p. 41, n.1.

patrons. Christina, daughter of Raba, granted land in St Brigit's parish 'which reaches to the city wall beyond the garden', while Fransigona's daughter granted land by the church of St Nicholas.

The intrusion of Anglo-Norman settlers, other than the great barons such as Strongbow or Raymond le Gros, is also evident especially in the south-western part beyond the town walls and around modern Thomas Street: Roger, brother of Haim, granted land in Krokkerestret;[116] Walter Camor, land in the parish of St John's hospital; William of Essex, land in St Werburgh's parish; and Simon de Saulo, land in St Martin's parish. One final interesting detail from the 1202 confirmation is the gift made by Earl Richard (Strongbow) and burgesses of Dublin of 'land beyond Holy Trinity graveyard from the corner of the market-place to the corner of John Bishop's land (*terra Johannis Episcopi*)'. John's name may not have been 'Bishop' but rather that he was John 'the Bishop', suggesting that he was head of a Jewish community in twelfth-century Dublin who was also a landowner.[117] This possibility requires more investigation as do the many other details contained in the 1202 confirmation and related earlier papal documents.

CONCLUSION

What can be deduced about the cultural identity and development of the urban landscape of Dublin from the church dedications and saints' cults of the eleventh and twelfth centuries? Just as the archaeology of the town is complex, so is its ecclesiastical landscape and much research needs to be undertaken using the extensive archaeological evidence and source material to fully comprehend Dublin's sacred geography.[118] It consists of many layers of dedications, some surviving into the modern era, others lost or usurped by later dedications.

On the basis of the evidence teased out here, one can speculate that when they arrived in Dublin the Vikings landed into an existing ecclesiastical landscape that consisted of churches which had been recently founded by adherents to the *céli Dé* customs. The main church was at Tallaght and other churches included Finglas, Clondalkin and Glasnevin. There is a possibility that the *céli Dé* had established a church at Dublin, or more correctly Áth Cliath, which would have been the main crossing over the Liffey on the road between Tallaght and Finglas. The memory of this pre-Viking ecclesiastical landscape survived in the dedications to Máel Ruain, St Michael, Cainnech

---

116 For whom, see Grace O'Keeffe, 'The merchant conquistadors: medieval Bristolians in Dublin' in Seán Duffy (ed.), *Medieval Dublin XIII* (Dublin, 2013), 116–38, at 122–6. 117 Marie Therese Flanagan, pers. comm.   118 Boazman, 'Material culture and identity in the southern hinterland of Hiberno-Scandinavian Dublin'.

and the reference in the annals and martyrologies to Siadail, abbot of Duiblinn. The next set of dedications is more speculative and depends on vague and late references to what could have been a Scottish/Irish Sea-influenced period of conversion. This period corresponds to that of the reign of Amlaíb Cúarán as king of Dublin and devotee of St Columba and his monastery of Iona. If Dublin's conversion emanated from Iona, then a dedication to Columba would surely follow, and perhaps even Mo-Luóc of Lismore in Scotland whose cult was also known in the Isle of Man. Equally, conversion of the Hiberno-Norse of Dublin would have required the foundation of a church in the town, and that church may have been the *Cell meic nÁeda* mentioned in *SGAC*, quite possibly located on or near the later church dedicated to St Patrick.

A constant feature of the development of medieval urban ecclesiastical landscapes in Britain and Europe was a dependence on the actions of kings and bishops who provided land and planned the sacred geography of many urban spaces. Sitriuc and Dúnán in the eleventh century, matched by Diarmait Mac Murchada and Lorcán Ua Tuathail in the twelfth, were to the fore in shaping Dublin's sacred geography. The founding of Christ Church, surrounded probably by an ecclesiastical quarter – or 'close' – in which an episcopal household resided, brought Dublin into line with towns elsewhere as did the new wave of dedications. Although important Irish saints – Patrick, Brigit, Kevin – had churches dedicated to them, an international panoply of saints also appeared, among them, Christ, the Virgin Mary, SS Peter, Paul, Nicholas and, significantly in a Norse context, St Olaf. By adopting these cults the citizens of Dublin had created a sacred geography similar to many towns in Britain, Scandinavia and northern Europe, and followed on a lesser scale in other Hiberno-Norse towns in Ireland, especially Limerick, Waterford and Wexford.

The apparent replication of a number of dedications (e.g., Peter, Paul, Olaf, Comgall) in the wider hinterland of Dublin raises the question of how early the bishops of Dublin began to organize a wider ecclesiastical landscape that went beyond the town's walls into its suburbs and beyond, a landscape that ultimately defined a bishopric. Tomás Ó Carragáin has argued that the stone churches of south Co. Dublin are a reflex of the progress in the eleventh century towards the creation of a bishopric.[119] Perhaps the relationship between the town's churches and those in rural areas was one of mutual dependence in that one provided a supply of priests, the other a supply of material goods for the bishop, his household and the town's priests. If the town's churches were originally associated with prominent urban families or, in the case of those dedicated to Irish saints, the property of Irish churches

---

119 Ó Carragáin, 'Church buildings and pastoral care in early medieval Ireland'.

(Armagh, Kildare, Glendalough, Tallaght), it seems that by the twelfth century, and most likely during the episcopacy of Lorcán Ua Tuathail, these churches were being appropriated by Christ Church and Holy Trinity Priory with the intention of organizing the town's parochial structure.[120]

The course taken by bishops of Dublin followed a trajectory similar to that of the Hiberno-Norse kings. They were open to ideas from abroad: indeed, in many instances they received their formation abroad and this is reflected in their choice of architectural styles, relics, saints' dedications and contacts. And while these external influences were considerable, from the beginning there existed a parallel tradition of fitting into the Irish ecclesiastical landscape. In reality, this had to be the case as the Hiberno-Norse of Dublin were fairly integrated into Irish society, by at least the tenth century. During the eleventh century Cologne and Canterbury played a part in integrating Dublin into western Christendom but an equally important role was played by Armagh in bringing the town into the fold of the Irish church. Dublin profited hugely from these external and Irish connections: when the Irish diocesan structure was finally formalized at the Synod of Kells in 1152, Dublin was named as one of the four metropolitan sees in Ireland.

---

120 Empey, 'Intramural churches and communities in Dublin'.

Why were there so few papal provisions in thirteenth-century Dublin?

THOMAS W. SMITH

Papal provision was a method of appointing clergy to benefices, or livings, by which the pope issued a letter charging an executor (usually the local prelate) to seek out a suitable vacant stipend and, if the candidate was suitable, to induct the cleric in question into possession of that church.[1] This innovation of the papacy – the appointment of clergy to benefices through provision mandates – first emerged in the twelfth century, but it was not until the early thirteenth century that it gained a strong foothold in the regional struggles for patronage between the bishops, kings and lay patrons of Europe.[2]

Driven both by papal nepotism and demand from native supplicants, the number of papal candidates installed through provision increased rapidly during the first half of the thirteenth century to become one of the main methods of appointment for medieval clergy. This invention exerted a disruptive effect on traditional methods of collation and fomented resistance from prelates and lay patrons who considered their hard-won rights of patronage to be under threat. But it was not simply bare-faced papal exploitation, as some scholars suggest.[3] The lack of a detailed exploration of

I wish to express my gratitude to the Leverhulme Trust for the award of an Early Career Fellowship at the University of Leeds (2017–20) to work on the rise of papal provision in thirteenth-century Britain, from which this chapter springs. My thanks to Dr Peter Crooks, Professor Séan Duffy, and the audience and delegates of the Friends of Medieval Dublin symposium in 2017 for their feedback on this paper. **1** On papal provision, see the classic studies by Hermann Baier, *Päpstliche Provisionen für niedere Pfründen* (Münster, 1911) and Geoffrey Barraclough, *Papal provisions: aspects of church history constitutional, legal and administrative in the later middle ages* (Oxford, 1935). For an overview of the state of research on provision, see Thomas W. Smith, 'The development of papal provisions in medieval Europe', *History Compass*, 13 (2015), 110–21. On the process of provision and the role of the prelate as executor, see Kerstin Hitzbleck, *Exekutoren: Die außerordentliche Kollatur von Benefizien im Pontifikat Johannes' XXII* (Tübingen, 2009) and Thomas W. Smith, 'Papal executors and the veracity of petitions from thirteenth-century England', *Revue d'histoire ecclésiastique*, 110 (2015), 662–83. On papal provision in thirteenth-century England, see now idem, 'The papacy, petitioners and benefices in thirteenth-century England' in Thomas W. Smith and Helen Killick (eds), *Petitions and strategies of persuasion in the Middle Ages: the English crown and the church, c.1200–c.1550* (Woodbridge, 2018), pp 164–84; Thomas W. Smith, 'The Italian connection reconsidered: papal provision in thirteenth-century England' in A.M. Spencer and Carl Watkins (eds) *Thirteenth Century England XVII* (Woodbridge, forthcoming). **2** See Baier, *Päpstliche Provisionen*, pp 1–15, 25–8. **3** See, for example, the interpretations in Christopher Harper-Bill, '"Above all these charity": the career of Walter Suffield, bishop of Norwich, 1244–57' in Philippa Hoskin,

the rise of papal provision in any European kingdom during the key period of growth in the thirteenth century means that there are many aspects of the operation and extent of papal provision that remain opaque or have been misunderstood.

One of the most significant uncharted areas is Ireland, and, specifically, Dublin, which bucked the apparent trend of expansive papal provision in the thirteenth century.[4] As such it represents a significant unexplained anomaly in the history of provision that goes some way to tempering the traditional narrative of papal provision as an unstoppable juggernaut. It is unclear what the importance of Ireland and Dublin was in the administration of papal provision in the Plantagenet dominions, how this intersection between the *ecclesia Hibernica* and its English and Roman counterparts functioned, and what its wider significance in high-medieval Insular ecclesiastical and political history was. Simply phrased, the question that this essay seeks to explore is: why were there so few instances of papal provision in thirteenth-century Dublin?

The large-scale influx of clergy from England to assume positions in Ireland's ecclesiastical hierarchy is an inescapable fact of Irish history after 1169, but to think exclusively in Insular terms is to risk misunderstanding the nature of the ecclesiastical politics of the thirteenth century. After the invention of papal provision in the twelfth century, and its rapid expansion in the first half of the thirteenth, competition for church benefices in Ireland and Britain no longer took place on a merely Insular basis: it became the focus of

Christopher Brooke and Barrie Dobson (eds), *The foundations of medieval English ecclesiastical history: studies presented to David Smith* (Woodbridge, 2005), pp 94–110, at p. 100; Christopher Harper-Bill, 'The diocese of Norwich and the Italian connection, 1198–1261' in John Mitchell (ed.), *England and the continent in the Middle Ages: studies in memory of Andrew Martindale* (Stamford, 2000), pp 75–89, at p. 87; Walter Ullmann, *A short history of the papacy in the Middle Ages* (London, 1972), pp 245–6; Bernard Guillemain, *La Cour pontificale d'Avignon (1309–1376): étude d'une société* (Paris, 1962), pp 104, 106; Hugh Mackenzie, 'The anti-foreign movement in England, 1231–1232' in C.H. Taylor (ed.), *Anniversary essays in mediaeval history by students of Charles Homer Haskins* (Boston MA, 1929), pp 183–203, at pp 186, 188, 189; Guillaume Mollat, *La collation des bénéfices ecclésiastiques sous les papes d'Avignon (1305–1378)* (Paris, 1921), pp 1–2, 321, 322. Others have criticized papal interference and encroachment, but on a more limited level: Agostino Paravicini Bagliani, *Il trono di Pietro: l'universalità del papato da Alessandro III a Bonifacio VIII* (Rome, 1996), pp 104–5; Pascal Montaubin, 'L'administration pontificale de la grâce au XIIIe siècle: l'exemple de la politique bénéficiale' in Hélène Millet (ed.), *Suppliques et requêtes: le gouvernement par la grâce en occident (XIIe–XVe siècle)* (Rome, 2003), pp 321–42, at p. 342. For an alternative view, see Barraclough, *Papal provisions*; and Smith, 'Development of papal provisions'.   4 There is a short overview of provision during the time of Avignon papacy, when the system was already juridically mature, in Urban Flanagan, 'Papal provision in Ireland, 1305–78' in James Hogan (ed.), *Historical studies III: papers read before the fourth Irish Conference of Historians* (London, 1961), pp 92–103. Flanagan's article is a valuable companion to the present essay and is very useful in providing an introduction to the later material, but it does not emphasize how unique

Irish, English, Italian and French clerics. This was a result of political developments that had a direct bearing on ecclesiastical life. In England, Wales and Ireland, the rise of papal provision coincided with King John's surrender of lordship over these kingdoms to the papacy in 1213.[5] After John's submission, the pope could exert influence not only as the head of the universal church but also as legal overlord. In England, the reign of Henry III also led to an influx of Poitevin and Savoyard favourites into the political arena who encouraged and supported even more candidates for church livings.[6]

These political developments changed the terms on which conflicts for ecclesiastical patronage were waged and led to increased provision of Italian and French clergy to church benefices in Britain and Ireland. Competition for benefices was now being played out on a truly international scale and the clergy had to fight off claims not only from their fellow countrymen but also Italian curialists and French favourites of the king.[7] The question is whether the struggle for benefices in Ireland evolved in the same way as that in England. King John's grant of 1213 had the same implications for Ireland and, like England, we would fully expect to trace the rapid rise of papal provision in the documentation regarding thirteenth-century Ireland.

The most sought-after quarry of benefice-hunters were the fattest stipends attached to cathedral chapters; it seems logical, therefore, to begin any exploration of papal provisions to Irish benefices in Dublin, where the focus, naturally enough, falls on the cathedral chapter. The city is famous for having two cathedrals: the church of Holy Trinity (Christ Church) and St Patrick's.[8] The peculiar circumstances in which there came to be two cathedrals within a stone's throw of each other in Dublin – and the rivalry that ensued – are treated masterfully in an article by Geoffrey Hand.[9] The key point of difference is that Holy Trinity had a monastic cathedral chapter, that is, its clergy lived as monks, and St Patrick's, which was founded later, in 1192, was a secular cathedral, that is, its clergy, or canons, did not withdraw themselves from the world, and performed a series of religious and administrative functions. The existence of monastic cathedrals was a peculiarity shared with England but not the rest of Europe, where secular chapters were the norm.[10] Churchmen 'on the make' were often secular clergy rather than monks and therefore sought appointment as canons to secular cathedrals – positions supported by benefices attached to their canonries called prebends. In comparison to benefices in parish churches, cathedral prebends were the most

Ireland was in the history of provision nor situate the material in a broader analytical framework.   **5** J.A. Watt, *The church and the two nations in medieval Ireland* (Cambridge, 1970), p. 84.   **6** Huw Ridgeway, 'King Henry III and the "aliens", 1236–1272' in P.R. Coss and S.D. Lloyd (eds), *Thirteenth Century England II* (Woodbridge, 1988), pp 81–92. **7** Smith, 'The Italian connection reconsidered'.   **8** On the two cathedrals, see Milne (ed.), *Christ Church*; and Crawford and Gillespie (eds), *St Patrick's*.   **9** G.J. Hand, 'The rivalry of the cathedral chapters in medieval Dublin', *JRSAI*, 92 (1962), 193–206.

sought-after type because they carried the largest stipends with the lightest pastoral loads.

As Margaret Murphy and Howard Clarke have separately observed, the foundation of St Patrick's as a secular cathedral was inextricably entwined with the Anglo-Norman conquest of Ireland from the 1170s onwards. The English king needed loyal, trained clergy who could carry out the mandate of the papal letter *Laudabiliter* to 'reform' the Irish church. Twelfth-century monks were thought to be not up to the task (and perhaps could not be trusted to elect royal candidates as archbishop to further the agenda of the English crown) and so a secular chapter composed of royal administrators was founded – a symbiotic relationship whereby the crown ensured its influence in Irish ecclesiastical life and its loyal servants received rich rewards.[11] As Hand wrote, St Patrick's was 'the largest and richest cathedral chapter of secular clergy in medieval Ireland' with some twenty or twenty-one prebends in the thirteenth century, as well as another two created from workarounds using the common store and the church of Donaghmore.[12]

Despite being the largest secular chapter in Ireland, the papal documentation presents a mixed picture of the wealth of the archdiocese of Dublin. On 29 January 1260, Pope Alexander IV granted Archbishop Fulk's petition that, since he (as archbishop) was a cathedral canon without a prebend, he might annex the prebend of Swords to his canonry and create a new prebend as a replacement, thus maintaining the same number of canons.[13] According to a valuation made in 1227, Swords was the second-most valuable benefice of St Patrick's, with a value of 100 marks (after the dean's prebend of Clondalkin, which was worth 120 marks).[14] The value of Swords appears to have remained fairly stable across the century, since the early fourteenth-century valuation listed it at 60 pounds (a mark being two-thirds of a pound).[15] For context, the next most valuable prebend was Lusk, worth 80 marks, and the majority of prebends brought in between 20 and 40 marks. As Hand

---

10 'Introduction' in Paul Dalton, Charles Insley and L.J. Wilkinson (eds), *Cathedrals, communities and conflict in the Anglo-Norman world* (Woodbridge, 2011), pp 1–26, at p. 2. 11 Margaret Murphy, 'Archbishops and Anglicisation: Dublin, 1181–1271' in James Kelly and Dáire Keogh (eds), *History of the Catholic diocese of Dublin* (Dublin, 2000), pp 72–91, at p. 84; Margaret Murphy, 'Balancing the concerns of church and state: the archbishops of Dublin, 1181–1228' in Terry Barry, Robin Frame and Katharine Simms (eds), *Colony and frontier in medieval Ireland: essays presented to J.F. Lydon* (London, 1995), pp 41–56; Howard Clarke, 'Cult, church and collegiate church before *c.*1220' in Crawford and Gillespie (eds), *St Patrick's*, pp 45–72, at pp 33–4. 12 Geoffrey Hand, 'The medieval chapter of St Patrick's Cathedral, Dublin: I. The early period (*c.*1219–*c.*1270)', *Repertorium Novum: Dublin Diocesan Historical Record*, 3 (1964), 229–48, at 229; Hand, 'Medieval chapter of St Patrick's', 234. 13 Charles Bourel de la Roncière et al. (eds), *Les Registres d'Alexandre IV*, 3 vols (Paris, 1895–1959), no. 3073; W.H. Bliss (ed.), *Calendar of entries in the papal registers relating to Great Britain and Ireland: papal letters, vol. I, AD 1198–1304* (London, 1893), p. 371. 14 *Reg. Alen*, pp 47–8; Hand, 'Medieval chapter of St Patrick's', 235. 15 *CDI*, v, p. 237.

observed, 'the Dublin deanery and Swords ... were surpassed only by the Salisbury deanery and one other prebend there'.[16]

Of the available prebends anywhere in the Insular world, therefore, Swords represented an enviable prize. This fact is not always obvious from the papal registers, which also record on 9 December 1289 that Pope Nicholas IV issued a document to Archbishop John of Dublin, on the petition of Otto de Grandson, allowing him to collect the first year's worth of fruits from all vacant benefices for three years, claiming that the income from his see had been decimated by war.[17] One should always treat petitioners' claims with a healthy dose of scepticism, especially where money is concerned, since these fleeting pleas of poverty are not representative of the normal value of the see.

If we hope to discover the status of Dublin's prebends in an international context, we need to compare them with the English cathedrals favoured by international pluralists. For the Irish church we have a set of valuations made in the early fourteenth century, and for England we have the slightly earlier, but closely contemporaneous, taxation of 1291–2.[18] Of course taxation figures need to be treated with care, since it was in the best interest of the clergy to underestimate the value of their benefices in order to pay less tax, but we can assume that the same forces of underestimation would have been at work in both surveys. The results are illuminating. The sum of the value of the deanery of Dublin was pegged at £316 17s. ½d.[19] Contrast this with the comparable figures available for the deanery of Canterbury, with a total value of £139,[20] the deanery of Rochester, valued at £443 13s. 4d.,[21] and that of St Paul's, London, worth £117 5s. 3d.,[22] and we see that Dublin was by no means impoverished: 'Alone among its sister-chapters', Hand writes, St Patrick's 'could stand comparison with the secular cathedral chapters of England'.[23] Indeed, with such a high value, Dublin must have been a very attractive proposition on the international benefice market.

It comes as a great surprise therefore, that, for the popes and their Italian curialists, the prebends of Dublin's two cathedrals, unlike their counterparts on the other side of the Irish Sea, represented an Insular hunting ground less commonly poached. We have surprisingly few records for the provision of

---

16 Hand, 'Medieval chapter of St Patrick's', 235.   17 Ernest Langlois (ed.), *Les Registres de Nicolas IV*, 2 vols (Paris, 1887–93), no. 1862; Bliss (ed.), *Calendar of entries in the papal registers*, p. 508.   18 *CDI*, v, pp 202–37, 237–323, and ix–xxi for the long list of corrigenda; see Geoffrey Hand, 'The dating of the early fourteenth-century ecclesiastical valuations of Ireland', *Irish Theological Quarterly*, 24 (1957), 271–4. The English *Taxatio* of 1291–2 can be consulted through the online database, at www.dhi.ac.uk/taxatio, accessed 4 July 2019. See J.H. Denton, 'The valuation of the ecclesiastical benefices of England and Wales in 1291–2', *Historical Research*, 66 (1993), 231–50.   19 *CDI*, v, p. 238.   20 *Taxatio*, www.dhi.ac.uk/taxatio/search?form=deanery&deanery=CA.CA.CA, accessed 17 May 2018.   21 Ibid., www.dhi.ac.uk/taxatio/search?form=deanery&deanery=RO.RO.RO, accessed 17 May 2018.   22 Ibid., www.dhi.ac.uk/taxatio/search?form=deanery&deanery=LO.LO.SP, accessed 17 May 2018.   23 Hand, 'Medieval chapter of St Patrick's', 229.

Italians to Dublin prebends until the middle years of the thirteenth century, when the system was already firmly established, utilized, and criticized on the other island. The first recorded papal provision mandate for Dublin is dated 23 August 1243.[24] The document, issued by Pope Innocent IV to Andrew de Mevanea (Bevagna), a papal subdeacon and clerk of Ottobon, cardinal-deacon of St Nicholas in Carcere – who already held the rectory of Sibson in Lincoln diocese – granted him a canonry in St Patrick's, Dublin, together with one in St Galeric, Cambrai, and the wardenship of St Angelo de Mevania in the diocese of Spoleto in Italy.

We must, of course, bear in mind that the papacy practised only selective registration of its documents, and hence the registers are not a complete record of papal correspondence.[25] Still, comparison with the surviving documentation for England paints a very different picture. Even accounting for the same selective registration practice of the papal chancery, we possess dozens of documents granting English benefices to papal kinsmen in the first quarter of the thirteenth century. These begin with a slow trickle of nine mandates during the eighteen years of Innocent III's pontificate (1198–1216) and increase exponentially under Honorius III to something approaching a torrent of twenty-three during his shorter reign of nearly eleven years (1216–27).[26] By the pontificate of Innocent IV (1243–54), these appointments to English benefices had become a flood. Therefore the utilization of provision to induct papal candidates in the kingdom of England was much more common than can be seen as regards the benefices of Dublin. And this is a surprise given that Dublin was under the same Plantagenet dominion as England, and the same papal overlordship following King John's grant of both England and Ireland to the papacy in 1213, and it provides our first indication that practice in Dublin stands out as distinct.

Though provision did not leave its mark on Dublin during the first half of the thirteenth century, the operation of the system, once it arrived in Ireland, was less tentative and displayed all the hallmarks of its development over the preceding decades in other European dioceses. The provision mandate for Andrew de Mevanea was followed by another letter, despatched by Innocent IV on 16 March 1249 to the archbishop and archdeacon of Cashel, which requested that they receive the papal nuncio Master John de Frosinone as a canon of Dublin, provided that he had not already been appointed to a benefice there via papal letter.[27] It is not known which prebend John acquired,

24 Élie Berger (ed.), *Les Registres d'Innocent IV*, 4 vols (Paris, 1884–1911), no. 82; Bliss (ed.), *Calendar of entries in the papal registers*, p. 199.   **25** On selective papal registration, see Harry Bresslau, *Handbuch der Urkundenlehre für Deutschland und Italien*, 2 vols (2nd ed. Leipzig, 1912–31), i, p. 121; Paul Rabikauskas, *Diplomatica pontificia* (6th ed. Rome, 1998), p. 82.   **26** For the provision documents issued by Innocent III, see Bliss (ed.), *Calendar of entries in the papal registers*, pp 4, 11, 16, 21, 22, 27, 36, 38. For those of Honorius III, see pp 47, 48, 49, 52, 56–7, 58, 59, 61, 68, 71, 73, 88, 89, 92, 106, 111, 114, 115, 116.   **27** Berger

but we know that he became successfully ensconced in the Church of Ireland because papal curialists then used him as their 'inside man' to facilitate the provision of further kinsmen.[28] On 3 February 1252, Innocent issued a mandate to John requesting that he provide another John, called *Rubeus*, a canon of Ferentino and son of one Rammanus, a knight of Ferentino, to a benefice in Ireland.[29] Presumably as a reward for this favour and to ensure that he carried out his duty, six days later the pope received John de Frosinone as a member of his papal chapel.[30] Almost exactly two years later, on 10 February 1254, Innocent called upon his man in Dublin again, this time issuing him with a mandate, at the request of Master Boethius, papal chamberlain, to provide the latter's nephew, Guy, a papal subdeacon and chaplain, to a cathedral prebend or failing that some other benefice in Ireland.[31]

These were typical strategies employed by pontiffs looking to advance their kinsmen and courtiers, and one could point to many cases from England of exactly the same thing. Once installed, the popes called upon such agents not only to facilitate the provision of other Italian clergy, but also to enforce unpopular legislation and generally act as representatives and informants. So this episode is entirely in keeping with the development of papal provision in England. What is so peculiar though is that, in stark contrast to the other island, this flurry of provision of Italians to Dublin benefices arrived so late and was so short-lived. Archbishop Alen's register – a collection of documents compiled much later in the sixteenth century, but which incorporates otherwise-lost material from our period – preserves grants made in 1245 and 1253 by Popes Innocent IV and Alexander IV, respectively, to the archbishop of Dublin protecting archiepiscopal collation rights and limiting the validity of papal provision documents.[32] This could suggest that more provision mandates arrived during this time of which no traces remain. Such petitions from prelates for the limitation of provision were quite common in England from the middle of the thirteenth century when the impact of the system was beginning to bite.[33] In the case of Dublin they follow quickly on from the provisions of Andrew de Mevanea and John de Frosinone in 1243 and 1252 and perhaps provide witness to concern in Dublin that more papal mandates would follow. Any such anxiety appears to have been unfounded, however: according to the evidence of the papal registers, it was only under Innocent IV that the papacy made a concerted effort to support its curialists using the churches of Dublin. After his pontificate, the papal documentation on this matter dries up.

(ed.), *Les Registres d'Innocent IV*, no. 4417; Bliss (ed.), *Calendar of entries in the papal registers*, p. 253.   **28** John is listed as a canon without a known prebend in H.J. Lawlor (ed.), *The fasti of St Patrick's, Dublin* (Dundalk, 1930), p. 191.   **29** Berger (ed.), *Les Registres d'Innocent IV*, no. 5809; Bliss (ed.), *Calendar of entries in the papal registers*, p. 278. **30** Berger (ed.), *Les Registres d'Innocent IV*, no. 5789.   **31** Berger (ed.), *Les Registres d'Innocent IV*, no. 7254; Bliss (ed.), *Calendar of entries in the papal registers*, p. 295.   **32** *Reg. Alen*, pp 70, 74–5.   **33** See Smith, 'The Italian connection reconsidered'.

Turning to other sources, we can glean a few more nuggets of information. A search in the *fasti* of St Patrick's for Italian clergy appointed through such means reveals no Italians among the six (or seven – the material is unclear) thirteenth-century deans,[34] none among the nine precentors,[35] apparently none among the nine chancellors (for two we only have initials),[36] none among the six treasurers,[37] and none among the eight archdeacons.[38] Added to this, there are sixty known prebendaries of St Patrick's. A sift of the evidence for these positions only turns up the aforementioned Andrew de Mevanea, who was awarded possession of the prebend of Kilmesantan and Kilbride after his provision to a canonry.[39] There are also forty-four canons listed without known prebends, and among their number we find only one, our other acquaintance, the papacy's fixer in Ireland, John de Frosinone.[40] Therefore, from a total of 142 (or 143) benefice-holders in St Patrick's, we can only positively identify two Italians. What we do find, however, at the end of our period are a number of canons apparently of French origin, probably installed through royal influence: Thomas de Montpellier as a possible occupant of Clonmethan in the late thirteenth century;[41] John de St Omer as the holder of Howth from 1275;[42] one Hugh de Vienne in possession of Monmohenock from 1276;[43] Iter Bochard or de Angoulême, who held Rathmichael from 1274 and Swords from 1277;[44] Louis de Savoy in possession of Tipper from 1277;[45] and Amadeus de Savoy who appears as a canon without a known prebend in 1298.[46]

Such few exceptions apart, there is a clear dominance of English clergy and royal servants. This material tallies with the lack of evidence for Italian providees in the papal registers and suggests that it is not a loss of documentation skewing our perception of the situation. As noted, it is striking that the actions of Innocent IV were so limited in comparison to his extensive use of provision in England (which aroused hostility and concerted complaints at the Council of Lyons), and that his hard-won provision of a handful of kinsmen did not set a precedent for his successors. One cannot point to another period of such intervention in the administration of Dublin prebends for the rest of the century. To place these examples in a longer temporal context, the number of recorded thirteenth-century provisions is much lower than those noted by Urban Flanagan, who turned up four instances of papal provisions to dignities and twenty appointments to canonries for the whole of Ireland between 1305 and 1378, finding most of his examples in Dublin.[47] Overall, then, the evidence presented here renders thirteenth-century Dublin a peculiarity of considerable significance, since, aside from this brief flurry of papal provisions in the middle of the century, the city bucks the trend of

---

34 Lawlor (ed.), *Fasti of St Patrick's*, pp 39–40.   **35** Ibid., pp 53–4.   **36** Ibid., pp 60–1. **37** Ibid., pp 67–8.   **38** Ibid., pp 75–7.   **39** Ibid., p. 123.   **40** Ibid., p. 191.   **41** Ibid., p. 99. **42** Ibid., p. 113.   **43** Ibid., p. 133.   **44** Ibid., pp 143, 155–6.   **45** Ibid., p. 168.   **46** Ibid., p. 192.   **47** Flanagan, 'Papal provision in Ireland', 100–1.

extensive and expansive papal provision of Italian curialists in England and elsewhere in Europe, and even elsewhere in Ireland.

Connected to this, and perhaps even more surprising is the fact that there is no correspondence preserved in the thirteenth-century papal registers relating to litigation and conflict over the possession of benefices in Dublin as a result of papal provision. Contrast this with England, where litigation was wielded as the main weapon in hundreds of recorded cases, creating a voluminous mass of documentation in the papal registers to do with appointing judges, hearing cases and pronouncing decisions.[48] One explanation might be that the extra distance separating Dublin and Rome curtailed the number of appeals to the curia. But we have a very large number of papal letters despatched to Ireland that testify to lively and entrenched contact between Ireland and Rome.[49]

More specifically, we can also point to a number of occasions when Dublin clergy transacted business at the papacy regarding benefices. On 15 October 1238, Archbishop Luke of Dublin successfully petitioned Pope Gregory IX for a licence to grant dispensations to two of his clerks so that they might hold two benefices each.[50] One of these clergymen appears to have been the archdeacon of Dublin, Master Richard de Garde, because a little less than a year later, on 1 September 1239, Gregory IX weighed in on a case involving Master Richard and his right of dispensation.[51] Through the archbishop of Dublin's papal licence, Richard had acquired a dispensation to hold a second benefice in Tonbridge, in the diocese of Rochester in England. The Hospitallers in England challenged Richard over possession of this benefice, but in his document of September 1239, Gregory quashed their objection. In the 1240s and 1250s, Innocent IV and Alexander IV both accepted similar petitions from the archbishop of Dublin and his canons granting them further dispensations and confirming pluralities of benefices. On 13 December 1244, Innocent permitted Luke to award another two dispensations to his clerks so that they might take possession of another benefice each.[52] Just over a decade later, on 30 September 1255, Alexander IV issued a letter to Master Geoffrey, precentor of Ferns Cathedral, which confirmed a dispensation to hold an additional benefice granted to him by the archbishop.[53] The following year, on 3 August 1256, Pope

---

48 See Smith, 'Papacy, petitioners and benefices', for a sample of such cases and the strategies employed by clerics in their efforts to secure and retain benefices.   49 Ample witness is supplied by the 467 extant papal documents concerning Ireland – themselves only a fraction of the total number of papal letters originally despatched – issued between 1198 and 1261: M.P. Sheehy (ed.), *Pontificia Hibernica: medieval papal chancery documents concerning Ireland, 640–1261*, 2 vols (Dublin, 1962), nos 32–497 (including no. 142a in the count).   50 Lucien Auvray (ed.), *Les Registres de Grégoire IX*, 3 vols (Paris, 1890–1910), no. 4579; Bliss (ed.), *Calendar of entries in the papal registers*, p. 177.   51 Auvray (ed.), *Les Registres de Grégoire IX*, no. 4923; Bliss (ed.), *Calendar of entries in the papal registers*, p. 183. 52 Berger (ed.), *Les Registres d'Innocent IV*, no. 818; Bliss (ed.), *Calendar of entries in the papal registers*, p. 210.   53 Bourel de la Roncière et al. (eds), *Les Registres d'Alexandre IV*, no. 994; Bliss (ed.), *Calendar of entries in the papal registers*, p. 325.

Alexander despatched a document to Master William de Cornerio, a canon of Dublin, permitting him to receive two benefices in addition to the two churches he held in Meath diocese.[54] A month later, on 6 September 1256, Alexander also confirmed a dispensation issued to the papal chaplain and canon of St Patrick's, Dublin, Master William de Cornet (apparently distinct from William de Cornerio), on account of the irregularity of his birth, thus allowing him to retain his canonry in Dublin.[55]

The point of this string of examples is that it proves that the clerics of Dublin were making use of the papal court as was normal throughout Europe. Such cases, especially that of Richard de Garde, where we can trace the archbishop's petition and the successful recipient, demonstrate that the register material for papal interaction with the Irish church is not completely deficient. This means that we can probably say with some confidence that the absence of evidence regarding papal provision and conflict is indeed evidence of absence. The most striking point about the case of Richard de Garde is that clergy in possession of Irish and English benefices were using the papal justice system to defend their English church possessions, but apparently not those in Dublin. This suggests that the very few papal documents issued regarding papal provision to benefices in Dublin reflect a difference in practice rather than source survival when compared with its English neighbours. We may need to speak in terms of two very different cultures of ecclesiastical politics when considering the place of Dublin in the wider context of the Plantagenet dominions.

What could be the reason for the existence of the very different ecclesiastical-political cultures in Dublin and England? The answer, almost certainly, is English political power in Dublin. As a number of scholars have pointed out, since the Anglo-Norman conquest of Ireland in the 1170s, the English crown had exerted great leverage over the benefices of Dublin through the appointment of a string of royal administrators as archbishop.[56] The archbishops of Dublin were forced to play a balancing act between their sacred and secular roles, made even more difficult, Margaret Murphy writes, by the fact that 'they were perceived by the crown to be its prime representatives in a newly-conquered land' and that 'the seat of their ecclesiastical office was also the power-centre of colonial government'.[57]

The late thirteenth- and early fourteenth-century papal registers, for instance, record a number of dispensations issued to royal clerks at the request of Edward I and Queen Eleanor, allowing these clerics to hold a string of

---

54 Bourel de la Ronciére et al. (eds), *Les Registres d'Alexandre IV*, no. 1440; Bliss (ed.), *Calendar of entries in the papal registers*, p. 333.   55 Bourel de la Ronciére et al. (eds), *Les Registres d'Alexandre IV*, no. 1465; Bliss (ed.), *Calendar of entries in the papal registers*, p. 334. 56 Murphy, 'Archbishops and Anglicisation'; Murphy, 'Balancing the concerns of church and state'.   57 Murphy, 'Balancing the concerns of church and state', p. 42.

benefices and cathedral prebends throughout England and in Dublin. To take but a pair of examples, on 2 October 1295, Pope Boniface VIII issued a dispensation, on the petition of Edward I, for Walter de Langton allowing him to reap the income from a quite incredible number of parish churches, along with prebends in the cathedrals of York, London, Lichfield, Wells, Dublin, and Chichester.[58] Similarly, on 7 July 1300, Boniface granted a dispensation, this time on the petition of Queen Eleanor, to her nephew, Master James, called 'de Yspania', allowing him to retain two parish churches along with the deanery of Pontefract Castle and prebends in the cathedrals of London, Salisbury, Lichfield, Wells, Lincoln, Dublin and Chester.[59]

We can also point to one occasion where the crown used the papacy's power of collation to further a royal candidate. In a letter issued by Nicholas IV on 18 July 1290, Queen Eleanor acquired a papal provision mandate, addressed to the bishop of London and the dean of Bayeux, to install one of her clerks in a canonry and prebend in Dublin.[60] That there is only a single instance of the crown's use of papal provision to install its clerks in Dublin benefices is peculiar, since by the end of the thirteenth century the king and queen of England were regularly using papal provision to appoint their followers to church stipends in England.[61] Royal influence in Dublin appears to have been so strong, perhaps unassailable, that the crown did not need to turn to the papacy to install its clerks in Dublin's benefices, as it did in England, but could rely almost exclusively on its own powers of patronage, knowing that it would not be challenged.

This leads us on to an important question that gathers a number of strands of this essay together. If papal provision was such a powerful weapon in the arsenal of the medieval cleric on the make elsewhere in Europe, if the benefices of Dublin were dominated by English clergy, and if the ecclesiastics of Dublin were familiar with the use of the papal curia in the search for justice and grace, why did native Irish clergy not apply for papal provision mandates so as to circumvent English royal power? An obvious answer does not present itself. Probably the Anglicization of the clergy of Dublin was so effective that it stifled any possibility of Irish resistance through papal documents.[62] But as I have argued elsewhere regarding England, we should be wary of framing debate on the struggle for benefices in the simple terms of one nationality pitted against another.[63] In England, opposition to papal providees does not seem to have arisen purely from the fact that many hailed from Italy: whether

58 Georges Digard et al. (eds), *Les Registres des Boniface VIII*, 4 vols (Paris, 1884–1939), no. 415; Bliss (ed.), *Calendar of entries in the papal registers*, p. 559.   59 Digard et al. (eds), *Les Registres des Boniface VIII*, no. 3691; Bliss (ed.), *Calendar of entries in the papal registers*, p. 589.   60 Langlois (ed.), *Les Registres de Nicolas IV*, no. 2949; Bliss (ed.), *Calendar of entries in the papal registers*, p. 515.   61 Smith, 'Papacy, petitioners and benefices', pp 168–9.   62 See Watt, *The church and the two nations*, pp 35–84.   63 Smith, 'The Italian connection

providees were Italian, French, or English appears to have mattered less than the fact that they embodied a threat to, and loss of, traditional patronage powers and rights of collation, and there was just as much resistance to English providees as to their Italian counterparts.

Although the situation in Dublin appears to be a simple case of English domination of cathedral prebends by virtue of royal influence over the foundation, we have to reimagine the struggle for benefices in broader European terms. As we have just seen above, Dublin prebends often made up impressive webs of pluralism, mostly concentrated in England, which spanned the Irish Sea with a single thread connecting them to Dublin. Another example of the international aspect of Dublin's prebends is furnished by one Master Thomasius. Thomasius was a canon of Dublin and the son of the Irish nobleman 'Maurice Gerold'.[64] On 4 April 1257, Alexander IV appointed Thomasius as a papal chaplain.[65] One can find a large number of such grants in the papal registers. What makes this letter special is that although Thomasius was a canon of Dublin he was resident in Orléans in France. This document thus exposes an aspect of Dublin's international connections that is often far from obvious. Although expatriates such as Thomasius appear to have been something of a rarity judging by evidence in the papal registers, it illustrates that the Dublin cathedrals did have international canons and connections. Taken with the examples of the Italian canons of Dublin examined earlier, Thomasius helps to situate the benefice market of Dublin in its broader European context, albeit not on the same scale as the English cathedrals.

We might also partly reconcile the evidence for international connections with the reality that the holders of benefices in Dublin were predominantly English clerics by looking abroad to wider European developments. The invention of papal provision changed the face of the struggle for benefices across Europe by intensifying rivalry for benefices. From the early thirteenth century, the English crown, which presided over territories in the Insular world and France, was not only competing against prelates and lay patrons to provide its clerks with a living, but also had to adapt to deal with the new international competition from the papacy. This probably exacerbated the extent to which the English crown perceived of and exploited Dublin as a secure source of stipends with little competition from Italy. Could this have created a divergent culture of competition for benefices, established through royal influence and the Anglicization of Dublin's cathedral chapters, where English and Irish clergy did not submit (or were even discouraged from submitting) supplications for

reconsidered'.   **64** Thomasius is listed as a canon without a known prebend, in Lawlor (ed.), *Fasti of St Patrick's*, p. 191. His father may have been Maurice fitz Gerald, 2nd baron of Offaly; as the latter had another son Thomas (father of John fitz Thomas, 1st earl of Kildare), Thomasius may have been illegitimate (Prof. Seán Duffy, pers. comm.). **65** Bourel de la Roncière et al. (eds), *Les Registres d'Alexandre IV*, no. 1871; Bliss (ed.), *Calendar of entries in the papal registers*, p. 345.

papal provision, and where papal provision mandates for Italians were resisted, so as to preserve the patronage powers of the English crown as the last safe haven from papal influence? Coupled with the royal political and ecclesiastical agenda of reform and control in Ireland, it represents an attractive explanation.

What conclusions can we draw, then, on the nature of papal provision in thirteenth-century Dublin, and can we begin to answer the question: why were there so few papal provisions in thirteenth-century Dublin? In charting the rise of papal provision in thirteenth-century Europe, Dublin is one of the most significant anomalies because it did not witness the same expansion of the system of provision that was common elsewhere in Europe. Indeed, it is perhaps ill-advised to speak in terms of a system of provision in Ireland at all, since Dublin is only recorded to have experienced a fleeting brush with the practice in the middle years of the century during the pontificate of Innocent IV, when papal provision in England reached new heights and engendered fierce opposition. Some spillover to Ireland, from one Plantagenet dominion to another, during this time was perhaps unavoidable. The installation of only a small handful of Italian providees, however, meant that they never established a community or gained a strong foothold as they did in England: as the records from England show, it was much easier to provide papal kinsmen to foreign churches when there were fellow countrymen present who could facilitate the process.[66]

So it is clear that papal provision did not take off in Dublin as it did on the other island. But why was provision such a rarity in Dublin when it grew exponentially in England, other parts of Ireland, and other European kingdoms? Why were there not non-resident Italian pluralists? Why did Irish and English clergy not acquire provision mandates when it was extremely popular among ambitious clergy in England? We can say with some confidence that there existed an alternative ecclesiastico-political culture in Dublin that mitigated against the use of papal grace. The motivation behind it can be sought in the Anglo-Norman invasion, which forever wrought asunder the political and ecclesiastical landscape of Ireland. The foundation of St Patrick's in 1192 established royal influence in Dublin through the appointment and reward of royal servants and the attempt to ensure that royal favourites were elected as archbishop. The aim of all this was to fulfil the king's agenda of ecclesiastical 'reform' and territorial conquest in Ireland. It was, to all extents and purposes, a 'closed shop'. It seems possible that the English secular and ecclesiastical powers deliberately fostered an environment hostile to the use of papal provision so as to preserve this irreplaceable pool of patronage and influence, almost untouched by the international competition from Italian curialists that was chipping away at their influence in England.

66 Smith, 'Papacy, petitioners and benefices', p. 171.

Writing about the late twelfth and early thirteenth centuries, J.A. Watt stated that there was a consistency in the papacy's attitude towards the crown's intervention in Ireland, which acknowledged 'the validity and reality of the king of England's lordship in Ireland'.[67] In the face of English royal dominance, and the tradition of papal acceptance and support of this political reality, it should perhaps be considered something of a success for the papacy that it managed to install any of its curialists at all. It is clear that Dublin represents an important chapter in the history of papal provision because it demonstrates that the new system of collation did not revolutionize ecclesiastical collation evenly throughout the West and that determined royal opposition in Dublin neutered the papacy's power to provide. In writing a new history of the rise of papal provision in thirteenth-century Europe, we must weigh carefully the geopolitical structures that permitted, fostered, or restricted its expansion, with the case of Dublin firmly in mind.

67 Watt, *The church and the two nations*, p. 84.

'The Pale at prayer': lived religious experience in Anglo-Norman Dublin's two cathedrals

JOHN WILLIAM SULLIVAN

In the study of medieval cathedrals, scholars can forget, as Alan Fletcher notes, that the buildings' primary purpose was to facilitate the worship of God.[1] Dublin's unusual arrangement of having two cathedrals within a ten-minute walk of each other inevitably, and justifiably, provokes discussion on issues of jurisdiction and ecclesiastical authority. Unfortunately, this often sidelines the devotional element of cathedral studies; the comparative element, too, frequently goes unexplored. Viewed in isolation, one can get the impression that Christ Church is where Dublin city prayed, and St Patrick's is where Dublin Castle prayed. This assessment is oversimplified at best, and requires further elaboration. This essay, therefore, proposes to modify this idea, and will comparatively analyse the lived religious experience of both cathedrals. Dublin city prayed at Christ Church, but worshippers ranged from Anglo-Norman merchant plutocrats to poor Irish pilgrims; Dublin Castle prayed at St Patrick's and the cathedral existed primarily as a colonial model, but the devotional life there was rich in its own right. Examined in this way, Dublin's two-cathedral dynamic shows a remarkable diversity of lived religious experience for a city of its size.

This essay will begin with a brief historiographical introduction and some context on the cathedrals' communities. Afterwards, it will examine, in order, an architectural schematic of Christ Church, St Patrick's devotion to Sarum and its colonial mission, Christ Church as a site of extensive lay patronage and pilgrimage, and finally St Patrick's Lady Chapel and its documentation. This combined analysis will form an overview of lived religious experience in each cathedral, and will demonstrate how each cathedral represented a distinct version of 'the Pale at prayer', to borrow Raymond Gillespie's phrase.[2]

A historiographical analysis of the lived religious experience of medieval Dublin's two cathedrals is essentially a commentary on the work of Alan Fletcher. He wrote the liturgical portions of both recent definitive histories of the cathedrals, and it is not an exaggeration to say that he is the foremost expert on the liturgical life of Christ Church and St Patrick's. Methodologically, his approach to liturgical studies with respect to St Patrick's is especially

---

1 Alan Fletcher, 'Liturgy in the late medieval cathedral priory' in Milne (ed.), *Christ Church*, pp 129–39, at p. 129. 2 Raymond Gillespie, 'Reform and decay, 1500–1598' in Crawford and Gillespie (eds), *St Patrick's*, pp 151–74, at p. 152.

significant. He advocates that music, liturgy, and architecture be understood holistically in order to prioritize a more complete understanding of cathedral life over narrower and more regimented analyses.[3] Also significant is the work of Geoffrey Hand, one of the few scholars to discuss the cathedrals *comparatively* as well as the only one to publish verbatim and unabridged samples of the Dublin Troper. A combination of these two authors' approaches reveals yet more insights on the cathedrals: Fletcher's holistic approach, coupled with Hand's comparative approach, provides a near complete window into what can usefully be termed 'lived religious experience' within medieval Dublin's two cathedrals. The subjects primarily examined here will be liturgy and its facilitation through architecture, relics, pilgrimage, chapels, bequests, and confraternities. With this methodology and prior historiography in mind, it is sensible to begin with some context on the communities of each cathedral.

Christ Church was within Dublin's walls, and St Patrick's was outside of them; this simple fact symbolizes the kind of communities that each cathedral housed, and by extension the lived religious experiences contained therein. Broadly speaking, Christ Church was the cathedral of the municipal government;[4] St Patrick's was the cathedral of the English ecclesiastical regime.[5] Christ Church held significantly more land in Co. Dublin, but St Patrick's was by a considerable margin the wealthiest cathedral in all of Ireland.[6] Both cathedrals had strong ties to the state. The Irish parliament frequently met in Christ Church, it was where Richard II secured the submission of prominent Irish lords during his abortive expedition to the country in 1394–5, and the pretender Lambert Simnel was famously crowned in the cathedral in 1487.[7] However, St Patrick's was in many respects a nexus of English control in Ireland, and – as will be examined later – the English crown held it in such high esteem that, when resident in Ireland in the early 1360s, Edward III's son Lionel of Antwerp worshipped there. Overall, Christ Church was the cathedral of guilds and mayors, and St Patrick's was the cathedral of high clerics and colonial administrators.

Just as important as the people who prayed in the cathedrals, however, were the spaces in which they prayed. Although architecture and liturgy are certainly related subjects in medieval cathedral studies, in the case of medieval Dublin they are inseparable. Of the two cathedrals, the architectural history of Christ Church is the more complex. Its several wildly controversial restorations, particularly in the nineteenth century, prompt Roger Stalley to contend that the medieval cathedral 'would have been barely recognizable as the building we

3 Alan Fletcher, 'Liturgy and music in the medieval cathedral' in Crawford and Gillespie (eds), *St Patrick's*, pp 120–48, at p. 120.   4 Gillespie, 'Reform and decay', p. 152. 5 Howard Clarke, 'External influences and relations, *c.*1220 to *c.*1500' in Crawford and Gillespie (eds), *St Patrick's*, pp 73–95, at pp 85–6.   6 Gillespie, 'Reform and decay', pp 152, 156.   7 James Lydon, 'Christ Church in the later medieval Irish world, 1300–1500' in Milne (ed.), *Christ Church*, pp 75–94, at p. 85.

know today'.[8] Even during the medieval period, Christ Church faced frequent change and innovation. Immediately preceding and following the Anglo-Norman conquest of Dublin in 1170, Christ Church was a cramped and liturgically cumbersome space; it would end the Middle Ages as a dynamic church, filled with smaller devotional areas, if still not particularly spacious.[9] These chapels will be discussed in greater detail later on, but it suffices to say for now that Christ Church was a better space for things like private worship and veneration of relics. Christ Church did carry over some aspects of its pre-Anglo-Norman design, though not many; reflecting Dublin's new inhabitants, post-conquest Christ Church was a south-western English building constructed by Bristolian architects using Cornish stone.[10] St Patrick's, however, was a far more direct example of an English religious building; it was in fact a carbon copy of one.

St Patrick's Cathedral was a nearly exact schematic replica of Old Sarum Cathedral (seat of the bishop of Salisbury); this facilitated the purest form of Sarum Rite, and essentially made St Patrick's an English cathedral on Irish soil. Liturgical manuscript studies show that Sarum use, a variant of the Latin Rite that originated in Sarum (modern Salisbury) and eventually became the ubiquitous English liturgical rite, was the normal rite found in those parts of Ireland that would become part of the Pale.[11] St Patrick's was crucial to its introduction to Ireland. That cathedral architects took design inspirations from each other was of course not unique to the situation of St Patrick's and Old Sarum; what distinguishes this particular arrangement was the extent of this inspiration. Michael O'Neill's overlay of St Patrick's and Old Sarum demonstrates that the dimensions of both cathedrals were essentially identical.[12] St Patrick's most prominent novelty, its tower, even seems to be a compensation for the fact that it lacked Sarum's westwork (a towering west-facing entrance section). Presumably St Patrick's might have copied even this were it not for the fact of the river Poddle making any further construction in that direction impossible;[13] hence, it was only logical to have its imposing westwork-substitute to the side. Devotion to Sarum was not unique to St Patrick's, as Christ Church also used Sarum Rite; however, Christ Church's organizational structure remained influenced by Irish custom. Lorcán Ua Tuathail (St Laurence O'Toole), archbishop of Dublin during the conquest, staffed Christ Church with Augustinian canons in an effort to use reformed Continental monasticism to remodel the monastic ways that had been so

---

8 Roger Stalley 'The architecture of the cathedral and priory buildings, 1250–1530' in Milne (ed.), *Christ Church Cathedral* (2000), pp 95–128, at p. 103.   9 Ibid., pp 95, 103. 10 Christine Casey, *Dublin: the city within the Grand and Royal Canals and the Circular Road with the Phoenix Park* (New Haven and London, 2005), pp 318–19.   11 William Hawkes, 'The liturgy in Dublin, 1200–1500: manuscript sources', *Reportorium Novum*, 2 (1958), 33–67, at 33.   12 Michael O'Neill, 'The architectural history of the medieval cathedral' in Crawford and Gillespie (eds), *St Patrick's*, pp 96–119, at p. 102.   13 Ibid., p. 101.

ubiquitous in early Irish Christianity.[14] In England, however, secular cathedrals were increasing in popularity;[15] as such, St Patrick's establishment as a secular collegiate church was no accident. In examining the documents of the cathedral's establishment, as well as documents concerning its connection to Sarum, St Patrick's status as a colonial ecclesiastical template becomes clear.

St Patrick's role as a colonial model for English spirituality is evident through analysis of the *Dignitas Decani*. This work consists of a collection of charters and other documents that range from the establishment of the collegiate church soon after the Anglo-Norman conquest through to the mid-sixteenth century. The *Dignitas Decani*'s first document is the charter of Archbishop John Cumin (1181–1212) establishing the cathedral. Archbishop John, believing Ireland to be a benighted place relative to the rest of Europe, announces the establishment of a collegiate church in order 'to provide for the simplicity of the Irish race'.[16] The charter of Archbishop Henry of London (1212–28) concerning the cathedral's governance continues this theme. He declares that the Irish church was, before the invasion, 'unrefined' and of 'lesser cultivation in sacred customs'.[17] The priests trained by this collegiate church are therefore to go out into Ireland and convert the Irish people to English religious custom; what better place to train such clerics, surely, than a replica of the cathedral that created the predominant English rite? Indeed, a late thirteenth-century item of correspondence between the two cathedrals survives, further demonstrating St Patrick's devotion to Sarum, again utilizing colonial language. 'We are determined', writes the chapter of St Patrick's, 'to regulate and run honourably our church … in a land waste, as it were, and hostile, according to your health-giving and approved statutes'.[18] This connection between liturgy and authority also implicitly appears in a 1216 bull by Pope Innocent III, in which the pope specifies the possessions of the cathedral alongside an injunction to use Sarum Rite.[19] Architectural evidence, too, suggests that St Patrick's served as a model for other churches in surrounding regions. A separate study by O'Neill has shown that the churches with a tithing relationship to St Patrick's emulated its architectural style, and that the cathedral was 'at the head of one stream of architectural influence in the Pale'.[20] Therefore, it is clear that St Patrick's was crucial in the establishment of English liturgical custom in Dublin as well as in the expansion of an

---

14 Geoffrey Hand, 'The rivalry of the cathedral chapters in medieval Dublin', *JRSAI*, 92:2 (1962), 193–206, at 194; see Bhreathnach in this volume, above.   **15** Hand, 'The rivalry of the cathedral chapters', p. 195.   **16** *The 'Dignitas Decani' of St Patrick's Cathedral Dublin*, ed. Newport White (Dublin, 1957), p. 1 (*simplicati gentis Hibernie providere*); the translation is that of the present writer.   **17** *Dignitas Decani*, p. 3 (*Hibernicana ecclesia rudis olim et in sacris institutionibus minus erudite*).   **18** Fletcher, 'Liturgy and music' in Crawford and Gillespie (eds), *St Patrick's*, p. 124.   **19** *Dignitas Decani*, p. 41.   **20** Michael O'Neill, 'St Patrick's Cathedral, Dublin, and its prebendal churches: gothic architectural relationships' in Seán Duffy (ed.), *Medieval Dublin V* (Dublin, 2004), 243–76, at p. 275.

English foothold in Ireland more broadly. Yet, for all that, Christ Church eclipsed St Patrick's in popular devotional importance.

Christ Church Cathedral was indisputably a more significant site for popular devotion than St Patrick's, and its rich devotional record deserves comment in some detail. The supreme source for devotional life at Christ Church is TCD MS 576. It contains an early sixteenth-century relic list prefacing the necrology, or Book of Obits, of the cathedral; quite literally stitched together with it is a thirteenth-century calendar and martyrology.[21] A serendipitous aspect of this odd arrangement is that it allows an examination of Christ Church's relic collection over the entire post-conquest and pre-Reformation period. Its first relic list is substantial, containing relics of Christ, several apostles, and saints both Insular and Continental. The only Irish saints listed, St Patrick and St Laurence O'Toole, are in a later hand; Raghnall Ó Floinn therefore dates their addition to the manuscript to sometime after Laurence's canonization in 1225.[22] This mid-thirteenth-century dating is key, as in the 1220s, according to the *Dignitas Decani*, St Patrick's was granted cathedral status; it then had that status reaffirmed by popes Honorius III and Gregory IX respectively.[23] Not even at this crucial juncture in its ascendant status, therefore, could St Patrick's Cathedral procure any of Christ Church's relics. In fact, it seems that St Patrick's had no relic collection whatsoever, besides those presumably necessary for the building's dedication.[24] In terms of relics, then, Christ Church surpasses St Patrick's by default and as a matter of fact its status as a house of relics was essentially unchallenged throughout the medieval period. Relics, of course, are relevant to a cathedral's lived religious experience in that they inspire veneration and pilgrimage; the nature of this pilgrimage is most visible in the later medieval period.

Christ Church Cathedral's late medieval relic list demonstrates a robust pilgrimage culture as well as a reincorporation of some aspects of Irish spirituality into the cathedral's lived religious experience. Moving on to Christ Church's early Tudor era relic list that precedes the Book of Obits, a marked increase in the amount of relics is visible. The most important relics are listed first; they are a cross that miraculously spoke, and the famed Bachall Ísu, a staff gifted to St Patrick by Christ.[25] Both of these, significantly, pre-dated the Anglo-Norman invasion.[26] In addition to the earlier relics, the list also contains a marked increase in Irish saints; more specifically, it lists the bones of Patrick, Columba, Brigid, and Laurence O'Toole.[27] That this list of relics expanded

21 Pádraig Ó Riain, 'The calendar and martyrology of Christ Church Cathedral, Dublin' in Gillespie and Refaussé (eds), *Medieval manuscripts*, pp 33–59, at p. 33.   22 Raghnall Ó Floinn, 'The foundation relics of Christ Church Cathedral and the origins of the diocese of Dublin' in Seán Duffy (ed.), *Medieval Dublin VII* (Dublin, 2006), pp 89–102, at p. 95. 23 *Dignitas Decani*, pp 9, 11.   24 Fletcher, 'Liturgy and music' in Crawford and Gillespie (eds), *St Patrick's*, p. 92.   25 Peadar Slattery, *Social life in pre-Reformation Dublin, 1450–1540* (Dublin, 2019), p. 192.   26 Ibid.   27 *The registers of Christ Church Cathedral, Dublin,*

over the course of the medieval period to include more Irish saints demon-strates that Christ Church warmed to Irish devotions over time. The presence of Columba and Brigid in particular shows this; they have more popular connotations, as opposed to Patrick and Laurence as the island's and archdiocese's patrons respectively. This relic collection inspired substantial pilgrimage; and pilgrimage was frequent enough that the Dublin Assembly had to issue a decree protecting pilgrims from harm in the late fifteenth century.[28] In addition to this relic list, church officials granted the faithful indulgences (remissions of sin) relating to Christ Church.[29] St Patrick's seems to have received no such indulgences, further indicating a lack of relics.

Beyond just pilgrims, however, the Dubliners themselves were integral to the devotional life of the cathedral, particularly through chantry chapels. The chantry chapels and bequests of Christ Church Cathedral show extensive lay involvement in religious life. With respect to chapels more broadly, such chapels that existed in Christ Church included St Laurence O'Toole's chapel, the Lady Chapel, the White Mary chapel, and the chapel of St Nicholas.[30] Concerning chantries, Peadar Slattery's definition of chantry is useful here. He defines it as a patronage-fuelled ecclesiastical institution that varied depending on the context; with respect to a chapel, he describes it as 'a fund that supported the building of a chapel, that chapel being known as a chantry chapel'.[31] The two most important chapels of that nature in Christ Church were the chapel of St Edmund and the chapel of the Holy Trinity.[32] These were the chapels of the city's military and merchant guilds respectively.[33] This chapel list is not exhaustive; the aforementioned architectural 'restoration' makes the interior layout of the cathedral somewhat difficult to know for certain.[34] Nevertheless, the chapels are evidence of Christ Church's patronage system, whereby guilds would exercise a kind of collective institutional piety by having a designated chapel. St Patrick's, meanwhile, seems to have had little guild-based contribution, the sole instance being a bequest from the guild of St George at the very end of the Middle Ages.[35]

Christ Church was also home to extensive individual patronage; the document that further elucidates this is the famed Christ Church Book of Obits. The latter is a priceless primary source for understanding the lived

ed. Raymond Refaussé with Colm Lennon (Dublin, 1998), p. 41.   **28** Slattery, *Social life*, p. 193.   **29** *CCD*, p. 58.   **30** James Mills, 'Sixteenth century notices of the chapels and crypts of the church of the Holy Trinity, Dublin', *JRSAI*, 10:3 (1900), 195–203, at 198–200. **31** Slattery, *Social life*, pp 184–5.   **32** Mills, 'Sixteenth century notices of the chapels and crypts', 198–200.   **33** Fletcher, 'Liturgy' in Milne (ed.), *Christ Church*, pp 132–3. **34** Derisive description of Christ Church's 'restorations' is a trend in Christ Church historiography at least a century old that continues to the present; see Mills, 'Sixteenth century notices of the chapels and crypts', 196; Stalley, 'The architecture of the cathedral', p. 96.   **35** Fletcher, 'Liturgy and music' in Crawford and Gillespie (eds), *St Patrick's*, p. 137.

religious experience of the cathedral; it represents a culture of active lay participation in the cathedral even beyond death. The Book of Obits is essentially a liturgical document for use by the canons, whereby clerics, members of the cathedral's Augustinian confraternity, and other important members of the community were commemorated in the liturgy each year on a particular calendar day.[36] Though many of the names are lay members of the confraternity, some gain their commemoration *ex officio*. One section of the text, for example, commemorates such worthies as Bishop Dúnán/Donatus (d. 1074), Archbishop Fulk de Sandford (d. 1271), and Edward IV (d. 1483).[37] Edward obviously gained his commemoration through his office, as did Donatus, who lived over a century before the Augustinians even came to Christ Church. Fulk in particular is clearly an *ex officio* commemoration, as he preferred St Patrick's enough to be the first archbishop buried there; the significance of this will be discussed in detail later. Nevertheless, the bulk of those commemorated are more ordinary Dubliners, of well enough means to afford a bequest but not necessarily of royal or even mayoral distinction. Most names listed are English; this is especially true of the canons, who often have western English toponyms typical of post-conquest Dublin such as one William of Shrewsbury.[38] All of this evidence, therefore, shows that the lived religious experience of Christ Church was thoroughly lay-involved. Lower-class Irish Gaels made pilgrimage to the cathedral to venerate relics of the saints, perhaps in particular those of native origin. In addition, the Anglo-Norman mercantile class, that held much of the power in Dublin, would have prayed at their guild chapels and participated in the confraternity. Scholars, however, have less of an understanding of lay devotion at St Patrick's but that cathedral's lived religious experience was, nevertheless, vibrant in its own way; and one can see this through an analysis of its Lady Chapel.

The documentation relating to patronage and chantry devotion at St Patrick's is sparse, but enough exists concerning its Lady Chapel to trace some idea of devotional life at the cathedral. Fletcher's work is again crucial here. He documents that St Patrick's housed the Lady Chapel as well as chapels to St Stephen, St Michael, St Paul, St Peter, and St John the Evangelist; the north transept of the cathedral, also, was eventually sectioned off to become the parish church of St Nicholas.[39] The Lady Chapel was the most significant chapel of the cathedral; not only is it the best documented, but the chapels to St Peter and St Stephen were, given their position in the cathedral, *de facto* sub-chapels within the Lady Chapel. Additionally, since both of St Patrick's transepts were sectioned off, Howard Clarke notes that the cathedral's layout

---

36 Colm Lennon, 'The Book of Obits of Christ Church Cathedral, Dublin' in Gillespie and Refaussé (eds), *Medieval manuscripts*, pp 163–83, at p. 164. 37 *Registers of Christ Church*, ed. Refaussé and Lennon, p. 56. 38 Ibid., p. 67. 39 Fletcher, 'Liturgy and music' in Crawford and Gillespie (eds), *St Patrick's*, p. 136.

'emphasized the linear dimension of the nave, quire, and Lady Chapel Sequence'.[40] O'Neill's overlay shows that the Lady Chapel was smaller than that of Old Sarum; this was one of St Patrick's few architectural deviations from Sarum.[41] Nevertheless, it seems to have been a place of considerable interest to clerics and laity alike. It was rebuilt shortly after its initial construction, and Fulk de Sandford was apparently proud enough of this reconstruction that he, the first archbishop buried in St Patrick's, still rests in St Peter's Chapel within it.[42] Two centuries thereafter, Archbishop Michael Tregury was himself buried in St Stephen's Chapel.[43] These burials demonstrate that, on either end of the Lady Chapel's medieval lifespan – and, indeed, on either end of the chapel itself – archbishops deemed it a prime space for their burial, clearly indicating its importance. Tregury's bequest to the chapel, as well as that of a thirteenth-century layman, helps to further explain the cathedral's liturgical life.

Devotional bequests to the cathedral, and to the Lady Chapel more specifically, show that St Patrick's had a network of elite patronage and that the Lady Chapel was likely one of the chief spaces for religious expression by these patrons. The first relevant bequest is the aforementioned one by Archbishop Tregury, who bequeathed a pair of organs 'for the celebration of the divine offices in St Mary's Chapel'.[44] Fletcher notes this, but confines it to a footnote, and does not emphasize its significance. The Lady Chapel, as mentioned, was not particularly large; the fact that Tregury felt it was even possible, let alone necessary, to house two organs within it suggests a sophisticated liturgical infrastructure, as will be discussed momentarily. The second relevant bequest concerns a man named William Godman. A landlord prominent enough to have the former mayor Walter Unred as one of his witnesses, he states that he will divert a rent receipt annually to light the Lady Chapel at Easter.[45] Fletcher discusses him as well but again perhaps does not perhaps fully recognize his importance. This grant by Godman is the sole instance in the entire *Dignitas Decani* of a layman gifting money to the cathedral for liturgical purposes. Other grants for which evidence exists elsewhere that do not necessarily involve the Lady Chapel are of a largely elite nature: deans, archbishops, and Lionel of Antwerp, chief governor of Ireland, all endowed masses for themselves or their loved ones.[46] Therefore, three things are clear; St Patrick's lacked as large a patronage network as Christ Church, those patrons that it did have were disproportionately of the highest elites, and the Lady Chapel was the premier focus of this patronage and devotion.

---

40 Howard Clarke, 'Cathedral, close and community, *c.*1220 to *c.*1500' in Crawford and Gillespie (eds), *St Patrick's*, pp 45–72, at p. 53.   41 O'Neill, 'The architectural history', p. 102.   42 Hugh Jackson Lawlor, 'The monuments of the pre-Reformation archbishops of Dublin', *JRSAI*, 47:2 (1917), 109–38, at 113.   43 *Register of wills and inventories of the diocese of Dublin in the time of Archbishops Tregury and Walton, 1457–1483*, ed. Henry Berry (Dublin, 1898), pp 25–6.   44 Ibid., p. 26.   45 *Dignitas Decani*, pp 94–5.   46 Fletcher,

And the sole liturgical manuscript that survives from St Patrick's indeed confirms the centrality of the Lady Chapel to its devotional life. Cambridge University Library, MS Additional 710, better known as the Dublin Troper, contains evidence for the Lady Chapel's sophisticated liturgy and St Patrick's elite confraternity. That Christ Church contained equally sophisticated liturgy and music is almost self-evident in the secondary literature at this point; its sumptuously decorated de Derby Psalter demonstrates this.[47] The Troper, however, is comparatively understudied. The text, the earliest parts of which date to the early to mid-fourteenth century, contains some compositions that are likely to be original to Dublin, many of which are Marian.[48] The sophistication and elaborateness of this liturgy puts it over a century ahead of its time.[49] It also, unsurprisingly, contains copious text from and references to Sarum.[50]

The portion of the manuscript listing confraternity members notably lists Lionel of Antwerp as a member.[51] This strongly suggests the prestige of the confraternity, and further analysis shows a mutual exclusivity with Christ Church. There is only one clear name in common between Christ Church's confraternity as listed in the Book of Obits and St Patrick's confraternity as listed in the Troper: Margareta Rochford.[52] There are three other close matches: John, Nicholas, and Richard Whyte.[53] However, the sheer popularity of this surname in medieval Dublin makes any direct link tenuous at best (in the Latin form *Albus*, the name appears in the Dublin Guild Merchant Rolls over one hundred times).[54] The Book of Obits itself even has four John Whytes listed, though only the John Whyte who was cook of the priory is explicitly listed as a confraternity member;[55] the Troper, as well, lists two John Whytts in St Patrick's confraternity.[56] Nevertheless, Lionel's membership and the fraternity's near-total exclusivity with Christ Church show that he and other elites could and did choose St Patrick's over Christ Church for their worship, presumably because of its relative Anglicization compared to its sister cathedral.

The Anglicization of the two cathedrals is a useful prism by which to understand the overall significance of this comparative approach. A combination of two key phrases by two separate authors, one originally relating to each

'Liturgy and music' in Crawford and Gillespie (eds), *St Patrick's*, p. 136.   **47** Alan Fletcher, 'The de Derby Psalter of Christ Church Cathedral, Dublin' in Gillespie and Refaussé (eds), *Medieval manuscripts*, pp 81–102, at pp 81–2.   **48** Fletcher, 'Liturgy and music' in Crawford and Gillespie (eds), *St Patrick's*, pp 131–3.   **49** Ibid., p. 133. **50** Geoffrey Hand, 'Cambridge University Additional MS 710', *Reportorium Novum*, 2 (1958), 17–33, at 21–5.   **51** Mary Clark and Raymond Refaussé, *Directory of historic Dublin guilds* (Dublin, 1993), pp 34–5.   **52** Hand, 'Additional MS 710', 27; *Registers of Christ Church*, ed. Refaussé and Lennon, p. 62.   **53** Hand, 'Additional MS 710', 27–8, *Registers of Christ Church*, ed. Refaussé and Lennon, pp 64, 75, 80 respectively.   **54** 'The Dublin Guild Merchant Rolls, *c.*1190–1256', transcribed by Philomena Connelly, https://databases. dublincity.ie/dmgr/surname_browse.php?startletter=a, accessed 1 February 2020. **55** *Registers of Christ Church*, ed. Refaussé and Lennon, pp 43, 46, 64, 70.   **56** Hand,

cathedral, demonstrates the significance of this analysis to medieval Ireland as a whole. Fletcher describes Christ Church's liturgical practices, specifically its commemoration of the city's prominent dead, as 'uniquely Dublinesque in colour'.[57] Such a description should also, through the Lady Chapel's Dublin unique compositions at the very least, extend to St Patrick's. Citing the unabashedly English nature of St Patrick's and its strong links with the English state, Raymond Gillespie declares that, by the Reformation, 'St Patrick's was no less than the Pale at prayer, sometimes literally so'.[58] Yet, no doubt that description also fits Christ Church, given its own strong association with the quite English city that was Dublin in the later Middle Ages. Taken together, then, St Patrick's was the Pale at prayer in theory, Christ Church was the Pale at prayer in practice, and both were uniquely Dublinesque in colour.

St Patrick's was thoroughly Anglicized, elite-centred, and loyal to a fault. It was, to clerical and governmental officials in the colonial administration, the ideal and the end goal of the Irish church. The residents of this ideal Pale, as emblemized by St Patrick's Cathedral, would worship identically to the English; they would be, as Clarke quips about the cathedral's clerics, 'more English than the English themselves'.[59] Christ Church, however, was the reality of the English ecclesiastical establishment in Ireland. It was Anglicized and elite, but not fully; English-speaking mayors venerated, alongside Irish-speaking pilgrims, the relics of thoroughly Irish saints like Columba and Brigid. It was loyal, but not fully; it required occasional symbolic pacification and even could host the coronation of a pretender king. St Patrick's was what the state wished the new church of the Lordship of Ireland to be; Christ Church was what that new church actually was.

Overall, this essay has shown that the lived religious experience of Christ Church Cathedral and St Patrick's Cathedral was more nuanced than simply being a cathedral for the people and for the elites respectively. Christ Church was the more active cathedral, and the one that better facilitated ways for both pilgrims from outside of Dublin and Anglo-Norman Dubliners to live their Christian faith; the sheer length of the Obits alone shows Christ Church to be a devotional centre. St Patrick's was indeed more of a top-down enterprise, and was a testing ground for the religious dimension of the Anglo-Norman colonial mission, but this does not invalidate the sophisticated and genuine ways in which its elite parishioners lived their faith. The chapels of Christ Church bustled with pilgrims, merchants, and soldiers; all of these groups were able to worship in ways unique to their purpose of visitation and profession. Though St Patrick's lacked the worship numbers of Christ Church, some of the Pale's most powerful attended and patronized services in the Lady Chapel; these services arguably surpassed in elaborateness, at least in some respects, anything

'Additional MS 710', 28.   **57** Fletcher, 'Liturgy' in Milne (ed.), *Christ Church*, p. 139.
58 Gillespie, 'Reform and decay', p. 157.   **59** Clarke, 'External influences', p. 86.

else seen in Britain and Ireland at the time. Though each cathedral served a distinct purpose, both were moulded by the complexities of the post-conquest city, and a simple elite-versus-popular dichotomy does a disservice to the richness of religious life experienced in the two buildings. Understood comparatively, these two cathedrals demonstrate that Dublin's high-level worship was certainly more colourful and diverse than its small population size would suggest.

Saints and skinners: excavations along the northern precinct of the abbey of St Thomas the Martyr, Dublin

PAUL DUFFY

INTRODUCTION

From November 2016 through to March 2018, archaeological test-trenching, open excavation and monitoring works were carried out at the site of what was Frawley's department store on Thomas Street in the Liberties area of Dublin, specifically, the houses and rear plots of nos 30, 32–36 Thomas Street (fig. 6.1). The excavations were carried out by IAC, in advance of redevelopment of the site, on behalf of Hattington Capital under licence to the National Monuments Service (No. 16E0054). The works were completed by a crew of between 14 and 20 archaeologists, generating an archive of 1,790 contexts, 5,802 photographs, 5,975 artefacts and 746 samples.

Extensive archaeological structures, deposits and features were identified and preserved by record over the course of these works. Abundant structures of seventeenth-, eighteenth- and nineteenth-century date were excavated including houses, industrial buildings, water pipes, wells and cisterns (fig. 6.2). The 'saints and skinners' of the title of this contribution refer to the two major medieval aspects of the site: the burial ground and northern precinct wall of the abbey of St Thomas the Martyr and a concentration of medieval plots immediately north of the precinct, several of which had been in use as tanneries in the thirteenth and fourteenth centuries.

The size and complexity of the excavations preclude full discussion here, and it must be highlighted that, while much post-excavation work has been completed, specialist analysis is ongoing on the numerous large assemblages of human skeletal remains, insect remains, plant macrofossil remains and the artefactual assemblage. This essay will therefore focus on the excavation results relating to the medieval abbey of St Thomas the Martyr and contemporary secular activities. It is envisaged that specialist reports on the human skeletal remains and the artefactual assemblages will form publication papers in their own right in later volumes of this series. The archaeology of the seventeenth century onwards, though touched upon briefly below, will ultimately be published elsewhere.

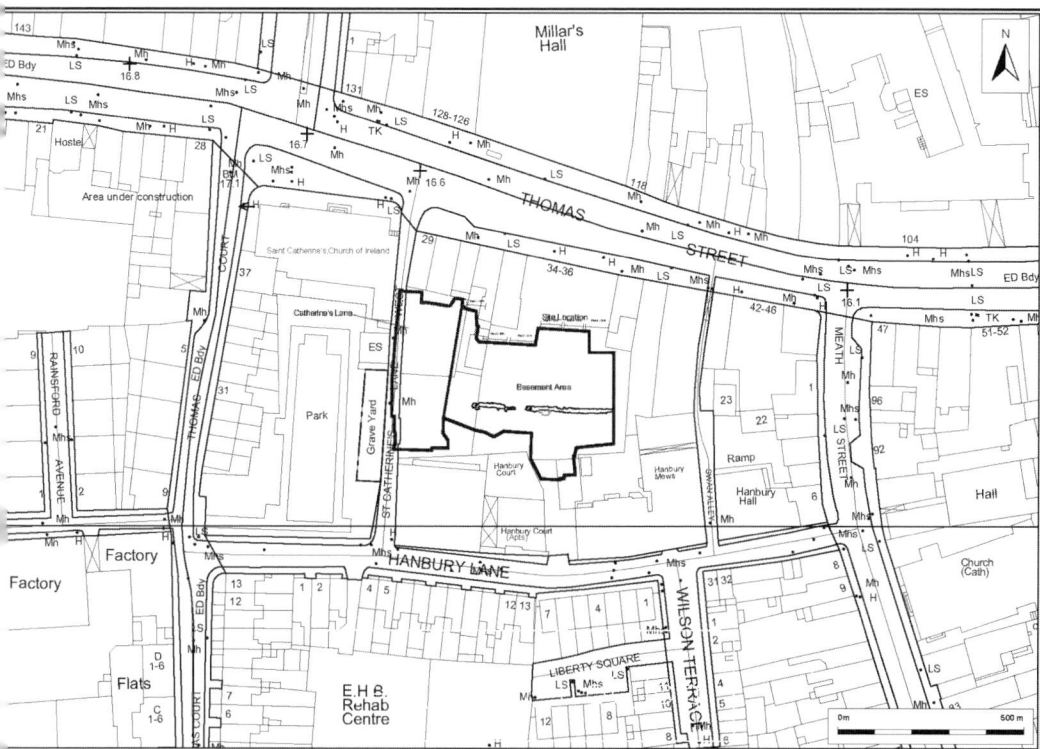

6.1 Site location

THE ABBEY OF ST THOMAS THE MARTYR

Numerous detailed academic papers on the subject of the abbey of St Thomas the Martyr (several in earlier volumes in this series) have been previously published,[1] culminating in a monograph commissioned by Dublin City

1 Aubrey Gwynn, 'The early history of St Thomas's Abbey, Dublin', *JRSAI*, 84:1 (1954), 1–35; Laureen Buckley, 'Health and status in medieval Dublin: analysis of skeletal remains from the abbey of St Thomas the Martyr' in Seán Duffy (ed.), *Medieval Dublin IV* (Dublin, 2003), pp 98–126; Claire Walsh, 'Archaeological excavations at the abbey of St Thomas the Martyr, Dublin' in Seán Duffy (ed.), *Medieval Dublin I* (Dublin, 2000), pp 184–202; A.L. Elliot, 'The abbey of St Thomas the Martyr, near Dublin' in Howard Clarke (ed.), *Medieval Dublin: the living city* (Dublin, 1990), pp 62–76; Lynda Conlon, 'Women in medieval Dublin: their legal rights and economic power' in Seán Duffy (ed.), *Medieval Dublin IV* (Dublin, 2003), pp 172–92; Cathal Duddy, 'The role of St Thomas's Abbey in the early development of Dublin's western suburb' in Seán Duffy (ed.), *Medieval Dublin IV* (Dublin, 2003), pp 79–98; Franc Myles, 'Archaeological excavations at the mill-pond of St Thomas's Abbey, Dublin' in Seán Duffy (ed.), *Medieval Dublin IX* (Dublin 2009), pp 183–212; Edmond O'Donovan, 'The growth and decline of a medieval suburb? Evidence from

6.2 Phased plan of archaeology on site

Council's Archaeology Section in 2017, authored by Dr Áine Foley.[2] The publication synthesizes the available information on the abbey as well as including some preliminary elements of the results of the excavations at Frawley's. The symposium organized to mark the launch of this monograph was itself an event of singular importance in the historiography of the abbey, bringing together not only the local community but a range of scholars in the field of medieval studies who presented papers on diverse aspects of the history, archaeology and architecture of the abbey.[3] While it suffices to point the reader in the direction of Dr Foley's monograph for the historical context of the abbey, several dates and key events are repeated here to facilitate discussion of the excavation results:

excavations at Thomas Street, Dublin' in Seán Duffy (ed.), *Medieval Dublin IV* (Dublin, 2003), pp 127–71.   **2** Áine Foley, *The abbey of St Thomas the Martyr, Dublin* (Dublin, 2017).   **3** These lectures and accompanying slides have been made freely available by History Hub: http://historyhub.ie/thomasabbey.

1177 Priory of St Thomas the Martyr founded by the serving justiciar, William Fitz Audelin, on behalf of Henry II as part of the latter's atonement for the murder of Thomas Becket, archbishop of Canterbury.

1192 Priory becomes an abbey, potentially marked by a programme of building works; St Catherine's Church founded.[4]

1227 Henry III requested by the abbot to lay the first stone of a new church.[5]

1250 Building stone destined for the abbey seized at Bristol by the king's stewards.[6]

1289 Fire destroys portions of the abbey buildings.

1392 Abbey attacked by mob led by the mayor, bailiffs and citizens of Dublin with some damage to the buildings.[7]

1497 Money given for the reparation of the monastic church of St Thomas.[8]

1538 Abbey surrendered by Abbot Henry Duff to the king on 25 July.

1543 An inquisition records a church with bell tower, a dormitory, a cloister, a hall with a tower, a solar and the King's Chamber in addition to two gardens, eight orchards, twelve acres of land and a watermill.

1634 Statement of John Smith records the presence of a 'great stone wall', a 'court' and a 'long garden plot' at Thomas Court.[9]

EXCAVATION RESULTS

The site comprised an area of approximately 1,820 square metres. Within the site boundary, a number of protected structures dating from the seventeenth to nineteenth century front onto the street. To the rear of these properties several buildings of twentieth-century date had been constructed on pile and groundbeam foundations. The area beneath this twentieth-century structure had been reduced by over 1m below the level of the ground along St Catherine's Lane. The excavation was divided into two distinct areas: a block parallel to St Catherine's Lane which was reduced to *c.*1.4m below the level of the modern laneway, and a larger area to the east, comprising the majority of the site footprint, which was reduced to *c.*3m below the previous ground level to accommodate a basement. It should be noted therefore that the archaeology along St Catherine's Lane was not fully excavated, significant deposits and

4 See Tadhg O'Keeffe's podcast, *St Thomas's Abbey and the history of Early English Gothic in Ireland,* at http://historyhub.ie/thomasabbey.   **5** Gwynn 'Early history', 20.   **6** Gwynn 'Early history', 20.   **7** On which, see Jones in this volume, below.   **8** '… Abbot John and the community of St Thomas enter into an agreement with Abbot Walter (Champfleur) of St Mary's, Philip Bermingham and James Aylmer concerning prayers to be said for the repose of the souls of Elizabeth Holywood, Alice Trevers, Walter Chever, Elizabeth Welles, John and William Chever, in return for money given for the reparation of the monastic church of St Thomas': Gwynn, 'Early history', 27.   **9** Henry F. Berry, 'Notes on a statement dated 1634, regarding St Thomas' Court and St Katherine's churchyard, *JRSAI,* 37:4 (1907), 393–6.

features being preserved *in situ* beneath the development. The phases of activity encountered on-site can be grouped into eight general phases:

Phase I   Eleventh–twelfth century: pre-priory/abbey burials.

Phase II   Twelfth–thirteenth century: abbey cemetery, abbey boundary ditch and adjacent secular plots/toft areas to the north.

Phase III Fourteenth–fifteenth century: abbey precinct wall and later phase of tanning/cess pits; beginning of garden-soil deposits.

Phase IV   Sixteenth century: timber-lined cess/tanning pit to north of precinct wall, stone-lined cess/tanning pits built into line of precinct wall on southern side, boundary walls along St Catherine's Lane; bulk garden-soil deposits across the northern portion of the site.

Phase V   Seventeenth century: tanning pits, timber water pipes, row of Dutch Billy-type structures fronting St Catherine's Lane. Several timber- and stone-lined tanning pits; bulk garden-soil deposits.

Phase VI   Eighteenth century: multiple redbrick boundary walls, structures, brick surfaces, cobbled surfaces, wells, waterpipes, timber water cisterns, timber tanning pits, a brick-built tanning pit, a brick-built lime-slaking pit.

Phase VII Nineteenth century: boundary walls, buildings, surfaces and an industrial complex along St Catherine's Lane comprising two coal-fired furnaces set into a sloping brick-floored sub-basement.

Phase VIII Twentieth century: yard surfaces, stone foundations, concrete pile clusters and concrete groundbeams; sewer pipes, water pipes and other services.

This contribution will confine itself to discussion of the first three phases of activity on-site.

The abbey precinct

The precinct wall

Early on in the excavations, a large east–west-running wall was discovered towards the southern end of the site. This wall survived for a length of 37.2m, was up to 2.3m wide (fig. 6.3) and stood to a maximum height of four courses, with an average height of 0.43m. The wall had been heavily impacted upon in several places by a modern concrete groundbeam, a modern test pit or refuse pit, an eighteenth-century well, a seventeenth-century wooden water pipe and a seventeenth-century stone-lined tanning pit. Two further stone-lined tanning/cess pits had been built into the line of the wall and all three pits had utilized robbed stone from the wall in their construction. The wall was entirely robbed out towards the western end of the site, the stone having been re-used

6.3 Section of precinct wall, facing east

in the foundation of a row of seventeenth-century houses fronting St Catherine's Lane, as well as in paved surfaces, a well and boundary walls.

It was soon obvious that this wall had acted as a barrier between the sanctified space of the graveyard of the abbey of St Thomas the Martyr to the south and an extended area of densely clustered and intercutting tanning and

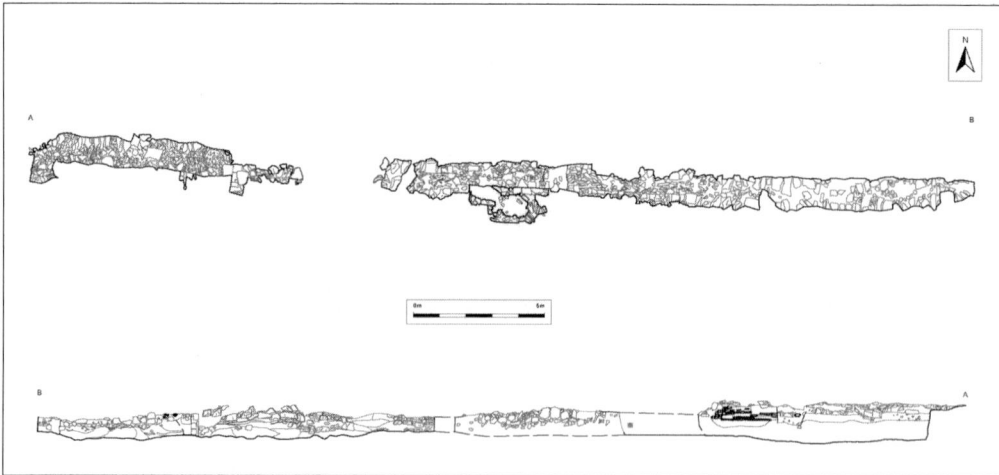

6.4 Plan and north-facing section of precinct wall

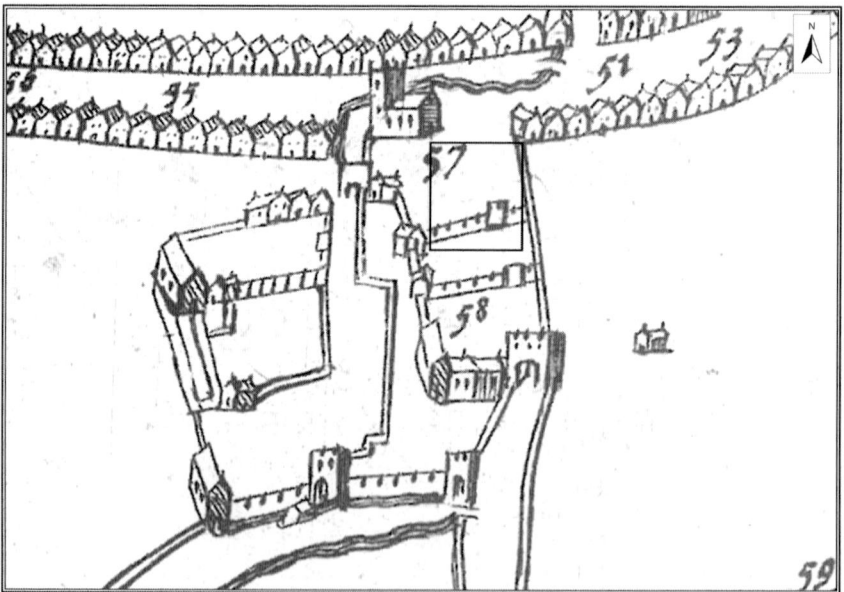

6.5 Extract from John Speed's map of 1610 showing northern precinct wall and inner precinct of St Thomas's abbey

cess pits to the north (fig. 6.4). This wall, in other words, was the outer precinct wall of the abbey of St Thomas as depicted on John Speed's map of 1610 (fig. 6.5). The wall was constructed of large to medium-sized slabs of limestone laid on the flat. The lower two courses of the wall comprised a clay-bonded plinth foundation up to 20cm wider than the upper courses which were bonded with a friable cream-coloured lime mortar. A total of 29 ceramic sherds were retrieved from within the fabric of the wall and immediately below it. These fragments suggest a construction date for the wall sometime in the late thirteenth to fourteenth century (see table 6.1).

Table 6.1 Types of ceramic and date-ranges from within and beneath the abbey precinct wall

Ceramic type	Date-range
Bristol–Redcliffe ware	Mid–13th to 14th century
Dublin-type ware	13th to 14th century
Dublin-type fineware	Late 13th to 14th century
Dublin-type cooking ware	Late 12th to 14th century
Chester-type ware	13th to mid–14th century
Dublin-type coarseware	Late 12th to mid–13th century
Dublin-type fineware	Late 13th to 14th century
Dublin-type cooking ware	Late 12th to 14th century
Saintonge mottled green glazed ware	13th to 14th century

The ditch

A shallow linear feature was identified paralleling this wall at an average distance of 2.8m from its northern edge. The ditch measured 34.9m long (though extensively cut and interrupted by later pits) with an average width of 1.5m. This feature appears to represent a boundary ditch or watercourse. The ditch was filled with a dense, sticky grey/blue clay. The ditched feature was severely truncated by multiple pits along its length (fig. 6.6). A total of 49 sherds of locally produced ceramic were retrieved from the fill of the ditch. These sherds suggest a date-range for the backfilling or silting of the ditch of early thirteenth to fourteenth century (see table 6.2). It is probable that this feature represents the original northern boundary of the abbey precinct.

Table 6.2 Types of ceramic and date-ranges from within the boundary ditch

Ceramic type	Date-range
Dublin-type cooking ware	Late 12th to 14th century
Dublin-type coarseware	Late 12th to mid–13th century
Dublin-type ware	13th to 14th century
Dublin-type fineware	Late 13th to 14th century

6.6 Boundary ditch (marked with ranging rods) and intercutting pits, facing north-west

The abbey cemetery

On the southern side of the precinct wall, a burial area was encountered extending across the width of the site. Previous excavation had identified graves immediately south-east of the site,[10] and it was presumed that the abbey graveyard was located to the south and east of the excavation area. However, excavation revealed a relatively even density of burials extending across the east–west axis of the southern portion of the site, totalling 142 interments. Many of these burials were truncated by later burials or post-medieval and modern features, and as a result a large quantity of disarticulated human remains was retrieved. The disturbed bone was usually reinterred with some care within later graves, sometimes laid out around the edges of the graves or placed upon the interred individual. While some localized areas exhibited higher-density burials with more frequent intercutting of graves, in the south-west and south, the distribution of burials was generally of moderate to low density. Perhaps this layout reflects the fact that the excavation area occurred at the outer limit of the cemetery.

10 Walsh, 'Archaeological excavations', p. 199.

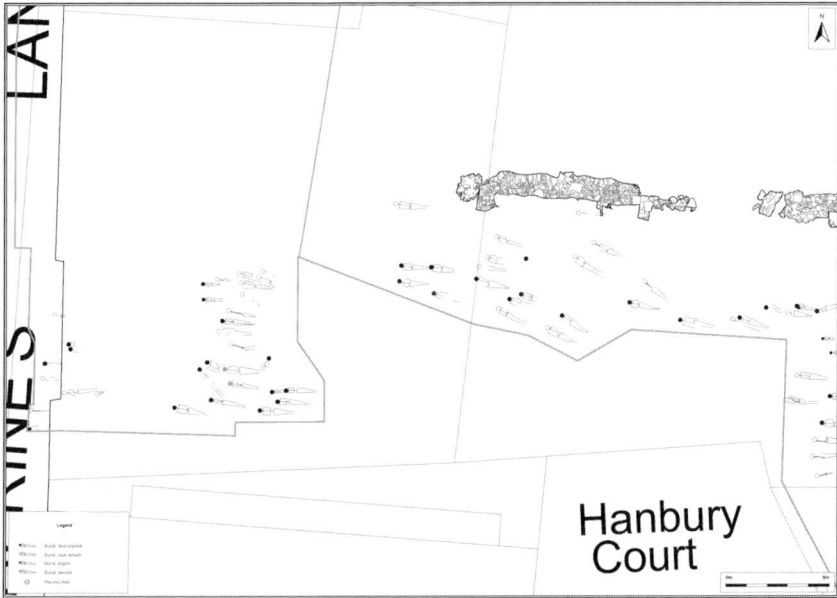

6.7a Western side of cemetery showing schematic plan of skeletons

6.7b Eastern side of cemetery showing schematic plan of skeletons

Generally, the graves were aligned west–east, with deviations towards the north aligned west-north-west–east-south-east and north-west–south-east (figs 6.7a and 6.7b). Grave goods were almost entirely absent and the cemetery

6.8 Disturbed slab–lined burial, facing west

soil was conspicuously devoid of ceramic or other artefactual material. No evidence for the use of coffins or shrouds was present; no coffin nails, shroud pins or other items from clothing or personal adornment such as buckles or buttons were found. Osteological analysis of the population is ongoing and it is hoped that the results of this work will form a future research paper to

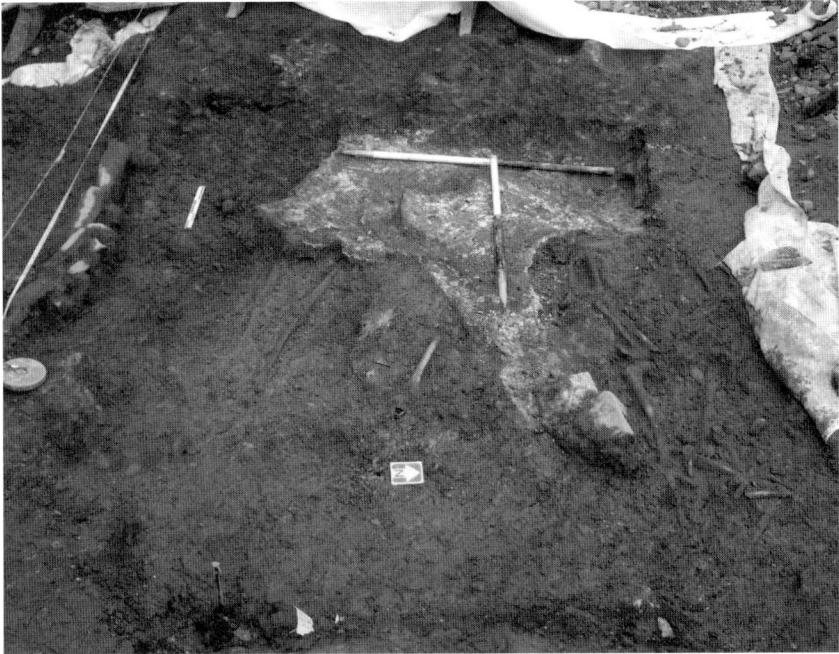

6.9 Possible plague pit with mortar covering several burials, facing west

complement work done on the adjacent population of 18 burials published by Laureen Buckley.[11] While exact demographic information is not currently available it is notable that the cemetery was open to all age categories, including infants, young and older children, adolescents, and adults of all ages and both sexes. Several burials had received specific attention in their burial and these are described below. At the time of writing, carbon 14 dating has been completed on five burials (see table 6.3). Further dates will follow.

Slab-lined burial
In the south-west of the site, an increased density of burials was observed. This higher density of graves appeared to be clustered around an individual who had been interred in a grave lined with rectangular blocks of limestone set on their edge (fig. 6.8). This slab-lined burial was the only example encountered and had been heavily disturbed by a charnel pit containing eight skulls. This later pit had removed the right arm, some of the right-side ribs and the skull of the individual. A small sherd of shell-edged ware retrieved from the fill of the charnel pit may suggest an eighteenth-century date for the disturbance, though it may also be an intrusive find. It is likely that one of the skulls re-interred in the charnel pit belongs to the individual buried in the slab-lined

11 Buckley, 'Heath and status'.

6.10 Pilgrim burial with perforated scallop shell on right arm

grave. Osteological analysis has shown that this possible male was a young middle adult at the time of death.[12] Surprisingly, the carbon 14 dating for this individual returned a date of AD 894–1146 (2 sigma–UBA 40201). This date-range clearly pre-dates the establishment of the priory by, at the very least, 31 years.

'Plague-pit' burials

A large, shallow, sub-square cut immediately to the north of the slab-lined burial was found to contain the remains of at least five individuals. This pit was covered by a layer of white lime mortar of varied thickness which lay directly on top of the skeletal remains (fig. 6.9). Given the jumbled nature of the burials within the cut and the fact that the mortar lay directly on the bones, this pit may represent a mass burial, or plague pit where bodies were interred quickly and sealed by a layer of lime which ultimately solidified once combined with the moisture in the bodies and surrounding soil. One of the individuals

12 Maeve Tobin, 'Report on osteological analysis of human remains from Thomas Street – Licence No. 16E0054' (unpublished report prepared by IAC Ltd, 2019).

6.11 Deviant burial with stone cobble inserted into mouth

from the pit – a young middle adult female – returned a date of AD 1040–1214 (2 sigma–UBA 40202).

Pilgrim burials
The only intentionally buried grave goods discovered in any of the interments consisted of two examples of perforated scallop shells retrieved from two older

Table 6.3 Initial round of carbon 14 dates from the cemetery

Context	Sample/ Skeleton	Context Description	C14 Result BP	1 Sigma Calibration	2 Sigma Calibration
C322	Sk. 20	Young middle adult possible male buried in a stone-lined grave.	1037 ± 40	AD 972–1028	AD 894–1146
C432	Sk. 29	Young middle-adult female buried in a cluster of graves (assoc.Sk.25–27) covered by a layer of mortar. Suggestion that they represent plague burials.	895 ± 31	AD 1048–1201	AD 1040–1214
C1778	Sk.142	Juvenile extended burial within southern limit of excavation. Aim to identify dating of cemetery expansion.	842 ± 29	AD 1165–1223	AD 1059–1263
C1520	Sk. 108	Older middle-adult male buried with a perforated scallop shell (over the lower left chest) indicating pilgrim status.	845 ± 22	AD 1169–1219	AD 1161–1249
C191	Sk. 1	Young child buried in a stone-lined grave.	812 ± 26	AD 1216–1257	AD 1170–1267
C1489	Sk. 98	Older middle-adult male buried with a perforated scallop shell (over the right upper arm) indicating pilgrim status.	809 ± 22	AD 1220–1254	AD 1190–1267

middle–adult male individuals (fig. 6.10). The positioning of the scallop shells, on the lower chest and over the right humerus, is suggestive of these items being sewn into garments or worn on a leather thong around the neck. The scallop shell is a symbol of St James the Apostle and such perforated scallop shells were used as pilgrim badges indicative of a pilgrimage to Santiago de Compostela in northern Spain.

Deviant burials
To the south of the slab-lined grave, two individuals were interred with rounded stones wedged in their mouths (fig. 6.11). These individuals appear to have been in middle adulthood at their time of death, with one identified as male and one as a possible female. These two burials represent the only obvious deviance from the normative burial practice in the cemetery population. At the time of writing, carbon 14 dates have yet to be returned from these individuals; however, this form of burial is very likely to date to the pre-Anglo-Norman period.

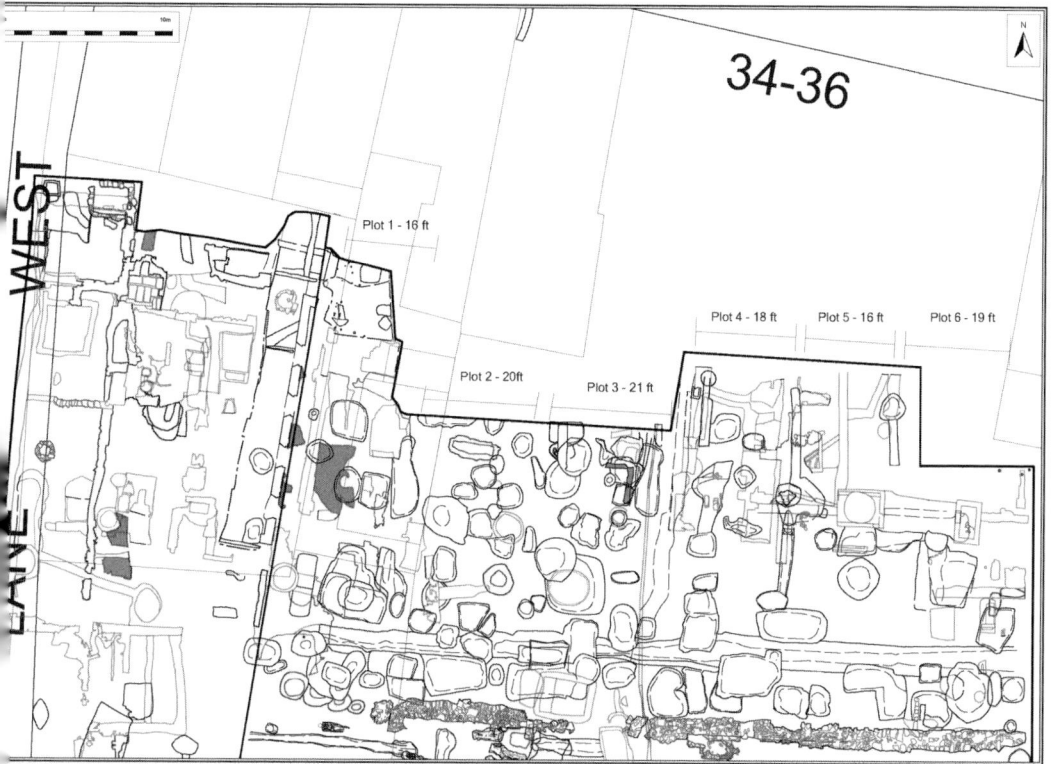

6.12 Plan of secular plots north of precinct wall

Secular plots

A series of six plots extended north from the precinct wall to the edge of excavation. These plots represent the rear toft areas associated with the houses that would have fronted onto Thomas Street in the medieval period. The plots, while not evident during excavation, can be traced in the finalized site plan with discontinuous, shallow linear features delineating the parcels of ground and many features respecting these divisions (fig. 6.12). The entire area to the north of the precinct wall was dominated by dense intercutting and interlocking pits of varying shape, size and depth. In addition to these pits, one plot contained a timber-lined well and a possible cereal-drying kiln.

A total of 68 pits were excavated in this area. Several of the pits were lined with a thick layer of blue-grey clay. No pits from this period were timber-lined and the majority seemed to rely on their depth relative to the water table to ensure they were watertight. In two instances, timber retaining walls built of posts and re-used planking/staves were constructed along a single side of a pit. This was particular to instances where a later pit cut through an earlier one and

6.13 Timber revetting in tanning pit, plot 5, facing north-west

the retaining wall was installed to prevent the slop from the earlier pit collapsing into the new cut (fig. 6.13). The pit morphologies included very large deep rectangular pits (*c.*3 x 2m x up to 3m deep) generally concentrated towards the southern end of the plots; large circular pits (*c.*2–3m diameter and 2–3m deep); large oval pits (*c.*2 x 1.5m x 1.5m deep) and smaller shallower square pits (*c.*1–2m square and up to 1m deep). Clustering of these pit types was also noted with instances of deep pits adjacent to or interlocking with small oval pits and large shallow rectangular pits, suggestive of a specific industrial purpose.

Not all of the pits respected the boundaries of the plots and this may suggest that the individual plots were amalgamated or that larger industrial areas emerged over time. The later mapping of the area presents a picture of such courtyards/open spaces between buildings. The most notable density of pits occurred within the *c.*2.5m-wide strip of land located between the abbey precinct wall to the south and the ditch to the north. Almost the entire surface area of this strip of land had been subjected to cutting and recutting from generally large pits. The pits in this area did not respect the plot boundaries discussed above.

The pits were filled for the most part with black noxious-smelling material. In several instances, green and brown foul-smelling organic deposits interspersed

6.14 Head of an oak paddle used to agitate tanning liquor

with layers of straw were encountered. The fills of the pits were rich in ceramic, leather and wooden artefacts as well as animal bone/horn-core and environmental remains. The head of a wooden paddle which was perforated with a series of holes to allow it to be drawn through liquid was retrieved from one of the larger pits along the eastern edge of the site (fig. 6.14). Such paddles were employed in the tanning process to agitate the tanning liquor that hides were placed in, indicating an industrial function. A double toilet seat was also recovered from a moderate-sized pit in the south-east area of the secular plots, illustrating that at least some of the pits were in use as latrines/cesspits (fig. 6.15). Whether this was the primary function intended for the pit or whether there was crossover in use at different stages of the lifecycle of the pits is explored further below. The toilet seat finds a parallel in an excavated example at Emmet Street, Trim, where a similar layout of rear plots and dense intercutting pits was encountered in a medieval suburban context, just outside of the town walls.[13]

13 Finola O'Carroll and Mandy Stephens, 'Trim Castle Lawn/Castle Street/Townsparks South carpark/Emmet Street, Trim, Meath Licence number: C121, C139, E2016', Excavations bulletin number 2006:1661: https://excavations.ie/report/2006/Meath/0016412/.

6.15 Double toilet seat from pit in plot 4

Soluble salts were prevalent across the site, and particularly in the areas of highest pit densities. These salts exuded out of artefacts, architectural stone and also the natural subsoil exposed to the air. The salts presumably derived from some function of the pits and were carried into the surrounding subsoil and deposits by the movement of rainwater and groundwater. It should be noted that the tawing process, discussed below, requires the use of alum, a double sulphate salt.

Environmental evidence
Samples were taken for analysis from all pits in order to understand further the nature of associated activities. The animal bone assemblage retrieved from the pits was found to contain relatively high numbers of cattle/goat horn-cores, many exhibiting chop marks indicative of the horn sheath being deliberately removed from the skull. Primary butchery waste was also present (butchered vertebrae, ribs, leg bones). The presence of horn-cores is an indicator for tanning activity on-site as the skins sold from the butcher to the tanner would have retained the head and, in some cases, the feet. There were, however, very infrequent phalanges of the domesticated species in the assemblage. The absence of lower leg bones and foot bones may be due to specific fellmonger practice, as some fellmongers removed the feet prior to selling on the

skins.[14] The absence of such waste would not rule out a tanning function at the site. In addition, a lot of primary butchering waste was retrieved from the pits from cattle, sheep/goat and pigs which may indicate the presence of a slaughterhouse. For the cattle, many of the bones relate to sub-adult animals.

Specialist analysis of the plant macrofossil assemblage has also been undertaken for several of the pits and provides further evidence for various processes with which the features may have been associated. The pits typically did not contain a high diversity of plants, which were unlikely to flourish within deposits of a high acidity that may have prevailed across the site. Bark fragments and acorns present in some of the pits are strong indicators for tanning. This evidence is spread across pits from different plots and not concentrated in a particular area (plots 1, 2, 5 and 6). Several of the larger pits also had clear indicators of cess (plots 2, 5 and 6), including fruit-stones (especially *prunus avium*, wild cherry).[15] This contrasts sharply with a sample taken from within the abbey precinct. This sample contained evidence for household and garden activities, a mix of charcoal and cereal grain/chaff. The grain was very abraded and seems to have been dumped from another source. A collection of garden produce – largely, vetches, chaff, carrot, celery, mustard, garlic, mint, herb-parsley, yarrow, charlock, fumaria and mercurialis – was recorded and it is interesting to note, in the context of a monastic garden, that most of these species would also have had medicinal properties. There is also a botanic collection of 'background noise' plants – ferns/bracken/heather/ sedges – all water-absorbing species that may have been brought to the site for padding/lining, etc. This has been interpreted as garden or orchard produce.[16]

Samples from the ditch were also processed. Many of the seeds were from grass and rushes, indicating waterlogged conditions and suggesting that the majority of the plant remains from this sample were found because these plants colonized the open feature. It should be noted that there was a strong concentration of fibrous plant material and some flax seeds identified, possibly indicating some small-scale textile enterprise at the site. Flax is used as an oil plant for culinary purposes but also for cloth making.[17]

A cesspit likely to date to the mid- to late sixteenth century (built into the precinct wall with robbed material from the abbey church) contained extensive indicators of cess material. Analysis of this material has provided a glimpse of the environment in the years immediately following the Dissolution of the abbey. Fruit stones dominated: *prunus spinose* (blackthorn); *prunus avium* (wild cherry); *malus* (apple); *strawberry* (Fragaria) and *Rubus idaeus* (raspberry) and *Rubus fruticosus* (blackberry); bilberry and flax were also found in small numbers. These

14 Patricia Stevens, 'Can we identify a tannery from waste products?' in Roy Thomson and Quita Mould (eds), *Leather tanneries: the archaeological evidence* (London, 2011), pp 187–91. 15 Susan Lyons, 'Report on plant macrofossil assemblage from excavations on Thomas Street' (unpublished report produced for IAC Ltd, 2019).   16 Ibid.   17 Ibid.

fruits are found in orchards, gardens and hedgerows. Wood fragments, *grasses/ bromus*, *poaceae*, *carex* (sedge) and *juncus* (rush) species were also recovered suggesting that fibrous plants were used to pad, line or quench odours.

Interestingly, from all samples, local urban vegetation signals were absent (or at least difficult to tease out from the occupation and domestic indicators). This could be as a result of the presumed acidic nature of the content of these features, but the lack of any pollutant species would imply that the site, while in use, was not left to become polluted.[18] This suggests that the site was quite open or cleared and any tree or low-lying species common to disturbed ground in urban areas were generally absent.

The medieval masonry

A total of 109 carved medieval masonry fragments were uncovered across the site. In all cases, the stones were retrieved from post-medieval demolition fills and re-used in walls dating from the seventeenth to the nineteenth century. The largest concentrations were retrieved from the stone lining of two cesspits of late sixteenth- or early seventeenth-century date. Specialist analysis of these stones is yet to be completed; however, the composition of the assemblage can be divided roughly along the following lines:

50%: grey/yellow grainy sandstone pieces which are mainly fragments of complicated window tracery exhibiting cusps, glazing channels and recurves potentially relating to trefoil or quatrefoil design (fig. 6.16). The stone is of uncertain origin and is similar to stone retrieved from St Audoen's which has tentatively been ascribed an Irish provenance.[19] There is a possibility, however, that fine grained sandstone was being imported from eastern Britain.[20]

40%: imported Dundry stone fragments, including some very finely carved sections of window tracery, voussoirs, jambs, mullions, a soffit from an internal (crossing?) arch, a gabled piece that may represent a portion of a shrine to house a relic of the saint,[21] and a very well-executed fragment displaying naturalistic, undercut foliage (fig. 6.17).

18 Ibid.   19 John Kelly, 'Appendix III – Building materials analysis' in Mary McMahon, *St Audoen's Church, Cornmarket, Dublin: archaeology and architecture* (Dublin, 2006), pp 119–22.   20 Further work is required to provenance this stone; however, a number of sources of sandstone, active in the medieval period, occur close to medieval trade routes across the Irish Sea. These include Egryn Sandstone from Cardigan Bay in Wales and sandstone from the Portishead formation near Bristol (I am indebted to Derek O'Brien for this information).   21 Paul Duffy and Tadhg O'Keeffe, 'A stone shrine for a relic of St Thomas Becket in Dublin?', *Archaeology Ireland*, 31:4 (2017), 18–23.

6.16 Laser scan of a selection of fragments of window tracery (courtesy of The Discovery Programme)

6.17 Fragment of Dundry stone with undercut carved foliage

6.18 Limestone double column base from a cloister arcade

5%:   dense, light grey limestone carved in a style consistent with the 'Perpendicular Style' Gothic from England (fig. 6.18).

5%:   miscellaneous stone including some fragments of granite and a single piece of red sandstone.

The type of stone employed appears to have a direct correspondence to the style of ornament, with the Dundry being used for what appears to be a late twelfth-/thirteenth-century form cognate with 'Early English Gothic' style of carving. The sandstone pieces with the abundance of cusps evident in the tracery belong to a later phase, known as 'Decorated Style Gothic' in England. These are likely to be fourteenth or fifteenth century in date, although a sixteenth-century date is also possible in an Irish context.[22] Limestone of possible local origin was used for the geometric designs which correspond to 'Perpendicular Style Gothic' likely dating to the sixteenth century.[23] The finely executed twin-column base from this period finds close parallel at the fifteenth-century cloister of Sligo Abbey. The stone assemblage therefore reflects a number of building/remodelling phases stretching from the early days of the abbey up to the final years prior to the Dissolution.

22 Harold Leask, *Irish churches and monastic buildings* (Dundalk, 1967), pp 124–8; Rachel Moss, 'Tales from the crypt: the medieval stonework of Christ Church Cathedral, Dublin' in Seán Duffy (ed.), *Medieval Dublin III* (Dublin, 2002), pp 95–114, at p. 98; Jim McKeon, 'St Nicholas's parish church, Galway: structural and architectural evidence for the high medieval period', *Journal of Irish Archaeology*, 18 (2009), 95–113.   23 Rachel Moss, 'Reduce, re-use, re-cycle: Irish monastic architecture *c.*1540–1640' in Roger Stalley (ed.), *Irish Gothic architecture: construction, decay and reinvention* (Bray, 2012), pp 115–60.

The artefact assemblage

A total of 5,975 artefacts were retrieved from the excavations, composed of, in the main, medieval and post-medieval ceramics. Post-excavation analysis of the finds is ongoing and the results presented below are confined to objects that further the broader interpretation of what functions were being carried out on-site. Again, it is hoped that, once finalized, the analysis of the artefact assemblage will form an independent publication.

Pottery
The vast majority of the medieval ceramics recovered during excavation (*c.*2,200) were of local origin, fabricated in Dublin (Dublin-type wares) or within the wider hinterland (Leinster cooking ware). The remainder were imports from England and continental Europe – mostly Flemish and French wares. Three ceramic masks/heads that once adorned jugs or similar vessels were recovered from different cess/tanning pits (fig. 6.19). One of these, imported from the Bristol area (Ham Green B; fig. 6.20), is a close parallel to the face on the spout of the knights jug on display at the National Museum of Ireland (Kildare Street), found during excavations at Wood Quay, from Bristol

6.19 Three ceramic heads retrieved from various pits

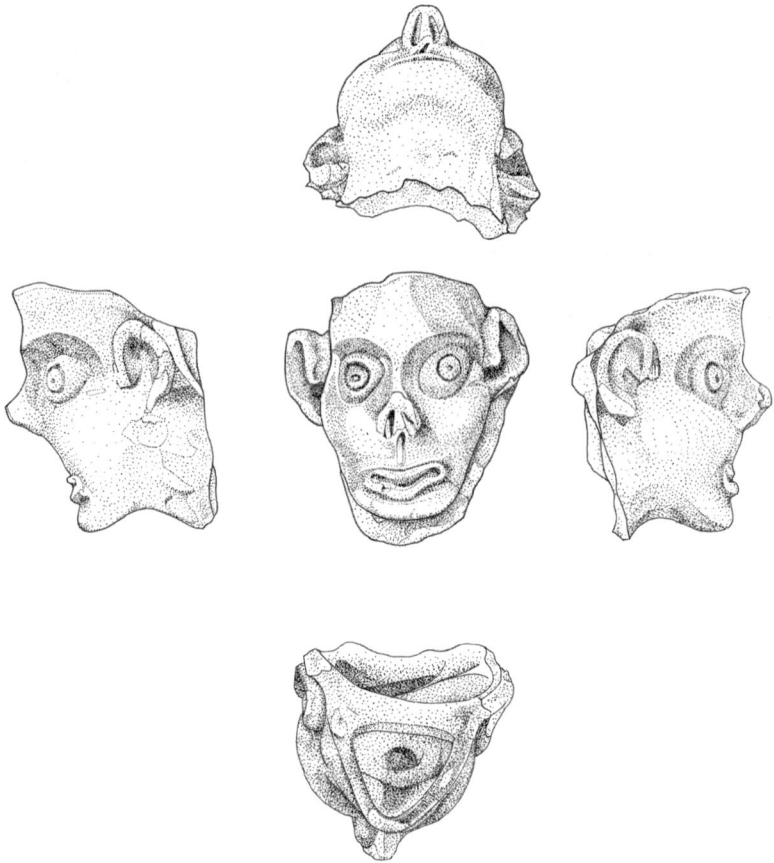

6.20 Illustration of Ham Green, ceramic head

Redcliffe.[24] A smaller and less naturalistically rendered head is of local origin (Dublin-type ware) while a third, smaller mask is from a French workshop and appears to be a simplistic representation of a bird's head with a beak-like projection/chin and applied clay pellets to form the eyes.[25]

Tile

A total of 787 medieval tile fragments were recovered. These comprised an even amount of floor tiles (393) and roof tiles (394). Of the floor tiles, 64 (16%) were two-colour tiles dating to the twelfth and thirteenth centuries

24 Clare McCutcheon, *Medieval pottery from Wood Quay, Dublin* (Dublin, 2006), pp 50–1.
25 Siobhán Scully, 'Ceramic report from excavations at Thomas Street (16E0054)' (unpublished report prepared for IAC Ltd, 2019).

6.21 Selection of two-colour tiles

(fig. 6.21). The tiles exhibited a wide range of motifs, including foliate patterns, trefoil patterns, stiff-leaf foliage as well as less frequent represent-ations of animals, including lions (3), a cockerel (1), and possible deer (1). Line-impressed floor tiles of late fourteenth-/fifteenth-century date were the most common with 196 examples retrieved (50%), with relief decorated tiles of sixteenth-century date representing 14% of the floor tile assemblage, the remainder being made up of undecorated glazed and non-glazed tiles. One border tile was found identical to those identified by Claire Walsh *in situ* within a tiled floor at the site of the abbey church. Interestingly, analysis has shown that the highest frequency of medieval tile was glazed roof tile (204) which represents 52% of the roof tile assemblage. The remainder were made up of unglazed roof tiles (40%), peg tiles (6.5%) and ridge tiles (1.5%). These roof tiles have a broad date-range spanning the thirteenth to sixteenth centuries.[26]

26 Joanna Wren, 'Medieval and post-medieval roof-tile', Appendix H in Clare McCutcheon, *Medieval pottery from Wood Quay, Dublin* (Dublin, 2006), pp 177–95, at pp 180–92.

6.22 Decorated leather knife-sheath

Leather
Ninety leather objects were recovered from the excavations. Of these, 72 are
artefacts including a decorated knife sheath (fig. 6.22), 26 shoes (fig. 6.23), a
bag, two straps, two binding strips and 40 unidentified objects and fragments.
There were also 18 items of leatherworking waste.[27] The knife sheath is very
similar to one found during excavations on the opposite side of Thomas Street,
suggesting a local production.[28] Several styles of shoe were retrieved from the
cess/tanning pits. All were medieval in date except for one shoe which dates to
the seventeenth century.

Evidence for leatherworking waste was retrieved from a single pit on-site
which dated to the sixteenth or seventeenth century. The pit contained a single
piece of primary waste arising from the initial trimming of hides during and
following tanning and currying; ten fragments of secondary waste, which
comprise the offcuts from cutting out pattern pieces and indicates the presence
of leather manufacturing trades such as shoemaking or the production of other
leather goods, and seven fragments of tertiary waste, which comprise the final
trimmings of the pattern pieces when they are being assembled into finished
goods.[29]

27 Siobhán Scully, 'Leather artefacts and leatherworking report from excavations at
Thomas St (16E0054)' (unpublished report prepared for IAC Ltd, 2019).   28 O'Donovan,
'Growth and decline', p. 158.   29 Scully, *Leather artefacts.*

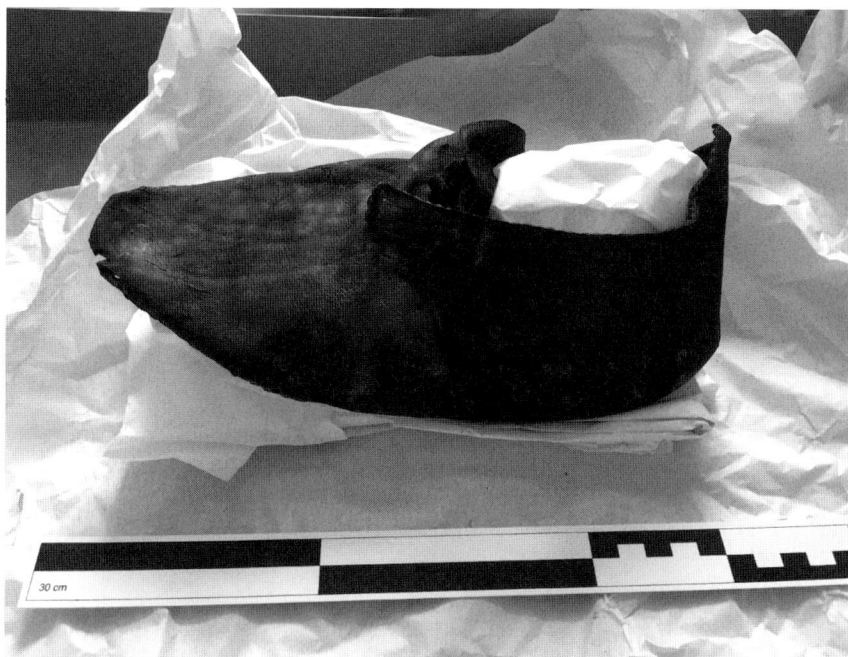

6.23 Medieval shoe

Metal

A total of 78 metal artefacts were recovered from the excavations at Thomas Street. The metals represented in the assemblage are copper alloy, iron, pewter and lead. The iron artefacts comprise 59% of the assemblage while the copper alloy artefacts represent 31% of the metal assemblage. There is only one pewter artefact in the assemblage, while the lead artefacts represent 9% of the assemblage. Of particular interest, given the potential for tanning activity on-site, was the retrieval of a possible iron awl which was recovered from the medieval garden soil immediately north of the precinct wall. Awls were most usually used for leatherworking, although they could have been used in woodworking, bone-working and other crafts. In leatherworking, they were used for piercing the leather.[30]

Wood

In addition to the wooden paddle and the toilet seat discussed above, three wooden lathe-turned bowls in various degrees of completeness were recovered from waterlogged deposits within cess/tanning pits. All three bowls were made

---

30 Siobhán Scully, 'Metal report from excavations at Thomas Street (16E0054)' (unpublished report prepared for IAC Ltd, 2019).

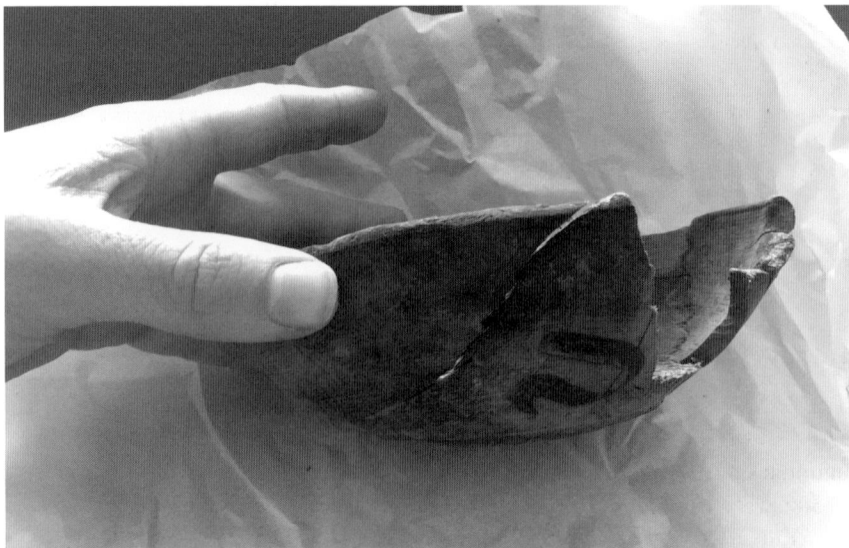

6.24 Lathe-turned ash bowl with branded manufacturer's mark

of ash.[31] The most complete example exhibits a seared brand on its exterior, presumably a manufacturer's mark (fig. 6.24). This mark is very similar to one visible on a lathe-turned wooden bowl on display at the National Museum (Kildare Street), found during Ó Ríordáin's excavations at Winetavern Street and dated stratigraphically to *c.*AD 1200.[32]

Glass
Discounting here the abundant post-medieval glass artefacts recovered (some of extremely high quality), three of the larger pits were found to contain multiple small fragments of medieval window-glass. One-hundred-and-eighty-four very small fragments of medieval window-glass were recovered from the excavations at Thomas Street. There is little evidence to suggest that window-glass was manufactured in Ireland during the medieval period.[33] Window-glass was being manufactured in England at this time, although it was considered an inferior product, and it is possible that the medieval window-glass from Thomas Street could have been imported from the Continent – the main sources of which were the parts of Burgundy and Lorraine which border the Rhine, Flanders and Normandy.[34]

31 Ellen O'Carroll, 'Timber identification from excavations at Thomas Street (16E0054)' (unpublished report prepared for IAC Ltd, 2019). 32 Breandán Ó Ríordáin, 'Excavations at High Street and Winetavern Street, Dublin', *Medieval Archaeology*, 15 (1971), 73–82; SMR: DU 018–020. 33 Jo Moran, 'The window-glass' in Miriam Clyne, *Kells Priory, Co. Kilkenny: archaeological excavations by T. Fanning & M. Clyne* (Dublin, 2007), pp 261–316. 34 Richard Marks, 'Window-glass' in John Blair and Niall Ramsay (eds), *English medieval*

Only one medieval window-glass fragment from Thomas Street is painted. It is of clear glass with red and black painting. The original design of the painting is unclear. Seventeen sherds of painted medieval window-glass were recovered from excavations at Dublin Castle. This glass was grisaille glass, that is, the design was patterned rather than figural and consisted mostly of foliage patterns. This painted medieval window-glass was thought to have dated from the mid-thirteenth to the fourteenth century.[35]

DISCUSSION

The abbey precinct

The ditch

Excavations at the Frawley's site have shown that the original precinct boundary of the abbey of St Thomas the Martyr was delineated by a ditch and presumably an inner bank from AD 1177, although it is possible that this ditch also fulfilled another function. The charter evidence from the unpublished register of the abbey has brought to light a reference to what appears to be a watercourse named the Lutteburne. A complicated system of water management was instituted in the mid-thirteenth century. This system saw water diverted into Dublin from the Dodder river via the artificial channel known as the city watercourse and along diverse culverts through St Thomas's Abbey and on to the walled city via the Glib Water and the city aqueduct.[36] Control of this water supply was one of the central points of dispute between the abbey and the citizens of Dublin. The course of the Glib Water is shown on Speed's 1610 map and de Gomme's 1673 map as running along the rear of the properties on the southern side of James's Street/Thomas Street from St James's Gate as far as St Catherine's Church. At this point it is shown to veer north to meet the roadway and turn east once more to run along the street itself as an open channel. The Glib Water then turns north into the hospital of St John the Baptist near what is now St John's Lane.

The charter of Gervase fitz Thomas Fating describes the location of 'my certain land in the parish of St Catherine of Dublin namely that which lies between the land of St Thomas and the land of Roger Ketell beside the horsemarket and contains in breadth twenty-one feet, and extends in length from the street as far as the water of Lutteburne'.[37] This charter makes it clear

industries: craftsmen, techniques, products (London and New York, 1991), pp 265–94, at p. 266.   **35** Siobhán Scully, 'Dublin Castle finds report' in Melanie McQuade, 'Excavations at Dublin Castle (11E0137)' (unpublished report for Archaeological Development Services Ltd, 2012).   **36** Henry F. Berry, 'The water supply of ancient Dublin', *JRSAI*, 1:7 (1891), 557–73; Val Jackson, 'The Glib Water and Colman's Brook', *Dublin Historical Record*, 11:1 (1949–50), 17–28; Olive C. Goodbody, 'The neighbourhood of the Glib river', *Dublin Historical Record*, 16:1 (1960), 1–8.   **37** RIA, MS 12 D 38 (unpublished Register of St

that the plot in question fronted onto Thomas Street and ran back as far as a watercourse of some kind. The name Lutteburne appears in one other later charter in the unpublished register as the Lotbourne where it is described as an orchard.[38] Given the eight orchards described within the abbey's holdings, it seems reasonable to assume that this Lutteburne was on the southern side of the street to the rear of the burgage plots.

While the horsemarket referred to in the text is known from other sources dating from the sixteenth century and is clearly somewhere on the route of Thomas Street, its exact address is uncertain.[39] However, Henry Berry has plausibly located the horsemarket to the west of the junction between Thomas Street and Francis Street.[40] This is significant as it suggests that, at one time, a watercourse ran to the rear of the plots on the southern side of Thomas Street on the eastern side of St Catherine's Church also.

The dating of Fating's charter is currently unclear and while it is likely to be of late thirteenth- or even fourteenth-century date there remains a possibility that this charter dates from pre-1244. Berry notes a deed of 1349 in Trinity College Library in which mention is made of land which extends from the street front of Thomas Street, south to a 'Pype Lane'.[41] This lane is mentioned again in another deed of 1426, described as a lane 'through which the water of the pipe of Dublin runs'.[42] This lane is represented to the rear of the plots extending south from James's Street on an estate map from 1703 where it is referred to as 'Back Lane'.[43] The line of the Lutteburne may therefore correspond to the location of the east–west-running ditch identified at the Frawley's site. An etymology for the name Lutteburne can be suggested as a compound of two Middle English words – 'leat' and 'burn'. 'Burn' is an old English/Lowland Scots term for a stream or watercourse while one of the Middle English meanings for the word 'leat' is a conduit. A 'leat' is also the term employed to describe the artificial watercourse that feeds a moat. In this sense, the Lutteburne may refer to the original ditch surrounding the abbey or a tributary of such which flowed with water. If, as suspected, the ditch identified during excavations represents the original northern boundary of the abbey precinct, constructed *c.*1177, it may have presented a pre-existing option for channelling water eastwards from the great Dublin water supply project of the mid-thirteenth century.

It is therefore proposed that the ditch excavated at the Frawley's site represents the northern precinct enclosure of the abbey, a feature that may have been incorporated into the original run of the watercourse known as the

---

Thomas), p. 77.   **38** Prof. Marie Therese Flanagan (pers. comm.).   **39** Clarke, *Dublin, Pt 1* (IHTA), p. 27.   **40** Henry F. Berry, 'Notes on an unpublished MS inquisition (AD 1258), relating to the Dublin city watercourse, from the muniments of the earl of Meath', *PRIA*, 24C (1902–4), 39–46, at 46.   **41** Berry, 'The water supply of ancient Dublin', 559. **42** Ibid.   **43** Neil Crimmins, 'A Dublin streetscape in 1703: an urban legacy of the Dongan estate', *Journal of the Irish Georgian Society – Irish Architectural and Decorative Studies*, 20

Glib Water/Pype Lane. Sometime in the later thirteenth or fourteenth century, this watercourse was diverted to run around the northern side of St Catherine's Church, down the centre of Thomas Street, leaving the stretch of the watercourse to the rear of the Thomas Street plots to silt up and ultimately be appropriated by the adjoining landholders as an extension to their plots. Mention of Pype Lane in the fifteenth and sixteenth centuries would, in this case, refer only to the surviving stretch of the original watercourse to the west of St Catherine's Church. Two potential reasons for redirecting the line of the watercourse suggest themselves. First, the citizens of Dublin may have taken increasing exception to their water passing through what, by the mid-fourteenth century, was surely becoming a densely populated graveyard to the rear of St Catherine's Church. Second, growing need for public access to the water may have prompted this diversion into the street to allow the public to use the water. In 1458, a record relating to the watercourse in Thomas Street describes the rights of public access in the following terms: 'the mayor and commons are to have, as of old, rights of easement such as washing and wringing'.[44]

The wall

There is little doubt that the stone-built wall encountered during the excavations represents the medieval wall delineating the northern precinct as depicted on Speed's map of Dublin in 1610. This wall corresponds very closely in morphology and manner of construction with an east–west-running wall excavated by Claire Walsh 120m to the south at Earl Street. Walsh has identified this feature as the southern precinct boundary wall of the abbey. The wall along Earl Street was constructed on the fills of a large, backfilled ditch. These fills were dated artefactually to the mid-fourteenth century and the wall therefore to the latter half of the fourteenth century.[45] Following infilling of the original ditch and construction of the wall at Earl Street, a smaller ditch was cut to parallel the wall, at a distance of *c.*1–1.5m. This differs slightly from the wall and ditch combination at the Frawley's site. No evidence for a large infilled ditch was found during excavations and it seems likely that the ditch paralleling the northern wall represents the original precinct boundary. The smaller size of the ditch on the northern side of the precinct may reflect the perceived level of threat here as opposed to the southern side of the precinct, which faced into open country running towards the Dublin/Wicklow Mountains, whereas the northern side faced onto a populous suburban area and the highway to the city.

The date-range of the ceramic sherds found within and directly below the northern wall also supports a construction date in the later thirteenth or fourteenth century. The artefactual evidence suggests that the northern ditch was backfilled sometime between 1260 and 1350. It seems likely therefore that an original boundary ditch surrounding the abbey was backfilled and the entire precinct walled, in a single event, or that these works were carried out within a relatively tight timeframe. The comparable wall of the prior's vill at the Augustinian foundation of Kells Priory in Co. Kilkenny has been dated to *c*.AD 1460.[46] Several precinct walls surrounding ecclesiastical foundations in Dublin have been partially excavated, including the Augustinian friary at Cecilia Street (*c*.1260),[47] St Peter's Church (*c*.fourteenth century),[48] St Michan's Church (fifteenth–sixteenth century)[49] and St Mary's Abbey (undated).[50]

While documentary evidence for the construction of the St Thomas's Abbey precinct wall has yet to be identified, reference to such a large building project may yet be found in the unpublished registers of the abbey, currently being transcribed and translated by Professor Marie Therese Flanagan. For the purpose of this contribution, however, historical events that may have prompted the construction of the precinct wall have been considered. These include the usual suspects such as the disruptive events of the Bruce Invasion (1315–18) and the Black Death (1348–50) and the rebellions of the Irish of the Dublin/Wicklow Mountains (later fourteenth century). While any or all of the above may have prompted the building project, the increasing tensions between the abbey and the town became a more immediate and pressing threat into the fourteenth century. This threat culminated in the well-documented, violent attack on the abbey by the citizens of Dublin, led by their mayor, which saw the attempted murder of the abbot, the widespread breaking of windows and the partial burning of the dormitory in 1392.[51] Such an aggressive attack perpetrated by the abbey's closest neighbours presents itself as a more immediate catalyst for a largescale construction event designed to seal the abbey lands off from the city.

Evidence that the northern wall may have still been standing in 1634 is contained within a very valuable document which provides an eyewitness account of the site and its surrounds. The document is a statement given by a lifelong resident of the area during the course of a title dispute. The author of the statement, John Smith, is therefore drawing on living memory of the area stretching conceivably back into the sixteenth century. Several particulars are worthy of note:

46 Clyne, *Kells Priory*, p. 53. 47 Linzi Simpson, '5–6 Cecilia St West', *Medieval Archaeology*, 41 (1997), 304–5; *c*.1260. 48 Tim Coughlan, 'Excavations at the medieval cemetery of St Peter's Church, Dublin' in Seán Duffy (ed.), *Medieval Dublin IV* (Dublin, 2003), pp 95–114. 49 Sinéad Phelan, 'The bank, the ditch and the water: Hiberno-Norse discoveries at Church Street and Hammond Lane' in Seán Duffy (ed.), *Medieval Dublin X* (Dublin, 2010), pp 165–97, at pp 180–1. 50 Emmett Stafford, *Report on archaeological test trenching at Dublin Corporation's Daisy Market, 01E711*, (unpublished report prepared by IAC Ltd, 2001). 51 Foley, *The abbey of St Thomas*, pp 67–8.

… from the backsyd of that house to the great stone wall joyninge to yor' honor's court theer was a long garden plott joyninge to my ffather's backsyd, one the est syd therof wherin did grow quynce trees and plum trees, of wch trees I have pulled some of the frutts of them many tymes and have eaten of them, and in the same plott of ground their was a great sestourn of stone, wch would contayne 20 barels of bai[r]lee or otts, or theraboutts for maltinge, as I have herd reported and bult by one John Luttrell of Dublin, mrchant, who was one of my godfathers, wch sestorn beinge made of long broad stones by direction of yor honorable ffather, I pulled down, and had those broad stones layed one the battelments of Kinge John's chamber, for gutter stones, then having noe lead thereon.[52]

Not only does this testimony illustrate that the precinct wall was at least partially standing in 1634, but it conveys a strong impression of extensive garden plots and orchards surrounding the houses, specifically the 'long garden' which would seem to extend, at least partially, across the Frawley's site in this period. This extensive and apparently open greenspace and groves of fruit trees fits very well with the widespread phase of deep garden soil that sealed the thirteenth- and fourteenth-century activity across the site.

The secular plots

Being the easternmost stretch of the *Slíghe Mhór*, Thomas Street represents one of the primary routeways of medieval Ireland. As the importance of the town grew, so did the traffic of imports and exports flowing from the city along this route, which is recorded at Thomas Street (*Vicus Sancti Thome*) by AD 1200.[53] Archaeological dating evidence from the vicinity of the Frawley's site suggests that formal burgage plots were laid out between the city walls and St Thomas's Abbey by the same date.[54] By the later fourteenth century there are records of houses fronting the street which were roofed with tiles,[55] reflected, perhaps, in the number of roof tile fragments uncovered during the excavations. The abbey was the biggest landlord in the area, its portfolio growing over the centuries as citizens bequeathed plots. The register of the abbey of St Thomas contains charters which give an indication of the types of tenants that were leasing land in the area. These include potters, plasterers, carpenters, glasswrights and several tanners, shoemakers and glove-makers.

52 Henry F. Berry, 'Notes on a statement dated 1634', 395. **53** Eric St J. Brooks (ed.), *Register of the hospital of St John the Baptist without New Gate, Dublin* (Dublin, 1936), no. 127. **54** O'Donovan, 'Growth and decline', p. 166. **55** Conlon, 'Women in medieval Dublin', pp 173–4.

Tanning or cess pits?

Evidence for at least six plots running from Thomas Street to the precinct wall was identified during excavations. The width of these plots is relatively consistent, ranging from 16 to 21 feet wide (*c.*5–6.5 metres). The density of the pits found within these plots corresponds to that seen on the northern side of the street, during excavations by Edmond O'Donovan immediately opposite the Frawley's site.[56] The majority of the pits excavated by O'Donovan were interpreted as cesspits, though some had been emptied of all organic material and backfilled with sterile clays.

As discussed above, the contents of a subset of the pits from the Frawley's site have been subject to environmental analysis,[57] and the results suggest that, far from representing features confined to a single purpose, some of the pits fulfilled a range of functions over time. Tanning activity has been inferred through artefactual and environmental evidence in plots 1, 2, 5 and 6. A function in the deposition of cess was identified in plots 1, 3 and 5; artefactual evidence (the toilet seat) in plot 4. Given the utilization of dung/faeces and urine in several stages of the tanning process, this uncertainty in function is not only unclear to the modern observer. In the thirteenth-century ribald Middle-English poem known as the *Satire on the people of Dublin* found among the so-called 'Kildare poems',[58] the tanners of Dublin (skinners) are accused of defecating in their own 'vats':

> Hail, you skinners with your poisonous vat! Whoever smells it is much distressed. When it thunders[59] you may void excrement therein. Misfortune on your manners, you cause the whole street to stink![60]

As has been illustrated, some of the pits with tanning indicators also have indicators for cess, implying a change of use over the course of the active life of the feature. The reference to the 'street' of skinners in the *Satire* is very likely to refer to the area of Thomas Street outside of the walls of the town:[61] given the noxious nature of the tanning process, this industry was often located away from the densest zones of habitation. Tanning pits with bark-rich fills have been excavated further east along the street.[62]

---

56 O'Donovan, 'Growth and decline', pp 140–1.   **57** This process is still ongoing and, unfortunately, at time of writing, no results from the analysis of insect remains has been completed.   **58** London, British Library, MS Harley 913; for English translation, see Angela M. Lucas (ed.), *Anglo-Irish poems of the Middle Ages* (Dublin, 1995). Text also available online (https://celt.ucc.ie//published/T300000-001/index.html).   **59** For which, read flatulence.   **60** Lucas (ed.), *Anglo-Irish poems*, ll. 79–82.   **61** Although, what is now Christchurch Place was known as Skinners' Row (*Vicus pellipariorum*) in the Middle Ages. **62** Judith Carroll, 'Excavations at 58–59 Thomas Street/Vicar Street and 63–64 Thomas Street, Dublin 8' in Seán Duffy (ed.), *Medieval Dublin XII* (Dublin, 2013), pp 161–88; Catriona Moore, 'Excavations bulletin 2018:291 – 61–62 Thomas St, Dublin, Licence No. 16E0367' (2018): https://excavations.ie/report/2018/Dublin/0027001/ (accessed 13 July 2019).

In attempting to understand the multiple shapes and sizes of pit excavated, some of which were clearly too shallow to fulfil a cess function, it is important to note that the process of tanning requires that the hides are subjected to a number of different processes prior to the prolonged immersion in tanning liquor. These different processes would conceivably have required the use of a number of different pits. The principal steps in the process are as follows:

- tanner acquires hides from the butcher who has cut all of the useful material from the animal.
- hides delivered with horns and hooves attached.
- tanner trims hides, washing blood, dung and any salt that may have been applied by the butcher.
- de-hairing of hides carried out by treating the hides with lime, wood ash solution or urine.
- when the hair was sufficiently loosened to the root, it was removed with a blunt, single-edged, two-handled knife.
- puering/bating followed, where the skins were immersed in either a warm solution of dog or bird excrement or of fermenting barley or rye.
- washing of the skins in water and rounding, i.e., dividing the skin into different quality parts.
- skins were then immersed in weak tanning liquor and moved around continuously in shallow pits called 'handlers' (as hides handled in and out of pits daily).
- once the colour was satisfactory, the hides were stowed in layaway pits where alternating layers of hides and tanning material were laid down and covered with water and left for a period of up to 12 months.
- once the hides were deemed ready, they were removed, washed once more and smoothed using a wooden 'setting pin'.
- finally, hides were hung up to dry slowly on tenters.[63]

It is therefore possible that a number of the pits or combinations of the pits represent 'handlers' while others may have been layaway pits and others used in de-hairing, etc. The weak tanning liquor used in the 'handlers' was likely siphoned from the larger layaway pits and adulterated with water. This process would not leave any bark residues in the pits, but the raised acidity could result in the reduced variation of plant species as illustrated in the plant macrofossil results.

Information from the Register of St Thomas provides further detail. In an undated charter, possibly dating to the late twelfth or early thirteenth century,

---

63 Allan Hall and Harry Kenward, 'Can we identify biological indicator groups for craft, industry and other activities?' in Peter Murphy and Patricia Wiltshire (eds), *The environmental archaeology of industry: symposia of the association for environmental archaeology*, no. 20

Rembold the son of John Tanner, for the yearly fee of two shillings and half a pound of cinnamon, 'confirmed to Alexander la Ware a certain land of 16 feet in the front without the new gate of Dublin between the High (*Magnum*) Street and the cemetery of the church of St Thomas, to wit, that land which we held of Master Hugh of the fee of St Thomas'.[64] Plot 1 and plot 5 at the Frawley's site were found to measure 16 feet in width,[65] and both run from the street-front to the cemetery of the church. Both plots have produced some evidence for medieval tanning and either could well be the plot referenced in the Rembold's charter. Another plot, 19 feet in width and 89 feet long, on the southern side of Thomas Street, was bequeathed in the later thirteenth century to the abbey with a proviso that the daughters of Roger the Tanner be provided for from the revenues.[66] That this charter was witnessed by a William the Currier, among others, provides a glimpse of a community of tradesmen operating in the Liberties area at this time.

Alum tawing

While, as discussed above, many of the pits at the Frawley's site may have played a role in the tanning process, there is another similar medieval industry, known from the historic record in Dublin but difficult to identify in the archaeological record.[67] Tawing involved processing hides using oils and salts such as alum and is associated with the production of supple, high-quality leather that is often white in colour. The process has been described as follows:

- the whittawyer acquires skin from butcher or fellmonger.
- skins are limed, un-haired and washed and then usually trampled in a barrel or tub together with a mixture of materials including alum and oil.
- the leather is then softened and dried and eventually sold (generally to the glover).
- the glover or other leatherworker, such as a shoemaker (*sutter*), converts the leather into a finished product.[68]

It has been noted in England that the activities of the fellmonger and the glover could, on occasion, be carried out by the same craftsman.[69] The *Satire* mentions tawing in the course of the following verse on the nuns of St Mary's del Dame in Dublin:

(Oxford, 2003), pp 114–30, at p. 124. **64** RIA, MS 12 D 38 (unpublished Register of St Thomas), pp 37–8. I am indebted to Dr Áine Foley and to Prof. Marie Therese Flanagan for their assistance in navigating the unpublished registers. **65** The imperial foot and the medieval measurement post-1200 are virtually the same unit. **66** RIA, MS 12 D 38, p. 86. **67** Hall and Kenward, 'Can we identify biological indicator groups', p. 124. **68** Umberto Albarella, 'Tawyers, tanner, horn trade and the mystery of the missing goat' in Murphy and Wiltshire (eds), *The environmental archaeology of industry*, pp 71–86, at p. 73. **69** Ibid., p. 72.

> Hail, you nuns of St Mary's house, God's ladies-in-waiting and his own spouses! You often 'treat your shoes amiss' [lose your virginity], your feet are very tender! Misfortune to the shoemaker who taws your leather [*tawith yure lethir*]![70]

While the double entendre is obvious, the association between shoemakers (sutters) and the act of tawing leather is clearly made.

The Middle English verb, *tauen*, is defined as preparing an animal skin for use, by dressing or treating it to produce a supple white leather.[71] This is taken up later in the poem when the sutters themselves come in for satire:

> Hail, you shoemakers with your many lasts! With your soft hides of wonderful animals, and afflictions and plaiting tools, leather-cutting tool and awls. Your teeth are black and horrible, filthy was that crowd.[72]

With the above in mind, the following record is of interest: in the late twelfth or thirteenth century Stephen Letteler confirmed to his sister Cristina a plot of land, held of the abbey but formerly held by William the Tanner, for the yearly rent of a pair of gloves.[73] Although gloves are quite commonly specified as rent in such deeds, in this instance it seems that the gloves were being produced on this plot, although no precise locational information is included. Similarly, Gervase fitz Thomas Fating in the late twelfth or thirteenth century granted a plot 21 feet wide (plot 2 at Frawleys measured *c.*20 feet wide) in the parish of St Catherine to Richard Faber for the yearly rent of a pair of white gloves.[74] Several other references to white gloves survive in the published register,[75] and their presence as a form of payment provides proof of tawing within the vicinity of the abbey from the twelfth/thirteenth century. There is a possibility that the abbey was profiting also by this industry, specifically in the form of parchment which was also a product of the tawing process. In this context, the widespread presence of soluble salts across the site would appear to be a strong indicator of the industrial use of alum, most likely in the tawing process, at the Frawley's site.

The abbey buildings

The building history of the monastery is difficult to piece together based on the scant evidence retrieved from the Frawley's site and other excavations.

---

70 Lucas (ed.), *Anglo-Irish poems*, ll. 49–52.   **71** Yoko Wada, 'The poem known as *Satire* from London, British Library, MS Harley 913: a new interpretation', *Bulletin of the Institute of Oriental and Occidental Studies*, Kansai University, 83–99, at 91 (accessed 13 July 2019 at https://www.kansai-u.ac.jp/Tozaiken/publication/asset/bulletin/46/kiyo4613.pdf). **72** Lucas (ed.), *Anglo-Irish poems*, ll. 73–7.   **73** RIA, MS 12 D 38, p. 86.   **74** Ibid., p. 77. **75** *Reg. St Thomas*, ed. Gilbert, pp 63, 64–5, 148, 385, 386.

However, as detailed above, three broad building phases are suggested by the recovered masonry fragments, supported by the presence of a range of floor tile typologies. These phases are provisionally put forward as follows:

- a late twelfth- to mid-thirteenth-century phase represented by carved Dundry stone fragments and two-colour floor tiles. A comparison between the moulding profiles of the Frawley's Dundry fragments and the fragments retrieved by Claire Walsh from within the footprint of the abbey church has identified a minimum of one match, indicating that at least some of the Frawley's stone came from the abbey church.[76]
- a fourteenth- to fifteenth-century phase, which saw extension to the abbey church or the remodelling of its principal windows, is represented by the frequent occurrence of sandstone tracery and also by the abundant line-impressed floor tile fragments.
- a fifteenth- or sixteenth-century phase is also represented by some pieces of geometrically carved limestone and small numbers of relief floor tiles.

Further subdivision of these phases can be proposed through analysis of the historic record. It is likely that building work started around 1177, when the priory dedicated to St Thomas was established by royal decree. Given that this act was part of the reparation agreed by Henry II with the pope, it is presumed that money would have been provided up front by the king to facilitate a building programme. The first monastic church would have been Romanesque in style. This would have involved either the construction of a church from scratch, or the refurbishment/expansion of a pre-existing chapel which is thought to have stood on the spot.[77] No Romanesque architectural fragments have been discovered. The elevation of the priory to the status of an abbey in 1192, apparently also the date at which the Victorine observance of the Rule of St Augustine was adopted, must have been accompanied by a programme of building, and there is a very strong argument that this was the first work of Gothic architecture in Ireland.[78] Some of the pieces of carved Dundry recovered at Frawley's may relate to this phase.

A third phase of building in the Anglo-Norman era is documented. Abbot Adam began the process of building a 'new church' in 1227, although it is unclear how fast work progressed. In 1251 the king ordered the mayor and bailiffs of Bristol to release or replace the stone which they had taken while it awaited transportation to Dublin for use in the construction of this church.

76 I am indebted to Claire Walsh for facilitating this comparative study.   77 Michael Staunton and Colmán Ó Clabaigh, 'Thomas Becket and Ireland' in Elizabeth Mullins and Diarmuid Scully (eds), *Listen, O Isles, unto me: studies in medieval word and image in honour of Jennifer O'Reilly* (Cork, 2011).   78 O'Keeffe, 'St Thomas' abbey and the history of early English Gothic in Ireland'; Duffy and O'Keeffe, 'A stone shrine', 20–3.

6.25 Dundry stone soffit from early thirteenth-century arch

This later building project is somewhat puzzling. Given that there was no move to a new site, it would have necessitated the removal of a church that was only a few decades old in 1227. Did it remain unfinished in 1251, almost a quarter of a century later, and had work been held up because stone was requisitioned in Bristol?

St Thomas's Abbey would certainly have had relics of Becket; the saint's relics were very widespread and not confined to monasteries that bore his name. The Dublin abbey is very likely to have possessed the most venerable type of relic – a corporeal relic, a part of the saint's body. It is possible that the 'new church' was either a great new east end to the existing church, built for the purpose of displaying a relic of St Thomas or a free-standing sepulchral monument, rather like that erected to the east of Ferns Cathedral. The possibility that some of the fragments of Dundry recovered during the excavations may have formed part of an elaborate stone shrine for such relics

6.26 Visualization of the type of window of which the cusped tracery may have formed part (courtesy of The Discovery Programme)

has been explored elsewhere.[79] Whatever the new building was, it was surely finished by 1240. Becket's feast day that year – the 70th anniversary – was marked by a great ceremony presided over by the archbishop of Dublin and illuminated by 800 wax tapers supplied by Henry III.[80]

The quality of the decoration of this phase of building is attested to in the jamb fragment with deeply undercut plant ornament. This is not stiff-leaf ornament, the type of ornament characteristic of early English Gothic and largely confined to capitals. The naturalism of its stalky asymmetry has better parallels in early thirteenth-century French Gothic (a reminder, perhaps, that St Thomas's community followed the monastic observance of a Parisian

79 Ibid.   80 Gwynn, 'Early history', 21.

monastery). Nevertheless, the moulding to which the plant is attached suggests a parallel in England, where, in the period of the so-called Decorated Style (from the mid-thirteenth century to the early fourteenth century), sculptors sometimes created naturalistic plants inspired by the earlier French models. The manner in which the plant on the St Thomas fragment sprouts from the jamb stone resembles, for example, sculpture on the doorway of Southwell Minster's late thirteenth-century chapter house. The Elder Lady Chapel (*c.*1220) at St Mary's Bristol-Redcliffe is also possibly a good comparison to this phase of building of the church of St Thomas's.[81] Another moulded stone potentially from this phase includes the soffit of an early thirteenth-century arch, the curvature of which suggests a very wide arch, possibly even from the crossing (fig. 6.25).

The refurbishment of the principal opes within the abbey church is suggested by the volume of cusped arch tracery recovered. This kind of remodelling was widespread in Irish churches and monastic buildings in the fourteenth century.[82] An examination of the tracery fragments by Dr Annejulie Lafaye facilitated by the Discovery Programme has resulted in a conjectural visualization of the type of window from which the tracery may have come (fig. 6.26). Another, less impressive voussoir of undecorated sandstone likely to date from this period of construction bears deep incisions of a type often found at castle and monastery gatehouses, resulting from sentries sharpening their bladed weapons on the stone.[83]

The retrieval of a column base and a few other fragments of likely sixteenth-century date shows that improvements to the monastic buildings were being undertaken right up to the Dissolution by Henry VIII in 1539.

The cemetery

Pre-abbey activity
The early dates retrieved for a number of burials in the western side of the cemetery were wholly unexpected and have prompted a reappraisal of the evidence and a change of direction in the research questions being pursued as the post-excavation work progresses. The date from the slab-lined burial and the potentially early dates for several other burials are, on balance, enough evidence to illustrate that Christian burial was taking place on the site, at the very least, 30 years in advance of the foundation of the priory (later, abbey) in 1177. There is also quite a possibility that some of the burials in the St Catherine's Lane area pre-date the priory by several hundred years. More

81 Roger Stalley, 'The Augustinians and their architecture', lecture presented at the St Thomas's Abbey Symposium 2017, available through History Hub at http://historyhub.ie/thomasabbey. 82 Leask, *Irish churches*, pp 124–8. 83 Paul Duffy, 'Point duty – evidence for a gatehouse at the abbey of St Thomas the Martyr, Dublin?', *IAI Newsletter Autumn 2018*, 18:2 (2018), 24–6.

confident statements to this effect will be possible following the second round
of dating. What is certain, however, is that these early dates have pushed
discussion of the cemetery from the secure and well-documented Anglo-
Norman period into the much greyer realm of early medieval Dublin. Of
particular interest are the two deviant burials, which, in light of the dating of
the slab-lined burial, are almost certainly early medieval. Chris Read excavated
two very similar examples from Kilteasheen, Co. Roscommon, and has
discussed them in the context of beliefs surrounding vampires, revenants or
ghosts which were believed to come back among the living, unless provisions
were undertaken to confine them in their graves. The Kilteasheen burials were
dated to between AD 661 and 784.[84] Full treatment of these Dublin burials will
follow final analysis; however, at this juncture, some attempt needs to be made
to explain this anomaly.

On current information, the earliest indication of a religious foundation on
the site is a reference to a chapel dedicated to St Thomas, along with a chaplain
and enclosed precinct *c.*1172–4.[85] This date comes from a story preserved in
the *Miracula S. Thomae*. In this account a certain Walter, fighting for
Strongbow in Ireland, left two horses 'which he had worn out in plundering
the region' within the sept/precinct (?) of the chapel of the Martyr Thomas,
near the city of Dublin. The horses were stolen, but the thief was miraculously
led back to the spot by the intervention of the Martyr.[86] The abbey of St
Thomas the Martyr was founded by William Fitz Audelin on behalf of King
Henry II in March 1177, almost a year after the death of Strongbow. This
reference, though tenuous, is the only documentary evidence known for an
earlier religious establishment on the site. Such a dedication makes sense given
the longstanding connections between Dublin and Canterbury as well as the
changing demographic of Dublin in this period to include large populations of
Bristol merchants and Anglo-Norman adventurers.

If, however, further dates are clustered more towards the ninth and tenth
centuries, a foundation of much earlier date will need to be considered. One
enigmatic fourteenth-century reference has been explored which mentions a
monastery of St Witteschan somewhere to the north of the mill pool of the
abbey of St Thomas:

> In the west part of Dublin, passing from the cathedral of St Patrick
> through the Coombe, to the pool of the house of St Thomas the Martyr,

84 Chris Read, 'Remembering where the bishop sat: exploring perceptions of the past at the
Bishop's Seat, Kilteasheen, Co. Roscommon' in Thomas Finan (ed.), *Medieval Lough Cé:
history, archaeology and landscape* (Dublin, 2010), pp 41–66, at p. 48.   85 'Miracula S.
Thomae', 6.128 in J.C. Robertson and J.B. Sheppard (eds), *Materials for the history of
Thomas Becket*, 7 vols, Rolls Series (London, 1875–85), i, pp 545–6; Staunton and O
Clabaigh, 'Thomas Becket and Ireland'.   86 *infra septa capellae martyris Thomae*, ibid.

> leaving the south gate of the monastery of Witeschan, and the Conelan towards the north, on the left hand.[87]

This otherwise-unknown monastery has been interpreted by Archdall as a thirteenth-century foundation of the friars of the sack or friars *de penitentia Jesu Christi*, disbanded in the early fourteenth century. A relict of this dedication to Witeschan is preserved in the name Weycesthame which is associated with a gate in the Coombe in the fourteenth century, transmuted to Washam in the seventeenth century.[88] The reference to the Conelon is also puzzling. Could either name preserve memory of an earlier, pre-Anglo-Norman foundation in the area?

There is also the sixteenth-century reference to a wayside chapel dedicated to Mo Lua which has been interpreted as a potential pre-Anglo-Norman/ Viking Age dedication located at the presumed intersection of the Slighe Mhór and the Slighe Midhluachra. The location of this intersection has been convincingly proposed as the intersection between Francis Street and Thomas Street, some distance to the east of the Frawley's site.[89]

One other foundation, thought to be the earliest church established in Dublin, is described in the sources as the church of the sons of Aedh (Cell Mac nÁeda) recorded in the eleventh- or early twelfth-century poem known as *Senchas Gall Átha Cliath*.[90] Previous suggestions for the location of this church have placed it in Cornmarket, potentially equating it with an earlier church at the current location of St Audoen's (though no pre-Anglo-Norman building was found during excavations).[91] The date for the slab-lined burial at Thomas Street represents the earliest date-range for a Christian burial in this part of the city and one of the earliest known Christian burials in the city as a whole. Located on a rise overlooking the Liffey, not far from the purported location of the 'ford of the hurdles' preserved in the name Áth Cliath, could the Thomas Street burials have an association with this early church?

Such speculation aside, it will be very difficult to definitively connect the burials to a historic foundation. It must also be considered that there is every chance that the burials were associated with a foundation that has evaded the historic record.

The abbey cemetery
The excavations have shown that the northern extent of the abbey cemetery is well-defined and burials were found to respect the precinct wall. Overcrowding

---

87 Mervin Archdall, *Monasticon Hibernicum*, revised edn, ed. P.F. Moran, 3 vols (Dublin, 1876), ii, p. 20.   88 Clarke, *Dublin, Pt 1* (IHTA), p. 21.   89 Ibid., p. 1.   90 *SGAC*, p. 45. 91 Clarke, *Dublin, Pt 1* (IHTA), p. 1; Mary McMahon, *St Audoen's Church, Cornmarket, Dublin: archaeology and architecture* (Dublin, 2006), p. 85.

does not seem to have been an issue along the northern part of the cemetery with very little intercutting encountered. The density was observed to increase slightly further south towards Hanbury Lane, and closer to the location of the abbey church, which is to be expected. The date-ranges retrieved so far support the view that the burials in this area relate to interments from the first 100 years of the foundation's life. Soon after, it appears that burials within the northern portion of the abbey precinct were discontinued and the area given over to gardening and groves of fruit trees.[92] The abbey cemetery may therefore have retracted in the fourteenth century to a smaller core which, as is usual with Augustinian foundations, is likely to have been to the east of the abbey church.

Notable burials

Two pilgrim burials from thirteenth-century levels were uncovered. Each burial contained a single scallop shell, a pilgrim souvenir from the shrine of St James at Santiago de Compostela. These burials represent the only known pilgrim burials from Dublin city or county, though a handful are known from across the country.[93] It is not certain if they were canons of St Thomas as the abbey graveyard was also used for burial by the wealthy lay population of Dublin. The identification of these pilgrims is all the more significant given the location of St James's pilgrim hostel at St James's Gate nearby. This is the traditional starting point in Ireland for the pilgrimage to Santiago de Compostela.

Due to the abbey's royal association, a number of notable personalities from the first generation of the Anglo-Norman era were buried in the abbey graveyard in the early years of the foundation. These include Hugh de Lacy (d. 1186), lord of Meath, his first wife Rohese of Monmouth (d. *c.*1180) of the famous Cambro-Norman family, and Basilia de Clare (d. 1186) who was the wife of Raymond (le Gros) fitz Gerald and sister to Richard de Clare (Strongbow). The case of Basilia is particularly interesting as she gave large grants to the church of St Thomas at Dublin which she describes as a place 'where she serves as a nun, and in which she desires to be interred'.[94]

Hugh de Lacy

The body of Hugh de Lacy is also of interest as it took a very circuitous route to the abbey. Firstly, following his decapitation in 1186 at Durrow during an ambush, both his head and body were taken by the Irish of Teathbha (in modern Co. Longford). The remains were retrieved by the de Lacy family a decade later following protracted deliberations. De Lacy's body was then

92 Lyons, *Report on plant macrofossil assemblage.*   **93** Louise Nugent, 'Pilgrimage and the Augustinians in medieval Ireland' in Martin Browne and Colmán Ó Clabaigh (eds), *Households of God: the regular canons and canonesses of St Augustine and of Prémontré in medieval Ireland* (Dublin, 2019), pp 215–34, at p. 233.   **94** Elliot, 'Abbey of St Thomas',

interred at Bective Abbey in the lordship of Meath, while the head was carried to the abbey of St Thomas to be interred close to his wife, Rohese. This resulted in a drawn-out dispute between the communities of Bective and St Thomas's which ultimately saw de Lacy's body reinterred at the abbey of St Thomas in 1205, almost twenty years after his death.[95] What body made it back from Teathbha in 1195 and whether it was the same body dug up a decade later and transported to Dublin are interesting questions; however, some indicators that might suggest reinternment may have been uncovered during the excavations at Frawley's. The slab-lined burial described above, with the early date, was truncated by a pit containing eight skulls. This pit cut through the location of where the skull in the slab-lined burial would have been. This pit was interpreted on-site as a later re-interment of skulls dug up during construction work in the area in the post-medieval period. However, the components of a headless body and a pit filled with skulls dug into this burial close to the position of the head could be described in a more creative way:

- a body is dug up from the Bective graveyard in 1205 a decade after its interment.
- either by accident or design, it is not the body of Hugh de Lacy, but an earlier burial dating to the foundation of the abbey (1177).
- it is buried in the cemetery of St Thomas the Martyr and subsequently an attempt is made to repatriate the head.
- however, nineteen years having elapsed, the skull is difficult to find and a selection of probable candidates are reinterred with the body.

Tempting as this reading is, the historical sources do not support it. Reference to the 'cross erected for the soul of the wife of Hugh de Lacy'[96] would suggest that de Lacy and his wife were buried towards the eastern end of the church.

Decline of the cemetery

A number of factors may have resulted in the decline of the abbey cemetery from the later twelfth century. These include the establishment of the parish church of St Catherine and associated graveyard in 1195 and the growing tension and later animosity between the citizens of Dublin and the abbey. It seems unlikely that the wealthy residents of fourteenth-century Dublin sought out the prestige of being buried in the king's foundation as much as the Bristol merchants and Anglo-Norman nobility did in the early days of the colony. Further, the excavations showed no clear division between the abbey graveyard and that of St Catherine's. It is possible that a divide exists beneath the western side of St Catherine's Lane, following the current graveyard wall (outside of

p. 64; *Reg. St Thomas*, ed. Gilbert, p. xiv.   **95** Colin Veach, *Lordship in four realms: the Lacy family, 1166–1241* (Manchester, 2014), p. 67.   **96** Ibid., p. 209.

the limit of excavation). Or it could be the case that a portion of the abbey graveyard was given over to the church at the time of its establishment, this becoming the burial place for the ordinary parishioners of St Catherine's parish. As illustrated below, the abbey graveyard had passed out of living memory by 1634 and quite probably well before then:

> For the buryll place or church yard bellonging to the aby, I do thinke that the churchyard now of St Katherin's church was their buriall place for strangers, and the rest buryed wthin the aby in severall places, whereof there was many vaults and darck places for that use. St Katherin's church is reputed to be a chapell of ease unto the aby of Thomas court, as I have herd often.[97]

CONCLUSIONS

Excavations at the Frawley's site have uncovered extensive evidence relating to the abbey precinct and graveyard and the adjoining secular plots throughout the twelfth to sixteenth centuries. Analysis of the archaeological findings, in conjunction with interrogation of the historical information, has enabled the proposal of several interpretations which may advance the understanding of broader patterns of development and activity in medieval Dublin.

It is proposed that the original boundary of the abbey was delimited by a ditch and bank arrangement, commonly employed to define monastic holdings in the twelfth and thirteenth centuries. From environmental evidence, the ditch appears to have carried water before clogging up over time, wetland species becoming established within the watercourse and along its verges. Some evidence for flax processing may suggest activity associated with textile production. This ditch, possibly known in the late twelfth/thirteenth century as the 'water of the Lutteburne/Lotbourne' ('leat stream'?), is likely to have been incorporated into the city watercourse/Glib water from *c.*1225. This stream was diverted to the north of St Catherine's Church sometime after 1348, plausibly to allow the residents of the liberty and town access to the water for public washing of clothes and, potentially, to prevent the city's water supply from passing through the active parish graveyard of St Catherine's Church.

At this time, the northern precinct boundary shifted *c.*2.5m to the south. Given the value of the leases of adjoining plots to the abbey, it is not inconceivable that the decision to move the boundary to the south may have had a commercial justification. The setting back of the boundary seems to have been followed immediately by an intensification of activity along the 2.5m wide strip immediately north of the wall. The wall was constructed in typical medieval

---

97 Berry, 'Notes on a statement dated 1634', 396.

fashion, with a broad foundation, interior and exterior facing and mortared upper courses of limestone slabs laid on the flat. It is likely that this wall was constructed in the mid- to late fourteenth century in line with the murage of other foundations around this time. Increasing hostility to the abbey, as much as its location on the western approaches to the city, may have provided the impetus for the construction of the wall in the later fourteenth century.

The dense clustering of pits of different shapes and depths in the plots backing off Thomas Street is suggestive of intensive industrial processes. However, the distinction between domestic cesspits and industrial tanning pits is difficult to ascertain in advance of the analysis of the insect remains. The changing use of the pits over time and the complicated relationship between tanning and excrement (as illustrated by the thirteenth-century poem known as the *Satire of the people of Dublin*) makes classification difficult to uphold. This duality of purpose is exemplified by the discovery in these pits of both an unequivocal tanning utensil and an undoubted toilet seat!

The carved masonry fragments provide the only tangible link to the abbey buildings and while much of the limestone used in post-medieval buildings and walls across the site was almost certainly quarried from the abbey buildings, the decorated stone provides a window on the phases of construction and refurbishment at the foundation.

Potentially the most significant findings have come for the excavation of the abbey cemetery which has yielded, not only extensive burials relating to the earliest phases of the abbey's life, but also evidence of pre-Anglo-Norman activity. These early dates may have a significant impact on current models used to explain the phases of development of Dublin city.

Given the scale of the excavation and the post excavation work remaining to be completed, it is expected that further specialist papers will follow and it is hoped that more definitive interpretations can be put forward in the near future.

To conclude, some additional dates for the timeline of the abbey of St Thomas are here proposed:

Pre–1100: graveyard (and potentially church) in existence.

*c.*1172:   pre-existing chapel (with chaplain) dedicated to Thomas Becket by citizens of Dublin.

1177:   priory established and lands encircled with a ditch, larger and more substantial to the south (the side exposed to Irish attack) and smaller to the north. The northern ditch carries water and may represent the 'Luttebrune' mentioned in a late twelfth-/ thirteenth-century charter.

1192:   elevation to abbey and significant building projects begun – some of the Dundry stone recovered may date to this period.

1225:   the 'Luttebrune' is tapped into for the purpose of carrying water from the city cistern to the west, towards St John's mill and the city.

1227: foundation stone laid in construction (extension?) of abbey church – the majority of the carved Dundry dates to this period.

*c.***1360:** the 'Luttebrune' stream east of St Catherine's Church is diverted into the thoroughfare of Thomas Street, becoming the Glib Stream, this potentially to facilitate access for citizens for public washing (as per reference in 1538). Intensification of tanning/cess pits along its former course.

*c.***1360–1400:** Construction of outer precinct wall, potentially in response to attack by mayor, bailiff and citizens of Dublin in 1392. Possible renovation of the abbey church at this time in the 'Decorated Style' Gothic, accounting for the extensive retrieval of high-quality sandstone pieces of cusped-arch window tracery.

1478: money given in reparation of the monastic church of St Thomas's may account for the few 'Perpendicular Style' limestone masonry pieces recovered, most notably the fifteenth-century cloister column base.[98]

*c.***1538:** quarrying of stone from the abbey church and buildings to line cesspits and tanning pits which begin to eat into precinct wall.

*c.***1650:** precinct wall levelled, largescale secular (tanning) activity established within abbey precinct.

ACKNOWLEGMENTS

From the pre-planning stage to the production of the final report, a project of this size necessarily benefits from the input and expertise of many hard-working archaeologists, consultants, specialists and public servants. While the specifics of each individual's contribution may be lost in the end result, all have left their imprint in some way, shaping the final product. For their varied and essential inputs into the process I would like to acknowledge the following people: Tim Coughlan, Ruth Johnson, Faith Bailey, Mairead Sweeney, Alan O'Raw, Rob Lynch, Emily Pigott, Femke Vleeshouwer, Siobhán Scully, Maeve Tobin, Dave Moore, Katie O'Mahony, Noirín Teahan, Andrew Finney, Neil Organ, Oscar Bulnes, Jacek Myrcha, Enda Lydon, Jane Whittaker, Mark Louth, Finbar O'Mahony, Brandon Walsh, Caroline McGrath, Christina Hughes, Ross Waters, Chris Coffey, John Parle, Niamh Milward, Ingela Wass, Rebecca Martin, James Purcell, Ellen O'Carroll, Susannah Kelly, Tadhg O'Keeffe, Roger Stalley, Ruth Carden, Susan Lyons, Linzi Simpson, Antoine Giacometti, Annejulie Lafaye, Gary Devlin, Aaron Deevy, Howard Clarke, Claire Walsh, Derek O'Brien, Áine Foley, Marie Therese Flanagan, with a particular and poignant thanks to the late Eileen Reilly for her expert, insightful and generous advice.

98 Gwynn, 'Early history', 27.

Blackpitts: Dublin's medieval tanning quarter

ANTOINE GIACOMETTI

INTRODUCTION

In 2004, an archaeological excavation took place at 48 New Street South, Dublin 8, in an area of Dublin known locally as 'Blackpitts'. The excavation identified over a hundred tanning pits dating from the late thirteenth to the seventeenth century. Back in the early 2000s, New Street was one of the largest and most extensive medieval leatherworking sites ever excavated in Ireland. Prior to this, archaeological evidence for medieval leatherworking had been either dumps of medieval leather objects, or individual small tanning pits. For example, the largest Irish deposit of medieval leatherworking evidence had come from Breandán Ó Ríordáin's excavations in the 1970s of a dump of waste at High Street in Dublin. This waste included shoe fragments dated to the twelfth and thirteenth centuries, leather sheaths, scabbards and satchels (Ó Ríordáin 1976); however, no actual tanning pits were found. A large quantity of medieval leather – again mostly shoes – was excavated by Claire Walsh on Patrick Street and Winetavern Street in the early 1990s (O'Rourke 1997, 163–78). Similar dumps were excavated in Waterford (McCutcheon and Hurley 1997, 161).

The first definitive medieval tanning pit in Dublin was identified in 1990 (pit 11, site B in Walsh 1997, 39). This was a fourteenth-century oak-stave and stone-lined tanning pit on Patrick Street. In 1993 a late fifteenth-century 'tanning house' at Ship Street Little was excavated, with a rectangular timber pit and three barrels (Simpson 2004, 43). Shortly afterwards pits containing tanning waste at 44–9 New Row South were interpreted as being tanning activity dating from the thirteenth or fourteenth century to the eighteenth or nineteenth century (Scally 1997, 11–13). In 2003, a number of what were possibly small medieval tanning pits were excavated on the Coombe (McQuade 2005).

The relatively limited archaeological evidence for medieval tanning before 2004 can be compared to the extensive evidence for late eighteenth- and nineteenth-century tanning complexes in Dublin 8, for example at Ardee Street (Myles 2005), James's Street (Bolger 2005) and Dolphin's Barn (Hayden 2002, 33–8) in the early 2000s. These eighteenth- and nineteenth-century tanneries were large, industrialized and well organized, whereas the medieval tanning sites were small, relatively rare, and often isolated. This did not fit the evidence from documentary sources, which suggested that Dublin had a thriving leather-making industry in the thirteenth century and that leather-making was an important medieval trade (O'Rourke 1997, 163; Webb 1929, 214).

Thus, the excavation of the large-scale medieval tanneries at New Street was significant, as the largest medieval leatherworking site excavated in Ireland, and indeed one of the largest in Ireland and Britain combined. As well as its size, the New Street site was also among the longest-lived leatherworking sites excavated in either Ireland or Britain, with evidence of continuous leatherworking dating from the late thirteenth to the late seventeenth century. In 2004, the only comparable published leather-making site was in the Greens in Northampton in England, excavated in the 1980s, which operated from the fifteenth to the seventeenth century (Shaw 1984; 1989; 1996).

In the last few years, however, much more evidence for large-scale and long-lived medieval tanning has been revealed from excavations in Dublin 8, most notably at Thomas Street in 2017 (see Duffy, this volume, above). More evidence for medieval tanning is emerging from excavations at Dean Street in 2017 (Collins 2018) and Francis Street in 2019 (McIlreavy, pers. comm., 2019). While New Street is probably no longer the largest and longest-lived medieval tanning site in Ireland, the findings from the excavation have become more relevant as comparable material is being discovered elsewhere.

LOCATION

The New Street site was situated at the corner of New Street and Fumbally Lane, in Dublin 8, at no. 48 New Street, a decommissioned service station and garage (fig. 7.1). A large modern development called Cathedral Court – so called because of its proximity to St Patrick's Cathedral – now occupies the site. A smaller road running behind the site is called Blackpitts. Prior to the excavation at New Street, it was unclear if the name Blackpitts had been derived from tanning pits, or from mass graves following a medieval epidemic (Herity 2001, 44; Murtagh 1973, 48). The findings from the excavation now strongly suggest that the place-name derives from the pits of black smelly tanning-solution that are the subject of this contribution. Indeed, this quarter of Dublin may have been known as Blackpitts from late-medieval times, hence the title of this paper.

TWELFTH AND THIRTEENTH CENTURIES

In the medieval period the site was situated next to Crosspoddle, which was the lowest point at which the river Poddle could be forded. Several important roads intersected here, and it was the location of an extramural gate and a medieval market (Clarke 1990, 57–8; McCullough 1989, 9; Manning 1998, 53).

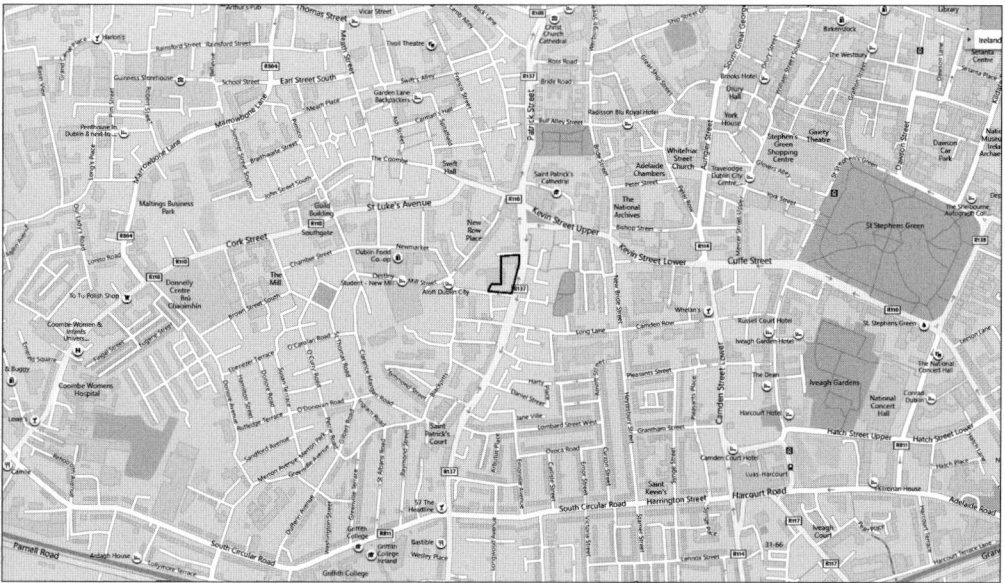

7.1 Site location

This area was already settled before the Anglo-Norman period: Crosspoddle may have held a number of pre-Anglo-Norman churches, and possibly formed an Irish suburb of the Hiberno-Norse town (Clarke 1998, 52; 1995, 92; McCullough 1989, 9, 14; Mills 1989, 31; Simpson 1997, 17).

There was no pre-twelfth-century material on the New Street site. The earliest archaeological evidence for activity was in the form of furrows and agricultural features, cesspits and drains. These would have been located behind houses on New Street and were dated to the late twelfth century and early thirteenth century, which is just after the Anglo-Norman capture of Dublin. In the thirteenth century Dublin expanded outside its Hiberno-Norse wall, and documentary sources record property plots along Thomas Street, Francis Street, Patrick Street and Kevin Street. New Street – 300m south of the city wall – is mentioned in documentary sources from 1218 (M'Cready 1982, 73).

PROPERTY BOUNDARIES

By the fourteenth century the character of the site had changed substantially. It was divided up into regular property boundaries defined by shallow ditches located 13–15m apart (fig. 7.2). The street-front of the property boundaries was missing as New Street had been widened, so there was no evidence on the site for medieval houses. Only the rear gardens or yards survived. These plot

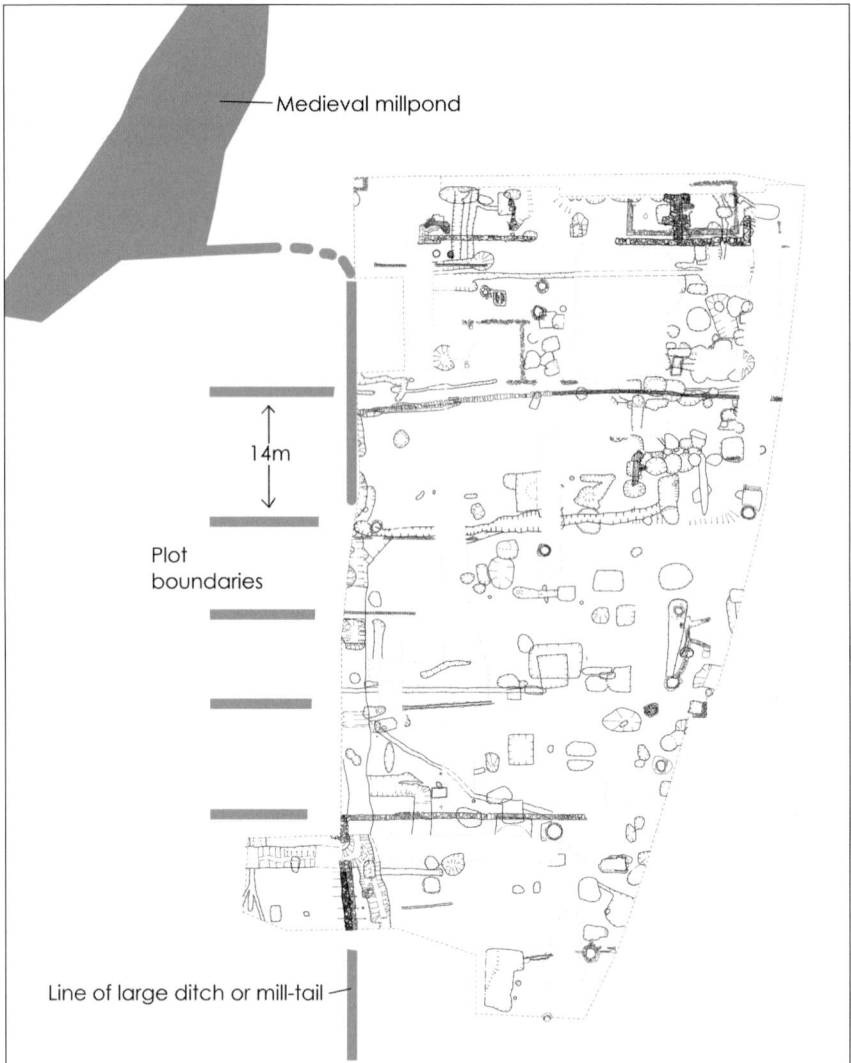

Medieval millpond

14m

Plot
boundaries

Line of large ditch or mill-tail

7.2 Medieval plot boundaries and mill tail

boundaries, established in the late thirteenth century, were frequently cut and
recut, and in later periods marked by walls, continuing in use all the way into
the eighteenth century. Even when the medieval boundaries did not survive,
clusters of tanning pits frequently respected their projected line.

Records of the medieval burgage plots laid out along Thomas Street, Bridge
Street and James's Street indicate that the street frontage generally measured
under 10m wide (Duffy 2001, 166–7), which is narrower than the plots at New

Street. However, the New Street plots are comparable to the 14m-wide
burgage plots excavated at the medieval village of Saggart outside Dublin
(McCarthy and Saunderson, pers. comm.), and perhaps reflect a suburban
arrangement of plots just outside the walled town. Although the medieval
property boundaries continued in use into the eighteenth century, they were
subdivided. The properties in the northern half of the site were subdivided
from the later medieval period, notably along one particular boundary which
became a laneway, named from at least the eighteenth century as Swift's Alley.
After 1640, evidence for plot subdivision was identified across the entire site,
which probably reflects the boom in Dublin's population after the mid-
seventeenth-century wars (Craig 1969, 86; McCullough 1989, 58). By the time
of Roque's 1756 map, the medieval plot divisions line up with laneways
separating groups of houses.

A POSSIBLE TAIL RACE

All the medieval plot boundaries drained into a large ditch that defined the
rear of the properties, and which was constructed in or around the late
thirteenth century. This ditch ran north to south and measured 2–3m in width
and up to 2m deep. It was located on a logical topographical boundary point,
running directly along the contour-line marking the high point of terrain that
sloped steeply down the Poddle river valley behind the properties to the west.
The ditch was filled in at the end of the medieval period, and the material
within the ditch contained medieval pottery dating from the late thirteenth to
the mid-fourteenth century, and fragments of medieval floor tiles with
parallels at St Patrick's Cathedral, Christ Church, Winetavern Street and
Meath Market. After it was backfilled, a wall was constructed along the top of
it. This medieval ditch marked a property boundary that lasted 700 years and
remains a property boundary today, forming the rear of the Cathedral Court
development.

Late-medieval documentary records indicate that ditches were dug off the
Poddle watercourse in order to serve tanneries, and legislation passed from the
fifteenth century onwards often required that these be filled in due to the
continuous flooding of the Poddle and contamination of the watercourse
(Ronan 1927, 45). The New Street ditch was backfilled in the late-medieval
period, at the same time as the tannery legislation, and the feature was initially
interpreted as a ditch dug by the tanners to provide themselves with water and
drainage. There is another possible function for the large ditch, however. A
medieval millpond on the bank of the Poddle was excavated directly north-
west of the New Street site (Lohan 1998, 45–6). The millpond was constructed
in the thirteenth–fourteenth century and backfilled in the fourteenth–fifteenth
century, which matches the dates for the construction and backfilling of the

New Street ditch. Based on the levels on the base of the ditch and its location, it does not appear to have functioned as a millrace, but it did run either into or out of the Poddle near the millpond, and may have functioned as a tail race or millpond overflow channel.

This ditch may have been part of a very large programme of waterworks carried out along the Poddle in the mid-thirteenth century, as the river was diverted around the liberties (Ronan 1927, 45; Joyce 1920, 452–3). Numerous mills, millraces and water channels were established along its new and old courses, and marked the edges of the liberties and ecclesiastical landholdings (Simpson 1997). Disputes about the mills and the watercourses that powered them are frequent in medieval texts, and in general involve monasteries and ecclesiastical manors (ibid.). Because the establishment of the New Street ditched watercourse – which was probably mill-related – could have been an essential component of the tanneries excavated at New Street, the question as to for whom the ditch was constructed is an important one: if the ditch was built as part of works associated with an ecclesiastical house, it is possible that the tanning quarter that subsequently grew up in this area was envisaged as part of that scheme.

TANNING PITS

Over one hundred tanning pits, or pits directly relating to leather-making, were excavated on the site, generally dating from the late thirteenth to the late seventeenth century. The latest two tanning pits, which were the only stone-lined pits, date to the start of the eighteenth century. The tanning pits were found in every plot and tended to be located in the eastern half of the plots, near the current New Street frontage. This would have been the location of the backyards of the original New Street buildings prior to the widening of the street. There was a concentration of pits in the north of the site in and around the laneway known as Swift's Alley. These pits respect the division of the site into property plots, and so the site should not be interpreted as a single tannery. Instead it must represent multiple tanners, perhaps living on New Street and working in their backyards or off lanes between groups of houses. In other words, a tanning quarter.

The most important discovery from the excavation is that there was almost no development or change in the tanning pits over time, either in their fills, shape, size, location or arrangement, from the medieval period to the seventeenth century. There is one exception: from approximately the sixteenth century onwards, there was a distinctive change in smell in the pits, and this might represent a change in the tanning-solution recipe, perhaps the use of a different wood either as a reaction to shortages, or technological progress. The only other observable change occurred at the very end of the eighteenth

7.3 Tanning pit – basic type

century. Only two pits were dated to the eighteenth century or later and they were completely different in style from the pre-1700 pits, being stone-lined and rectangular.

Three distinct types of pre-1700 tanning pit (identified by function on the basis of tanning material in the fill) were identified on the site. The first type was the most common: the 'basic' tanning pit (fig. 7.3). These were located in clusters, or on Swift's Alley in distinctive rows, of intercutting pits. Both circular and square pits were used in even ratios in every time-period and in almost every plot. They measured approximately 1–2m in width and 1m in depth. The basic tanning pit clusters were often associated with small drains that led from one side of a pit, and that could have regulated the level of water in the pits. Documentary sources suggest that this sort of pit was sometimes called a 'handling pit', where hides were swished around in progressively stronger solutions until they reached the right colour or level of tanning.

The second type was rarer, and comprised larger and deeper pits (over 2m in width and over 1m in depth), again with an equal ratio of circular and square shapes. These had different fills from the basic pits, and in some cases they were associated with specific processes such as de-hairing or long-term

7.4 Tanning pit – rinsing

7.5 Tanning pit – lining

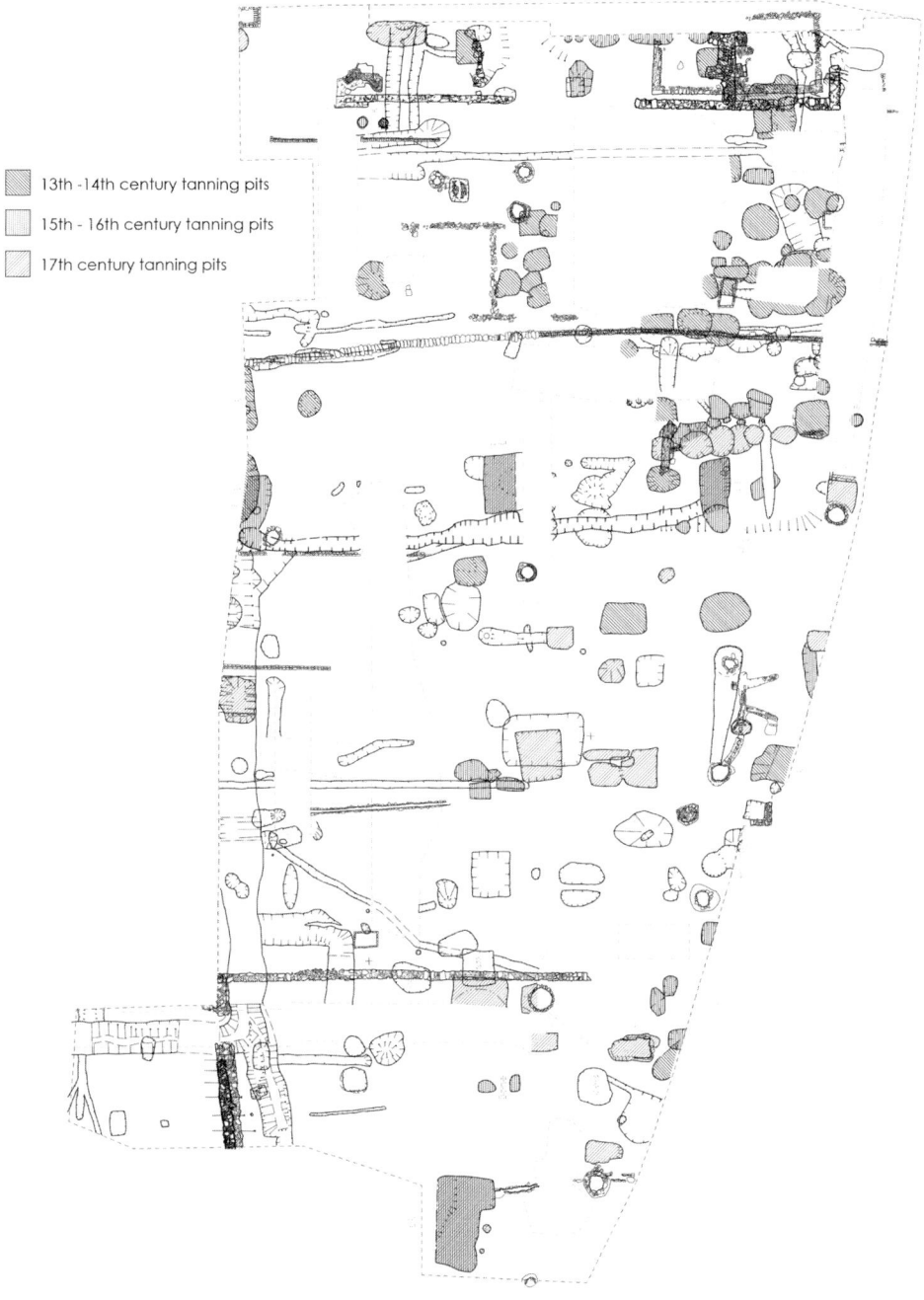

13th -14th century tanning pits

15th - 16th century tanning pits

17th century tanning pits

7.6 Tanning pits phased

tanning (layaway pits). Some of these pits were very similar to medieval cesspits excavated at other sites, except for their fills, and it is likely that some of them may have started out as cesspits and were later used as tanning pits, or vice versa.

The third type of pit was broad and shallow, and these are interpreted as rinsing pits (fig. 7.4). These were always located at the plot boundaries and were directly associated with drains or ditches, presumably to provide a steady supply of water. One of these pits was associated with numerous postholes and stakes inside and around it, which may have supported a frame for laying out the hides for rinsing. These pits were found in every plot and in every time-period. One of the distinct differences between this type of pit and the previous two was that all the 'rinsing pits' had multiple phases of use, with evidence for their reuse over centuries, rather than the single-use tanning pits.

The tanning pits did not have clear evidence of lining. This was considered unusual in 2004, as eighteenth- and nineteenth-century tanning pits generally have evidence for lining, but now that more medieval tanneries have been excavated in the last few years, the absence of lining evidence at New Street fits with similar evidence at other sites. At New Street there was some evidence for clay lining, and some evidence for timber lining on one or more sides (fig. 7.5), or more rarely stone lining on one or more sides, but this was not consistent. Several pits were excavated that were the same size and shape as tanning pits, and their bases had been stained with tanning-solution, but they contained no tanning material, which might possibly suggest that a lining had been removed in one piece after the pits were used. Overall, the thirteenth- to seventeenth-century tanning pits at New Street (fig. 7.6) displayed a variety of informal and temporary lining techniques, which is in contrast to eighteenth- and nineteenth-century tanneries in the Liberties.

ANIMALS AND BONES

The butchering and skinning of animals prior to tanning was represented on the site by the very large animal bone assemblage. The animal bone assemblage associated with tanning deposits was analyzed separately to that associated with non-tanning contexts. Tanning deposits were dominated by cow bones (38%), followed by sheep/goat (24%), calf (12%), pig (8%), kid (7%), horse (6%), piglet (5%), deer (2%) and foal (1%). Many of the animal bones displayed evidence of butchery and skinning. The proportions were consistent for every phase from the thirteenth to the seventeenth century, with a slightly higher proportion of cow in the earlier (medieval) phases, and the difference generally being made up by a higher proportion of young animals in the post-medieval period. It will be interesting to compare these proportions to those from the recently excavated medieval tanneries at Thomas Street and Dean Street to see if geographical specializations of leather tanning can be discerned. This would seem to be the case, based on early analysis of the Thomas Street bone (see Duffy above).

The hides of young animals, which were well represented on the bone assemblage from tanning contexts, could also be used for making vellum, which is a fine parchment used in the production of documents and books. The location of the site next to St Patrick's Cathedral might have encouraged a market for vellum. The percentage of juvenile animals rose over time: 15% in the thirteenth and fourteenth centuries, 20% in the fifteenth and sixteenth centuries, and was highest at 22% in the seventeenth century. The largest relative quantities of juvenile animal bone were concentrated in the two southernmost plots, which had the smallest number of definitive tanning pits, but which had multiple pits containing no leather artefacts, no leather cuttings, and no oak-bark chippings. It is likely that a specialist tanning process was carried out here involving juvenile animals, perhaps the manufacture of supple leathers, such as for gloves or slippers, rather than vellum, which in any case had generally been replaced by paper by the seventeenth century.

DE-HAIRING

The de-hairing process was represented at New Street, although not by the presence of the lime pits commonly found in excavations of eighteenth- and nineteenth-century tanneries. Large fragments of limestone debris found at medieval tanning sites in the York area have been interpreted as relating to de-hairing using lime (MacGregor 1998, 15). While limestone rubble was also commonly found in the seventeenth-century tanning pits at New Street, it is more likely to have resulted from the demolition of nearby buildings used to backfill the pits.

Several of the excavated pits smelt strongly of ammonia, derived from urine, and these may have been de-hairing pits. Other pits smelt so toxic that they were probably full of the combination of chicken and dog dung used in 'bating', 'puring' or 'mastering' de-hairing pits (Thomson 1998, 5–7). Fragments of eggshell found in these pits can be interpreted as representing the most durable element of the sweepings of henhouses used in bating solutions, as interpreted at a medieval tanning site at Pavement in York (MacGregor 1998, 15).

Barley seeds and small fruit seeds identified in several of the tanning pits could be interpreted as part of de-hairing or pre-tanning skin-treatment solutions. Historically skins could be subject to 'raising' or 'drenching' in fermented barley (Thomson 1998, 8), or soaked in elderberry liquid (MacGregor 1998, 15), but at New Street the evidence for de-hairing using 'bating' and urine was more convincing. No evidence was identified for the use of salt or alum tanning, which is a process in which the skin is tanned with the hair still attached. This is interesting as the contemporary tannery excavated in Thomas Street is believed to have carried out alum tanning (see Duffy above).

THE TANNING PROCESS

The active ingredient in the tanning process is the astringent tannin, derived from vegetable matter, which draws liquids out of organic material. Tannins are present in coffee and red wine. Tannins can be extracted from most vegetable matter, but the most common and concentrated source historically and archaeologically is tree-bark (MacGregor 1998, 16). Oak-bark was the most commonly used vegetable tanning agent, and indeed in *c.*1300 all other agents were prohibited in Colchester. All the New Street tanning pits contained a thick layer of chipped tree-bark near their bases, which was identified as alder and oak, and it was this bark layer that provided the principal method for identifying a pit as a tanning pit. The tree-bark had been ground to different thicknesses in different pits, which would have allowed for varying strengths of the tanning-solution, in the same way as grinding coffee more finely allows for a stronger brew.

Hides were immersed in the pits in solutions of bark and water for a period of six to eighteen months (Shaw 1984, 242), being cycled through the various solutions, and moving on to progressively stronger ones. A number of wooden paddles that were probably used to stir the tanning-solution in the pits were found on the site. A wooden shovel was also identified (fig. 7.7), perhaps used to dig the pits, or to fill them with bark chippings. Once the hide had gone through this cycle it would no longer rot, and became a piece of leather.

CURRYING

The preparation of the tanned hide into a workable piece of leather was called 'currying'. After tanning, the skin was washed and carefully dried, which probably occurred at New Street in the broad shallow rinsing pits. A slicker and beam were often used to squeeze out the remaining liquid. A slicker could take the form of a smooth rod or round-edged slab of glass, and one of these was found during the excavation. The leather was then stretched on a beam and the currier would work and shape the skin with a special knife. A creaser from this final phase was identified in an excavation next door at Fumbally Lane (Lohan 1998, 309). Three bags of suede-like flesh shavings from the currying process were recovered from New Street, demonstrating that currying was taking place on site.

Several of the unidentified pits on the site had a fishy smell, and the fill had a noticeably greasy sheen. Fish bones were also identified. It is possible that

04E1286:797:1

04E1286:133:48   04E1286:493:1

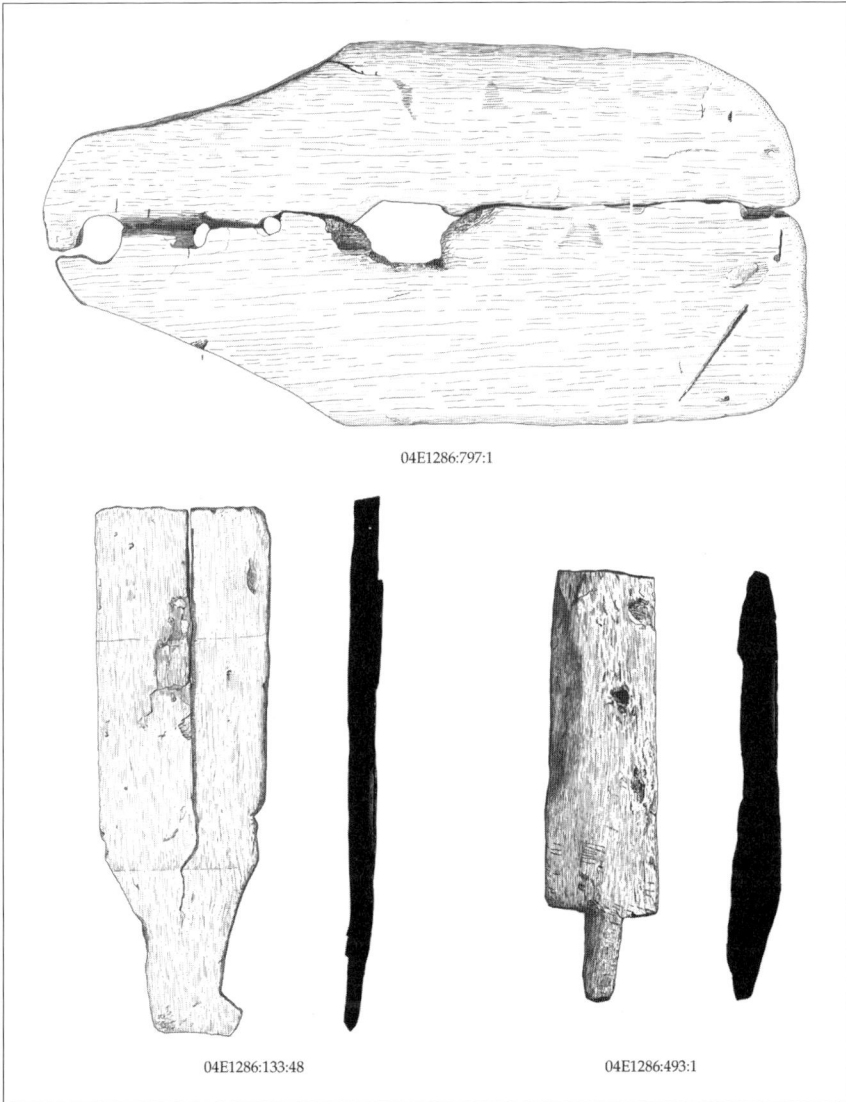

7.7 Wooden shovel and paddles

these pits were related to a process of using fatty fish oils to tan very fine leathers (Thomson 1998, 7) or treat finished fine leather. Similarly, 'neatsfoot oil' derived from cattle metapoidals (lower leg bones) is also used in currying or 'chamoising' (Serjeantson 1989, 141; Scally 1997, 12) and may also have been produced on the site.

BONE-WORKING

It might be expected that the bone-working crafts and leatherworking crafts would operate together, as both use different parts of the same animal. However, there was no evidence for bone-working at a craft level at New Street. The worked bone artefacts recovered during the excavation included

0   5cm

7.8 Find – wooden spoon

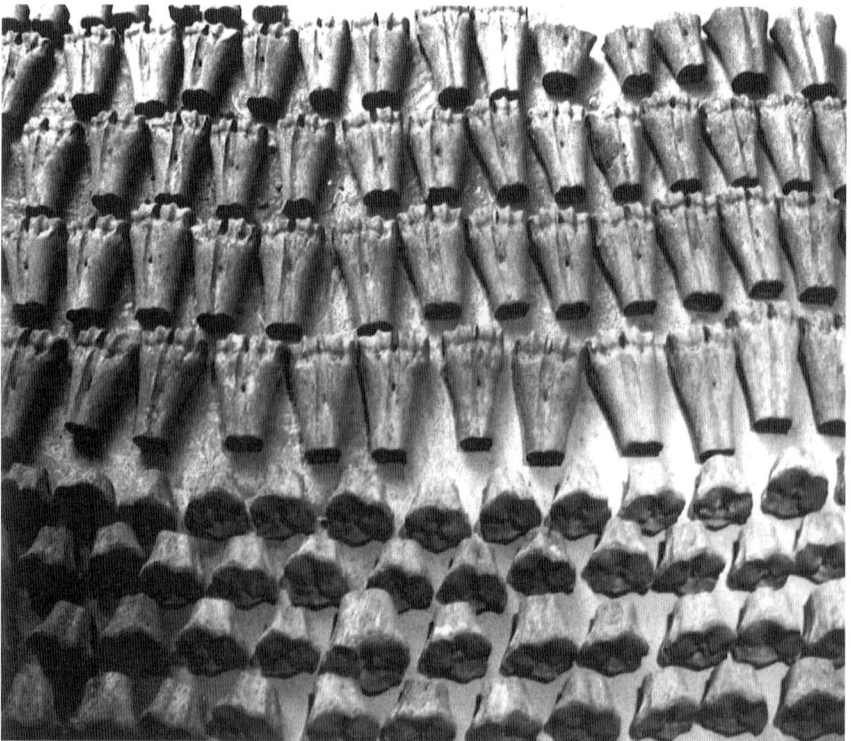

7.9 Find – bone offcuts

pins, needles, weaving tools and a stamp, all of which were roughly made and were probably casual tools made as needed by the leatherworkers (fig. 7.8).

A number of small pits, possibly disused tanning pits, were packed with very specific parts of cattle bones: the distal and proximal ends of cattle metapoidals (fig. 7.9). The middle part of the bone was absent, and indeed these bone elements were very rare on the site. This suggests that the middle part of cattle leg bones was systematically removed, probably by tanners, and sent to a bone-worker, for example for comb manufacture. Very similar deposits were identified in the medieval tannery at Southampton and in Muster in Germany (MacGregor 1998, 17–18), and interpreted similarly. At New Row a similarly large proportion of metapoidal cattle bones was interpreted as evidence for the production of 'neatsfoot oil' for currying fine leathers (Scally 1997, 12), and in this regard it is interesting that the locations of most of the New Street metapoidal offcuts matched the locations of the unusual tanning pits that contained the highest proportion of juvenile bone.

SWIFT'S ALLEY

The greatest concentration of tanning activity from every period was located either side of one of the northern plot boundaries, which later became a laneway called Swift's Alley. This laneway appears to be marked, unnamed, on de Gomme's 1673 map and again on Brooking's 1728 map, and is first named on Rocque's 1756 map (fig. 7.10). On the site, the lane was defined by a stone-lined drain, which cut a medieval drain. Based on the arrangement of late-medieval tanning pits arranged in well-defined rows either side of the drain, the laneway most likely dates back to the late-medieval period. The tanning pits along Swift's Alley were of particular interest because they were arranged in distinctive rows from the fourteenth to the seventeenth century, which demonstrated an exceptionally strong continuity of tanning practices and organization from the late-medieval to early post-medieval period.

The most interesting artefacts were also found in the Swift's Alley tanning pits, including an amber bead, sixteenth-century Nuremburg *jetons*, lathe-turned wooden bowls, numerous wooden pins probably used for stretching leather, and the seeds of exotic fruit such as fig. The seventeenth-century tanning pits along Swift's Alley also contained a large amount of glazed ridge tile, which may represent the refurbishment and re-roofing of the New Street and Swift's Alley houses following the damage caused by the 1640s wars. The remains of two buildings were also excavated off Swift's Alley, including a two-phase seventeenth-century structure with back-to-back fireplaces. The first phase had almost no foundation and was not very solid, while the second phase, dated by ceramics to *c.*1700, sat on the reused wooden timbers of the earlier building, which is a recurring pattern around the Blackpitts area.

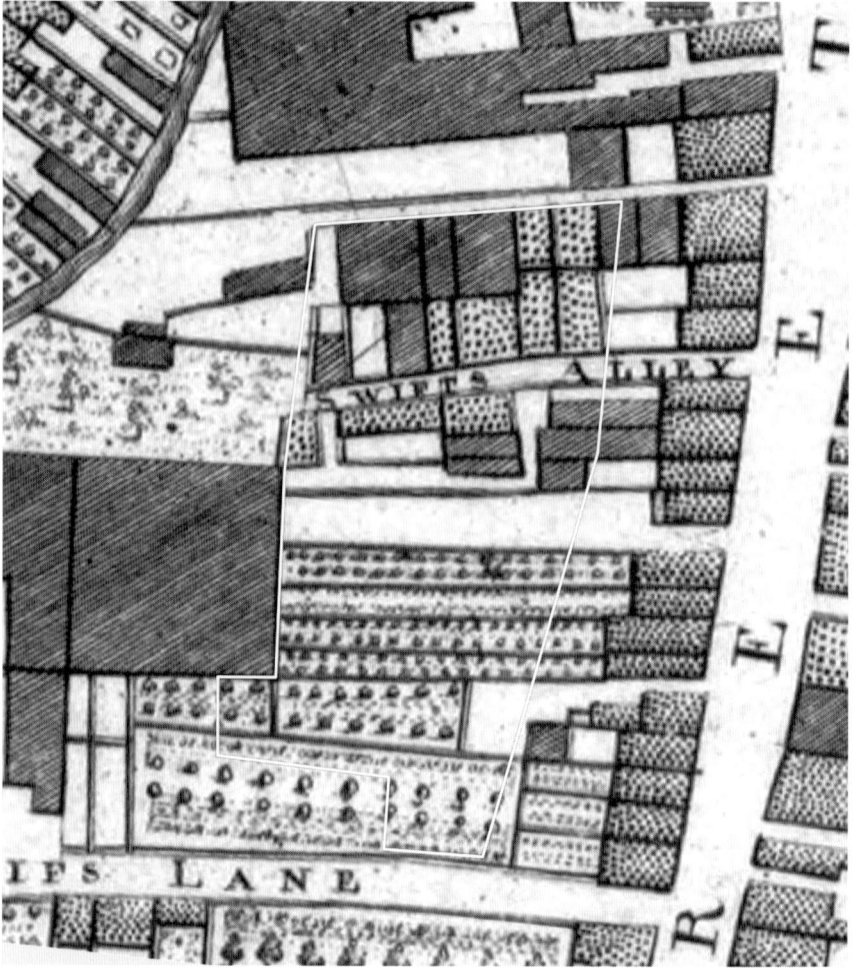

7.10 Rocque 1756 map showing Swift's Alley

COBBLING AND GUILDS

The tanning pits along Swift's Alley contained evidence for cobbling, in the form of a large amount of fragments of leather shoes and leather shoe-offcuts (fig. 7.11). Twenty-nine semi-complete shoes were analyzed by Nicholl and divided into nine different shoe types representing the full range of styles from the medieval to the early modern periods. There are several examples of shoe parts which have been cut down to provide material for children's footwear. Both Irish brogue and Continental-style shoes were identified, and the assemblage is comparable to shoes found on archaeological sites at Mill Street,

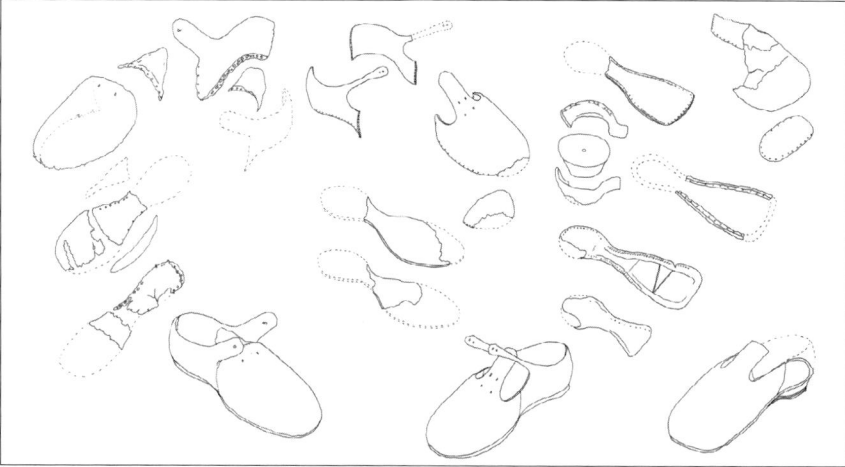

7.11 Find – shoes

Kevin Street, Chancery Lane and Dean Street in Dublin 8 (Nicholl, pers. comm., 2019). The shoe remains were indicative of the repair or modification of shoes, rather than their manufacture. Considering that every single step of the leatherworking process – from the skinning and deboning of the hide, de-hairing, washing, tanning, and currying (Reed 1972; Serjeantson 1989) – was represented on the site, it is unusual that no definitive evidence for shoe manufacture (as opposed to repair) was identified.

Perhaps this is evidence of the influence of guilds. The tanners of Dublin were granted a charter by King Edward I in 1289 and formed one of the oldest guilds in the city (Webb 1929, 214). By 1735, five of the guilds represented at the common council of the city were leatherworkers: these were the tanners, curriers, glovers, shoemakers and saddlers (Webb 1913, 14). Medieval British guild records suggest that tanners, curriers and shoemakers were separated into different crafts, and different guilds, and that the three could not work together (MacGregor 1998, 16; Thomson 1998, 8). At New Street, tanners and curriers do appear to have been working together, which does not fit with historical records of guilds. However, the suggestion that shoe manufacture, and bone-working, do not appear to have taken place on the site, may indicate guild influence. This raises the question of what archaeological evidence would look like for guild organization in a site such as this.

DECLINE OF THE TANNERIES

The Irish tanning industry was in decline by the second half of the eighteenth century, as suggested by a pamphlet written in 1773 urging tanners to adopt new improved methods (John Nicholl, pers. comm., 2014). More sophisticated tanning techniques were being used in England, and the Irish tanners were falling behind. There is some evidence that the tanners at the New Street site attempted to modernize, reflected by two stone-lined pits dated to the first half of the eighteenth century (fig. 7.12). These two pits were similar to tanning pits found at larger and later leatherworking sites in Dublin, and were among the last tanning pits in use on the site. Local competition for leather manufacturing was growing, as demonstrated by the numerous archaeological investigations in the vicinity of the New Street site that have revealed extensive tanneries dating to the eighteenth century. Like at Northampton, these 'modern' tanneries were large, laid out in an organized system, and the tanning pits were formally lined. They represent a modern approach to tanning. The Dublin tanning industry as a whole was becoming industrialized, and small cottage-industry producers, such as those on New Street in the Blackpitts tanning quarter, were being out-produced.

THE COTTAGE-INDUSTRY TANNING TRADITION

The layout, organization, and form of the late thirteenth- to seventeenth-century tanning remains at New Street South are in sharp contrast to previously excavated eighteenth- and nineteenth-century tanneries, both in Dublin city and abroad. The evidence from the excavation suggests that tanning pits at New Street were dug as they were needed and informally lined, with perhaps only a few open at any one time in each plot as at Exe Bridge and at High Street in Exeter (MacGregor 1998, 22). The 'Blackpitts tanning quarter' is best visualized as comprising several small household tanneries and cobbling workshops in adjoining plots, rather than as a single organized tannery of an industrial nature. The tanning pits would have been situated behind the houses fronting New Street, in which the leatherworkers may have lived and sold their wares.

The strong evidence for continuity of leatherworking and tanning on the site from the late thirteenth to the late seventeenth century is important. This continuity is evident in the organization of different leatherworking processes in specific plots, and in specific locations within each plot over time, as well as in the continuity of traditional processes and ways of working. One of the reasons this continuity is important is because it crosses the transition from the medieval to the early-modern period, which is generally placed in the mid-sixteenth century by archaeologists.

This transition marks a time of enormous political, religious and societal change in Ireland and abroad, particularly in elite spheres. It is of interest that this great change is not reflected at the Blackpitts leatherworking quarter. Instead, the site demonstrates a significant change in the late seventeenth

7.12 Tanning pit, eighteenth-century type

century, with the decline and collapse of the cottage-industry leatherworking quarter and subsequent expansion of leatherworking at an industrial scale outside of the site. This period of fundamental change in material culture saw the emergence of new manufacturing bases and production of new goods for export, and the exponential growth of Dublin as a manufacturing centre and as the seat of central government (McNeill 2007, 12). It may be that the late seventeenth-century societal and economic shifts were more significant for non-elites living and working at the edges of Dublin, or at least among leatherworkers in Blackpitts. These excavation findings can thus demonstrate how different periods of social and economic change are reflected differently at different scales of analysis within Dublin.

BIBLIOGRAPHY

Bolger, T. 2004 'Archaeological assessment and impact statement, 48 New Street, Dublin 8'. Unpublished report dated 9 June 2004, Margaret Gowen and Co.

Bolger, T. 2005 'Archaeological excavation at 36–39 James's Street, Dublin 8, 01E1034 ext.', Unpublished report, Margaret Gowen and Co.

Clarke, H.B. 1990 *Medieval Dublin: the making of a metropolis*. Dublin: Irish Academic Press.

Clarke, H.B. 1995 'Myths, magic and the Middle Ages: Dublin from its beginnings to 1577'. In idem (ed.), *Irish cities*, pp 82–95. The Thomas Davis Lecture Series. Cork and Dublin: Mercier Press and RTE.

Clarke, H.B. 1998 '*Urbs et suburbium*: beyond the walls of medieval Dublin'. In Manning 1998, pp 45–58.

Collins, A. 2018 'Excavation summary for 16E0080 Dean Street'. In Bennett (ed.), www.excavations.ie, reference 2018:11.

Craig, M. 1969 *Dublin, 1660–1860: a social and architectural history*. Dublin: Riverrun.

Duffy, C. 2001 'The western suburb of medieval Dublin: its first century', *Irish Geography* 34:2, 157–75.

Giacometti, A. 2005 'Preliminary excavation report of 48 New Street, Dublin 8, 04E1286'. Unpublished excavation report, Arch-Tech.

Hayden, A. 2002 'Rivers and industry: archaeology on the Coombe bypass and Cork Street realignment roadworks, Dublin 8, 93E0066 and 01E0614'. Unpublished report dated February 2002, Archaeological Projects Ltd.

Herity, M. 2001 *Ordnance survey letters, Dublin*. Dublin: Four Masters Press.

Joyce, W. St John 1920 'The old city water supply'. In idem (ed.), *The neighbourhood of Dublin*, 3rd edn. Dublin: M.H. Gill.

Lohan, K. 2008 'Archaeological excavation at Fumbally Lane, Dublin 8, 05E0585'. Unpublished excavation report, Margaret Gowen and Co.

Manning, C. 1998 *Dublin and beyond the Pale: studies in honour of Patrick Healy*. Bray: Wordwell.

McCullough, N. 1989 *Dublin: an urban history*. Dublin: Anne Street Press.

MacGregor, A. 1998. 'Hides, horns and bones: animals and interdependent industries in the early urban context'. In E. Cameron (ed.), *Leather and fur: aspects of early medieval trade and technology*, pp 11–26. London: Archetype Publications.

M'Cready, C.T. 1982 *Dublin Street names, dated and explained*. Dublin: Carraig Books.

McCutcheon, S.W.J. and Hurley, M.F. 1997 'Insula North'. In M.F. Hurley, O.M.B. Scully and S.W.J. McCutcheon (eds), *Late Viking Age and medieval Waterford: excavations 1986–1992*, pp 154–63. Waterford: Waterford Corporation.

McNeill, T.E. 2007 'Where should we place the boundary between the medieval and post-medieval periods in Ireland?'. In A. Horning, R. Ó Baoill, C. Donnelly, and P. Logue (eds), *The post-medieval archaeology of Ireland 1550–1850*, pp 15–23. Irish Post-Medieval Archaeology Group Proceedings 1. Bray: Wordwell.

McQuade, M. 2005 'Archaeological monitoring and excavation at 105–109 the Coombe, Dublin 8, 03E0207'. Unpublished excavation report, Margaret Gowen and Co.

Mills, J. 1889 'Notices of the manor of St Sepulchre, Dublin in the fourteenth century', *JRSAI*, 9, 119–26.

Murtagh, M. 1973 'Walking around the Liberties'. In E. Gillespie (ed.), *The Liberties of Dublin*. Dublin: E. and T. O'Brien.

Myles, F. 2005 'Stratigraphic report for 24–26 Ardee Street, Dublin 8, 03E0315'. Unpublished excavation report, Margaret Gowen and Co.

Ó Ríordáin, A.B. 1976 'The High Street excavations'. In B. Almqvist and D. Greene (eds), *Proceedings of the seventh Viking Congress, Dublin, 15-21 August 1973*, pp 135–40. Dublin: Royal Irish Academy/Viking Society for Northern Research.

O'Rourke, D. 1997 'Leather finds'. In Walsh 1997, pp 163–78.

Reed, R. 1972 *Ancient skins, parchments and leathers*. London and New York: Seminar Press.

Ronan, M.V. 1927 'The Poddle river and its branches', *JRSAI*, 57, 39–46.

Scally, G. 1997 'Report on archaeological excavation at 44–49 New Row South, Dublin 8, 96E0342'. Unpublished excavation report, Margaret Gowen and Co.

Serjeantson, D. 1989 'Animal remains and the tanning trade'. In D. Serjeantson and T. Waldron (eds), *Diet and craft in towns*, BAR British Series 199. Oxford.

Shaw, M. 1996 'The excavation of a late fifteenth- to seventeenth-century tanning complex at The Green, Northampton'. *Post-Medieval Archaeology*, 30, 63–127.

Shaw, M. 1989 'Early post-medieval tanning in Northampton, England', *Archaeology*, 40.2, 43–7.

Shaw, M. 1984 'Northampton: excavating a sixteenth century tannery', *Current Archaeology* 8, no. 91, 241–4.

Simpson, L. 1997 'Historical background to the Patrick Street excavation'. In Walsh 1997, pp 16–33.

Simpson, L. 2004 'Excavations on the southern side of the medieval town at Ship Street Little, Dublin'. In S. Duffy (ed.), *Medieval Dublin V*, pp 9–51. Dublin: Four Courts Press.

Thomson, R. 1998 'Leatherworking processes'. In E. Cameron (ed.), *Leather and fur: aspects of early medieval trade and technology*, pp 1–10. London: Archetype Publications.

Thomson, R. 1981 'Leather manufacture in the post-medieval period with special reference to Northamptonshire', *Post-Medieval Archaeology*, 15:1, 161–75.

Walsh, C. 1997 *Archaeological Excavations at Patrick, Nicholas and Winetavern Streets, Dublin*. Dingle: Brandon.

Webb, J.J. 1913 *Industrial Dublin since 1698 & The silk industry in Dublin: two essays*. Dublin: Maunsel.

Webb, J.J. 1929 'The guilds of Dublin', *Irish Ecclesiastical Record*, ser. 5, 34, 332–4.

Dragons, giants and beautiful women: medieval Dublin in the European imagination

CAOIMHE WHELAN

The dragon, giant and beautiful woman of this essay's title refer to the literary depictions found in perhaps the most popular and widely circulated of the Arthurian romances – *Tristan and Isolde*. The Tristan story dates not later than the twelfth century and scholars identify three early written versions of the narrative: one (now lost) probably written by a man named Thomas – sometimes called Thomas d'Angleterre – at the court of King Henry II of England (1154–89); a translation from French into German undertaken *c.*1170–90 by Eilhart von Oberg, vassal of Henry, duke of Saxony, whose second wife, Matilda (b. 1157), was the daughter of Henry II and Eleanor of Aquitaine (d. 1209); and an Anglo-Norman version of the Tristan narrative *c.*1160–90 ascribed to the poet Béroul.[1]

The narratives are considered to be Arthurian because, late in some of the versions' reception history, they become part of King Arthur's world, but they begin life as a separate tradition. Few medieval legends were as enduring as that of the tragic love story of the knight Tristan from the court at Cornwall in south-west Britain and the princess Isolde of Dublin. The story of the greatest knight of his age who finds in Ireland the woman he will love and lose remains an enduring staple of a tragic love affair and the struggle between responsibilities and desires. Perhaps the story's most famous legacy is the influence it had on the story of Lancelot, Guinevere and King Arthur, which was likely inspired by the love triangle between Tristan, Isolde and King Mark.

Various versions of the Tristan story circulated in manuscript in the Middle Ages in Europe, initially in French and later translated into local vernacular languages, and it also appears in other artistic forms in Britain and on the Continent.[2] The story was famously retold in Germany in the 1850s by Richard Wagner in his opera *Tristan und Isolde*, which opens as Tristan and Isolde travel from Ireland to Cornwall, and the narrative is punctuated with flashbacks from their time in Ireland.[3] This version reintroduced the legend to a modern audience and, moreover, is heralded as opening a new chapter of

1 See Joan T. Grimbert, 'Introduction' in eadem (ed.), *Tristan and Isolde: a casebook* (London, 1995), pp xiii–cii. 2 See, for instance, Joan T. Grimbert, 'The matter of Britain on the Continent and the legend of Tristan and Iseult in France, Italy and Spain' in Helen Fulton (ed.), *Companion to Arthurian literature* (Oxford, 2009), pp 145–59; for Italy, see pp 151–4. 3 For Wagner and the later interest in the story in Germany, see Grimbert, 'Introduction' in

modern music. More recently, the story has enthralled a movie-going public in the film *Tristan + Isolde* (2006), directed by Kevin Reynolds with James Franco and Sophia Myles respectively in the title roles. Remaining recognizable throughout the ages, the legend tells the story of Tristan's life, his early adventures, his days at the court of his uncle, King Mark of Cornwall, and his interactions with Ireland: fighting a giant, a dragon and embarking on a calamitous love affair where he competes with Mark for the love of the Irish princess Isolde, and his later life in Brittany with another Isolde.

As it modulates between languages and artistic representations, the narrative twists and turns with subsequent additions and omissions serving to alter various aspects of the narrative but not the overall story. This essay will blend literary, artistic and historical sources not generally considered together – when writing about either medieval Dublin or this legend – to explore, first, how the legend may reflect twelfth-century ideas about Ireland's relationship with Britain, and second, ways that this story was reimagined in various media in the fourteenth and fifteenth centuries, subliminally transmitting messages about Ireland to communities throughout Europe.[4]

A GIANT WALKS INTO A BAR

The medieval precursor to stereotypical violent and drunken Irish Paddies in Britain was the stereotypical strong, warlike Irish knights and kings who roamed Britain, causing trouble. The giant that appears in the Tristan tale, Morant or Moraunt, is the brother of the queen of Dublin, heroic champion of the Irish, and the man who appears at the court of King Mark of Cornwall to demand the annual tribute of gold and children which, in the legend, England owes to Ireland (whether Mark was king of Cornwall or of England depends on the version of the narrative consulted). Morant is likely a form of the common Irish names Muirchertach or Murchad – an appropriate selection when choosing an Irish-sounding name for the legend's fearsome Irish champion. His status as a giant indicates not only his fierceness in battle but also suggests a level of wildness that makes the Irish feared by all (bar, of course, our hero, Tristan). Morant's defeat, at the hands of the untried knight Tristan, marks a turning point in relations between Ireland and Cornwall and it seems that by extension it may symbolize the dawning of an era of supremacy for England.

Nothing is quite so simple when the Irish are involved. An injury inflicted on Tristan by the Irish champion confounds England's leeches and he takes to the sea with his harp to die. Dragged by the currents to Dublin, he conceals his

eadem (ed.), *Tristan and Isolde*, at pp liv–lx.   **4** The essay will explore representations in what are now Great Britain, Germany and Italy, entities that do not equate with medieval

identity and finds a welcome at the Irish court while Princess Isolde and/or her mother Queen Isolde (varying across the versions) nurse him back to health.[5]

Ireland's champion may have been defeated, but Ireland is still a force to be reckoned with. Casting Ireland as a place of healers was not just the work of imagination. It drew on a long tradition of Ireland as a place with powerful healing properties. The great Anglo-Saxon scholar Bede wrote in the mid-eighth century that a drink made from the scrapings of books from Ireland could heal serpent poison.[6] Geoffrey of Monmouth, in his *Historia regum Britannie* (*History of the kings of Britain*, *c.*1138), wrote that Stonehenge was relocated from Ireland to Britain by Merlin and he praised the healing qualities of the structure. At the start of the thirteenth century, this trope of the stones of Stonehenge imbuing rainwater with healing properties which could be used for bathing had appeared in Layamon's *Brut*, one of the first major works produced in Middle English:[7]

> for ich what a wærc; mid wundere bi-stonde.
> for þat weorc stondeð; inne Irlonde.
> Hit is a swiðe sellic þing;
> þat woerc is of stane; swulc ne beoð oðer nane.
> swa wid swa is weorlde-riche; nis nan weorc his iliche.
> þa stanes beo[ð] muchele; mahten heo habbeoð.
> þa men þe beoð un-hal; heo fareð to þan stane.
> & heo wasceð þene stan; & þer-mide baðieð heore ban.
> umbe lutle stu[n]de; heo wurðeð al isunde.[8]

> for I know a work with wonder encompassed;
> far the work standeth in Ireland.
> It is a most surprising thing,
> it is named the Giant's Ring;
> the work is of stone, such another there is none,
> so wide as is the world's realm is no work its like.

polities, but are used here for geographic convenience.   **5** For an analysis of the variation in presentation of the women's healing powers and where that knowledge and power ultimately comes from in Thomas's version (no judgement on the ability to harm or heal), the thirteenth-century prose Romance of *Tristan* (drawn from divine power but with the potential to be misused), and Gottfried's version (medicinal skills not magic), see April Harper, 'The image of the female healer in Western vernacular literature of the Middle Ages', *Social History of Medicine*, 24:1 (April 2011), 108–24, at 113–15.   **6** Bede, *Ecclesiastical history of England*, Book 1, i.   **7** For the origins of Stonehenge in Ireland, see Keith Busby, *French in medieval Ireland, Ireland in medieval French: the paradox of two worlds* (Turnhout, 2017), pp 366–8.   **8** *Layamon's Brut edited from British Museum MS. Cotton Caligula A.IX and British Museum MS. Cotton Otho C.XIII*, ed. George L. Brook and Roy F. Leslie, *EETS*, OS 250, 277, 2 vols (London, 1963–78), ii, p. 446, ll. 8573–80.

> The stones are great, and virtue they have;
> the men who are sick they go to the stones,
> and they wash the stones, and therewith bathe their bones;
> after a little while they become all sound![9]

Those at the court in Ireland in the Tristan narrative are not presented as barbarians. They have considerable skills but they are particularly amazed by Tristan's musical skill which surpasses their own. Princess Isolde is eager to learn and becomes Tristan's pupil. In this way the Irish appear open to the apparently 'superior' culture that Tristan offers in the same way that they will soon rely on his military prowess to protect them from danger. Once Tristan's wounds have healed, he returns to King Mark, waxing lyrical about the beauty of the Irish princess, Isolde. Before long he is ordered to return to Ireland in order to secure her hand in marriage for his monarch. This proposed marriage alliance has the potential to reinforce the altered balance of power of Cornwall/England over Ireland. Of course, this is not going to be quite so simple to achieve.

THERE BE DRAGONS

The Dublin to which Tristan returns is a city in turmoil. As the first extant English translation of the Tristan narrative (in the early fourteenth-century romance *Sir Tristrem*) tells it:

> Out of Deuelin toun / Þe folk wel fast ran / In a water to droun / So ferd were þai þan. / For doute of o dragoun, / Þai seyd, to schip þai wan / To hauen þat were boun. /
>
> *(Sir Tristrem, 1409–15).*[10]
>
> Out of Dublin town / the folk so fast ran / into the water to drown / so scared were they then. / For fear of a dragon / they said they were going to a ship / to the port they were bound.[11]

As terrified Dubliners flee from the dragon, Tristan resolves to defeat the beast and win the hand of the princess Isolde. Medieval bestiaries associate dragons with the devil. Whether or not there is a religious element involved in Tristan's

---

https://quod.lib.umich.edu/c/cme/LayCal/1:86?rgn=div1;view=fulltext.   **9** *Layamon, the 'Arthurian' portion of the Brut*, trans. Frederic Madden, *Middle English series* (Cambridge, Ontario, 1999), p. 45.   **10** This romance survives in a single copy dating to the 1330s in Auckinleck Advocates MS 19.2.1, fos. 281r–99v, National library of Scotland; the entire manuscript has been edited by David Burnley and Alison Wiggins in 2003 and can be accessed at: http://auchinleck.nls.uk/index.html.   **11** Present writer's translation.

fight, dragons are appropriately monstrous foes for the great heroes to face even if they are not usually associated with Ireland. Tristan's victory allows the knight to receive his reward of the princess's hand and symbolizes Ireland's need for the English court's protection. The tale began with England owing Ireland tribute for Irish dominance but now the roles have been reversed and the Irish require the hero of a king in England to come to their aid.

The dynastic marriage that should secure this relationship is not unproblematic. Stories involving beautiful women rarely run smoothly. When Isolde discovers that Tristan is responsible for her uncle's murder she contemplates taking vengeance by killing him while he is bathing. Eventually, she relents and lets the handsome knight live. That threat has barely passed when they set sail for England with a vial of magic potion that Isolde's mother has made to ensure that Isolde and the man she has agreed to marry, King Mark, fall in love. During the voyage, however, Tristan and Isolde (joined, in the Middle English version, by Tristan's dog), accidently drink the love potion and properly set in motion the love triangle that will consume them.

This is, by any standards, a rather fanciful story. But there may be some broad historiographical brush strokes hidden within the romance narrative.[12] Might the Irish champion in the Tristan narrative, Morant or Moraunt, be loosely based on someone like the powerful Muirchertach Ua Briain (1050–1119), king of Munster, *de facto* king of Ireland from 1088 until 1118, and one-time king of Dublin? Muirchertach was the dominant figure in late eleventh- and early twelfth-century Ireland and his court appears to have served as a safe haven for Welsh dynasts such as Gruffudd ap Cynan of Gywnedd and Cadwgan ap Bleddyn and the latter's son Owain, of Powys, all of whom sought temporary respite in Ireland from Anglo-Norman aggression back home.[13] Muirchertach also provided a haven in Ireland to the Anglo-Norman lord of Pembroke, Arnulf de Montgomery. The Welsh chronicle, *Brut y Tywysogion*, records that in 1101 Arnulf sent Gerald of Windsor (grandfather of Gerald of Wales, the cleric who would chronicle the English invasion of Ireland in the 1160s) to Ireland to secure the hand of the daughter of 'Murcard [Muirchertach Ua Briain] King of Ireland' along with military support against King Henry I of England.[14] Arnulf's rebellion against Henry and his marriage

---

12 For a useful account of the Irish elements within the early Tristan versions in a French context, see Busby, *French in medieval Ireland*, pp 337–61.   13 For Muirchertach's court as a safe haven, see Seán Duffy, 'The 1169 invasion as a turning-point in Irish–Welsh relations' in Brendan Smith (ed.), *Britain and Ireland, 900–1300: Insular responses to medieval European change* (Cambridge, 1999), pp 98–113, at pp 100–3; for Muirchertach, see Anthony Candon, 'Muirchertach Ua Briain, politics, and naval activity in the Irish Sea, 1075 to 1119' in Gearóid Mac Niocaill and Patrick F. Wallace (eds), *Keimelia: papers in memory of Tom Delaney* (Galway, 1988), pp 397–415; and Seán Duffy, '"The western world's tower of honour and dignity": the career of Muirchertach Ua Briain in context' in Damian Bracken and Dagmar Ó Riain-Raedal (eds), *Ireland and Europe in the twelfth century: reform and renewal* (Dublin, 2004), pp 56–73.   14 Edmund Curtis, 'Murchertach O'Brien, high-king

to the daughter of a king of Ireland may offer a loose model for the Tristan narrative, a nod to the dangers of alliances between Irish kings and ambitious knights.

Muirchertach is widely thought to have commissioned, *c.*1103–11, the pseudo-historical narrative called *Cogadh Gáedhel re Gallaibh* ('The War of the Irish against the Foreigners'), which offered a propaganda account of events in the ninth and tenth centuries, celebrating his great-grandfather, Brian Boru, and glorifying his dynasty. That work's mix of history and legitimizing fiction may find a faint echo in the Tristan narrative that paints an evocative picture of dominance and alliances spanning the Irish Sea.

The most damaging of alliances from an Irish perspective between Ireland and Britain came with the submission of King Diarmait Mac Murchada (1110–71) to King Henry II. Mac Murchada became Henry's vassal in return for aid regaining his lost territory in Leinster, an action that resulted in the invasion beginning in the late 1160s. Henry II would struggle to contain the ambitions of many of the Anglo-Norman knights who campaigned on his behalf in Ireland, including those of 'Strongbow', Richard de Clare, sometime earl of Strigoil and Pembroke (d. 1176), who was involved in perhaps the most famous diplomatic marriage in medieval Ireland when, in 1170, he married Aífe, daughter of Diarmait MacMurchada.

The name Tristan has been identified as a version of 'Drust', a Pictish name found in the Welsh sources.[15] If Tristan represents a hero with Welsh connections (who eventually alters the balance of power between Ireland and England), might he represent Welsh involvement in Ireland? The fictional character of Tristan may stand as an exemplary model of knighthood: he resists the rebellious barons at Mark's court who urge him to marry the Irish princess and seize the throne for himself. Tristan's loyalty, however, is not always secure: at times he yields to temptation to seize Isolde (or Ireland) for himself. This love story is about a lust for power as much as love for an individual. The Tristan narrative is not telling the history of Ireland and Britain but it may serve as counter-factual historical fiction illustrating the dangers of 'what if' using stock characters and scenarios drawn from the recent past which would likely have been known to at least some of its early audience in Britain. It seems possible that those shaping the Tristan narrative knew that situations of the type they were suggesting here between kings in Ireland and knights from Britain were not beyond the realm of possibility.

of Ireland, and his Norman son-in-law, Arnulf de Montgomery, circa 1100', *RSAI*, 51 (1921), 116–34.   **15** For an overview of the Pictish, Irish and Breton traditions evident in the Tristan material, see Helaine Newstead, 'The origin and growth of the Tristan legend' in Roger Sherman Loomis (ed.), *Arthurian literature in the Middle Ages: a collaborative history* (Oxford, 1959), pp 112–33; for the Celtic analogies and sources, see chapters by W.J. McCann, 'Tristan: the Celtic and Oriental material re-examined' and Leslie W. Rabine, 'Love and the new patriarchy: Tristan and Isolde' in Grimbert (ed.), *Tristan and Isolde*, pp

DUBLIN: TOPOGRAPHY AND LEGENDS

Those familiar with the topography of medieval Dublin will recognize that the Dublin princess, Isolde, shares her name with a tower – Isolde's Tower – today situated on modern Essex Quay/Lower Exchange Street (originally called 'Isolde's Lane'). This round tower, situated at the north-eastern extremity of the fortified city, was one of Dublin's major defensive structures and the first tower at the entrance point that seafarers would encounter when approaching by sea. The foundations of the tower have been dated to the mid-thirteenth century, which makes it later than the original Tristan legend.[16] Whether the lane gave the name to the tower or the tower to the lane, it is clear that this area of Dublin had a long-standing connection to a woman by the name of Isolde although it is unlikely that this was the fictional Isolde of Tristan fame.

The first identified reference to Isolde's Tower appears to be the granting of it, by the mayor and commonalty of Dublin, to the clerk William Picot around 1275. The earliest reference to 'Chapelizod' in west Dublin – another location that might share a connection to Isolde – is a little earlier, in 1216.[17] Breandán Ó Ciobháin and Seán Duffy have suggested that these topographical features are named after a member of a prominent Dublin landowning family, the Bissets, who arrived in Dublin from Scotland in the late twelfth century.[18] Isolda, wife of Henry Bissett who died in 1208, held lands near Chapelizod, and about 1205, Isolda appears to have been a mistress of John (d. 1216), lord of Ireland, who would become king of England in 1199.[19] Some of the earliest extant versions of the Tristan story date to the latter half of the twelfth century when Isolda was alive – Gottfried's version, for instance, is thought to be composed in 1210 – and it may be that she was named after this fictional heroine.

The view of unstable kingship threatened by power-hungry barons combined with the story's interest in England's control over Ireland suggest that searching for inspiration for a reworking of this story in John's reign

---

3–36 and pp 37–74. On the Welsh versions, see Rachel Bromwich, 'The Tristan of the Welsh' in Rachel Bromwich, A.O.H. Jarman, and Brynley F. Roberts (eds), *The Arthur of the Welsh: the Arthurian legend in medieval Welsh literature* (Cardiff, 1991), pp 209–28. **16** Linzi Simpson, *Excavations at Isolde's Tower, Dublin* (Dublin, 1994), p. 4; see also, Nuala Burke, 'Dublin's north-eastern city wall: early reclamation and development at the Poddle-Liffey confluence', *PRIA*, 74C (1974), 113–32. **17** Simpson, *Excavations at Isolde's Tower*, p. 7; Busby, *French in medieval Ireland*, p. 358; See *CARD*, i, p. 95; *The Irish cartularies of Llanthony prima and secunda*, ed. E. St John Brooks (Dublin, 1953), p. 252. **18** Simpson, *Excavations at Isolde's Tower, Dublin*, p. 4; Seán Duffy, 'The lords of Galloway, earls of Carrick, and the Bissets of the Glens: Scottish settlement in thirteenth-century Ulster' in David Edwards (ed.), *Region and rulers in Ireland, 1100–1650: essays for Kenneth Nicholls*, Cork Studies in Irish History, 4 (Dublin, 2004), pp 37–50. **19** Busby, *French in medieval Ireland*, p. 360; Sidney Painter, *The reign of King John* (Baltimore, 1949), pp 234–5. For John's reputation as a lady's man and seducer of noble women, see Ralph V. Turner, *King*

might prove fruitful.[20] Indeed, John's title as lord of Ireland may find its literary parallel in, first, Tristan's defeat of the giant-hero of Ireland resulting in the halting of the payment of tribute from England to Ireland and, second, through his diplomatic marriage to Isolde of Ireland, which symbolically brought Ireland further under his dominion. Along with his connection to a woman named Isolda, John was married to two women named Isabella. In 1189, John married Isabelle, countess of Gloucester and in 1199, before he became king, the marriage was annulled so that in 1200 John could marry Isabelle of Angoulême, an heiress betrothed to Hugh de Lusignan; John's refusal to appear at the court of Philip II of France when prompted to explain his actions started a war. Moreover, John's quest to fund his war resulted in a revolt by the English barons in 1215–16, which aimed to subject him to the rule of law and resulted in his grant of Magna Carta. The presence of two fictional characters named Isolde, one in Ireland and one in Brittany (the latter whom Tristan marries) seems remarkably curious given the parallels in John's life. Could the historic Isabelle be the inspiration for the epitaph '*la belle Isole*' that is applied in some versions? Might a version of the old Tristan story be rewritten at the Angevin court in this period with John in mind?

In this period, the elite in Britain consumed romances in French and if a politically inclined raconteur who knew their Irish history sought to influence court opinion, producing such a romance might have been a logical (if somewhat dangerous) option. Scholarship has long suggested that the inspiration for the narrative was based on a Cornish source and Cornwall has its own topographic features related to the story. Again, this may offer a connection with John who was granted the county of Cornwall by his father, Henry. Literary representations of historical personages, events and places are notoriously difficult to pin down and the earliest surviving versions of the story (which may have had oral antecedents) are usually at some remove from any original. What is clear, however, is that the presence of a high-profile 'Isolde' of Ireland and this remarkably enduring narrative with a prominent woman of the same name, both linked to kings of England, may have contributed to the early interest in this story.

Little has been identified to date that demonstrates interest in this story in Ireland or medieval Dublin. This is likely to be due, in part, to the difficulty in identifying medieval romances circulating in medieval Ireland (other than those in the rich corpus of the Gaelic tradition). It would, however, be surprising if the story was not known in Ireland, at least within the English colony in Ireland, whose cultural appetite tended to reflect that of England. Since at least the sixteenth century, connections have been made between

John: England's evil king? (London, 2005), p. 166.   **20** Geoffrey of Monmouth's *Historia regum Britannie* is thought to have been partly composed during the tumultuous civil unrest of King Stephen's reign (1135–54).

8.1 Paris, Bibliothèque National de France, MS f. fr.112 fo 74r

places in Dublin relating to the name Isolde and the literary Isolde, though these efforts likely represent the perception of a connection rather than a true historical link. In this way, they may very well reflect a medieval oral tradition connecting these two Dublin Isoldes in popular legend.

Intriguingly, one of the illustrations in a deluxe manuscript of a French Lancelot-Grail text with abridged Tristan interpolations, dated to 1470, presents the scene where a dying Tristan strumming his harp sails in a small sailboat into Dublin (fig. 8.1). In the illustration he is watched by a male crowned figure (presumably the king) and female figure (presumably Isolde). They watch Tristan's arrival from the square window of a round tower on the shore standing out against a distant landscape of rolling hills with rows of trees

– approximately representing the position of Isolde's Tower (the only round mural tower in Dublin) in relation to the port and its hinterland.[21]

This illustration, found in a French manuscript owned by the bibliophile Jacques d'Armagnac (1433–77), duc de Nemours and later Comte de Castres, presents a comprehensive miniature cycle offering visual reminders of the various Arthurian narratives combined in this manuscript.[22] The varying depictions of this scene, and other episodes from Tristan's adventures in Ireland across the extensive manuscript corpus that deals with the Tristan narrative, are likely drawn from the imagination of individual artists, perhaps based on a textual description or a suggestive exemplar rather than eye-witness knowledge.[23] Though most probably drawn from an artist's mind, the fact that this particular miniature in the Paris manuscript appears to offer a relatively good representation of the medieval entry point by sea to the city makes it tempting to suggest that the archetype is based on familiarity with Dublin.

The historical references to the tower and Chapelizod offer little to link the historical locations with the legend, but a number of sixteenth-century historians do just that. The Dublin-based Welsh churchman and scholar, Meredith Hanmer, in his *Chronicle of Ireland* (1571) explained the connection, setting the story in the distant past:

> Mare King of Cornwall anno 459 married with Label Isode that bilt Isodes Chappell (or Chappell Isode) and Isodes Tower in Dublin, shee was the King of Irelands daughter.[24]

Hanmer expounds on the story of Tristan later in his chronicle and also adds a reference to Chapelizod:

> In Dublin vpon the wall of the Citie, is a Castle called Isod'towre, and not farre from Dublin, a Chappell with a Village named Chappell-Isod: the originall cause of the name I doe not finde, but it is coniectured, that her father King Anguish, that doted on her, builded them in remembrance of her, the one for her recreation, and the other for the good of her soule.[25]

21 For a discussion of this illustration in relation to music, see Mary Beth Winn, 'Tristan's harp in the Prose Tristan', *Early Music*, 45:2 (May 2017), 171–83. 22 The scholarship on depictions of Arthurian narratives is vast; the most important study remains Laura Hibbard Loomis and Roger Sherman Loomis, *Arthurian legends in medieval art* (New York, 1938). For the most extensive study of this manuscript BNF MS f fr.112, see esp., Susan A. Blackman, 'A pictorial synopsis of Arthurian episodes for Jacques d'Armagnac, duke of Nemours' in Keith Busby (ed.), *Word and image in Arthurian romance* (New York, 1996), pp 3–37. 23 See, for instance, the description of Tristan's arrival at Dublin quoted from the *Tristano Riccardiano* below. 24 Meredith Hanmer, 'Chronicle of Ireland' in James Ware (ed.), *The historie of Ireland, collected by three learned authors viz. Meredith Hanmer doctor in divinite: Edmund Campion sometime fellow of St John's Colledge in Oxford: and Edmund Spenser Esq* 2 (Dublin, 1633; repr. 2 vols, Dublin, 1809), p. 16. 25 Hanmer, *The chronicle of*

Writing a few years later, in a chronicle produced for Raphael Holinshed's *Chronicles of England, Scotland and Ireland*, the Dubliner Richard Stanihurst also confidently proclaimed that this tower, village and fountain ('Isolde's Font') near the Phoenix Park were connected to Isolde. In the 1577 edition of this work (which remains unchanged in the chronicle's subsequent 1587 edition) he explains that:

> There ſtandeth néere the caſtle, ouer againſt a voyde rowme, called Preſton his Innes, a tower, named, Iſoudes tower. It tooke the name of La Beale Iſoude, daughter to Anguiſhe, king of Irelande. It ſéemeth to haue béene a Caſtle of pleaſure for the kinges to recreat thē ſelues therin. Which was notvn like, conſidering that a meaner tower might ſerue ſuch ſingle ſoale kinges, as were at thoſe dayes in Irelande. There is a village harde by Dublynne, called of the ſayde La Beale, Chappell Iſoude.²⁶

This nomenclature connecting the characters from the legend and specific locations in Ireland may have appealed to these men, both antiquarians and interested in the history of Dublin. Stanihurst in particular, being from an old Dublin family, is likely to have had access to legends and stories circulating orally in sixteenth-century Dublin.²⁷ It is likely that – whatever the historical links, if any, between Tristan's Isolde, Isolda Bisset, and the topography of Dublin – the story of Tristan and his adventures in Ireland was known in Ireland in the late Middle Ages.

THE EUROPEAN DIMENSION

In the legend, Tristan is eventually banished to Brittany by King Mark, and he builds a palace that he decorates with images of his beloved Isolde of Dublin. Now married to a woman who shares Isolde's name but whom he does not love, he manages to infuriate both his wife and his brother-in-law with his inability to forget about his Irish paramour. The literary creation of images of Isolde that Tristan uses to recall their story is mirrored in the real-world creation of

Ireland, 1571, pp 104–5; for the story, see pp 103–5.   **26** *Holinshed's chronicles of England, Scotland, and Ireland*, 1.2, ch. 3. For a parallel online edition of this source, see 'The Holinshed Project' http://www.cems.ox.ac.uk/holinshed/index.shtml.   **27** A comparable sixteenth-century echo might be that made by Thomas Herron who suggested that Edmund Spenser had Dublin in mind as a backdrop for his imagined city Cleopolis, 'city of fame', which appears in his epic poem *The Faerie Queene* (first published in 1590); Thomas Herron, 'Edmund Spenser's "Cleopolis" and Dublin' in John Bradley, Alan J. Fletcher and Anngret Simms (eds), *Dublin in the medieval world: studies in honour of Howard B. Clarke* (Dublin, 2009), pp 448–56. I am grateful to Dr Herron for supplying me with a copy of his article.

8.2 Representation on tile of Tristan teaching Isolde to harp from Chertsey Abbey (V&A Museum C.347-1927; Ceramics, Room 138, Harry and Carol Djanogly Gallery, case 1, shelf 8; photo © V&A Museum)

countless visual representations of the lovers and their adventures across Europe.[28] One use for visual representations of this popular secular story had a moralizing function in a religious context. The scene where the lovers try to meet secretly at court – the Tryst scene – where Isolde's suspicious husband is hiding in a tree to spy on them, is used in misericords in Chester and Lincoln Cathedrals to represent God's ability to see all human actions and serve as a check to the actions of those who meditate on this episode from the romance in

28 For studies on the artistic representation, see, Julia Walworth, 'Tristan in medieval art' in Grimbert (ed.), *Tristan and Isolde*, pp 255–300.

8.3 Rendering of the Chertsey tile piecing together broken fragments to show the original picture, 'After Shurlock, Tristram teaches Isolt to harp', from R.S. Loomis, *Illustrations of medieval romance on tiles from Chertsey Abbey* (Urbana, 1916), fig. 21

a religious context.[29] This particular scene was frequently used as an *aide memoire* in various media to represent this well-known story in its entirety, drawing attention as it did to the illicit nature of their love and their responsibility for their own actions.[30] Another famous English representation of the story is found in the remarkable tile sequence of Chertsey Abbey, dated to the

29 G.L. Remnant and Mary Désirée Anderson, *A catalogue of misericords in Great Britain* (Oxford, 1998), xxxiii. Surviving misericords in Ireland are considerably less extensive. The only surviving medieval misericords from Ireland are the twenty misericord carvings in Limerick Cathedral which are drawn from the bestiary tradition where animals represent moral characteristics or a spiritual message; on this see, Roger Stalley, 'Limerick misericords' in Rachel Moss (ed.), *Art and architecture of Ireland: volume I, Medieval art and architecture c.400–1600*, 5 vols (Dublin and New Haven, 2015), 321–2. **30** See, for instance, Lydia Yaitsky Kertz, 'Shadows and reflections: Tristan and Isolde in manuscripts and ivory', *Word & Image*, 30:2 (April–June 2014), 131–54.

8.4 Hanging of wool and gilded leather, *c.*1370–1400, of the Tristan legend (V&A Museum, item 1370–1864, Medieval & Renaissance, Room 10a, Françoise and Georges Selz Gallery, case WW; photo © V&A Museum)

late thirteenth century. Thirty-five scenes from the Tristan narrative are represented here on red and white clay tiles (figs 8.2–3).[31]

Further afield, a remarkable and eye-catching wall-hanging from northern Germany represents the Tristan narrative in storyboard form on striking chequered red and blue background – a relatively cheap way of making eye-catching designs (fig. 8.4).[32] The appliqué hanging (now measuring 109cm x 256.5cm) has twenty-two scenes, a number of which depict a castle, presumably representing Dublin. One of the scenes appears to depict King Angus emerging with his horse and hound from his castle and encountering the dragon which is threatening his land and which Tristan will later kill. The fight itself is rendered through a series of tableaux on the wall hanging.

These artistic depictions, dated *c.*1370 on account of the costumes, are based on one of the oldest-preserved Tristan narratives, the *Tristant* (*c.*1170) of Eilhart von Oberg who translated the story into Middle High German. More

---

31 R.S. Loomis reproduced the tiles in *Illustrations of medieval romance on tiles from Chertsey Abbey* (Urbana, 1916); see also, W.R. Lethaby, 'The romance tiles of Chertsey Abbey', *Walpole Society Annual*, 2 (1912–3), 69–80. 32 See Sarah Randles, 'Heraldic imagery in the embroidered Tristan narratives' in Elizabeth Archibald and David F. Johnson (eds), *Arthurian literature XXXII* (Cambridge, 2015), pp 165–86, at pp 173–5; see also, James Rushing, 'The medieval German pictorial experience' in William H. Jackson and Silvia A. Ranawake (eds), *The Arthur of the Germans: the Arthurian legend in medieval German and Dutch literature* (Cardiff, 2000). For a comparison of the Tristan story in embroidery and text, see Alan Deighton, 'Visual representations of the Tristan legend and their written sources: a re-evaluation', *Tristania: A Journal Devoted to Tristan Studies*, 20 (2000), 59–92 (with thanks to Dr Stuart Kinsella for supplying me with a copy of this article).

crude representations of the seat of the king and his family in a standard
medieval castle are found in a mid-thirteenth-century illustrated manuscript
from Germany that generally dedicates full-page panel illustrations to tell the
story pictorially.[33] These depictions present visual impressions of the medieval
Dublin mentioned in the story. This is a Dublin residing in the imagination, a
place of adventure where dragons still roam, and magic still lingers. It is the
Ibernia fabulosa (fabulous Ireland) recalled by Ruggiero, a character in
Ludovico Ariosto's *Orlando Furioso* (1532), whose flying horse brings him on a
scenic journey over Ireland.[34] The representations of the city found in these
artistic creations are figurative, not literal. But they are, nonetheless, a vision
of Dublin that has travelled beyond Ireland and brought a small part of the
legend of the medieval city to a European audience.

Another artistic representation, from the late fourteenth century, this time
of the individual characters, was made for the brothers Niklaus and Franz
Vintler when they redecorated their spectacular Castel Rocolo (Schloss
Runkelstein) – later owned by Emperor Maximilian I who restored the
artworks – in the Southern Tyrolean Alps situated near Bolzano in what today
is the most northerly region of Italy. Some of the frescos on the summer house
and loggia leading to the castle depicted Tristan and Isolde of Ireland, this
time, following the story as told by Gottfried of Strassburg.[35] There was
considerable interest in literary accounts of Tristan in the various city-states
which comprised what is now Italy. Almost one quarter of the extant Old
French versions of the French-language *Tristan en Prose* circulated or were
copied in Italy.[36] The *Tristan en Prose* also served as the source for a vernacular
mid-thirteenth- to fourteenth-century Tuscan-Umbrian version of the story,
known as the *Tristano Riccardiano*, and in the early fourteenth century it was
used to create Venetian vernacular versions known as the *Tristano Veneto* and
the *Tristano Corsiniano*.[37] These works offered a European audience a literary

---

33 Tristan MS 1, Bayerische Staatsbibliothek Munchen, Cod. Germ. 51; the illustrations
on the panels on fo. 46v depict Tristan approaching Dublin by boat and later being healed in
the castle, while below it shows him teaching Isolde; an illustration on fo. 67r shows Tristan
fighting and subduing the dragon. Other scenes in Ireland are also depicted, including (on
fo. 76r) Isolde standing over Tristan threatening to kill him in vengeance for killing her
uncle.   34 For an interesting study of attitudes to Ireland in Renaissance Italy (although it
makes no reference to the Tristan story), see Eric Haywood, *Fabulous Ireland Ibernia
fabulosa: imagining Ireland in Renaissance Italy* (Oxford, 2014); for a study of *Orlando*, see
chaps 4 and 5.   35 For a summary of some of the material and scholarship, see Gloria
Allaire, 'Arthurian art in Italy' in Gloria Allaire and F. Regina Psaki (eds), *The Arthur of the
Italians: the Arthurian legend in medieval Italian literature and culture* (Cardiff, 2014), pp
205–32, at pp 210–12.   36 For a list and discussion of the twenty-six manuscripts of the
Tristan en Prose circulating in Italy, see Marie-José Heijkant, 'From France to Italy: the first
Tristan texts' in Allaire and Psaki (eds), *The Arthur of the Italians*, pp 43–7; for a list of
manuscripts of translations and adaptations of the *Tristan en Prose*, see Heijkant, 'From
France to Italy', pp 47–8.   37 For the *Tristan Veneto*, the most important of the northern

depiction of Dublin in their vernacular, as evidenced by the scene when the gravely ill Tristan arrives at the port of Dublin and is rendered as follows in the *Tristano Riccardiano*:

> Now the tale tells that Tristan and Governal had been at sea for nine months. And if anyone should ask me where Tristan ended up, I will say that he arrived in Ireland at the court of King Anguin (*Languis*), the brother-in-law of Morholt (*l'Amoroldo*), who had died of the wound that Tristan had given him. Once Tristan's ship was secured he took his harp and began to play. It was nearly dawn, and he played so sweetly that King Anguin heard it in his own chamber. And hearing the sound of the harp, it seemed to him so sweet that he rose from his bed, dressed, and went to the window, which gave out over the seaport, and there he stayed for as long as Tristan played.[38]

The popularity of this tale in Italy is evident not only through the surviving manuscripts of these works and others such as the *Tristano Panciaticchiano* and the important Tuscan *Tavola Ritonda*, but also through the other artistic representations mediated through these vernacular texts.[39] The *Tavola Ritonda* was an early fourteenth-century Tuscan version (now extant in ten fourteenth- and fifteenth-century manuscripts), which served as the inspiration for a remarkable patterned, quilted linen cloth made in Sicily in the mid-to-late fourteenth century. Figurative renderings of the narrative, accompanied by raised capitals in Sicilian dialect based on *La Tavola Ritonda*, were outlined in brown thread.[40] It has been suggested that two Tristan quilts found separately today were once part of the same very large piece that is considered by scholars to be either a bedspread or a tapestry, possibly a bedchamber hanging.[41] One is

Italian texts, see Heijkant, 'From France to Italy', pp 53–5. **38** *Italian literature II: Tristano Riccardiano*, ed. and trans. Regina Pasaki (New York, 2006), pp 44–5: [22] 'Or dice lo conto ke Tristano e Governale istetterono in mare mens; .viiij. E.sse alkuno mi domanderae là ove arivoe Tristano, io dirae k'arivoe, inn-Irlanda a la ko[r]te de.rree Languis, lo quale iera kognato de l'Amoroldo, il quale morio de la fedita ke Tristano igli diede. E.ddappoi ke la nave di Tristano fue aconc[ia] , ed egli sì prese l'arpa e incomincioe a sonare. Ed iera presso a giorn[o] essonoe tanto dolcemene, ke lo ree Languis, l'udie infino ne la kamera sua. E intendendo lo suono dell'arpa, parvelli tanto dolce a udire ke si levoe del retto e vestisi e venne a la finestra, la quaele è sopra lo porto del mare, e quivi istette tanto quando Tristano sonò.' **39** For an account of the *Tristano Panciaticchiano* and the *Tavola Ritonda*, see Heijkant, 'From France to Italy', pp 50–2 and 55–6 respectively. **40** For the text, see Anne Shavers (ed. and trans.), *Tristan and the Round Table: a translation of La Tavola Ritonda*, Medieval and Renaissance Texts and Studies, 28 (Binghmanton, 1983). **41** For the development of the scholarly discussion on the bedspread/tapestry debate, see Sarah Randles, 'One quilt or two? A reassessment of the Guicciardini quilts in the Victoria and Albert Museum and the Museo del Bargello' in Robin Netherton and Gale R. Owen-Crocker (eds), *Medieval clothing and textiles*, 5 (Woodbridge, 2009), pp 103–27, at pp 94–7; see also, pp 124–7. Allaire dismisses scholarship which has claimed it as a bedspread and refers to it as 'a single wall hanging', in 'Arthurian art in Italy', p. 222.

8.5 The Tristan Quilt, *c.*1360–1400 (V&A Museum item no. 1391–1904, Medieval & Renaissance, Room 9, Dorothy and Michael Hintze Gallery, case 1; photo © V&A Museum)

today found in the Victoria and Albert Museum in London (item 1391–1904; 320x287cm), the second in the *Museo Nationale del Bargello* in Florence (247x207cm).[42]

42 The first important scholarly study of the quilts is that of Pio Rajna, 'Intorno a due artche coperte con figurazioni tratte dale storia di Stistano', *Romania*, 42 (1913), 517–79; for a more recent study, see Randles, 'The Guicciardini quilts'; for the Bargello portion which was recently restored, see Rosanna Caterina Proto Pisani, Marco Ciatti, Susanna Conti and Maria Grazia Vaccari, *La 'coperta' Guicciardini: il resauro delle imprese di Tristano, problem di*

8.6 Ceiling of the *Sala Magna* (*c.*1377–80), Steri Palazzo Chiaramonte, Palermo, Sicily. Photograph by F. Vergara Caffarelli, Palermo-Florence 2009 from survey of the ceiling by the Representation Department of the University of Palermo; reproduced by permission of Centro Regionale per l'Inventario, la Catalogazione e la Documentazione grafica, fotografica, aerofotogrammetrica, audiovisiva (CRICD), U.O.VIII.

The coat-of-arms of the Guicciardini family appears on a shield held by Tristan.[43] It has been suggested that the quilt was created to celebrate the 1395 wedding of the important Florentine Guicciardini and Acciaioli families who were influential in southern Italy, but there is no definitive proof of this link.[44] For our purposes, it is the representation of Dublin on the V&A Tristan quilt that is of most interest (fig. 8.5). One of the six scenes displays the title: '*Sitati de Irlandia*' in the right-hand corner while a large and fanciful castle takes up most of the space before the border, presumably showing an entirely imagined view of medieval Dublin, or the palace of the king, as Rajna described it: '*il palazzo reale di re Languis*'.[45] Five heads appear within the edifice, two crowned figures – presumably the king and his wife the queen – look from the top of one tower and a smaller figure peers out from a floor below (possibly the sly steward who will attempt to claim Tristan's victory for himself and claim the hand of the princess Isolde). Isolde herself, without a crown, peers from a balcony off a campanile adjacent to a church; the second female figure in the floor below likely represents her loyal maidservant, Brangane.

The depictions are obviously not accurate representations of buildings in Dublin, but they offer a fascinating glimpse of an imagined Ireland in medieval

conservazione e restauro, 27 (Florence, 2010).   **43** For a discussion of Tristan's arms and the potential political message within the battles depicted, see Kathryn Berenson, 'Political partisanship in the Tristan furnishings', *Uncoverings*, 39 (2018), 9–46; for the seven embroidered Tristan depictions from the medieval and early modern period, see Randles, 'Heraldic imagery in the embroidered Tristan narratives'.   **44** Randles suggests the quilt may have been made up to a decade before this marriage took place: 'Heraldic imagery in the embroidered Tristan narratives', p. 179.   **45** Rajna, 'Intorno a due arche coperte con

Sicily, another island conquered by the Normans. This evocative artwork was not the only representation of this famous story in Sicily: the wooden painted ceiling of the *Sala Magna* (1377–80) in the Palazzo Chiaramonte Steri in Palermo also shows a series of scenes from the Tristan story including the knight battling the dragon, and later embracing Isolde who reaches down to him from the ramparts of her castle, rendered in the style of the palazzo itself (fig. 8.6).[46] A later scene depicts a dramatic embrace by Tristan and a crowned Isolde as they sail across the choppy sea while four sailors struggle with the sail in the background, reflecting the daring of the lovers embarking on this dangerous journey. It is clear that many of the artists drew from their imagination and their own surroundings rather than from any extensive knowledge of Ireland. For many, Ireland likely served as a far-off location in a popular adventure story, a place where strange and heroic daring deeds of knights and princesses could still occur.

CONCLUSION

As historical fiction, the Tristan story could play a little with the representations of characters and places, but those hailing from the island of Ireland do not come out looking any worse than other communities in the narrative. The reality is that the story of Tristan panders to some extent to the stereotypes. Fiery and tempestuous, fierce fighters, slave-owners, famed healers and good musicians, the Irish of the Tristan story are neither real nor entirely fictional. The best fiction plays with things that are known, reinventing them anew and imbuing them with new purpose. The narrative of the Tristan story has remained an enduring example of exceptional storytelling precisely because it both reflects and reinvents the history of Ireland, renegotiating the relationship between Ireland and Britain. In spite of the central role Ireland and Dublin plays in the Tristan tradition, it remains an imagined place, vividly brought to life through the remarkable number of visual depictions, all over Europe, of aspects of the narrative, showing the remarkable endurance of a good story.

---

fiurazioni tratte dale storia di Tristano', p. 555.   **46** For the Tristan cycle in the *Sala Magna* ceiling specifically, and in the wider context of the Palazzo Chiaramonte ceiling paintings more generally, see, Licia Buttà, 'Storie per governare: Iconografia giuridica e del potere nel soffitto dipinto della sala magna del palazzo Chiaromonte Steri di Palermo' in Licia Buttà (ed.), *Narrazione, exempla, retorica. Studi sull'iconografia dei soffitti dipinti nel medioevo mediterraneo*, caracol edizioni (Palermo, 2013), 69–126, esp. 92–7. For an overview of the entire ceiling, see the encyclopedic study by Francesco Vergara Caffarelli, *Il Soffitto dello Steri di Palermo: Rilievo fotogrammetrico digitale a cura di Francesco Vergara Caffarelli*, CRICD (Palermo, 2009).

St Sepulchre's palace: new perspectives from recent excavations

ALAN R. HAYDEN

INTRODUCTION

Monitoring of the removal of the concrete surface of the courtyard of Dublin's St Sepulchre's palace in early 2019 revealed medieval stone walls and deposits immediately below it. Limited excavation and recording of the structures demonstrated that they formed a central part of the palace and prove that its original layout differed significantly from that previously suggested (O'Donovan 2003).

ARCHAEOLOGICAL AND HISTORICAL BACKGROUND

The palace of St Sepulchre was erected south-east of what was then St Patrick's Church (raised to cathedral status in 1212) in an area described, before 1186, as *cros gort*, 'cross field' (Gilbert 1897, 48–9; McNeill 1950, 16) (fig. 9.1). The palace was reputedly built by the first Anglo-Norman archbishop of Dublin, John Cumin (archbishop from 1181, but who only arrived in Dublin in 1184); however, it is only first attested historically in 1216 when the 'archbishop's house and buildings at St Sepulchre's, with the buildings and appurtenances' are mentioned (McNeill 1950, 38–9). Parts of the palace grounds were damaged in 1317 as a result of incursions by troops defending the city from the threatened assault by Edward and Robert Bruce. Much of the southern suburbs of the city were also razed at this time and never fully rebuilt, attested to archaeologically by excavations at the adjacent site to the east (Simpson 2008) and further west on Kevin Street (Hayden 2018). St Patrick's Cathedral was damaged at this time and the palace itself also appears to have suffered. A description of the palace from shortly afterwards, in 1326, is the most complete we have of the medieval site and mentions that it consisted of a 'stone hall badly roofed with shingles, a chamber annexed to the said hall, a kitchen and a chapel, roofed but all of no value as in disrepair' (McNeill 1950, 170).

The arrival of the Black Death in Dublin in 1348 resulted in a further depopulation of the southern suburbs, which had not recovered from the 1317 burning. This facilitated the clearance and enclosure by the archbishops of more ground around the palace and adjoining areas. Excavations east of St

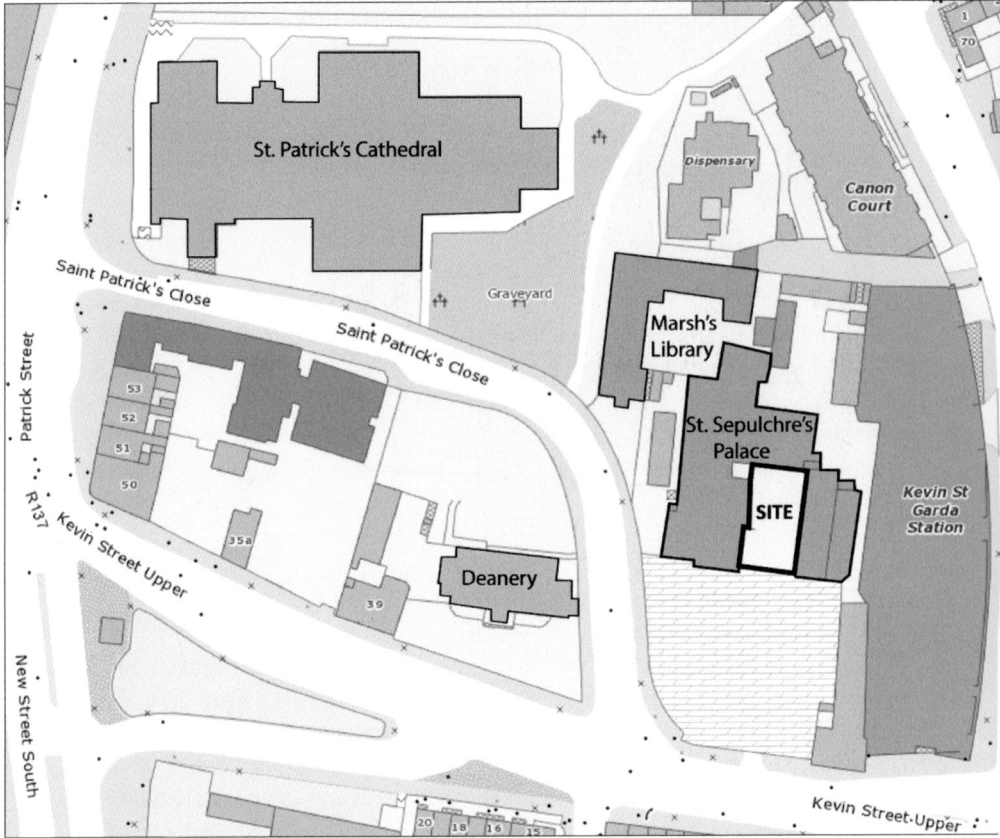

9.1 The location of the former palace and of the area of the courtyard assessed

Sepulchre's have shown that the curving enclosure depicted there on Speed's map of 1610 (fig. 9.2) originated in the later medieval period (Simpson 2008). Speed's map also shows castellated walls surrounding the palace and cathedral and the chancellor's manse on the south side of Kevin Street. Part of the wall around the latter was recently revealed by excavation (Hayden 2018, 9). There are further mentions of the kitchens in the palace in 1213–28, of the great hall in 1395, and of the chapel in 1367, 1425 and 1497. However, at some stage after this the chapel appears to have gone out of use or was demolished as Archbishops Narcissus Marsh and William King both mention around 1700 that there was no chapel in the palace.

A gaol or prison is mentioned in 1302 (*CJRI, 1295–1303*, 398–9), in 1377 (*CPR, 1377–81*, 55) and in 1504 (McNeill 1950, 254–5). It lay between the palace and the deanery; the position of the latter, to the west of the palace, was the same in the medieval period as today. The construction of an almshouse is also attested in 1504 and in the following year between the prison and the

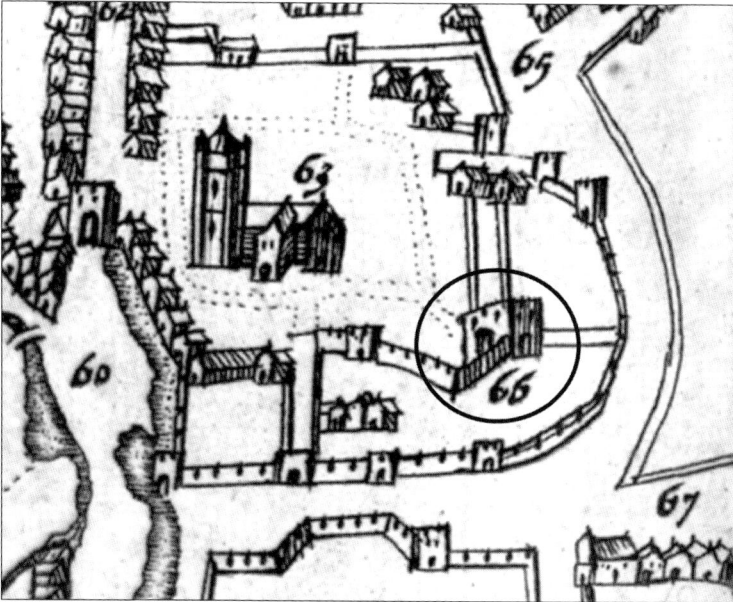

9.2 Extract from Speed's map (1610) with St Sepulchre's palace highlighted. Note the late medieval castellated walls surrounding much of the lands of St Patrick's

deanery (McNeill 1950, 258–9). It is again mentioned in 1553 (*CPR Ire., Hen. VIII–Eliz.*, 314).

Ware (1705, 13) states that Archbishop Huge Inge repaired the palace. However, it appears this was purely on the evidence of a doorway topped with a plaque bearing the date 1523 and arguably decorated with Inge's coat of arms in the western wall of the palace. During the sixteenth century the palace was several times seized and held by the secular authorities. The viceroy, Lord Grey, moved in in 1539 but was soon ejected. During the reign of Edward VI (1545–53) a later lord deputy lived there but with Mary's accession it was returned to the archbishop. However, after Elizabeth came to the throne it was seized in 1558 by the lord deputy, the earl of Sussex (Monck Mason 1820, 153). It was given over to the new reformed Church of Ireland by the 1570s when it was described as 'an abode well pleasantly sited as gorgeously builded' (Miller and Power 1979, 50). Archbishop Adam Loftus resided there at this time and died there in 1605.

Speed's map of 1610 (fig. 9.2) is the earliest representation we have of the palace. It shows it as a great square block with an entrance on the west. Unfortunately, none of the other surviving seventeenth-century maps give any details of the buildings on the site. In 1664 the palace was described as 'decayed, ruinous and in need of repair' (*Cal. S.P. Ire., 1663–5*, 368). However, in the same year Archbishop Michael Boyle (1663–79) received the sum of

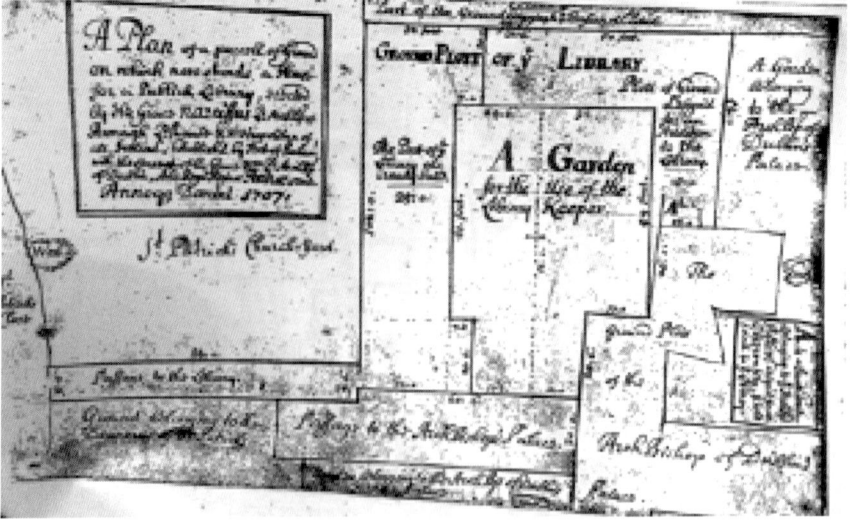

9.3 1707 plan of Marsh's Library showing the small tower north of the medieval vaulted structure and the existence of the new north range of the palace

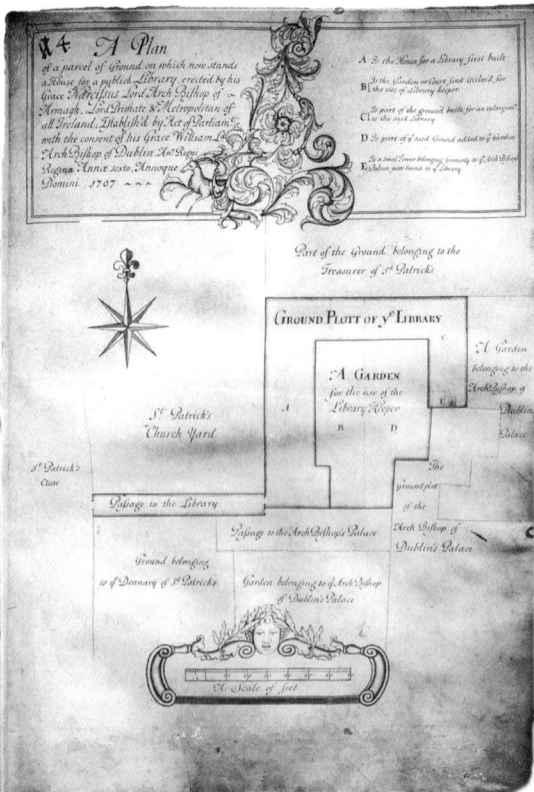

9.4 1707 plan of Marsh's Library showing the small tower north of the medieval vaulted structure and the existence of the new north range of the palace

9.5 Extract from Brooking's map (1728) showing Marsh's Library and St Sepulchre's palace

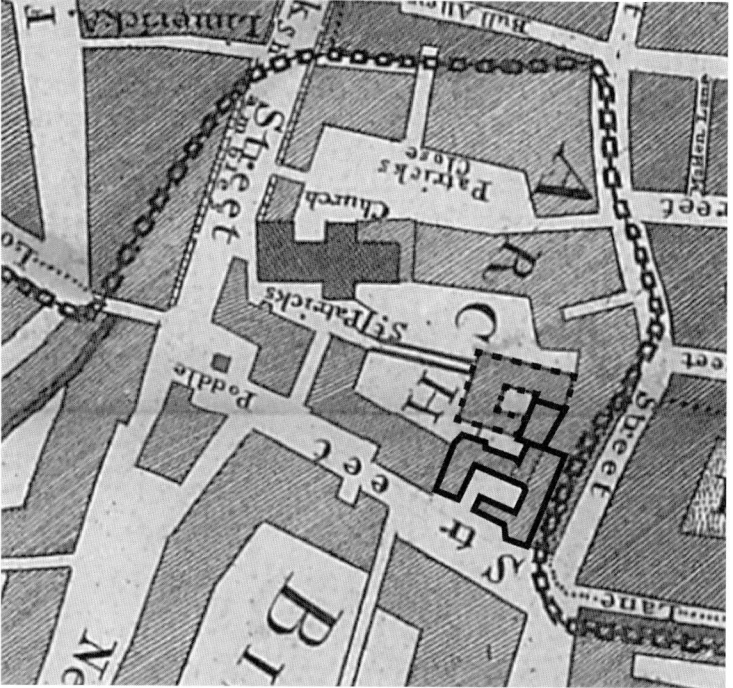

9.6 Extract from Rocque's map (1756) showing Marsh's Library and St Sepulchre's palace

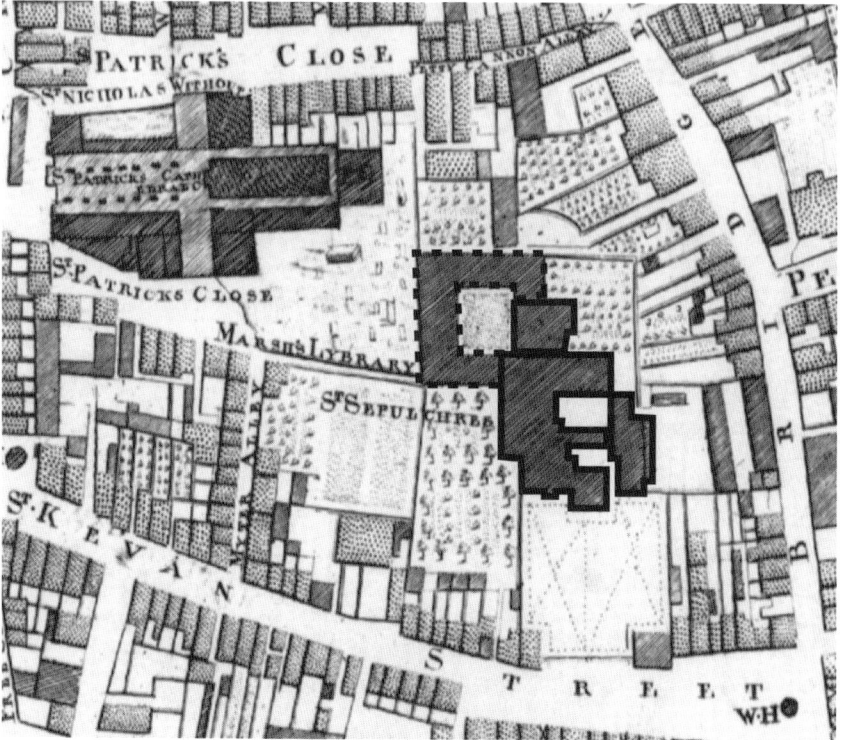

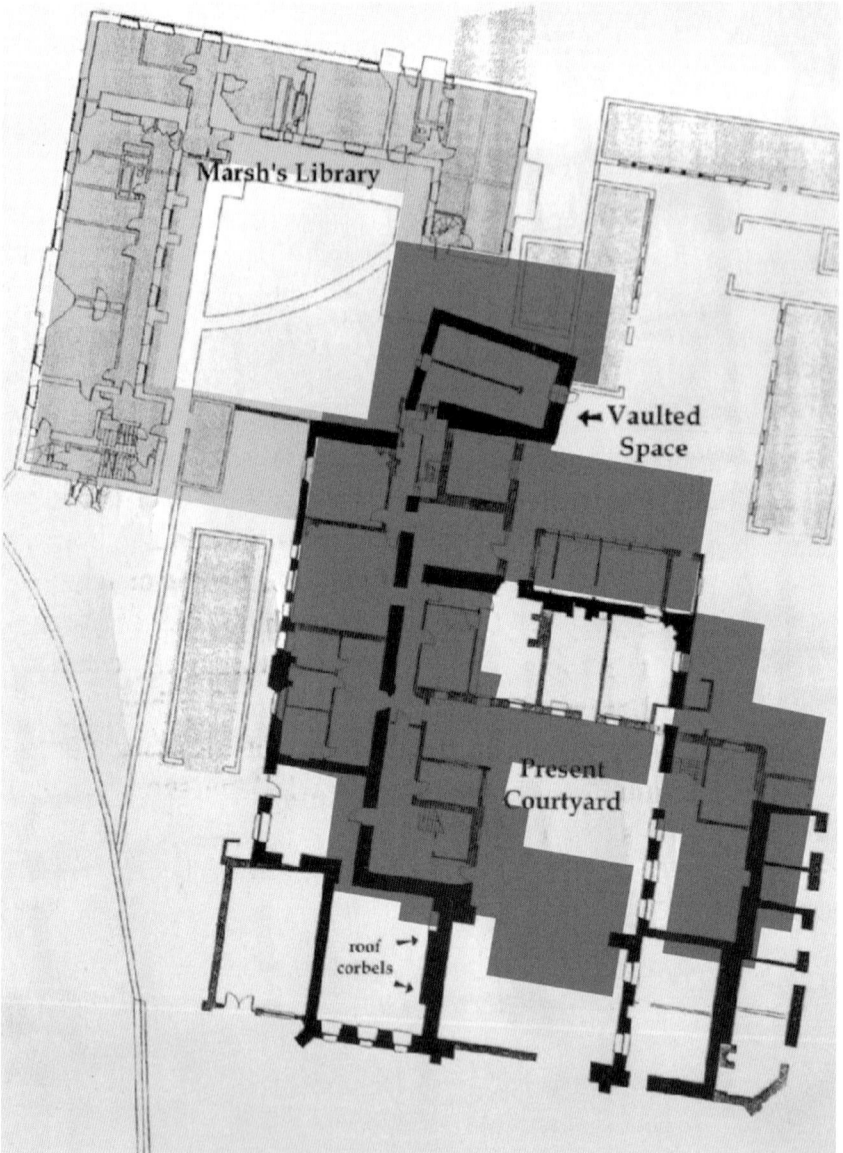

9.7 Rocque's 1756 map aligned on modern plan

1000l. and 'very much repaired and beautified the Palace of St Sepulchre'. This
was the start of a phase of an almost total rebuilding of the palace, which was
completed by the succeeding archbishops Francis Marsh (1682–93), Narcissus
Marsh (1694–1703) and William King (1703–29). The re-edification effectively
involved the almost total removal of the original late twelfth-/early thirteenth-

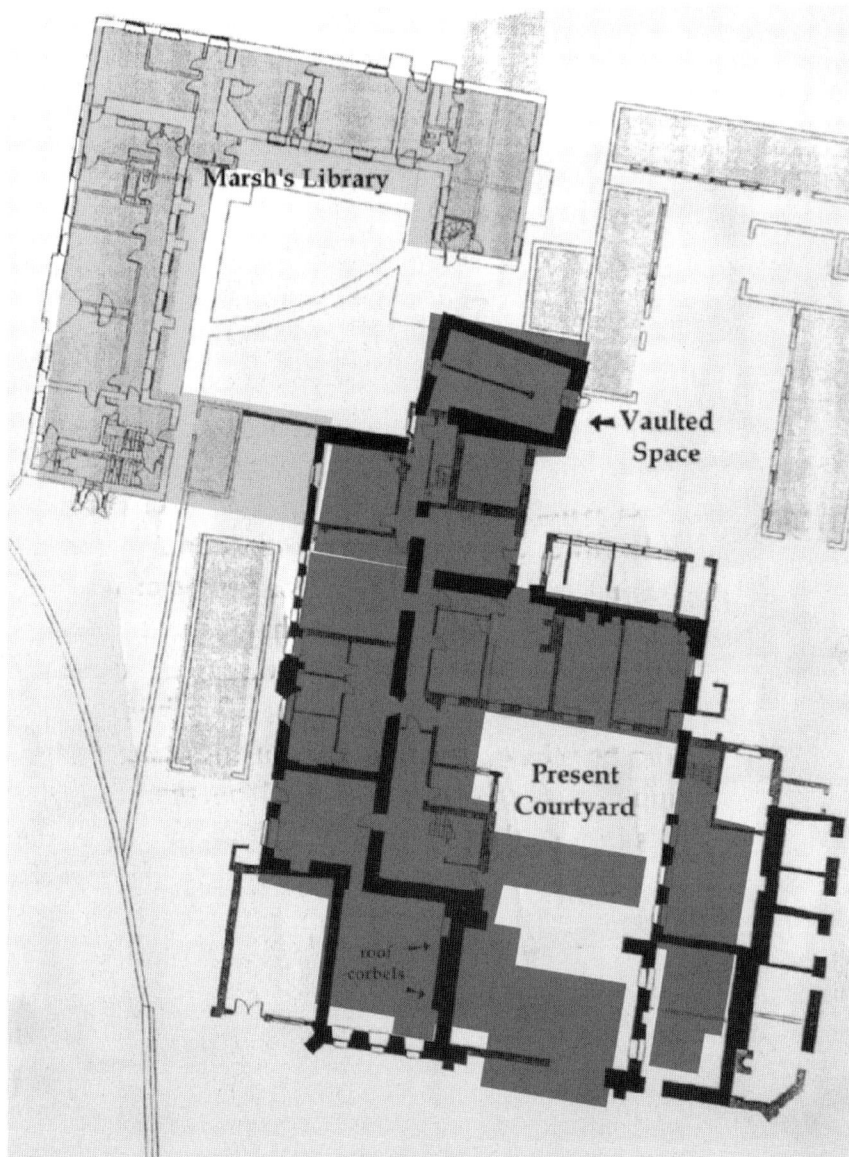

9.8 Rocque's 1756 map divided into Library and palace and each separately aligned on the modern map

century buildings. The new buildings are partly shown on two plans from 1707 (figs 9.3 and 9.4), with varying degrees of accuracy on Brooking's map of 1728 (fig. 9.5) and Rocque's map of 1756 (figs 9.6–9.9), and in a watercolour of 1765 by Gabriel Beranger (fig. 9.10), which appears also to show the last remnants of some of the earlier buildings.

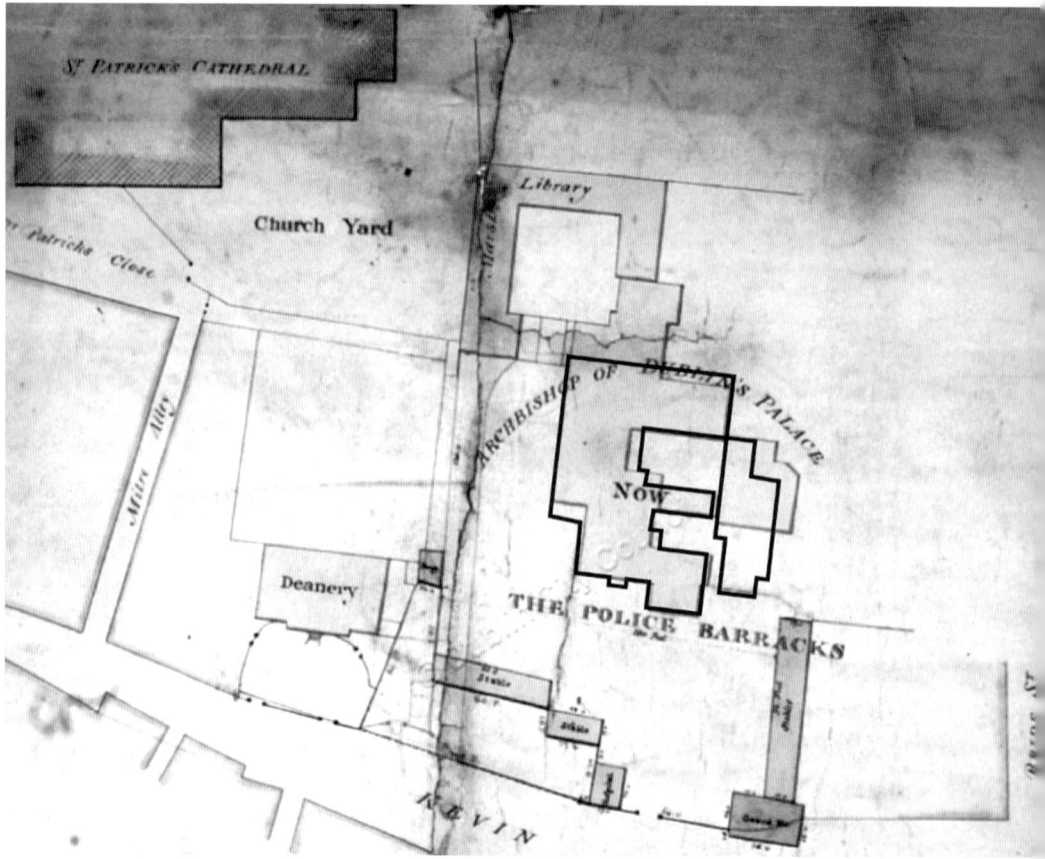

9.9 Rocque's realigned 1756 map overlain on 1824 Wide Street Commissioners' plan (WS/maps/503/1–5)

Brooking's map of 1728 (fig. 9.5) is inaccurate, as it shows the palace too far west in relation to Marsh's Library and also shows it stretching all the way down to the Kevin Street frontage. However, in the overall shape depicted – buildings arranged around three sides of a courtyard with a narrow building across the southern side – it does echo what is shown on Rocque's more detailed map of 1756 (fig. 9.6). However, Rocque's map is also not without its problems. Overlaying it on a modern plan reveals that the palace is shown too far to the north where it is jammed into Marsh's Library (fig. 9.7). However, if Rocque's plans of the palace and library are separated and that of the palace is moved southwards, then it lines up closely with the modern plan (fig. 9.8) and also with the buildings shown on an 1824 Wide Street Commissioners' map (fig. 9.9). Such inaccuracies are not unknown on Roque's various maps; he usually depicts individual buildings accurately but does, at times, show the juxtaposition between buildings with far less precision.

9.10 Gabriel Beranger, The archiepiscopal palace, Dublin. Watercolour, 22.7 x 28.7cm, signed G.B. Del 1765 (National Library of Ireland)

In 1804, the archbishop moved to new premises (what is now Newman House) on the south side of St Stephen's Green and the palace became a barracks for the 41st Regiment. At some time in or after 1834 the former palace was sold to the Dublin Metropolitan Police becoming one of the earliest police stations in these islands. The site has remained a police station ever since. The alterations made to the former palace during the later eighteenth and nineteenth centuries are partly visible in the buildings themselves, on the Wide Street Commissioners' map from 1824 (fig. 9.9) and on the OS first edition 6" map of 1848 (fig. 9.11). Later works are visible both on the site and on later editions of the OS maps (fig. 9.12).

The buildings that survive on the site today are a mix of late medieval, late seventeenth-, eighteenth-, nineteenth- and twentieth-century elements (fig. 9.13). In recent years, several architectural surveys of the complex have been conducted (Gibney 2001; Gowen 2007; Moss et al. 2015) and an attempt was made to reconstruct its original medieval layout (O'Donovan 2003). Archaeological investigations were also undertaken of the east side of the site in advance of the construction of a new Garda station on Bride Street (Simpson 2004; Gowen 2007a). The features more recently revealed under the courtyard demonstrate that the medieval palace is likely to have been of a somewhat different plan and layout to that previously suggested.

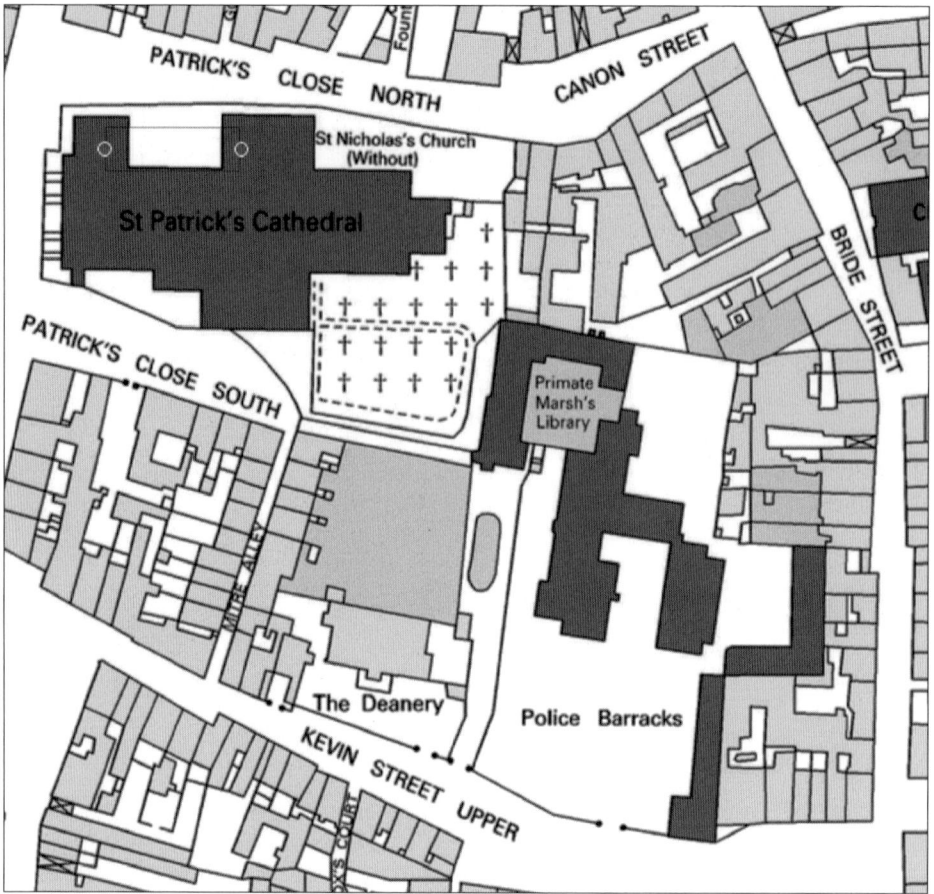

9.11 OS 1st ed. 6″ map (1848)

MONITORING AND EXCAVATION

The 100mm-thick modern concrete surface (F01) of the courtyard (apart from
that on the small outshot at its north-west side) was removed in March 2019.
This revealed the tops of a number of medieval and later stone walls and
deposits containing medieval pottery. Following consultation with the National
Monuments Service, the yard was archaeologically cleaned down by hand and a
few small areas were excavated to varying degrees to facilitate the recording
and interpretation of the features and deposits revealed. There was no
intention to fully excavate the site, as this was neither feasible in the timeframe,
nor necessary at this stage. The surface of subsoil was revealed only in limited
areas. It lay 300–350mm below the modern surface of the northern end of the
yard but sloped downwards lying 450mm below the modern surface of the

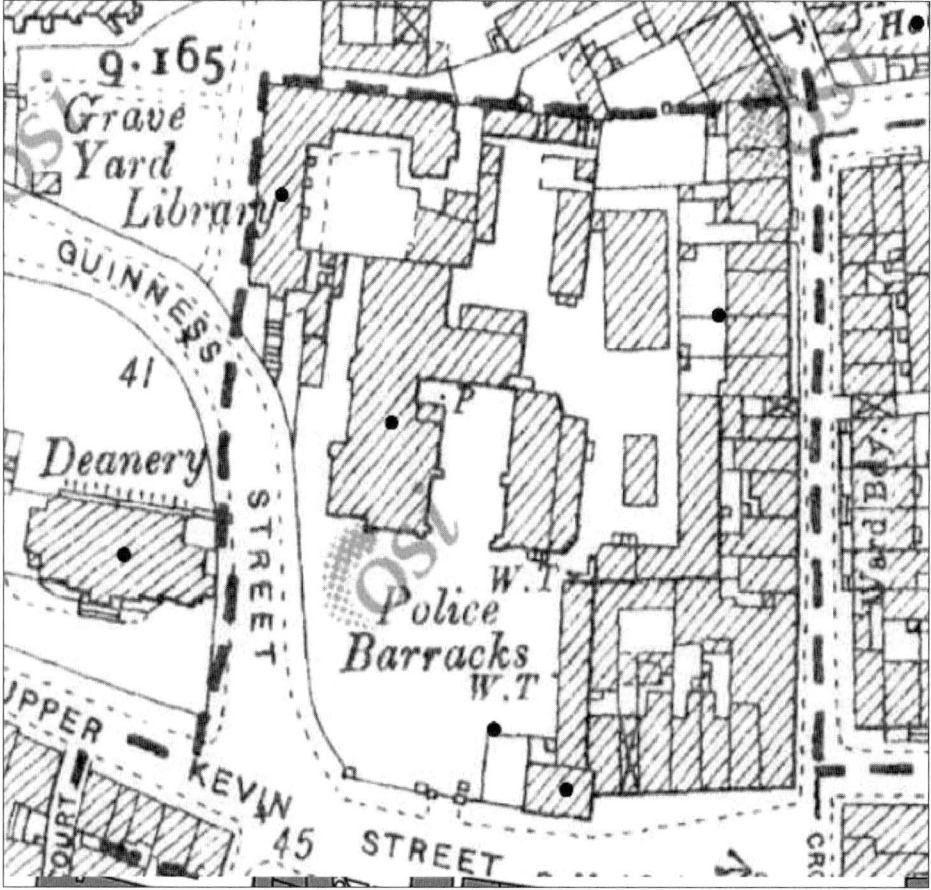

9.12 OS 1880–1911 map

9.13 Composite photograph of the south façade of the palace today. The changes of the last 150 years can be seen by comparing this view with that shown by Beranger in 1765 (fig. 9.10)

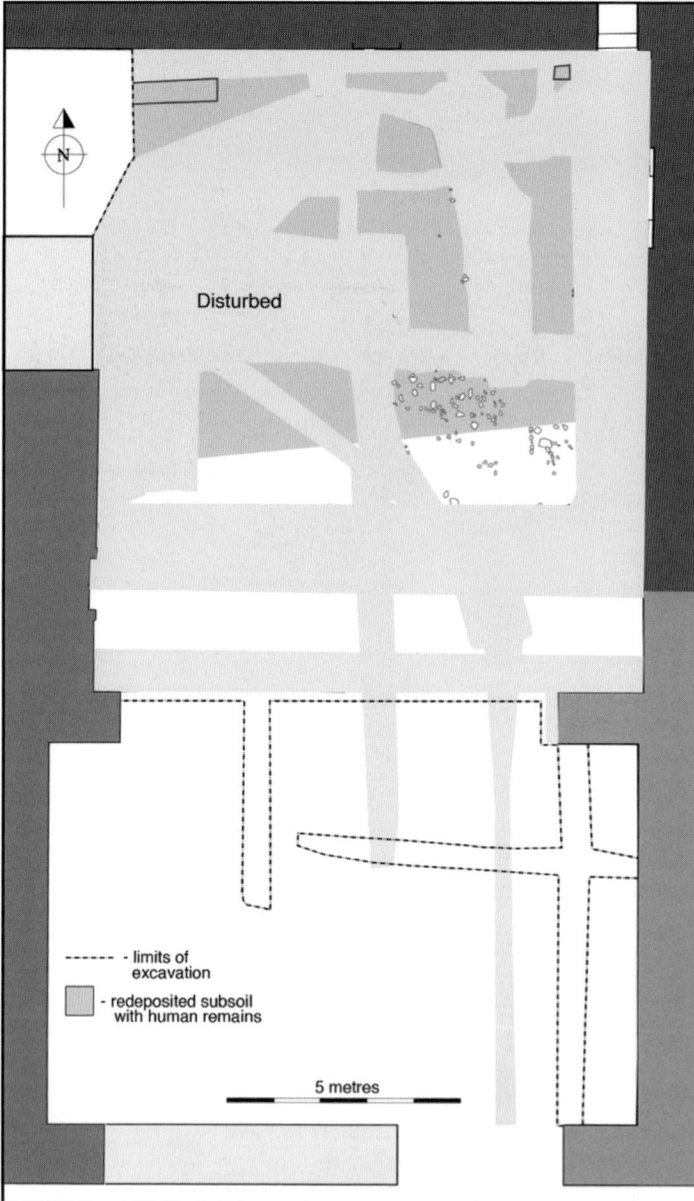

9.14 Location of excavated area of redeposited subsoil (F02) that contained human remains

Disturbed

------ - limits of
          excavation

- redeposited subsoil
  with human remains

5 metres

south end of the yard. Where it was encountered in the northern third of the site, it was very soft and evidently disturbed. More compact and undisturbed subsoil was revealed in the southern two thirds of the yard.

The site had also been heavily disturbed in relatively recent times. There were many lines of pipes and several manholes and chambers cut down into the underlying deposits and structures. Some of the drains contained ceramic

9.15 Human remains from redeposited subsoil (F02)

pipes and were of early twentieth-century date; however more were of late twentieth or early twenty-first-century date, as they contained plastic Wavin pipes. These were installed without archaeological supervision or monitoring. Medieval deposits also directly underlay the modern concrete surface of the yard. There were no eighteenth- or nineteenth-century yard surfaces or deposits present. These also appear to have been removed in recent times, most likely when the concrete surface was laid down. Again this work was undertaken without any archaeological involvement.

Early graveyard

In the northern third of the site, the softer subsoil was overlain by a 100–250mm-thick layer of redeposited subsoil (F02) (fig. 9.14). This was excavated in two small areas at the north-east and north-west corners of the site and in both locations it contained fragments of disarticulated human bone and sherds of medieval pottery (fig. 9.15). This layer is likely to have been the spread-out upcast from the excavation of the foundation trenches for the walls (F03–05) built on the site in the late twelfth century (see below).

In drainage works in the courtyard in 1926 three human burials (two adults and a child) were found close to the 'east door', probably that at the north-west corner of the courtyard. These, the disturbed state of subsoil and the presence of the layer of redeposited subsoil (F06) containing fragments of human bone confirms that the site was a burial ground at an early stage and before building works began in the late twelfth century.

The late twelfth-century palace

Three wide lime-mortar bonded, stone wall footings, forming the north (F03), east (F04) and south (F05) sides of a substantial medieval building (which measured 9.0m north–south by a minimum of 15m E–W internally), with another medieval building to its east – evidenced by a clay floor (F11) and burnt deposits (F10) – all constructed on subsoil, were revealed in the northern third of the courtyard (figs 9.16–9.20). The footings survived to a

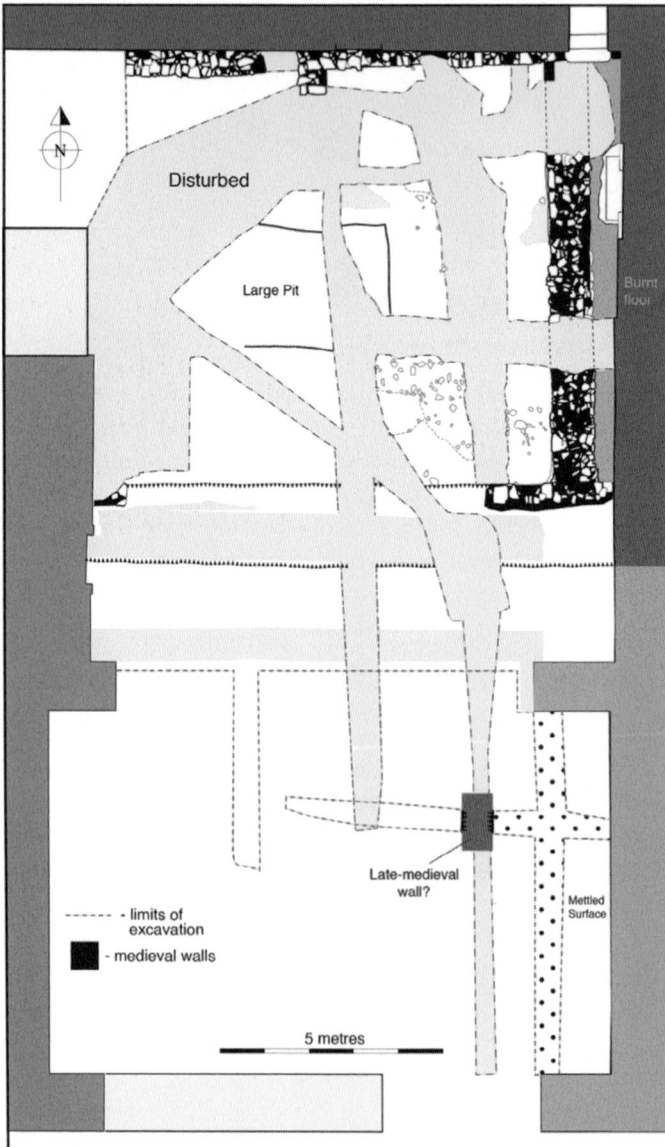

9.16 Plan of uncovered medieval and later medieval structures

9.17 The north wall (F03) of the great hall

9.18 The east wall (F04) of the great hall and west wall of the kitchens

maximum height of one course (200mm) above subsoil and their tops lay as little as 150mm below the modern ground surface. The mortar bonding the walls had largely decayed and only the tan-coloured sand and up to 7mm-diameter pieces of limestone aggregate survived. There were no traces of a projecting footing on any of the surviving masonry and it is possible that it lay at a higher level than that which survived, perhaps suggesting that the larger building had a suspended timber floor at a higher level than that which remained.

The northern wall (F03) (fig. 9.17) had been cut down to just above the top of its footing, at least by the late seventeenth century when it served as a footing for the block of buildings that currently forms the north side of the courtyard. The later wall ran at a slightly different angle to the medieval footing beneath it. Part of what may have been a buttress survived on the southern face of the early wall. Its west side was partly removed by a modern drain. Although the east end of this wall did not survive later disturbance, short lengths of robber trenches showed that the wall was originally linked to

9.19 Oxidized floor (F11) and burnt deposits (F10) in the kitchens

the eastern wall uncovered, but that it also extended beyond it to the east. The eastern wall (F04) measured 1000mm in width (fig. 9.18). Its top lay *c.*200mm below the modern ground surface and its base lay 500mm lower down. Its east side was abutted by a clay floor (F11) covered in an 80–100mm thickness of ash and charcoal fragments (F10) (fig. 9.19), which also overlay a 1400mm-long and 200mm-wide section of the eastern face of the wall, perhaps suggesting the former existence of a wide but shallow fireplace. At its southern end the wall turned to the west and east. The southern wall (F05) was evidenced largely by a 1700mm-wide robber/construction trench (F08) and only a short length of the northern side of the masonry footing survived linked to the eastern wall (fig. 9.20). The wide robber/construction trench had vertical sides and measured 600mm in depth but was only excavated to base at its east and west ends. The robber trench had been partly reused as the foundation trench for a narrower late seventeenth-/early eighteenth-century wall (F16), which itself was later demolished and partly robbed out.

Within the larger building two spreads of mortar (F07) identical to that bonding the walls survived on top of the redeposited subsoil at the east side and at the centre of the north side of the site, attesting that this was the construction level of the wall. The mortar might also have underlain the base of further, long gone, structural elements of the building. The burnt deposits (F10) in the building at the east side of the site contained sherds of Dublin Fine Ware, and overlay a clay floor that lay 200mm below the surviving top of

9.20 The surviving part of the south wall (F05) of the great hall and robber trench (F08) over it

the wall. The floor of this building hence lay at a lower level than the floor of the main building. A 100–150mm thick spread of mortar lumps, ash, clay and stone rubble (F02) overlay the easternmost spread of mortar (F07) and the layer of redeposited subsoil (F06) and covered much of the interior of the eastern side of the larger building. An identical layer also overlay the burnt deposits (F09) east of the eastern wall (F04) where they were cut through by the foundation of the building currently forming the eastern side of the courtyard. The top of part of a large rectangular pit filled with similar material (F12) was revealed in the north-west quarter of the site cut down through the redeposited subsoil layer to a depth of at least 500mm (fig. 9.16); the pit was not bottomed.

A 300mm-thick deposit of identical material (F13) – top at 200mm below modern ground level – was also revealed filling a 200mm-deep depression along the east side of the southern corner of the site. The lower-lying area was floored with a mettled surface (F15) laid on subsoil (figs 9.16 and 9.21–9.23). The west side of the mettled surface appeared to be defined by a north–south-aligned robber trench (F14) but only a short section was revealed, as a live 4"-Wavin pipe lay in the robber trench and prevented its excavation. The wall may be part of a square building shown here on Roque's map of 1756 (figs 9.8–9) and in Beranger's illustration of 1765 (fig. 9.10) and it and the mettled surface are likely to have been of later-medieval date. To the west of the line of the possible wall subsoil was overlain by modern rubble.

9.21–9.23 Buttresses (left and right) and wall (bottom left) at south-west side of the site cutting through the layer of late seventeenth-century demolition refuse (F13)

The demolition deposits both within the building (F02) and at the south-east corner of the courtyard (F13) contained a range of medieval finds (figs 9.28–32): Dublin Fine Ware ceramics, early thirteenth-century roof tiles, early thirteenth-century moulded Dundry stone fragments, a thirteenth-century two-colour ceramic floor tile, a fourteenth-century lime-impressed ceramic floor tile, and a fourteenth-/ fifteenth-century false-relief ceramic floor tile. However, a number of sherds of mid-seventeenth- to mid-eighteenth-century North Devon Gravel Tempered Ware and the stem of a seventeenth-century wine glass (fig. 9.34) were also found in these deposits, attesting that they had been laid down in the second half of the seventeenth or very beginning of the eighteenth century. These deposits suggest that the standing medieval buildings were extensively demolished in the later seventeenth or early eighteenth century. The demolition work clearly also involved the wholesale removal of earlier deposits, reducing the ground level of the site considerably; no late-medieval or post-medieval deposits survived and the late twelfth-century levels lay directly beneath late seventeenth- or early eighteenth-century material.

The late seventeenth/early eighteenth century

Two parallel east–west-aligned walls were built crossing the middle of the courtyard in the late seventeenth or early eighteenth century (figs 9.24 and 9.25). The northernmost (F16) of the pair was built in the south side of the robber trench of the southern medieval wall revealed. This wall was itself largely robbed out to ground level but parts of its foundations with an offset on its north side survived. The wall was composed of limestone rubble masonry bonded by a hard, white lime mortar that contained small fragments of brick and limestone aggregate. There were also large fragments of red brick and a reused Dundry-stone window-mullion in the fabric of the wall (fig. 9.26). The wall extended west beneath the late eighteenth-/early nineteenth-century doorway of the building defining the west side of the modern courtyard (fig. 9.25). The southern wall (F17), which measured 600mm in width was also largely robbed out at a later time but its 250mm-deep lime-mortar-bonded, redbrick footings survived in places. These walls appear to be the remains of a narrow corridor, which linked the east and west blocks and is shown on maps dating from 1728, 1756 and 1824 (figs 9.5 and 9.9).

The building on the northern side of the modern courtyard was also added at the same time on top of the demolished northern wall of the larger medieval building. Its fenestration suggests a date around 1700; it is shown on two maps dating to 1707 (figs 9.3 and 9.4). The modern render had been removed from a short section of the wall of the building revealing the masonry of this wall (fig. 9.36). It is partly composed of large and natural rectangular limestone blocks which are clearly of medieval date but badly relaid. The masonry also included fragments of reused Dundry stone.

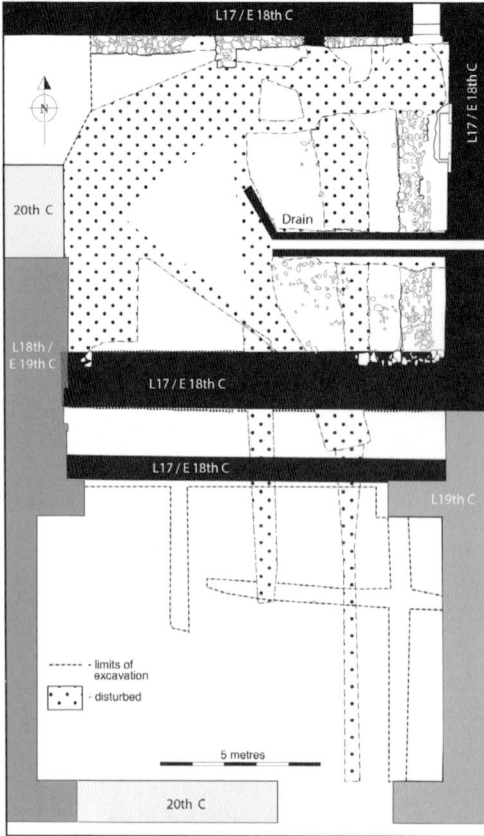

9.24 Plan of late seventeenth-/early eighteenth-century and later features

9.25 Late seventeenth-century wall (F16) at west side of site

9.26 Brick fragments and reused Dundry stone mullion in fabric of wall (F16)

The building on the northern half of the eastern side of the courtyard was also likely added at the same time although its fenestration suggests that its upper floor may have been rebuilt in the later eighteenth or nineteenth century. A drain (F18) with a 350mm-wide internal channel, built at the same time as the building, extended west for a distance before it either widened out or more likely joined a second north–south-aligned drain (fig. 9.27). The sides of the drain consisted of limestone masonry bonded with a hard white lime mortar. The top of the side walls of the drain were flat and level and it clearly was originally capped with limestone flags, all of which had been previously removed.

The later eighteenth and nineteenth centuries

The building at the west side of the courtyard was evidently added after the east–west-aligned corridor was demolished between 1824 and 1848 and was further extended northwards in the late nineteenth or early twentieth century. The buildings on the southern half of the east side of the courtyard and the buttresses against them were also added in the nineteenth century. All were cut through the layer of demolition debris but the northernmost buttress may be the latest of these structures as its foundation lay at a higher level than those of the other walls (figs 9.21–9.23). The buttresses are also not shown on the 1848 map (fig. 9.11) but are indicated on later OS maps (fig. 9.12). Two 500mm-wide and 300–500mm-deep drainage trenches, one (F20) aligned east–west, the other (F19) north–south, were cut into the north-east quarter of the courtyard probably in the later nineteenth century. The backfill of both contained substantial numbers of small limestone cobbles, which probably derived from the late seventeenth- to eighteenth-century yard surface, which was very likely removed in the twentieth century when it was replaced by the modern concrete surface.

There is a substantial two-meter diameter, stone-lined well in the outshot at the north-west side of the modern courtyard. It is covered over by the modern concrete yard surface but is accessible by a manhole. Its size and position suggest it is of nineteenth-century date but no part of it or its construction trench was revealed by the works on the site.

Modern

Drainage works in the courtyard in 1926 are mentioned and may refer to the lines of ceramic pipes and manholes uncovered. Quite a number of more recent drains, which contained modern, orange plastic Wavin pipes and gullies and manholes were also laid in the courtyard in modern times. These were cut deep into the medieval deposits and features and disturbed substantial areas. It is likely, as mentioned above, that the eighteenth- and nineteenth-century yard surfaces were also removed at the same time. None of these works appear to have been archaeologically monitored and, most unfortunately, neither were the recent restoration works undertaken by the Office of Public Works within the complex, with the exception of the excavation and monitoring in the courtyard, which is the subject of this report.

THE FINDS

Pottery

A total of nineteen sherds of medieval pottery and four sherds of post-medieval pottery were uncovered. All the pottery from medieval contexts consisted of medieval Dublin-type glazed and unglazed wares. Further residual sherds of these wares, along with those of seventeenth-century Irish, Dutch and North Devon wares, were uncovered from a number of later seventeenth-century contexts. All of the pottery is of commonly found types.

9.28 Fragments of Dundry stone roll mouldings with flat-topped keel on the arris

Dundry Stone

Four fragments of Dundry stone were uncovered from the demolition rubble (F02) within the larger building and that overlying (F13) the mettled surface at the south-east corner of the site. Three were fragments of vertically tooled, 60–70mm diameter, engaged roll mouldings with a flat-topped keel on the arris (fig. 9.28). The fourth fragment had three diagonally tooled faces, two of which were set at right angles while the third was at a 45-degree angle. Dundry stone was imported and used in Ireland from the late twelfth century (Waterman 1970, 65) and the flat-topped keel moulding on the three small engaged rolls suggests they date to the late twelfth to early thirteenth century.

Floor tiles

Five sherds of medieval ceramic floor tile were uncovered from the late seventeenth-century demolition deposits (F02) and (F13). Two were heavily worn and unclassifiable. The remaining sherds consisted of a single example of a two-colour tile decorated with a lion rampant (fig. 9.29), a type L46 or L47 line-impressed tile and a small fragment of a false-relief tile (fig. 9.30). Two-colour tiles were in use and made in Ireland from *c.*1230 onwards. While their usage in England continued up until the sixteenth century, in Ireland they were largely replaced by line-impressed tiles by *c.*1330 (Eames and Fanning 1988, 23–32). The lion rampant on the two-colour tile found is a common motif used on these tiles and generally similar but not identical examples are previously known from St Patrick's Cathedral and other sites. The line-impressed tile found is most likely of fourteenth-century date and is of a type previously known from a number of sites in Dublin (including St Patrick's Cathedral and Swords Castle) and further afield. The fragment of the false-relief tile is of a previously unknown type but is too small to reconstruct the

9.29 Two-colour ceramic floor tile

9.30 Line-impressed ceramic floor tile and false-relief ceramic floor tile

design. It dates to sometime between the fourteenth and early sixteenth century (Eames and Fanning 1988, 44–50).

Roof tiles

Eight fragments of medieval and two fragments of post-medieval roof or ridge tiles were found in the late seventeenth-century demolition deposits (F02) and (F13). While only one certain ridge tile was uncovered (fig. 9.32), the remaining fragments (fig. 9.31) are more than likely to have been from ridge tiles, although without a surviving part of the top of the tile it is not possible to identify whether the fragments derive from ridge or roof tiles. The triangular cresting on the definite medieval ridge tile fragment (fig. 9.32) is typical of an early thirteenth-century date (J. Wren, pers. comm.) and the incised curved line on another medieval fragment is also a commonly-used decorative devise. The two sherds of post-medieval tile were made in North Devon gravel tempered ware and are of a type imported in large numbers in the seventeenth century.

Decorative plaster

A piece of early decorative plasterwork was found in the backfill of the robber trench (F08) over the southern wall (F05) of the larger medieval building (fig. 9.33). It has a slightly concave back and is composed of quite crude and

9.31 Medieval ceramic roof tiles

9.32 Triangular crested ridge tile

9.33 Fragment of early decorative plaster

coarse lime mortar with inclusions up to 5mm across. The moulded decoration is heavily worn and unclear but its context suggests it dates to before the end of the seventeenth century but it could be as early as the sixteenth century.

Wine glass

A fragment of the air-twist stem of a wine glass (fig. 9.34) was found in the late seventeenth-century demolition debris (F13) at the south side of the site. The decoration was made by stretching out and twisting air bubbles placed close to the surface of the stem. While this technique is attested in Venice from the sixteenth century onwards, it only first appeared in English-produced glass in the mid-eighteenth century (www.mark littler.com/18th-century-english-glass). The context from which the stem derived appears to be of late seventeenth-century date and hence the glass is likely to be of Continental and probably Venetian origin.

9.34 Late seventeenth-century air-twist wine glass stem

Button

A plain, flat, steel button was found in the backfill of the robber trench (F08) over the southern wall of the great hall. The button is probably not much earlier than the later seventeenth century.

Human remains (fig. 9.15)

Eighteen fragments of human bone (from cranium, ribs and scapula) were found in the layer of redeposited subsoil (F02) at the north end of the site. This layer was likely the upcast from the excavation of the foundation trenches of the original palace and so the burials represented by the remains are of pre-Anglo-Norman date.

RESURFACING THE COURTYARD

After the completion of the archaeological assessment of the site a method to resurface the area was agreed with the National Monuments Service and was installed under archaeological supervision. The proposed scheme and the methodology adopted for its installation was designed so ensure that no damage would be done to the surviving deposits and structures but also that anything installed or built could be removed at a later date without damaging them.

DISCUSSION

The recently revealed structures and deposits, although of limited extent, are of significance and, combined with a review of previously known evidence, appear to indicate that the medieval palace was located and laid out somewhat differently than previously suggested.

The previously suggested layout of the medieval palace

O'Donovan (2003, 260–5) attempted to reconstruct the layout of the medieval St Sepulchre's palace and concluded that it consisted of two L-shaped blocks of buildings arranged around a central courtyard (fig. 9.35). However, the methodology used to reach this layout was flawed in some respects and the results of the recent excavation show that her conclusions were incorrect. O'Donovan suggested, perhaps not unreasonably, that the thicker walls on the site were likely to be medieval and the narrower ones later. However, the recent works have shown the inaccuracy of this assumption, at least in some cases. For example, the north wall of the present courtyard is narrow and of late seventeenth- or early eighteenth-century date but it sits on top of the medieval wall (F03) recently found, while the east wall of the courtyard is wide but is clearly of late seventeenth- or early eighteenth-century date, as it is part of a building erected over the truncated medieval structures recently encountered. The excavations also clearly showed that O'Donovan's proposed south range did not exist. The buttresses, which she suggested were stumps of its wall, are clearly of nineteenth-century date and there were no traces of a medieval wall or the foundation trench for a wall crossing the southern third of the present courtyard between them.

O'Donovan also attempted to reconstruct the original geometrical layout of the palace but she noted that 'the wall widths pose some problems'. In fact, the geometrical basis O'Donovan suggests does not work at all well in relation to the standing buildings; several walls and the corners of buildings do not line up with her scheme. It is extremely odd that the mason – who must have been of some repute considering the importance of his client, and who laid out and built the palace – would have made so many and such basic errors. Roger Stalley and Kevin O'Brien discovered in the near contemporary donjon of Trim Castle, Co. Meath, that the geometry dictated not only the location but

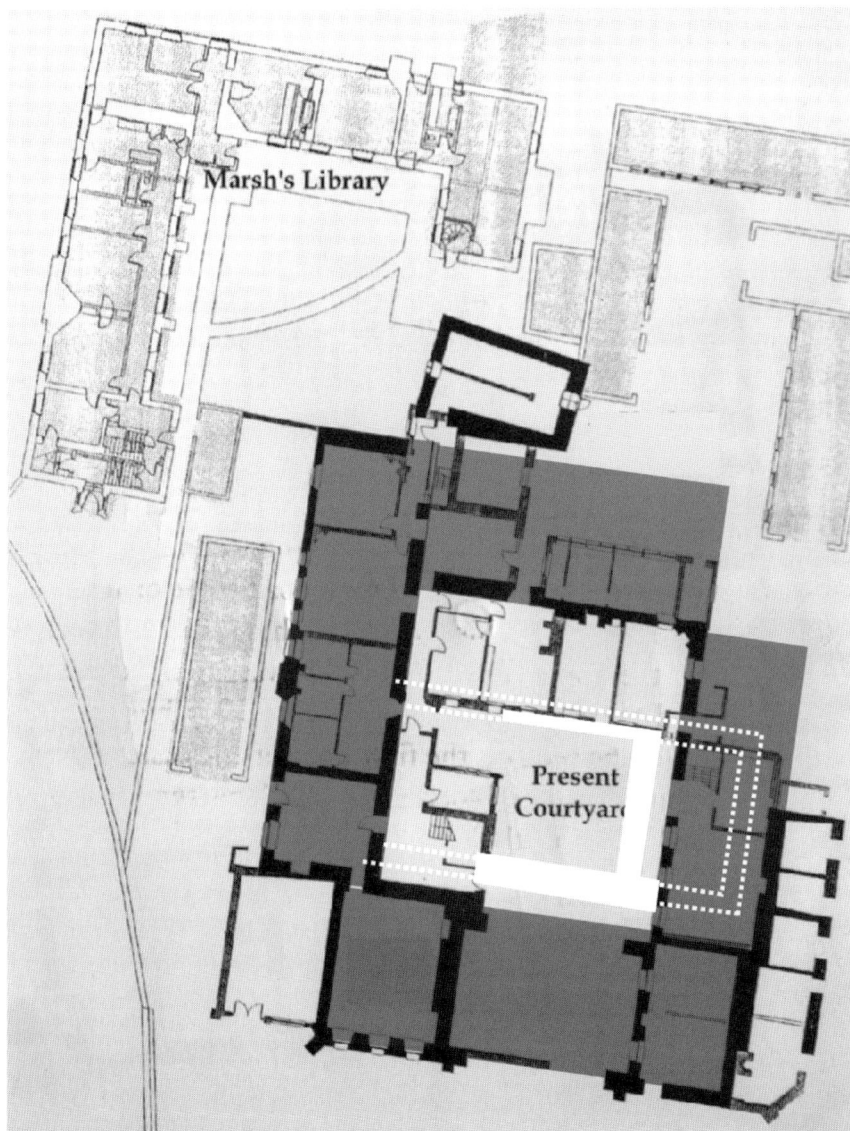

9.35 O'Donovan's suggested layout of the medieval palace (2003, 260-5) and the position of the buildings recently uncovered (outlined in white)

also the thickness of the walls and also the positions and widths of the doors and windows (Hayden 2011, 59); all the structure was most carefully laid out and built. Of course, the recent discovery of the medieval buildings within O'Donovan's proposed central courtyard (fig. 9.35) proves beyond doubt that her reconstruction is not accurate.

An alternative suggestion

An alternative plan and layout can be suggested if the results of the recent excavations are combined with a re-evaluation of the previously known evidence. The earliest surviving depiction of the site is on Speed's map of 1610 (fig. 9.2). It appears to show the building as a great square block with an entrance at its west side. A generic 'building' is shown on the Down Survey map of 1655 but no details of the buildings are shown on the other surviving late seventeenth-century maps. Later cartographic sources only show the palace after it had been largely rebuilt in the later seventeenth and early eighteenth centuries and are of little use in determining the medieval layout of the site.

The medieval palace

Apart from the recently revealed walls there is little medieval masonry visible within the standing buildings, which largely date from the late seventeenth to early twentieth century – in this context 'medieval' means anything between the later twelfth and the later sixteenth century, as it is more often than not impossible to date what remains precisely. Part of the render had been removed from the wall of the building framing the northern side of the courtyard, revealing the masonry of which the wall was composed (fig. 9.36). It included several large and naturally sub-rectangular limestone blocks, which are typical of those used to build twelfth- and thirteenth-century buildings in Dublin. However, they were clearly relaid, and badly. The masonry also included several pieces of reused Dundry stone. Many more pieces of Dundry stone have been found in test-trenching on the site and in other works including a number of late twelfth- or early thirteenth-century pieces unearthed in the recent excavations. Combined with the early thirteenth-century ridge tile recently found, they confirm the historical reference to the existence of the palace by at least 1216.

A number of other features within the standing buildings are suggestive of the presence of the earlier structure (fig. 9.40). There is a 2.3m-wide buttress on the west wall of the palace (fig. 9.37). The masonry of which at least its exterior is composed is clearly of seventeenth- or eighteenth-century date. However, its position is interesting as it lines up precisely with the northern medieval wall (F03) recently discovered and it is wide enough to encase medieval masonry. The wall to its south has a pronounced batter, which would not be expected in a seventeenth- or eighteenth-century domestic building. There are corbels at first-floor level on the internal face of this wall and corresponding ones on the wall to its east (fig. 9.38). Unfortunately, all of these are painted or plastered over and cannot be closely dated; if they were not made of granite, then the dressing used on them may be datable. These

9.36 Medieval stones and Dundry stone reused in the later wall at the north side of the courtyard

9.37 Buttress and battered wall in west side of palace

9.38 Corbels on west side of room, in west side of palace

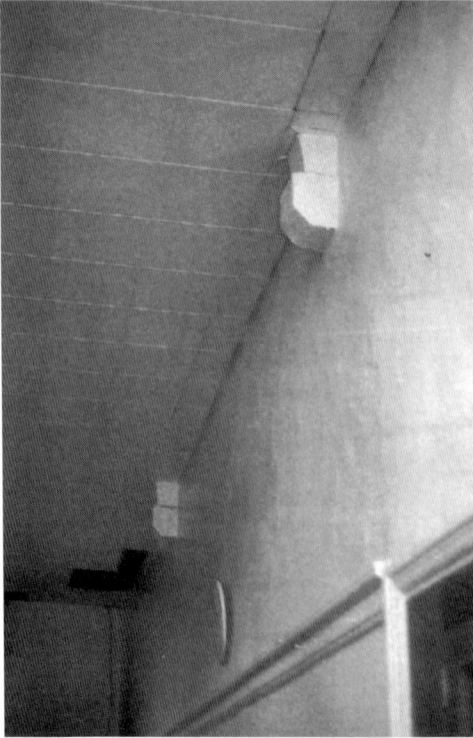

9.39 Corbels at first floor level in building at south-west side of courtyard

features combined, however, do suggest the presence here of a building predating the later seventeenth century. There are also corbels formerly visible high up in the east wall at first-floor level of the building at the south-west side of the modern courtyard (fig. 9.39). These appear to have supported a high open roof over this floor. This again is something which would not be expected in a seventeenth-/eighteenth-century domestic setting and they might also suggest the presence here of something earlier.

Gabriel Beranger's 1765 watercolour (fig. 9.10) of the south façade of the palace appears to match well with what survives today (fig. 9.13) and with Rocque's map (fig. 9.6) and the 1824 map (fig. 9.9). The building Beranger shows on the left, which is the south end of the late seventeenth-/ early eighteenth-century west range, is depicted containing a high relieving arch broken through to insert two late seventeenth-/ early eighteenth-century windows. The arch suggests that there originally was a large ope beneath it. High buttresses are also shown at the corners of the building; the one on the right appears to include offsets at what would have been ground- and first-floor level. Taken together these features are suggestive of the previous existence of a building to the south of that shown.

The remainder of the southern façade of the palace is shown composed of three sections of stone wall with a high arch in each, interrupted by a gabled structure protruding to the south. The right-hand end of the top of the arcaded wall is shown broken, which is a commonly used convention in eighteenth-century illustrations to indicate an old or ruined structure. Archbishop King, writing in the early eighteenth century, also describes this wall as 'ancient' (TCD, MS 1995–2008/1057; MS 1995–2008/1072; RCBL, MS 88, no. 3d). No evidence was uncovered during the recent excavations of a corresponding wall to the north of the arcaded wall. The arches shown on the south face of the wall would also be most unusual on the external face of a building and they are clearly internal features. They would have carried the roof over the bays, each of which would have contained a large window; the north wall of the thirteenth-century hall excavated in Trim Castle provides a close parallel (Hayden 2011, 198). The presence of this wall suggests that there formerly was a range of buildings south of the present palace, which were demolished probably in the late fifteenth century or at least before the mid-eighteenth century.

Late-medieval contraction and expansion

There is also evidence of some of the later-medieval structures built on the site (fig. 9.40). The square, stone-walled building Beranger shows protruding through the line of the arched wall (fig. 9.10) is clearly the square block shown by Rocque and on the 1824 map (fig. 9.9). It looks like it post-dates the ruinous arched wall but could itself be of later-medieval date. It is a curious structure

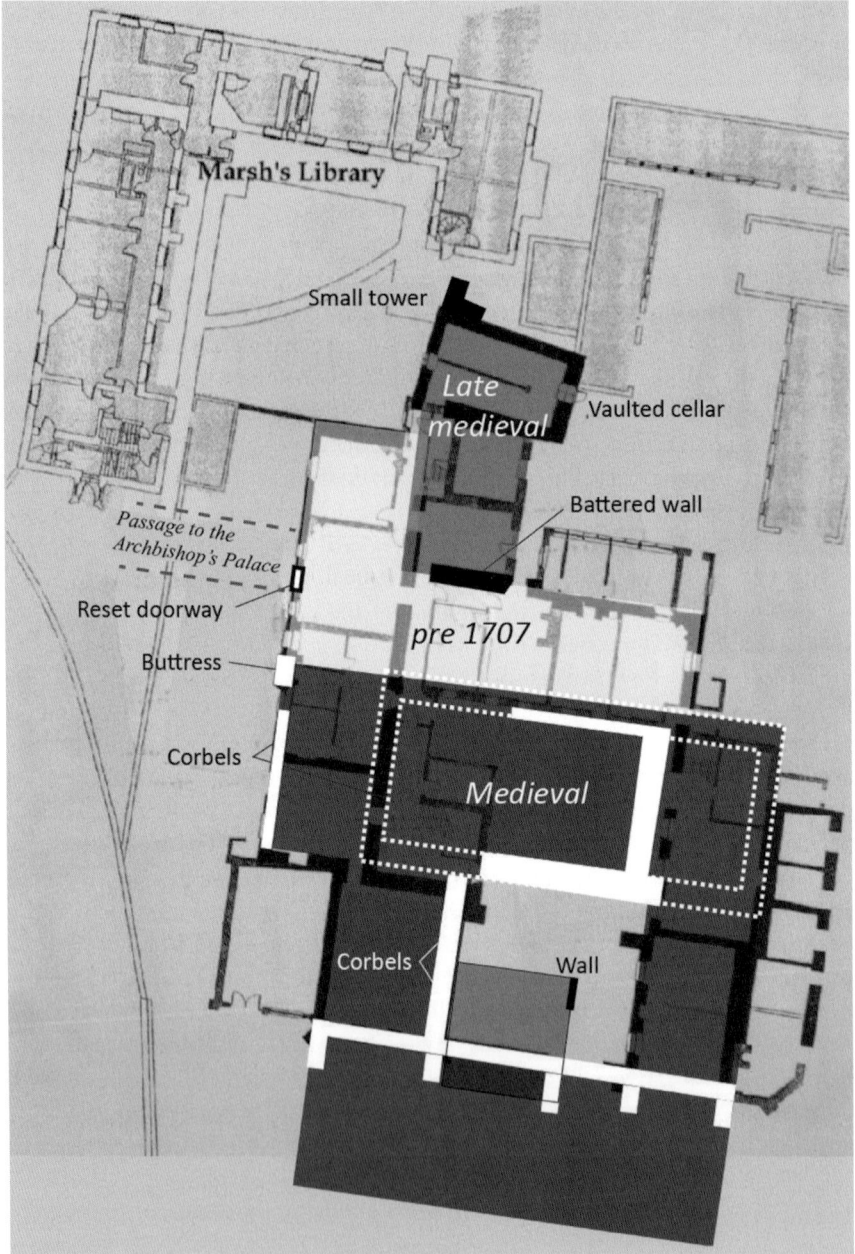

9.40 Location of surviving medieval, late-medieval and pre-1707 parts of the palace

and is composed of elements of differing dates. It contains a possibly fifteenth-century, almost ogival, pointed arch with a somewhat clumsy, classically inspired doorway inserted into it. The structure is topped with a clearly later brick gable of late Elizabethan or Jacobean style. There is also a small doorway to the right of the building leading into the courtyard precisely where the recently uncovered mettled surface lay. The two tall narrow chimneys that are shown on the right of the illustration appear to be of late Elizabethan or Jacobean type. They were also clearly built cutting through the early arched wall and would have stood on the end of a building south of the smaller medieval building recently uncovered at the east side of the courtyard.

An almost ogival, wicker-centred vault survives in the cellar of a building at the north side of the palace (fig. 9.40). Plank centring was generally used to form arches and vaults in the twelfth and thirteenth centuries, with wicker centring coming into use in the later fourteenth century and continuing through into the early sixteenth century. Plank centring again reappears and was used from the sixteenth century onwards. The wicker centring and the ogival form of the vault suggests a late fourteenth- to early sixteenth-century date for the structure. This building containing the vault is laid out on a different alignment to the palace and so may always have been a separate structure. However, there are doorways in the north-west and south-west corners of the structure, suggesting it communicated with other buildings not now visible. The northern doorway opened into a small tower, possibly a stair turret, which is shown on the 1707 plans (figs 9.3 and 9.4). The south doorway would have opened into a building now absent. There is, however, a wall with a pronounced batter on its south face just to the south, which is suggestive of the presence here of another building or buildings. However, it is not known how extensive this was and all that can be said of it as regards date is that it pre-dates the late seventeenth-/early eighteenth-century redevelopment of the palace. It would be expected that if the southern range of buildings had been demolished, as suggested by Beranger's illustration, then they must have been replaced by buildings elsewhere to compensate for the loss of space within the palace. These possible buildings north of the medieval palace may have provided the required additional space.

Sixteenth- and early seventeenth-century additions

Both Archbishop Inge (although on dubious evidence: see above) and Archbishop Alen (in 1529 (O'Donovan 2003, 260)) are credited with the repair of the palace in the early sixteenth century. An almshouse was erected to its west in 1504 and, as noted above, Beranger's illustration (fig. 9.10) also shows a brick gable and chimney of late Elizabethan or Jacobean style. Other works of this era are also evidenced by the fine early sixteenth-century doorway at the west side of the palace (fig. 9.41) and by the discovery of many masonry fragments bearing identical mouldings to the doorway, which suggest at least the replacement of doorways and windows in the palace. The surviving

9.41 The fine early
sixteenth-century doorway
at the west side of the palace

doorway is topped by a plaque bearing the date 1523 and what might be the
arms of Archbishop Huge Inge (1521–8). However, it stands in what otherwise
appears to be a later wall and it is probable that it was reset here after having
been removed from elsewhere in the palace. This is further suggested by a
second plaque above the doorway which bears the date 1723 and appears to
mark the contribution made by Archbishop King (1703–29) to the rebuilding
of the palace.

As previously stated, various Lords Deputy seized and resided in the palace
during the sixteenth century and in 1570 is was described as 'an abode well
pleasantly sited as gorgeously builded' (Miller and Power 1979, 50).
Archbishop Adam Loftus, a person of immense standing and importance, also
resided in the palace in the later sixteenth century and died there in 1605. It is
difficult to see why these individuals would have lived in the palace if it had not
been extensively refurbished in a contemporary style. With the absence of the
original south range, if there had not been additional buildings, it would have
been extremely cramped accommodation. It would be expected, for example,

that there must have been a long gallery somewhere within the sixteenth-century complex and there is clearly no room for such in the earlier structure. Clearly then, within the palace at this time there may well have been an additional range or ranges of buildings, of which we have little or no evidence today. The most likely location for these would have been north of the medieval palace where there is a suggestion of buildings attached to that containing the vaulted cellar. Indeed, it is not impossible that there may have been an additional courtyard there surround by ranges of buildings on its west, north and east sides.

The late seventeenth century onwards – a new palace

In 1664, the palace was described as 'decayed, ruinous and in need of repair' (*Cal. S.P. Ire, 1663–5*, 368) and Archbishops Michael Boyle (1663–79), Francis Marsh (1682–93), Narcissus Marsh (1694–1703) and William King (1703–29), completely rebuilt the palace over the following half-century. The full details of this need not concern us here. As revealed by the recent excavations these works involved the almost total removal of the original late twelfth-/early thirteenth-century buildings. These new buildings and later additions made in the eighteenth to twentieth centuries are evidenced by the standing structures and on the various surviving maps and illustrations (figs 9.5–9.12) and are discussed in detail by Moss et al. (2015, 6–14). These works included the acquisition of lands to the south of the palace on Kevin Street to create a new entrance and gardens on the south; the admittedly slender evidence appears to suggest that the entrance previously lay at the west side of the palace.

CONCLUSIONS

It is clear that very little of the actual structure of the medieval to early seventeenth-century palace visibly survives above ground. However, the available evidence could be reinterpreted to suggest that the original medieval palace lay in a slightly different location than previously suggested and consisted of at least a quadrangle of buildings around a small open courtyard; the latter being the southern half of the present courtyard. In the late fifteenth or sixteenth century, if not before, the palace may have been extended northwards, possibly to compensate for the loss of the original southern range of buildings. Speed's map of 1610 suggests that the palace at this time was a large square or rectangular block with the entrance on the west. The medieval palace appears to have been almost completely demolished to ground level or below during the extensive rebuilding works undertaken between the 1660s and 1720s, while the last standing section of old work, the north wall of the putative southern range, was demolished in the later eighteenth century.

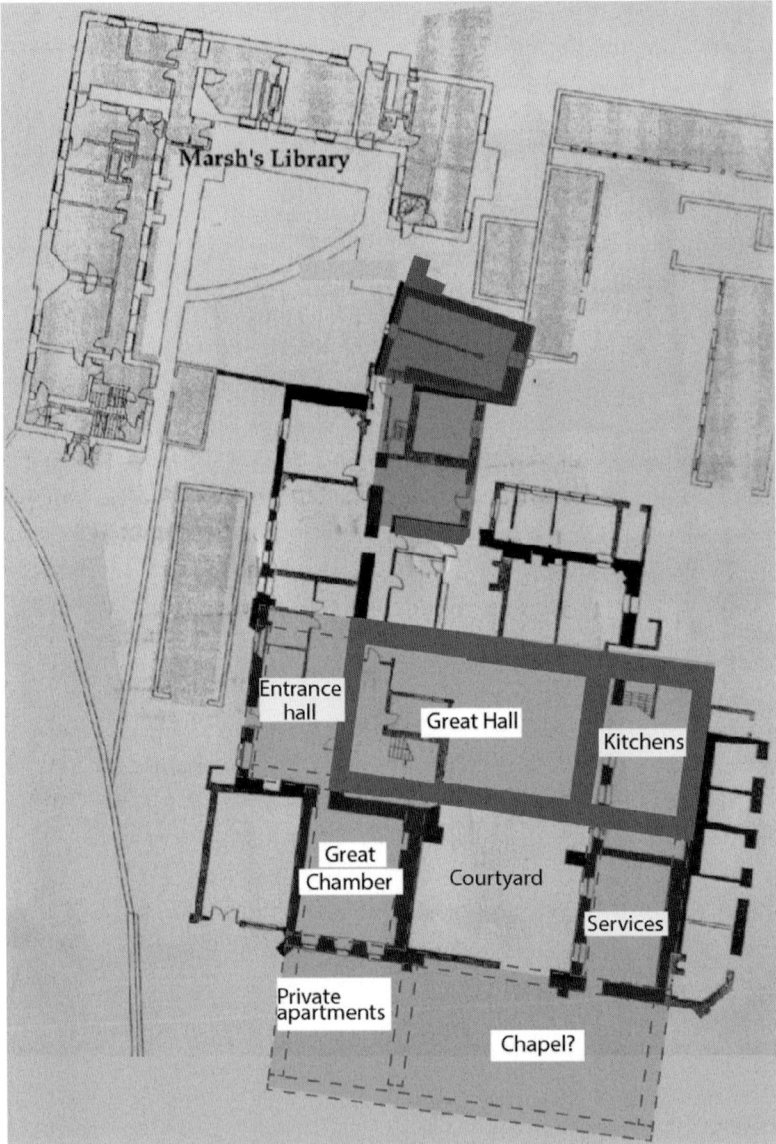

9.42 The possible layout of the medieval palace

Although brief and somewhat formulaic, the 1326 description of the palace as 'a stone hall badly roofed with shingles, a chamber annexed to the said hall, a kitchen and a chapel, roofed but all of no value as in disrepair' (McNeill 1950, 170), is the most complete that survives. This description can be combined with the known or possible medieval structures that survive to speculate about the internal layout and use of the medieval palace (fig. 9.42).

The large size (9m in width by at least 15m in length) of the main building recently revealed suggests that it may have been the great hall of the palace mentioned in 1326. It likely had a suspended timber floor that did not survive and would have been open to its great timber roof. The possible large fireplace and burnt deposits in the building to its east could suggest it was the kitchens. As a medieval great hall was used for feasts, kitchens were usually located close by, as can be seen for example in the thirteenth-century great halls in the castles at Trim and Adare. There was possibly a building to the west of the hall evidenced by the buttress, battered wall and corbels at ground-floor level. This may have been an entrance hall, which would have contained an anteroom or screens passage and controlled public access to the great hall and other parts of the palace. As noted, Speed's map suggests that the entrance to the palace lay at its west side and, as also stated above, it was only in the eighteenth century that a southern entrance appears to have been created.

The 1326 description mentions 'a chamber annexed to the said hall'. This chamber is of course the great chamber of the complex. Great chambers can be found in many medieval castles and great houses and were the main living and dining space used by the lord. While feasts would have been held in the great hall, the great chamber would have been used for everyday dining. It was here too that the lord would have retired from events held in the great hall for private meetings, where he entertained visitors and conducted much of the administration of his estates. It was also where much of his retinue would have slept at night. In many medieval houses that had a great hall at ground-floor level, the great chamber lay close by but at first-floor level. The corbels high up in the building at the south-west side of the present courtyard might indicate that this was the great chamber 'annexed' to the great hall and open to the roof as typically expected.

The great chamber also usually gave access to the lord's private apartments: solar, bed chamber, wardrobe, closet, etc. If the great chamber was where it is suggested, then these private apartments would have been located at first-floor level in the south-west corner of the palace. This would have allowed the maximum benefits of the natural heat and light from the sun which was a most important factor in providing comfort to those residing in a cold medieval building. Placing the great chamber and private apartments at first-floor level would also have allowed for the location of public or semi-public offices and administration space at ground-floor level beneath them in a location immediately accessible from the entrance hall.

The last structure mentioned in the 1326 description is the chapel. It is clear that this must have been a substantial space as it was used for the ordination of priests (O'Donovan 2003, 258–9; Moss et al. 2015, 5) and so was not simply a small private chapel. Chapels or churches usually required a great east window to light the altar and interior. There is only one location where the chapel would fit in the layout speculated here and that is in the eastern part of the south range. The 'ancient' arcaded wall shown in Beranger's 1765 watercolour might then have been the north wall of this chapel containing large windows overlooking the courtyard and matching windows on its south side. The chapel is mentioned historically several times up to 1497. However, at some time after that it disappears, as both Narcissus Marsh and William King mention that there was no chapel in the palace and that they intend to rectify the situation. As noted above, Beranger's illustration shows what is likely to be a square late-medieval building seemingly built into what might have been the ruined chapel and so this might reflect the historical evidence for the demise of the chapel.

Beranger's watercolour also shows an Elizabethan or Jacobean brick chimney atop an older structure at the south-east corner of the palace. It doesn't take a great leap of faith to suggest that this building may have been a further part of the early service range containing the kitchens at the east side of the palace.

The archbishops of Dublin also possessed another palace at Swords Castle (also built by John Cumin) and later ones at Tallaght and Rathfarnham Castle. These, however, were laid out on quite different plans to that suggested at St Sepulchre's. There are many more medieval episcopal and archiepiscopal palaces surviving in Ireland, Britain and further afield. They follow a wide variety of plans but there are a number where the buildings are arranged around a courtyard in the manner in which, it is suggested here, St Sepulchre's was laid out. Two palaces in particular (as previously noted by O'Donovan 2003, 272–5), both built by Bishop Roger of Salisbury in the early twelfth century at Old Sherbourne and Old Sarum Castles, and Lamphey palace in St Davids in Wales (fig. 9.43), appear to be of very similar plan to the suggested layout of St Sepulchre's.

It must be emphasized that the layout suggested here for the medieval St Sepulchre's palace is largely speculative, as it is clear there is little actual surviving structural evidence. It is very possible that either the medieval palace was larger than evidenced or was expanded northwards during the late-medieval period. It was also almost certainly extensively rebuilt, refurbished or altered during the sixteenth century. There is also, however, very little surviving evidence of these works. Hopefully future test excavation, geophysical prospection or render removal, etc., might shed further light on the early history of the development of the palace.

The Gardaí are scheduled to vacate the site in about three years' time and move to new premises. It is planned that the former palace at that stage may be used for some form of heritage or cultural functions. This could provide an opportunity to lift the paving slabs to re-expose the medieval walls of the great hall and kitchens. Very little of the original height of these walls survives and

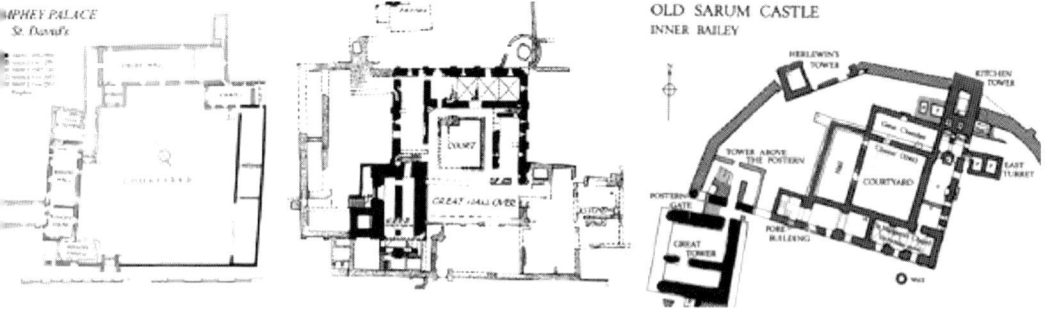

9.43 Plans of medieval episcopal palaces laid out around a central courtyard: St Davids (*left*), Old Sherbourne Castle (centre) and Old Sarum Castle (right)

they also lie very close to the modern ground surface, so they are very vulnerable. It would therefore be preferable that they are conserved. This might require archaeological excavation of the area, which would be a valuable contribution to the understanding of the history and development of the palace. These walls are also the only known surviving parts of the medieval palace and deserve to be displayed or marked in some way. There might also be an opportunity at that stage to excavate test trenches in the carpark outside the south side of the courtyard to determine whether anything remains of the possible southern range of medieval buildings. The medieval ground here slopes more steeply down to the south than the present ground level and there could be up to a metre of deposits there above subsoil. This, and the fact that this area was not built on in the eighteenth century, could well mean that more archaeological deposits and more of the medieval structure survives underground here than elsewhere.

BIBLIOGRAPHY

Eames, E. and Fanning, T. 1988 *Irish medieval tiles*. Dublin: Royal Irish Academy.

Gibney, A. 2001 'The cathedral precinct: St Patrick's, St Sepulchre's palace and Marsh's Library'. Unpublished report for the Office of Public Works.

Gilbert, J.T. 1897 *Crede Mihi. The most ancient register book of the archbishops of Dublin before the Reformation*. Dublin.

Gowen, M. 2007 'Kevin Street Garda Station: architectural assessment of buildings'. Unpublished report for the Office of Public Works.

Gowen, M. 2007a 'Kevin Street Garda Station archaeological impact statement for the proposed development of the eastern side of Kevin Street Garda Station'. Unpublished report for the Office of Public Works.

Hayden, A.R. 2011 *Trim Castle, co. Meath: Excavations 1995–8*. Archaeological Monography series: 6. DoAHG. Dublin.

Hayden, A.R. 2018 'Preliminary report on archaeological excavations at Kevin St, Dublin 8: 15E0033'. Unpublished report lodged with the National Monuments Service.

Jackson, V. 1975 'The palace of St Sepulchre', *DHR*, 28:3, 82–92.

McNeill, C. (ed.) 1950 *Calendar of Archbishop Alen's register, c.1172–1534.* Dublin.

Miller, L. and Power E. (eds) 1979 *Holinshed's Irish chronicle: the historie of Irelande from the first inhabitantion thereof unto the year 1509 collected by Raphale Holinshed and continued till the yeare 1547 by Richarde Stanyhurst.* Dublin.

Monck Mason, W. 1820 *The history and antiquities of the collegiate and cathedral church of St Patrick.* Dublin.

Moss, R., Casey, C., O'Donovan, D. and Malin, N. 2015 'St Sepulchre's palace, Kevin Street'. Unpublished report for the Office of Public Works.

O'Donovan, D. 2003 'English patron, English building? The importance of St Sepulchre's archiepiscopal palace, Dublin'. In S. Duffy (ed.), *Medieval Dublin IV*, pp 253–78.

Simpson, L. 2004 'Archaeological evaluation of a site including the east side of the Kevin Street Garda Station to the rear of 41–7 Bride Street and 35–47 Bride Street, Dublin 2'. Unpublished report lodged with Dublin City Council and National Monuments Service.

Simpson, L. 2008 'Kevin Street Garda Station, 35–47 Bride Street, Dublin'. *Excavations* 2008:394.

Ware, J. 1705 *The antiquities and history of Ireland.* Dublin.

Waterman, D. 1970 'Somerset and other foreign building stone in Ireland, c.1175–1400'. *Ulster Journal of Archaeology* 33, 63–75.

www.marklittler.com/18th-century-english-glass (accessed 13 April 2019).

The parliamentary subsidy in fifteenth-century County Dublin and the men who collected it

BRIAN COLEMAN

The parliamentary subsidy was the principal form of taxation in late medieval Ireland. It took the form of a grant agreed on behalf of the landholders of the county by their parliamentary representatives, either on the basis of an agreed total (divided in set proportions among the counties, the cities, and what were called 'crosslands' belonging to the church), or – as was increasingly the case as the fifteenth century progressed – on the basis of a fixed sum on each ploughland.[1] By the late fifteenth century the general subsidy was the most important source of crown revenue in Ireland, forming a vital part of efforts to fund the government and the defence of the nascent Pale at a time when financial support from England had reached its nadir.[2]

Assessing and collecting the subsidy was a significant undertaking, involving large numbers of individuals across the four 'obedient shires' of Dublin, Louth, Meath and Kildare. This essay examines that undertaking as it relates to Co. Dublin from the beginning of the reign of Henry IV to the end of that of Henry VII (1399–1509), looking not only at the subsidy, but also at the men who assessed and collected it, and those who paid it (or, in some instances, attempted not to). This examination sheds light on the subject of the subsidy itself and also illuminates aspects of the social and ethnic character of Co. Dublin in this period, revealing not only the large number of individuals who played a role in royal government but also the wide variety in their social status. Perhaps most strikingly it provides evidence for a small but growing number of men of Gaelic Irish background playing an active role in local government in the heart of the English Pale.[3]

---

1 The ploughland or carucate was a standard unit of land measurement, consisting (in the ideal) of 120 medieval acres, which themselves varied in area depending on factors including the quality of the soil in question. In Dublin a medieval acre roughly corresponded to 2½ or 3 modern acres: James Mills, 'Tenants and agriculture near Dublin in the fourteenth century', *JRSAI*, 21 (1890), 39–52, 56; A.J. Otway-Ruthven, 'The organization of Anglo-Irish agriculture in the Middle Ages', *JRSAI*, 81 (1951), 1–13, at 3.   2 James Lydon, *The lordship of Ireland in the Middle Ages* (2nd edn, Dublin, 2003), pp 184–93.   3 Cf. Sparky Booker, *Cultural exchange and identity in late medieval Ireland: the English and Irish of the four obedient shires* (Cambridge, 2018), p. 9 and passim.

THE PARLIAMENTARY SUBSIDY

The origins and evolution of the parliamentary or general subsidy have been discussed in detail by M.V. Clarke and D.B. Quinn.[4] Clarke traced the rise of the subsidy over the course of the fourteenth century, in the face of much opposition from the inhabitants of the lordship of Ireland, and concluded that by the end of the century the parliamentary subsidy had largely replaced the local or regional subsidies from which it first took shape. Quinn continued the study of the subsidy into the early sixteenth century, by which time it was effectively a permanent annual tax. Whereas in the late fifteenth century each subsidy had been granted individually by the Irish parliament for the year in which the parliament had been held, under Henry VII parliament was persuaded to assent to longer-term grants (five or ten years) during which fixed sums were to be raised annually, without the need for further parliamentary approval.[5] In contrast to other forms of Irish revenue, the subsidy was increasing in value in the last decades of the fifteenth century, apparently as a result of increasing tillage as more land was brought under the plough in Ireland.[6]

Direct taxation was not the norm in the Middle Ages and (prior to the last decades of the fifteenth century at least) each general subsidy was granted on a case-by-case basis by the Irish parliament for a specific purpose. The subsidy was intrinsically linked to defence. It was in most cases granted by parliament for hiring and maintaining soldiers.[7] A specific number of soldiers to be raised might be specified, as in 1473 when 160 marks (i.e., a little over £100, a mark being two-thirds of a pound) were to be levied on Dublin, Meath, Kildare and Louth to pay for a retinue of 160 archers and 63 spearmen.[8] Local subsidies might be raised for a variety of purposes, though almost all were at least tangentially connected to defence. Subsidies were granted to raise the reward for the capture of an outlaw, the ransom of tenants abducted by the Irish, and the maintenance of watchmen in border areas.[9] Other local contributions included the payment of 'O'Connor's wages' (protection money paid by the English of Meath) and similar 'black rents'.[10] Less frequently, subsidies might

4 M.V. Clarke, 'William of Windsor in Ireland, 1369–76' in L.S. Sutherland and May McKisack (eds), *Fourteenth century studies by M.V. Clarke* (Oxford, 1937), pp 146–241; D.B. Quinn, 'The Irish parliamentary subsidy in the fifteenth and sixteenth centuries', *PRIA*, 42C (1934–5), 219–46. **5** Quinn, 'Irish parliamentary subsidy', 226; Steven Ellis, 'Parliament and community in Yorkist and Tudor Ireland' in Art Cosgrove and J.I. McGuire (eds), *Parliament and community: Historical Studies XIV* (Belfast, 1983), pp 43–68, at p. 54. **6** Steven Ellis, *Defending English ground: war and peace in Meath and Northumberland, 1460–1542* (Oxford, 2015), pp 45–51. **7** Richardson and Sayles, *The Irish parliament in the Middle Ages* (Philadelphia, 1964), pp 233–4. **8** *Stat. rolls Ire. Edw. IV*, ii, pp 130–7. **9** *Stat. rolls Ire. Edw. IV*, i, pp 610–13; *Stat. rolls Ire. Ric. III to Hen. VIII*, pp 72–5; *Register of John Swayne, archbishop of Armagh and primate of Ireland 1418–1439*, ed. D.A. Chart (Belfast, 1935), p. 184. **10** British Library, Royal MS 18C xiv, fos. 41, 174; Quinn, 'Irish

be raised for more quotidian purposes that were held to be for the common good – such as the construction of a harbour at Rush by the earl of Ormond's tenants there.[11]

By far the greatest number of local subsidies for which record survives were granted for the construction (or reconstruction) of tower houses at strategic locations.[12] Generally, these castle subsidies were granted at the request of the individual building or intending to build the tower house. The usual sum to be levied in support of construction from the county concerned was £10 (although there were exemptions), according neatly with the well-known acts of parliament of 1428 and 1430 which granted that sum to anyone undertaking to construct a tower house of specified dimensions in Co. Louth and in the four obedient shires respectively.[13] Others had grants of a particular sum on every ploughland. These ranged from 8*d.* on every ploughland in Meath in 1447 up to 4*s.* 4*d.* on every ploughland in Rathdown thirty years later.[14] The higher sums would appear to be cases where defensive needs were particularly pressing.[15] Other grants included building materials and labour, as in 1461 when Thomas Plunkett was given permission to fell trees in the park of Trim for fuel and timber for the construction of a tower house at Corranford, or in 1480 when Robert Preston, Lord Gormanston, was to have a cart from every ploughland within three miles of Ballymadan to help him draw stones and sand for the construction of a tower there.[16]

Subsidies for the construction of tower houses were less common in Dublin than in Meath, Louth and Kildare. Grants in the other three counties tended to be in the nature of what modern political jargon terms a 'public-private partnership'. The process typically involved a petition made to parliament by the landowner building or intending to build a tower, and parliament then granting a subsidy to be levied on the county in support of construction. In Dublin, only two grants follow this pattern. The first was the subsidy on Rathdown in 1477, mentioned above, in aid of the reconstruction of the Walsh castle at Jamestown (par. Kilgobbin), which had been taken and partially destroyed by the O'Byrnes and O'Tooles.[17] The second was the grant to Robert Preston of labour services in aid of the construction of a tower at Ballymadan. Both these grants were to be levied on a small area – the first on the barony of Rathdown, and the second on the immediate neighbourhood of Ballymadan. A not dissimilar grant was made to John Bennet, citizen (later mayor) of Dublin, in the 1460s when he was granted the town of 'Baltire' (possibly Ballinteer?) for

parliamentary subsidy', 220; Ellis, *Defending English ground*, p. 64.   11 Quinn, 'Irish parliamentary subsidy', 220.   12 See, for example, *Stat. rolls Ire. Hen. VI*, pp 284–7; *Stat. rolls Ire. Edw. IV*, i, pp 6–7, 22–3, 64–5 and passim; ii, pp 122–3, 286–7, 516–19 and passim. 13 *Stat. rolls Ire. Hen. VI*, pp 16–17, 32–5, 284–7; *Edw. IV*, i, pp 64–5, 146–7, 148–9, 368–9, 396–9, 742–3; ii, pp 122–3, 710–11, 714–17; cf. *Edw. IV*, i, pp 22–3 (£40), 608–11 (£20). 14 *Stat. rolls Ire. Hen. VI*, pp 106–9, 126–9; *Edw. IV*, ii, pp 516–19.   15 *Stat. rolls Ire. Edw. IV*, i, pp 22–3; ii, pp 516–19, 764–5.   16 Ibid., pp 6–7; ii, pp 852–3.   17 *Stat. rolls Ire.*

60 years, on condition of building a tower there.[18] The area was stated to be 'a common place for the Byrnes and Tooles to lie in [from which] they would sally forth to Clondalkin and all the country round'.[19]

Jamestown Castle was right on the frontier, located on the main pass from Dublin south-east into the Wicklow mountains. It was thus a key part of the defensive system of the south Dublin marches or borderlands. Even so, the commons of the county of Dublin appear to have been reluctant to offer anything beyond the minimum support necessary for its reconstruction. Only those left most exposed by the destruction of the castle – the commons of Rathdown, together with the religious foundations holding extensive lands there – were to contribute to the subsidy. The commons of Dublin appear to have been unwilling to contribute to castle subsidies that were not of the most pressing defensive urgency. In 1459, they agreed to a subsidy on the county as a whole to raise £10 for the construction of a castle at Cork 'on the *boher* of Bray' (Cork Great and Cork Little, bar. Rathdown) to control 'the most common road for the O'Byrnes ... coming from day to day into the marches of the said county'.[20] This of course bears direct comparison with Jamestown.

Similar to this grant was a rather larger project of fortification begun in 1455. In that year the commons agreed to a subsidy of 140 marks (just over £90) on the county to fortify the bridges at Kilmainham and Lucan, and to construct a tower to control 'the ford by the pier of Saint Mary's Abbey' by which 'sundry Irish enemies and English rebels' had entered Fingal by night. Those overseeing the subsidy and the subsequent works included the greater part of the leading gentry of Dublin.[21] The works were still not completed eight years later, when the baronies of Castleknock, Balrothery and Coolock were ordered to provide cartloads of stone for the construction of the tower 'begun at the bridge of Kilmainham ... in resistance of thieves prowling by night'.[22] It is likely that the relative security of Fingal – almost certainly the most populous half of the county – lessened the incentive for a large part of the commons of Dublin to contribute to castle-building in the county. This comparative security was reflected in other acts made for the defence of the four counties. The retinue of archers and spearmen raised in 1473 was to be

Edw. IV, ii, pp 516–19.   **18** *Stat. rolls Ire. Edw. IV*, i, pp 320–1.   **19** *Stat. rolls Ire. Edw. IV*, ii, pp 444–7.   **20** *Stat. rolls Ire. Hen. VI*, pp 632–5.   **21** Ibid., pp 402–5. Christopher St Laurence, kt, lord of Howth, was one of the assessors of the subsidy, while the surveyors of the workmen included former, serving, and future sheriffs Richard Mareward, kt, Robert St Laurence, esq., Reginald Talbot, esq., John Woodlock, esq. and Thomas Field, esq. In addition, Robert Burnell, kt, served as one of the auditors to hear the account of the subsidy. For an overview of these men's place in the society of fifteenth-century Dublin, see Brian Coleman, 'County office and county society in Dublin and Meath, *c.*1399–*c.*1513' (PhD, University of Dublin, TCD, 2017), passim, but particularly Appendix: sheriffs of Dublin 1399–1513.   **22** *Stat. rolls Ire. Edw. IV*, i, pp 262–5. On this occasion James Blakeney, gentleman, future sheriff of the county, and John Field, former justice of the peace, had power to levy carts to draw stones, while Blakeney and Robert St Laurence were quartered on Kildare, Meath and Louth but not on Dublin 'except only at such times that as the sheriff of the county shall bring them, under his survey, for the prosperity of the said county'.[23]

WHO PAID THE SUBSIDY?

The question of who actually paid the subsidies, and in what form, is difficult to answer from the surviving evidence. The subsidy was a land tax and as such might reasonably have been expected to fall on the landowner. The frequent petitions, preserved in the statute rolls, of landowners seeking to have their lands assessed at a lower rate support such a conclusion.[24] But other petitions make it clear that the burden was shared, at least in part, by their tenants. In 1475 both Roland FitzEustace and Christopher Barnewall had reductions in the assessment of their lands; Roland because the greater part of his tenants at Rathcarran had left and the remainder proposed to leave 'through fear of the payment of the money for each ploughland to be granted now in the said Parliament', and Christopher because the rate of subsidy for which his lands at Assey (in Co. Meath) were liable meant that he could not find any tenants to occupy them.[25] Grants of subsidy are usually said to be upon the county or counties concerned, without further detail. Occasionally a longer version is given: 'upon the commons', 'upon the lords and commons', or 'upon the gentry (*gentilx*) and commons' of the county.[26] In 1467, parliament made arrangements for auditors to hear the account of a 360 mark subsidy on the freeholders, gavellers and chattellers (*de lez franktenauntes gauillers et catallers*) of Meath.[27] A similar formula had been used in 1450, when a subsidy for the construction of a castle in Kildare was to be paid by 'all manner of men, freeholders, gavellers, exempted and not exempted, within the said county'.[28]

Gavellers were tenants who held either at will or by copyhold.[29] The dower assigned to Anastacia, widow of David Wogan, knight, in 1418 included several parcels of land held by gavellers ranging in size from just over two acres up to 27 acres, at rents of roughly one shilling per acre.[30] Chattellers are a more difficult class to identify, but they would appear to have been a fairly humble class of leasehold tenant.[31] The gavellers and chattellers are clearly

to hear the account of the master of works.   **23** *Stat. rolls Ire. Edw. IV*, ii, pp 130–7.
24 *Stat. rolls Ire. Edw. IV*, i, pp 194–7, 203; ii, pp 150–5, 345.   **25** *Stat. rolls Ire. Edw. IV*, ii, pp 274–7, 282–3.   **26** *Stat. rolls Ire. Hen. VI*, pp 16–17; *Edw. IV*, i, pp 176–9; 468–9. **27** *Stat. rolls Ire. Edw. IV*, i, pp 430–3. Berry translates *catallers* here, uniquely, as 'graziers'. Elsewhere he prefers to leave the word untranslated. There is nothing to indicate why graziers should be preferred.   **28** *Stat. rolls Ire. Hen. VI*, pp 284–7.   **29** *Reg. Alen*, pp 176, 179.   **30** CIRCLE, Cl. 1 Hen. VI, no. 3 (here 'gavel-land' is used as a translation for '*gavelar*'; this should probably read as denoting a section of the rental pertaining to this form of tenure, rather than an individual parcel of land).   **31** 'Chattel-interest' in *Oxford English dictionary* [http://www.oed.com/view/Entry/30963]; 'Cat/allarius' in R.E. Latham (ed.),

distinguished from the lords, gentlemen and commons who granted the sub-sidy, almost always occurring together in grants of subsidy which specifically included contributions by those 'exempt and non-exempt', suggesting that their inclusion was the exception rather than the rule.[32] They were not among the electors of knights of the shire and consequently they were not represented by the parliamentary commons which consented to grants of taxation.

The account of William Darcy, undertreasurer of Ireland, for the year ending 18 October 1502, includes his account for the 13s. 4d. subsidy on each ploughland in Louth, Kildare, Dublin and Meath, with a breakdown of the sums collected.[33] From the payments received it is clear that most of the parcels of land contributory to the subsidy in Dublin were (or were assessed as being) a ploughland or half a ploughland in extent, and were thus the lands of the gentry or the wealthy yeomanry, but some contributions were consistent with a quarter or even a sixth of a ploughland. These smaller payments cannot however be taken as evidence of contribution to the subsidy by the lower orders. A payment of only 2s. 4d. was given for the *mons* of Howth, a possession of the St Laurence family, members of the Irish peerage, while 2s. 3d. were paid for Dardistown, belonging to the upwardly-mobile Berminghams of Baldongan.[34]

Darcy's account includes payments for 37 parcels of land in the county of Dublin. Many of these, including several parcels assessed at half a carucate (carucate being another name for a ploughland), are known to have been the principal estates of leading gentry families. James Cruise, sheriff of Dublin in 1509, paid £1 in total for two ploughlands at Naul, Flacketstown and Mallahow (bar. Balrothery).[35] Darcy accounted for 6s. 8d. of subsidy from Cappoge (bar. Castleknock) which was the estate of Robert Bath, sheriff of Dublin in 1507. Oldcamysh (now Kimmage) was a possession of the Barnewalls of Drimnagh, another leading county family.[36] 6s. 8d. was charged on these lands, with another 6s. 8d. on Drimnagh itself. Contributions were also received from Belgard, Rathcreedan and Balgriffin, estates of the Talbot, Sherlock and Burnell families respectively, each of whom provided at least one sheriff of Dublin in the late fifteenth century.[37] The lands contributing to the

Revised medieval Latin word-list (London, 1965), p. 75. For further discussion on this point, see Coleman, 'County office and county society', pp 259–61.   **32** *Stat. rolls Ire. Edw. IV*, i, pp 430–3.   **33** National Library of Ireland, MS 761, pp 328–32; Ellis, 'An English gentleman and his community: Sir William Darcy of Platten' in Vincent P. Carey and Ute Lotz-Heumann, *Taking sides? Colonial and confessional mentalités in early modern Ireland* (Dublin, 2003), pp 31–2.   **34** NLI, MS 761, p. 330; F. Elrington Ball, *The judges in Ireland, 1221–1921* (2 vols, London, 1926), i, p. 193; Dardistown was certainly in Bermingham possession by 1516 (Griffith (ed.), *Cal. inquisitions*, Hen. VIII, no. 67). For further discussion on the fortunes of this family, see Coleman, 'County office and county society', pp 69–70, 169–72.   **35** Griffith (ed.), *Cal. inquisitions*, Hen. VIII, no. 26.   **36** *Stat. rolls Ire. Edw. IV*, ii, pp 486–9.   **37** Coleman, 'County office and county society', Appendix: sheriffs

subsidy in Co. Dublin were thus the estates of the gentry of the county, although it is impossible to determine what portion of the payment was passed on by the landowners to their tenants.[38]

RESISTANCE

Evidence of organized resistance to the subsidy in the fifteenth century is relatively scarce; but as the petition of Christopher Barnewall cited above makes clear, it could be (or could at least be presented as) a significant burden on stretched landowners. The limited available evidence on the subject indicates that in the early sixteenth century the wealthiest members of the Pale gentry might have an income in the region of £80–£120 per annum.[39] While a payment of 13s. 4d. (two-thirds of a pound) does not seem excessive in that context, it may well have seemed so to their less wealthy peers, particularly when they found themselves paying these sums on an annual basis. We might note in support that 13s. 4d. was the average price of a draft horse during the reign of Edward IV, as we shall see in a moment.

The parliament rolls feature numerous petitions from members of the gentry to have the assessment of their subsidy reduced. Thus in 1463 Peter Travers, who was then a favourite of royal government (having backed the Yorkist cause in the Wars of the Roses) petitioned parliament that his manors of Baldongan and Courtlough had been considered as a single ploughland 'in all past subsidies which were granted to the lieutenants of this land', until Sir Robert Burnell and other assessors appointed in Dublin had 'lately within these eight years … negligently and unadvisedly' assessed Baldongan as constituting a single ploughland in itself.[40] In many cases these petitions reflect individuals taking advantage of favourable political winds for personal advantage rather than organized resistance to payment.

Probably more typical of the disgruntled taxpayer are the frequent references to the forcible liberation of livestock impounded by the collectors to ensure payment. Thus in 1472 Thomas White and John Conlan, collectors in the barony of Balrothery, complained that Robert Preston of Gormanstown had seized a draft horse worth 13s. 4d. which they had taken for 4s. 8d. of the

---

of Dublin, 1399–1513.   **38** Examples from Meath suggest that in some instances at least the men physically handing over the money for the subsidy were the tenants and not the landowners, but that they were to be given an allowance for this payment out of the rent owed to the landowner (*Stat. rolls Ire. Edw. IV*, i, pp 176–9). For further discussion on this point, see Coleman, 'County office and county society', pp 262–3.   **39** Coleman, 'County office and county society', pp 13–14; Ellis, 'William Darcy of Platten', p. 29; *State Papers, Henry VIII* (11 vols, London, 1830–52), ii, pp 476–7.   **40** *Stat. rolls Ire. Edw. IV*, i, pp 194–7. For Travers's political connections, see Coleman, 'County office and county society', pp 68–70.

subsidy assessed upon Ballymadan.[41] In the same year Simon White of Corrstown (on the Howth peninsula) and Dermitius Corvicer of Santry (to whom we shall return), collectors in the barony of Coolock, complained that Peter Coolock, gentleman, had deforced them of a horse worth 13*s*. 4*d*. for 4*s*. 8*d*. of the said subsidy in contempt of the king, while the same day James Keating, knight, prior of the Hospital of St John of Jerusalem in Ireland, had deforced the same collectors of another.[42] The formulaic nature of these entries suggests that these were not the spontaneous actions of over-taxed landlords but were instead a recognized part of the process of challenging one's tax assessment. The parliamentary rolls support this. Several petitioners who were granted a reduction of their subsidy assessment were explicitly authorized to deforce collectors of any livestock seized for their old subsidy.[43]

In border regions aggrieved landlords might go one further. In 1460, the commons of Dublin complained to parliament that 'Henry Walsh of Carrickmines, gentleman, from day to day oppresses and destroys the liege people of the King'. Henry's oppressions included seizing the cattle of a collector who had the temerity to distrain one of Henry's tenants to pay his share of the subsidy.[44] Henry Walsh was the head of one of the south Dublin 'marcher' families whose position on the frontier encouraged a more direct approach to the problems of government and defence.[45] To his south-east, other frontier lineages might go yet further. In 1470, the commons of the barony of Newcastle in Dublin petitioned parliament seeking to have the collectors of the baronies discharged of the subsidy due for 'Harold's Country', the southernmost part of the barony, which lay in the upland marches of the county, 'which Harold's Country is in rebellion, and no man dares to go there to distrain for any subsidy … for fear of their lives or of being made prisoners and delivered to the Irishmen'.[46] Nonetheless, from the surviving evidence, it would appear that such actions were the exception, and as we shall see even the Harolds and other frontier families would occasionally play a role in the collection of subsidies.

While there was no doubt a great deal of passive or more-or-less active resistance that we can no longer glimpse, it would appear that the payment of the subsidy was generally accepted. Doubtless the immediate vicinity of the frontier made taxation more palatable. The diversion of part of the subsidy towards the fees of the knights of the shire – that is, the parliamentary representatives of the commons whose job it was to approve the subsidy – no

---

41 National Archives of Ireland, Record commission calendars of the memoranda rolls (RC series 8), RC 8/41, p. 328. The imbalance between the value of the animal and the amount owed suggests that the animal was taken as security for payment, rather than being taken in lieu of money. **42** Ibid., pp 328–9. **43** See, for example, *Stat. rolls Ire. Edw. IV*, i, pp 378–81, 794–7; ii, pp 54–5, 250–1, 810–13. **44** *Stat. rolls Ire. Hen. VI*, pp 766–9. **45** Christopher Maginn, 'English marcher lineages in south Dublin in the late Middle Ages', *IHS*, 34, no. 134 (Nov. 2004), pp 113–36. **46** *Stat. rolls Ire. Edw. IV*, i, pp 666–9.

doubt greased the wheels somewhat.[47] Doubtless more of the subsidy found its way into the coffers of families like the Harolds. Finally, the reduced charges on gentlemen's demesne lands no doubt helped secure the consent of the majority – or rather, the majority of the people who mattered.[48]

ASSESSORS AND COLLECTORS OF THE SUBSIDY IN DUBLIN

The assessors of the subsidy, the men who determined what was or was not a ploughland for subsidy purposes, tended to be the leading men of the county, the men who served as sheriff or justice of the peace.[49] Often they included the men who had been the counties' parliamentary representatives that approved the subsidy in the first place, as in June 1420 when the assessors of the subsidy granted to the earl of Ormond included Stephen Howth and Richard Tyrell, the knights of the shire who had assented to the subsidy.[50] The same is true of John Walsh and John Woodlock, who were among the assessors of another subsidy granted the following year.[51] In later grants of subsidies the responsibility for appointing assessors and collectors was generally given to the knights of the shire and clerical proctors attending parliament, while in some cases the knights of the shire were specifically given the role of assessors.[52] It may well be that the service of the knights of the shire as assessors of the subsidy to which they had assented (as in the subsidies of 1420 and 1421) was the standard practice.[53] Given that the assessment touched directly on the financial interests of the great landowner, it is not difficult to understand why the position was one generally reserved to the county's elite.

From the mid-fifteenth century there appears to have been a movement towards increasingly standardized, written assessments for each county which were used for successive subsidies, a development that can be glimpsed in the 1463 petition of Peter Travers (cited above) to have his assessment lowered from the level of the 1455 assessment.[54] It can be seen more clearly still in 1477 when, in response to a petition from John Barnewall, the clerk and keeper of the rolls of chancery was ordered to 'withdraw and put out of the said new

---

47 *Stat. rolls Ire. Edw. IV*, ii, pp 672–3. For further discussion on this point, see Coleman, 'County office and county society', pp 271–2.   48 For example, *Stat. rolls Ire. Edw. IV*, i, pp 794–7. For discussion of the exemption of the demesne lands of the gentry from the subsidy, see Coleman, 'County office and county society', pp 263–7.   49 Coleman, 'County office and county society', p. 275 (and passim).   50 *Parliaments and councils of medieval Ireland*, eds H.G. Richardson and G.O. Sayles (Dublin, 1947), pp 141–2, 158–9. 51 Richardson and Sayles, *Parliaments and councils*, pp 179–80.   52 For example, *Stat. rolls Ire. Hen. VI*, pp 456–7; *Edw. IV*, ii, pp 130–7, 672–3; *Ric. III to Hen. VIII*, pp 74–7. 53 Thomas Bacon, knight of the shire for the liberty of Meath in 1421, was not among the assessors of the subsidy granted at that parliament; but he is the exception among the knights for the liberty and cross of Meath 1420–1: Richardson and Sayles, *Parliaments and councils*, pp 137–8, 171–4.   54 Coleman, 'County office and county society', pp 270–3;

extent' the assessment for some of his lands at Kimmage.[55] Here we have
clear evidence of the existence of a detailed extent of lands in Co. Dublin
overseen by the officials of the royal government, to change which required
parliamentary sanction. Presumably copies of this assessment might be made
available to those appointed to collect subsidies in Dublin. This development,
attested equally well in other counties, no doubt explains the lack of any named
assessors of subsidy for the last decades of the fifteenth century: they were no
longer necessary to the collection of the subsidy.[56]

The job of physically collecting the subsidy was far more widely spread
across the society of Co. Dublin than that of assessment. It was the means
by which by far the greatest number of individuals played their part in
government in late medieval Ireland. A new team of collectors was appointed
for each subsidy. After 1421, every known subsidy saw two collectors appointed
for each barony in the county, and for a relatively defined (though not
unvarying) list of lordships that made up the crosslands – the very extensive
lands and liberties of the archbishop and the two cathedrals which were treated
as a separate unit to the county, with collectors nominated by the cathedral
chapters.[57]

It has been possible to recover the names of some 210 individuals who
served as collectors in the county or crosslands of Dublin between 1399 and
1513.[58] By far the greatest number of the known collectors of subsidies date
from the reign of Henry VII (August 1485 to April 1509), at the very end of our
period. In part this is due to the chance survival of material; but it is also the
period for which the subsidy was most fully established – being, in effect, a
permanent tax.[59] The large number of individuals named as collectors in this
period, together with the fact that comparatively few are named more than
once, suggests that the true number of those who served as collectors of
subsidies during the reign of Henry VII alone was considerably higher. The
preponderance of names from the reign of Henry VII must be borne in mind
in our analysis of the number and social and ethnic background of the
collectors of subsidy. However, the existence of another block of collectors
from 1420 and 1421, together with chance survivals throughout the century,

Stat. rolls Ire. Edw. IV, i, pp 194–7.   **55** *Stat. rolls Ire. Edw. IV*, ii, pp 486–9.   **56** Coleman,
'County office and county society', pp 270–3.   **57** Richardson and Sayles, *Parliaments and
councils*, pp 133–4, 138–9.   **58** To the names of the lay collectors could be added the names
of the collectors for the clergy of the diocese of Dublin, which have been preserved for the
three subsidies of 1420–1 and for the years 1495–6, 1498, 1499, 1500 and 1508. Without
exception these men were themselves clerics, such as John Brennan, vicar of Donabate,
whose letter to undertreasurer William Hattecliff, probably written in late 1495, gives us a
rare surviving glimpse of the actual business of collecting and handing over the money
raised. Given their very different social position, these clerical collectors have been
excluded from the analysis of the social and ethnic background of the collectors below:
Richardson and Sayles, *Parliaments and councils*, pp 137, 155–6, 173–4; RC 8/43, pp 95–6,
137, 189–90; BL, Royal MS 18 C xiv, fos. 7, 9, 43v–44v. For Brennan's letter, see BL, Royal
MS 18 C xiv, fo. 7.   **59** Quinn, 'Irish parliamentary subsidy', 226.

allows us to provide some balance. Crucially, many of the same families served as collectors of subsidies in the 1420s and the 1490s.[60]

In the first decades of the fifteenth century most of the men appointed as collectors of subsidy for Co. Dublin were from leading gentry families of the county. John Tyrell, who served as collector in June 1420, was presumably a close relation of Walter Tyrell, then sheriff of the county, and Richard Tyrell, assessor of both the subsidies granted in that year.[61] Others however were from much less prominent families. Simon Coolock was one of three men elected collectors of 9*d.* upon every carucate in Dublin to pay the wages of footsoldiers heading north to reclaim Ulster from the Scots and Irish in August 1404.[62] Coolock was apparently the only member of his family to hold office in Co. Dublin in the later Middle Ages, as were the two men elected with him, William Bossard and John Montgomery.[63]

The subsidy granted by the representatives of the county to the earl of Ormond in October 1421 is the last recorded subsidy for which collectors were appointed for the county as a whole. Each subsidy thereafter apparently had collectors appointed for each barony. Some of these men were members of the county elite. James Cruise, collector in Balrothery in 1495 and 1498, was sheriff of the county eleven years later.[64] Robert Talbot of Belgard, sheriff of the county in 1498, was collector in Newcastle in the same year.[65] Robert Barnewall of Drimnagh, who had been sheriff of Dublin in or before 1495, was collector in Newcastle in 1499.[66] Yet these men were the exception. Robert Talbot was the only member of his family to serve as a collector, despite the fact that his family, the Talbots of Feltrim and Belgard, were heavily involved in county government throughout the fifteenth century, with at least three generations of the family holding the office of sheriff.[67] The same is true for James Cruise. No member of the Burnell family served as a collector, despite their frequent appearance in the more prestigious offices of sheriff, justice of the peace, or assessor of subsidies.[68] Neither of the members of the Fitzwilliam family who served as collectors of subsidy in our period were heads of that family, although one, John Fitzwilliam of Jobstown, was head of a cadet branch. Although Robert White of Killester was appointed several times as an assessor of subsidy in the early fifteenth century, no member of his family

---

60 See appendix below; examples of such families include Tyrell, Luttrell (Castleknock), Woodlock (Castleknock), Bailey, Goodman, Lawless (Shankill), Chamberlain (Finglas), More (Finglas).   **61** RC 8/38, p. 3; CIRCLE, Cl. 9 Hen. V, no. 45; Richardson and Sayles, *Parliaments and councils*, pp 141–2, 159; Áine Foley, 'The sheriff of Dublin in the fourteenth century' in Seán Duffy (ed.), *Medieval Dublin XII* (Dublin, 2012), pp 283–8; Coleman, 'County office and county society', Appendix: sheriffs of Dublin, 1399–1513.   **62** CIRCLE, Pat. 5 Hen. IV, no. 84.   **63** CIRCLE, Pat. 3 Hen. IV, no. 61; Coleman, 'County office and county society', pp 280–1.   **64** RC 8/43, pp 93, 284, 286; CIRCLE, Pat. 24 Hen. VII, no. 8. **65** RC 8/43, pp 93, 97, 156.   **66** *Letters and papers illustrative of the reigns of Richard III and Henry VII*, ed. James Gairdner (London, 1863), ii, p. 307.   **67** Coleman, 'County office and county society', pp 57–8.   **68** Ibid., pp 75–80.

served as a collector, although several men from families that may have been cadet branches were appointed.[69] There is thus a clear distinction between the county elite and the great majority of the men who served as collectors of subsidies. In all, only five of the 210 individuals who are recorded as collectors of subsidies are also recorded as having served as sheriff in the county.

So who were the men who served as collectors? Many came from families that, while not as prominent as the Talbots of Belgard, were clearly part of the gentry of the county. Such families often provided several collectors over the course of our period. The Woodlock family provided collectors of subsidy in Castleknock in 1434 and again in 1498. John Woodlock was a knight of the shire and assessor of subsidy for the county in 1421. His namesake was sheriff of the county *c.*1475.[70] Perhaps slightly further down the social scale, but still recognizably part of the gentry, were men like John Pippard of Balrothery, who was collector for Balrothery in 1499. John, or his namesake, was among the electors of the coroners of Dublin in 1485.[71] Other families that provided both electors of officers and collectors of subsidies, without apparently holding county office themselves, included the Chamberlain family of Finglas who provided collectors for Finglas in both 1421 and 1498, as well as an elector of the sheriff, Peter Travers, in 1465.[72]

Others who do not appear among the few surviving records of election of officers also appear to have been from families of at least local importance. Many of our collectors come from families that appear frequently as jurors on inquisitions held in the county during the reign of Henry VIII, on which they sat alongside leading members of the county gentry. Richard English of Baldwinstown (par. Garristown), collector of subsidy in Balrothery in 1500, was presumably a close relation of James English of Baldwinstown, juror at the inquisition post mortem of Thomas Mareward at Dublin in November 1515.[73] William Nott of Baldwinstown, who also served as a juror at that inquisition, was presumably a close relative of Robert Nott of Garristown, collector in Balrothery in 1495 and 1499, and of Thomas Nott, one of the electors of Peter Travers as sheriff in 1465.[74] The family gave their name to Nutstown in the parish of Ballymadan.

As electors of sheriffs, they should in theory have been comfortably within the gentry community of the county. And yet in January 1499 Robert Nott of Garristown, 'merchant', who was presumably identical with our collector, was fined for contempt for infringing rules controlling the purchase and sale of

69 John White of Parnelstown, collector in the crosslands north of the Liffey in 1402, Thomas White of Corbally, in the barony of Balrothery, and Simon White of Correston (on the Howth peninsula) in Coolock, both in 1472, and William White of Courtlough in Balrothery in 1499.   70 Coleman, 'County office and county society', pp 220–2.   71 RC 8/43, p. 9.   72 RC 8/41, pp 61–5.   73 Griffith (ed.), *Cal. inquisitions*, Hen. VIII, no. 3. 74 RC 8/41, pp 61–5.

hides, hardly the mark of a gentleman's lifestyle.[75] William Nott and James English of Baldwinstown were jurors for the inquisition post mortem of Robert Talbot of Belgard in May 1525, when their fellow jurors included Christopher Holywood of Artane, head of a leading county family.[76] Collectors from similar families included Richard Lock of Colmanstown (par. Newcastle), collector of subsidy for Clondalkin in the crosslands of Dublin in 1499 and 1508, who was a fellow juror of English, Nott and Holywood at the May 1525 inquisition. These families were thus men of some local importance, who could expect to have their judgement called on in matters touching landholding in the county. They were members of what has been called the parish – in contrast to the county – gentry.

The line separating the poor gentleman from the prosperous peasant could be quite blurred and it seems certain our collectors included both. The sheer number of families that provided collectors of subsidies – over 160 – makes this practically certain, especially given that the great majority of the surviving names of collectors date to a comparatively short period in the late fifteenth and early sixteenth centuries. In 1508 Thomas Rath of Athgoe, husbandman, William Lock of Colmanstown, husbandman, and John Donyll of Saggart, husbandman, entered into a bond for good behaviour for £40.[77] John Donyll of Saggart, with his Irish surname, was collector in Newcastle that year. William was presumably a close relation of Richard Lock of Colmanstown who was appointed collector of subsidies for Clondalkin in that year.

The title of husbandman accorded to these men indicates (at best) a relatively well-off peasant, and these men were clearly not considered to be among the local gentry. John Donyll's fellow collector in Newcastle was Richard Russell 'the elder', who had served in the same capacity in 1499. He too is called husbandman when he entered into a bond for good behaviour in the same year.[78] The most prominent officer from the Russell family in the fifteenth century was William Russell, subserjeant of Balrothery in 1472, an office that was by no means indicative of gentry status.[79] The Russell family, then, were a family whose members approached, but generally fell short of, the line separating the gentry from the wealthier peasantry. Apart from Richard, two other members of the family served as collectors of subsidy at the close of the fifteenth century. John Russell was collector in Newcastle in 1498, while Stephen Russell of Goddamendy (par. Mulhuddart) was collector in Castleknock in the same year. It is likely that the great majority of our collectors, whose families are otherwise invisible in the record, were of similar status to the Russell family – men of some immediate importance in their locality, but no more than that.

---

75 RC 8/43, p. 113.   **76** Griffith (ed.), *Cal. inquisitions*, Hen. VIII, no. 24; For Holywood, see Coleman, 'County office and county society', pp 47–8, 79 and passim.   **77** RC 8/43, pp 263–4.   **78** RC 8/43, pp 264.   **79** Coleman, 'County office and county society', pp 226–7.

Some of our collectors came from a group of families otherwise not well-represented among Dublin officeholders but who were nonetheless an important part of the political and military equilibrium in the region. These were the Archbold, Harold, Lawless and Walsh families, classified (whatever their ultimate ethnic origin) as leading English marcher lineages of the south Dublin borderlands.[80] Occupying land in the foothills of the Dublin mountains, they were in direct contact and perennial conflict with the Gaelic Irish of Leinster. Weakening royal authority, the challenges of pastoral agriculture and 'march' or frontier warfare, and interaction with the Irish contributed to the evolution of a distinct society. By the fifteenth century these marcher families had in important respects diverged from the more recognizably 'English' society of the lowlands. In the fourteenth century the justiciar or chief governor of Ireland had overseen the election of Walter Harold and Matthew Archbold as captains of the Harolds and Archbolds respectively.[81] These elections exactly mirrored the election of John O'Byrne as captain of the O'Byrnes.[82] As with the Irish, hostages were taken from the marcher lineages to ensure their good behaviour.[83] They were not above plundering their lowland neighbours when the opportunity arose. A particularly spectacular raid occurred in August 1463, when William Harold, esquire, 'a fugitive [who] keeps no certain residence in any place', raided Balally, Dundrum, Mulchanstown and Leopardstown in south Dublin, killing eight of the king's subjects and stealing 200 head of cattle, 40 draught horses and 100 sheep.[84]

The marcher family that had progressed least far along the route of what might cautiously be termed 'Gaelicization' was the Walsh family of Carrickmines. They might expect to play an occasional role in the governance of the county – certainly when it concerned their *patria* in the frontier.[85] Henry Walsh of Carrickmines was one of those given a commission to summon and organize labourers from the southern baronies of Newcastle and Rathdown to throw up earthworks for the defence of the county's southern march in 1460. This was the same Henry who was accused of harassing collectors of subsidies in that very year.[86] No members of the Archbold, Harold or Lawless families appear in county office during the fifteenth century, but they did each provide collectors of subsidy. Thomas *Carraghe* Lawless was collector for the crosslands of Shankill for each of the three subsidies of 1420–1. His

---

80 Maginn, 'English marcher lineages', pp 113–36.   81 Edmund Curtis, 'The clan system among English settlers in Ireland', *English Historical Review*, 35:97 (Jan. 1910), 116–20, at 116–17; Robin Frame, *Colonial Ireland, 1169–1369* (2nd end, Dublin, 2012), p. 142. 82 Curtis, 'Clan system', pp 117–17; Maginn, 'English marcher lineages', p. 123.   83 Frame, *Colonial Ireland*, p. 142.   84 *Stat. rolls Ire. Edw. IV*, i, pp 66–9.   85 For examples of the use of *patria* or *pays* for the lands – or perhaps dominions – of the marcher families, see *Stat. rolls Ire. Edw. IV*, i, p. 666 ('*pais de harrold*'); BL, Royal MS 18 C xiv, fo. 223v ('*in patriam Theolbaldi Walsh*').   86 CIRCLE, Pat. 3 Hen. VI, no. 128; Robin Frame (ed.), 'Commissions of the Peace in Ireland, 1302–1461', *AH*, 35 (1992), 1–43, at 13; *Stat. rolls Ire. Hen. VI*, pp 756–9.

descendant John (sometimes rendered as Shane) Lawless was the sole collector for Shankill for the subsidies of 1496, 1498, 1499 and 1500. Richard *More* Archbold was collector in Rathdown in 1498, 1499 and 1508, while Maurice Walsh of Kilgobbin (head of a cadet branch of the family of Carrickmines) was collector there in 1500.

The only member of the Harold family to be named as a collector was John Harold of Tallaght, collector in the crosslands there in 1500. Tallaght lay just to the north of 'Harold's Country', which extended 'from Saggart to Kilmashogue (par. Whitechurch, bar. Rathdown)'.[87] However, John may have been from a comparatively lowly branch of the family. He is almost certainly identical with 'John Harroll Smyth' who had been collector in Tallaght in 1498; if this identification is correct, then it is quite possible that 'smith' here represents an occupation, rather than a surname. The petition of the commons of Newcastle to the Irish parliament in 1470 concerning Harold's Country has already been noted; parliament ordained that the collectors of Newcastle were to be discharged of the subsidy due for Harold's Country and two collectors were to be specifically appointed to collect the same.[88] While no names of collectors for Harold's Country have survived, it is likely that any collectors so appointed (if the ordinance actually ever had affect) would have been members of the Harold marcher lineage.

Although the 1470 petition does not name the individuals in Harold's Country who were inclined to kill collectors or sell them to the Irish, it is difficult to imagine that the culprits were any other than the Harolds themselves or their close associates. The petition sheds light on the role of the marcher lineages in the collection of subsidies. As Englishmen in the eyes of the law, and the leading men of their localities, they were the sort of men who might be expected to exercise a role in the levying of the subsidy on their families, tenants and neighbours; but perhaps more importantly they were also the only men who could exercise such a role. They could, if they so chose, make the collection of the subsidy difficult or impossible. It seems likely that the cooperation of the marcher lineages in the collection of the subsidy would have had to be bought, perhaps at the cost of a portion of the subsidy collected. Nonetheless, it would appear that their appointment as collectors was effective and not merely notional: John Lawless is recorded as paying a mark (13*s*. 4*d*.) for the subsidy of Shankill in February 1496.[89]

GAELIC IRISHMEN AS COLLECTORS

One fact that is immediately striking upon reading the names of the collectors of subsidy in Co. Dublin is the presence of a number of men of unambiguously

87 *Stat. rolls Ire. Edw. IV*, i, pp 666–9.   88 Ibid.   89 BL, Royal MS 18 C xiv, fo. 44.

Gaelic Irish origin, in stark contrast to all the other offices of royal government in the county. Fully thirty-seven of the collectors can be assigned with confidence to this category.[90] Another collector, William Mac Thomas *Og* (if this is Irish *óg*, 'junior') of Dalkey, may have been of English descent but clearly came from an Irish-speaking *milieu*. The same may have been true of collectors from the English marcher lineages such as Shane and Thomas *Carragh* Lawless (*carrach*, 'scabby') and Richard *More* Archbold. Against these must be balanced men like Jenkin ('Little John') Horsley of Swords, collector in Swords, and John alias Jenkyn Granger, collector in Rathcoole, whose nicknames suggests they came from an area where English remained the main language.

The Irish collectors were doubtless well-integrated members of local society. Most of them have English (or Anglicized) first names (the great majority being John, William and Patrick – although the prevalence of the latter among men with English surnames may in itself be an indicator of cultural exchange). Eight however do not – Dermitius or Dermot Corviser of Santry, collector in the barony of Coolock in 1472; Dermot Mannyn (Ó Mainnín?), collector in the lordship of St Sepulchre's; Donald(us) Curran (Ó Corráin?) of Diswellstown, collector in the barony of Castleknock; Donald *gromagh* (*gruaimeach*, gloomy?) O'Kelly (Ó Ceallaigh) and Donald Omoren (Ó Murcháin?) of Clondalkin, collectors in the crosslands of Clondalkin; Donald Carpenter of Finglas, collector in the crosslands of Finglas; and Donald O'Nolan (Ó Nualláin) of Shankill in the crosslands of Shankill, all in 1499; and Dermot Bay (*buidhe*, 'yellow-haired'?) of Rathcoole, collector in Rathcoole in 1500. It will be observed that these all occur very late in the century. It is striking that only two unambiguously Gaelic names – Diarmaid and Domhnall – are borne by our collectors. It seems likely that a wider variety of Irish names lies hidden by the John, Patrick and William of the exchequer Latin. Nonetheless, the existence of a number of officers of royal government in Co. Dublin with unambiguously Gaelic names provides some striking evidence for a rise in 'relatively unanglicized Irish people' among the English society of late fifteenth-century Dublin.[91]

The majority of our Irish collectors (all but nine) were collectors for the crosslands, where collectors appear on the whole to be of comparatively lower status than those of the county. It may be significant that Gaelic Irishmen were

---

90 Surnames in italics in the appendix below. This figure excludes a number of individuals whose surnames are ambiguous but may well indicate Gaelic origins, such as Thomas Begge and Patrick Devenysh of Ballymore, John Begge of Baluske, John Rabo, and Hugh and William More of Finglas. Men with occupational or placename surnames, such as John Cabra, also fall into this ambiguous category; they too have been excluded from the figure above. The Duff family has also been excluded as they appear to have been of English origin or at least 'functionally English' from the period immediately following the conquest: Coleman, 'County office and county society', pp 83–7.   91 Booker, *Cultural exchange and*

also well represented among the clerical collectors of Dublin.[92] The role of the church in facilitating a place for Irishmen in 'English' society has been demonstrated by Sparky Booker.[93] Nonetheless there are also a number of unambiguously Gaelic collectors among the collectors for the county, including Dermot Corviser of Santry, collector in the barony of Coolock in 1472.

Dermot's surname is occupational. He, or his immediate ancestors, are likely to have been corvisers or cordwainers, that is, shoemakers or leather-workers.[94] This was a trade in which Irishmen were particularly prominent, even in the Pale, by the late fifteenth century. Furthermore, Dermot may possibly have been actively trading in Dublin. In 1472 (the same year Dermot was collector in Coolock) a Dermot Cornell, 'tanner', was admitted to the franchise of Dublin.[95] Cornell is not a Gaelic name, but its combination with an unmistakeably Gaelic first name here strongly suggests that Cornell is a misreading – or perhaps a deliberate misrepresentation, on the family's part – of Dermot's surname. This Dermot was admitted to the franchise having served his apprenticeship, and so was probably a young man. It is tempting to suggest that he was the son of our collector. Although this is simple conjecture, his involvement in the leather trade makes a connection to Dermot Corviser very possible. Only seven years earlier, in 1465, the Irish parliament had ordered Irishmen dwelling among the English to take on a suitably English surname. Among the surnames suggested by the Act were colours, such as White, town names, such as Sutton, and trade names. It appears likely that Dermot Corviser was among those who had obeyed this ordinance.[96]

Dermot *Corvisarium* of Santry appears again in 1479, when he was involved in a plea of debt against Thomas Byrsall of Howth.[97] Howth is in the barony of Coolock, and it is at least possible that this suit was connected to Dermot's role as collector of subsidies, in which case he may have served as collector more than once. It is even possible to suggest Dermot's 'real' surname. In 1508 the collectors in Coolock included William 'Morg'h' of Santry. His surname should probably be read as a version of Murchadh.[98] William is the only other man described as being 'of Santry' among the collectors of the barony. It seems at least possible that Dermot and William represent the same comparatively

identity, p. 94.   **92** Richardson and Sayles, *Parliaments and councils*, pp 137, 155–6, 173–4; RC 8/43, pp 95–6, 137, 189–90; BL, Royal MS 18 C xiv, fos. 9, 43v–44v.   **93** *Cultural exchange and identity*, pp 115–30.   **94** Dermot is in fact called 'Cornicer' (horn-worker?), but this is almost certainly a misreading on the part of the record commissioners: RC 8/43, pp 328–9.   **95** *The Dublin city franchise roll, 1468–1512*, ed. Colm Lennon and James Murray (Dublin, 1998), p. 6; *CARD*, i, p. 348; Booker, *Cultural exchange and identity*, p. 241.   **96** Donald Carpenter of Finglas, collector of Finglas in 1499, is another example of an Irishman bearing an English trade name.   **97** Steven Ellis (ed.), 'The common bench plea roll of 19 Edward IV (1479–80)', *AH*, 31 (1984), 19–60, at 40. My thanks to Dr Sparky Booker for drawing this and the Dermot Cornell reference to my attention.   **98** For a similar rendering of Murchadh, see Booker, *Cultural exchange and identity*, p. 241.

prominent family of Irish origins in Santry. So Dermot Corviser may just possibly have been Diarmaid Ó Murchadha.

Prominent among the surnames of Irish origin borne by our collectors is Finn. Three members of the Finn family are named as collectors in Tallaght between 1498 and 1500 – Geoffrey in 1498, David Finn of Tallaght in 1499, and Richard Finn of Tallaght in 1500. Thomas Finn of Tallaght was collector there eight years later. Another member of the family, Patrick Finn 'of Meurath' [?], was collector in the lordship of St Sepulchre's in 1499, while earlier in the century Patrick Finn was appointed collector in Shankill of the subsidies granted to James Butler, earl of Ormond, in June and December 1420. The family were clearly well established in Tallaght at the close of the fifteenth century, with at least three contemporary family members being of sufficient local prominence to be appointed collector. It is possible that the family's roots in Tallaght – whether under the moniker of Finn (which may be Irish *fionn*, 'white, fair-haired'), White or Albus – may have been very deep.[99] One of the two collectors in the barony of Newcastle in 1500 was Patrick White. He is described as 'of Fynnyston' (Finnstown, par. Esker). It seems probable that Patrick has a good claim to be a seventh member of the Finn family named among the collectors of subsidy in fifteenth-century Dublin, albeit that his family (or his branch of the family), further from the march, had conformed more closely to the parliamentary ordinance on acceptable surnames.

It is clear that this family were long established in English areas – albeit on the march – and thus it is questionable to what extent they can be considered as 'functionally' Irish or were taken by their neighbours to be English. They had close links with the church. William Finn was vicar of Rathmore in 1500, when he was collector of the clerical subsidy in the deaconry of Ballymore, while Thomas Finn of Rathkenny, administrator of the goods of John Coleman, chaplain, in 1472 may also have been in holy orders.[100] Nonetheless it is noteworthy that they do not feature elsewhere in royal service as officers. The Finn family, together with Dermot Bay (*Buidhe*?), reflect the use of colour (nick?)names in Irish that may have prompted the Irish parliament to suggest English colour names as an alternative to Gaelic names in the Pale maghery (the still relatively Anglicized parts of the four 'obedient shires'). No collectors are named for Tallaght in the subsidy indentures of 1420–1, the collection of the subsidy there apparently being the responsibility of the collectors named for Clondalkin and Rathcoole.[101] Had Tallaght been assigned its own collectors,

---

99 For further discussion on this family, and their potential antecedents at the time of the conquest, see Coleman, 'County office and county society', pp 296–8.   100 RC 8/43, p. 190; *Register of wills and inventories of the diocese of Dublin, in the time of Archbishops Tregury and Walton, 1457–1483*, ed. Henry F. Berry (Dublin, 1898), pp 48–9.   101 Richardson and Sayles, *Parliaments and councils*, pp 133–4, 161–2, 181–2.

it seems reasonably possible that a member of the Finn family might have been among them. An Irish surname would not have been an impediment, as John Dermot was appointed as one of the collectors in Clondalkin and Rathcoole for each of the three subsidies granted to Ormond.

Thus in the late fifteenth and early sixteenth centuries a number of men with unambiguously Gaelic names served as collectors of subsidies, the only office in Dublin for which this is the case. Gaelic surnames turn up earlier – and more frequently – among the collectors of the crosslands, but they are also represented among the collectors for the county by the reign of Edward IV (1461–83). Gaelic surnames are joined in the later part of the fifteenth century by unambiguously Gaelic first names. This provides striking evidence for the existence of a small but increasingly prominent group of Gaelic Irishmen occupying positions of at least local importance in the heart of the English Pale, just as that term was coming into use. These men worked alongside their English neighbours in the joint – though perhaps unwelcome – endeavour of financing the defence of English Ireland against 'Irish enemies and English rebels'.

The general subsidy, the primary source of royal income in Ireland by the late fifteenth century, was the means by which a very large number of individuals and families had experience of, and took part in, the process of local government. Much more so than other comparatively humble offices, such as that of subserjeant of a barony, it drew on a wide body of men whose importance is unlikely to have extended beyond their immediate locality. These men might be members of lesser gentry families, who might on occasion take part in the higher level of local government as electors of knights of the shire, sheriffs, and coroners. However, they might equally belong to yeoman families like the Russells of Newcastle. While a few men served as both collectors in their baronies and as sheriff of the county, there is in general a very pronounced division between the individuals and families that provided collectors and the county elite who supplied the assessors of subsidies and might expect a position on commissions with subsidy-raising powers. The business of collecting the subsidy thus took in a wide cross-section of the society of Co. Dublin, from the marcher lineages of the south of the county to the yeoman farmers of Garristown, from the lords of Howth to John Harold Smyth (or rather the smith?) of Tallaght, and taking in, uniquely among the offices of English government in Dublin, men of unambiguously Gaelic Irish background.

APPENDIX

ASSESSORS AND COLLECTORS OF SUBSIDY IN DUBLIN, HENRY IV
TO HENRY VII (1399–1509)[102]

Assessors:[103]	
1. 1 June 1402[104]	Thomas Mareward, sheriff of Dublin; Christopher Holywood; Thomas Serjeant; Thomas Howth; John Owen
	Appointed 'to assess 40 m[arks] that the commons of Co. Dublin granted to be levied from them, to be spent in the marches of the said county, for the salvation of the said marches.'
2. June and December 1420[105]	Stephen Howth; John Owen; Richard Tyrell; Robert White of Killester
	Assessors of the subsidy granted by the commons of Co. Dublin to the earl of Ormond, June 1420. The same team of assessors was appointed to assess a second subsidy in December following.
3. October 1421[106]	Richard Bermingham; John Owen; John Walsh of Surgalstown; John Woodlock
	Assessors of the subsidy granted by the commons of Co. Dublin to the earl of Ormond, October 1421.
4. February 1434[107]	John Walsh of Surgalstown; William Field
	Assessors of a subsidy of 5s. 8d. on each ploughland.
5. 1455(?)[108]	Sir Robert Burnell 'and others'
	Assessors of the subsidy within the county of Dublin.
6. 1473[109]	John, archbishop of Dublin; James, prior of Holmpatrick; Walter, abbot of St Mary's; William, prior of Holy Trinity; William, prior of St John in Dublin; William, prior of All Saints near Dublin; Master John Allen, dean of Dublin; Robert St Laurence, lord of Howth; Robert Dowdall, knight; John Burnell, gentleman; John Barnewall, gentleman; Philip Bermingham, gentleman; Thomas Dowdall, gentleman; William Foster, gentleman
	Empowered to assess on county, clergy and cross of Dublin such sums as they or the better part of them shall think fit, and to appoint collectors for the same, to be employed in hiring soldiers to attend on John Talbot, sheriff, as their captain, or any other sheriff for the time being.

102 A note on names: names (including placenames) have been given their modern spelling in instances where this is not in doubt (e.g., Kilshane instead of Kylshane; Surgalstown instead of Surgoteston; Field instead of de la Felde, etc.); elsewhere the spelling is left as presented in the record.   103 Note that this list excludes local subsidies and those for specific projects of fortification.   104 CIRCLE, Pat. 3 Hen. IV, no. 249.   105 Richardson and Sayles, *Parliaments and councils*, pp 142, 159.   106 Ibid., p. 180.   107 NAI, M. 2675 (Delafield MS), p. 55. From the record it is unclear whether Walsh and Field were assessors for the whole county or only for the barony of Castleknock. Given the absence of any other reference to barony-level assessors in fifteenth-century Co. Dublin, and given that Walsh had previously been an assessor for the county, the former seems the correct reading.   108 *Stat. rolls Ire. Edw. IV*, i, pp 194–7. Date uncertain. In 1463 Peter Travers, esq., complained to parliament that 'within these eight years ... Sir Robert Burnell and others, who were made assessors of the subsidy within the county of Dublin' incorrectly assessed his lands at Baldongan as comprising a full ploughland.   109 *Stat. rolls Ire. Edw IV*, ii, pp 138–9. This

Collectors:		
1. December 1401[110]	Richard Mylys; Walter Field; Robert Ballygoodman [Goodman]; John Waterville of Rathcreedan Collectors of 40 crannocks of wheat and 40 of oats granted by the commons of Dublin to Thomas of Lancaster.	
2. 1402[111]	**Crosslands of Dublin:** Alexander Taylor of Swords; Richard Barrett of Finglas; John White of Parnelstown Elected as collectors of 20 marks which the commons of the crosslands of Dublin on the Fingal side of the water of Anilyffy [Liffey] granted in aid of the sustenance of 240 foot for one quarter of a year.	
3. 1404[112]	William Bossard [Bossher?]; Simon Coolock; John Montgomery Elected collectors of subsidy of 9*d.* on every carucate voted by commons of Dublin for force to reclaim the parts of Ulster.	

4. June 1420[113]	**County of Dublin:**
	 Robert Luttrell; John Tyrell; John Walsh
		Crosslands of Dublin:
		 Ballymore:
		     John Purcell; Nicholas Austin
		
		 Clondalkin and Rathcoole:
		     Robert Hendy; John Wilput; John *Dermot*[114]
		
		 Finglas:
		     Walter Breakspear; William Nottingham
		
		 St Sepulchre:
		     John Bailey; Nicholas Barnewall
		
		 Shankill:
		     Thomas *Carraghe* Lawless; Patrick *Finn*
		
		 Swords:
		     William Alger; John Barron junior; William Comyn

5. December 1420[115]	The same collectors as in June, except in Co. Dublin and Swords where:	
	County of Dublin: Robert Luttrell; John Brown of Lusk	**Crosslands of Dublin:** Swords: William Alger; William Comyn

commission clearly stands apart as their role as assessors is secondary to their power to determine the level of subsidy or subsidies to be raised to meet these extraordinary costs. **110** CIRCLE, Pat. 3 Hen. IV, no. 61.　**111** Ibid., Pat. 3 Hen. IV, no. 250.　**112** Ibid., Pat. 5 Hen. IV, no. 84.　**113** Richardson and Sayles, *Parliaments and councils*, pp 133–4, 142. **114** Italics are used to indicate Gaelic names (and nicknames).　**115** Richardson and Sayles, *Parliaments and councils*, pp 159, 162.

Collectors: *(continued)*		
6. October 1421[116]	**County of Dublin:** John Luttrell; Robert Luttrell; Richard Tallon	**Crosslands of Dublin:** Ballymore: Nicholas Austin, provost of Dunlavin; James Lupin, provost of Ballymore Clondalkin: John *Dermot*; Robert Hendy; Edward Shillingford; John Wilput Finglas: Thomas Chamberlain of Ferdromyn;[117] John Haws; Hugh More[118] St Sepulchre: John Max; John *Omaille* [Ó Máille?]; John Rabo Shankill: Thomas *Carraghe* Lawless; William Read; Thomas Reban Swords: John Bailey of Lusk; Walter Francum; John Puddynge[119]
7. December 1423[120]	County of Dublin *or* Barony of Castleknock: Robert (*or* John) Luttrell Collector of a subsidy granted to James Butler, earl of Ormond, by the commons of Co. Dublin at a great council before the same, December 1423.	
8. February 1434	Barony of Castleknock: John Luttrell; Nicholas Woodlock Collectors of a subsidy of 5s. 8d. on each ploughland.	
9. 1472[121]	Barony of Balrothery: John *Conlan* of Walshillys [Walshestown?]; Thomas White of Corbaly Barony of Coolock: *Dermot Cornicer [Corviser]* of Santry; Simon White of Corrstown Collectors of a subsidy granted to Thomas, earl of Kildare.	
10. Easter term, 1495[122]	**County of Dublin:** Barony of Balrothery: Robert Nott; John Pippard Barony of Castleknock: John Fowle; Richard Tyrell Barony of Coolock: Christopher Holywood; John Long Barony of Newcastle: John Cabra; John Stephens	**Crosslands of Dublin:** Swords: William Long; John White

116 Ibid., pp 180, 182.   117 Possibly Baldrumman, par. Lusk?   118 Possibly the Irish patronymic Ó Mórdha or adjectival nickname *Mór* ('senior') or it may simply be the English surname Moore.   119 This may be a corruption of the Irish name Paidin which gives us surnames like Padden and MacFadden, or it may simply be English Pudding.   120 NAI, Ferguson collection of memoranda roll extracts [Ferguson MS 2–4], iii, fos. 20–1. The record refers to the collector alternatively as Robert and John Luttrell. His bailiwick is not specified and could be either the county, as in earlier subsidies, or the barony, as in all later subsidies. In October 1424 he complained to the exchequer that one David Stakeboll of Castleknock broke his arrest of a rick (*tassus*) of wheat taken for 3s. 1d. of subsidy on the half carucate called 'Britaghesland'.   121 RC 8/41, pp 328–9.   122 BL, Royal MS 18 C xiv, fos. 74–74v.

Collectors: *(continued)*		
11. Michaelmas term (?), 1495[123]	Barony of Balrothery: Walter Bermingham; James Cruise Barony of Coolock: Patrick Caddell; Walter Howth Barony of Newcastle: Robert Barnewall; Robert Talbot	

12. Michaelmas term 1495/Hilary term 1496[124]	**County of Dublin:**
	Barony of Castleknock: Thomas
	    Woodlock
		Crosslands of Dublin:
		Ballymore: John Fitz Robert of
		    Ballymore
		Clonmethan: Laurence Brown
		Clondalkin: Thomas Walsh
		Dalkey: Patrick Wever
		Finglas: William More of Finglas;
		    John Cowper
		Lusk: Richard Saunder; Richard
		    Mayler
		Rathcoole: Patrick Lawless
		St Sepulchre: Patrick Blake;
		    Richard Gerrard; Walter *Oge*
		Shankill: John Lawless
		Swords: John Jordan; Richard
		    Heyward
		Tallaght: Richard Fitz William

13. Easter term 1496.[125]	**Crosslands of Dublin:** Clonmethan: William *Rogan* Finglas: John Bailey; Walter Bailey Lusk: Thomas *Nele*; Robert Rousse [Russell] Portraine: Thomas Bermingham	
14. 1497(?)[126]	**Crosslands of Dublin(?):** Tallaght(?): Maurice Eustace of Tallaght	
15. 1497–8(?)[127]	Barony of Castleknock: Roger Duff; Thomas Woodlock	

123 Ibid., fos. 84v–5. Assignment made of sums raised by them, Michaelmas 1495. In February 1496 they paid in sums of the subsidy in several portions: ibid., fo. 42v. While they are not specifically named as collectors for Michaelmas term, the consistent appointment of pairs of collectors, and lack of overlap with the Easter collectors, suggests that they represent a separate set of appointments to no. 10 above.   **124** Ibid., fos. 42, 43v–44v, 57, 61. These collectors made payments to the exchequer in the early part of 1496. Given the different bailiwicks involved, it is possible that this entry and no. 11 above, or indeed (with the possible exception of Castleknock, which has different collectors named in each instance) this and no. 10 above, should be grouped together as one. New collectors are named for Easter term 1496: see no. 13 below.   **125** BL, Royal MS 18 C xiv, fo. 73. Payments received or to be received from them are assigned to Nicholas Turnor, second justice of the common bench, in Easter term. They are specifically referred to as 'collectors of the cross[lands] of Finglas [etc.] of Easter term'.   **126** NAI Ferguson Coll., iii, fo. 222. In 13 Hen. VII (1496–7) Maurice Eustace of Tallaght was collector of subsidy. It is likely (but not certain) that he was collector for the crosslands in Tallaght.   **127** RC 8/43, p. 106. Date uncertain but likely 1498 or 1497. A memorandum among the rolls for Michaelmas 14 Hen. VII (1498) records evidence of Woodlock and Duff coming to the exchequer court

Collectors: *(continued)*		
16. Michaelmas term 1498[128]	**County of Dublin:** Balrothery: James Cruise; John Dillon of Gralagh Castleknock: John Cristyn of Kilsallaghan; Stephen Russell of Godamenthe [Goddamendy] Coolock: David Heghern of Mote near Kyllegh [Killeek]; Richard Heghern of Surgalstown Newcastle: John Russell of Newcastle; Robert Talbot of Belgard Rathdown: Richard Archbold	**Crosslands of Dublin:** Ballinteer: John Fitz Henry; John Fitz Robert Clondalkin: James Thomyn of Clondalkin; John Venables of Clondalkin Clonmethan: William Ley of Oldtown Dalkey: William Webbe Finglas: John Bailey of Kilshane; John Chamberlain of Finglas Lusk: Walter England of Collinstown; Thomas Paris of Lusk Portraine: Henry Walsh of Portraine Rathcoole: James Granger; William *Lalor* [Ó Leathlobhair?] St Sepulchre: William *McKeyn* [Mac Aodháin?]; Laurence Sex Shankill: *Shane* [Seán] Lawless Swords: John Hore of Swords; William *Kelly* [Ó Ceallaigh] of Moreton Tallaght: Geoffrey *Finn*;[129] John Harroll Smith
17. Easter term 1499[130]	**County of Dublin:** Balrothery: William White of Curtelagh [Courtlough]; Simon Mounfeld of Garristown Castleknock: John Eliot of Correston; *Donald Curryn* [Ó Cuirín?] of Diswellstown Coolock: John *Kenane* [Ó Cianáin?] of Mablieston [Mabestown?]; Maurice Dowoke [misreading for Coolock?] of Dunbro Newcastle: Robert Barnewall of Drimnagh; Richard Bagot [Baggot] of Esker Rathdown: Richard Archbold	**Crosslands of Dublin:** Ballymore: James Ballard of Ballymore; Patrick *Obulgyn* [Ó Buadhacháin?] of the same Clondalkin: *Donald Omoren'* [Ó Murcháin?] of Clondalkin; *Donald Gromagh OKelly* [Domhnall Gruaimeach Ó Ceallaigh] of the same Clonmethan: Robert Sendell of Moreton Dalkey: William Webbe of Dalkey John Lawless of Shankill Finglas: Patrick *Kenne* [or possibly Thenne?] of Finglas; John Palmer of Broghan Lusk: James Mellon [O Mealláin?] of Ballough; Robert Butler of Lusk Portraine: Henry Brown of Portraine Rathcoole: Patrick Ashe of Rathcoole; Patrick Leche of the same St Sepulchre: *Derm[ot] Mannyn* [Ó Mainnín?] of New Street; William Owen of Patrick's Street Swords John Count of Swords; Thomas Darcy of Balketh Tallaght Patrick Tyrell of Tallaght; Patrick *Curran* [Ó Corráin?] of the same

concerning their efforts to collect Thomas Bermingham's contribution for half a carucate in Little Cabragh: RC 8/43, 106–11. Different collectors are named for Castleknock in Michaelmas term 1498 (see no. 16 below). **128** RC 8/43, pp 93–5. **129** As noted above, this may be from *fionn* ('fair-haired') or it may be a patronymic surname like Ó Finn. **130** RC 8/43, pp 135–7.

Collectors: *(continued)*		

18.
Michaelmas
term, 1499[131]
	County of Dublin:
	Balrothery: Robert Nott of
	  Garristown; John
	  Pippard of Balrothery
	Castleknock: Richard
	  Aylward of Stagube
	  [Astagob]; James Scott
	  of Bay
	Coolock: Thomas Cowyll
	  [Cowell] of Harristown;
	  John Lounsby of
	  Kylbarroke
	  [Kilbarrack]
	Newcastle: Richard
	  Russell of Newcastle;
	  Richard Grete of
	  Crumlin
	Rathdown: Richard *More*
	  Archbold; Thomas
	  Godeman [Goodman]
		Crosslands of Dublin:
		Ballymore: Thomas Begge;[132] Ed[ward] *Bannyn*
		  [Ó Banbháin?] of Ballymore
		Clondalkin: Richard Lock; William Taverner of
		  Clondalkin
		Clonmethan: John Kayser of Wyanstown
		Dalkey: James White of Dalkey
		Finglas: *Donald* Carpynder [Carpenter] of
		  Finglas; John *Kelly* of Kilshane
		Lusk: Richard Whithede [Whitehead] of Lusk;
		  David Pavy of Collinstown
		Portraine: Henry Brown of Portraine
		Rathcoole: Thomas Harry [FitzHenry?];
		  Andrew Water[s?] of the same
		St Sepulchre: Patrick Grange of Newstreet;
		  Patrick *Finn* of Meurath [?]
		Shankill: John Lawless of Shankill
		Swords: John Heyward; William Arnold of
		  Swords
		Tallaght: David *Finn*; Henry Brown of Tallaght

19. Easter
term, 1500[133]
	County of Dublin:
	Balrothery: Thomas
	  Gamoll of Ballycarryke
	  [Balcarrick]; Richard
	  English of
	  Baldwinstown
	Castleknock: William
	  Luttrell of Tyrellstown;
	  William Bragges of
	  Dunsink
	Coolock: Nicholas Dullard
	  of Balgriffin; Thomas
	  Wynter
	Newcastle: James Highern'
	  of Galrotheston;
	  Patrick White of
	  Fynnyston'
	  [Finnstown]
	Rathdown: Maurice Walsh
	  of Kilgobbin; James
	  Godeman [Goodman]
	  of Ballylaghnan'
	  [Loughlinstown]
		Crosslands of Dublin:
		Ballymore: John Fleming of Ballymore; Henry
		  Gamagh [*geamchaoch*, 'purblind'?] of the
		  same
		Clondalkin: John *Galmole*[134] of Clondalkin;
		  Patrick *Curryn'* [Ó Corráin?] of the same
		Clonmethan: John Heyward of Clonmethan
		Dalkey: William Webbe of Dalkey
		Finglas: William More of Finglas; John Palmer
		  of Broghan
		Lusk: John *McLane* [Mac Laidhghinn?] of
		  Courduff; Nicholas Bulloke [Bullock] of
		  Lusk
		Portraine: John Begge of Baluske [Ballisk]
		Rathcoole: *Dermot Bay* [Buidhe, 'yellow-haired'?]
		  of Rathcoole; Patrick Coton' of the same
		St Sepulchre: William Scolok[135] of New Street;
		  Laurence Sex of the same
		Shankill: John Lawless of Shankill
		Swords: Roger Brown of Swords; Robert
		  Passemer of Sawcereston' [Saucerstown]
		Tallaght: Richard *Finn* of Tallaght; John
		  Harrold of the same

131 RC 8/43, pp 162–4.   132 May possibly be Irish *beag*, 'little'.   133 Ibid., pp 187–9.
134 The surname appears Irish, perhaps something like Mac Gilla Mhichil; there is a
Galmoylestown in Co. Westmeath.   135 This is probably from Irish *scológ*, 'student',
'servant', 'ecclesiastical tenant', but might be the English surname Scurlock.

Collectors: *(continued)*		
20. Michaelmas term 1508[136]	**County of Dublin:** Balrothery: John Edvard [Edward or perhaps Eylward/Aylward?] of Baldwinstown; William Butyrley [Bitterley, Butterley] of Kynnaw'd [Kinoud?] Castleknock: Richard *Regan* [Ó Riagain] of Corrstown; Maurice Brokton of Damaleston [Damastown?] Coolock: Robert Hayvard [Heyward] of Coolock; William *Morg'h* [Ó Murchadha?] of Sauntrief [Santry] Newcastle: John *Donyll* [Ó Domhnaill?] of Tassagard [Saggart]; Richard Russell of Newcastle the elder Rathdown: Richard *More* Archbold	**Crosslands of Dublin:** Ballymore: Patrick Devenysh of Ballymore Clondalkin: Roland Sherref of Clondalkin; Richard Lock of Colmanstown Clonmethan:[137] Richard Allen of Clonmethan Dalkey: William *McTomas Ooge* ['son of Thomas junior'] of Dalkey Finglas: John Archbold of Finglas; John Palmer of Broghan Lusk: Thomas *Oklyn* [Ó Claoin?] of Lusk; Henry Dandon [Daundon] of the parish of Lusk Portraine: William Lawless of the same Rathcoole: Nicholas Wise of Rathcoole; John Morice [Maurice] of the same St Sepulchre: Nicholas Tanner of New Street; John Locum of Calyn Shankill: *Donald ONolan* [Ó Nualláin] of Shankill Swords: Jenky [Jenkin] Horsoly [Horsley] of Swords; Andrew Smyth of Balheary Tallaght: Thomas *Finn* of Tallaght; John Fythwyllam [Fitz William] of Jopiston [Jobstown] Tipperkevin: William *McKnawyn'* [Mac Cnáimhín?] of Tipperkevin

136 RC 8/43, pp 275–7.   **137** Richard Allen of Clonmethan is listed as a third collector for Finglas, but this seems likely to be in error as no collector is listed for Clonmethan.

Late medieval footwear and leather finds from Chancery Lane, Dublin

JOHN NICHOLL

INTRODUCTION

The leather assemblage from Chancery Lane was originally uncovered by excavation in 2002 by Claire Walsh and details of the excavation were subsequently published in an earlier volume in this series (Walsh 2009, 9–30). Among the finds recovered was a large assemblage of leatherworking material. These leather artefacts were recovered from the lower levels of an infilled quarry, located in Area D in the north-east corner of the site. Within the quarry itself, the majority of the finds were recovered from the lowest level, F64, a water-logged, soft, brown silt, and F56, a deposit of organic silt in the southern area. A small number of leather finds was recovered from F57 and F55 in the northern part of the quarry. Other finds from these levels also included large quantities of medieval and post-medieval pottery (ibid., 13–15). Of particular significance though is the presence of both Irish-style brogues and English or Continental-style shoes in the assemblage, especially in level F64.

COBBLING SCRAP

The finds could best be described as cobbling scrap and consisted mainly of footwear parts from both brogues and shoes as well as complete examples of both. The largest cluster, recovered from F64, included 51 complete or partial vamps with six different vamp tongue styles along with right and left quarters, backparts, latchets, soles, heel lifts, fragments of straps, handles and belts. All the pieces were very worn and damaged prior to being discarded and some had been cut down for reuse as repair parts. None of the triangular off-cut pieces, which remain when new soles are being cut out from a sheet of leather and are typical of shoemaking, were present. It is tempting to consider this material as the refuse of a single cobbling workshop located in the near vicinity. The other three fills, F56, F55 and F57, contained a total of eleven leather finds, some of which may have been redeposited from elsewhere.

MEDIEVAL FOOTWEAR – TURNSHOES

In the medieval period, all footwear was made using the turnshoe method of construction. The commonest style consisted of a one-piece, wrap-around upper with a single sole and an optional rand. Sometimes, small triangular or rectangular inserts were used to fully close the medial side seam. Lengths of leather thong were used for lacing. A narrow strip of leather, known as a rand, was sometimes stitched between the upper and sole to improve the water tightness of the seam. The stitching medium was generally waxed linen thread although, sometimes, animal sinew or leather thonging were used.

The shoes themselves were made inside out before being soaked and turned right-way-round. In this way, the stitching, which is the most vulnerable part of the shoe is placed on the inside where it is protected from wear-damage (Grew and de Neergaard 1998, 44–51).

The early fourteenth century saw the development of a new type of shoe in Britain and on the Continent with uppers consisting of separate vamp and quarters and fastened with latchets using laces or thong as opposed to the prevailing pattern of sole with one-piece upper. The rand became broader and was no longer optional and it continued to be placed between sole and upper. The construction method continued to follow the turnshoe tradition. A find of such a shoe from St Denis in France, which was dated to AD1325, was consider by Goubitz to be an *archetypical* example which he classified as a Lace-tied latchet shoe type 130 (Goubitz 2001, 281–7).

Shoes continued to be made for the left and right foot and became more decorative. It becomes possible to speak of shoe fashions with footwear being an essential part of dress and costume as a display of status and wealth. Contemporary manuscript illustrations such as those on the Waterford Charter Roll give some idea of the variety of shape, colour and decoration of footwear (Walton 1992, 7).

LATE MEDIEVAL FOOTWEAR – TURNSHOES TO SHOES

During the early to mid-sixteenth century further changes in shoe fashions took place. Slip-on style shoes with uppers of vamp and quarters and no latchets became popular in England. The numerous examples recovered from the wreck of the *Mary Rose*, the flagship of Henry VIII that sank in 1545, shows the popularity of this type of shoe with the crew (Gardiner 2005). The rand became broader and was used by shoemakers to attach a second sole to the shoe, giving rise to what is known as the turn–welt shoe.

As the century progressed, this turn–welt process of manufacture was further refined and developed into the welted shoe. The rand, which had been placed between the upper and sole of the turnshoe was now located outside the upper. This simple repositioning allowed the shoe to be made right-way-out and the turnshoe method of construction was abandoned. Shoes were now made on a last and by the end of the century they were being closed and secured on the foot with latchets and laces. The uppers consisted of four separate parts, a vamp with right and left quarters, which were joined together with two side seams and a heel seam and a continuous welt, which ran around the lasting margin of the shoe. The latchets, which had been separate parts in the earlier turnshoes, were now integral extensions of the upper edges of the quarters.

A final innovation was the development of the heel, which was facilitated by the use of multiple sole layers. Originally, the heel was a simple wedge pegged to the treadsole. The use of a welt allowed a second sole to be added and the heel was inserted between the two. Gradually the spring heel was developed, which consisted of a number of wedges or lifts stacked one above the other, located between the soles and secured in place with wooden pegs. To simplify the construction process, shoemakers developed the straight shoe, a symmetrical design, which was not specifically intended for the right or left foot and became the norm from 1600 to 1800 (Swann 1982, 7–15).

BROGUES AND SHOES

However, to properly understand the significance of the leather finds from Chancery Lane it is necessary to distinguish between two differing traditions of footwear manufacture, which began to become apparent in the late medieval period in Ireland, namely, the brogue and the shoe. The two traditions co-existed in medieval Ireland and were of little significance when all shoemakers used the turnshoe method of manufacture. What distinguished them was the use of a single length of leather thong to join the sole and upper of a brogue, and a waxed end of linen thread to assemble a shoe. Following the development of the welted and heeled shoe in the late sixteenth and early seventeenth centuries, the difference between the two traditions came to reflect the differences between the dress styles of the Gaelic Irish and the English settlers.

A.T. Lucas, in his paper 'Footwear in Ireland', traces some of the discussion in the State Papers as to whether Irish brogues could be used *in lieu* of English shoes to equip English armies campaigning in Ireland, the brogues being a cheaper option to supply but one which threatened to barbarize the appearance of the English soldier (Lucas 1956, 351–61). Lucas also developed a typology of Irish footwear in which he classified this lace-tied latchet-style shoe as Type 5 and identified it with the 'brogue' (from Irish *bróg*, 'shoe') of literary and documentary texts to distinguish it from the English or Continental shoe. At the time, he was limited to an examination of stray bog finds which led him to conclude that this type of composite shoe with a separate sole and upper was a late introduction into Ireland during the seventeenth century and most likely influenced by outside fashions (ibid., 378–87). However, the Dublin excavations of the 1970s revealed examples of composite footwear from medieval levels, which were broadly in line with similar examples from Britain and the Continent (Wallace 2016, 276–8).

More recently, the excavations at Deer Park Farms, Co. Antrim, and at Drumclay crannog, Co. Fermanagh, have shown the composite style of footwear manufacture to be of even earlier date in Ireland. The leather finds from Deer Park Farms included evidence for footwear consisting of soles with rounded heels and uppers of a separate vamp and backpart which dated to the ninth century (Neill 2014, 368–83). The subsequent excavations at the Drumclay site revealed evidence for Lucas Type 5 shoes at medieval levels. A number of extremely well-made boots were also recovered from the lowest levels of the crannog. These composite boots were comprised of separate vamps, wrap-around backparts with toggle fastenings, complete rands and separate soles with pointed V extensions at the heels. A further detail worth noting is the use of a single length of leather thong, in an undulating S-type stitch, to close the seams of both the boots and the brogues as opposed to any other stitching medium. Such finds suggest the development of a style of footwear manufacture in Ireland in the early medieval period, which continued thereafter, and which pre-dates its development in Britain and on the Continent (Nicholl 2016).

DISCUSSION OF THE LEATHER FINDS

As already mentioned, the bulk of the leather finds came from the lowest fill of the quarry, F64, at the southern end and contained both brogues and shoes and almost 200 off-cut pieces of footwear. F56 overlay this level and yielded four incomplete brogues, including one in a child's size. In the northern sector of the quarry, F57 yielded a single example of an almost complete adult-sized brogue as well as an almost complete heeled shoe. The upper fill, F55, yielded fragments of a shoe as well as a single example of a hybrid shoe, which combined features of both the brogue and the shoe. In all, there were five complete brogues, three in children's sizes and two in adult sizes, as well as ten almost complete examples. Of the almost complete brogues, three were in children's sizes and seven in adult sizes as well as a further six incomplete soles, which suggests a total number of twenty-one brogues recovered. This is by far the largest assemblage of Irish brogues recovered from any excavation in Ireland to date.

In addition to the brogues there were three complete adult-sized shoes recovered as well as twelve almost complete shoes of which, four were in children's sizes and eight in adult sizes. A further eleven isolated shoe vamps were also found in addition to two mules (discussed below), two shoes with one-piece uppers and heels and a single example of a slip-on shoe (Nicholl 2004).

An account of a brogue-maker at work in Tralee, Co. Kerry, in the late 1830s makes reference to a *gréasaí Gaelach* or brogue-maker and a *gréasaí Gallda* or shoemaker and the fact that the brogue-makers considered themselves to be of a more ancient trade than the shoemakers (Hall 1840, 188–90). This distinction would also appear to have been used by the guild merchant in Dublin which would allow 'country shoemakers' access to the city markets when city shoemakers' prices were considered to be too high and to the detriment of the citizens (Webb 1929, 108). Brogues were consistently cheaper to manufacture than shoes (Lucas 1956, 359–62).

The brogues

The brogues demonstrated a standardized approach to their construction with what could be termed a consistent 'parts list', which comprised of the following: a vamp; a single backpart; a short length of insert between vamp and backpart side seams; a triangular shaped heel stiffener of thin leather; two lace tabs/latchets with either a single or two pairs of lace holes at each terminal; a single or bifurcated lace of thin leather; a wide continuous rand; two soles of thin leather placed flesh side to flesh side. There are examples of both straight and right/left sole patterns in the assemblage. There are four different tongue styles among the brogues and this is the only real variation that suggests the passage of time and changes in fashion.

02E1694:64:32 is a good example of a child's brogue and is almost complete with only the right latchet/tab missing. It shows very heavy wear-damage and the soles are worn through at the heel and tread. However, this allows the construction details to be clearly seen. The brogue was made as a turnshoe. The sole is composed of two layers of thin leather stitched flesh to flesh with grain/flesh stitches at the sole/upper seam. A wide rand was stitched between the soles and uppers and this folded outwards, along the seam, to protect it from wear. Where the seam has separated, a continuous length of leather thong can be seen in a serpentine S stitch securing the uppers, the rand and the soles with grain/flesh stitching. The uppers consist of vamp and a single-piece backpart with a heel stiffener at the heel. The top-edge of the backpart slopes upwards from the side seam towards the heel and two latchets were attached with a length of thong. A thin insert of leather was stitched into the side seams

11.1 Child's brogue with sole worn through (Photo: J. Nicholl)

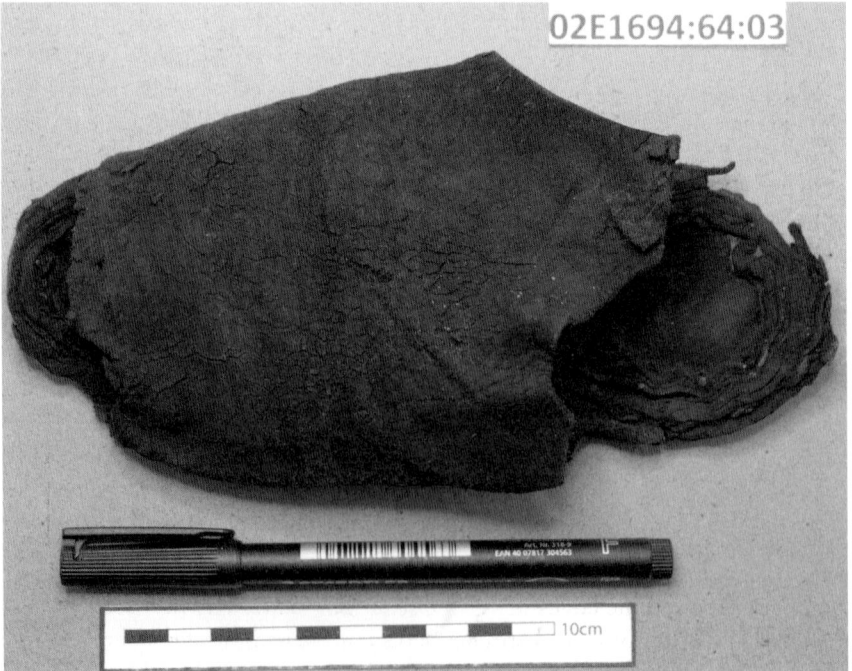

11.2 Child's brogue with backpart removed, heavy wear-damage to toe (Photo: J. Nicholl)

11.3 Adult's brogue showing constituent parts (Photo: J. Nicholl)

and latchet seams to strengthen them. A closed seam with grain/flesh stitches was used for all the seams of the brogue. The latchets were secured with a thong lace through single lace holes. The lace was also threaded through a pair of small slits cut into the instep of the vamp at the base of the tongue.

02E1694:56:06 (fig. 11.1) would appear to have been worn – indeed, all six examples of children's brogues have been very heavily worn and damaged through use – even though the brogue had become too small for the child's foot. The soles are worn through and the backpart appears to have been crushed flat and worn from being walked on.

02E1694:64:03 (fig. 11.2) has its sole in better condition but the backpart has been cut away to convert the brogue to a mule and allow for further wear after its owner had outgrown it.

02E1694:64:25 (fig. 11.3) is an adult-sized brogue which, like the others in the assemblage, is simply a larger example of the children's sizes, equally worn with some evidence for conversion to mules as well. Its vamp would appear to have been reused or repaired. The original sole seam has been cut away and the vamp reattached by stitching down through the rand. A line of rough stitch holes runs around the edges where the seam was made. The heel area was also repaired and a row of tunnel stitches across the waist indicates where a clump patch was attached. Such excessive wear and conversion suggests either a considerable level of poverty or a scarcity of leather or both.

11.4 Complete backpart assembly of a brogue with latchets and lacing thong *in situ* (Photo: J. Nicholl)

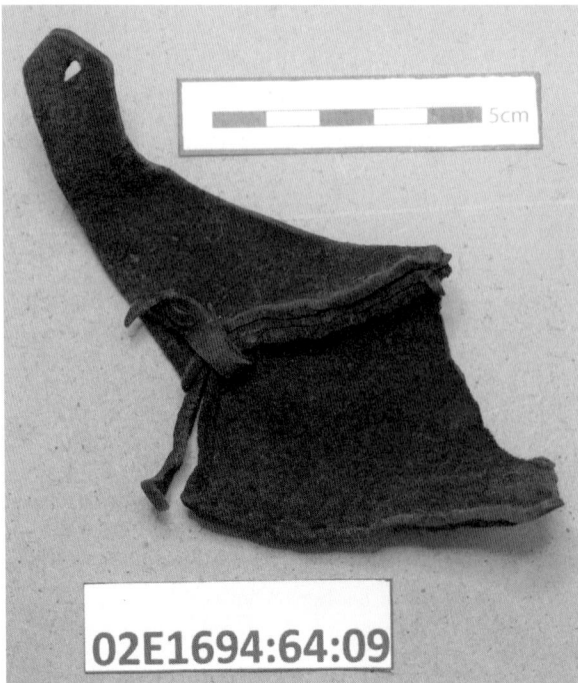

11.5 Detailed view of backpart wing showing latchet seam with insert (Photo: J. Nicholl)

02E1649:64:19 (fig. 11.4) is a complete brogue backpart assembly that has separated from its vamp. The bifurcated lacing thong remains *in situ* on the right latchet and the seams are reinforced with strips of knotted thong as already described. The backpart rises above the back of the heel to form a tab to facilitate putting the brogue on the foot.

02E1649:64:09 (fig. 11.5) is a right backpart wing and a good example of latchet construction. The closed seam between the latchet and backpart is intact and the insert strip is clearly visible. The three parts are further secured with a strip of knotted thong, which may have helped to locate the parts during assembly. This detail was also noted on the side seams of a number of early medieval boots from Drumclay crannog (Nicholl 2016).

The shoes

Unlike the brogues, which show little variation in design, there are a number of different shoe patterns, which reflect changes of fashion in the sixteenth and early seventeenth centuries. As with the brogues, there are a number of examples of children's shoes, of which three are complete and four incomplete. The children's shoes are simply smaller versions of adult shoes with the same style and number of component parts.

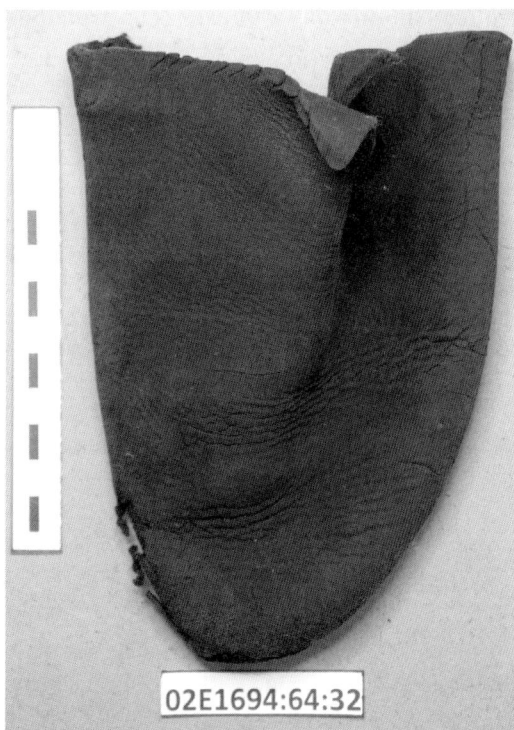

11.6 Vamp of early sixteenth-century slip-on shoe (Photo: J. Nicholl)

02E1694:64:32

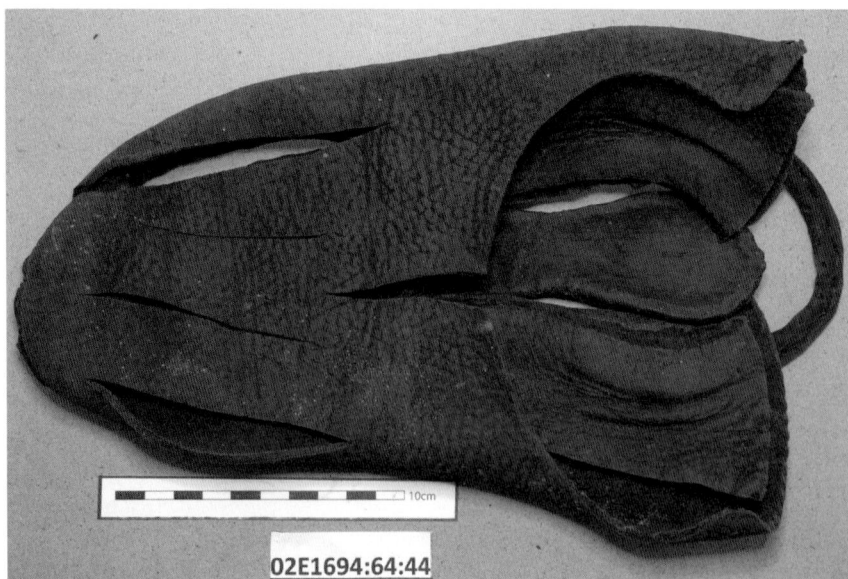

11.7 Shoe with slashed vamp – decorative or medicinal? (Photo: J. Nicholl)

02E1694:64:32 (fig. 11.6) is an intact vamp of an early to mid-sixteenth-century slip-on shoe of turnshoe construction. The shoe upper was originally made of two parts, the vamp and backpart. The side seams were stitched to the backpart using a butted seam. The grain/flesh awl holes along the sole seam appear to be grouped in pairs rather than at regular intervals. There is no vamp tongue and a short slit cut into the vamp at the instep facilitated putting the shoe on the foot. Between the edge of this slit and the top of the side-seam, a series of small cuts have been made in the leather along the upper edge to give a decorative, feathered effect. In Volken's classification of shoe styles, this style of shoe is classified as Style DD and dated to the first half of the sixteenth century (Volken 2012, 298). A number of examples were recovered from the *Mary Rose* wreck which sank in 1545 and are classified as Type 2.1 shoes with straight-throated vamps without wings (Gardiner 2005, 66). In Derrick's *Images of Ireland*, published in 1581, the depiction of 'Donolle obreane the messenger' shows the watching English infantry wearing a similar type of shoe (McClintock 1943, 36).

02E1694:64:42 and **02E1694:64:44** are variations on Volken's Style V, a mid-sixteenth-century shoe style with a one-piece upper, seamed at the heel (Volken 2012, 68–9). **64:44** (fig. 11.7) is an especially interesting example. It is a welted shoe with traces of a heel-lift impression and the quarters are reinforced on the inside with two lining pieces. The vamp has been slashed

11.8 Detail from Derrick's *Image of Ireland* (1581) depicting Sir Henry Sidney wearing slashed shoes

with four long cuts running from the instep to the toe. A long slit has also been cut in the centre of the vamp at the instep to facilitate putting on the shoe. The vamp instep has been further decorated with three punched motif patterns. The quarter linings are heavily worn and slightly flattened from wear. Slashed shoes were fashionable in the late sixteenth century as a way of displaying coloured hose and stockings. A further image from Derrick's *Images of Ireland* depicts Sir Henry Sidney wearing slashed shoes as he receives the submission of Turlough O'Neill (McClintock 1943, 38) (fig. 11.8).

Mules

Fashionable footwear is further represented by two examples of elaborately decorated mules. Mules were worn by both men and women and generally for indoor wear. The vamps could be made from a combination of embroidered textiles or soft leather and were worn by individuals of high status and wealth. Mules are commonly depicted footwear in portraits of the sixteenth and seventeenth century.

11.9 Mule with incised decoration on vamp (Photo: J. Nicholl)

02E1694:64:04 (fig. 11.9), the first of the Chancery Lane examples, was of welted construction and the vamp is decorated with a pattern of incised crosses. This vamp is made from two layers of thin goatskin leather placed flesh side to flesh side. The two layers were whip stitched across the instep. The incised cross motifs may have been embroidered.

02E1694:64:41 (fig. 11.10), the second example, has an intact insole and the remnants of a welt and heel cover. The insole seat shows traces of a decorative herringbone pattern, which may have been dyed. The vamp was originally made from two layers of thin leather, which were stitched flesh side to flesh side. The instep was again whip stitched across vamp throat. Only fragments of the outer layer remain and this outer layer may have been dyed. The grain pattern is indistinct but is probably goatskin. Most of welt remains and the heel cover is complete, but the heel is missing. In this case the heel was probably made of wood and similar to examples recovered from Mill Street in Dublin (Nicholl 2017). The mules were originally very finely made and both suggest a level of wealth and comfort.

There are three further examples of stacked heels of the early 'spring heel' style where several lifts of leather were sandwiched between the inner and outer soles. Shoes of similar construction were recovered from excavations at the early Jamestown settlement in North America and can be dated to 1607 (Saguto 2007, 144–50).

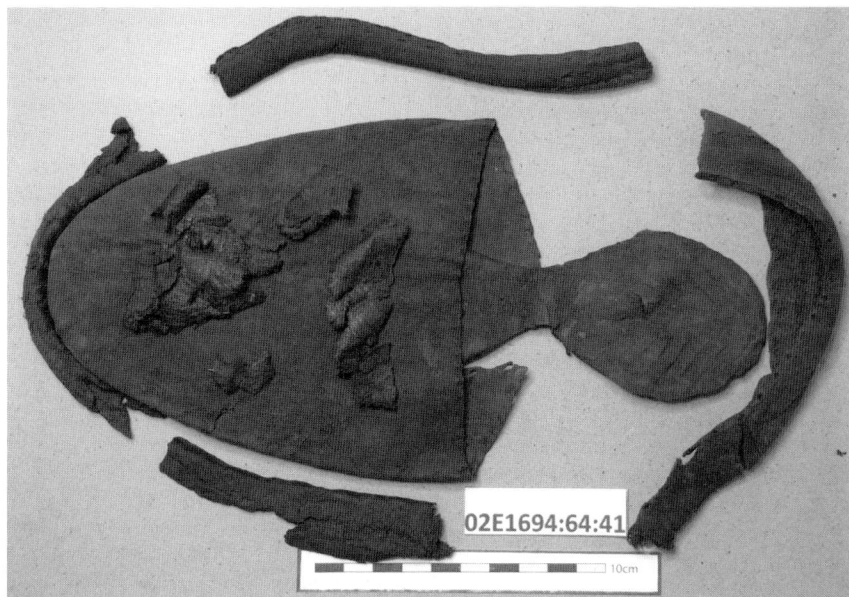

11.10 Mule with decorated insole (Photo: J. Nicholl)

Hybrid shoe

02E1694:55:01 (fig. 11.11) combines elements of both brogues and shoes. The upper is constructed with a vamp and separate right and left quarters seamed at the heel. This seam is stitched from the outside with thread using grain/edge stitches. The side seams are stitched on the inside, also with thread and using flesh/edge stitches. The single sole with a broad rand is stitched with a length of thong using a serpentine S stitch. A shorter length of flat thong is used to stitch a heel stiffener inside the heel seam. The side seams are low and the vamp has a long narrow tongue, which is typical of shoes of late sixteenth-century date. There are two pairs of holes at the base of the tongue, one of which may have been used to secure a shoe rose and could be taken as an indication of fashion consciousness. Shoe roses were a popular fashion from the 1590s to the 1620s. The roses were made from narrow lengths of decorative lace and arranged into floral head shapes, which came to be known as shoe roses. The roses, which were worn by men and women, were deliberately made to complement the costume of the wearer and were secured to the tongue of the vamp (Swann 1982, 12). Decorative shoe roses are a common feature of portraits of the nobility of the period, such as the portrait of James I and Anne of Denmark by Renold Elstrack *c.*1610 (Ribiero 2005, 24).

Examples of this type of hybrid shoe, combining elements of shoes and brogues, have been recorded from New Street in Dublin (Nicholl 2004) and

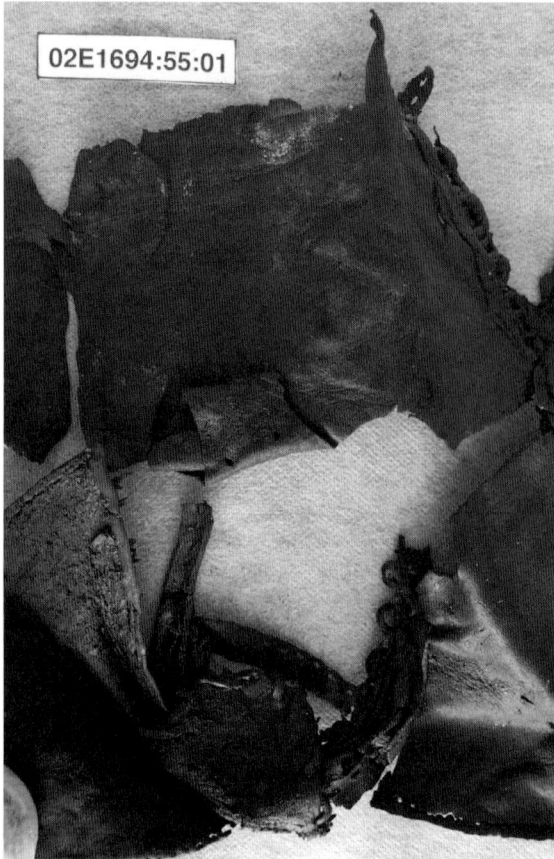

02E1694:55:01

11.11 Detail of hybrid shoe/
brogue (Photo: J. Nicholl)

also from the abandoned, early seventeenth-century plantation settlement of
Salterstown, Co. Derry (Neill 1991). Such footwear suggests that the brogue-
maker and the shoemaker were familiar with each other's work. It might also
suggest they worked in close proximity or collaborated in producing a product
where the shoemaker assembled the uppers and the brogue-maker attached the
sole.

Foot ailments

There are four examples of deliberate cuts being made to adult-size shoes and
child-size brogues. The adult shoe has already been mentioned as a possible
high-fashion item, which would be in keeping with the slashed vamp, which is
stamped with a decorative motif. However, the deep cut at the instep might
suggest another interpretation for the slashing. It is possible the shoe was made
for an injured and swollen foot with the slashing intended to relieve pressure
on a swollen or deformed toe joint. A second shoe, **02E1694:64:38** (fig. 11.12),

11.12 Shoe with slashed vamp to ease pressure on injured toe (Photo: J. Nicholl)

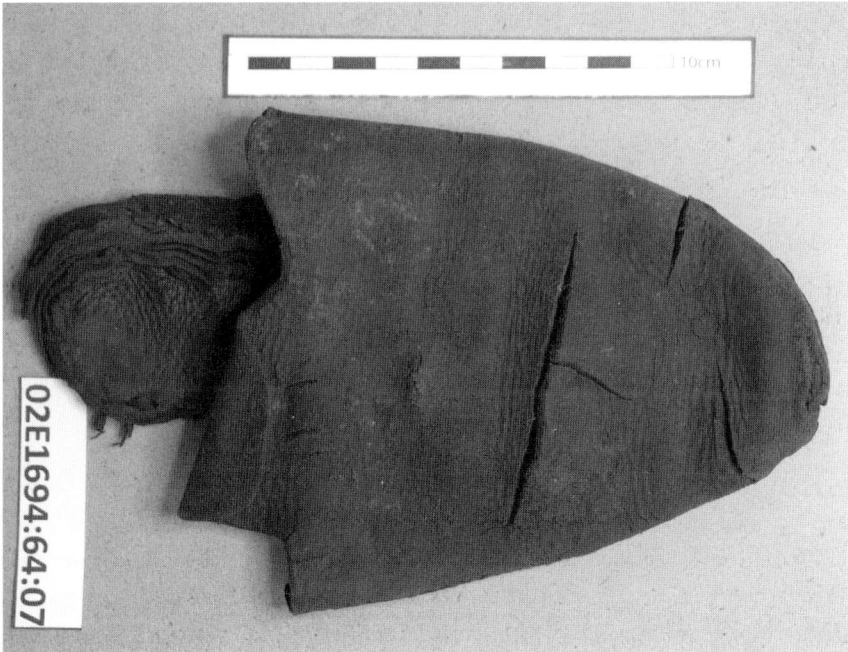

11.13 Brogue with slashed vamp for a swollen foot (Photo: J. Nicholl)

has three slits cut into the vamp over the area of the big toe joint to relieve pressure at this point. The child's brogue, **02E1694:64:27**, has a triangular piece removed from the vamp which would have allowed the toe joint to protrude. The sole also has heavy wear-damage at the tread, which suggests the condition of 'hammer toe' from consistently wearing narrow and tight shoes (Grew and de Neergaard 1988, 105–11). A second brogue, **02E1694:64:07** (fig. 11.13), also in a child's size, has three large transverse cuts across the vamp and the backpart had been removed. The largest cut is across the instep and the other two are on either side of the toe area. They would appear to have been made to relieve pressure on an injured foot, which was swollen across the instep. The leather of the vamp still retains the impression of the swelling.

Brogue and shoe laces

All of the brogues and shoes in the assemblage were secured with either textile laces or leather thonging and examples of both survive. Two shoes, **02E1694:64:02** (fig. 11.14) and **02E1694:64:05**, have a short length of textile lace *in situ* through holes in the narrow latchets of the left and right quarters. **02E1694:64:22** (fig. 11.15) contained the remnants of three shoes, including a complete example of a textile shoelace. It appears to be of finely woven silk, which was folded and twisted to form a point at each end for threading through the lace holes on the latchets and vamp. It is probable that these

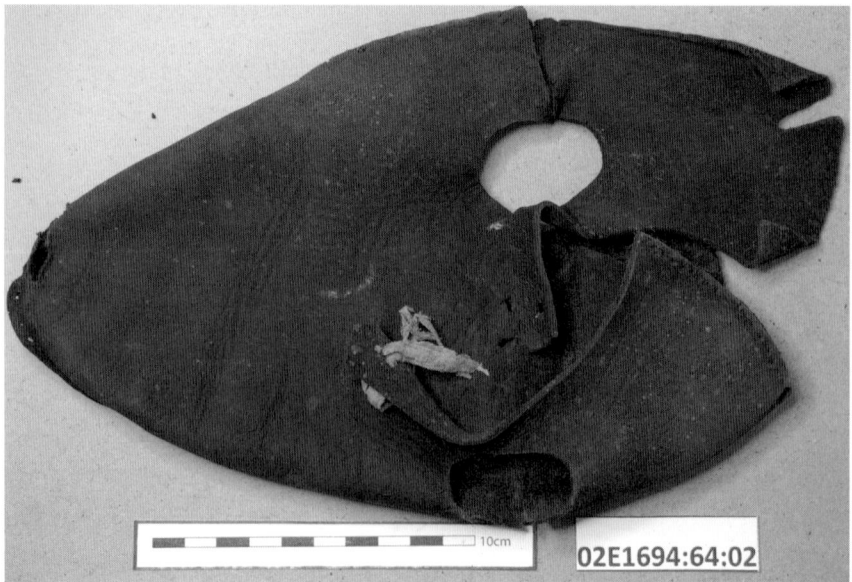

11.14 Shoe with fragment of lace *in situ* on latchet (Photo: J. Nicholl)

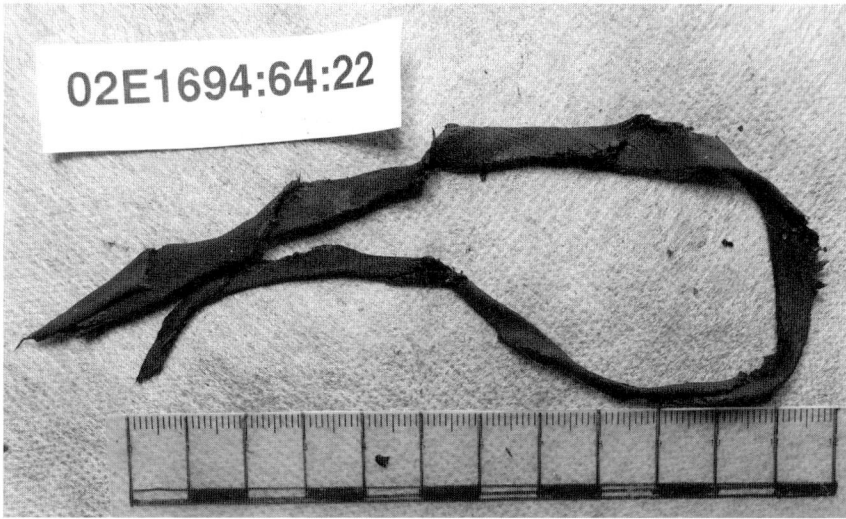

11.15 Shoe lace (Photo: J. Nicholl)

terminals were fitted with copper alloy aiglets, which are now no longer attached. The brogues were laced with bifurcated thonging, which passed through paired holes in the latchet terminals and on the vamps. **02E1694:64** retains its thonging lace *in situ* through paired holes in the right latchet.

CONCLUSION

The shoe finds from the Chancery Lane quarry are typical of similar finds from elsewhere in Dublin and further afield in Britain, the Continent and settlements in North America, such as Jamestown, Virginia. They are clearly in keeping with the fashions of the period. However, the most interesting aspect of the leather assemblage is the large number of brogues present. To date, the Chancery Lane brogues represent the largest number of brogues recovered from a single site in Ireland. They are clear evidence of the continuation of an indigenous tradition of footwear manufacture over a long period in Ireland. The presence of both children's and adult's sizes adds to their significance. The extremely worn and repaired nature of the brogues suggests a significant level of poverty and offers a glimpse of the hardships of life for some of the population of Dublin in the late sixteenth and early seventeenth centuries.[1]

1 I would like to express my gratitude to Claire Walsh for giving me access to the Chancery Lane excavation archive and for answering all of my many questions.

BIBLIOGRAPHY

Goubitz, O. et al., 2001 *Stepping through time: archaeological footwear from prehistoric times until 1800*. Zwolle: Foundation for Promoting Archaeology.

Grew, F. and de Neergaard, M. 1988 *Shoes and pattens*. London: Boydell Press.

Hall, Mr and Mrs 1840, *Ireland: its scenery, character etc.*, vol. 1. London.

Lucas, A.T. 1956 'Footwear in Ireland', *Journal of the County Louth Archaeological Society*, 13:4, 309–94.

McClintock, H.F. 1943, *Old Irish and Highland dress*. Dundalk: Dundalgan Press.

Neill, M. 2014 'The leather objects'. In C.J. Lynn and J.A. McDowell (eds), *Deer Park Farms: the excavation of a raised rath in the Glenarm Valley, Co. Antrim*. Northern Ireland Archaeological Monographs 9. Belfast: The Stationery Office/Northern Ireland Environmental Agency.

Neill, M. 1991 'The Salterstown leather report'. In O. Miller, 'Archaeological investigations at Salterstown, County Londonderry, Northern Ireland'. PhD University of Pennsylvania.

Nicholl, J. 2017 'More than just mud at the bottom of the pond', *Archaeology Ireland* 31:1, 33–7.

Nicholl, J. 2004 'The leather finds from Chancery Lane, Dublin'. Unpublished leather finds catalogue, for Archaeology Projects Ltd.

Nicholl, J. 2016 'The leather finds from Drumclay Crannog, Co. Fermanagh'. Unpublished specialist report, Dept. of Communities, NI.

Sagudo, D.A. 2007 'Footprints on the past'. In D. Montgomery et al. (eds), *1607: Jamestown and the New World*, chap. 21. Williamsburg: The Williamsburg Foundation.

Swann, J. 1982 *Shoes*. London: Batsford Ltd.

Volken, M. 2013 *Archaeological footwear: development of shoe patterns and styles from prehistory till the 1600s*. Lausanne.

Wallace, P. 2016 *Viking Dublin: the Wood Quay excavations*. Dublin: Irish Academic Press.

Walton, J. 1992 *The royal charters of Waterford*. Dublin: Criterion Press.

Walsh, C. 2009 'An early medieval roadway at Chancery Lane: from Duibhlinn to Ath Cliath?'. In S. Duffy (ed.), *Medieval Dublin IX*, pp 9–30. Dublin: Four Courts Press.

Webb, J.J. 1925 *The guilds of Dublin*. Dublin: Three Candles Press.

From mayor of Dublin to barons of Scrine: the Mareward family in Ireland, *c.*1360–1564

RANDOLPH JONES

INTRODUCTION

Previous volumes of this series have carried essays on Dublin's urban elite and the transformation of some its families from a mercantile background to county gentry.[1] The following essay concentrates on the Mareward family, which rose to prominence in the last quarter of the fourteenth century.[2] Although the Marewards probably came from an English gentry background to begin with, the foundation of its success rested on two marriages contracted by its founder in Ireland. This advanced him from a man-at-arms and minor officeholder, to country gentleman and prominent citizen within a short period of time. The Mareward family maintained its close connections with both Dublin county and city until 1487. Thereafter, it struggled to maintain itself, thanks to the early deaths of successive heads, the long periods spent by their underage heirs as wards, and ultimately its failure to produce enough male offspring to guarantee its own survival.

The present writer started collecting these notes several years ago but had difficulty untangling the first four members of the family – thanks to their all being called Thomas! Previous writers have often conflated them to two, sometimes one person, arising from the fragmentary nature of the surviving evidence. It is largely due to the repertory of the Irish exchequer memoranda rolls, compiled under the direction of William Lynch in the late 1820s, that it has proved possible to separate them and trace the line of descent from their founder member until firmer ground is reached in the mid-fifteenth century. It is for this reason that this essay concentrates primarily on the first five generations. The long decline of the family through the sixteenth century has been narrated elsewhere. To help place each individual, their descent back to the founder of the family is given in the header of each subsection.

---

1 Charles Smith, 'Patricians in medieval Dublin: the career of the Sargent family' in Seán Duffy (ed.), *Medieval Dublin XI* (Dublin, 2011), pp 219–28; Brian Coleman, 'Urban elite: the county and civic elite of later medieval Dublin' in Seán Duffy (ed.), *Medieval Dublin XV* (Dublin, 2016), pp 293–304.   2 Initially rendered in the sources as Maureward and Mawreward, eventually transforming into Mareward, the version preferred in the article, and then into Marward, Marwood and other variants.

Thomas I (d.1395)

Thomas, the founder of the Mareward family in Ireland, was probably the younger son of Sir John Maureward of Goadby Marwood, Leicestershire. Sir John died in 1346, leaving a sixteen-year old heir, William, and so it is feasible he may have produced other sons before he died.[3] The arms of the Maureward family in England were *azure, a fess argent between three cinquefoils or*.[4] The Irish branch bore the same arms, but with different tinctures.[5] The English branch failed in the male line when Sir John's grandson, Sir Thomas Maureward, died in 1424, leaving an heiress Philippa, married to Sir Thomas Beaumont.[6]

Thomas probably arrived in Ireland as a man-at-arms in the retinue of James Butler, second earl of Ormond, when the latter was appointed justiciar in 1359. On 6 April 1360, Ormond appointed Thomas seneschal of the king's manors in Co. Dublin, but on 1 December 1361 he was replaced by Walter Somery, who came to Ireland in the retinue of the recently arrived Lionel, duke of Clarence, the king's second son and his lieutenant in Ireland.[7] Nothing further is heard of Thomas until November 1368, when he served during a 20-day expedition against the O'Nolans led by Thomas de Burley, prior of Kilmainham and chancellor of Ireland. The other retinue leaders were James Butler, earl of Ormond, Sir Robert de Preston, Sir Robert Holywode, Eustace de Leawe, Sir Robert Tyrrell, baron of Castleknock, Sir James de la Hyde, Patrick and Robert de la Freigne, John Troye, clerk, William de Carlell, clerk, Dermot McMurrough, William fitz William, Walter Harold, Henry Walsch, John Calf and William Orory. Unfortunately, neither the size of the individual retinues, nor the sums paid to their captains (from which they could be calculated), are known.[8]

In 1373/4, Thomas was distrained for allegedly receiving 10 marks from Thomas bishop of Ferns, which the latter owed John de Troye, who died indebted to the king.[9] Thomas was also nominated one of John de Asteley's attorneys in Ireland, when the latter had letters enrolled at Westminster on 6 February 1374.[10] In a muster roll dated 18 October 1374, Thomas was twice

3 *Calendar of inquisitions post mortem and other analogous documents preserved in the Public Record Office*. vol. VIII, Edward III (London, 1913), p. 469.   **4** William Burton, *The description of Leicestershire: containing matters of antiquity, history, armoury, and genealogy*, 2nd edn (Lynn, 1777), pp 108 and 198–9.   **5** Sir Bernard Burke, *The general armory of England, Scotland, Ireland, and Wales; comprising a registry of armorial bearings from the earliest to the present time* (London, 1884), pp 659 and 665. Vert, a fess between three cinquefoils, or.   **6** J.S Roskell, L. Clark, C. Rawcliffe (eds), *The history of parliament: the house of commons 1386–1421* (1993).   **7** Áine Foley, *The royal manors of medieval County Dublin: crown and community* (Dublin, 2013), p. 201, quoting NAI RC 8/27, pp 578–9 and RC 8/28, p. 91; Philomena Connolly, 'Lionel of Clarence and Ireland, 1361–1366' (PhD, TCD, 1994), p. 307.   **8** NLI, MS 761, fo. 255.   **9** College of Arms, MS Ph 15170, p. 99 (Exch, mem. roll, 48, 49 Edw. III, m. 47.).   **10** *CPR 1370–74*, p. 407. Asteley had been listed as a man-at-arms serving in the retinue of Sir William Windsor, a former lieutenant of Ireland, now its governor and keeper.[11] Windsor was then based at Castledermot, campaigning against the Leinster Irish.[12] Thomas appears to have been new to the retinue, for he was not listed in an earlier muster roll dated 18 February 1374.[13]

On 1 February 1375, Thomas appointed John fitz Raymond Feypo and William Frere as his attorneys in Ireland.[14] Two days later he was granted letters of protection as he was going to England on the king's service.[15] The reason for his intended journey is not known, but the Irish parliament met in Dublin on 20 January and failed to grant Windsor a subsidy. It is possible that Thomas was to have been part of a delegation to the king's council in England to report on the situation in Ireland and to plead for more money. The king responded on 30 March, sending Windsor 2000 marks by the hands of Robert Eure and Thomas Holhurst, promising to send the balance of £11,213 6s. 8d. he owed in back pay for Windsor's indentured retinue of 200 men-at-arms and 400 archers within three weeks.[16] However, it is unlikely that Thomas went to England, because on 11 February 1375, Windsor appointed James Butler, earl of Ormond, Hugh Cromp and Thomas to seek out any merchants in counties Dublin, Meath, Louth, Cork, Limerick, Kilkenny, Waterford and Wexford who had avoided prisage on wines landed in Ireland, by obtaining letters patent from the prince of Wales, certifying that they had paid this duty in the prince's duchy of Cornwall.[17] This was followed on 20 March by two more commissions, one appointing John More, Geoffrey Gallan and Thomas to search all ships in the ports of Dublin, Dalkey and Clontarf for any grain exported out of Ireland contrary to the ordinances, and another appointing John More, Nicholas Serjeant, the mayor of Dublin and Thomas, to search for any grain held in the city, arrest any citizens or merchants who were found to be hoarding it, and release it for sale in the market at a reasonable price.[18]

Soon after Thomas's arrival in Ireland, he married Katherine, the second surviving daughter of Sir Francis Feypo, baron of Scrine (Skreen). When Sir Francis died in 1363, he was succeeded by his son John, a minor, whose wardship was granted to Thomas Marnham and William Roshalle.[19] Despite

serving in Ireland in the retinues of various justiciars since the 1350s.   11 TNA, E101/33/34, from the AHRC-funded 'The soldier in later medieval England online database', at www.medievalsoldier.org.   12 CIRCLE, CR 48 Edw. III, §73, 86, 210 and 211. 13 TNA, E101/33/35.   14 CIRCLE, PR 49 Edw. III, §14 (RCH 90/14).   15 CIRCLE, PR 49 Edw. III, §16 (RCH 90/16).   16 A.J. Otway-Ruthven, *A history of medieval Ireland* (London, 1968), pp 304–5; Philomena Connolly, 'Financing expeditions to Ireland, 1361–1376' in James Lydon (ed.), *England and Ireland in the latter Middle Ages: essays in honour of Jocelyn Otway-Ruthven* (Blackrock, 1981), p. 116; H.G. Richardson and George Sayles, *Parliaments and councils of medieval Ireland*, vol. I (Dublin, 1947), pp 55–6. Both Eure and Holhurst are listed in the 1374 muster rolls serving as men-at-arms in Windsor's retinue. 17 CIRCLE, PR 49 Edw. III, §206 (RCH 95/205).   18 CIRCLE, PR 49 Edw. III, §207 and 214 (RCH 95/206 and 96/213).   19 *Calendar of fine rolls 1356–68*, pp 260 and 281.

being underage, John was already married to a lady called Juliana, as Sir Francis had granted them both a carucate of land in Scrine before he died.[20] John seems to have gained his majority by 15 February 1372, when the seneschal of Meath was ordered to summon him to parliament, though not as a peer.[21] John seems to have died in 1375, with his title and lands in Co. Meath passing to his nearest male relative, John fitz Nicholas Feypo. How John fitz Nicholas was related to John fitz Francis is not known, but he may have been a first cousin. However, the manor of Santry (*Sauntreff*), which Sir Francis held in Co. Dublin directly from the crown in return for 40s. scutage paid each time royal service was proclaimed, does not seem to have been entailed in the male line. As a result, when their brother John died, Santry passed to his four sisters: Joan, married to Sir Robert Beverley; Katherine, married to Thomas Mareward; Ela or Alice, married to John Freignes; and Margaret, who was then unmarried. On 20 November 1375, the barons of the Irish exchequer ordered the sheriff of Meath to distrain the four sisters and three husbands, in the mistaken belief that they were the inheritors of all of Sir Francis's lands. Similar instructions were also sent to the sheriff of Dublin to distrain them for payment of relief on Santry. Their homage for the same was respited until Easter 1376, presumably on payment of a fine.[22]

By this time, Katherine Feypo was dead. Sometime between 5 May 1373 and 1 June 1375, Thomas married Cecilia, the widow of Richard Heygreve, twice mayor of Dublin.[23] Heygreve died childless, leaving all his premises in Dublin to his wife for the term of her life, with remainder to the confraternity of St Katherine, in the church of St Michael in the High Street.[24] Heygreve's property included a lease on the parcel of Santry held by Joan Feypo (Katherine's sister), comprising one messuage and one-and-a-half carucates of land in return for an annual rent of seven marks. Although Thomas and Celia subsequently intruded into this parcel, on the alleged basis that Heygreve's lease was for a term of years, rather than for his life, it was subsequently seized into the king's hands, because Joan had alienated it to Heygreve without a royal licence. It was also alleged that Heygreve was illegitimate and his property should have been escheated to the crown when he died because he had no heir.[25] On 22 May 1375, Thomas was granted temporary custody of Joan's lands and on 1 June pardoned for his previous intrusion.[26] The king seems to

20 College of Arms, MS Ph 15173, p. 39 (Exchequer memoranda roll, 3 Hen. IV). **21** CIRCLE, CR 46 Edw. III, §123 (RCH 84/114).   **22** College of Arms, MS Ph15170, p. 342 (Exch. mem. roll, 49, 50 Edw. III, m. 63).   **23** J. Gilbert Smyly, 'Old deeds in the library of Trinity College – III', *Hermathena*, 69 (1947), no. 90; RCH 92/113. Heygreue, Hegreue, Hygreue and Hegrue, appear to be various renditions of the place-name Haygrove, a village near Bridgwater in Somerset, with which Dublin and other east coast ports had trading links.   **24** CIRCLE, PR 18 Ric .II, §50 (RCH 152/50).   **25** CIRCLE, PR 49 Edw. III, §113 (RCH 92/113).   **26** CIRCLE, PR 49 Edw. III, §87 (RCH 92/87); Benjamin William Adams, *History and description of Santry and Cloghran parishes, county*

have retained them under the Statute of Absences, because Joan was living in England.[27] Her husband Sir Robert Beverley, constable of Newcastle McKinegan during the justiciarship of Sir Thomas Rokeby, seems to have returned to England soon after the arrival in Ireland of Lionel, duke of Clarence, and died there in the early 1370s.[28] Joan subsequently married one Roger Rale and on 26 June 1376, as the wife of such, she was granted letters of protection and general attorney under the Irish great seal, as she was about to go overseas. She probably returned to Ireland temporarily after the death of her brother John in an attempt to protect her share of his lands.[29] As well as Joan's parcel of Santry, Thomas also retained that of his former wife, Katherine Feypo, thanks to the practice known as 'courtesy of England'. Thomas obtained a further interest when he and Philip fitz Eustace were granted custody of one messuage and one carucate of land in Collinstown (*Colyneston and Towaneston*), formerly held by John Crump on 15 July 1384.[30] The rents and services due from these lands were later held by Thomas's descendants.

As a member now of Co. Dublin's gentry, Thomas began to serve in several administrative capacities. On 22 December 1375, he was one of those charged by the governor, Sir William Windsor, to elect two of their number to send to England as representatives of the county.[31] It was hoped that if the county representatives from Ireland had to face the king in person, they would be more amenable to voting a local subsidy, for the support of Windsor's administration.

On 12 May 1378, Thomas was appointed keeper of the peace in the barony or cantred of Clondalkin.[32] On 20 October of the same year, he was one of the two justices appointed to keep the ordinances and statutes relating to workmen and labourers in Co. Dublin. He apparently heard cases in his own seat, for in the following year, he heard one in Santry, fining the mayor and bailiffs of Dublin 100s. for not returning a writ to him.[33]

Thomas was elected sheriff of Co. Dublin in November 1378. As such, he proffered at the exchequer during the Michaelmas term of 1379. In November of the same year, Thomas and five other men sought compensation for accompanying the justiciar, Alexander Balscot, bishop of Ossory, to Baltinglass with 128 men-at-arms, archers and hobelars, where the bishop parleyed

Dublin (London, 1883), p. 22, NAI, Lodge MS 19, no. 201. **27** *Cal. fine rolls, 1356–68*, p. 260. **28** Philomena Connolly (ed.), *Irish exchequer payments 1270–1446* (Dublin, 1998), pp 459, 468, 471, 479, 486, 504, 506; Frederick Devon (ed.), *Issue roll of Thomas de Brantingham, bishop of Exeter, lord high treasurer of England; containing payments made out of his majesty's revenue in the 44th year of king Edward III, AD 1370* (London, 1835), pp 393, 434. **29** CIRCLE, PR 49 Edw. III, §123–4 (RCH 93/123–4). **30** CIRCLE, PR 8 Ric. II, §25 (RCH 119/16); Adams, *Santry*, p. 49. **31** Maud V. Clarke, 'William of Windsor in Ireland 1369–1376', *PRIA*, 41C (1932–4), 128. **32** College of Arms, MS Ph15171, pp 97 and 140 (Exch. mem. roll, 3, 4 Ric. II, mm. 16 and 53). **33** CIRCLE, CR 3 Ric .II, §33 with the lieges of counties Carlow and Kildare for three days, as well as McMurrough, O'Nolan, O'Byrne and O'Toole.[34] Because of this service, Thomas was excused from rendering his account at the exchequer as the former sheriff of Dublin, thanks to a letter from the justiciar dated 25 January 1380, stating that Thomas had been with him on the king's service.[35] On 8 March 1382 Thomas was appointed one of the keepers of the peace for the county. He was appointed again on 8 May 1389.[36] On 20 January 1386, he was also appointed the seneschal of the king's manor of Crumlin, Co. Dublin.[37]

Thomas's marriage to Cecilia Heygreve also gave him the wherewithal to cut a dash among Dublin's civic elite and was probably admitted as a citizen soon afterwards.[38] He certainly had joint control of her property, as seen by a lease they made together on 10 June 1392 to Adam Piers, chaplain, of a messuage in Rupell Street (otherwise Rochelle Street, now Back Lane), formerly held by Heygreve.[39] Thomas also acquired property of his own within the city. In 1374, one Richard de Kerrdeyff granted him a messuage in Picottislane, St Michael's parish (Schoolhouse Lane, off High Street).[40] Thomas is also mentioned in a rental compiled on 31 May 1382, as holding a tenancy within the city, formerly held by Robert Fold, for a pair of gilt spurs or 12*d*. rendered annually to the archbishop of Dublin.[41] On 28 July 1385, Thomas was granted by the mayor and commonalty of Dublin for life, the Pool mill (in Ship Street Little), together with its appurtenances, for an annual rent of 13*s*. 4*d*. in silver.[42] On 'the fourth Friday after the Nativity' (20 January) 1391, they also granted him a messuage lying outside the gate of St Patrick's (in Patrick Street) for an annual rent of 12*d*.[43]

Thomas's acceptance within Dublin society is demonstrated by William de la Chaumbre, archdeacon of Dublin, nominating him as one of his attorneys in Ireland while he remained in England for one year. The letters were enrolled at Westminster on 28 February 1376.[44] He also began to appear on document witness lists as one of Dublin's prominent citizens after the names of the mayor and bailiffs.[45] From Michaelmas 1384, Thomas served as one of the two bailiffs of the mayor, Roger Bekeford.[46] In the following year, he sat on a jury empanelled to hear a long-running dispute on the 'tollboll', a tax-in-kind on

(RCH 107/30); Adams, *Santry*, p. 83.   **34** CIRCLE, CR 3 Ric. II, §12 (RCH 106/9). **35** College of Arms, MS Ph15171, p. 97, 114 and 141 (Exch. Mem. Roll, 3, 4 Ric. II). **36** CIRCLE, PR 5 Ric. II, §206 (RCH 115/206); PR 12 Ric. II, §242 (RCH 142/241). **37** CIRCLE, PR 9 Ric. II, §219 (RCH 127/219).   **38** *CCD*, no. 247.   **39** *CCD*, no. 775. **40** *CCD*, no. 730.   **41** James Mills, 'Notices of the manor of St Sepulchre, Dublin, in the fourteenth century', *JRSAI*, 9:78 (1889), 123; *CCD*, no. 730.   **42** *CARD*, i, pp 125–6. **43** *CCD*, no. 255. The printed calendar has 'Friday, 4th day after the Nativity, 14 Richard II', which is probably an error, as the fourth day after Christmas in 14 Richard II (1390) was a Thursday. The city's quarter assembly meetings were normally held the fourth Friday after the feast days of Michaelmas, Christmas, Easter, and St John's Day.   **44** *CPR 1374–77*, p. 252.   **45** *CCD*, no. 247.   **46** Smyly, 'Old deeds III', no. 102.

ale brewed in the city traditionally due to the abbot and convent of St Thomas the Martyr.[47] On 9 January 1386, Thomas was also one of the citizens appointed to oversee the collection and expenditure of ferry tolls for the repair of the city's single bridge over the river Liffey, which had collapsed in the previous year.[48]

At Michaelmas 1389, Thomas was elected mayor of Dublin for the ensuing year and appointed Thomas Cusake and William Wade as his two bailiffs.[49] During his term in office, Sir John Stanley, the justiciar, led an expedition to St Mullins, Co. Carlow, for which he recruited several Dublin citizens into his retinue, including Thomas and his son, as men-at-arms. On this occasion, Thomas senior led a small retinue of eight archers.[50] Further military service occurred in 1392, when Thomas stayed with his men for six days at Naas, resisting Irish enemies, for which he was later reimbursed 40s.[51]

Thomas was elected mayor of Dublin for a second time at Michaelmas 1392. His bailiffs were Thomas Donewith and Ralph Ebb.[52] Shortly after his election, Mareward allegedly attacked the abbey of St Thomas the Martyr with a mob,[53] after he and John Drake had been bribed by Richard Totterby and other canons from the abbey. Their alleged intention was to eject or kill John Sergeant, Totterby's rival as abbot. During the disturbances, some of the abbey's windows were broken, personal possessions stolen (mainly arms and armour), and at least one man killed. Although the justiciar, James Butler, earl of Ormond, sent men to quell the riot, the mob ignored them and recovered several of their fellows who had been detained by the justiciar's men.[54] Despite the accusation of wrongdoing, it seems that Mareward's action was legitimate, but probably got out of hand in its execution. On 26 September 1392, the king sent individual writs to Ormond as justiciar, the mayor and bailiffs of Dublin, and the sheriffs of counties Dublin, Kildare and Meath, ordering them to arrest Sergeant for offending against the Statute of Provisors, because Sergeant had obtained his office by travelling to Rome, seeking papal bulls to displace Totterby, who had been elected abbot by the convent in Dublin with

47 Henry F. Berry, 'Proceedings in the matter of the custom called tollboll, 1308 and 1385. St Thomas's Abbey v. some early Dublin brewers, &c.', *PRIA*, 28C (1910), 171. 48 *CARD*, i, pp 26–7. 49 H.F. Berry, 'Catalogue of the mayors, provosts and bailiffs of Dublin city, AD 1229 to 1447' in Howard Clarke (ed.), *Medieval Dublin: the living city* (Dublin, 1990), p. 161. 50 TNA E101/41/18 m. 10, from 'The soldier in later medieval England online database', at www.medievalsoldier.org; Otway-Ruthven, *Medieval Ireland*, p. 322. 51 CIRCLE, CR 16 Ric. II, §14 (RCH 150/14). 52 In published works, the mayor for this year is usually referred to as *John* Mareward, but no one with that name ever served as bailiff of the city, a prerequisite to becoming mayor. It is possible that the abbreviation 'Tho.', as it clearly appears in Harris' MS 13 mentioned in the following footnote, has been misread by Archdall as 'Jno.'. 53 On which, see Duffy in this volume, above. 54 Mervyn Archdall, *Monasticon Hibernicum; or, An history of the abbeys, priories, and other religious houses in Ireland* (London, 1786), p. 194; NLI, Harris MS 13, fos. 185–7. This Ormond was the son of the one mentioned previously.

the king's licence.[55] The matter was probably exacerbated by the city's dispute over the tollboll and other payments due to the abbey from its fee-farm, which had fallen several years into arrears. Only William Fitzhugh, a London goldsmith, was charged over the incident, and then for allegedly receiving 100 marks' worth of items stolen by Totterby from Sergeant, to raise the 40 marks with which he allegedly bribed Mareward and Drake. Fitzhugh quickly received a pardon.[56] Certainly, Mareward's standing with Ormond does not seem to have been affected for, on 30 November 1392, he and William Spaldyng, admiral of Ireland, were ordered to arrest several individuals attempting to leave the country without the king's licence.[57]

Thomas was mayor again for a third and final term from Michaelmas 1394, during which Richard II, king of England, lodged in the city from November 1394 to March 1395. As mayor, Thomas was one of the witnesses in Dublin Castle, when Donnchadh O'Byrne submitted to the king in person on 18 February 1395.[58] Thomas must have died shortly afterwards, because Thomas Cusake was elected as his replacement sometime before 1 September 1395, to complete his year in office.[59] Mareward may have died before 26 April 1395, when the king granted the messuages and tenements of the late Richard Heygreve, both within and without Dublin city, to the value of £10, to the prior and convent of Holy Trinity at Christ Church. Heygreve had bequeathed them in his will to the confraternity of St Katherine in St Michael's Church, after the death of his wife Cecilia, contrary to the Statute of Mortmain without obtaining the king's licence first. His property was therefore considered forfeited to the crown. This anomaly probably came to light after the death of Thomas.[60] At Michaelmas 1396, on the manucaption of Nicholas Macclesfeld and Thomas Mareward junior, Cecilia was given a day to appear before the barons of the Irish exchequer to account for the debts of her late husband Thomas Mareward senior, 'late mayor of Dublin'.[61]

Despite the king's grant of Heygreve's property to Holy Trinity Priory, it seems that Cecilia still retained her life interest in it, which she eventually granted to the prior and convent in 1404. This included premises in Patrick Street, Rupell Street, Francis Street, Cook Street, High Street, Scarlet Lane (near Isolde's Tower), Ram Lane 'beside the Polgate' (junction of Werburgh and Bride Street), and in Oxmantown. In return, Cecilia received a rent of 20 marks per annum for the remainder of her life, to be drawn from the possessions of the convent.[62] Around this time, the prior recorded in his psalter

55 *CCR 1392–96*, pp 16–17.   **56** James Graves (ed.), *A roll of the proceedings of the king's council in Ireland, for a portion of the sixteenth year of the reign of Richard the Second*, AD *1392–93* (London, 1877), p. 35.   **57** Ibid., pp 53–4. The printed calendar gives the mayor's given name as John.   **58** Edmund Curtis, *Richard II and the submissions of the Irish chiefs* (Oxford, 1927), p. 152.   **59** Cusake witnessed a document as mayor on 1 September 1395: *CARD*, i, p. 125.   **60** CIRCLE, PR 18 Ric. II, §50 (RCH 152/50); *Reg. Alen*, pp 229–30.   **61** College of Arms, MS Ph15172, p. 280 (Exch. mem. roll, 21–22 Ric. II).   **62** *CCD*, nos

that he had paid Cecilia for the Christmas term, 46*s*. 2*d*.[63] Cecilia eventually died in 1416 and as a 'sister of our congregation', was commemorated in the convent's book of obits with nine lessons under the date 18 April (XIV Kal. Jun.).[64]

Thomas II (d.1414), son of Thomas I and Katherine Feypo

Thomas II was probably born in the late 1360s, if he was old enough to serve as a man-at-arms in Sir John Stanley's retinue in 1389. On his father's death in 1395, Thomas inherited his mother's parcel of the manor of Santry. Thomas seems to have spurned a civic career and pursued the life of a country gentleman instead and the responsibilities that went with it. Thomas was subsequently elected as sheriff of Co. Dublin by his peers and was confirmed in the said office by the king on 3 May 1400.[65] One of his first acts was to return a writ into the Irish exchequer stating that, as the king's farmer, his father had held Joan Feypo's parcel of the manor of Santry and that he now had custody of the same. He therefore distrained himself of the issues due to the king.[66]

Thomas was sheriff again on 28 February 1402, when he was appointed with four others to levy the hearth tax known as 'smoksilver'. This tax was used to pay for the wages and expenses of the watch that secured the county marches from attacks by the Leinster Irish.[67] On 5 April of the same year, still as sheriff, Thomas was appointed with John Oweyn and Robert Tyrrell, to assess and array all men within the county and crosslands of Dublin, to see that they were properly equipped with arms and horses appropriate to their lands, and to lead them on the marches. His commission to levy the hearth tax was also confirmed on the same day.[68] On 1 June 1402, Thomas and others were also appointed to assess and levy the 40 marks granted by the commons of the county to be spent on defending the marches.[69] Three days later he was appointed one of the keepers of the peace for the county.[70] Although Thomas was heavily involved in defending the marches during a period of heightened tension in the first half of 1402, it is not known whether he took part in the mayor of Dublin's victory over the Leinster Irish, which took place near Bray on 11 July. Playing such a vital role in the county's defence, he probably did.[71]

On 16 May 1405, Thomas was pardoned for 'all intrusions, abatements, alienations, etc., and undue liveries by him, his ancestors or tenants, in and of

268 and 269. **63** Geoffrey J. Hand, 'The psalter of Christ Church, Dublin (Bodleian MS Rawlinson G. 185)', *Reportorium novum: Dublin diocesan historical record*, 1:2 (1956), 321. **64** Raymond Refaussé with Colm Lennon (eds), *The registers of Christ Church Cathedral, Dublin* (Dublin, 1998), p. 57. **65** CIRCLE, PR 1 Hen. IV, §61 (RCH 156/59); Adams, *Santry*, p. 83. **66** NAI, EX 2/4, fo. 111. **67** CIRCLE, PR 3 Hen. IV, §235 (RCH 165/235). **68** CIRCLE, PR 3 Hen. IV, §227 (RCH 165/227). **69** CIRCLE, PR 3 Hen. IV, §249 (RCH 166/249). **70** CIRCLE, PR 3 Hen. IV, §246 (RCH 166/246). **71** Randolph Jones, 'The battle of Bray, 11 July 1402', Friends of Medieval Dublin

the two parts of the manor of Santry or in any parcel of said manor, until ratification of his estate therein'.[72] It seems that Thomas had permanently acquired his aunt's, Joan Feypo's, parcel of the manor, perhaps on her death in that year. It is not clear what happened to the third part of the manor. This may have been the third part traditionally given as dower to the widow of the former holder, but it was probably still held by Sir Francis Feypo's third daughter, Ela or Alice, and her descendants (there seems to be no further mention of Sir Francis's fourth daughter Margaret, and her share probably went to her three elder sisters). By this time, the fortunes of the Mareward family had changed significantly due to Thomas inheriting the title 'baron of Scrine' and the lands in Co. Meath that went with it.

The early history of the Feypo family has been covered in some detail by Elizabeth Hickey down to the lifetime of Sir Francis.[73] When Sir Francis's son and heir John died *c.*1374, he was succeeded by John fitz Nicholas Feypo as the new baron. In 1385, John fitz Nicholas was given licence for several chaplains to grant him, his wife Matilda, and the heirs of his body, the manors of Scrine and Kilcarne, which were both held of the earl of March, a minor then in the king's hands, as of his manor of Trim, with remainder to Luke Feypo, John fitz Henry Feypo, and their heirs male, with a final remainder to the right heirs of Sir Francis Feypo.[74] On 14 October 1403, however, John fitz Nicholas obtained another licence to change the succession to the heirs male of his body, with remainder to Thomas Mareward senior and his heirs male, and then the right heirs of Sir Francis Feypo.[75] Less than three weeks later, John fitz Nicholas was dead, having died on 2 November and his lands were seized into the hands of the king because of debt. A subsequent inquisition found that a Richard Feypo had entered them.[76] Temporary custody was granted on 10 November to Sir Thomas Cusak and Hugh Banent, clerk, while the lands remained in the king's hands.[77] Yet on 9 May 1404, Thomas Mareward was pardoned for his intrusion into those lands and he formally took possession of them from that date for a fine of £20.[78]

Mareward's succession to the Feypo inheritance did not go unchallenged, for later in the same year, Richard Feypo petitioned the king in England to grant him the goods and chattels that John fitz Nicholas had bequeathed to him on 8 March 1403, but which had been seized by Sir Laurence Merbury,

'Milestones of Medieval Dublin' lecture, 8 November 2016, https://www.academia.edu/33946987/2016_The_Battle_of_Bray_11_July_1402.   **72** NAI, RC 8/33, p. 218; College of Arms, MS Ph15174, p. 177 (Exch. mem. roll, 8 Hen. IV, m. 19).   **73** Elizabeth Hickey, *Skryne and the early Normans: papers concerning the medieval manors of the de Feypo family in Ireland in the 12th and early 13th centuries* (Trim, 1994).   **74** CIRCLE, PR 9 Ric. II, §29 (RCH 123/29).   **75** CIRCLE, PR 5 Hen. IV, §13 (RCH 176/13).   **76** College of Arms, MS Ph15173, p. 51 (Exch. mem. roll, 5 Hen. IV, m. 28).   **77** College of Arms, MS Ph 15173, p. 134 (Exch. mem. roll, 7 Hen. IV, m. 46); ibid., p. 307 (ibid., 9 Hen. IV, m. 36).   **78** NAI, RC 8/33, p. 217; College of Arms, MS Ph 15173, p. 176 (Exch. mem. roll, 8 Hen. IV, m. 19).

treasurer of Ireland for a debt of 20 marks John fitz Nicholas owed to the crown. Richard Feypo also petitioned for an enquiry to be made into the apparent misdemeanours of the said treasurer, together with Thomas Mareward.[79] On 12 January 1405, the king sent a commission, to Richard Rede and Sir Thomas Cusak,

> to enquire about diverse extortions and oppressions and other trespasses and crimes committed against the king's lieges Luke Feypowe, Richard Feypowe, Barnabas Cusak and John Cusak of the county of Meath in Ireland by Laurence Merbury, treasurer of Ireland, and Thomas Mareward and others of Ireland in the same county.[80]

It would therefore seem that the male members of the Feypo family believed that they had been cheated out of their inheritance, and that Thomas Mareward was the prime culprit. John fitz Nicholas may have agreed to the change in succession because he was financially embarrassed. As well as being indebted to the king, he also owed the abbot of St Mary's, Dublin, 10 marks, in part payment of which he pledged a golden *zone* (belt or girdle) with the abbot on 16 May 1401, to raise a loan of 100*s*. from a Dublin merchant.[81] John fitz Nicholas also sold a silver cup to William Symcok of Drogheda worth 4 marks in repayment of a debt that John owed him. This was done in John's manor of Kilcarne, shortly before his death.[82] It therefore seems that Thomas took advantage of John fitz Nicholas's impecuniosity to change the order of succession in his favour, possibly in return for unspecified debts being written off.

Thomas's succession seems to have been challenged yet again by Luke Feypo and Mathilda Beures, John fitz Nicholas's widow, who subsequently married Richard Lynham.[83] On 9 April 1406, Stephen Bray, James Uriell and Nicholas Savage were appointed to hear an assize of novel disseisin that Thomas Mareward had arraigned against Richard Lynham and others concerning tenements in Scrine and Kilcarne.[84] This was followed by a similar appointment on 23 June to hear a case against Luke Feypo.[85] It appears, that Thomas Mareward successfully fended off both challenges, for on 14 January 1408 he was pardoned all intrusions, in and of the manor of Scrine and of one messuage, one mill, three carucates, 24 acres meadow, 40 acres pasture, 10 acres moor in Kilcarne, by him or his ancestors, and of all issues and profits, fines and amercements due the king, who ratified his estate therein.[86]

79 J.L. Kirby (ed.), *Calendar of signet letters of Henry IV and Henry V (1399–1422)*, HMSO (London, 1978), p. 219.   **80** *CPR 1401–5*, p. 509.   **81** NAI, Ferguson Collection iii, p. 1 (Exch. mem. roll, 7 Hen. IV, m. 14).   **82** College of Arms, MS Ph 15173, p. 88 (Exch. mem. roll, 7 Hen. IV, m. 24). Ibid., p. 144 (ibid., m. 57).   **83** College of Arms, MS Ph 15173, p. 66 (Exch. mem. roll, 6 Hen. IV).   **84** CIRCLE, PR 7 Hen. IV, §151 (RCH 184/149).   **85** CIRCLE, PR 7 Hen. IV, §152 (RCH 184/150).   **86** College of Arms, MS Ph 15173, p. 302 (Exch. mem. roll, 9 Hen. IV, m. 34).

Nevertheless, it appears that Thomas came to some kind of settlement with Richard Lynham and Matilda, because on 31 January 1408, he paid 13s. 4d. for a licence to enfeoff them both with eight messuages and 150 acres of land in Kilcarne.[87] This may have represented Matilda's dower.

In 1410, Thomas also faced a further challenge from St Mary's Abbey in Dublin when he installed his own candidate, John White, into the vicarage of Skreen's parish church of St Columba, when the previous incumbent died on 4 May. His right to do so was successfully challenged by the abbot in the court of common pleas, who successfully proved that the advowson had been granted to the abbey by a previous Feypo baron of Scrine.[88]

In the exchequer year commencing Michaelmas 1411, the sheriff of Meath was ordered to distrain Thomas for two parts of his lands in Scrine, because he had been absent from them since the year before. Unfortunately, the reason for Thomas's absence is not recorded and nothing further is known of this matter.[89] Thomas was certainly back in Ireland, when he was killed on 10 May 1414 at the battle of *Cill Echain*, possibly Killagh, near Delvin, Co. Westmeath,[90] when the English of Meath were defeated by Murrough O'Connor Faly and others.[91] He left a son and heir, also called Thomas. His widow, Joan Pettit, was granted a licence on 12 April 1415, to marry whom she pleased.[92] Brian Coleman has suggested that she subsequently married Walter Tirrell, later mayor of Dublin, on the basis that Walter and his wife Joan were pardoned intrusion into various lands in Santry and the vicinity in 1419, which may have been part of her dower.[93] Joan seems to have died *c.*1447, when temporary custody of her lands was awarded to person or persons unknown.[94]

Thomas III (d.1419), son of Thomas II, son of Thomas I and Katherine Feypo; and his sons, Thomas IV (d.1434) and Robert (d.1439)

On 17 July 1414, Thomas III was pardoned for all intrusions into the manor of Scrine, Kilcarne, Ballymulghan and two parts of the manor of Santry, which were released to him in return for a fine of six marks.[95] On 26 June 1417, he was one of several signatories to a letter sent to the king by the members of an afforced council which met in Naas, in support of Sir John Talbot, the

87 CIRCLE, PR 9 Hen. IV, §66 (RCH 188/38).   88 *CStM*, i, p. 244.   89 College of Arms, MS Ph 15173, p. 439 (Exch. mem. roll, 13–14 Hen. IV).   90 See Pádraig Ó Riain et al. (eds), *Historical dictionary of Gaelic placenames*, fascicle 3, Irish Texts Society (London, 2008), p. 166, *s.n.* 'Ceall Each'.   91 'Henry Marlborough's Chronicle of Ireland' in *Ancient Irish histories* (2 vols, Dublin 1809), ii, p. 25; *AFM*, iv, p. 817; College of Arms, MS Ph 15174, p. 566 (Exch. mem. roll, 4 Hen. V, m. 57). For the background to the battle, see Randolph Jones, 'Lost and found: a missing exchequer issue roll of 1414 rediscovered' at https://beyond2022.ie/wp-content/uploads/2018/06/5.-Archive-Fever-Lost-and-Found.pdf. 92 CIRCLE, PR 3 Hen. V, §20 (RCH 210/20); NAI, Lodge MSS vol. 19, p. 205.   93 Coleman, 'Urban elite', p. 298.   94 College of Arms, MS Ph 15174, p. 131 (Exch. mem. roll, 26 Hen. VI). 95 CIRCLE, PR 2 Hen. V, §36 (RCH 204/32); NAI, Lodge MSS, vol. 1, p. 357.

lieutenant of Ireland, who was in dire need of money and threatening to return to England to obtain it.[96] By 22 September 1419, Thomas III was dead, when custody of his lands was granted to John Charneles, the escheator of Ireland, during the minority of his son and heir, also called Thomas, with the exception of nine marks rent payable annually from lands in Ballymun and Silloge, which were confirmed to John Burnell on 18 December 1419.[97] On 28 April 1421, the marriage of Thomas IV was granted to Stephen Bray, chief justice of the king's bench, but Thomas was dead by 15 December 1434, when custody of his lands was granted to Christopher Bernevall, the treasurer of Ireland, during the minority of Robert, Thomas IV's brother and heir.[98] Once again, the head of the Burnell family sought confirmation of his nine marks rent out of Ballymun and Silloge. It seems that Robert was married to Bernevall's daughter, for Bernevall was later accused of causing livery to be granted to Robert, even though he was still a minor, to the great financial loss of the king.[99] This daughter may have been one Thomasina who, with her subsequent husband Alexander Ever, was still holding one third of the manor of Scrine, in 1467, probably as part of her dower.[100] However, by 9 May 1439, Robert was dead, when livery of his lands was granted to his uncle, Richard Mareward, the younger brother of Thomas III.[101]

Richard (d.1473), son of Thomas II, son of Thomas I and Katherine Feypo

Richard Mareward was first married to Joan, daughter and heiress of William Ashbourne, by whom they had two sons, Richard and William and a daughter Agnes. Richard's father-in-law was the great-grandson and ultimately the heir of Sir Elias Ashbourne (d.1356), a former chief justice in Ireland.[102] William does not seem to have been Elias's direct heir, only inheriting his lands after the death of a John Ashbourne junior.[103] William was pardoned for his intrusion into these lands on 26 March 1407, when they were released to him.[104] He did not live long to enjoy his inheritance, for he seems to have died

96 Henry Ellis, *Original letters, illustrative of English history; including numerous royal letters: from autographs in the British Museum, and one or two other collections, second series*, vol. 1 (London, 1827), p. 62.　**97** Joseph Hunter, *Rotuli Selecti ad res Anglicas et Hibernicas spectantes, ex Archivis in Domo Capitulari West-Monasteriensi, deprompti* (London, 1834), p. 76; RCH 215/21; Adams, *Santry*, p. 36; Paul Dryburgh and Brendan Smith (eds), *Handbook and select calendar of the sources for medieval Ireland in the National Archives of the United Kingdom* (Dublin, 2005), p. 181. Burnell's rent had been granted in perpetuity to his grandfather by Sir Francis Feypo in return for a fixed sum.　**98** CIRCLE, PR 13 Hen. VI, §11 (RCH 256/11).　**99** M.C. Griffith, 'The Talbot–Ormond struggle for control of the Anglo-Irish government, 1414–47', *IHS*, 2:8 (Sept. 1941), 396.　**100** College of Arms, MS Ph 15175, p. 230 (Exch. mem. roll, 10 Edw. IV, m. 14).　**101** College of Arms, MS Ph 15174, p. 85 (Exch. mem. roll, 17 Hen. VI, m. 30).　**102** William, son of Roger, son of Sir Thomas, son and heir of Sir Elias Ashbourne.　**103** College of Arms, MS Ph 15173, pp 322 and 331 (Exch. mem. rolls, 9 Hen. IV and 11 Hen. IV, m. 9).　**104** College of Arms, MS Ph

before 10 August 1415, when his lands were temporarily held by John Talbot of Feltrim and John Walsh of Dublin.[105] This may have been because William had been declared an outlaw the year before, for failing to present himself before the king's bench in Ireland.[106] A William Ashbourne, who was sworn in as the deputy escheator of Ireland on 1 September 1422, may have been a short-lived son.[107] It is not known when Richard and Joan were married, but he was probably in control of her lands before he inherited those of his nephew Robert, baron of Scrine, in 1439.

Joan died before 1451, when her husband was still holding her lands in Coultry (*Collveleston*) and Ashbournerath, courtesy of England.[108] Richard also held Pickerstown (*Pycotston*), *Glasclod*, Kinoud (*Kynaird*) and Barberstown (*Barbedoreston*) through her, for which he paid the archbishop of Dublin the chief rent of 4s. on 10 September 1454, for the forthcoming Michaelmas and Easter terms.[109] On 4 March 1454, Richard also released to Nicholas Dowdall, citizen and merchant of Dublin, a messuage in St Audeon's parish, lying near the Bullring. The messuage had previously been held by his late father-in-law. As this property was later granted to the religious guild of St Anne of Dublin, Richard's deed is now preserved among its muniments with his wax seal still attached. Unfortunately, the impression is poor, but it seems to depict a shield charged with three cinquefoils. Whether there is a fess separating the three cinquefoils is not clear.[110]

Soon after coming into his Mareward inheritance, Richard began serving in several administrative capacities. His election as sheriff of Co. Dublin by the commons of the county was confirmed by the king on 5 December 1442.[111] Although not sheriff at the time, he participated in Richard, duke of York's campaign against the O'Byrnes in August 1449, during which he was knighted at Kiltimon, along with several others. He was the only member of his family to receive this honour. York was also the heir of the Mortimer family, from whom Mareward held the manor of Scrine.

Richard seems to have served as sheriff of Co. Dublin again in 1454/55: during the Michaelmas term 1455, he was called upon to account for the profits of the county, before the barons of the exchequer, as the late sheriff.[112] By a statute passed by the Irish parliament on 17 October 1455, Richard and two others were appointed to supervise the construction of a tower, together with a wall twenty perches long and six-foot high, near to the existing wall of

15174, p. 143 (Exch. mem. roll, 29 Hen. VI, m. 18).   **105** Henry F. Berry, 'History of the religious gild of St Anne, in St Audeon's church, Dublin, 1430–1740, taken from its records in the Haliday collection, RIA', *PRIA*, 25 (1904–5), no. 134; College of Arms, MS Ph 15174, p. 608 (Exch. mem. roll, 8 Hen. VI, m. 69).   **106** CIRCLE, PR 2 Hen. V, §46 (RCH 204/41).   **107** CIRCLE, PR 10 Hen. V, §6 (RCH 180/6).   **108** College of Arms, MS Ph 15174, p. 143 (Exch. mem. roll, 29 Hen. VI, m. 18).   **109** *Reg. Alen*, p. 241.   **110** Berry, 'Gild of St Anne', nos. 35 and 36.   **111** College of Arms, MS Ph 15174, p. 97 (Exch. mem. roll, 21 Hen. VI, m. 5).   **112** College of Arms, MS Ph 15174, p. 167 (Exch. mem. roll, 35

St Mary's Abbey, Dublin. This was intended to protect the ford over the river Liffey, near to the abbey's pier, which was used by Irish enemies to cross at night-time and raid Fingal.[113]

On 8 November 1458, Richard's election as sheriff for the ensuing year was confirmed by the king. During this term, he took advantage of a statute passed in the Irish parliament on 17 October 1455 to claim £10 from the profits and first issues of the county to help him meet the cost of maintaining men on the marches in defence of the county as sheriff.[114] Richard was elected sheriff again on 4 December 1470, but on this occasion he refused to take the oath on the grounds that he was exempt from holding this office against his will, because he was a citizen of Dublin, then living within the city, thanks to a charter granted by Edward III in 1334. Richard's reluctance to serve on this occasion may have been due to his age. His claim was upheld, and he was exonerated from taking the oath by the barons of the exchequer.[115]

In the exchequer year commencing Michaelmas 1459, Richard found it necessary to produce letters patent before the same court pardoning him all intrusions into Santry as the brother of Thomas Mareward, baron of Scrine. In a nineteenth-century calendar of the exchequer memoranda roll for this year, the place and date of attestation of these letters is given as Dunboyne on 18 December 3 Henry V, i.e., 1415. However, this may be a mistake, for Richard's brother Thomas III was still alive in that year, having been pardoned a similar intrusion into two-thirds of the same manor the year before. Other than the fact that the date may be incorrect (the repertory clerk initially indicated in his calendar entry that the monarch was Henry VI, but corrected this to Henry V), the only other possible explanation is that Thomas decided to provide for his younger brother, by granting him his interest in Santry. With Richard's ultimate inheritance of his brother's title of baron of Scrine in 1439, Santry would have returned once more into the possession of the main line of the Mareward family.[116]

Early in the reign of Edward IV, Richard took possession the manor of Rathconnell and its appurtenances from Richard Chambre, who had defaulted on loans owed to him. Yet, despite a legal judgment confirming this possession, the manor was still held by Chambre and his adherents, the Darcys, Petits and others, by force. Richard therefore sought redress from the Irish parliament held in 1464, which ordered Chambre to appear before the king in chancery in the quinzaine of Easter to prove his title to the manor, with the threat of outlawry if he failed to do so.[117]

Hen. VI, m. 21).   113 *Stat. rolls Ire. Hen. VI*, pp 403–5.   114 College of Arms, MS Ph 15174, pp 175 and 181 (Exch. mem. roll, 37 Hen. VI, m. 36).   115 College of Arms, MS Ph 15175, p. 229; NAI, Ferguson Collection iii, p. 225; William Lynch, *The law of election in the ancient cities and towns of Ireland traced from original records. With fac-simile engravings and an appendix of documents* (London, 1831), p. 46 (Exch. mem. roll, 10 Edw. IV, m. 11).   116 College of Arms, MS Ph 15174, p. 189 (Exch. mem. roll, 38 Hen. VI, m. 27).   117 *Stat.*

In 1466/7, Richard, together with the other electors of Robert Bath of Laundeston, late sheriff of Dublin, made a fine in the court of exchequer for the issues and profits of the county for the period 29 January 1462 to 28 February 1463, due to Bath's failure to account.[118]

Prior to the parliament held in 1468, Walter Prendregast, the vicar of St Columba's Church in Skreen, who had been installed by the abbot of St Mary's, Dublin, in 1410, died. In his place, Richard unilaterally installed his own candidate, Richard Fychet. Mareward apparently did so in ignorance of the fact that the advowson to the church belonged to the abbot, who successfully recovered it once again through the law courts.[119] Richard's acknowledgment of the abbot's right may have been the substance of a charter tested by John Cheever, chief justice of the chief place, on 28 February 1472, and enrolled in the now lost chartulary of the abbey.[120]

By now Richard was probably quite old and his thoughts turned to settling his worldly affairs. On 8 February 1467, Thomas Norreis and John Sprotte, chaplains, settled on Richard and his second wife Alson or Alice Petite, the two parts of the manor of Santry, with its appurtenances, for the term of their two lives. Then, on 21 August 1469, Richard granted to Richard Stanyhurst, merchant of Dublin, the annual rent of twenty marks from all his messuages and lands in Mochekilcarne, Co. Meath, in return for eighty marks that Mareward owed him. The reason for the debt is not known, but Stanyhurst was married to Mareward's daughter Agnes.[121] As we have seen before, by this time Richard claimed he was living in Dublin city itself. On 15 October 1472, Richard also granted James Ailmer a life pension of 20s. per annum, to be levied from his lands and tenements in Little Kilcarne, Co. Meath. Again, the reason for the grant is not known, but James may have been a long-term retainer of Richard's. Then, over a three-week period in late March and April 1473, Richard and Thomas Norreys, chaplain, conveyed to three other chaplains, all his messuages, lands, tenements, rents and services in Ballymun, comprising 180 acres, as of his demesne in Santry, to Richard Stanyhurst, his wife Agnes and their descendants, with remainder to the abbot and convent of St Mary's, Dublin, if Richard and Agnes had no children.[122] Richard Mareward was still alive on 6 April 1473, when he sealed the quitclaim to this transaction, but by 29 April of the same year, he was dead. On that date an inquisition was held before the barons of the exchequer, with the result that Richard's lands in Santry were seized into the king's hands because his heir was then a minor, despite his widow Alson having a life interest in the same. Nevertheless, in the

rolls *Ire. Edw. IV*, i, pp 203–5.   118 College of Arms, MS Ph 15175, p. 212 (Exch. mem. roll, 6 Edw. IV, m. 11).   **119** *Stat. rolls Ire. Edw. IV*, i, pp 451–5.   **120** *CStM*, ii, p. 24. **121** Smyly, 'Old deeds in the library of Trinity College – IV', *Hermathena*, 70 (Nov. 1947), no. 169.   **122** Ibid., nos. 172; ibid., 'Old deeds in the library of Trinity College – V', *Hermathena*, 71 (1948), nos. 173–5; Adams, *Santry*, p. 38.

following year, Alson successfully petitioned the Irish parliament for the two parts of Santry manor to be restored to her.[123]

Walter I (d.1487), son of William, son of Richard, son of Thomas II, son of Thomas I and Katherine Feypo

As both of Richard's sons predeceased him, he was succeeded as baron of Scrine by his grandson Walter. His mother was Matilda Bath, who lived until 25 October 1514.[124] As Walter was a minor, all his lands were seized into the king's hands. Temporary custody was subsequently granted to a person unknown.[125] This may have been Robert St Lawrence, Lord Howth (d. 1487), whose daughter, Margaret, Walter later married. In 1479, Walter was 21 years of age and was granted livery of his manors of Scrine and Kilcarne, but not Ballymolghane, which was now held by William Cusak. Walter was also granted livery of the two parts of Santry, except for Stormanstown (*Sturmeyneston*), held by his mother as part of her dower, and Ballymun (*Balicore*), held by Richard Stanyhurst and his wife Agnes. On the same occasion, Walter was granted possession of his grandmother's lands in Brackenstown, Coultry (*Colwellestown*) and Ashbournerath, Co. Dublin.[126] On 22 October 1479, he was admitted as a citizen of Dublin, the reason being 'according to justice'.[127] A charter of Walter's, dated 8 June 1481, was subsequently entered into the chartulary of St Mary's Abbey, Dublin, and was probably a confirmation by him that the advowson of the parish church of St Columba's in Skreen belonged to the abbot.[128] In 1481/2, Walter was granted licence of absence from Ireland for four years.[129] The purpose is not known, but it may have been to study law in England. By 2 February 1485, he was back in Ireland when he paid 15*d*. in the court of the exchequer to respite his homage for the manors of Scrine and Santry.[130] He did the same again on 3 October 1485.[131] Some time prior to November 1486, Walter, together with Richard Bruyn and John Clerk, had goods to the value of £40 stolen from them by the people of Yorkshire. This was one of several assaults and thefts committed against Dublin merchants in England, which the mayor and commons of Dublin complained about, petitioning the Irish parliament for redress because they could not get satisfaction through the courts in England. It is interesting to hear that Walter was actively involved in commerce, although whether he was actually accompanying his goods when they were

---

123 *Stat. rolls Ire. Edw. IV*, ii, pp 249–51.   **124** Griffith (ed.), *Cal. inquisitions*, p. 1.   **125** College of Arms, MS Ph 15175, p. 251 (Exch. mem. roll, 18 Edw. IV, m. 3).   **126** *Stat. rolls Ire. Ric. III to Hen. VIII*, pp 318–9; College of Arms, MS Ph 15175, p. 256 (Exch. mem. roll, 19 Edw. IV, m. 16).   **127** Colm Lennon and James Murray (eds), *The Dublin city franchise roll, 1468–1512*, (Dublin, 1998), p. 13.   **128** *CStM*, ii, 24.   **129** College of Arms, MS Ph 15175, p. 269 (Exch. mem. roll, 21 Edw. IV, m. 13).   **130** NAI, RC 8/33, fos. 398v–399; College of Arms, MS Ph 15175, p. 281 (Exch. Mem. Roll, 2 Ric. III, m. 4).   **131** BL, Add MS 4793, fo. 149 f (Exch. mem. roll, 1 Hen. VII, m. 15).

stolen is not known.[132] This is the last we hear of Walter, because he died on 6 November 1487, leaving his three-year-old son and heir, Thomas, and a daughter Eleanor.[133] How Walter died is not known, but it occurred during a period of uncertainty in Ireland, following the coronation of Lambert Simnel in Dublin as king of England in May 1487, and before the earl of Kildare and the other lords temporal and spiritual of Ireland resumed their allegiance to Henry VII in July 1488.

Thomas V (d.1504), son of Walter I, son of William, son of Richard, son of Thomas II, son of Thomas I and Katherine Feypo

The lands of the Mareward family once again fell into a long period of custodianship. This time, they were probably granted to Sir Roland Fitzeustace of Harristown (d. 1496), Lord Portlester and treasurer of Ireland. He was also the father-in-law of Gerald FitzGerald, earl of Kildare, who at the time of Walter's death was acting as the lieutenant of the boy-king crowned in Dublin as 'Edward VI'. Thomas later married Sir Roland's daughter, Maud, by whom he had a son and heir, James.[134] Thomas died on 10 February 1504, while he was still a minor, never receiving livery of his own lands.[135]

James (d.1534), son of Thomas V, son of Walter I, son of William, son of Richard, son of Thomas II, son of Thomas I and Katherine Feypo

James was only two years old at the time of his father's death and on 20 June 1518 custody of his lands were granted to Sir William Darcy of Platten, who married him to his granddaughter, Maud, the daughter of his son George.[136] James was given livery of his lands in 1525/6, but he did not live long to enjoy them.[137] He was murdered on 14 September 1534 by his wife's lover, Richard FitzGerald, brother of the ninth earl of Kildare, during the rebellion of his nephew, Thomas FitzGerald, lord of Offaly (Silken Thomas).[138] Maud subsequently married Richard FitzGerald, who was later attainted and executed for his part in the rebellion. She then married Sir Thomas Cusack of Cushinstown and Lismullen, the lord chancellor.[139]

---

132 Sir William Betham, *The origin and history of the constitution of England, and of the early parliaments of Ireland* (Dublin, 1834), pp 381–4; David B. Quinn, 'The bills and statutes of the Irish parliaments of Henry VII and Henry VIII', *AH*, 10 (1941), 79–81.   133 John Lodge, *The peerage of Ireland: or, A genealogical history of the present nobility of that kingdom*, iii (Dublin, 1789), pp 186–7.   134 Lodge, *Peerage*, iii, pp 186–7.   135 Griffith (ed.), *Cal. inquisitions*, pp 2–3.   136 Lodge, *Peerage*, iii, p. 187; College of Arms, MS Ph 15175, pp 335, 354 (Exch. Mem. rolls, 22 Hen. VII, m. 4 and 8, 9 Hen. VIII, mm 23 and 36).   137 College of Arms, MS Ph 15175, p. 368 (Exch. mem. roll, 17 Hen. VII, m. 14).   138 Griffith (ed.), *Cal. inquisitions*, pp 58–60.   139 Paul Walsh, 'Janet Marward 1562–1629' in idem, *Irish leaders and learning through the ages: essays collected, edited and introduced by Nollaig Ó Muraíle* (Dublin, 2003), pp 134–40.

Walter II (d.1564), son of James, son of Thomas V, son of Walter I, son of William, son of Richard, son of Thomas II, son of Thomas I and Katherine Feypo

James left an underage heir, Walter. He was granted livery of his lands on 20 February 1555. In August 1559, he was granted a licence to leave Ireland to study abroad for five years. Yet by 8 May 1564, he was dead, when the wardship, marriage and custody of the lands of his two-year-old daughter and heiress, Janet, were granted to John Fitzwilliam. A stone memorial to Walter, his mother Maud Darcy, his first wife Margaret Plunket and their daughter Janet, was set up in 1611 by his half-brother John Cusack in the parish church of Skreen. It is only one of two monuments to any member of the Mareward family in Ireland that survives today and bears their arms, *a fess between three cinquefoils*.[140]

Janet (d.1629), daughter of Walter II, son of James, son of Thomas V, son of Walter I, son of William, son of Richard, son of Thomas II, son of Thomas I and Katherine Feypo

Janet was the last of the Marewards. She was abducted by force in 1573 and subsequently married to William Nugent, the younger brother of the then Lord Nugent. In 1577, William was granted livery of her lands, and began calling himself Lord Scrine.[141]

Murwode / Marwood of Drogheda

A junior branch of the family may have established itself in Drogheda by the reign of Henry VII, but how it was related to the barons of Scrine is not known, if at all. During the Trinity term of 1497, a William Murwode of Drogheda, together with Nicholas Salman, John Feld and others of the same place, put Thomas Sharpe clerk, in their place against the king in a plea of contempt before the barons of the exchequer.[142] By Michaelmas of the same year, William was the mayor of Drogheda.[143] A William Marwood served in the same office from Michaelmas 1508.[144]

---

140 Ibid., pp 139–40; Thomas J. Westropp, 'The churches of Dunsany and Skreen, County Meath', *JSRAI*, 4:3 (1894), pp 231; Elizabeth Hickey, 'A description of the Marward stone at Skryne and a discussion on John Cusack who sculptured it', *Ríocht na Mídhe*, 5:3 (1973), 50. The other monument is an inscription in Rathmore church commemorating Sir Alexander Plunket (d.1503) and his wife Ann Marward (d.1485), probably the sister of Walter I. Lord Walter Fitzgerald, 'Rathmore (St Lawrence's church and burial ground)', *Journal of the Association for the Preservation of the Memorials of the Dead, Ireland*, 7:1 (1907), pp 432–3.   **141** Walsh, *Irish leaders*, pp 134–40.   **142** BL, Add MS 43769, fo. 76v.   **143** BL, Add MS 4793, fo. 151f.   **144** BL, Add MS 4793, fo. 154v.

CONCLUSION

The Mareward family, a junior branch of the same family in England, were latecomers to the Irish scene, arriving here in the mid-fourteenth century. Two deaths and two fortuitous marriages enabled Thomas I, the founder of the Irish family, to become almost simultaneously a country gentleman with a seat close to Dublin city and a prominent citizen of the same. Initially, he seems to have preferred the former, holding many responsible positions in the county, before taking up the latter. He subsequently became mayor of the city three times, dying in office during the very year when the king in person, Richard II, was residing in Dublin.

His son, Thomas II, continued the role of country gentleman, and thanks to his descent from his deceased mother, Katherine Feypo, became titular baron of Scrine, which came with several lands in Co. Meath. As well as the result of dynastic accident, he seems to have achieved this goal by persuading the last impecunious baron of the Feypo family, on his deathbed, to change the order of succession from the male line to that of the heirs general of Sir Francis. Nevertheless, Thomas had to fight off subsequent legal challenges to his succession from those he managed to dispossess.

The family received a temporary setback, when Thomas II was killed in battle in 1414. This was followed by the death of his son and successor, Thomas III, just five years later. There then followed a twenty-year period during which the Mareward lands were held in temporary custody by others as his sons, Thomas IV and Robert, followed each other to the grave without heirs of their bodies. The succession then reverted to their uncle Richard, brother of Thomas III, who had already made his way in the world thanks to his marriage to the heiress of the Ashbourne family. It appears that he was closely connected to the city before he inherited the family title and lands in counties Meath and Dublin. Although he was a citizen of Dublin, he chose not to seek office within the civic administration and contented himself with performing the roles expected of a country gentleman. Nevertheless, later in life he chose to live in the city itself, with his daughter Agnes marrying a prominent citizen, Richard Stanyhurst, who became mayor in 1489.

Richard's long tenure as head of the family resulted in his grandson, Walter I, being his successor. Although a minor when he succeeded in 1473, he gained livery of his lands six years later. Walter was the last Mareward known to have held the citizenship of Dublin, being admitted in the year he reached his majority. Unfortunately, Walter died young in 1487, resulting in a series of minorities which led to the family not playing its accustomed role within counties Dublin and Meath. Indeed, during the 160 years the Mareward family held the title baron of Scrine (1404–1564), their lands were in wardship for 94 of them, or 59%. During the 91-year tenure of the last four generations of the family (1473–1564), they were in wardship for 74, or a remarkable 81%. Indeed, during this period, the succession itself hung by a single tenuous thread, remarkable only due to the fact that the barons were able to marry and produce a male heir before their majorities were reached. As a result, the inheritance of each successive heir was significantly reduced by the continual need to provide dowers for each of the young widows of their predecessors, amounting to one third of their lands and issues being temporarily lost on each occasion. Some of these widows seemed to have lived long, passing their dower lands into the control of husbands they subsequently married.

It is noteworthy perhaps that two of the last four barons who reached their majorities died during periods of political unrest within Ireland: Walter I in 1487, during the time when Gerald FitzGerald, earl of Kildare, recognized the title of the pretender 'Edward VI' as king of England and Ireland, and James in 1534, during the rebellion of the Great Earl's grandson, Silken Thomas. This suggests perhaps that, during the period of the Kildare hegemony at least, the Mareward family sided with its opponents and paid the ultimate price for this during periods of crisis.

***

Since writing the above, the following 1446 grant made by Richard Mareward, baron of Scrine, to the abbot and convent of St Thomas the Martyr near Dublin has come to light. My thanks to Dr Áine Foley who shared with me this transcript from RIA MS 12 D 38, p. 43v.

Be it Known to all by these presents that I Richard the son & heir of Thomas Marward Baron of Scrine have remitted & released & altogether for me & my heirs for ever have quitted claim to the Abbot & Convent of the House of St Thomas the martyr near Dublin & their successors, all my right & claim which I had or have or in any manner can have, in a certain tenement in St Thomas Street & in the parish of St Katherine of Dublin; the which tenement lies between the tenement of the vicar of the church of St Patricks of Dublin on the western side & the land of the said Abbot & Convent of the Monastery of St Thomas on the eastern side, & the street of St Thomas to the north, and the orchard & land of the said abbot & convent on the south; in which tenement I confess the said abbot & convent to be now in full seizin, so that neither the aforesaid Richard or my heirs nor any other in my name can in future demand or challenge my right or claim in the aforesaid tenement but that I and they may be entirely excluded by these presents for ever from any action & remedy at law therein. And I the aforesaid Richard & my heirs will warrant, acquit & defend for ever the aforesaid tenement to the aforesaid abbot & convent & their successor for us & our heirs. In testimony of which thing I have put my seal [——] Dated the twentieth day of the month of May in the twenty fourth year of the reign of King Henry the Sixth.